THE CONSUMER CREDIT ACT
ACT
A Students' Guide

For Catherine

THE CONSUMER CREDIT ACT
ACT
A Students' Guide

by

R. M. GOODE, O.B.E., LL.D.

*Solicitor, Crowther Professor of Credit and Commercial Law
and Dean of the Faculty of Laws
Queen Mary College, University of London*

3396308

LONDON
BUTTERWORTHS
1979

This work is reprinted from Goode:
Consumer Credit Legislation

ENGLAND:
Butterworth & Co. (Publishers) Ltd.
London: 88 Kingsway, London WC2B 6AB

AUSTRALIA:
Butterworths Pty. Ltd.
Sydney: 586 Pacific Highway, Chatswood, NSW 2067
Also at Melbourne, Brisbane, Adelaide and Perth

CANADA:
Butterworth & Co. (Canada) Ltd.
Toronto: 2265 Midland Avenue, Scarborough, M1P 4S1

NEW ZEALAND:
Butterworths of New Zealand Ltd.
Wellington: 77–85 Customhouse Quay, Wellington

SOUTH AFRICA:
Butterworth & Co. (South Africa) (Pty.) Ltd.
Durban: 152–154 Gale Street, Durban.

USA:
Butterworth & Co. (Publishers) Inc.
Boston: 10 Tower Office Park, Woburn, Mass. 01801

©

Butterworth & Co. (Publishers) Ltd.

1979

ISBN 0 406 21165 5

This book is sold subject to the Standard Conditions of Sale of Net Books and may not be re-sold in the U.K. below the net price fixed by Butterworths for the book in our current catalogue.

Typeset by CCC, printed and bound
in Great Britain by William Clowes,
Beccles and London

Preface

The forerunner to this book, published under the title *Introduction to the Consumer Credit Act 1974*, was produced at some speed in order to satisfy the immediate need for an introductory guide to a complex and far-reaching piece of legislation.   The lapse of nearly five years before the appearance of this new work is due primarily to my own natural indolence, encouraged by a sympathetic Government whose lethargic programme for implementing the Act reflects a satisfying awareness of the problems of authorship.

Nevertheless, there has been considerable activity since 1974.   The licensing system is fully operative and, indeed, renewals of licences are already coming up for consideration; regulations have been made covering a range of matters, including exempt agreements, computation of the cost of credit, variation of agreements and credit reference agencies; and several important sections of the Act dealing with other topics have been brought into force, such as the provisions relating to the creditor's liability for the defaults of the supplier and the reopening of extortionate credit bargains.   In addition, other legislation has been enacted bearing on credit and supply transactions, of which the most significant example is the Unfair Contract Terms Act 1977.

In this work (which also features as Division I of my looseleaf publication *Consumer Credit Legislation*) the old book has been substantially expanded, partly to reflect a more considered analysis of the Act and partly to provide by way of background a picture of the major classes of credit institution, the principal types of credit, the instruments employed and the legal characteristics of each credit form.   The contents of what was previously Chapter 25 (Other Duties of the Director) have been absorbed into a new chapter dealing with the administration of the Act.   A complete new chapter is devoted to the concept of credit, a fundamental question on which the Act itself offers little guidance.   The treatment of the creditor's liability for misrepresentations and breaches of contract by the supplier has been considerably enlarged so as to deal more fully with the common law aspects of the supply contract and to depict the main features (and some of the difficulties) of the Unfair Contract Terms Act.   Finally, the complex subject of rate computation and disclosure is examined in detail in a lengthy new chapter.   The result is that, with the addition of other chapters dealing with a range of different topics, the work now contains eight new chapters, namely:

Chapter 2—The Consumer Credit Institutions
Chapter 3—The Instruments of Consumer Credit
Chapter 4—The Common Law Setting
Chapter 6—Administration of the Act
Chapter 8—The Concept of Credit
Chapter 13—Rate Computation and Disclosure
Chapter 32—Agreements with a Foreign Element
Chapter 35—Consumer Credit in the EEC

The aim throughout has been to set the statutory provisions in the context of prevailing practice and to illustrate the underlying policy and functional approach of the legislation, as well as the problems of interpretation raised by the Act and the practical difficulties in giving effect to some of the provisions. The work can no longer be properly described as a mere introduction, and the title has been altered to reflect the change.

I am indebted to my colleague Mr. John Yelland for many helpful ideas. My warm thanks are also due to Butterworths editorial staff for their painstaking labours in connection with the publication; and, once again, to Mrs. Anne Lyons for compiling the admirable index.

May 1979

R. M. Goode
Faculty of Laws,
Queen Mary College,
London

Preface to Introduction to the Consumer Credit Act 1974

"He that practiseth usury goeth to Hell; and he that practiseth it not tendeth to destitution." Thus spoke Benvenuto da Imola some six hundred years ago, neatly pinpointing one of the many problems with which the Committee on Consumer Credit, under its outstanding chairman Lord Crowther, had to grapple during the two and a half years preceding the publication of its Report in March 1971.

The Consumer Credit Bill, having fallen with the advent of the General Election in February, rose like a phoenix from the ashes of the previous Administration and after many vicissitudes reached the statute book on 31st July 1974, a date that will be indelibly engraved on every financier's heart. The Act implements almost in their entirety those recommendations of the Crowther Committee relating to the reform of the law of *consumer* credit. The equally radical proposals of the Committee for restructuring of the general law affecting security in personal property, strongly influenced by Article 9 of the American Uniform Commercial Code, have not as yet been adopted. They are receiving further study from the Government, which is expected in due course to engage in consultations with interested parties. There can be little doubt of the need for reform of English personal property security law, which remains in a parlous state and is certainly no model to offer to Britain's partners in Europe.

The consumer credit industry is complex and sophisticated. It offers a wide range of credit facilities, and utilises an extraordinary diversity of legal instruments—hire-purchase, conditional sale, credit sale, rental, trading checks, credit cards, secured and unsecured loans and overdrafts. Hitherto, each of these legal forms has been subjected to different rules of law. One set of statutes has regulated hire-purchase and instalment sales contracts; another set has governed loans and security. Some hybrid forms, such as check trading and credit cards, have occupied a twilight zone, stealing within the penumbra of the Moneylenders Acts whilst never conclusively subjugated by them. Certain lenders, notably banks, have been free altogether from the shackles of moneylending legislation.

The Consumer Credit Act, when fully operative, will sweep away this fragmented legislation, replacing it with what is probably the most advanced, and certainly the most comprehensive, Code ever to be enacted in any country in the sphere of consumer credit. The Act draws into its net all types of consumer credit, of whatever legal form, and applies to them and to consumer hire a comprehensive licensing system, to be administered by the Director General of Fair Trading, and a detailed set of provisions regulating the conduct of business, entry into agreements and the rights and duties of the parties. The old legalistic distinctions between loan credit and sale credit are discarded, and all forms of consumer credit are subjected to a unified system of control, save only for such variations in treatment as reflect differences of practical importance in the nature, function and mechanics of the various types of credit.

It cannot be said that the Consumer Credit Act is a simple enactment. To expect simplicity in the regulation of activities so complex and variegated would be to ask the impossible. What is important is that the underlying concepts shall be soundly based and logically expressed. The draftsman, faced with formidable problems of analysis and presentation and obliged to engage in massive amendment in the short period allowed by the Parliamentary timetable, has performed his task with consummate skill. Many of the defects in the original version of the Bill have been eliminated. These included a small omission that would have resulted in the repeal of all the existing legislation before most of the new statutory provisions had been brought into force, thus producing a glorious interregnum in which creditors' rights would be altogether free of statutory control! Happily (or otherwise, depending on your viewpoint) this was picked up at an early stage, together with various other points of difficulty, so that whilst the Act remains far from perfect it is none the less both sound and imaginative, and when backed by regulations should substantially achieve the desired objectives. A brief historical introduction to the Act will be found in chapter 1, and a bird's eye view of the statutory provisions in chapter 2.

This book is designed to meet the immediate needs of an introductory guide to what is undoubtedly a most complex piece of legislation. Necessarily, therefore, it has been written at speed, and though reasonably detailed it does not purport to be an exhaustive analysis of the new Act, which requires closer acquaintanceship and reflection over a period of time before the many underlying problems and subtleties begin to surface. Within this limitation I have endeavoured to provide not a literal translation of the statutory provisions—which could be done by the intelligent reader himself and might leave him just as mystified at the end—but an insight into the structure of the Act, the purpose and significance of its elaborate classification of credit agreements and the impact of the various provisions on specific types of transaction. To that end, I have treated the various aspects of regulation in an order somewhat different from that adopted by the draftsman, examining these in the sequence in which they would normally appear in a typical transaction, whilst at the same time bringing together widely separated sections that require to be read in conjunction. Wherever possible, I have indicated not merely the general effect of a statutory provision but its particular relevance to different types of consumer credit agreement, illustrating this with numerous examples.

Whilst the Act itself is obviously the central feature of the book, many of the statutory provisions can only be understood in the context of the existing law, whether the common law or another statute. Moreover, the Act does not provide a complete code of rights. Other statutes confer rights on parties to a credit agreement, or restrict the exclusion of liability under such an agreement, and the common law also imposes certain restraints on freedom of contract. I have therefore woven into the analysis of the Consumer Credit Act concise expositions of the remedies for breach of duty available at common law, the common law doctrine of fundamental breach and the rule against penalties, and have summarised relevant provisions of various statutes, including the Misrepresentation Act 1967, the Trade Descriptions Act 1968 and the Supply of Goods (Implied Terms) Act 1973. I have also given as detailed a picture as I can of the likely shape of regulations to be made under the Act, in the light of the very informative White Paper on the *Reform of the Law on Consumer Credit* and such other information as was available to me. The regulations will be phased, and it is the intention to keep the book up to date with supplements as appropriate.

A number of provisions of the Consumer Credit Act reproduce, albeit in somewhat different form, existing provisions of the Hire-Purchase Act 1965. These I have analysed in such detail as is appropriate for a book of this kind. For a comprehensive study of the current hire-purchase legislation, and of the common law rules governing hire-purchase, instalment sale and leasing agreements, the reader is referred to my text book *Hire-Purchase Law and Practice* (2nd Edition), where these are exhaustively examined.

As so often in the past, my warm thanks are due to Mr. C. McNeil Greig, Director of the Hire Purchase Trade Association, for his illuminating comments on various problems and for supplying me so rapidly with details of amendments to the Bill which due to printing problems were not available through the ordinary channels. Mr. Derek Hyde, the Assistant Secretary of the Department of Prices and Consumer Protection having charge of the Bill, was kind enough to read the proofs and save me from various errors I should otherwise have committed. His remarkable mastery of the statutory provisions has been of the greatest value to me, and I am deeply grateful. I should also like to thank my colleague, Mr. John Yelland, who performed a similar proof-reading service and whose lively and penetrating comments on the proofs, and on the Bill itself, have been most helpful.

For the typing of the manuscript, carried out impeccably at lightning speed, my warm thanks are due first to my wonderfully efficient secretary Mrs. Wendy Mann, and secondly to Mrs. Kathleen Gerroll and Mrs. Mary Griffin of the Rushgrove Secretarial Agency.

Finally, I should like to thank the publishers, Messrs. Butterworths, for the efficiency and speed with which they handled the production of the book; and to add a special word of appreciation to the printers, Messrs. Butler and Tanner, who laboured with such skill and perseverance to ensure its prompt publication.

The Consumer Credit Act is a landmark in the regulation of consumer credit which is likely to influence developments not only in this country but overseas. It is also a further monument to Geoffrey Crowther, whose inspired chairmanship of the Committee on Consumer Credit brought the reform of consumer credit law to fruition.

October 1974   R. M. Goode

Table of Contents

Contents

LIST OF TABLES

Chapter — Para.

Table of Statutes

References in this Table to *"Statutes"* are to Halsbury's Statutes of England (Third Edition) showing the volume and page at which the annotated text of the Act will be found.

Paragraph numbers printed in bold type indicate where the section of an act is set out in part or in full.

Table of Statutes

Table of Cases

In the following Table references are given to the English and Empire Digest showing where a digest of the case will be found

A

B

PARA.

1. How it all Began

Early history

For nearly 800 years consumer credit as a subject of regulation was almost entirely ignored by successive monarchs, by Parliament and by the common law. Apart from enactments controlling usurious loans and the activities of pawn-brokers, the intervention of the legislature prior to 1854 was virtually non-existent. The courts themselves stood back and, though willing on occasion to grant relief to the hard-pressed baronet's son who had mortgaged his inheritance, saw little reason to interfere with freely concluded contracts. "The Chancery mends no man's bargain", said Lord Nottingham in 1676, and few dissented from so self-evident a truth. Indeed, the primary concern of the law in the field of credit was not to protect the debtor from his creditor but to ensure that a person did not defeat his creditors at large by secret transfers of his assets to a third party. This was less of a problem in the early days of English law, when the pledge was almost the only recognised form of security and possession of the chattel thus passed from debtor to creditor. But when the law came to accept the non-possessory chattel mortgage as a valid form of security, the matter became more serious, for a person might mortgage his goods to secure an indebtedness but, being left in possession, obtain credit on the faith of his apparent ownership, and the mortgage would then be set up against his creditors when they came to secure satisfaction from the debtor's estate. This led to the passing of the Fraudulent Conveyances 1571, which rendered void conveyances in fraud of creditors. A transfer of goods unaccompanied by possession was almost invariably treated by the courts as fraudulent, a rule firmly established in *Twyne's Case* in 1602. [1]

The Bills of Sale Acts

In 1854, the first Bills of Sale Act was passed, requiring registration of written bills of sale (in the same year, removing with one hand what had been given with the other, Parliament abolished all existing usury legislation). With the new registration system, courts were able to take a somewhat less jaundiced view of bills of sale, for an unregistered bill was void against creditors. [2]

The Act of 1854 was amended in 1866 and eventually replaced by the Bills of Sale Act 1878. Fours years later the 1878 Act was supplemented by the Bills of Sale Act (1878) Amendment Act 1882, which not only dealt with certain further problems confronting a bankrupt's creditors—in particular, the ability of a trader, under the rule in *Holroyd* v. *Marshall*, to mortgage his after-acquired stock in trade, leaving nothing for the general body of creditors—but for the first time recognised that the debtor himself needed a measure of protection against the grantee of the bill. Hence a requirement that a mortgage bill of sale be in accordance with a statutory form, and duly witnessed; the prohibition of a bill of sale over after-acquired property (which is the reason why, with certain exceptions, an individual cannot grant an effective floating charge); and the outlawing of certain other contractual provisions considered offensive. The Bills of Sale Acts, amended in 1890 and 1891, remain with us to this day. [3]

The Moneylenders Acts

Apart from the Bills of Sale Acts and pawnbroking legislation, the lenders of money enjoyed an unparalleled era of freedom and prosperity between 1854 and 1900, and serious abuses resulted. Trickery and extortion were rampant and borrowers suffered misery and hardship through ruthless enforcement of security. The Report of the House of Commons Select Committee on Money-Lending, published in 1898, showed that one lender had admitted charging on occasion interest at rates as high as 3,000 per cent, while another confessed that to avoid the notoriety likely to result from his activities he had traded under no less than 34 different aliases. It was therefore scarcely surprising that two years later the first Moneylenders Act was passed, providing for registration (but not licensing) of moneylenders and empowering the courts to re-open harsh and unconscionable moneylending transactions. The Act of 1900, though a step in the right direction, was not a very effective piece of legislation. The absence of any licensing system meant that control of moneylenders was left to the civil courts, acting on the individual initiative of an aggrieved borrower. But most borrowers in the category for whose protection the Act was designed were unlikely to be able to afford the luxury of legal representation, even if they would otherwise have been willing to involve themselves in litigious procedures. [4]

The Money-lenders Act 1900 had a further curious weakness, the full impact of which was not to become apparent for some considerable time. Instead of delineating the boundary of protection for the debtor according to the purpose, size or type of the transaction or the status of the debtor (in particular, whether the debtor was a company or an individual), the Act concentrated on the status of the lender. Lending by a moneylender was within the Act; lending by an exempted category such as a bank was not. Conversely, the Act, though designed as a source of consumer protection, was not confined to consumer transactions. It applied equally to commercial loans, even if to registered companies. This situation was to continue unchanged for the next 74 years. [5]

Moneylending legislation, after amendment of the 1900 Act in 1911 was substantially strengthened by the passing of the Moneylenders Act 1927, which substituted annual licensing for registration and imposed severe restrictions on methods by which a moneylender could seek business. In particular, he was not permitted to employ agents or canvassers or to send out unsolicited circulars or advertisements, and even the right to advertise in newspapers was closely circumscribed. The loan contract had to be evidenced by a note or memorandum in writing and a copy supplied to the borrower; and other detailed requirements were imposed. Unfortunately, the 1927 Act, though going a considerable way towards protection for the small borrower, also seriously inhibited legitimate business transactions. Those engaged in granting commercial loans who were not bankers or otherwise within an exempt category were controlled by the Act in the same way as the small loan business; and since the slightest infraction of a minute technicality would render a loan irrecoverable, with no power in the court to grant relief, very sizeable loans—sometimes as high as £50,000 or more—might be placed at risk through a technical defence by a corporate borrower which was wholly lacking in merit. [**6**]

These difficulties with moneylending legislation had two consequences. First, they were a major factor in the development of instalment selling and hire-purchase, a form of credit which by-passed the Moneylenders Acts. Secondly— and this was a post-war development—they led companies to explore other methods of escape, particularly by the formation of banking companies, so that a completely new system of secondary banking developed, enjoying the same immunity from the Moneylenders Acts as was possessed by the clearing banks. Initially, these banks suffered the disadvantage that there was no official machinery by which their banking status could be established for the purpose of the Moneylenders Acts without their having to prove such status in a court of law. This was to some extent remedied by s. 123 of the Companies Act 1967, which empowered the Board of Trade to issue a certificate on application that the applicant could properly be treated as carrying on the business of banking for the purpose of the Moneylenders Acts. Early applicants who thought that such certificates were designed to allow non-banking hire-purchase companies to obtain a recognition of banking status were speedily disillusioned. The Board of Trade insisted that banking activities had to be carried on which fulfilled the criteria for banking laid down by the Court of Appeal in *United Dominions Trust, Ltd.* v. *Kirkwood*, [1966] 2 Q.B. 431, [1966] 1 All E.R. 968 and also satisfied other, rather imprecise, criteria developed by the Board to ensure that certificates were limited to companies that were reputable and financially sound. Even so, s. 123 certificates were granted too freely in the early years of the new system, and following serious abuses by certain s. 123 banks, applications for certificates were temporarily frozen in April 1973, pending the formulation of much more stringent criteria, which came into operation in August of that year. It was during this period that the government asked leading finance houses to adhere to a Voluntary Code providing for such matters as disclosure of the true rate of borrowing, a cooling off period and restrictions on sales by mortgagees. What constitutes the business of moneylending has never been exhaustively determined, but both check trading and the issuance of credit cards would seem to involve the lending of money. See further para. [**95**]. [**7**]

Instalment sale and hire-purchase

English law in the credit field has always been characterised by a sharp distinction between the regulation of loan credit on the one hand and that of sale credit on the other. The lending of money, as we have seen, was subject to usury legislation prior to 1854, and from 1900 was controlled by the moneylending legislation referred to above. The rights of the mortgagee under a written chattel mortgage, or security bill of sale, were governed by the Bills of Sale Acts 1878 and

1882 and by the small amending Acts of 1890 and 1891. But the sale of goods on credit has never been considered as constituting a loan in English law and thus did not attract the operation of the Moneylenders Acts. Similarly, the reservation of title under a conditional sale or hire-purchase agreement is not a security for a loan and is thus outside the Bills of Sale Acts. [8]

The general statute dealing with contracts of sale is the Sale of Goods Act 1893, which *inter alia* sets out a range of implied terms in favour of the buyer. This enactment was originally a permissive statute in that the parties were free to contract out of its provisions. The Supply of Goods (Implied Terms) Act 1973, in addition to introducing modifications into the statutory implied terms, drastically altered the *laissez-faire* approach of the 1893 Act by making void clauses in consumer sales and consumer hire-purchase agreements purporting to exclude or restrict the terms implied under the 1893 Act, and by rendering such clauses unenforceable even in non-consumer transactions to the extent that they were unreasonable. This part of the 1973 Act has been repealed and replaced by the more wide-ranging provisions of the Unfair Contract Terms Act 1977. These various provisions have been reinforced by the Consumer Transactions (Restrictions on Statements) Order 1976, as amended by the Consumer Transactions (Restrictions on Statements) (Amendment) Order 1978, which *inter alia* makes it an offence to incorporate in a consumer sale or hire-purchase agreement exemption clauses that are void under the 1977 Act. [9]

The common law status of hire-purchase agreements is outlined in Chapter 4. Suffice it to say at this stage that at common law a hire-purchase agreement is not a contract of sale and thus falls outside the scope of the Sale of Goods Act and the provisions of the Factors Act 1889 dealing with sale contracts. However, with the advent of hire-purchase legislation the treatment of hire-purchase and conditional sale was largely assimilated. [10]

The first enactment dealing specifically with hire-purchase was the Hire-Purchase and Small Debt (Scotland) Act 1932. England followed with the Hire-Purchase Act 1938, which was subsequently amended by the Hire-Purchase Acts 1954 and 1964 and later replaced in a consolidating enactment, the Hire-Purchase Act 1965. The 1965 Act applied to all hire-purchase and instalment sale agreements under which the hire-purchase price or total purchase price did not exceed £2,000 (since raised to £5,000) and the hirer or buyer was not a body corporate. It contained provisions regulating the formalities of contract, the right of cancellation of a hirer or buyer signing the agreement elsewhere than at appropriate trade premises, the non-excludable terms implied in favour of the hirer or conditional buyer and a range of matters designed for his protection, including a prohibition against enforcement of a right to recover the goods from him when one-third of the hire-purchase price or total purchase price had been paid or tendered and the agreement had not been terminated by him. [11]

The advertising of goods as available for disposal on hire-purchase or instalment sale was regulated by the Advertisements (Hire-Purchase) Act 1967, a measure that represented a consolidation of the Advertisements (Hire-Purchase) Act 1957 and amendments made to that Act by the Hire-Purchase Act 1964. [12]

In addition, there have been several provisions of different statutes dealing with the effect of a wrongful disposition of goods held by the disposer on hire-purchase or conditional sale. These are still in force. Section 9 of the Factors Act 1889 and s. 25 (2) of the Sale of Goods Act 1893 provide in effect that in given

4

conditions the delivery of goods by a conditional buyer to a *bona fide* purchaser can pass title to that purchaser, even though the conditional buyer has not yet become the owner. These provisions never applied to hire-purchase agreements, and were also made inapplicable to conditional sale agreements within the Hire-Purchase Act 1965, an exemption continued by the Consumer Credit Act in paragraphs 2 and 4 of the Fourth Schedule. [**13**]

By Part III of the Hire-Purchase Act 1964 (which is still in force) a disposition of a motor vehicle by a hirer under a hire-purchase agreement or a buyer under a conditional sale agreement, if made to a *bona fide* private purchaser without notice of the hire-purchase or conditional sale agreement, was made effective to transfer to the purchaser the title of the person who had let the vehicle on hire-purchase or agreed to sell it on conditional sale. This was so whether or not the hire-purchase or conditional sale agreement was within the limits of the Hire-Purchase Act 1965. [**14**]

Finally, by s. 1 of the Emergency Laws (Re-enactments and Repeals) Act 1964—embodying in permanent statutory form powers originally conferred by regulation 55 of the Defence (General) Regulations 1939—the Board of Trade (later the Department of Trade and Industry and now the Department of Prices and Consumer Protection) was empowered to make orders restricting the disposal of goods by way of hire-purchase or instalment sale. Such orders (which do not apply to loan contracts) were designed not as a measure of consumer protection but to protect the economy from becoming overheated by inflationary tendencies supposedly generated by consumer credit. The orders provided minimum down-payments and maximum payment periods for hire-purchase and instalment sale agreements covering a range of goods—mainly, though not exclusively, consumer goods. Rental agreements were regulated by parallel orders requiring advance rentals and controlling the period of hire and spread of rental payments. The orders current at the time of the Crowther Report (referred to below) were the Hire-Purchase and Credit Sale Agreements (Control) Order 1969 and the Control of Hiring Order 1969. These were revoked in July 1971 but were restored on the 18th December 1973 as the Hire-Purchase and Credit Sale Agreements (Control) Order 1973 and the Control of Hiring Order 1973. The orders currently in force are the Control of Hiring Order 1977 and the Hire-Purchase and Credit Sale Agreements (Control) Order 1976, as amended by the Hire-Purchase and Credit Sale Agreements (Control) (Amendment) Orders 1977 and 1978. Unlike their predecessors, these orders do not apply to the supply of goods for the purpose of or in the course of the trade or business of the hirer or buyer, a relaxation which has generated an enormous increase in business, particularly in the field of car leasing and contract hire. [**15**]

The Crowther Report

The Committee on Consumer Credit, under the chairmanship of Lord Crowther, was appointed in September 1968, when it embarked on what was to become the most wide-ranging review of consumer credit ever undertaken in this country—indeed, the first comprehensive government study of this important subject. For various reasons the Committee felt it impracticable to examine the law of consumer credit in isolation—particularly since the Bills of Sale Acts and the Moneylenders Acts were not confined to consumer transactions—and they extended their study to encompass the general legal framework within which the granting of credit and the taking of security were required to operate. The Committee's Report, published in March 1971, covered the entire field of consumer credit in Britain. After discussing at length the social and economic implications of credit and recommending that terms control (see para. [**15**]) should be abolished, the Report proceeded to a detailed evaluation of the law relating to credit transactions. The Committee concluded that the existing law was gravely defective, the most serious weaknesses being the following:

  (a) *The regulation of transactions according to their form instead of according to their substance and function.* This was reflected in the sharp distinction drawn between loans for the purchase of goods and the extension of credit by deferment of the price under a hire-purchase or instalment sale agreement. One set of statutes governed the lending of money, another the taking of security for repayment. Sale credit, however, was not considered to involve the making of a loan, and the reservation of title was not in law equated with a security interest, so that hire-purchase and instalment sale transactions were altogether outside the above two sets of statutes and were regulated independently by a third set, whose provisions were completely different.

  (b) *The failure to distinguish consumer from commercial transactions.* Thus, the Moneylenders Acts, though designed as a measure of consumer protection, were equally applicable to loans to companies for business purposes. Similarly, the Bills of Sale Acts, though not according protection to companies, did not draw any other distinction between consumer and commercial transactions.

  (c) *The artificial separation of the law relating to lending from the law relating to security for loans.* In particular, there was no link between the Bills of Sale Acts and the Moneylenders Acts, Parliament having evidently failed to appreciate that the security for a loan was an integral part of the loan transaction itself.

  (d) *The absence of any rational policy in relation to third party rights.* Thus, the buyer under a conditional sale agreement (but not a hirer under a hire-purchase agreement) could in certain circumstances pass a good title to an innocent third party under the Factors Act 1889, but not if the conditional sale agreement was within the Hire-Purchase Act 1965. Both a conditional buyer and a hirer under a hire-purchase agreement could pass a good title to a *bona fide* private purchaser of a motor vehicle, pursuant to Part III of the Hire-Purchase Act 1964. The grantor of a duly registered mortgage bill of sale could not transfer a good title under either of the above Acts. Quite apart from these anomalies, there was no official machinery for registering the reservation of title under a conditional sale or hire-purchase agreement.

  (e) *Excessive technicality.* The slightest infraction of the Moneylenders Acts, however technical, would deprive the lender of his right to recover the loan, however large. Similarly, infringement of the fearsome technicalities of the Bills of Sale Acts might invalidate the security.

  (f) *Inadequate protection for the consumer in credit transactions.* This was due to various factors, in particular:

6

   (i)   the distinction previously mentioned between sale credit and loan credit;

   (ii) the absence of statutory control of the cost of credit in transactions outside the Moneylenders Acts;

   (iii) the absence of any requirement that the consumer should be informed of the true cost of borrowing;

   (iv) the absence of any legal requirement to give a rebate for early settlement;

   (v) the use of negotiable instruments to defeat defences that the consumer might otherwise have been able to raise;

   (vi) the total freedom of rental transactions from legislative control;

  (vii) inadequate protection for those entering into contracts of guarantee and indemnity in relation to consumer credit transactions;

 (viii) the absence of any effective machinery for enforcing compliance with the legislation. [**16**]

The Crowther Committee considered the law to be so unsatisfactory that it was useless to tinker about further with piecemeal amendments. They therefore recommended repeal of the entire range of existing legislation affecting credit and security in personal property—the Hire-Purchase Acts, the Bills of Sale Acts, the Moneylenders Acts, etc—and their replacement by two new enactments which would clearly distinguish between rules of general application and rules for consumer credit transactions, viz:

  (*a*) a Lending and Security Act, which would apply across the board, would rationalise the treatment of security interests and conflicts between secured parties, would establish a security register and would facilitate legitimate business transactions;

  (*b*) a Consumer Sale and Loan Act, which would harmonise the treatment of all forms of consumer credit, including consumer rental transactions, thus applying a uniform code to sale and loan credit agreements, with strengthened protection for the consumer and proper enforcement through a licensing system operated by a Consumer Credit Commissioner. [**17**]

The Government's response to the Crowther Report

Despite the overwhelmingly favourable reactions to the Crowther Report, both from the credit industry and from consumer organisations, the government's initial response was muted. This was understandable, since the Department of Trade and Industry wanted time to work out in more detail the implications of the recommendations. Some 15 months elapsed before the government was induced to break its silence as the result of a debate initiated by Baroness Phillips in the House of Lords. In the course of this, it became clear that whilst the government accepted nearly all the recommendations of the Report in relation to *consumer* credit, it was firmly reserving its position on the more fundamental proposals for restructuring of the basic law of lending and security generally.

> "Central to the Committee's proposals in this field is their proposed register of security interests. We can so far find no convincing evidence that, were such a register to be established,

it would be sufficiently used to justify its existence ... If the proposal for a register is in question, the basis of many other of the Committee's suggestions must also be questioned. For example, complex rules to govern third party rights, which the Committee began to draft but did not complete, are predicated on the existence of such a register. It is by no means certain that, when fully elaborated, such rules would be less complex and easier to understand than the present rules, which are based partly on Statute and partly on precedent. If no register were to be established, the Committee's proposals for third party rights would fall and we would either have to leave the law as it now stands or work out a new set of rules using the Committee's principles as a starting point" (Earl of Limerick in *H.L. Debates*, 28th June 1972, cols. 974–975). [18]

The author's answers to this reasoning have been fully deployed elsewhere (see "Credit Law—The Case for Reform", *Credit*, March 1973, p. 12). Suffice it to say that at the time the above statement was made, there were already no less than seven different registers of security interests in force; and within a matter of weeks the Minister's own Department proceeded with legislation for the creation of an eighth, the Register of Aircraft Mortgages! [19]

The Voluntary Code

Having accepted the recommendations of the Crowther Committee in relation to consumer credit the Government nevertheless recognised that it would take a little time to prepare legislation, and was anxious to take more immediate steps to alleviate concern that had built up concerning certain consumer loan practices. A particular target was the second mortgage market, which had attracted considerable opprobrium on various grounds. Brokers advertised loans as if they were principals when in fact the true lenders standing behind them were s. 123 banks. High-pressure salesmanship was applied to house owners to borrow money against the substantial equity in their houses resulting from the great increase in property values, and since the lenders were recognised as banks for the purpose of the Moneylenders Acts none of the constraints imposed by these enactments applied, so that lenders were free to use agents and canvassers (some of whom were of doubtful repute) to engage in the doorstep peddling of credit. Charges were misrepresented or stated in misleading fashion, interest being quoted in terms of a flat rate (see para. [479]) and without taking account of additions made in the form of "administration" or "service" charges, brokerage and survey fees; and in many cases the overall cost of credit was extremely high, if not extortionate. [20]

Accordingly in February 1973 the Government announced the introduction of a Voluntary Code which it expected those lending to the public to observe pending the introduction of legislation to implement the Crowther Report. The Code (still operative) sets out general guidelines for loans to individuals, dealing with disclosure of the cost of credit (expressed both as an amount and as a true percentage rate) and with brokerage commission, and separate guidelines applicable to loans to individuals secured on land, designed to provide a cooling-off period in which the borrower can withdraw from a transaction without charge, coupled with certain restrictions on the mortgagee's remedies in the event of the mortgagor's default. [21]

The White Paper

In September 1973, after extensive discussions with interested parties and the dissemination of a number of consultation papers, the government produced a White Paper on the *Reform of the Law on Consumer Credit* (Cmnd. 5427). In this, the government indicated its intention of implementing by legislation virtually the whole of the Crowther Committee's recommendations on consumer credit law, with certain additional safeguards for the consumer that had been shown to be necessary as the result of experiences after the publication of the Report. Two particular deviations from Crowther were the increase in the financial limits for protection from a total purchase price of £2,000 to an *advance* of £5,000—reflecting a substantial drop in the value of money since the Crowther recommendations were formulated—and considerably stronger protection for hirers under hiring contracts. In most other respects, the White Paper closely followed the Crowther Report. The White Paper was a particularly useful document in that it not only depicted in the text the scope of the forthcoming Consumer Credit Bill but also set out in Appendices much of the proposed content of regulations to be made under the Consumer Credit Act, including mathematical formulae for statement of the cost of borrowing in terms of a true percentage rate. [**22**]

The White Paper also set out the government's latest thinking in regard to the Committee's proposals for the fundamental restructuring of the general law of credit and security in the Lending and Security Act.

> "The Committee's proposals are for radical reform in a complex field and their implementation would require another major Bill, central to which would be the establishment of a Register of Security Interests and detailed priority provisions depending upon its existence and use. The government accept that there are aspects of the existing law in this field which cause difficulty, but they do not have sufficient evidence either of a need for such major recasting of existing law on new principles or of general support for the particular solution proposed by the Committee. They intend to institute consultations with those most closely concerned in the light of the situation existing after passage of the Consumer Credit Bill" (para. 14). [**23**]

The Consumer Credit Act

The government lost no further time in proceeding with the consumer credit legislation, i.e. Stage 2 of the Crowther proposals. The White Paper had been published in September 1973. By the beginning of November a Consumer Credit Bill had been presented, running to some 96 pages. The Bill was widely welcomed on both sides of the House for the clarity of its drafting and the comprehensive nature of its provisions. It was accepted as a non-controversial, non-partisan measure, and all parties pledged their support for its speedy enactment. By the beginning of February 1974 it had completed its Committee Stage in the House of Commons and the wind looked fair for a speedy passage through its remaining stages, when, in the light of the prevailing economic crisis and a decision by the members of the National Union of Mineworkers to give their Executive a mandate for a strike, the government called a general election, Parliament was dissolved and the Consumer Credit Bill, with 88 other measures, was lost. However, almost immediately after the election, the new administration reintroduced the Bill in substantially the same form in the House of Lords and it was passed as the Consumer Credit Act on 31st July 1974. [24]

Impact on existing legislation

Table 1 shows the structure of consumer credit legislation prior to the Consumer Credit Act 1974. Table 2 depicts the dramatic changes effected by the Act. The old sale credit/loan credit dichotomy disappears completely, and with it the institution-based character of lending legislation. Under the Consumer Credit Act the status of the lender become largely irrelevant. What matters is the nature of the business being carried on and, as regards the control of specific transactions, the amount of credit advanced and whether the debtor/hirer is a body corporate or an individual. For Tables 1 and 2 see paras. [26]–[28] on pp. 11–13. [25]

Whilst some part of the Act came into force on the day of its passing (31st July 1974), most of its provisions were left to be brought into operation in stages by orders made by the Secretary of State, different days being appointed for the commencement of different provisions. Progress has been painfully slow and after five years little of the Act is yet operative apart from the licensing system. [29]

When fully operative, the Act will repeal the Hire-Purchase Act 1965, the Advertisements (Hire Purchase) Act 1967, the Moneylenders Acts 1900–1927 and the Pawnbrokers Acts 1872–1960, replacing them with a new and comprehensive structure of regulation covering all forms of consumer credit. Thus has begun the first phase of the reform of English credit law, which has been characterised by an unusual degree of parliamentary bi-partisanship. The Crowther Committee, set up by a Labour Government, reported to a Conservative administration. The latter introduced the Consumer Credit Bill, which was continued and completed by its Labour successor. The Act is influencing developments not only here but abroad. It has been closely studied in America and the Commonwealth and forms the basis of an EEC draft Directive on Consumer Credit which the Commission has recently submitted to the Council. But Phase 1 of Crowther, the reform of the general legal framework underpinning secured transactions in personal property, has yet to come. Meanwhile, the Bills of Sale Acts and all the anomalies created by other statutes in relation to third party rights in secured transactions will continue to cause hardship and injustice and to restrict our ability to influence the adoption in Europe of a modern personal property security law. The task of modernisation is not an easy one, and formulation of detailed rules will require extensive study and consultation. Nevertheless, it is hoped that it will not be too long before work can be put in hand with a view to implementation of this most important part of the Crowther recommendations. [30]

The new legislative structure

It may be helpful at this point to summarise the structure of legislation affecting credit when the Consumer Credit Act has been brought fully into force.

(a) *Licensing and enforcement*

The Consumer Credit Act requires those carrying on a consumer credit, consumer hire or ancillary credit business to be licensed. The licensing system is now fully operative and is described in detail in Chapter 11.

TABLE 1. STRUCTURE OF CONSUMER CREDIT LEGISLATION PRIOR TO THE CONSUMER CREDIT ACT 1974

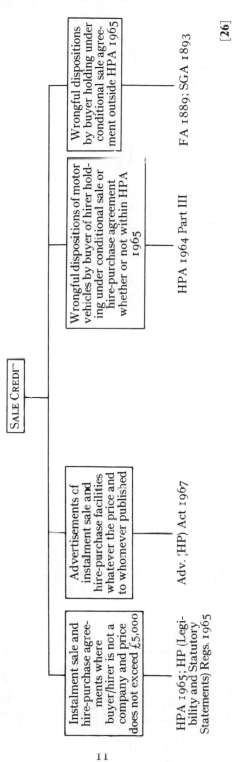

Instalment sale and hire-purchase agreements where buyer/hirer is not a company and price does not exceed £5,000	Advertisements of instalment sale and hire-purchase facilities whatever the price and to whomever published
HPA 1965; HP (Legibility and Statutory Statements) Regs. 1965	Adv. (HP) Act 1967

SALE CREDIT

Wrongful dispositions of motor vehicles by buyer of hirer holding under conditional sale or hire-purchase agreement whether or not within HPA 1965	Wrongful dispositions by buyer holding under conditional sale agreement outside HPA 1965
HPA 1964 Part III	FA 1889; SGA 1893

[26]

TABLE I—*cont.*

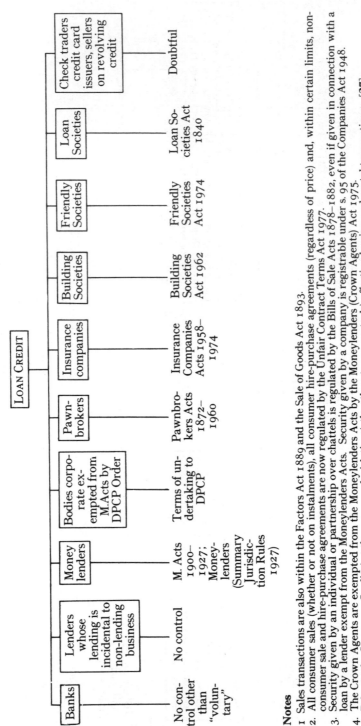

			LOAN CREDIT					
Banks	Lenders whose lending is incidental to non-lending business	Money lenders	Bodies corporate exempted from M.Acts by DPCP Order	Pawnbrokers	Insurance companies	Building Societies	Friendly Societies	Loan Societies	Check traders credit card issuers, sellers on revolving credit
No control other than "voluntary"	No control	M. Acts 1900–1927; Moneylenders (Summary Jurisdiction Rules 1927)	Terms of undertaking to DPCP	Pawnbrokers Acts 1872–1960	Insurance Companies Acts 1958–1974	Building Societies Act 1962	Friendly Societies Act 1974	Loan Societies Act 1840	Doubtful

Notes

1. Sales transactions are also within the Factors Act 1889 and the Sale of Goods Act 1893.
2. All consumer sales (whether or not on instalments), all consumer hire-purchase agreements (regardless of price) and, within certain limits, non-consumer sale and hire-purchase agreements are now regulated by the Unfair Contract Terms Act 1977.
3. Security given over chattels is regulated by the Bills of Sale Acts 1878–1882, even if given in connection with a loan by a lender exempt from the Moneylenders Acts. Security given by a company is registrable under s. 95 of the Companies Act 1948.
4. The Crown Agents are exempted from the Moneylenders Acts by the Moneylenders (Crown Agents) Act 1975.
5. Prior to the Consumer Credit Act there was no legislation (other than terms controls) affecting leasing and rental transactions. **[27]**

TABLE 2. STRUCTURE OF CONSUMER CREDIT LEGISLATION AFTER THE CONSUMER CREDIT ACT 1974

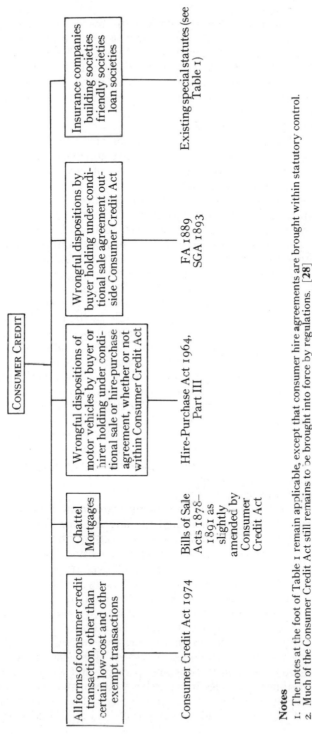

CONSUMER CREDIT

All forms of consumer credit transaction, other than certain low-cost and other exempt transactions	Chattel Mortgages	Wrongful dispositions of motor vehicles by buyer or hirer holding under conditional sale or hire-purchase agreement, whether or not within Consumer Credit Act	Wrongful dispositions by buyer holding under conditional sale agreement outside Consumer Credit Act	Insurance companies building societies friendly societies loan societies
Consumer Credit Act 1974	Bills of Sale Acts 1878–1891 as slightly amended by Consumer Credit Act	Hire-Purchase Act 1964, Part III	FA 1889 SGA 1893	Existing special statutes (see Table 1)

Notes

1. The notes at the foot of Table 1 remain applicable, except that consumer hire agreements are brought within statutory control.
2. Much of the Consumer Credit Act still remains to be brought into force by regulations. [**28**]

13

(b) *Seeking business*

Advertisements of credit facilities will now be controlled not by the Advertisements (Hire-Purchase) Act 1967 (which the Consumer Credit Act repeals) but by the Consumer Credit Act itself and regulations under it. This will also regulate canvassing, the issue of quotations and other methods of obtaining business (see Chapter 12). The Consumer Credit Act is not, of course, the only enactment affecting advertisements (see paras. [**439**]–[**441**]).

(c) *Rights of the parties* inter se

The rights of the parties to consumer credit agreements (including pledges to pawnbrokers), consumer hire agreements and linked transactions, and of sureties under contracts of guarantee and indemnity given in relation to such agreements, will be regulated by the Act and regulations, which will also control the taking and enforcement of security. All forms of consumer credit will be covered, and the Moneylenders Acts and Pawnbrokers Acts will be repealed. There is one aspect of the rights of the parties which will continue to be controlled by other legislation. Terms implied in favour of a person acquiring goods under a hire-purchase or instalment sale agreement are prescribed not by the Consumer Credit Act but, in the case of sale, by the Sale of Goods Act 1893, as amended by the Supply of Goods (Implied Terms) Act 1973, and, in the case of hire-purchase, by the 1973 Act. Contractual provisions purporting to exclude or limit such implied terms, or to qualify the remedies for their breach, are vulnerable under the Unfair Contract Terms Act 1977; and the inclusion of clauses made void by the Act is an offence (see para. [**439**]). What the Consumer Credit Act does is to give the debtor who has a claim for misrepresentation or breach of contract against the supplier a similar claim, in given conditions, against a connected lender, whether the supply contract relates to goods or to services (see Chapter 16). Moreover, the security provisions of the Consumer Credit Act do not entirely displace other legislation (*e.g.* the Bills of Sale Acts and the property statutes) affecting the rights of the parties to a secured transaction.

(d) *Rights of third parties*

The Consumer Credit Act is not, on the whole, concerned with the impact of a hire-purchase or conditional sale agreement or security on the rights of third parties into whose hands the goods or other security may pass. Thus, conflicts between the owner or conditional seller and one who purchases from the hirer or conditional buyer are governed by common law rules, by s. 9 of the Factors Act 1889, s. 25 (2) of the Sale of Goods Act 1893, Part III of the Hire-Purchase Act 1964 and certain provisions of the Torts (Interference with Goods) Act 1977. However the Consumer Credit Act (re-enacting in this respect the provisions of the Hire-Purchase Act 1965) excludes conditional sale agreements within the Act from the scope of the above-mentioned provisions of the Factors Act and Sale of Goods Act (see Fourth Schedule, paras. 2 and 4) and also in certain circumstances excludes hire-purchase agreements and conditional sale agreements within the Act from the scope of certain provisions of the Law of Distress Amendment Act 1908 and the Bankruptcy Act 1914

(Fourth Schedule, para. 5 and 6). In other respects, the Consumer Credit Act is silent on third party rights in relation to such agreements. Similarly, the efficacy of mortgage and other security interests *vis-à-vis* third parties, and the priority of successive security interests, continues to be governed largely by rules of common law and equity and by the Bills of Sale Acts and property statutes, though the Consumer Credit Act does have some impact in this area through various provisions dealing with ineffective securities (see paras. [**774**]–[**776**]).

(*e*) *Fair trading*

The powers of the Director General of Fair Trading under Parts II and III and Schedule 6 of the Fair Trading Act 1973 remain applicable to consumer credit transactions and practices as much as to other forms of consumer trading. Indeed, in relation to consumer credit business there is a considerable overlap between the powers of the Director under the Fair Trading Act and his powers under the Consumer Credit Act. However, the definition of "consumer" in s. 137 (2) of the Fair Trading Act 1973 confines consumer transactions within that Act to those in which the recipient of the goods or services does not receive or seek to receive them in the course of a business carried on by him. Thus, whilst a consumer credit agreement entered into by a partnership as debtor is within the Consumer Credit Act if for credit not exceeding £5,000, it would not be a consumer transaction for the purposes of the Fair Trading Act 1973.

(*f*) *Terms control*

In relation to hire-purchase and instalment sale agreements, requirements as to down-payments and maximum payment periods for certain categories of goods are prescribed by the Hire-Purchase and Credit Sale Agreements (Control) Order 1977, as amended; and the Control of Hiring Order 1977 imposes in relation to hiring agreements covering designated categories of goods requirements as to advance rentals and as to the period of hire and spread of rentals over the hire period. These orders are made under the Emergency Laws (Re-enactments and Repeals) Act 1964, and operate quite independently of the Consumer Credit Act. [**31**]

2. The Consumer Credit Institutions

The diversity of credit institutions

One of the major problems involved in the enactment of comprehensive legislation regulating consumer credit is the great diversity of credit-granting institutions and ancillary credit organisations. Moneylenders and pawnbrokers have been in business since time immemorial. Banks are a more recent phenomenon, though still of respectable antiquity. In the commercial sector, several organisations that are now essentially financial in character originated as trading entities which, as part of their services to clients, advanced surplus funds or otherwise extended credit. Among these were the merchant adventurer (the progenitor of the modern merchant bank), the factor and the finance house. Only the last, however, came to extend its credit-granting activities into the consumer sector, initially through hire-purchase and instalment sale but expanding in more recent times to a variety of other forms of credit, including personal loans and revolving credit. These are described in the next chapter. [**32**]

Table 1, set out in para. [**34**], shows the principal types of organisation concerned with commercial credit, Table 2, set out in para. [**35**], shows those engaged in consumer credit. As will be seen, some institutions, notably banks and finance houses, straddle the two sectors. The Consumer Credit Act principally affects the institutions shown in Table 2, but since credit to sole traders and partnerships is within the Act where not exceeding £5,000 (see Chapter 7), some institutions whose activities are confined to credit for business will also fall within the statutory control. [**33**]

[continued on p. I/17]

TABLE 1. PRINCIPAL INSTITUTIONS GRANTING COMMERCIAL CREDIT

Clearing banks	Merchant banks	Insurance companies	Finance houses	Semi-public institutions	Credit insurance and guarantee organisations	Investors
	Accepting houses — Others		Instalment sale — Lease — Loan	ICFC — FCI — Agricultural Mortgage Corporation	ECGD — Confirming houses — Bad debt insurers	Institutional investors — The public

17

TABLE 2.   PRINCIPAL INSTITUTIONS GRANTING CONSUMER CREDIT

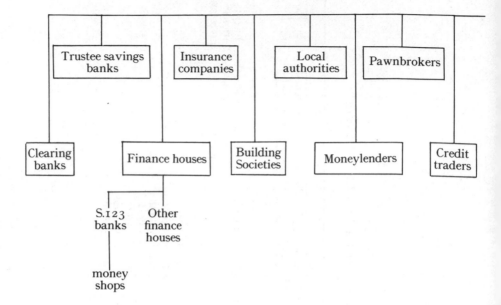

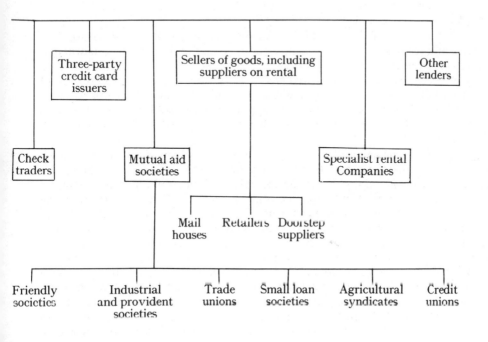

[**35**]

1. THE GRANTORS OF CONSUMER CREDIT

Banks

The incursion of the clearing banks into the consumer credit sector is a relatively recent development, symptomatic of the more aggressive marketing tactics of the clearers over the last decade. Credit for the consumer is extended by way of overdraft, personal loan and credit card. The characterisation of each of these forms of credit is described in Chapters 3 and 4. In addition, banks have an indirect interest in consumer credit through the acquisition of finance houses, and at the present time almost every major finance house is controlled by one of the large banks. [**36**]

There is no meaningful statutory definition of a bank or a banker. Such enactments as do offer a definition generally state that a banker is one who carries on the business of banking; but to this factual description some statutes add either a requirement or a facility to obtain official recognition of banking status for the purpose of that or some other enactment. The result is that this country, though almost unique in permitting a person to set up business as a banker without a licence or other authorisation, has nevertheless developed a legal hierarchy of banks, the effect of which is that whilst the carrying on of a banking business *as such* requires no official approval, the right to undertake certain types of activity controlled by statute and associated with banking (advertising for deposits, maintaining secret reserves, and the like) is limited to those enjoying official banking status for the purpose of the statute in question. The tests applied to determine acceptability for recognition are not officially published and vary widely according to the purpose for which this is required, recognition under some enactments being relatively difficult to obtain whilst under others it is more readily granted. But as regards deposit-taking institutions, radical changes have now been made by the Banking Act 1979. [**37**]

So far as credit-granting activities are concerned, the importance of banking status is that it gives total exemption from the Moneylenders Acts. This will, of course, become progressively less significant as the Moneylenders Acts are phased out by regulations which bring corresponding provisions of the Consumer Credit Act into force; but at present the greater part of the Moneylenders Acts, apart from licensing, is still operative, so that banking status remains important. [**38**]

In *United Dominions Trust, Ltd.* v. *Kirkwood*, [1966] 2 Q.B. 431, [1966] 1 All E.R. 968, the Court of Appeal held that the essential characteristics of banking were (i) the taking of deposits from customers on loan for the purpose of employing the borrowed monies as the bank's own funds; (ii) the issue of cheques to customers to enable them to draw money, and the honouring of cheques so drawn; (iii) the collection of cheques for customers; and (iv) the maintenance of current accounts to record drawings and collections. For full details of this decision, and of ancillary factors tending to establish the carrying on of a banking business, see R. M. Goode, *Hire-Purchase Law and Practice* (2nd Edn.), pp. 103 *et seq.* and Supplement. [**39**]

Section 123 of the Companies Act 1967 provided machinery by which official certification of banking status for the purpose of the Moneylenders Acts could be obtained from what is now the Department of Trade; and the Department established various criteria for dealing with applications (see R. M. Goode *op cit.*, Supplement, para. [116]). But the Consumer Credit Act provides no exemptions for banks as such, and when the Moneylenders Acts are repealed, s. 123 of the Companies Act will become inoperative. In practice, s. 123 certificates are now virtually unobtainable. Certification under s. 123 has never been obligatory; its effect is to preclude a challenge to the lender's banking status under the Moneylenders Acts, and without it the onus is on the lender to show that he is in fact carrying on the business of banking within the exemption. [**40**]

The trustee savings banks have now also entered the consumer credit field, having for the first time become able to carry on the full range of banking business by virtue of s. 9 of the Trustee Savings Banks Act 1976. [**41**]

Finance houses

The term "finance house" is not a term of art and has no distinct legal meaning, nor is it easy to define it in a business sense. Until relatively recently, the main function of finance houses was to extend credit under hire-purchase and credit sale agreements, and indeed it is not so long ago that they were termed "hire-purchase companies". In recent years, finance houses have extended into a complete range of credit activities, including personal loans (by those qualifying as bankers or otherwise exempt from or complying with the Moneylenders Acts) and revolving credits. Much of the consumer credit extended by finance houses is supplier-connected in that the business is introduced to it by a dealer or retailer with whom the finance house has an arrangement. The typical form of supplier-connected credit is that involved in motor vehicle hire-purchase business. [**42**]

More recently, finance houses have endeavoured to move away from supplier-connected credit of this kind, which involves the payment of commission to the dealer, a factor tending to force up the finance charge to the customer compared with other forms of credit. One way in which finance houses have been able to avoid the burden of dealers' commission is by lending to the customer direct. This, of course, allows loans at a cheaper rate but has the disadvantage that the finance house then has to maintain a network of branches in order to establish the necessary contact with prospective borrowers. A newer development is the involvement of finance houses in supplier-connected *revolving* credit under which the finance house takes over budget and option accounts opened by a store in favour of its customers and, as a necessary corollary to its purchase of the accounts, undertakes not only the financial burden of the credit extension but also the accounting responsibility, so relieving the store of a heavy administrative load. The incentive for the finance house is that, instead of paying a commission as in the case of fixed-sum motor vehicle credit, it buys the accounts at a discount and in addition retains the whole of the credit charge for its own benefit. The participating store gains from the substantial increase in the volume of business generated by the credit facilities. [**43**]

As we shall see, the distinction between supplier-connected credit and unconnected credit is crucial in determining the responsibility of banks and finance houses under the Consumer Credit Act when the supplier fails to carry out his contract with the customer. [**44**]

Insurance companies, building societies and local authorities

In relation to the extension of credit to the consumer, these three institutions share the characteristic that their advances are primarily to finance the purchase, repair or improvement of dwelling houses, and are secured by a first mortgage on the property concerned (building societies, in particular, are in general prohibited by s. 32 (1) of the Building Societies Act 1962 from advancing money on second mortgage except where the first mortgage is in favour of the society). Since local authority and building society mortgage transactions are almost entirely exempt from the Consumer Credit Act (s. 16 (1)—and see para. [312]), as are most advances by insurance companies (see para. [312] *et seq.*) they are not considered further. For a description of the principal types of mortgage, classified by repayment method, see para. [86]. [45]

Retailers

An important source of consumer credit is the retail trade, which extends credit in a variety of forms covering both fixed-sum credit (e.g. under hire-purchase and credit sale agreements) and revolving credit (through budget and option accounts). Sometimes the burden of the credit facility is carried by the retailer itself, more frequently the retailer elects to improve its cash flow by coming to an arrangement with a finance house to buy its paper or accounts under block discounting or similar arrangements (see Chapter 3). [46]

Moneylenders and pawnbrokers

These now represent a relatively insignificant source of consumer credit. As regards licensing, canvassing and the re-opening of extortionate bargains, they are already controlled by the Consumer Credit Act. In most other respects, they continue for the moment to be regulated by the Moneylenders Acts 1900–1927, in the case of moneylenders, and the Pawnbrokers Acts 1872–1960, in the case of pawnbrokers. [47]

Credit traders

Credit traders (formerly known as Scotch drapers, tallymen or credit drapers) are doorstep sellers who sell by instalments. They have little significance today as a source of credit. [48]

Check traders

Check trading, which developed in the latter part of the nineteenth century, is a form of three-party credit under which trading checks or vouchers of stated denominations are issued by the check trader to its customers for use in shops and stores that have previously agreed with the check trader to accept its checks. The customer pays the check trader the face value of the check plus charges by instalments, with a small downpayment, and the shop or store in question accepts the checks in payment of the price of goods to their face value, receiving payment subsequently from the check trader less a discount. Originally, trading checks were for small amounts repayable by twenty weekly payments collected from the customer's house by one of the check trader's collectors—a convenient, if somewhat expensive, system of financial budgeting for the customer—while the stores derived benefit from increased business and the check trader received his income partly from the customer, partly from the store through the discount. Recent years have seen a growth in the issue of hire-unit vouchers payable over longer periods by monthly instalments, payment being made by the customer to the check trader direct or through the customer's bank. Check trading remains a significant form of consumer credit extension, particularly in the north of England. [49]

Credit card issuers

There are broadly two types of credit card, the "t and e" (travel and entertainment) card, which is not intended as an instalment facility but is simply a convenient method of obtaining credit on open account to be settled monthly (examples are Diner's Club and American Express) and cards which allow the customer an instalment payment facility attracting a monthly credit charge (examples are Access and Barclaycard). Credit cards may also be classified as two-party, involving merely the creditor and the debtor, and three-party, in which the supplier of goods or services is a third party. The two-party card is in essence an in-house card offered, for example, by certain retail establishments to their customers on terms that the customer can use the card to make purchases up to a given limit within the issuing store or members of the group to which it belongs, payment being made within a given period after the rendering of a monthly statement, with or without an option to pay by instalments. The three-party credit card fulfils much the same functions, and operates in much the same way, as a trading check, except that the cardholder is not necessarily given the facility of paying by instalments. [50]

A bank credit card also fulfils the functions of a two-party card in that it can be used to draw cash from the issuer and from other banks co-operating with the issuer in the scheme. Where banks collaborate in a credit card scheme, they usually set up a service company to administer it. For example, Access is administered by the Joint Credit Card Company, a company set up by the three clearing banks initiating the scheme, which does not itself extend credit but simply acts as the administrative agent for the participating banks, sending out statements, collecting in payments and making credits and debits to the accounts of the banks and stores involved. [51]

Credit cards should be distinguished from cheque guarantee cards, which merely constitute an undertaking by the issuing bank to persons at large that if a cheque is given and the card produced the cheque will be honoured if it does not exceed the limit on the card (at present £50). [52]

Mutual aid societies

Together, the various types of mutual aid society make a significant contribution to consumer credit. The most important, in financial terms, are the friendly societies and the industrial and provident societies. Friendly societies are mutual aid and insurance societies which collect voluntary subscriptions from members for the purpose of providing financial assistance for members and their families. They are now regulated by the Friendly Societies Act 1974, which also applies to certain other types of mutual benefit society, such as benevolent societies and working mens' clubs. Registered friendly societies are exempt from the Moneylenders Acts, and certain classes of consumer credit agreement are exempted from the Consumer Credit Act by regulations under that Act when entered into by friendly societies named in the regulations (see paras. [**315**] *et seq.*). [**53**]

Industrial and provident societies are mutual trading co-operatives. They are registered under the Industrial and Provident Societies Acts 1965–1975. Such societies, unlike friendly societies, do not enjoy exemption from the Moneylenders Acts. They do, however, receive special statutory treatment so far as the taking of security is concerned in that an instrument creating or evidencing a fixed or floating charge on assets of the society is not a bill of sale for the purpose of the Bills of Sale Act if an application for recording of the charge is made in accordance with the requirements of the Industrial and Provident Societies Act 1967 (*ibid.*, ss. 1(1), 8 (2)), and debentures issued by a society registered under the Acts creating in favour of a bank a floating charge on property which is farming stock within the meaning of Part II of the Agricultural Credits Act 1928 may be registered as an agricultural charge and are not to be treated as bills of sale within the Bills of Sale Acts (Agricultural Credits Act 1928, s. 14). [**54**]

Loan societies registered under the Loan Societies Act 1840 are now of small importance. Of greater potential significance are credit unions, mutual aid societies whose members are linked by some common bond—residence in a particular locality, employment in the same store or factory, subjection to some common misfortune—and whose primary object is the provision of financial assistance to members through loans at interest, utilising for this purpose interest-bearing deposits made by members. The credit union movement in Great Britain has not begun to achieve the significance enjoyed by its counterparts in North America and the Antipodes but has at least developed to the point where the Government has thought it desirable to enact legislation in the shape of the Credit Union Act 1979. [**55**]

2. ANCILLARY ORGANISATIONS

The activities of the credit-granting institutions are serviced by a range of credit intermediaries and other ancillary credit organisations without which it would be extremely difficult for the consumer credit market to function effectively. Five principal categories of ancillary organisation are listed in the Consumer Credit Act and a description of each of these will be found in Chapter 31. [**56**]

3. FINANCE AND TRADE ASSOCIATIONS

The consumer credit industry is served by a number of finance and trade associations who act in various ways to protect the interests of their members and to provide services or facilities designed to enhance the smooth running of business. Among these may be mentioned the Finance Houses Association, Eurofinas, The Consumer Credit Trade Association and HP Information Ltd. The Finance Houses Association encompasses most of the major finance houses and represents its members in discussions and negotiations with Government, the EEC and other outside organisations. Much of the work of the Association concerns existing and projected legislation and EEC Directives likely to affect the business activities of its members. The Finance Houses Association is itself a member of the European Federation of Finance House Associations (Eurofinas), which collates information concerning credit legislation and statistics in the various countries in which its members are based. Eurofinas also acts as a channel of communication between its members and the EEC. [**57**]

The Consumer Credit Trade Association (formerly the Hire Purchase Trade Association) performs for its members functions similar to those of the Finance Houses Association, but the membership largely comprises retailers engaged in consumer credit, with a small number of manufacturers, professional persons and others. [**58**]

HP Information Ltd. is a non-profit making company set up by the Finance Houses in 1938 for the purpose of recording hire-purchase agreements entered into by finance houses relating to motor vehicles and associated goods. The company maintains a highly efficient record system which depends on the co-operation of its subscribers in notifying agreements entered into and discharged by settlement. Thus if a person holding a car on hire-purchase seeks to dispose of it to a motor dealer who subscribes to HP Information Ltd., a telephone enquiry will quickly reveal that the vehicle is the subject of an undischarged hire-purchase agreement. [**59**]

The service is not in fact confined to vehicles held on hire-purchase but extends to those purchased on credit sale or by means of personal loans. These last two classes do not, of course, involve any title retention or security over the vehicle and thus have no bearing on title disputes as such. Registration has, however, been found useful, first in alerting members to a disposition by the buyer/borrower which may trigger off an acceleration clause in the agreement and secondly as a general record which assists the police in tracing stolen vehicles. [**60**]

Although HP Information Ltd. is a purely private agency, it has received a measure of statutory recognition in that under the Removal and Disposal of Vehicles Regulations 1968, as amended, a local authority cannot exercise its statutory right to dispose of an abandoned vehicle without first making enquiries of HP Information Ltd. in an endeavour to trace the vehicle. [**61**]

Failure to record an agreement with HP Information Ltd. does not of itself estop a finance house from asserting its title to a motor vehicle against a third party, even if he acquires it in good faith, nor does it expose the finance house to an action for damages for negligence (*Moorgate Mercantile Co., Ltd.* v. *Twitchings*, [1977] A.C. 890, [1976] 2 All E.R. 641), and presumably the effect must be the same where incorrect particulars are registered. [**62**]

3. The Instruments of Consumer Credit

This chapter examines the principal forms of consumer credit arrangement and the typical procedures used and the parties involved in each. [**63**]

Sale credit and loan credit

It has been remarked earlier that case law and legislation prior to the Consumer Credit Act divided credit into two broad groups, sale credit and loan credit. Into the former fell agreements in which the credit took the form of deferment of the price of goods or services supplied, typical examples being conditional sale, hire-purchase and credit sale agreements. The latter category comprised all credit extended in loan form, including personal loans and overdrafts. Certain types of arrangement did not fit very easily into this twofold classification, since they partook of the nature both of sale and of loan. Among these were check trading, credit cards and budget and option accounts (in America termed revolving charge accounts). The first two almost certainly belong to the loan category, the last to the sale category, but there is no English authority on the point beyond an unreported county court decision holding that check trading was moneylending (*Premier Clothing and Supply Co., Ltd.* v. *Hillcoat* (1969), 13th February (Newport (Mon.) County Court)). [**64**]

As we shall see, the sale credit/loan credit classification is formal rather than functional and it has been abandoned in the Consumer Credit Act. But before turning to classifications that are more meaningful in business terms, we shall briefly describe the characteristics of each of the above kinds of agreement and the documentation and mechanics involved in typical transactions. [**65**]

Hire-purchase and instalment sale

A hire-purchase agreement is an agreement for the hire of goods with an option (but no obligation) to purchase (see further para. [**94**]). A conditional sale agreement is an agreement for the sale of goods under which the passing of the property to the buyer is deferred until payment of the price or performance of some other stipulated condition. In practice, the term is applied almost exclusively to agreements providing for payment by instalments. To constitute a contract of sale the agreement must, of course, be one which by its terms commits the buyer to

26

buy as well as the seller to sell; but in the consumer credit sector the distinction between hire-purchase and conditional sale is of little importance in that the buyer under a conditional sale agreement is given the same statutory right to terminate the agreement as is a hirer on hire-purchase. A credit sale agreement is a contract of sale providing for payment by instalments (s. 1 (1) of the Hire-Purchase Act 1965 specifies five or more instalments as an ingredient of the definition), but without any provision deferring the transfer of title to the buyer. In effect, hire-purchase and conditional sale are forms of secured credit (though retention of title is not technically a security so far as the law is concerned) whilst credit sale is unsecured. [**66**]

Hire-purchase and instalment sale facilities may be extended directly by the retail supplier, but in larger-unit transactions, particularly motor vehicles, boats and light aircraft, it is common for a finance house to be brought in as the credit provider. Thus a motor dealer, D, will have an arrangement with a finance house, F, by which F will provide hire-purchase facilities for customers of D wishing to acquire cars from him on hire-purchase terms. D will be given a stock of F's forms of hire-purchase agreement. An intending hirer, H, will sign the agreement, pay D the required deposit and receive a copy of the agreement in exchange, and the signed agreement, embodying a proposal form or schedule setting out details of the intended transaction and personal data concerning H, will be forwarded by D to F with a request to purchase the vehicle from D and let it to H under the hire-purchase agreement. At this stage there is no contract, merely an offer by H to take the car on hire-purchase. If F approves the transaction it will buy the vehicle from D (paying him the cash price less the deposit in D's hands), sign the hire-purchase agreement and notify H of its acceptance of the proposal. H will pay the specified instalments direct to F. The total sum payable by H to F will comprise the balance of the cash price, any additional sums payable for installation, insurance and the like and a finance charge calculated by reference to the amount of F's outlay. D will receive from F, in addition to the balance of the cash price, an agreed percentage of the finance charge as his commission for the introduction. He may or may not be required to give recourse, that is, to undertake responsibility for payment of the instalments, or alternatively to repurchase the vehicle, in the event of H's default. [**67**]

A similar mechanism is used where the car is to be bought outright with a personal loan from F (see para. [**72**]). [**68**]

With small-unit transactions, it is administratively burdensome and uneconomic for finance houses to engage in "direct collection" hire-purchase along the lines described above. Their involvement in the bookkeeping and collection of relatively small instalments is justified only where the arrangement is one under which they *receive* a discount from the supplier instead of paying him commission. For such cases, F's arrangement with D is that, D having supplied the goods on hire-purchase or instalment sale in the first instance, F will buy batches of agreements from D at regular intervals under the terms of a master block discounting agreement, paying D the collection value of the discounted agreements (i.e. the amount remaining payable under them) less an agreed discount. Block discounting is usually conducted upon terms that D will give recourse in the event of default by the debtors under the discounted agreements. [**69**]

The involvement of finance houses in the purchase of revolving credit accounts is discussed in para. [**73**]. [**70**]

Rental

A rental, or hiring, agreement is not, of course, a form of credit in the strict sense, since the hirer merely has the use of the goods without the option of becoming the owner. A finance house may supply goods on rental but its involvement will more usually take the form of discounting rental agreements entered into by the retailer. The characteristics of different forms of rental agreements are discussed in Chapter 25. [**71**]

Personal loan

The term "personal loan" is generally used to denote a fixed-term consumer loan by a bank or finance house repayable by instalments. It may be either a purchase-money loan (that is, a loan for the purchase of goods or services where the lender controls the application of the loan to its intended purpose, e.g. by making payment direct to the supplier) or a non-purchase-money loan. In the motor vehicle field, the personal loan is used as an alternative to hire-purchase or credit sale, the customer being introduced by the motor dealer to the finance house, in return for a commission, the only difference being that instead of the customer acquiring the vehicle on hire-purchase he buys it outright for cash advanced by the finance house by way of a payment direct to the dealer, the customer repaying the loan by instalments which combine principal and interest. [**72**]

Revolving credit

In the last decade there has been a sharp increase in the volume of revolving credit, that is, credit in which, instead of receiving a fixed advance repayable in a lump sum or by instalments, the customer is given a credit limit and is free to draw on his account as and when he chooses so long as his indebtedness does not rise above the limit. The particular characteristic of revolving credit is that it is facultative, i.e. the customer need not utilise the credit at the outset (or indeed at all) but may draw on the facility when it suits his convenience. As a consequence, interest is not precomputed but accrues only on drawings as they are made. Each drawing reduces the available credit line, but each repayment *pro tanto* restores it, so that instead of creditor and debtor having a fixed-term contract which (in the absence of default) will inevitably end with settlement, a revolving credit arrangement keeps them in a continuous relationship which may last indefinitely. This, of course, is not only convenient to the customer but attractive to the creditor for it encourages a continuous flow of dealings. [**73**]

Like fixed-sum credit, revolving credit may be purchase-money or non-purchase-money. [**74**]

(i) *Purchase-money revolving credit*

A typical agreement is the *budget account*. A department store agrees to open an account for a customer into which he will make regular monthly payments. He is given a credit limit—usually fixed as a stated multiple of the monthly payment—and is required to pay for his purchases within a specified period after the rendering of a statement, a monthly charge being levied. There is a variety of charging methods. For example, under the "closing balance" method the charge is computed as a percentage of the balance outstanding at the end of the monthly billing cycle, regardless of the dates on which purchases or repayments during the billing cycle are made (for a description of other methods, see R. M. Goode (ed.), *Consumer Credit*, pp. 55 *et seq.*). With prudent use, a customer can obtain a month's free credit by making all his purchases on the first day of the cycle and paying for them on the last. [**75**]

A variant of the budget account is the *option account*, a combination of an open account and a budget account. At the end of the monthly cycle the customer is given the option of paying the account in full without charge or of paying a minimum monthly sum with charges geared to the closing debit balance. [**76**]

The operation of these revolving charge accounts does, of course, impose a heavy administrative burden on the store concerned, and in recent years it has become increasingly common for a store or group of stores to come to an arrangement with a finance house to take over the accounts by purchase at a discount, the finance house not only maintaining the accounts and dealing with collections but also undertaking responsibility for the initial credit evaluation of customers. [**77**]

A third, increasingly dominant, form of purchase-money revolving credit is the *credit card*. A bank or other card issuer reaches agreements with retail outlets by which the retailers agree to allow cardholders to purchase goods or services on production of the card. When the customer buys goods with the use of the card, he signs a slip confirming the purchase, and this enables the store to claim payment from the card issuer. Batches of invoices and slips are sent by each participating store to the issuing bank daily, and against these daily payments are made to the credit of the store's account with the bank, a periodic discount charge being levied by the bank. A monthly statement is rendered to the cardholder who must (if there is no arrangement permitting payment by instalments) pay within a stipulated time after the rendering of the statement, no interest being levied if he pays within this period. The agreement between issuer and cardholder may give the latter the option of paying by instalments, in which case a cardholder exercising the option will be debited with interest at, say, 2% per month, calculated on the balance outstanding at the end of each month. [**78**]

(ii) *Non-purchase-money revolving credit*

The archetype is the *bank overdraft*. The customer is given a credit limit up to which he is permitted to overdraw on his account, drawings being by cheque in the same way as for a current account in credit, and interest being payable on a daily balance from time to time outstanding, at a rate geared to the bank's base rate. In theory, sums outstanding on overdraft are usually repayable on demand; in practice, banks will not terminate a facility without reasonable warning, though they may require prompt measures to reduce an overdraft where they consider that in the light of prevailing circumstances the amount is too high. [**79**]

Another form of non-purchase-money revolving credit is the bank credit card, insofar as this is used not for the purchase of goods or services but for the drawing of cash. [**80**]

Check and voucher trading

This has already been described (see para. [**49**]). [**81**]

Security for advances

English law provides three forms of security, the pledge, the mortgage and the charge. A pledge is a delivery of goods, or of documents of title to goods or to money (i.e. instruments) by way of security. Necessarily, therefore, the pledge is confined to assets capable of physical delivery. The pledgee has a legal possessory interest which carries with it an implied right of sale in the event of default (*Re Hardwick, ex parte Hubbard* (1886), 17 Q.B.D. 690), but he does not acquire a general property in the asset. Pledges taken by pawnbrokers are regulated for the most part by the Pawnbrokers Acts, but these are prospectively repealed by the Consumer Credit Act. [**82**]

A mortgage of chattels, by contrast with a pledge, involves the transfer of ownership to the creditor by way of security, upon the express or implied condition that there will be a retransfer to the debtor on redemption. Delivery of possession to the creditor is not an essential ingredient of a mortgage. It follows that almost all classes of asset, tangible and intangible, are capable of being mortgaged. Endowment policies are a common form of security in the consumer credit field.
[**83**]

The charge, or hypothecation, does not involve the transfer either of possession or of ownership to the creditor, but is simply a right to have the proceeds of the asset applied to the debt it secures in priority to the claims of other creditors. Again, almost all classes of asset are capable of being charged. The charge is the creature of equity and there is thus no such thing as a legal charge on goods. Written mortgages and charges on chattels given by an individual are governed by the Bills of Sale Acts, and since the statutory form of bill of sale involves a transfer of ownership, security conforming to the Acts must take the form of a mortgage, not a charge. Because of the technicalities of the Bills of Sale Acts, the bill of sale is not a widely used form of security. Mortgages or charges of goods by a company are outside the Bills of Sale Acts but are registrable under section 95 of the Companies Act 1948, which also applies to certain other categories of charge, including charges over book debts. [**84**]

Though much of the Law of Property Act 1925 applies equally to personalty, interests in land are subjected by the Act to special rules. A mortgage of land no longer takes the form of a transfer of the fee simple, or assignment of the leasehold term, with a proviso for retransfer on redemption. Only two forms of legal mortgage are now permissible, namely a mortgage by demise for a term of years absolute (i.e. a lease) or a charge by way of legal mortgage. The latter is by far the most convenient and common. The chargee does not in fact possess a legal estate but has the same rights and remedies as if he did. [**85**]

The greater part of financial assistance for house purchase is provided on long-term mortgage by building societies, but a significant role is also played by insurance companies and local authorities. There are several types of mortgage in use (see Fisher and Lightwood's *Law of Mortgage* (9th Edn.), p. 30), but the main division is between repayment mortgages and endowment mortgages. Under a repayment mortgage, the borrower repays the principal by instalments over the stipulated credit period, and interest is either charged on the balance outstanding at the end of each year (or other agreed period) or combined with principal in the computation of instalments. In the latter case interest is usually spread in a manner approximating to the actuarial method, so that the interest reduces as principal outstanding diminishes, most of the early repayments going in discharge of interest rather than principal. In the case of an endowment mortgage, the mortgagor secures the principal by taking out an endowment policy with an insurance company, the policy maturing at the date on which repayment of the mortgage is due, and assigns the policy to the building society as security. The mortgagor pays the premiums on the policy but makes no repayments of principal, merely keeping up the interest on the mortgage. When the policy matures, the proceeds are paid to the building society in discharge of the principal sum. The Consumer Credit (Total Charge for Credit) Regulations create some difficulties for lenders in relation to this type of mortgage, in that the whole of the premium on the endowment policy may have to be brought into account in computing the total charge for credit, notwithstanding that this reflects a substantial capital element (see para. [**520**]). It is likely that the regulations will be changed to deal with this. [**86**]

A considerable amount of non-purchase-money finance is provided on the security of property, either by deposit of the title deeds or land certificate, where there is no previous mortgage, or by a second mortgage if the property is already charged. The Consumer Credit Act favours first mortgages, particularly local authority and building society mortgages, but second mortgage lending some years ago attracted a considerable opprobium (see para. [**20**]) and exceptions enjoyed by first mortgage lenders from some of the provisions of the Consumer Credit Act have for the most part been denied to the second mortgage market. [**87**]

The functional classification of consumer credit

As previously observed, the distinction between sale credit and purchase-money-loan credit is formal rather than functional. To the customer it is a matter of indifference whether he pays for a motor car by credit sale or purchase-money loan. The law may distinguish between deferment of the price and the grant of a loan but in commercial terms the distinction is meaningless. [**88**]

The three really significant distinctions (as recognised by the Consumer Credit Act) are between supplier-connected credit and unconnected credit, between fixed-sum credit and revolving credit and between secured and unsecured credit. Supplier-connected credit (which the Act terms debtor-creditor-supplier credit) denotes credit extended either by the supplier himself or by a third party pursuant to or in contemplation of arrangements with the supplier. The business *nexus* between creditor and supplier (where they are not the same) is, *inter alia*, of crucial importance in identifying those classes of transaction for which the creditor is to carry legal responsibility for the defaults of the supplier, a matter discussed in some detail in Chapter 16. Entirely different considerations apply in the case of unconnected (or in the language of the Act, debtor-creditor) credit. [**89**]

Equally important is the distinction between fixed-sum credit and revolving credit (which the Act terms "running-account credit"). Revolving credit has distinctive features which make it inappropriate to subject it to precisely the same rules as those governing fixed-sum credit (see para. [**272**]). [**90**]

The remaining classification—secured and unsecured credit—is self-explanatory. Secured credit (including for this purpose credit secured by retention of title under hire-purchase or conditional sale agreements) gives the creditor greater protection and exposes the debtor to a correspondingly greater risk. Hence the need for distinct rules as to the taking and enforcement of security, and the restriction of exemptions from the Act so as to exclude secured credit transactions from some categories of exemption (see Chapter 21). [**91**]

4. The Common Law Setting

In this chapter we shall briefly describe some of the more important common law rules of particular relevance to consumer credit, with especial reference to hire-purchase transactions. For a comprehensive analysis, the reader is referred to the author's separate work, *Hire-Purchase Law and Practice* (2nd Edn. 1970, with Supplement 1975) and to Professor A. G. Guest's *Law of Hire Purchase* (1966, with Supplement 1969). For a comparative analysis, see R. M. Goode (ed.) *Consumer Credit* (1978), which embodies *inter alia* papers by distinguished contributors from eight jurisdictions presented at the Colloquium on Consumer Credit held by the United Kingdom National Committee of Comparative Law at the University of Southampton in September 1977. [**92**]

The characterisation of the credit agreement

There are various reasons why it may be important to determine the legal characterisation of a credit agreement. Legislation may impose licensing requirements or other constraints on some types of business but not on others (for example, the Moneylenders Acts, so far as still in force, apply to the business of moneylending but not to hire-purchase or instalment sale, which has hitherto been governed by separate legislation in the form of the Hire Purchase Acts); the treatment of third party rights may be affected by the nature of the credit agreement (for example, wrongful dispositions by a conditional buyer may be effective to pass a good title to an innocent third party under s. 9 of the Factors Act 1889 or s. 25 (2) of the Sale of Goods Act 1893, neither of which applies to dispositions by hirers); and certain types of agreement are considered to constitute a security so as to require registration whereas others are not (for example, a chattel mortgage is registrable as a bill of sale if given by an individual and under s. 95 of the Companies Act 1948 if given by a company, whereas a reservation of title under a hire-purchase or conditional sale agreement is not in law a security device and thus does not attract registration requirements). [**93**]

Hire-purchase, as previously remarked, is to be distinguished from conditional sale in that the hirer has an option, not an obligation, to buy, whereas the essence of a contract of sale is that the buyer has the same obligation to buy as the seller to sell. The distinction between sale and hire-purchase was established some 84 years ago in the celebrated House of Lords decision in *Helby* v. *Matthews*, [1895] A.C. 471. The effect is that neither the Sale of Goods Act nor any other enactments insofar as they relate to sales of goods apply to hire-purchase agreements, and as just mentioned an innocent third party cannot acquire a title from a hirer under s. 9 of the Factors Act or s. 25 (2) of the Sale of Goods Act. To avoid classification as a contract of sale, the agreement must be so framed as to avoid a commitment to purchase. This may be achieved in one of two ways. The hirer may be given the right to terminate the agreement before it has run its full course. Alternatively, the hiring agreement may be for a fixed period, with no power of termination, if at the end of the period of hire the hirer is required to pay a further sum which is not purely nominal in order to acquire title. The absence of the right to terminate is not material in such a case, for even if the hiring agreement does run its full course the hirer is not thereby committed to paying the full price. [**94**]

Certain types of credit agreement are not so easy to classify. Check trading has been held to constitute moneylending (see para. [**64**]), and the same is probably true of the three-party credit card arrangement. On the other hand, a department store operating a budget or option account is probably not lending money but making a series of sales on a running account (see *N. G. Napier, Ltd.* v. *Patterson*, 1959 S.C. (J.) 48, a Scottish decision). [**95**]

Security
The different forms of security and their basic legal characteristics have been dealt with in the previous chapters (paras. [**82**] *et seq.*). [**96**]

Duties of the supplier of goods
The terms implied in favour of the hirer of goods under a hire-purchase agreement (title, correspondence with description, fitness, merchantable quality) are broadly the same as those implied in favour of the buyer under a contract of sale pursuant to the Sale of Goods Act, except that in the case of hire-purchase the owner is required to have a good title at the time of delivery of the goods to the hirer (*Mercantile Union Guarantee Corporation, Ltd.* v. *Wheatley*, [1938] 1 K.B. 490, [1937] 4 All E.R. 713), whereas on a contract of sale the implied condition of title is not required to be satisfied until the time when the property is to pass to the buyer under the contract (Sale of Goods Act, s. 12 (1) (*a*)). So far as consumer transactions are concerned, ss. 8–11 of the Supply of Goods (Implied Terms) Act 1973 have for the most part assimilated hire-purchase to sale as regards implied terms; but the hirer remains entitled to invoke any wider common law rules (s. 15 (5)) including that concerning title, and in addition he is not bound by the strict sale of goods rules as to deemed acceptance of the goods but will, it seems, lose his right to reject defective or non-conforming goods only if he has elected to affirm the contract with knowledge of the breach or if some other event occurs which at common law would extinguish his right to treat the contract as repudiated. [**97**]

Exemption clauses designed to exclude or restrict the supplier's liabilities or the buyer's remedies for breach of the supply agreement have long been controlled by a battery of judicial devices—the *contra proferentem* rule, a finding that the clause was not contained in a contractual document or was overridden by an oral warranty, the doctrines of fundamental term and fundamental breach—but the powers of the court have now been greatly strengthened by the wide-ranging provisions of the Unfair Contract Terms Act 1977 (see paras. [**665**] *et seq.*). [**98**]

The dealer as agent of the finance house

At common law there is no general rule that a dealer to whom a hire-purchase agreement is concluded with a finance house is the agent of the finance house. In determining the dealer's position, regard must be had to the particular facts of each case, and to the nature of the act in question and the stage at which that act is performed. In the words of Pearson L.J. in *Mercantile Credit Co., Ltd.* v. *Hamblin,* [1965] 2 Q.B. 242 at p. 269, adopted by the majority in the House of Lords in *Branwhite* v. *Worcester Works Finance, Ltd.,* [1969] 1 A.C. 552, [1968] 3 All E.R. 104:

> "There is no rule of law that in a hire-purchase transaction the dealer never is, or always is, acting as agent for the finance company. In a typical hire-purchase transaction the dealer is a party in his own right, selling his car to the finance company, and he is acting primarily on his own behalf and not as general agent for either of the two parties. There is no need to attribute to him an agency in order to account for his participation in the transaction. Nevertheless the dealer is to some extent an intermediary between the customer and the finance company, and he may well have in a particular case some *ad hoc* agency to do particular things on behalf of one or the other or it may be both of those two parties."

Thus, at common law the dealer who makes a representation which induces his customer to enter into the hire-purchase agreement would not appear to do so as agent of the finance company (though he may incur a personal liability for fraud or on a collateral contract) nor is the dealer the agent of the finance house for the purpose of taking a pre-contract deposit, though if the finance house subsequently enters into the hire-purchase agreement it will be deemed to have received the deposit in a balance of account with the dealer and may thus be liable to repay it to the hirer if he lawfully cancels the transaction or on some other ground has a right of recovery for total failure of consideration (*Branwhite's* case). Equally, the dealer has no ostensible authority to vary or terminate a hire-purchase agreement on behalf of the finance company or to receive a notice of termination from the hirer. On the other hand the dealer will in general be the finance house's agent for the purpose of receiving notice from the hirer withdrawing from a proposed hire-purchase agreement (*Financings, Ltd.* v. *Stimson,* [1962] 3 All E.R. 386, [1962] 1 W.L.R. 1184) and of delivering the goods to the hirer after the agreement has been made (see the passage in *Branwhite* cited above). [99]

The common law rule was substantially altered by the Hire-Purchase Acts, and has been whittled down still further by the Consumer Credit Act (see Chapter 17).

[100]

Creditor's responsibility for defaults of supplier

Where the creditor and the supplier are not the same, the common law treats the supply contract and the credit agreement as quite distinct, and will rarely allow a breach of one contract to affect the rights and duties of the parties under the other. Thus if a motor vehicle is purchased with the aid of a purchase-money loan from a finance house, and the vehicle is defective or fails to accord with the contract description, the buyer's remedy at common law is against the supplier alone. He has no claim against the finance house, nor even a right to withhold payment of instalments pending the remedying of the defects. Similarly, the contract between a credit card issuer and the cardholder is independent of the contract between cardholder and supplier, and a breach of the latter does not, at common law, entitle the cardholder to sue the issuer or to withhold repayments or assert a set-off. [**101**]

Again, the position has been changed by legislation, partly by provisions in s. 56 of the Consumer Credit Act which make the supplier the agent of the finance house for certain purposes (so that the supplier's default is attributed to the finance house) and partly by s. 75 of the Act, which in a debtor-creditor-supplier transaction exposes the creditor to liability for misrepresentations and breaches of contract on the part of the supplier (see Chapter 16). [**102**]

Creditor's remedies on default

Where the debtor defaults, the creditor can recover sums accrued under the agreement, with any stipulated interest, as a debt, and, if the breach has caused additional loss, may recover damages for it. The creditor may also, subject to statute, invoke any contractual provision accelerating liability, and may terminate the agreement and repossess the goods where the agreement so provides or where the debtor's breach is so grave or persistent as to be repudiatory. The creditor appears to have almost complete freedom at common law to stipulate the events that are to attract a right to terminate a hire-purchase agreement, including the hirer's bankruptcy (*McEntire* v. *Crossley Bros., Ltd.*, [1895] A.C. 457; and *cf. Re Apex Supply Co., Ltd.*, [1942] Ch. 108, [1941] 3 All E.R. 473), though there is a county court decision to the effect that a clause providing for termination on bankruptcy is contrary to general principles of bankruptcy law (*Re Piggin, Dicker* v. *Lombank, Ltd.* (1962), 112 L. Jo. 424), and the point is perhaps open to be taken despite *McEntire* v. *Crossley Bros., Ltd.* inasmuch as it was not specifically argued in that case. [**103**]

On termination the owner can recover arrears of rent and interest, plus damages for any specific breach of the agreement (e.g. failure to repair). But this will not necessarily compensate the owner, for he has the goods thrown back on his hands with no certainty of being able to realise them for a sum sufficient to recoup the outstanding balance of the hire-purchase price. So it has become common to insert a minimum payment clause in a hire-purchase agreement requiring the hirer to pay a further sum in the event of the owner's termination for default. Excessive minimum payment stipulations soon led the courts to strike these down as penalties, and eventually the position was reached that even a clause providing for full credit for the proceeds of sale of the goods against the unpaid balance of the hire-purchase price was held penal, partly because it did not allow a discount for the resultant acceleration of the payment obligation, partly because its intended effect was to put the owner in the same position as if the agreement had run its full course, an objective considered inconsistent with the right to terminate given to the hirer by the agreement (*Anglo-Auto Finance Co., Ltd.* v. *James*, [1963] 3 All E.R. 566, [1963] 1 W.L.R. 1042). The difficulties with this argument have been discussed by the author elsewhere (see *Hire-Purchase Law and Practice* (2nd Edn.) pp. 393 *et seq.*). [**104**]

Somewhat anomalously, recovery of the discounted balance of the hire-purchase price, less the proceeds of the repossessed goods, is allowed where the hirer's breach is repudiatory (see para. [**884**]); and the weight of authority indicates that the rule against penalties does not apply at all where the event that makes the minimum sum payable is the hirer's voluntary termination of the agreement (see R. M. Goode, *op. cit.*, pp. 387 *et seq.*). [**105**]

It is fair to say that minimum payment clauses have caused the courts anxiety on additional grounds external to the agreement, particularly because all too often the repossessed goods have been sold for substantially less than the sum they could reasonably have fetched. It remains an open question whether, in deciding what sum ought to be credited to the hirer as the proceeds of sale, the court should take the retail price or the price on sale to the trade. Finance houses are not equipped to sell at retail and are thus perforce constrained to sell to the trade either by private treaty or at auction. Probably no universal rule can be laid down; the question is simply whether the finance house has acted reasonably in all the circumstances. [**106**]

Credit sale and loan agreements usually contain an acceleration clause by which, in the event of default in payment of an instalment within a specified time or the commission of some other breach, the whole outstanding balance of the price or loan is immediately to become due and payable, and to carry interest at a stated rate. In principle, this is unexceptionable; but where the outstanding balance is not merely of principal but comprises an interest or charge component, the agreement should provide for rebating of the interest or charges, for otherwise interest will in effect be charged in respect of a period when the debtor does not have the use of the money (the principal having been called up), and the contractual provision will be vulnerable to attack as a penalty. But if the unaccrued interest is duly rebated, there is no reason why interest should not be stipulated to run thereafter on the outstanding principal called up by the acceleration clause. As to rebate computations generally, see Chapter 20. [**107**]

Debtor's relief against forfeiture

As will be seen, the Consumer Credit Act gives the court wide powers to grant a debtor relief against the consequences of default. Quite independently of the statutory provisions, the court has an equitable jurisdiction to grant relief against forfeiture of monies paid and of other rights, and thus to order restoration of a terminated contract. But this relief is given only in stringent conditions and the power has rarely been successfully invoked. See para. [**840**] and R. M. Goode, *Hire Purchase Law and Practice* (2nd Edn.), pp. 379 *et seq.* [**108**]

5. The Structure and Phasing of the Act

The legislative process

A major difficulty in grappling with a substantial new enactment is to be able to see the wood for the trees, to get a picture of the structure of the statute, the ground it covers and the objectives it seeks to attain. To a considerable extent this difficulty results from our parliamentary procedure. The general principles of proposed legislation may be embodied in consultation papers distributed for comment to interested parties, but the convention of Parliament precludes publication of a Bill before it has been introduced into one of the Houses of Parliament. The result is that no opportunity for informed comment on the Bill itself is available until it has begun its journey through Parliament, and by this time the structure of the Bill has crystallised and the ability to make sensible changes is correspondingly restricted. What happens is that as the Bill proceeds, more and more weaknesses and practical difficulties come to light as a result of examination by those in business or elsewhere who are going to have to work the legislation, and since the exigencies of the parliamentary timetable do not usually permit the government to scrap the original Bill and start afresh, these deficiencies have to be dealt with by speedy *ad hoc* amendment during the passage of the Bill. All too often the result is that what started as a relatively simple, coherent structure became distorted by a mass of detailed drafting, losing much of its original clarity of style and orderliness of arrangement. [**109**]

It is a tribute to the skill of the draftsman of the Consumer Credit Act that his creation, widely praised for its lucidity and originality when the Bill was first introduced, managed to withstand the pressures of the parliamentary procedure as well as it did. Nevertheless, the Act in its final form has undoubtedly been affected by the large number of amendments found necessary after it had first been introduced. From a solid 96 pages at its inception it doubled in length, finally embodying a massive 193 sections and five schedules. The purpose of this short chapter is to strip away the foliage and provide a bird's eye view of the framework of the Act, showing its various divisions. Each of these will be examined in more detail in subsequent chapters. [**110**]

The framework of the Act

The Act is divided into 12 parts, as follows:

Part   I—Director General of Fair Trading
Part   II—Credit agreements, hire agreements and linked transactions
Part   III—Licensing of credit and hire businesses
Part   IV—Seeking business
Part   V—Entry into credit or hire agreements
Part   VI—Matters arising during currency of credit or hire agreements
Part VII—Default and termination
Part VIII—Security
Part   IX—Judicial control
Part   X—Ancillary credit businesses
Part   XI—Enforcement of Act
Part   XII—Supplement [**111**]

Even from this bare list of headings, a picture begins to emerge. The Act is designed to provide a comprehensive code regulating the consumer credit and consumer hire industry and almost every aspect of a credit granting operation, from advertising at one end to the consequences of default at the other. All those engaged in the business of granting consumer credit will have to be licensed, as will those carrying on various forms of ancillary credit business, such as credit brokerage and debt collecting. The licensing system will be administered by the Director General of Fair Trading (hereafter referred to as the Director), who is made responsible for overall superintendence of consumer credit and for central enforcement of the Act and regulations made under it. His functions, and those of the Weights and Measures authorities responsible to him, will be discussed more fully in Chapter 6 and 25. Strict controls are imposed on methods of seeking business—advertising, canvassing and the giving of quotations. Detailed provisions are made—and further provisions will be made by regulations—as to the form and content of consumer credit and consumer hire agreements and as to information and documents to be supplied to debtors and hirers. Rights of cancellation are given, broadly along the lines previously prescribed by the Hire-Purchase Act 1965, though with significant changes. The creditor's rights in the event of default are closely circumscribed so as to safeguard the debtor or hirer against unfairness or hardship, and various restrictions are imposed on repossession of goods and on enforcement of securities. Particularly strict are the provisions regulating the enforcement of land mortgages given to secure a regulated agreement. Finally the court is given the widest powers to control enforcement of an agreement, to modify the agreement and to re-open extortionate credit bargains. [**112**]

In short, what the Consumer Credit Act does is to replace the previous fragmented legislation with a unified code governing all forms of consumer credit and consumer hire, with a battery of provisions for the protection of the consumer backed up by powerful enforcement machinery. [**113**]

It is important to remember that detailed though the Act is, it does not represent the whole story. The Act provides for a whole range of subordinate legislation and administrative controls—regulations, orders, directions, general notices and the like—to be made by the Secretary of State or the Director. The proposed content of the regulations was set out in the Appendices to the White Paper previously referred to on *Reform of the Law on Consumer Credit*, but it is clear that consequent on extensive consultations with the industry and other interested parties major changes will be made. [114]

How to read the Act

The usual approach of a person confronted with new legislation is to begin with section 1 and to go on steadily (or otherwise!) to the end   We shall not employ that method in this book. The draftsman of an Act has reasons of his own for planning the sections in a given sequence, but the adoption of that sequence is not necessarily the best for the reader, particularly since various sections at the end of an Act have an uncomfortable habit of controlling those which appear at the beginning. For this reason, we shall not start with the first section. Instead we shall devote the next three chapters to a discussion of the administration and scope of the Act and some basic concepts and definitions (for the Act creates a whole new legal terminology) before examining the forms of control which the Act imposes on the consumer credit industry and the various ways in which it seeks to protect those entering into a consumer credit or consumer hire transaction. [115]

As a preliminary we should observe two interesting features of draftsman-ship. The first is the collection of definitions in s. 189. This is an extremely useful device. Section 189 not only gives definitions of its own but also indicates all the other sections in which definitions appear. When reading the Act it is essential to refer continually to s. 189, because even words that might be assumed to have a meaning that was self-evident—such as "creditor", "pre-existing arrangements", "security", and the like—are specially defined. The second interesting technique adopted by the parliamentary draftsman is the use of examples to illustrate some of the new terminology adopted in the Act. These examples are contained in the Second Schedule, and reference should be made to see what the draftsman had in mind when coining expressions (and there are several of them) that have not hitherto found place in an English statute. [116]

The Consumer Credit Act falls broadly into two halves. One half contains what might be called transactional provisions, that is, provisions which come into effect on the making of an agreement and regulate the rights of the parties to the agreement. The other half is concerned with the general regulation of the consumer credit industry (through licensing, restrictions on seeking business and use of the elaborate enforcement machinery provided by the Act), without having any direct impact on specific contractual relationships. But as we shall see in the next chapter, the definition of a "regulated agreement", which goes to the heart of the Act, not only fixes the transactional boundaries of the Act but is also relevant in determining the applicability of its general regulatory provisions. The principal exceptions are the provisions relating to extortionate credit bargains, the impact of which is not limited to regulated agreements (see para. [305]). [117]

Phasing of the Act

Because of the complex machinery necessitated by the Consumer Credit Act and the intricacy of the matters to be covered by the regulations under it, the Act is being brought into operation in stages, each stage awaiting either the establishment of the requisite administrative procedures or the formulation of

39

regulations.   Progress has been pitifully slow, and even now, some five years after the Act was enacted, the greater part of it remains to be brought into force. Indeed, so ponderous has been the advance towards implementation of the will of Parliament that in 1978 the Government felt constrained to raise from £2,000 to £5,000 the limits of application of the Hire-Purchase Act 1965, which the Consumer Credit Act had prospectively repealed! See the Hire-Purchase (Increase of Limit of Value) (Great Britain) Order 1978. [**118**]

The first major phase, concerned with licensing, has been completed, and indeed the first batch of licences have already come up for renewal. Opportunity has also been taken to deal with matters concerning credit references and credit reference agencies and certain other matters of a relatively minor nature. The second phase will be devoted primarily to the seeking of business (advertising, quotations, and the like), but again will encompass certain other aspects, such as rebates for early settlement, statements of account, etc. The third, and in some respects the most important, phase will cover the form and content of contract documents.

Repeals to be effected by the Act are being similarly phased so that as each stage of the Act is brought into force with supporting regulations, corresponding provisions of existing enactments and statutory instruments will be repealed and revoked. Thus, the licensing provisions of the Moneylenders Acts and Pawnbrokers Acts were to have been repealed on the day appointed for the licensing of consumer credit businesses (1st October 1977), though for administrative reasons the repeals in question were brought forward two months (see para. [**328**]); and the coming into force of documentation regulations will spell the end of the provisions of the Moneylenders Acts, Hire-Purchase Acts and regulations relating to contract documents. [**119**]

The present state of effectiveness of the Act is conveniently set out in a circular issued by the Office of Fair Trading on the 8th March 1977. It should be borne in mind that some parts of the Act, though technically in force, have little or no impact until triggered off by some other provisions not yet operative. [**120**]

The transitional provisions of the Act (Sch. 3) are discussed in Chapter 33. [**121**]

6. The Administration of the Act

1. THE ADMINISTRATIVE AND ENFORCEMENT AGENCIES

The distribution of control

Responsibility for the application and enforcement of the Act is divided among five principal organs:—

(i) The court.
(ii) The Secretary of State for Prices and Consumer Protection, acting through the Department of Prices and Consumer Protection.
(iii) The Director General of Fair Trading, acting through the Office of Fair Trading.
(iv) The persons appointed for the hearing of licensing appeals.
(v) The local weights and measures authorities, acting through their trading standards/consumer protection officers. [**122**]

The court

The court—which in the context of the Consumer Credit Act usually denotes the county court (see s. 189 (1))—plays a central role in the enforcement of the statutory provisions. Apart from its normal function as the arbiter of statutory interpretation, the court is given wide powers to control the exercise of creditors' remedies, to grant relief to debtors against the consequences of default and to re-open extortionate bargains. Moreover, there are numerous cases in which an agreement can be enforced against a debtor only on an order of the court. In some of these cases, the court has power to grant the creditor dispensation from the consequences of infringing the Act. For a detailed description of the court's powers, see Chapter 30. [**123**]

The Secretary of State

The authority having the primary power of regulation is the Secretary of State, who may make a range of orders, regulations and directions under the Act, as well as procedural directions under the Consumer Credit Licensing (Appeals) Regulations 1976. In general it may be said that:

(i) *orders* define or redefine the limits of the statutory provisions (e.g. orders under s. 16 as to exempted agreements, s. 43 (5) as to exempted advertisements and s. 181 as to determination of monetary limits);
(ii) *regulations* constitute mandatory requirements which impose positive and specific duties (e.g. as to the computation and disclosure of the total charge for credit the form and content of advertisements and contract documents and the provision of rebates for early settlement);
(iii) *directions* prescribe procedure or administrative action (e.g. directions by the Secretary of State to the Director under s. 2 or procedural directions under the Consumer Credit Licensing (Appeals) Regulations 1976.) [124]

The Secretary of State possesses certain additional functions under the Act, notably the approval of fees to be charged by the Director (s. 2 (4)), the receipt of annual reports from the Director (Fair Trading Act 1973, s. 125 (2), as amended by Consumer Credit Act, s. 5), the receipt of complaints that the functions of a local weights and measures authority under the Acts are not being properly discharged in any area, the setting up of a local inquiry to investigate such complaints and the receipt and publication of the report of the person holding the inquiry (s. 161 (4), (5)). [125]

The Director General of Fair Trading
    The office of the Director General of Fair Trading was created under s. 1 of the Fair Trading Act 1973, the Director being appointed by the Secretary of State for a term or terms not exceeding five years at a time. The Director is the head of the Office of Fair Trading and is responsible for the general administration and enforcement of the Fair Trading Act, which covers three main fields: monopolies and mergers, restrictive trade practices and consumer protection. A separate Division of the Office of Fair Trading is allotted to each of these areas. [126]
    Consumer credit was not originally envisaged as falling within the Director's remit, though his powers under the Fair Trading Act are certainly wide enough to embrace several aspects of consumer credit. The Crowther Committee had recommended the appointment of a Consumer Credit Commissioner and this was provided for in the original Consumer Credit Bill. But by the time the revised version of the Bill came to be introduced (the original Bill having been lost as the result of the election in February 1974), second thoughts had prevailed as to the wisdom of a separate office of Consumer Credit Commissioner, and under the revised Bill the functions that would have been allotted to the Commissioner were instead added to the existing functions of the Director General of Fair Trading. To deal with these a further Division was set up within the Office of Fair Trading, headed by the Director of Consumer Credit, who, though acting under the overall direction of the Director General, is *de facto* the person primarily responsible for overseeing the Consumer Credit Act. [127]
    Two of the most important functions of the Director are administration of the licensing system and supervision of enforcement of the Act. These duties are

spelled out in s. 1 (1) of the Act, which provides as follows:

"It is the duty of the Director General of Fair Trading ('the Director')—

(a) to administer the licensing system set up by this Act,

(b) to exercise the adjudicating functions conferred on him by this Act in relation to the issue, renewal, variation, suspension and revocation of licences, and other matters,

(c) generally to superintend the working and enforcement of the Act, and regulations made under it, and

(d) where necessary or expedient, himself to take steps to enforce this Act, and regulations so made."

But crucial though these functions are, they are by no means the sole functions of the Director. Other important duties are imposed on him by ss. 1 (2) and 4. There is some overlap between these and the wide-ranging functions conferred on the Director by the Fair Trading Act in field of consumer protection, particularly under ss. 2 (4), 14 and 17. [**128**]

By s. 1 (2) of the Consumer Credit Act:

"It is the duty of the Director, so far as it appears to him to be practicable and having regard to the national interest and the interests of persons carrying on business to which this Act applies and their customers, to keep under review and from time to time advise the Secretary of State about—

(a) social and commercial developments in the United Kingdom and elsewhere relating to the provision of credit or bailment or (in Scotland) hiring of goods to individuals, and related activities; and

(b) the working and enforcement of this Act and orders and regulations made under it."

The reference to the national interest envisages that the Director shall have regard to the effect of consumer credit on the national economy, thereby obliquely involving him in the assessment of the effect of terms control operated under the hire-purchase and hiring control orders (see para. [**15**]). Additional functions may be conferred on the Director by the Secretary of State (s. 2 (1)), who may give general directions indicating considerations to which the Director should have particular regard in carrying out his functions under the Act, and specific directions on any matter connected with the carrying out by the Director of those functions (s. 2 (2)). [**129**]

Section 4 requires the Director to arrange for the dissemination, in such form and manner as he considers appropriate, of such information and advice as it may appear to him expedient to give to the public in the United Kingdom about the operation of the Act, the credit facilities to him and other matters within the scope of his functions under the Act. This is an extremely important aspect of the Director's work, enabling the Director to engage in activities designed to educate the consumer in relation to credit matters (a task the need for which was emphasised in the Crowther Report) and to provide information to Citizens' Advice Bureaux and other advisory organisations which can be passed on by them to members of the public consulting them. The Office of Fair Trading has published a series of booklets for the guidance of the public dealing with different aspects of the Consumer Credit Act. In addition the Office has produced various guidance notes for specific professions and trades, e.g. accountants, chartered surveyors, valuers, chartered auctioneers, estate agents, etc., and motor dealers. These guidance notes draw attention to the particular impact of the Act on members of these professions and trades. [**130**]

Under s. 125 (1) of the Fair Trading Act 1973, the Director is required, as soon as practicable after the end of the year 1974 and of each subsequent calendar year, to make to the Secretary of State a report on his activities, and the activities of the Advisory Committee and of the Commission, during that year. Each such report must include a general survey of developments during the year to which it relates, in respect of matters falling within the scope of the Director's duties under any enactment (s. 125 (2)), including, of course, the Consumer Credit Act, and must set out any directions given to the Director under s. 2 (2) of the Consumer Credit Act during that year (Fair Trading Act, s. 125 (2) as amended by Consumer Credit Act, s. 5). [**131**]

Hence the functions of the Director are partly executive, partly administrative and partly judicial. In the exercise of his judicial functions he is a tribunal under the general supervision of the Council on Tribunals (Tribunals and Inquiries Act 1971, s. 1 and 1st Schedule, as amended by the Consumer Credit Act 1974, s. 3), but the Council has no jurisdiction over the Director's working, decisions or procedure in the exercise of executive functions (*ibid.*, s. 19 (4)).
[**132**]

The regulatory powers of the Director relate principally to the operation of the licensing provisions (examined in detail in Chapter 11) and the grant of dispensations from certain of the statutory provisions, e.g. from Part V of the Act (covering formalities of contract, withdrawal and cancellation), relief from the consequences of trading without a licence and directions for an alternative procedure under s. 160 for the supply of information to business consumers by credit reference agencies. These powers take a bewildering variety of forms several of which appear to differ from each other only in name. [**133**]

(i) *Authorisations*

These are shown in licences issued under the Act and state the activities authorised under the licence and the name or names under which the licensee may carry on a business. For authorisations to unlicensed traders see (iv) and (vi), *post.* [**134**]

(ii) *Determinations*

These are decisions directly relating to *inter alia* the grant, refusal, variation, suspension or revocation of a licence, the exemption of certain overdraft agreements from the prohibition in s. 49 as to soliciting and the exclusion of certain classes of agreement from Part V of the Act. [**135**]

(iii) *General Notices*

These are notices of acts and decisions of the Director (whether quasi-judicial or purely administrative) published for the information of those likely to be affected by the acts or decisions concerned. Among matters that have been the subject of a general notice are the contents of the public register to be maintained by the Director, the form of licence applications and supporting information, the fees payable for a licence and the granting of group licences. Some general notices have a regulatory effect, so that the acts or decisions which they announce can become operative only on the publication of the general notice. Thus fees and forms of application to the Director can only be such as are specified in a general notice (see ss. 2 (4), 6 (2)), so that the general notice itself is an operative instrument. In other cases a general notice does not have such a regulatory effect but is simply the prescribed machinery for making known acts done and decisions taken by the Director. Examples are general notices relating to the issue, variation, suspension, revocation and renewal of group licences (ss. 22 (8), 29 (6), 31 (6)) and all matters requiring to be entered in the register (s. 35 (2)). Here the decision or act of the Director precedes and is evidenced by the general notice. Exactly when the act or decision (e.g. a renewal of a group licence) takes effect is not spelled out in the Act, but presumably it is when the Director has taken some formal step to manifest the act or decision in question, as by notification of a party affected or by entry in the register.

General notices must, by definition, be published (see s. 189 (1)), but it is for the Director to decide the time and manner of publication suitable for securing that the notice is seen within a reasonable time by persons likely to be affected by it (*ibid.*).

[**136**]

(iv) *Orders*

These are similar in effect to determinations. The Director can make an order *inter alia* that agreements made by a trader when unlicensed shall be treated as though he had been licensed (ss. 40 (1), 148, 149). [**137**]

(v) *Notices*

A notice by the Director is a notice to a specific party, as opposed to a general notice. Thus the Director must give notice to an applicant for a licence that the Director is minded to refuse an application or grant it in terms different from that applied for (s. 27 (1)); to a person whom the Director proposes to exclude from a group licence, that he is so minded (s. 28); to a licensee whose licence the Director proposes to vary, suspend or revoke, that he is so minded (ss. 31 (2), 32 (2)); to a licensee who has given notice of changes under s. 36, that the Director requires him to furnish specific information (ss. 36 (6)). Notices are purely administrative and do not themselves have any regulatory force, though they may operate to fix a time from which the period allowed for an appeal or the performance of some other act begins to run. [**138**]

(vi) *Directions*

Section 32 (5) empowers the Director, on revoking or suspending a licence, to give directions authorising a licensee to carry into effect agreements made by him before the revocation or suspension. Presumably such directions need not be confined to designating the agreements to which the authorisation in question relate but may prescribe such conditions and procedures as the Director thinks appropriate. [**139**]

(vii) *Other acts*

Several acts which the Director is empowered to do are not given any of the above labels. Thus, the Director does not make an order or determination for the grant of a licence, he simply issues a licence. He does not order suspension or revocation, but merely suspends or revokes. [**140**]

(viii) *Decisions*

The Director is required to ensure that the register records particulars of decisions given by him under the Act, and any appeal from these decisions (s. 35

45

(2)). The word "decisions" is not defined but presumably embraces all the other categories listed above except general notices and acts which are not determinative in character. [141]

For a comprehensive list of the Director's functions and of general (i.e. non-specific) directions and determinations made and general notices issued by him see Part VI. [142]

By s. 183 of the Consumer Credit Act, the Director may vary or revoke any determination or direction made or given by him under the Act, other than Part III or Part III as applied by s. 147. Within s. 183 are for example, directions under ss. 60 (3) and 101 (8) and determinations under ss. 64 (4) and 74 (3). [143]

Appointed persons and advisers

Appeals to the Secretary of State from a determination of the Director mentioned in s. 41 of the Act are governed by the Consumer Credit Licensing (Appeals) Regulations 1976, examined in Chapter 11. Such appeals may in certain cases be dealt with by the Secretary of State without a hearing. Where the appeal is to be disposed of by a hearing, then unless it is to be heard by an officer of the Secretary of State, which is unlikely to be the case save in exceptional circumstances (see para. [418]), it will take place before an "appointed person" either alone or with other appointed persons (reg. 10). An appointed person is a person appointed by the Secretary of State to hear such appeals and to report them to the Secretary of State. Appointed persons are drawn from a panel set up by the Secretary of State. Members of the panel are appointed to it because of their wide experience of business, administration or law. Their appointment is part-time only. [144]

On any particular appeal to be disposed of by a hearing it will be for the Secretary of State to decide how many panel members should be appointed to hear the appeal, and who those members should be. Selection will obviously depend on the nature of the appeal and the circumstances of the case. Where a difficult point of law is involved it will no doubt be considered desirable to appoint a lawyer. Where the question turns on business practice, different considerations may apply. [145]

The Secretary of State is empowered by reg. 19 (2) of the Consumer Credit Licensing (Appeals) Regulations to appoint any person to give the appointed person advice on a matter of law or on any other matter relating to the appeal.
[146]

Trading standards/consumer protection officers

Whereas the overall responsibility for enforcement of the Act lies with the Director, enforcement at local level will largely be left to the local weights and measures authorities (see Chapter 33). They in turn will usually act through officers formerly known as weights and measures inspectors, who still carry this title when exercising their statutory functions under the Weights and Measures Acts but are now, with the increase in the range of their duties, more commonly described as trading standards officers or as consumer protection officers. Since the weights and measures inspector does not as such have a statutory status for the purpose of the Consumer Credit Act, it is open to the local authority to arrange for local enforcement of the Act and regulations by trading standards officers who are not weights and measures inspectors. [**147**]

In operating the licensing system the Director will be heavily dependent on information received from trading standards officers. There is already an elaborate system in operation by which trading standards officers collect weekly from Citizens' Advice Bureaux information on consumer complaints, integrate this with their own data on such complaints and send the details forward to the Office of Fair Trading. The trading standards officers will also keep the Office of Fair Trading informed of local practices and of intended prosecutions, notice of the latter being a statutory obligation under s. 161 (2) of the Act (see para. [**1063**]). In the early stages of licensing, applicants for licences were required to send notice of their applications in form CC 11/75 to the trading standards officers for the areas in which they intended to carry out the licensed activity, but this requirement was abandoned in November 1976 (see further para. [**367**], *post*). The trading standards officers act as agents of the Office of Fair Trading in holding licence application forms and licensing publicity material and in disseminating leaflets prepared by the Office of Fair Trading informing the consumer of his rights and the trader of his duties. [**148**]

Consumer advice powers of local authorities

By s. 201 (8) of the Local Government Act 1972, a local weights and measures authority may make, or assist in the making of, arrangements to provide advice to or for the benefit of consumers of goods and services within the area of the authority. This is a very useful provision upon which many authorities have acted. [**149**]

2. THE REGISTER MAINTAINED UNDER THE ACT

The Register and its contents

The Director is required by s. 35 of the Act to establish and maintain a register containing particulars relating to licences and applications therefor, together with such other matters (if any) as he thinks fit, and to give general notice of the various matters required to be entered in the register, (see para. [**330**]). The register was established on the 2nd February 1976, and the required particulars are set out in General Notice No. 5 dated 29th January 1976. [**150**]

The register is arranged alphabetically under the names of the applicants for licences and existing licences. The particulars entered in it will take the form of a photocopy of the document or registrable part of the document, containing the particulars in question, in much the same way as in the case of particulars filed in the Company Registry. Thus, particulars of an application for a standard licence will be entered by filing on the register a photographic copy of the front page of the application form (CC 1/75) covering the answers to questions 1–6 (see further on this para. [**353**], *post*). [**151**]

Location of the Register

The register itself is maintained at Chancery House, 53 Chancery Lane, London WC2A 1SP. Photographic copies of the register were initially kept in Belfast and

Edinburgh, with a public enquiry point at Cardiff which was to have had a full copy of the register at a later date. However, with increasing constraints on public expenditure the public register facilities at Edinburgh, Belfast and Cardiff were withdrawn from the 1st November 1976. [152]

Searches and copies

The register is open to the public and, on payment of the appropriate fee, may be inspected between the hours of 10.00 am and 3.30 pm on any day other than a Saturday, Sunday or public holiday. The fee is 10p for each file of entries inspected. An index listing applicants and licensees by their name and business name can be examined free of charge. By using this index, the person making the search can see whether a file exists on the person or organisation in which he is interested. Certified and uncertified copies of any entries may be obtained, the fee being 20p per sheet for uncertified copies and 40p for each sheet of copies certified by the Director. An additional fee of 50p is charged for each copy sent by post. [153]

Amendment and removal of entries

Since the register is essentially a register of documents rather than of facts, so that there is no "entry" other than that which is embodied in the filed documents, no amendments are made as such to the file. All that happens is that a document recording the change is put on the file, with the previously filed document being retained as being part of the file until the time comes for it to be removed. It is understood that entries will be maintained in the file for six years. [154]

7. When the Act Applies

General scope of the Act

In determining the boundaries of control established by the statutory provisions, it is necessary to distinguish four principal objects of regulation First, there are the primary contracts on which the Act is centred, namely consumer credit agreements and consumer hire agreements. These are collectively termed regulated agreements. Then, there are other contracts of various kinds ancillary to consumer credit and consumer hire agreements, though themselves capable of constituting regulated agreements in certain conditions. Among these are guarantees, indemnities and "linked transactions". Next, the Act has provisions which do not concern specific contracts but regulate the general conduct of business, whether by creditors or owners or by those conducting some ancillary credit business, e.g. credit brokerage. These provisions include licensing requirements, advertising controls, restrictions on canvassing and other methods of seeking business, and rules affecting some of the operations of credit reference agencies. Finally, there are various sections dealing with administration and enforcement of the Act and penalties for breach. [155]

The ambit of control varies according to the object of regulation, but the control criteria are closely linked through the unifying factor of the regulated agreement. The rest of this chapter is devoted to the limits of control of transactions, with particular reference to consumer credit and consumer hire agreements. [156]

The regulated agreement

A basic definition is that of the *regulated agreement*. The regulated agreement is the key to an understanding of the scope of the Act. We shall discuss the meaning of "regulated agreement" shortly. Its importance lies in the fact that:

(a) all regulated agreements are governed by the requirements and restrictions of the Act;

(b) transactions linked to regulated agreements—e.g. associated sale, maintenance or insurance contracts—are affected by the Act in various ways;

(c) security provided in relation to regulated or linked agreements is controlled by the Act;

49

(*d*) those wishing to carry on the business of granting credit under regulated agreements must be licensed by the Director;

(*e*) those wishing to carry on an ancillary credit business, the definition of which is in effect tied closely to that of the regulated agreement, must be licensed by the Director.

It will be apparent, as mentioned in para. [**117**] that the definition of "regulated agreement" is relevant to the overall applicability of the Act, not merely to the operation of its transactional provisions. [**157**]

A regulated agreement is a consumer credit agreement or consumer hire agreement which is not an exempt agreement (ss. 189 (1), 8 (3), 15 (2)). A *consumer credit agreement* is an agreement between an individual ("the debtor") and any other person ("the creditor") by which the creditor provides the debtor with credit not exceeding £5,000. In fact, the Act does not lay out the definition of consumer credit agreement in quite this way. It starts by defining a *personal credit agreement* as an agreement between an individual ("the debtor") and any other person ("the creditor") by which the creditor provides the debtor with credit of any amount (s. 8 (1)). It then goes on to say that a consumer credit agreement is a personal credit agreement by which the creditor provides the debtor with credit not exceeding £5,000 (s. 8 (2)). The reason why the term "personal credit agreement" was introduced in the Act was that at certain points in the Act (e.g. ss. 10 and 11) it was desired as a matter of drafting to use a phrase that would denote an agreement having the characteristics of a consumer credit agreement but without the financial limitation. Hence the insertion of "personal credit agreement" is a pure drafting device. The Act is concerned only with those personal credit agreements that lie within the £5,000 ceiling and thus constitute consumer credit agreements. However, this figure may be increased or reduced by statutory instrument laid before and approved by each House of Parliament (s. 181). A *consumer hire agreement* is an agreement made by a person with an individual (the "hirer") for the bailment of goods which (*a*) is not a hire-purchase agreement and (*b*) is capable of subsisting for more than three months and (*c*) does not require the hirer to make payments exceeding £5,000 (s. 15 (1)). Again, the figure of £5,000 may be increased or reduced in the manner above mentioned. The ingredients of a consumer credit agreement and a consumer hire agreement are examined in detail below. It should not be assumed that because the Act uses the phrase "consumer credit" it is confined to domestic transactions. As we shall see, the word "consumer", if taken at face value, is misleading, since a considerable number of commercial transactions are caught by the Act. Moreover the transactional provisions of the Act are not entirely restricted in impact to regulated agreements or agreements associated with actual or prospective regulated agreements. In particular:

(i) all credit agreements, of whatever amount, where the debtor is an individual (as defined—see para. [**172**] are subject to the provisions of the Act relating to extortionate credit bargains (see Chapter 30);

(ii) the Secretary of State is empowered to make regulations as to agreements entered into in the course of a business of credit brokerage, debt-adjusting or debt-counselling (s. 156), and though for the most part such businesses are by definition linked to the provision of credit under regulated agreements, this is not always the case (see, for example, s. 145 (2) (*a*) (ii) and para. [**998**]. [**158**]

The consumer credit agreement encompasses every conceivable form of consumer credit—hire-purchase, conditional sale, credit sale, check trading, credit card issuing, budget accounts, unsecured loans and overdrafts, mortgage transactions, pledges and indeed any form of contractual credit that one can conceive. Moreover, it is not confined to the supply of land or goods under credit arrangements; the provision of services and facilities on credit is equally within its scope (see Chapters 8 and 26). The term "credit" covers non-instalment as well as instalment credit. But regulations under s. 16 (5) of the Act exempt unsecured debtor-creditor-supplier agreements under which the credit is repayable by not more than four instalments (see para. [310]). This removes from the scope of the Act a large amount of account credit and at the same time renders academic some of the more difficult questions arising as to the meaning of "credit" (see Chapter 8). [159]

Purpose of use irrelevant

The task of deciding who is to qualify as a "consumer", and what is to constitute a "consumer" transaction, for the purpose of protective legislation is far from easy. Indeed, the answer will usually vary widely according to the type of protection sought to be provided and the underlying purpose of the legislation. Moreover, different facets of a transaction may demand different control criteria. The Crowther Committee identified no less than nine forms of classification as worthy of consideration (see Crowther Report, para. 6.2.17), including the size of the credit, the rate of interest charged, the status of the debtor and the purpose for which the credit is required, and in one way or another the Consumer Credit Act utilises every one of these classifications, and others besides—an indication of the complexity of the subject. [160]

In other legislation, Parliament has usually adopted the "purpose of use" test in distinguishing between consumer and commercial transactions. Thus both the Supply of Goods (Implied Terms) Act 1973 and the Unfair Contract Terms Act 1977 identify a consumer purchase as a purchase of goods of a type ordinarily supplied for private use or consumption where the purchaser does not buy or hold himself out as buying them in the course of a business. The Crowther Committee rejected the purpose of use test as a basis for overall transactional control, because of the difficulty that a lender would face in knowing the purpose for which the loan was intended, concluding that the test was too vague and subjective to form an acceptable basis for defining the limits of the projected legislation (see Crowther Report, paras. 6.2.18–6.2.19). The Committee's own approach was to identify protected transactions by reference to the size of the credit and the status of the debtor (i.e. bodies corporate would be excluded from protection). [161]

The Consumer Credit Act adopts the view of the Crowther Report in rejecting purpose of use as a general control criterion, and as advocated by the Report it utilises two basic tests, a financial ceiling (limiting the Act to transactions where the credit or total rental commitment does not exceed £5,000) and the non-corporate status of the debtor. However, the EEC draft Directive on Consumer Credit now before the Council uses the purpose of use test with no financial ceiling, though it is intended that governments of member States shall be free to negotiate individually with the Commission as to the upper and lower limits of control. [162]

Before we proceed to a detailed analysis of the definitions of consumer credit agreement and consumer hire agreement it is worth drawing attention to changes introduced by the Act in its description of the parties. [**163**]

"Creditor"; "debtor"

As has been mentioned earlier in this chapter, the term "credit"in the Consumer Credit Act covers not merely loan credit but every other form of financial accommodation. "Creditor" and "debtor" are given correspondingly extended meanings. "Creditor", as defined by s. 189 (1), "means the person providing credit under a consumer credit agreement or the person to whom his rights and duties under the contract have passed by assignment or operation of law, and in relation to a prospective consumer credit agreement, includes the prospective creditor." "Debtor", under the same provision, "means the individual receiving credit under a consumer credit agreement or the person to whom his rights and duties under the agreement have passed by assignment or by operation of law, and in relation to a prospective consumer credit agreement includes the prospective debtor." Thus "creditor" and "debtor" now embrace the seller and buyer of goods disposed of under an instalment sale agreement and the owner and hirer of goods on hire-purchase. Included in the definition are assignees and also transferees by operation of law, e.g. the trustee in bankruptcy or personal representative of the creditor or debtor. By a drafting slip s. 189 (1), when referring to assignees, speaks of the person to whom rights *and* duties have passed by assignment. Literally construed, this part of the definition would be largely nugatory, since as a matter of contract law an assignment transfers rights but does not relieve the assignor of his duties to the other contracting party or entitle that party to enforce such duties against the assignee. It is thought that this is a case where the court would construe "and" as "or", thus maintaining the sense of the definition as more accurately provided in s. 58 (1) of the Hire-Purchase Act 1965. [**164**]

"Owner"; "hirer"

The words "owner" and "hirer", hitherto used in the Hire-Purchase Acts to denote the parties to a hire-purchase agreement, are now confined to simple hiring agreements. "Owner", under s. 189 (1), "means a person who bails or (in Scotland) hires out goods under a consumer hire agreement or the person to whom his rights and duties under the agreement have passed by assignment or operation of law, and in relation to a prospective consumer hire agreement, includes the prospective bailor or person from whom the goods are to be hired." "Hirer", by the same section, "means the individual to whom goods are bailed or (in Scotland) hired under a consumer hire agreement, or the person to whom his rights and duties under the agreement have passed by assignment or operation of law, and in relation to a prospective consumer hire agreement includes the prospective hirer." The comments made in para. [**164**] are equally applicable here. [**165**]

1. REGULATED CONSUMER CREDIT AGREEMENT

The elements of the statutory definition

The statutory definition of a regulated consumer credit agreement embodied in

s. 8 of the Act possesses six ingredients, namely:

    (*a*) an agreement between two parties;
    (*b*) one of whom, "the debtor", is an individual;
    (*c*) and the other, the creditor, is "any other person";
    (*d*) by which the creditor provides the debtor with credit;
    (*e*) not exceeding £5,000;
    (*f*) the agreement not being an exempt agreement.

To these six essential elements of a regulated consumer credit agreement we may now add a seventh, namely that the agreement is made on or after the 1st April 1977 (Consumer Credit Act 1974 (Commencement No. 2) Order 1977, art. 2 (1)). [**166**]

"Agreement"
    The word "agreement", picturesquely defined in an old case as a copulation of two or more minds, means not merely a mutual understanding but a contract, that is, an agreement which produces a legal relationship. To be within the Act, the contract need not be formal. It may be made by an exchange of letters, by word of mouth or even by implication from conduct. It need not be an enforceable contract (for example, the fact that one of the parties may not enforce it for want of a written memorandum prescribed by other legislation does not negate the existence of the contract); but it must be valid in the sense of possessing the minimum attributes required to produce a legal relationship, namely *consensus ad idem* and consideration, i.e. a *quid pro quo* for a promise, the *quid pro quo* taking the form either of a counter-promise or of performance of some act. [**167**]
    In most cases, the need to determine whether a particular form of arrangement constitutes a contract arises not so much from the Consumer Credit Act as from the desire of the parties to know where they stand as a matter of general contract law. If there is no contract the provisions of the Act as to formalities of a contract, for example, do not come into operation, but immunity from these provisions in such a case is of no importance, since *ex hypothesi* there is no enforceable agreement in any event. Unless at least one of the parties seeks to assert the existence of a contract (an issue to be resolved not by the Consumer Credit Act but by the general law of contract) the question whether there is indeed a contract on which the Consumer Credit Act can bite is largely academic. Nevertheless, for certain purposes it may be important to determine whether a particular arrangement generates a contract so as to give rise to a regulated agreement. For example, if a bank agrees to give a customer an overdraft facility up to a stated figure and the customer subsequently draws a cheque which takes his overdraft over the agreed limit, does the bank's decision to honour the cheque constitute a separate agreement which requires compliance with the formalities of the Act in order to be enforceable or is it merely a voluntary waiver (as regards that particular cheque) of the credit limit fixed when the facility was opened? The answer to this particular question is to be found partly in banking law and partly in the Consumer Credit Act itself and is given in para. [**264**]; but the question suffices to make the point that it may be necessary for the purposes of the Consumer Credit Act, as well as of general contract law, to determine whether a particular act or series of acts constitutes a contract. What is regulated by the transactional provisions of the Act is not the provision of credit as such but the provision of credit *under an agreement*. The

question is whether the prospective creditor has bound himself to give credit, not whether the prospective debtor has bound himself to take it. Indeed, an agreement by a prospective debtor to enter into a regulated agreement is void (s. 59 (1)), though a mere option to him to take credit is outside s. 59, even though binding the prospective creditor. An agreement to provide a line of credit constitutes a credit agreement if the lender has committed himself to giving this facility, whether or not the borrower chooses to use it; but in most cases the provision of a line of credit is merely an offer which the lender can withdraw at any time before the borrower has accepted it by utilising the facility, and even thereafter can be revoked by the lender except so far as already utilised (see para. [**169**]). *A fortiori*, a mere letter of intent indicating a willingness to provide a line of credit or other facility without commitment is not a credit agreement. [**168**]

Some documents, though labelled "agreement" and signed by both parties, do not in fact possess contractual force at the time of their execution, since they do not themselves embody any specific transaction but simply lay down a set of "if" provisions, i.e. standard terms which are to govern future dealings between the parties if and when these occur. In other words, the stipulations in the document as to the provision of credit constitute a continuing offer by the prospective creditor to extend credit on the specified terms, the offer to be accepted by the prospective debtor by use of the facility, thus generating a series of unilateral contracts each of which is governed by the standard terms. This is true of virtually every form of revolving credit facility, whether it be an overdraft, a budget account, an option account or a credit card arrangement. The fact that it *is* a facility and not a commitment by the debtor to take the credit means that no contract comes into existence until the facility is utilised, and up to that time the debtor is free to withdraw, as also is the creditor unless by a separate promise supported by consideration he has undertaken to keep the facility available. Each time the debtor uses it he makes a separate acceptance of the creditor's continuing offer, generating a distinct contract governed by the standard or master agreement, but leaving both parties free to withdraw as regards future transactions. [**169**]

Thus an "agreement" for an overdraft facility crystallises into a contract every time the customer issues a cheque drawn on his account; the opening of a budget or option account for a customer of a store imposes no liability either on him or on the store at the time the account is opened but attracts a contractual commitment on both sides when the customer makes a purchase (assuming that he has not meanwhile received notice terminating the facility), the commitment continuing on the customer's side until all the goods bought have been paid for, whilst the store remains free to terminate the facility as to future purchases. [**170**]

In short, an "agreement" for revolving credit is in effect an umbrella for future credit transactions which would otherwise have been designated as fixed-sum credit, and until at least one such transaction has been effected the revolving credit agreement has no legal significance in relation to the provision of credit, though it may have effect as a bilateral contract for other purposes, as where a credit card agreement requires the cardholder to hold his card in safe keeping (see also s. 84 and paras. [**247**], [**828**]). The point is material for the purpose of determining when a consumer credit agreement comes into existence, a question that may be important for a variety of reasons (see para. [**239**]), including fixing the time when credit is deemed to have been provided, a matter discussed in the next chapter (para. [**248**]). There are, however, various situations in which the Act will operate in relation to an inchoate agreement. See, for example, s. 57, discussed in paras. [**585**] *et seq.* [**171**]

"Individual"

"Individual" is defined in s. 189 (1) as including a partnership or other unincorporated body of persons not consisting entirely of bodies corporate. Hence the only type of debtor excluded from the protection of the Act is a body corporate, that is, an association or body constituting a distinct legal entity and having perpetual succession and a common seal. Companies registered under the Companies Acts are bodies corporate, as are corporations created by royal charter or by special Act of Parliament (including public corporations like the B.B.C. and London Transport) and corporations sole, such as bishops and certain Ministers of the Crown. A registered industrial or provident society is by virtue of its registration a body corporate (Industrial and Provident Societies Act 1965, s. 3) and is thus not protected by the Consumer Credit Act. On the other hand, friendly societies and trade unions (whether registered or not) are not bodies corporate and each of these qualifies as an "individual" for the purpose of the Act. The word "individual" likewise covers an unincorporated club and an unincorporated charity. Only bodies corporate are excluded from protection; and even a body corporate can invoke the Act as a debtor where it is joined as debtor with an individual in a consumer credit agreement (s. 185 (5)). [**172**]

"Person"

Except where s. 16 of the Act (relating to exempted agreements) applies, it is only the status of the *debtor* that is relevant in determining whether the Act is applicable. The Act bites on credit agreements between "an individual" as debtor and "any other person" as creditor; and by the Interpretation Act 1978, s. 5 and Sch. 1, unless the contrary intention appears "person" includes a body of persons corporate or unincorporate, and thus embraces individuals, partnerships and other unincorporated associations, bodies corporate and indeed every form of entity known to the law. [**173**]

"Provides"

The Act speaks of "an agreement by which the creditor provides the debtor with credit". The word "provides" is not the happiest choice, since it suggests that the financial accommodation is to be furnished at the time of the agreement, whereas it is clear that what the Act means is an agreement for the provision of credit, whether the credit is to be provided at the time of the agreement or at a later date. [**174**]

"Credit"

Section 9 (1) of the Act provides that "credit" includes a cash loan and any other form of financial accommodation. This may seem straightforward enough, particularly as elaborated by s. 9 (3) and (4). But the concept of credit is peculiarly elusive, so much so that we shall devote the whole of the next chapter to its elaboration. [**175**]

"Not exceeding £5,000"

The Act is restricted to agreements under which the credit to be provided does not exceed £5,000. The meaning of the phrase "credit not exceeding £5000" is by no means as simple as it appears, and indeed may cover some transactions where there is no credit limit at all. The phrase is examined in detail in Chapter 8. [176]

Exempt consumer credit agreements

Certain agreements that would otherwise fall within the definition of a regulated consumer credit agreement are designated as exempt agreements. These are analysed in chapter 10. [177]

2. REGULATED CONSUMER HIRE AGREEMENT

The elements of the statutory definition

The statutory definition of a regulated consumer hire agreement was set out in para. [158] It possesses eight essential ingredients:—

- (a) an agreement between two parties;
- (b) one of whom, "the hirer", is an individual;
- (c) and the other, "the owner" (see s. 189 (1)), is "a person";
- (d) by which goods are bailed to the hirer;
- (e) without an option to purchase;
- (f) the agreement being capable of subsisting for more than three months;
- (g) being an agreement which does not require the hirer to make payments exceeding £5,000;
- (h) and is not an exempt agreement.

As in the case of the consumer credit agreement, we may now add a ninth element, namely that the agreement is made on or after the 1st April 1977 (Consumer Credit Act 1974 (Commencement No. 2) Order 1977, art. 2 (1)). [178]

The words "agreement", "individual" and "person" have been examined earlier in relation to consumer credit agreements, and as they have the same meaning for consumer hire agreements they need no further explanation. "Owner"and "hirer" are explained in para. [165]. Exempt hire agreements are dealt with in Chapter 10. [179]

Goods

By s. 189 (1) of the Act, "goods" has the meaning given by s. 62 (1) of the Sale of Goods Act 1893, namely chattels personal other than things in action and money. Whether an article which is to be installed on land or in a building is to be regarded as a chattel or as part of the land or building depends on the intention of the parties. If it is intended to be let for use and enjoyment as a distinct chattel, then except where it has already become a fixture by the time of the agreement (see *infra*) it will constitute goods under the agreement. If it is supplied for incorporation into the building as a fixture, the agreement will not be for the bailment of goods. Where at the time of the agreement the article is so firmly embedded as to be incapable of severance without material damage to the article or to the land or building to which it is annexed, it will constitute a fixture regardless of the intention of the parties, and the agreement will thus not be one of bailment. For a more detailed discussion of the topic, see R. M. Goode, *Hire-Purchase Law and Practice* (2nd Edn.), pp. 36–39 and Chapter 32. [**180**]

A lease of land together with goods in consideration of a single rental issuing out of the land (as in the case of a furnished letting) is not a consumer hire agreement (see para. [**301**]). [**181**]

No option to purchase

The agreement must not be a hire-purchase agreement. This means that it must not confer on the hirer an option to buy the goods (see the definition of "hire-purchase agreement" in s. 189 (1), and the description of hire-purchase in para. [**94**]). [**182**]

"Capable of subsisting for more than three months"

The agreement must be capable of subsisting for more than three months. This characteristic is fulfilled by any hiring agreement other than a hiring agreement for a fixed term not exceeding three months with no option to either party to renew beyond the three-month period. If the agreement is for an indeterminate period (e.g. is a periodic hiring such as from week to week or month to month until terminated by a prescribed period of notice) or if it is for a fixed period not exceeding three months but an option to renew beyond the three months is given to one party or the other, the hiring is capable of subsisting for more than three months for the purpose of s. 15. [**183**]

Payments not to exceed £5,000

To be a consumer hire agreement within the Act the agreement must not require the hirer to make payments exceeding £5,000. To see whether this condition is fulfilled one looks at the hirer's minimum legal commitment, taking account of any contractual right given to the hirer to terminate the agreement. If the hirer can limit his commitment to £5,000 (e.g. by exercising a power of termination before more than £5,000 rentals have accrued due) the agreement is a consumer hire agreement (given fulfilment of the other conditions) even if the hirer has power to incur a total rental liability exceeding £5,000 by exercising a right to renew the agreement or by declining to exercise a contractual right of termination that would restrict his liability to £5,000. [**184**]

So far the position is clear enough. Slightly more difficult is the case where the terms of the agreement are such that the total rental *may* go above £5,000 without the hirer having the right to prevent it. There are various ways in which this might occur. The agreement may empower the owner to increase the rent on notice to a level which will take the total above £5,000. Alternatively he may give the right to serve a notice of increase only upon the occurrence of certain events external to the contract, e.g. a change in tax or bank base rate. A further alternative is that the agreement provides for automatic increase in the rent upon the occurrence of some external event (e.g. of the kind described above) without the necessity for any notice or other act by the owner. Again, the agreement may include a provision for a rebate of rentals geared to the residual value of the goods at the end of the hiring period, a fact not known when the agreement is made. [**185**]

Fortunately the difficulties raised by these cases are more apparent than real. In deciding what the agreement "requires" for the purpose of determining its status, one looks at the facts at the time the agreement is made, not at the events which subsequently occur, unless those events, having been stipulated in the contract, are bound to occur and to take place at a time already determined when the agreement is entered into. The ultimate effect of the agreement may be to impose on the hirer a total liability in excess of £5,000, but in the various cases mentioned above this is due not to the force of the agreement alone but also to later events not predictable with certainty at the time of its making. It is true that s. 15 (1) (*c*) is couched in the negative, so that instead of the onus being on the owner to show that the agreement *does* require payment in excess of £5,000, it is for the hirer to show that it does *not* so require. But there is no problem here. The agreement does not, as seen at the time of its making, require the hirer to make payments in excess of £5,000; it merely requires him to make payments which may or may not exceed that figure. [**186**]

In computing the hirer's minimum rental liability, the statutory right of termination conferred by s. 101 must be ignored, since that section does not come into operation until it has first been established that the hiring agreement is a consumer hire agreement within the statutory definition. This point is brought out by the parliamentary draftsman in example 20 in Sch. 2. [**187**]

3. PARTIALLY REGULATED AGREEMENTS

A consumer credit or consumer hire agreement which is not an exempt agreement under s. 16 is regulated by the Act; but certain classes of regulated agreement are exempt from certain specific provisions of the Act. Into this category fall small agreements (see para. [**190**]); non-commercial agreements (see para. [**192**]); multiple agreements (see para. [**296**]); certain purchase-money agreements secured by a land mortgage (see chapter 15); agreements for overdrafts (see para. [**593**]); and pledge of documents of title (see para. [**197**]). These may conveniently be termed "partially regulated agreements". [**188**]

4. SMALL AGREEMENTS

There are special provisions as to small agreements. As defined by s. 17, these are regulated consumer credit agreements where the credit does not exceed £30 and regulated consumer hire agreements which do not require the hirer to make payments exceeding £30. There are three qualifications. The definition does not embrace conditional sale or hire-purchase agreements. These do not qualify as small agreements, however small the credit. Secured transactions are likewise outside the definition, except where the security is limited to a guarantee or indemnity. In this connection, the wide definition of "security" in s. 189 (1) should be noted. Finally, the provisions of the Act cannot be evaded by the device of breaking up a transaction involving credit over £30 into two or more small agreements between the same parties at or about the same time, or by arranging that part of the transaction is split off into a separate agreement which, though not between the same parties, substitutes for either party an associate of that party, as defined by clause 184 (see s. 17 (3), (4)). [**189**]

In determining whether an agreement is a small agreement within s. 17 the figure to be taken (except in the case of consumer hire agreements) is the amount of the credit. This will be dealt with in detail in the next chapter, but may be tabulated as follows:

Nature of Agreement	*Figure to be Taken*
Credit sale	Total price less deposit and charges
Credit card	Credit limit
Check trading	Face value of checks less downpayment
Unsecured loan	Amount of loan, excluding components of credit charge

In the case of consumer hire agreements, the total amount to be paid by the hirer must not exceed £30. This would appear to exclude from the small agreement category (i) consumer hire agreements for an indefinite period (*e.g.* weekly or monthly), however low the periodic rental, unless the hirer has a right to terminate before he becomes committed to a rental in excess of £30; and (ii) consumer hire agreements for a fixed period under which, though the total rent for the period cannot exceed £30, the owner has an option to renew for a further period or periods which may take the total rental above £30. On the other hand, if the option to renew is purely with the hirer, rentals payable on the renewal would be excluded in deciding whether the £30 limit has been exceeded. [**190**]

Small agreements (of which illustrations are given in examples 16, 17 and 22 in the Second Schedule to the Act) enjoy exemption from the whole of Part V of the Act, except ss. 55 and 56, where the agreements are debtor-creditor-supplier agreements for restricted-use credit (s. 74 (2)). These terms are explained in para. [**273**] *et seq.* Suffice it to say at this stage that within this exemption fall, for example, small credit sale, check trading and credit card transactions. All these are exempt from the formalities of contract (other than disclosure requirements prescribed by regulations under s. 55) and from the cooling off provisions. In addition, the duty to supply a copy of the executed agreement and any document referred to in it on issue of a new credit token (s. 85 (1)) does not apply in relation to a small agreement of any kind (s. 85 (3)). Further, a creditor under a small agreement is not affected by ss. 78 (4) and (5) relating to the automatic duty to supply periodic statements of account (see s. 78 (7)). On the other hand, small agreements remain controlled by the provisions of Part IV of the Act regulating the seeking of business (see Chapter 12) and by the provisions requiring the creditor or owner to supply information to the debtor or hirer on request (ss. 77, 78). Moreover, the restrictions on remedies for default, including termination, apply to small agreements, which are likewise governed by the whole of Part IX of the Act, relating to judicial control and the re-opening of extortionate credit bargains.
[**191**]

5. NON-COMMERCIAL AGREEMENTS

The transactional provisions of the Consumer Credit Act are primarily aimed at the trader or other professional credit grantor. Accordingly many of the statutory provisions are made inapplicable to a non-commercial agreement, that is, a consumer hire agreement not made by the creditor or owner in the course of a business carried on by him (s. 189 (1)). It is important to note that in order for an agreement to be a non-commercial agreement it must not be made by the creditor or owner in the course of *any* business carried on by him, whether or not that business relates to the granting of consumer credit or consumer hire facilities. Hence, if, for example, a solicitor regularly makes loans to clients in the course of his practice, the fact that this credit-granting facility is purely ancillary to a professional activity not otherwise concerned with consumer credit is irrelevant: the loan agreement will not qualify as a non-commercial agreement. On the other hand, a person is not to be treated as carrying on a particular type of business merely because occasionally he enters into transactions belonging to a business of that type (s. 189 (2)). So consumer credit agreements entered into as creditor by a solicitor who makes only occasional loans in the course of his business would satisfy the test for a non-commercial agreement, as, of course, would loans he makes in a purely private capacity. It is for the creditor to prove that an agreement is a non-commercial agreement. [192]

Non-commercial agreements are exempt from Part V of the Act, other than s. 56 (see s. 74 (1)) and thus are not governed by any formal requirements or by the cooling off provisions. The creditor under a non-commercial agreement cannot incur any liability under s. 75 (1) (see s. 75 (3)). In other words he does not, in Crowther terms, incur the liability of a connected lender. He is also exempt from the duty to supply information to the debtor or a surety under ss. 77–79 and 107–110 of the Act. Normally the debtor under a regulated agreement which requires him to keep goods to which the agreement relates in his possession or control must supply the creditor with information as to their whereabouts after receipt of a written request (s. 80 (1)); but this duty is excluded in the case of a non-commercial agreement. Other provisions of the Act inapplicable to non-commercial agreements are ss. 40 (1), 82, 103, 112 and 114. Moreover, although the Act does not say so directly, a creditor whose activity is restricted to granting credit under non-commercial agreements need not be licensed, since it follows from the definition of a non-commercial agreement (see para. [192]) that he is not carrying on a consumer credit or consumer hire business. [193]

6. OTHER CATEGORIES

Multiple agreements
These are considered in paras. [296] *et seq..* [194]

Purchase-money land mortgages
Certain types of purchase-money land mortgage are exempted from some of the statutory provisions. These are dealt with in Chapter 15. [195]

Overdrafts
Debtor-creditor agreements for overdrafts are exempted from Part V of the Act (except s. 56) where the Director so determines (s. 74 (1) (b), (3)). Such determination may be made subject to such conditions as the Director thinks fit, but may not be made unless the Director is of opinion that it is not against the

interests of debtors (s. 74 (3)). However, if the creditor is a recognised bank or a licensing deposit-taking institution, the Director must make a determination unless he considers this would be against the public interest (s. 74(3A), added by the Banking Act 1979). [**196**]

Pledges of documents of title

Sections 114–122, relating to pledges, do not apply to pledges of documents of title or bearer bonds (s. 114 (3) as amended by the Banking Act 1979). The phrase "documents of title" is not defined but in this context denotes documents of title to goods (see para. [**783**]). Whereas documents of title to land are documents indicative of ownership, this is not necessarily so in the case of a document of title to goods. It suffices that it is a document used in the ordinary course of business as proof of the possession or control of goods or as authorising (by delivery with any necessary indorsement) the holder of the document to transfer or receive the goods represented by it (see *Ramdas Vithaldas Durbar* v. *S. Amerchand & Co.* (1916), 85 L.J.P.C. 214, at p. 216; and *cf.* Factors Act 1889, s. 1 (4)). A bill of lading is a document of title to the goods represented by it, so long as the goods remain under the shipowner's control, even though the goods have arrived at the port of destination and have been received from the ship into a warehouse (*Barclays Bank, Ltd.* v. *Customs and Excise Commissioners,* [1963] 1 Lloyd's Rep. 81). A letter of trust, or trust receipt, taken by a bank as a condition of releasing pledged documents of title is indicative of the bank's continued control of the goods but is not, it is thought, a document of title since it is not ordinarily transferred by indorsement or delivery and the goods remain represented by the bill of lading released against the trust receipt. A delivery order has in one case been held a document of title (*Ant. Jurgens Margarinefabrieken* v. *Louis Dreyfus & Co.,* [1914] 3 K.B. 40) but the reasoning is untenable and the decision can be justified only on the basis that the delivery order in question was indorsed by the warehouse and handed to the intended transferee, so that it became analogous to a warrant by the warehouse itself (see, for example, *Laurie and Morewood* v. *John Dudin & Sons,* [1925] 2 K.B. 383). Even a warehouse or dock warrant or receipt will not usually be considered a document of title unless the warehouse or dock company is created by special Act of Parliament which provides that its warrants are to constitute documents of title, as in the case of the Port of London and the Mersey Docks. A car registration book is not a document of title (*Joblin* v. *Watkins and Roseveare* (Motors), *Ltd.,* [1949] 1 All E.R. 47; *Pearson* v. *Rose and Young, Ltd.,* [1951] 1 K.B. 275, [1950] 2 All E.R. 1027, nor is an invoice or a certificate of completion of a hire-purchase agreement. [**197**]

Hire-purchase and conditional sale agreements

Within the classification previously discussed, and elaborated in the next chapter, the statutory provisions apply across the whole field of consumer credit, so that in the main no distinctive significance attaches to hire-purchase and conditional sale agreements as such, and in the greater part of the Act these forms of contract do not receive specific mention. There are, however, provisions which apply exclusively to hire-purchase and conditional sale agreements. Thus (i) they are excluded from the definition of "small agreement" (s. 17 (1)); (ii) only goods comprised in a hire-purchase or conditional sale agreement can become protected goods so as to attract the prohibition in s. 90 (re-enacting the Hire-Purchase Act 1965, s. 34) against repossession without a court order; (iii) prohibition of entry into premises for the purpose of repossessing goods is confined to goods comprised in a hire-purchase or conditional sale agreement (s. 92 (1)); (iv) special provisions (re-enacting those of the Hire-Purchase Act 1965) give a hirer on hire-purchase and a buyer on conditional sale a right to terminate the agreement (s. 99), restrict his liability on termination (s. 100), regulate the powers of the court (s. 133) and deal with proof of adverse detention (s. 134). [**198**]

"Hire-purchase agreement" is defined in s. 189 (1) in terms rather wider than those of s. 1 (1) of the Hire-Purchase Act 1965, fully analysed in the author's work *Hire-Purchase Law and Practice* (2nd Edn.), pp. 54–60. In particular, a provision in the agreement for the passing of the property to the hirer suffices to make the agreement a hire-purchase agreement even if the event stipulated as causing the property to pass is not the voluntary act of the owner or hirer but the happening of some other specified event. Hence the type of agreement which the court in *R. v. R. W. Proffitt, Ltd.*, [1954] 2 Q.B. 35, [1954] 2 All E.R. 798 declined to hold a hire-purchase agreement would fall within the new statutory definition. The meaning of "conditional sale agreement" is the same as in s. 1 (1) of the Hire-Purchase Act 1965, except that it is no longer confined to goods but extends to land. [**199**]

Contracts with a foreign element

As a rule, United Kingdom legislation is construed so as to avoid giving it extra-territorial effect. One might, therefore, expect that the Consumer Credit Act would be held inapplicable to transactions concluded abroad. However, the width of the Act, and the provisions relating to linked transactions, make it impossible to say that a transaction concluded abroad cannot attract the statutory provisions in some way. A good example is the credit card issued by a United Kingdom bank under a credit-token agreement and usable abroad. The debtor might utilise the card to make a foreign purchase. That purchase would no doubt be governed by the law of the country where it was made, but it does not follow that the United Kingdom bank would on that account avoid the liability under s. 75 that would ordinarily arise if the supplier's performance was defective. Indeed, the court would very probably take the view that since (by definition) the debtor-creditor-supplier agreement involved an existing or prospective arrangement between the bank and the foreign supplier who had agreed to accept the card, there was no reason why the bank should not accept the ordinary liability of a connected lender, particularly as the cardholder might have great difficulty in securing redress from the foreign supplier. [**200**]

With a view to resolving problems that may arise with transactions involving a foreign element, the Secretary of State is empowered by s. 16 (5) (c) to exclude from the scope of the Act agreements "having a connection with a country outside the United Kingdom." The regulations made under this provision are dealt with in Chapter 10. [**201**]

8. The Concept of Credit

The notion of credit is central to the Consumer Credit Act, yet there is almost no legal literature or case law offering guidance as to what constitutes credit or what is meant by instalment credit. This is not as surprising as it might appear, for prior to the Consumer Credit Act English statute law did not embody any global concept of credit but merely controlled specific credit forms, namely moneylending, pawnbroking, hire purchase and instalment sale. But now that the legislation has been broadened to encompass all forms of credit and all types of supply transaction, whether involving land, goods, services or facilities, an appreciation of the concepts of credit and instalment credit becomes crucial to an understanding of the Act and Regulations. [**202**]

1. WHAT CONSTITUTES THE PROVISION OF CREDIT

The statutory definition
"Credit" is defined in section 9 of the Consumer Credit Act, which provides as follows:—

> "(1) In this Act 'credit' includes a cash loan, and any other form of financial accommodation.
> (2) Where credit is provided otherwise than in sterling it shall be treated for the purposes of this Act as provided in sterling of an equivalent amount.
> (3) Without prejudice to the generality of subsection (1), the person by whom goods are bailed or (in Scotland) hired to an individual under a hire-purchase agreement shall be taken to provide him with fixed-sum credit to finance the transaction of an amount equal to the total price of the goods less the aggregate of the deposit (if any) and the total charge for credit.
> (4) For the purposes of this Act, an item entering into the total charge for credit shall not be treated as credit even though time is allowed for its payment."

The crucial phrase is "financial accommodation", but before looking at this we must first dispose of a few preliminary points. [**203**]

63

"Includes"

Prima facie a statutory provision by which a given word "includes" certain meanings is to be interpreted either as illustrating the meaning of the word or as enlarging its meaning beyond that which it would ordinarily bear, and is not to be read as providing an all-embracing definition (see *Dilworth* v. *Stamps Commissioner*, [1899] A.C. 99, *per* Lord Watson at pp. 105–106). But this is not necessarily the case. The context in which the word "include" is used may indicate that it is intended to denote a comprehensive definition (see *ibid.*). It is submitted that, subject to s. 9 (3) (which probably does not enlarge the definition anyway), the opening words of s. 9 (1) should be interpreted as if they read "means and includes", and that accordingly the word "credit" does not comprehend anything which is not a form of financial accommodation. [**204**]

"Cash loan"

By s. 189 (1), "cash" includes money in any form. We need not spend any time on this since, as the draftsman of the Act has pointed out in his own work on the subject, any form of credit which is not a cash loan is covered by the wide residuary category "any other form of financial accommodation", and nothing turns on which limb of the definition is involved (see F. A. R. Bennion, *Consumer Credit Control*, para. 1 §720A). Suffice it to say that a payment need not be made direct to the debtor to constitute a loan. Payment at his request to a third party also constitutes a loan to the debtor provided that it is an express of implied term of the payment that the debtor shall make repayment. [**205**]

"Financial accommodation"

At this stage we are concerned only with what constitutes financial accommodation. How one computes the figure to be taken as the amount of the credit is discussed later (paras. [**254**] *et seq.*). As a generalisation, we can say that between them "cash loan" and "any other form of financial accommodation" cover all the forms of credit described in para. [**159**]; and s. 9 (3) makes it clear that hire-purchase is included. This is to avoid a possible argument that hire-purchase is not credit since the hirer is merely hiring goods, with an option to buy, and is paying the hire-rent as he goes along, so that there is no deferred indebtedness generating credit. [**206**]

Which brings us to the crucial element of debt deferment. This is the essence of credit, and features explicitly in two American definitions. Section 103 (e) of the Federal Truth in Lending Act states that the term "credit" means

> "the right granted by a creditor to a debtor to defer payment
> of debt or to incur debt and defer its payment".

The same idea is adopted, in somewhat expanded form, in s. 226·2 of Regulation Z, made under the Truth in Lending Act, which defines credit as

> "the right granted by a creditor to a customer to defer payment
> of debt, incur debt and defer its payment or purchase property
> or services and defer payment therefor".

Hence the obverse of credit is not debt *simpliciter* but debt deferred; and the obverse of instalment credit is not instalment debt as such but debt repayable by instalments at least one of which is deferred. This, however, merely rolls the problem back a stage; for we still have to consider what constitutes debt, when debt is considered to be incurred and what amounts to deferment of debt. [**207**]

The ingredients of credit

The task of defining credit becomes easier if we break the concept down into its constituent parts. Building on the phrase "financial accommodation" and on the ideas implicit in the other definitions given above, we can postulate that credit involves:

(*a*) the receipt of a benefit;
(*b*) attracting a contractual duty of payment;
(*c*) in money;
(*d*) the duty to pay being contractually deferred for a significant period of time after the contractual date for the provision of the benefit. [**208**]

Receipt of benefit

The debtor must, of course, have received some benefit in order to incur an indebtedness; but so far as the Consumer Credit Act is concerned, it does not matter whether the benefit provided is land, goods, documents, money, choses in action, services or facilities. The provision of any of these on deferred payment terms constitutes the giving of credit. [**209**]

What is less clear is the stage at which benefit is to be considered furnished for this purpose. The question is crucial in that credit implies the provision of a benefit in advance of a duty to pay for it. Put another way, credit involves payment in arrear   but in arrear of what? The time when the asset or service is physically received? Or the (earlier) date on which the supplier contracts to provide it? We revert to this question in paras. [**213**] *et seq.* [**210**]

Contractual duty of payment

There are two aspects to this element. First, if the recipient of the benefit has no duty to pay for it, then he is not a debtor and it cannot be said that credit is being extended to him. Thus an undertaking to make a gift is not an extension of credit, nor is the gift itself. Equally, a purchase of book debts is not a credit transaction, for though the buyer receives a financial benefit (the price) it is not repayable; and the law draws a clear distinction between a purchase of debts and a loan on the security of debts (see para. [**230**]). Secondly, the payment must be due under a contract and not, for example, in quasi-contract by way of restitution. This is because debt, and thus credit, is essentially contractual in nature. Indeed, without a contract the test of a right to deferment of payment could not be satisfied. [**211**]

In money

"Financial accommodation" implies deferment of a debt and thus of a money obligation. Accordingly a payment made for services to be performed in the future does not constitute credit (though the giving of the services in return for a deferred payment would constitute the grant of credit by the provider of the services). Similarly, an agreement for exchange, or barter, is not a credit agreement, since no *financial* accommodation is involved. On the other hand, an instalment sale in which there is a part exchange does entail a financial accommodation, for the primary obligation of the buyer is to pay a money price, and even though part of this is satisfied by delivery of the part-exchange goods, there remains a money balance in respect of which the seller's agreement to defer payment constitutes an extension of credit. Indeed, even what appears at first sight to be a pure barter may on examination be found to involve a money obligation, as where A sells B a car for £500 to be paid in one month's time but agrees to accept B's caravan in full discharge of the price. [**212**]

Contractual deferment of the payment obligation

As a preliminary point, what the Act deals with is not credit as such but the provision of credit under an agreement. Hence the material fact is not when payment is actually made or when the goods or services to which it relates are actually supplied but what is the contractual time for payment and supply. In other words, credit for the purpose of the Act involves the *contractual* deferment of debt. If a person takes credit without having been granted it—as where he is slow in paying his dentist's bill or his solicitor's account—there is no extension of credit within the Consumer Credit Act. Even if the supplier agrees to a delay in payment, there is no credit agreement unless he receives consideration for consenting to the delay, as by stipulating for interest. But if such consideration is furnished, a credit agreement comes into existence. For example, if the customer of a bank overdraws without prior arrangement and a bank agrees to honour the cheque, this is by implication an acceptance of an offer from the customer to pay charges in accordance with normal banking practice, and a contract results. The position is otherwise if the bank refuses payment. Similarly, if a person allows delay in settlement of a debt without binding himself to grant time to the debtor, there is no agreement for credit. This is so whether the delay in the demand for payment arises from inadvertence or inactivity—as where the supplier is simply dilatory in sending out his accounts—or is an intentional indulgence, as where the supplier agrees to allow further time to pay or to accept payment by instalments. Only where this deferment is not just an indulgence but contractual is there an agreement for credit; and, again, to establish a contract it is necessary to show that the supplier received some consideration for agreeing to the delay. Conversely, an agreement by which payment is to be made significantly after the contractual date for the supply of the specified goods or services does not cease to be a credit agreement merely because the supply is made late and thus coincides with or follows after the contractual, or the actual, date of payment. [**213**]

The real difficulty concerns the reference point to be taken for the purpose of determining whether debt is in fact being contractually deferred. Deferment presupposes some earlier point in time at which the debt would have been payable but for the contract. The general principle is thus clear enough. Debt is deferred, and credit extended, whenever the time fixed for payment by the contract is significantly later than the time at which payment would have fallen due in the absence of a contrary contractual provision (the import of "significantly later" is discussed in para. [**221**]). But as will be seen from some of the following illustrations, the principle may be easier to state than to apply.

There is no great problem with loan indebtedness, for deferment of debt is inherent in a loan contract, and for this purpose it is immaterial whether the loan takes the form of a cash payment to the debtor or a payment to a third party at his request, including a payment made under check trading or credit card arrangements. We need not discuss loan transactions further. The tricky questions arise in relation to indebtedness taking the form of a price obligation, the indebtedness arising from a supply transaction relating to land, goods, services or facilities, where the creditor is the supplier himself. [**214**]

Prepayment for goods

Charles, the proprietor of a mail order house, sends a catalogue through the post to Derek advertising a washing machine at a price of £300, available on eight weeks' delivery, but payment of the full price to be made with order. Derek places an order, enclosing a remittance for £300, and shortly afterwards receives from Charles an acknowledgement and confirmation of order. [**215**]

This is plainly not a credit transaction. Derek receives no benefit of any kind in advance of payment. Indeed, there is never a moment at which he is a debtor at all; if anyone is receiving "accommodation" it is Charles. But the agreement would still not constitute a credit agreement, even with Derek as creditor and Charles as debtor, for Charles's obligation is not a financial one. [**216**]

Layby sale

Charles, a retailer, agrees to sell a washing machine to Derek for £300. Derek cannot afford to pay this sum all at once, while Charles is not willing to relinquish possession of the washing machine until payment. On the other hand, Derek is anxious to clinch the deal now, before the price rises. So a layby sale is agreed (an arrangement sometimes met in this country and not uncommon in Australia), by which Charles agrees to reserve a washing machine for Derek, who will pay by instalments over a period of six months, collecting the machine upon completion of payment. [**217**]

This case is similar to the first, the only difference being that Derek, instead of avoiding the incurring of a debt by paying in advance, contracts to pay by instalments and thus becomes a debtor. But has he been granted credit? This depends on whether the contract of sale provides for the deferment of his indebtedness. It is thus necessary to ask when payment would have fallen due if the time of payment had not been stipulated by the contract. The answer is to be found in s. 28 of the Sale of Goods Act, which makes it clear that unless otherwise agreed payment and delivery are concurrent conditions, so that the seller must be ready and willing to give possession of the goods in exchange for the price. Since Derek is obliged to pay the full price before he can obtain possession, the provision for payment by instalments does not constitute deferment of a debt, but on the contrary means that the payment obligation is advanced. [**218**]

It would make no difference if Charles were to appropriate a particular washing machine to the contract at the outset; nor would it affect the matter if the contract were to provide that Derek should pay a charge over and above the cash price. The mere levy of a financial impost in addition to the cash price does not convert the transaction into a credit transaction, for Derek is not being granted credit, he is merely paying for the privilege of having goods set aside and held for him until he is able to take delivery. This case indicates that a contract is not a credit contract merely because it provides for payment by instalments. [**219**]

Discount for cash

Where goods are sold upon terms that the buyer will receive a discount for cash, the contract of sale constitutes a credit agreement, for it implies that the buyer has the option of settling the amount later, *e.g.* on the normal monthly open account basis. The fact that the buyer has the option to pay cash, and thus need not avail himself of the credit option, is irrelevant, for as we have seen from the previous chapter (para. [**168**]) the question is whether the creditor has bound himself to give credit, not whether the debtor has bound himself to take it. [**220**]

Straight cash sale

Where goods are sold on cash terms, with no provision for delayed payment, the agreement is not, of course, a credit agreement, since delivery and payment are contemporaneous. This is the case where I buy goods in a store and hand over the money at the same time as I take my purchases. Suppose, however, that on presenting my goods at the cash desk I find I have left my wallet at home, and that as I am a regular customer the cashier lets me take the goods on my agreeing to call later that day with the money. It would be straining language to call this a credit transaction, even if we were to treat the fractional extension of time for payment as contractual rather than as a mere indulgence. Contemporaneity is necessarily relative and a *precisely* simultaneous exchange is rare (do we count the minute that elapses between the time I hand over the money in a shop and the time it takes the shop assistant to wrap the goods and pass them over the counter?). [**221**]

Hence we must use some common sense and treat a debt as deferred only where the contractual period of deferment is significant, that is, where payment is not to be made on the same occasion (in a broad sense) as that of the purchase to which it relates. [**222**]

Supply of services and facilities

When we come to the supply of services (and for brevity the term "services" is hereafter used to include facilities, except where otherwise indicated), we must differentiate between a contract for the provision of services on a single occasion and a contract for continuing services to be paid for in stages or at prescribed intervals. More precisely, we must distinguish an *entire* contract, under which performance and payment are indivisible, from a severable contract, under which performance is to be divided up by portions of work or periods of time, each portion or period to be separately paid for. [**223**]

(i) *Entire contracts*

I engage a decorator to paper and paint all the rooms in my house for the total sum of £1,000 to be paid on completion of the work. In entering into the contract I am, of course, incurring a debt; and because the work is likely to take the decorator some days to complete I am receiving a measure of benefit in advance of my payment obligation. Nevertheless this is not a credit agreement, for even if the contract were silent as to the time of payment the contractor could not claim his money until he had finished the job. Accordingly, my agreement with the decorator does not involve any contractual deferment of debt. [**224**]

Of course, if my contract had provided that I was to pay the decorator within 14 days of issue of a certificate by my architect confirming satisfactory completion of the work, the indivisibility of the contract would not prevent it from being a credit agreement, for there is here a clear gap between the normal time for payment (i.e. completion) and the time fixed by the contract. [**225**]

Suppose that the contract does not specify any *time* interval between completion and payment but merely provides that payment is to be made on completion, subject to the issue of the architect's certificate that all is in order. This is not a credit agreement, for although in the nature of things a few days, at least, is likely to elapse between completion and the issue of the architect's certificate, the contract is not providing for the deferment of the debt as such but is merely stipulating a non-temporal condition precedent to payment. [**226**]

(ii) *Severable contracts*

Let us now take the case where the contract is severable. For example, I engage a kitchen designer to design and instal a kitchen for the total sum of £4,000, of which 20% is to be paid on completion of drawings, 60% on arrival of the units at the house and the balance on completion. This may seem like an instalment credit contract, but in truth it does not involve either the extension of credit or payment by instalments. On the contrary, I am paying as I go along. Each stage of performance encompasses a contract within a contract, and each stage is to be paid for in a lump sum as and when it is completed. Accordingly the payment obligation is not being deferred to a time later than it would otherwise fall due. On the contrary, if there were no provision (express or implied) for stage payments, I should be entitled to withhold the entire contract sum until completion of the whole of the works. [**227**]

The same applies to contracts for services divisible by time. If I enter into a 12-month maintenance contract, by which I agree to pay a company £10 a month at the end of each month to service my photocopying equipment, I commit myself to a series of payments, but they are not instalments and I am not being given credit. Payment by instalments presupposes a contractual liability which is being discharged in stages. But each of the payments I am required to make relates to a different stage. At the end of every month I have to make a payment for the servicing facility available to me during that month. Within the overall severable maintenance contract, there are in effect twelve one-month entire contracts. The payment I have to make at the end of the second month is not the second instalment of a sum due in respect of the first two months but is a single payment attributable exclusively to the second month. The fact that I am paying for each month in arrear does not mean that I am receiving credit, for an individual month is not apportionable. The monthly service charge does not accrue day by day but is earned only on expiry of the month. [**228**]

In short, a severable contract is not for our purposes different in principle from an entire contract, but it may be viewed as equivalent to a series of entire contracts governed by uniform terms and coming under the umbrella of the overall severable contract. This point is important when we come to consider what constitutes a contract for payment by instalments, and in particular, what the Consumer Credit (Exempt Agreements) Order 1977 means when it speaks of agreements under which the number of payments to be made by the debtor does not exceed four. [**229**]

Purchase of debts

The purchase of debts does not constitute an extension of credit to the buyer, for he has no repayment obligation. For this reason a blockdiscounting agreement by which a finance house agrees to buy a dealer's receivables owing under hire-purchase, instalment sale or rental agreements is not an agreement for the provision of financial accommodation, for though the economic object of the transaction is to assist the dealer's liquidity the law draws a clear distinction between a sale of debts and a loan on the security of debts (see R. M. Goode, *Hire-Purchase Law and Practice* (2nd Edn.) pp. 98–99, 660–661) and only the latter is within the definition of "credit" under the Consumer Credit Act. Even if the seller guarantees payment by the debtors, no financial accommodation is involved, since his recourse liability is not for *repayment* of the price but for *payment* of the guaranteed debts; and the giving of a guarantee does not in itself constitute the provision of financial accommodation (see para. [236]). Moreover, the Court of Appeal has held that if a blockdiscounting agreement is entered into providing for the sale of hire-purchase debts, the fact that the parties subsequently choose to operate the agreement in a manner substantially different from that originally envisaged does not convert the transactions entered into under it into loan transactions, for the blockdiscounting agreement continues to govern the rights of the parties in its original form unless and until modified by a contractual variation (*Lloyds and Scottish Finance, Ltd.* v. *Prentice* (1977), 121 Sol. Jo. 847, reversing the decision of Mocatta J. at first instance, but now awaiting the decision of the House of Lords). [230]

Mutual dealings on current account
We now come to a slightly more complex problem, namely the case where the parties engage in mutual dealings recorded in a running account, so that, depending on the balance of trade between them at any given time, first one, then the other, is in debit. For example, a stockbroker buys and sells shares for a client on the basis of monthly settlement. Purchases are debited to the client's account, sales credited. Sometimes the client's account is in credit, sometimes in debit. Is the agreement between them a credit agreement, and if so, who is the creditor and who the debtor? The answer would seem to be that the agreement *is* a credit agreement, each party being both creditor and debtor, in that each binds himself to wait until the monthly settlement before collecting any balance due to him. Fortunately, such an arrangement will usually come within the four-instalment exemption (see para. [320]), thus avoiding what might otherwise have been a serious problem in complying with the Act. (Incidentally, though there is a running account between the parties, the case is not one of running-account credit within the meaning of the Consumer Credit Act but, curiously enough, is an agreement for fixed-sum credit— see para. [270]). [231]

Hire of goods
Even if the Act had made no special provision for consumer hire agreements, a hiring agreement would not normally constitute a credit agreement. This is because, in accordance with the principle discussed earlier, a rental agreement is either an entire contract, where rent is to be paid as a single sum on or before expiry of the hire period (so that there is no debt deferred) or because it is a severable contract in which the hirer pays for each rental period on or before the end of that period (so that again no question of debt deferment is involved). It would be possible to construct a rental agreement so as to involve the provision of

credit, e.g. by giving the hirer the option to pay a lump sum rental for a single-period contract by instalments (for each instalment would then be attributable to the contract as a whole, and thus to periods prior as well as subsequent to the due date of payment); but the Consumer Credit Act makes separate provision for consumer hire agreements and clearly intends that the categories of consumer credit agreement and consumer hire agreement shall be mutually exclusive for the purposes of the Act. [**232**]

Lease of land

For the same reason, a lease of land at a rack-rent is not normally a credit agreement even where rent is expressed to be payable in arrear, i.e. at the end of each rental period, for this does not involve deferment of the payment obligation beyond the date when it would otherwise fall due. The position is otherwise, of course, if a premium is exacted and as a term of the agreement time is allowed for its payment. Similarly, an agreement for assignment of a lease will be a credit agreement if the premium payable by the assignee is contractually deferred to a date later than that on which the assignment is to take effect. [**233**]

Deferred payment under agreements to assign

This brings us to a further question, namely the temporal reference point to be taken where an agreement to assign an asset is to be, or may be, followed by an assignment at a later date. Suppose, for example, that A agrees to assign to B for £2,500 book debts to the value of £3,000, payment of the £2,500 to be by two equal monthly instalments, and as a term of the agreement B undertakes to execute a formal assignment of the debts to A if called upon to do so. If the date of the agreement to assign is taken as the supply point, and the instalments are payable wholly or in part after that date, A is clearly extending credit to B. If, on the other hand, the relevant date is the formal assignment (i.e. the document which, if followed by written notice of assignment to the debtor, will constitute a statutory assignment under s. 136 of the Law of Property Act 1925) then the date of supply is uncertain and indeed the supply may never take place at all because A may not find it necessary to call for the formal assignment. Again, what is the position where A agrees to assign a lease to B? Is the supply point the date of the agreement or the date of the assignment? [**234**]

The answer would seem to depend on the date on which it is intended that the assignee shall be given beneficial enjoyment of the asset to be assigned. In the case of the book debts, this would usually be the date of the agreement to assign. In the case of an agreement to assign a lease, on the other hand, it is the assignment, not the agreement to assign, that would normally be the supply point. Similarly in a contract of sale of land, the relevant date would be the conveyance, not the contract of sale, and a provision for payment of the purchase price by instalments would not make the contract a credit agreement unless at least one instalment fell due after the contractual completion date. [**235**]

Guarantees and indemnities

An interesting question is whether accommodation by way of guarantee constitutes the extension of credit. If, for example, a bank agrees to lend its name to a bill for the accommodation of its customer, or to honour a cheque under a cheque guarantee card or to enter into some other form of guarantee at the customer's request, is this a form of financial accommodation for the purpose of the Consumer Credit Act? It is thought that the answer is no. The Act deals separately with suretyship agreements, which are embraced in the term "security instrument" and constitute a "security" as defined by s. 189 (1). It is scarcely likely that the Act intended that one and the same obligation should constitute at the same time a granting of credit and a security for payment of such credit, particularly since consumer credit agreements and security instruments are separately regulated by the Act. In any event, the exemption under the "four-instalment" rule (see para. [320]) will for the most part make the question academic. [236]

The position would appear to be the same where what is provided is an indemnity rather than a guarantee. [237]

2. THE TIME FACTOR IN THE PROVISION OF CREDIT

The credit agreement and the credit provision

Given that a credit agreement exists, it may be relevant to know when it was created and when credit under it is to be deemed to have been provided. It is important to observe the distinction. As we saw in an earlier chapter (para. [168]), a credit agreement comes into existence as soon as the creditor binds himself to grant credit, whether or not the debtor binds himself to take it and whether or not he does in fact take it, though in the great majority of cases the creditor will not become bound until the debtor either agrees to use the credit or does in fact use it, for it is usually one or other of these acts which furnishes the consideration necessary to make the creditor's promise binding. On the other hand, although, in the language of the Act, it is the creditor's entry into the agreement which is said to "provide" the credit, it is plain that what is meant is simply that the agreement *makes provision* for the giving of credit, either at the time of the agreement or at a later date (and see para. [248]). When the credit is in fact to be furnishèd pursuant to the agreement is thus a question quite separate from that concerning the time when the agreement itself comes into existence. [238]

When is the agreement created?

There are several reasons why it may be important to know the exact point of time at which a consumer credit agreement comes into being. First, there must be a contract in existence before the transactional provisions of the Act relating to credit agreements can bite. For example, an agreement is not a regulated agreement unless made on or after 1st April 1977; and the liability imposed by s. 75 of the Act on the creditor in a debtor-creditor-supplier transaction is confined to cases where the agreement is made on or after 1st July 1977. Secondly, until there is a contract either party is free to withdraw from the transaction. Thirdly, it is necessary to know the time of making of the contract in order to ascertain at what moment the statutory rights and duties triggered off by entry into a regulated agreement (formalities of contract, cancellation, etc.) become operative. [239]

The normal, though by no means the invariable, sequence of events leading up to a consumer credit agreement relating to goods is that the prospective debtor makes an offer to the prospective creditor to buy goods or take them on hire-purchase, as the case may be, and this offer is subsequently accepted by the creditor. In order to produce a binding contract, acceptance must be intimated to the offeror either by express communication of acceptance to him or by some other act equivalent to such communication, e.g. delivery of the goods to which the agreement relates. For example, in the case of a hire-purchase agreement with a finance house, the prospective debtor's signature of the hire-purchase document and its delivery to the dealer for transmission to the finance house do not bind the debtor at that stage, nor is he bound even after despatch of the document to the finance house, since he has merely made an offer which has yet to be considered by the finance house. That offer will usually be accepted by signature of the agreement by the finance house and the acceptance will be considered complete by communication to the debtor when a letter of acceptance, or a copy of the contract showing that it has been signed by the finance house, is put in the post to the debtor or where acceptance is conveyed to him in some other manner, as by telling him face to face or even on the telephone or by procuring delivery of the goods to him. Similarly, an applicant for a loan may be asked to sign a form of application and to send this back to the prospective lender. Such an application is merely an offer and it is for the prospective lender to decide whether to accept the offer by notifying the prospective borrower that the loan will be granted. [**240**]

On the other hand, the practice of some financiers (particularly in the case of cash loans) is to make a formal loan offer themselves, the prospective borrower being requested to signify his acceptance of the terms by counter-signing and returning the offer document or by signing and returning a copy of it. [**241**]

English contract law does not in general recognise the binding nature of a promise as such, though promises may be enforceable outside a contract, as where they are under seal or where they are promises to make a gift which equity will treat as perfected because the promisor has knowingly stood by and allowed the promisee to incur expenditure on the promised asset in reliance on the promise, thus generating what is commonly referred to as proprietary estoppel. A contract involves a bargain, a promise for which the promisor exacts a price, taking the form either of a counter-promise or of performance of a designated act. Contracts of the former type are termed bilateral, or synallagmatic; contracts of the latter, unilateral. [**242**]

The types of contract described in para. [**240**] are bilateral, meaning that they involve a commitment on both sides to perform an act in the future. The consideration for one party's promise is not immediate performance of the stipulated *quid pro quo* by the other but simply a promise to perform. The contract is thus said to be executory since it consists on both sides of promises as yet unfulfilled, the parties becoming bound the moment the promises are exchanged. [**243**]

To be contrasted with this is the unilateral contract, so called because only one party undertakes a commitment, the consideration being not a counter-promise by the other party but actual performance by him. The latter therefore never *promises* anything, since the consideration is actual performance and it is by performance (or at any rate, by the commencement of performance) that he accepts the promisor's offer. In other words, in a unilateral contract the creation of the contract coincides with acceptance by performance on the part of the offeree. The offeree does not promise to perform; he either performs or he does not. Until he performs, there is no contract at all. After he has performed, nothing remains to be done by him. [244]

An example of the unilateral contract is an agreement to provide an overdraft facility (indeed, it is in the nature of any facility that there is no commitment by the offeree to utilise it, so that the contract is almost invariably unilateral). A bank agrees to allow its customer to overdraw up to a stated amount. This "agreement" by the bank constitutes a continuing offer which remains open until withdrawn prior to acceptance and which the customer accepts each time he overdraws his account. Hence each drawing on the account when it is not in credit constitutes a separate acceptance and thus generates a separate contract, the consideration for the bank's promise to honour the cheque being the customer's express or implied undertaking to repay the advance with interest. If the customer, without authority, overdraws beyond the agreed limit, this is not an acceptance of the bank's offer (since the offer is limited to the agreed credit ceiling) but a request to the bank to honour the further drawing (i.e. an offer by the customer to repay the bank with interest if it honours the further cheque), which the bank impliedly accepts by payment. It is at this point that the contract comes into existence as regards the excess overdraft. (However, for the purpose of the Consumer Credit Act such a contract is deemed to be part of the original credit agreement and does not constitute a separate agreement attracting the formal requirements of the Act or the cancellation provisions—see para. [300]). [245]

Other examples of a unilateral contract are credit card agreements and agreements for the operation of a budget or option account. [246]

A contract does not necessarily have to be wholly unilateral or wholly bilateral. Indeed, it might be more precise to speak of unilateral and bilateral promises rather than contracts. A contract may be unilateral as to some promises, bilateral as to others. For example, a bank issuing a credit card to its customers will do so upon a set of standard terms, most of which relate to the manner in which the facility is to be used and the payment obligation to the customer as and when he uses the facility. To this extent, the contract is unilateral since it does not become operative except as and when the bank's continuing offer is accepted by use of the facility. But there may be provisions which impose duties on the customer before use of the facility, these being triggered off by some separate act of acceptance, such as signature of the card. For example, the agreement may provide that upon signing the card the customer must undertake responsibility for its safe custody and will be liable for loss suffered by the bank if the card is later stolen and misused (the Act now imposes restrictions on such liability—see para. [828]). This part of the contract is bilateral. By signing the card the customer creates a contractual bailment and promises to keep the card safely, the consideration for this promise being the grant of the facility to use the card. [247]

At what time is credit deemed to have been provided?

This question is relevant primarily for the purpose of computing the credit period and thus the effective rate of charge and the rebate to which the debtor will be entitled in the event of an early settlement. The question is discussed in the context of the Consumer Credit (Total Charge for Credit) Regulations 1977 at paras. [249] *et seq.* We should emphasise here that what is under discussion is not the actual date of provision of credit but the contractual date of provision. In other words, at what time will credit be deemed to have been furnished to the debtor if the contract provisions are carried out? In general, the relevant time is the time fixed by the contract for the supply of the benefit to the debtor, whether the benefit takes the form of a cash loan or the provision of goods, services, or facilities. If this is specified as a definite time, then it is that time which marks the provision of credit, as where the contract provides for money to be lent or goods to be delivered on a specified date. Where the benefit is to be provided on or before a given date which is at the discretion of the creditor, the date so specified is the relevant date; and where the benefit takes the form of a facility which the debtor can utilise at a time of his own choosing, the relevant date is the earliest date at which he is entitled to utilise the facility. These rules are reflected (though not quite as precisely or unambiguously as they might be) in Regulation 2 (2) of the Consumer Credit (Total Charge for Credit) Regulations 1977. [**248**]

3. PAYMENT BY INSTALMENTS

Instalment payments under the Act and regulations

The Act and regulations contain various provisions dealing with agreements under which payment is required to be made by the debtor otherwise than in a single sum. Sometimes the reference is to payment "by instalments", more usually it is to cases where "the number of payments to be made by the debtor" does not exceed a stated figure, e.g. four. There is a reference to payment by instalments in the definition of "credit sale agreement" in s. 189 (1) of the Act, though what purpose the definition serves is not clear for the term defined nowhere features in the body of the Act. Section 71 deals with a credit repayable by instalments, and the meaning of "instalment" is thus material in applying that section. Of potentially greater importance are (1) the provisions of the Consumer Credit (Exempt Agreements) Order 1977, which provide exemptions for fixed-sum credit agreements under which the number of payments to be made by the debtor does not exceed four and running-account credit agreements where there is no more than one payment to be made in respect of each payment period; and (ii) the provisions of the Consumer Credit (Total Charge for Credit) Regulations 1977, which (*inter alia*) prescribe rules for calculating the effective rate of credit, the rule varying according to the time and manner in which the credit is made repayable. [**249**]

What, then, constitutes a "repayment of credit" and what is meant by an instalment? [**250**]

"Repayment of credit"

The word "*re*payment", which is strictly applicable only where what the debtor receives is a loan rather than deferment of the price, should here be construed as including "payment" under a contract for the supply of goods or services on credit. Not every payment by the debtor in reduction of the principal amount of his indebtedness is a repayment of credit, but only those payments which go in reduction or discharge of a *deferred* debt obligation. A contract providing for payment by instalments is not on that account alone an instalment *credit* contract;

75

it will be so only if at least one of the instalments is payable after the date on which it would otherwise have accrued due, normally the date of supply of the goods or services to which the contract relates. All this follows from the concept of credit as contractual deferment of debt. [**251**]

It must be emphasised that the time when the debtor actually makes his payment is irrelevant; what matters is whether the indebtedness to which the payment relates is or is not a deferred indebtedness. If I buy goods under an agreement which provides for payment of the price of instalments commencing one month after delivery and choose to make the first payment before the goods have been despatched, then although my payment precedes the extension of credit to me it is nevertheless a repayment of the credit for it is paid by way of settlement of a deferred debt, namely the first instalment falling due after delivery. Conversely, if the price is payable in advance of delivery, the fact that in breach of my contract I fail to pay until after the goods have arrived does not convert the contract into a credit agreement, nor does my late payment constitute a repayment of credit, for no contractual extension of credit has taken place. [**252**]

"Instalment" and "number of payments"

If we ignore the anomalous case of the credit sale definition in s. 189 (1) of the Act where "instalments" denotes payments of the purchase price, the word "instalment", "payment" or "repayment", when used in reference to payments by the debtor, denotes a payment or repayment which is wholly or partly in respect of credit. That is to say, a payment which does not in any way go towards discharge of the deferred part of the indebtedness, i.e. the "financial accommodation", is not a payment for the purpose of the relevant section or regulations. This may be very material in applying the "four-instalment" exemption embodied in art. 3 (1) (*a*) of the Consumer Credit (Exempt Agreements) Order 1977, which exempts from the Act an unsecured debtor-creditor-supplier agreement for fixed-sum credit under which the number of payments to be made by the debtor does not exceed four, "payment" meaning "a payment comprising an amount in respect of credit with or without any other amount". For illustrative examples, see Chapter 10, paras. [**320**] *et seq*.). [**253**]

4. COMPUTING THE AMOUNT OF THE CREDIT

Items excluded

"Credit" denotes the amount of the loan or other financial accommodation extended, not the amount which the debtor has to pay. Hence interest and other items entering into the total charge for credit do not form part of the credit, a point made explicit by s. 9 (4) of the Act; and a down-payment by the debtor is likewise excluded from the computation of the credit, whether the agreement is a hire-purchase agreement (the case specifically mentioned in s. 9 (3) of the Act) or any other form of instalment credit agreement involving a deposit. For the purpose of s. 9 (3) "deposit" means any sum payable by a debtor or hirer by way of deposit or down-payment, or credited or to be credited to him on account of any deposit or down-payment, whether the sum is to be or has been paid to the creditor or owner or any other person, or is to be or has been discharged by a payment of money or a transfer or delivery of goods or by any other means (s. 189 (1)). [254]

Since an item entering into the total charge for credit is not to be treated as credit *even though time is allowed for its payment* (s. 9 (4)), the definition of "total charge for credit" is of crucial importance. This definition is given in the Consumer Credit (Total Charge for Credit) Regulations 1977, a complex set of regulations analysed in detail in Chapter 13. Suffice it to say for the present that as a general rule "credit" is confined to the actual financial accommodation received by the debtor and excludes expenses generated by the credit transaction itself and not reflected in any corresponding benefit to the debtor. These expenses are (with some exceptions) classified as part of the total charge for credit, for they are expenses which the debtor would have avoided if he had not taken credit and accordingly their payment by the creditor cannot be said to have conferred a benefit on the debtor. Such expenses may include legal fees, survey and valuation costs, insurance premiums, stamp duties and Land Registry fees. The fact that the creditor likewise does not benefit from these is irrelevant, for what is involved is the cost of the debtor, and not the benefit of the creditor. [255]

Indeed the regulations go further, in that even where expenditure of a kind from which the debtor benefits, e.g. insurance, is laid out by the creditor and forms part of the sum repayable by the debtor by instalments, it will as a general rule be caught up in the total charge for credit and will thus be excluded from the computation of the credit itself. [256]

The rule that the credit charge is excluded in computing the amount of the credit applies whether the charge is an add-on charge or is a discount deducted at the outset from the agreed amount of the loan. Thus, on a loan of £500 repayable with interest of £100 by 12 instalments of £50, the credit is £500. The interest of £100 is not part of the credit. If a lender makes an advance of £500 for a year at a discount of 10 per cent. deductible at the outset, the real amount of the loan, representing the amount of the credit for the purpose of the Consumer Credit Act is £450, and the remaining £50 is the credit charge. Hence if in this case the borrower gives a post-dated cheque for £500, care must be taken not to treat the face value of the cheque as the amount of the credit since it includes a £50 interest charge which must be excluded in computing the credit. (Instruments other than a cheque are prohibited—see s. 123 and para. [794]). [257]

"Credit not exceeding £5,000"

The Act is restricted to agreements under which the credit does not exceed £5,000. Where credit is provided otherwise than in sterling, it is to be treated for the purposes of the Act as provided in sterling of equivalent amount (see s. 9 (2)). [258]

In a fixed-sum credit transaction the amount of credit is relatively (!) easy to calculate. In the case of a loan, it will be the amount of the loan. In the case of a hire-purchase or instalment sale agreement it will be the total price of the goods less the aggregate of the down-payment and the total charge for credit. It will be evident from this that the increase in the financial ceiling of the Act compared with the Hire-Purchase Act 1965 is much greater than a mere jump from £2,000 to £5,000, for the Hire-Purchase Act ceiling was fixed by reference to the total price. [259]

The effect of s. 9 (4), and of the definition of "total charge for credit" in the Consumer Credit (Total Charge for Credit) Regulations 1977, on the computation of the credit is illustrated by the following example.

> A finance house lets goods on hire-purchase at a total purchase price of £8,650 made up as follows:
>
> | | |
> |---|---:|
> | Cash price, including VAT | £7,500 |
> | Insurance premium under compulsory insurance with company nominated by finance house | £150 |
> | Charges | £1,000 |
> | Total | £8,650 |
>
> The required down-payment is £2,500.

The credit is £5,000, i.e. £8,650 − (£2,500 + £1,150). The agreement is therefore a regulated consumer credit agreement within the Consumer Credit Act since the credit does not exceed £5,000. The total charge for credit is £1,150, i.e. £1,000 plus the insurance premium of £150. The insurance premium is part of the *charge* for credit and does not form part of the credit itself (even if not paid direct to the insurance company but given to the debtor to enable him to pay the insurance company himself), despite the fact that it represents an amount laid out in the first instance by the finance house and included in the total figure repayable by instalments. The position would be otherwise if entry into the insurance contract were voluntary or if, though the insurance were compulsory, the buyer were left free to choose his own insurer. In either such case, the premium would then form part of the credit, making the amount of the credit £5,150 and thereby placing the agreement outside the Consumer Credit Act. [**260**]

So far, we have confined ourselves to *fixed-sum credit*. Special provisions apply to *running-account credit*. This is defined in s. 10 (1) (see para. [**269**]) and illustrated in examples 15, 16, 18 and 23 in Sch. 2 to the Act. In essence it means a revolving credit, that is a credit which entitles the debtor to make drawings up to an agreed credit limit on the basis that, whilst each drawing on the account reduces the credit available, the credit is *pro tanto* restored by payments which the debtor makes in reduction of the debt. Within this category are revolving loan accounts (such as overdrafts), credit card arrangements and store budget accounts. It is necessary for the Act to deal separately with running-account credit because, in contrast to fixed-sum credit, the amount of the credit which will actually be utilised is not known at the outset since this depends on the extent to which the debtor chooses to draw on his account. Section 10 (3) of the Act provides that these running-account credit transactions will be deemed within the £5,000 ceiling if:

(a) the credit limit does not exceed £5,000 (for the definition of "credit limit", see para. [**264**] below); or

(b) whether or not there is a credit limit, and if there is, notwithstanding that it exceeds £5,000,

   (i) the debtor is not enabled to draw at any one time an amount which, so far as (having regard to s. 9 (3)) it represents credit, exceeds £5,000, or

   (ii) the agreement provides that, if the debit balance rises above a given amount (not exceeding £5,000), the rate of the total charge for credit increases or any other condition favouring the creditor or his associate comes into operation, or

(iii) at the time the agreement is made it is probable, having regard to the terms of the agreement and any other relevant considerations, that the debit balance will not at any time rise above £5,000.

But if an agreement contains a term signifying that in the opinion of the parties s. 10 (3) (*b*) (iii) does not apply to the agreement, it is to be taken not to apply unless the contrary is proved (s. 171 (1)). [**261**]

The three categories listed in (*b*) above require some explanation. Category (i) is reasonably clear. If at any time the debtor cannot draw more than £5,000, the agreement is within the Act, however high the credit limit. In deciding whether the debtor can draw more than £5,000 at any one time, one must exclude such part of the permitted drawing as represents an item in the total charge for credit, e.g. sums payable under compulsory maintenance or insurance contracts as described in paras. [**517**], [**522**]. In many cases, this point will not arise in relation to drawings by the debtor, since the sums payable under the contract in question will be paid direct by the lender to the supplier of the maintenance service or the insurance company, and category (i) is concerned with the character of drawings by the debtor, not payments by the lender. Even if the lender is to pay such amounts direct to the borrower himself, leaving him to pay the servicing or insurance company, it is unlikely that a stipulation as to the amount of the drawing at any one time will distinguish between the loan element and the credit charge element. Categories (ii) and (iii) are designed to prevent evasion and to ensure that a stated credit limit in excess of £5,000 is not illusory. Where the agreement provides for the rate of the credit charge to increase, or for any other condition favouring the creditor or his associate (as defined by s. 184) to come into operation, if the debit balance rises above £5,000 or any lower figure, the credit will be deemed not to exceed £5,000. Notice that an agreement providing for an increase in interest if drawings exceed £5,000 is still within the financial ceiling of the Act. It is not sufficient to allow the debtor to draw up to £5,000 without an increase in interest rate. If the application of the Act is to be avoided, he must be allowed to draw at least some amount (however small) in excess of £5,000 without alteration of the terms in favour of the creditor. If the increase in interest rate does not become operative until the overdraft exceeds £5,001 then the agreement is taken outside category (ii). If the boundary is fixed at exactly £5,000, the agreement remains governed by the Act. Category (iii) (which *prima facie* does not apply if the agreement includes a term signifying that in the opinion of the parties it is inapplicable—s. 171 (1))—is illustrated by example 7 in the Second Schedule to the Act.

EXAMPLE 7

Facts: J is an individual who owns a small shop which usually carries a stock worth about £1,000. K makes a stocking agreement under which he undertakes to provide on short-term credit the stock needed from time to time by J without any specified limit.

Analysis: Although the agreement appears to provide unlimited credit it is probable, having regard to the stock usually carried by J, that his indebtedness to K will not at any

79

time rise above £5,000. Accordingly the agreement falls
within s. 10 (3) (*b*) (iii) and is a consumer credit agreement.
[**262**]

In many cases, no difficulty will arise in relation to category (iii). The problem
area is in the provision of running-account credit for a debtor whose drawings are
likely to be near the £5,000 boundary. The wording of s. 10 (3) indicates that the
presumption is in favour of the creditor—i.e. the onus is on the debtor to show that,
though the credit limit exceeds £5,000, the agreement falls within category (iii)
because of the probability that the debit balance would not at any time rise above
£5,000. For this purpose, the probability has to be tested at the time the agreement
is made, not in the light of subsequent events. In so providing s. 10 (3) (*b*) (iii)
avoids the inconvenient result that a single running-account credit agreement (and
for the purpose of the Act there is a single agreement concluded when the facility
is first opened, not a series of agreements constituted by the separate drawings)
would be within the Act one day, outside it the next and back within it a few days
later, depending on the probability from day to day of the future debit balance.
Hence the section provides in effect that if, at the time the facility was opened with
a credit limit in excess of £5,000, there was no probability that the debit balance
would be restricted to £5,000, the agreement will be outside the Act regardless of
the fact that the debtor's regular utilisation of the facility subsequently drops down
to or below the £5,000 ceiling. Such a situation is not within the mischief against
which s. 10 (3) of the Act is aimed. [**263**]

By s. 10 (2), "credit limit" means, as respects any period, the maximum debit
balance which, under the credit agreement, is allowed to stand on the account
during that period, disregarding any term of the agreement allowing that maximum
to be exceeded merely temporarily. The words referring to the maximum debit
balance being temporarily exceeded were apparently inserted to meet the wish of
the banks to clarify the effect of a bank deciding to honour a cheque drawn by its
customer in excess of the previously agreed credit limit. If, when the account is
first opened providing for a limit of £5,000, there is a term of the agreement
permitting this limit to be temporarily exceeded, such provision will not take the
agreement outside the Consumer Credit Act. In practice, this situation will rarely
arise, since the typical case—and that to which the banks were drawing attention—
is the temporary excess drawing which has not previously been arranged but
which the bank, to protect its customer's credit, decides to honour, on the basis that
it will then ask its customer to take prompt steps to bring his overdraft down to the
agreed limit. However, as the result of other provisions of the Act, s. 10 (2) also
applies to this latter situation. It is generally accepted as a matter of banking law
that the drawing of a cheque by a customer in excess of an agreed limit constitutes
a request to the bank to honour the cheque, in consideration of payment of normal
overdraft charges. This request represents an offer which the bank accepts by
payment of the cheque, thus giving rise to a new agreement varying the original
overdraft agreement. Under s. 82 (2) this latter agreement has the effect of
revoking the original agreement and combining its provisions with those of the
new agreement, so that in effect there is a single new agreement providing for an
overdraft limit, with a temporary excess above that limit. Although this excess is
for a fixed amount, s. 18 (5) provides that the term permitting the temporary excess
is not to be treated as a separate agreement or as providing fixed-sum credit in

respect of the excess. The result is that s. 10 (2) operates in relation to the new agreement as a single agreement for running-account credit, and despite payment of a cheque which takes the customer's overdraft above £5,000, the credit limit is deemed to remain at £5,000 and the entire overdraft agreement (as notionally reconstituted under s. 82 (2)) is within the Act, though it does not again attract the provisions of Part V, other than s. 56 (see s. 82 (4) and para. [**728**]). [**264**]

9. The Classification of Agreements under the Act

The purpose of classification

The Consumer Credit Act has many interesting and original features. Not the least of these is the new terminology coined by the draftsman in a highly successful endeavour to encompass not only the extraordinary diversity of forms of consumer credit currently used but also forms not yet conceived which may one day appear on the English financial scene. To a great degree, the classification of agreements made by the Act is modelled on that put forward in the Crowther Report. The language has changed (sometimes for the worse!), the Crowther concepts have been crystallised and refined and the classification has been fuller and more complex in the light of practical problems thrown up by detailed drafting and by consultation with interested parties. But in essence, the framework of regulation is modelled closely on Crowther; and if at first sight the structure created by the Act seems confusing, a perusal of the relevant paragraphs of the Crowther Report will throw light on the policy underlying the new classification of agreements and the reason why it was found necessary to draw distinctions that may on first impression appear to serve no useful purpose. An explanation of these matters will be given in the ensuing paragraphs. [265]

We have previously discussed the regulated agreement—meaning broadly an agreement which is regulated by the Act—and have seen that this divides into two primary groups, the consumer credit agreement and the consumer hire agreement. It was not found necessary to make any further subdivision of consumer hire agreements in definitional terms and we can accordingly leave this on one side, and concentrate on the consumer credit agreement. Here the position is more complex. Whilst hiring has only one legal form, the rest of consumer credit, as we have seen from Chapter 3, covers a very wide range of different instruments. Some are concerned exclusively with loans of money unconnected to the purchase of specific goods or services. Others do not, as a matter of law take a loan form at all but involve the deferment of the price of goods under a hire-purchase or instalment sale contract or the deferment of the price of services. Yet others are of a hybrid character, being neither loans in the traditional sense nor ordinary sales or hire-purchase agreements. Into this category fall check trading and credit card arrangements. Some forms of credit involve a loan of an amount fixed at the outset, creating an indebtedness which is reduced by successive payments until it is altogether extinguished, as in the case of the fixed loan, the hire-purchase agreement and the credit sale agreement. Other forms of financial accommodation contemplate a continuing relationship between creditor and debtor through a revolving credit of indefinite duration by which, instead of the credit being used once for all, it is utilised at the pleasure of the borrower up to the agreed limit, and is *pro tanto* restored by payments made in reduction of the debt. Into this category fall bank overdrafts and credit card arrangements. Some forms of purchase-money credit are made by independent lenders having no contact with the supplier, as where a clearing bank lends a customer money to buy a motor car. Others are made by financiers pursuant to a regular business relationship with the supplier, from whom they may get much of their business. An example of this type of agreement is the hire-purchase agreement for a motor vehicle concluded between a finance house and a hirer through the medium of a motor dealer. [**266**]

It is to reflect these functional differences that the Consumer Credit Act, building on the Crowther Report, has jettisoned the old sale credit/loan credit dichotomy and has in its place enacted what may at first sight appear to be an over-elaborate structure and classification of agreements. The particular strength of the Consumer Credit Act is that for the first time in the history of English credit law, Parliament has abandoned a legal structure based on differences in legal form and has instead produced a pattern of regulation which classifies transactions according to their function and effect. [**267**]

The classification that we are about to tackle is contained in Part II of the Act. This should be read in conjunction with:

(*a*) the illustrative examples in Schedule 2 to the Act;

(*b*) the list of definitions in s. 189, some of which refer back to definitions in Part II whilst others are provided by s. 189 itself;

(*c*) the White Paper, and in particular the Introduction to the Appendices, including, in paragraph 4 of that Introduction, the tabulation of consumer credit agreements under the new nomenclature. [**268**]

Fixed-sum credit and running-account credit

The statutory definition of these terms is to be found in s. 10, which provides as follows:

"(1) For the purposes of this Act—

(*a*) running-account credit is a facility under a personal credit agreement whereby the debtor is enabled to receive from time to time (whether in his own person, or by another person) from the creditor or a third party cash, goods and services (or any of them) to an amount or value such that, taking into account payments made by or to the credit of the debtor, the credit limit (if any) is not at any time exceeded; and

(*b*) fixed-sum credit is any other facility under a personal credit agreement whereby the debtor is enabled to receive credit (whether in one amount or by instalments).

(2) In relation to running-account credit, "credit limit" means, as respects any period, the maximum debit balance which, under the credit agreement, is allowed to stand on the account during that period, disregarding any term of the

agreement allowing that maximum to be exceeded merely temporarily.

(3) For the purposes of section 8 (2), running-account credit shall be taken not to exceed the amount specified in that subsection ("the specified amount") if—

    (*a*) the credit limit does not exceed the specified amount; or

    (*b*) whether or not there is a credit limit, and if there is, notwithstanding that it exceeds the specified amount,—

        (i) the debtor is not enabled to draw at any one time an amount which, so far as (having regard to section 9 (4) it represents credit, exceeds the specified amount, or

        (ii) the agreement provides that, if the debit balance rises above a given amount (not exceeding the specified amount), the rate of the total charge for credit increases or any other condition favouring the creditor or his associate comes into operaton, or

        (iii) at the time the agreement is made it is probable, having regard to the terms of the agreement and any other relevant consideration, that the debit balance will not at any time rise above the specified amount."

The language of s. 10 (1) (*a*) is not free from difficulty, for though the phrase "credit limit (if any)" implies that there may be a running-account facility without a credit limit, yet if the ingredient of a credit limit is removed the definition is left suspended midway though an uncompletable sentence. However the basic idea is simple enough. Running-account credit is synonymous with revolving credit. As noted earlier (para. [**261**]) the essential ingredient of running-account credit is that the debtor has a *facility*, a line of credit which is taken up by drawings but *pro tanto* restored by repayments, the debtor being free to draw as and when he chooses as long as he does not exceed his limit, and the facility continuing indefinitely unless and until terminated by either party. The most common examples are the bank overdraft, the credit card and the budget account. All credit other than running-account credit is fixed-sum credit. Into this category fall hire-purchase, conditional sale and credit sale agreements, check and voucher trading transactions, fixed loans (as opposed to overdrafts) and the like. Full definitions of running-account credit and fixed-sum credit are given in s. 10 (1) of the Act and illustrated in Sch. 2, but in essence they are as described above, subject only to the addition that to be within running-account credit or fixed-sum credit, the credit must be one which is provided by a personal credit agreement as defined by s. 8 (1). This has already been discussed in para. [**158**]. [**269**]

The phrase "running-account credit" is not an altogether happy one for it does not adequately convey the revolving character of the transaction. The mere fact that there is a running account (i.e. a current account) between the parties and that under the agreement between them payment is made in arrear does not make the agreement one for running-account credit, for a current account does not by itself establish the existence of a continuous credit line. Hence the running account set up between, for example, a newsagent and his customers for newspapers delivered and paid for at monthly intervals stems from a fixed-sum agreement, not a running-account agreement, for at the end of each month the customer is required to settle his account in full and does not enjoy the right to keep the account in debt within an agreed ceiling. Yet such arrangements do not fit very happily into the concept of fixed-sum credit either, for no fixed-credit figure is established at the outset; and but for the fact that most such agreements are exempt under the four-instalment rule (see para. [**320**]), it would probably have been necessary to allocate them to a distinct category. [**270**]

Most "agreements" for running-account credit are in their inception standing offers by a prospective creditor which crystallise into a series of unilateral contracts as a result of use of the facility, each drawing or purchase constituting a separate act of acceptance generating a distinct contract governed by the terms of the standing offer (see paras. [**169**] *et seq.*). [**271**]

What is the relevance of the distinction between running-account credit and fixed-sum credit? First, as has already been mentioned, running-account credit is subject to special rules for the purpose of determining whether a transaction is within the £5,000 ceiling (see paras. [**261**] *et seq.*). Secondly, the criteria for exemption of agreements from the Act under the Consumer Credit (Exempt Agreements) Order 1977 vary according to whether the agreement is a fixed-sum or running account agreement (see para. [**320**]). Thirdly, the debtor in a running-account credit provided under a regulated agreement has an *automatic* right to receive statements of account at least once a year and, where the agreement provides for periodic payments by the debtor, a statement of the state of the account at the end of every period in which there has been a movement in the account (s. 78 (4)). This is in addition to the right to a statement on request which is conferred in relation both to running-account and fixed-sum credit (ss. 77, 78 (1)–(3)), though the information that can be called for by the debtor under these sections and by a surety under ss. 107 and 108 is somewhat different for running-account credit than for fixed-sum credit. Fourthly, where an actual or prospective regulated agreement has two or more debtors, the duty under s. 185 (1) to supply each of them with periodic statements of account under s. 78 (4) can, as regards any of them, be dispensed with by him by a dispensing notice given under s. 185 (2). Finally, the requirements as to information to be given by the creditor in advertisements, quotations and agreements necessarily differ according to whether the document in question deals with fixed-sum credit or running-account credit. For example, the cost of borrowing expressed as a percentage rate cannot be given in the same way for running-account credit as for fixed-sum credit, since the effective rate will depend on the manner in which the debtor uses the facility. Accordingly in the case of running-account credit, what will be required is not the actual rate that the debtor will pay (which will not be known at the outset) but the basis of calculation of the period rate and the effective annual equivalent of the period rate on the basis of annual compounding. Rate disclosure is discussed separately in Chapter 13. [**272**]

Restricted-use credit and unrestricted-use credit

Section 11 (1) of the Act defines a restricted-use credit agreement as a regulated consumer credit agreement:

(a) to finance a transaction between the debtor and the creditor, whether forming part of that agreement or not, or

(b) to finance a transaction between the debtor and a person (the "supplier") other than the creditor, or

(c) to refinance any existing indebtedness of the debtor's, whether to the creditor or another person.

An unrestricted-use credit agreement is any other class or regulated consumer credit agreement (s. 11 (2)). This subsection would have been more logically placed after, rather than before, s. 11 (3), for s. 11 (1) is not by itself sufficient to carry the concept of restricted-use credit but merely identifies the purpose of the credit, and it is only s. 11 (3) that makes the distinction between a restricted-use credit agreement and an unrestricted-use credit agreement meaningful. By section 11 (3) an agreement is not a restricted-use agreement if the credit is in fact provided in such a way as to leave the debtor free to use it as he chooses, even though certain uses would contravene that or any other agreement. On the other hand by s. 11 (4) an agreement may fall within s. 11 (1) (b) although the identity of the supplier is unknown at the time the agreement is made. [**273**]

In essence, then, restricted-use credit is credit extended to finance a particular purchase or transaction and provided in such a way that the creditor can ensure its application to the purchase or transaction in question. The word "transaction" is not defined but is very wide in scope and embraces all forms of supply, whether relating to land, goods, documents, services or facilities. [**274**]

The first type of restricted-use credit covered by para. (a) of s. 11 (1) is where the creditor is himself the supplier, the credit taking the form of deferment of the price of the land, goods, services etc., the subject of the supply. In cases within this category, the supply agreement and the credit agreement are telescoped into one. Examples are hire-purchase, conditional sale, credit sale (including budget and option account arrangements), the sale of land where part of the price is left outstanding on mortgage, the supply of services on credit (but not rental agreements nor agreements for the provision of services to be paid for in stages or at periodic intervals as provided, for these are not credit transactions—see paras. [**228**] *et seq.* [**275**]

The second category of restricted-use credit, covered by s. 11 (1) (b), is where the supplier is a third party and the creditor controls the application of the credit to the intended supply contract either by paying the supplier direct (as where a finance house makes a personal loan for the purchase of a car and sends a remittance for the price direct to the motor dealer) or by furnishing the debtor with a token, such as a credit card or voucher, which can only be used by a supplier or suppliers designated by the creditor. In such cases, the credit agreement and the supply agreement are two distinct contracts, the former being between creditor and debtor, the latter being between debtor and the third-party supplier. The character of the supply transaction is irrelevant to the status of the credit agreement as a restricted-use agreement. Usually the supply contract will be a cash sale financed by the restricted-use credit agreement; but it may itself be a restricted-use credit agreement (e.g. a hire-purchase agreement between debtor and creditor A where the downpayment is advanced by creditor B by a payment direct to A) or a rental agreement (where the amount of the advance rental is lent by creditor to debtor and paid directly to the owner of the rented goods). [**276**]

The third category of restricted-use credit agreement, covered by section 11 (1) (c), is a refinancing transaction. This itself sub-divides into two, the refinancing of agreements between debtor and creditor and the refinancing of the debtor's indebtedness to a third party. As an example of the first case, debtor owes creditor money under a hire-purchase agreement and to accommodate debtor, who is in temporary financial difficulties, creditor agrees to reschedule the outstanding payments over a long period. Alternatively, debtor owes creditor sums under several credit agreements and it is agreed to consolidate the contracts into a single agreement providing for payment of the total indebtedness by agreed instalments. As an example of the second case, debtor owes money to various third parties and creditor assists debtor by paying the sums due to those third parties, agreeing to accept from the debtor at a later date, whether by instalments or otherwise. [**277**]

If the contractual method of providing the credit is one which does not enable the creditor to control its application to the intended purpose but gives control to the debtor, the credit is unrestricted-use credit even though the debtor may have contracted to utilise the loan for a designated purpose. It would seem that only two forms of unrestricted-use credit agreement are possible. The first is that which provides for credit in the form of a money payment to or at the direction of the debtor. The second is where the credit agreement is entered into for the purpose of financing a transaction to which the debtor is not a party at all, as where a parent borrows money to pay for goods or services to be furnished to his child under a contract concluded between that child and the supplier. In such a case, the credit agreement is an unrestricted-use credit agreement even if the creditor controls the application of the advance to its intended purpose by paying the supplier direct. This is because the definition of "restricted-use credit" in section 11 (1) is confined to an agreement to finance a transaction or indebtedness *of the debtor*, and thus does not embrace agreements financing the indebtedness of a third party. [**278**]

The restricted-use/unrestricted-use classification may be relevant in determining whether a transaction is a linked transaction (see s. 19 (1) (c) (iii)), and is material for various other reasons. The advertising of restricted-use credit facilities where the goods or services are not at that time offered for cash by the person advertised as the supplier is an offence (s. 45). Restricted-use credit agreements to finance the purchase of land and to be secured by a mortgage on that land are exempt from the special procedure prescribed for land mortgage transactions which is designed to give the debtor an opportunity to withdraw (see para. [**577**]). The cancellation provisions are modified in some respects as regards debtor-creditor-supplier agreements for restricted-use credit; and again, the disclosure requirements to be imposed by regulations are likely to vary according to whether the credit is restricted-use or unrestricted-use credit. [**279**]

Debtor-creditor-supplier agreement and debtor-creditor agreement

We come now to what is perhaps the most important, and certainly the most difficult pair of labels in the classification, namely debtor-creditor-supplier agreements and debtor-creditor agreements. Actually, the difficulty is visual rather than conceptual. Debtor-creditor-supplier credit is simply another, and less elegant, name for what the Crowther Committee termed a connected loan, that is to say, a loan extended by the supplier himself (e.g. by deferment of the price under a hire-purchase or instalment sale agreement) or by a connected lender in the sense of a lender having a pre-existing arrangement or contemplating a future arrangement with the supplier. The Crowther Report advanced compelling reasons for distinguishing connected from unconnected loans.

> "Where goods are bought for cash provided by an independent
> lender there is no reason to regard the sale as any different
> from a normal cash sale, or to treat the loan as other than a
> normal loan. Where, however, the price is advanced by the
> seller or a connected lender the sale and loan aspects of the
> transaction are closely entwined. The connected lender and
> the seller, where not the same person, are in effect engaged in
> a joint venture to their mutual advantage, and their respective
> roles cannot be treated in isolation" (para. 6.2.24). [**280**]

The Crowther Report set out three areas in which the distinction was
significant. First, unconnected loans at interest not exceeding 2½ per cent. above
Bank Rate were to be exempt from the proposed consumer credit legislation. This
exemption features, in slightly modified form, in paragraph 3 (1) (c) of the Consumer
Credit (Exempt Agreements) Order 1977 (see para. [**322**]). Secondly, restrictions
against contracting out of terms implied in favour of the buyer in an instalment
sale were to apply equally to a sale for cash advanced by a loan from a connected
lender. This has disappeared as a relevant factor, since exemption clauses in all
consumer sales, even if for cash, were brought within the Supply of Goods (Implied
Terms) Act 1973, and are now controlled by s. 6 of the Unfair Contract Terms Act
1977, which renders void provisions purporting to exclude or restrict such implied
terms or remedies for their breach. Thirdly, the connected lender was to be liable
for misrepresentations made by the supplier in antecedent negotiations and for
defects in goods or services purchased by the buyer with the aid of the connected
loan. This idea is retained in extended form in s. 75 of the Consumer Credit Act,
discussed in Chapter 16. [**281**]

(i) *Debtor-creditor-supplier agreement*

It is now necessary to look a little more closely at the definition of debtor-
creditor-supplier agreement in section 12 of the Act, which provides as follows:

> "A debtor-creditor-supplier agreement is a regulated consumer
> credit agreement being—
>> (a) a restricted-use credit agreement which falls within
>> section 11 (1) (a), or
>> (b) a restricted-use credit agreement which falls within
>> section 11 (1) (b) and is made by the creditor under
>> pre-existing arrangements, or in contemplation of
>> future arrangements, between himself and the sup-
>> plier, or
>> (c) an unrestricted-use credit agreement which is made
>> by the creditor under pre-existing arrangements
>> between himself and a person (the "supplier") other
>> than the debtor in the knowledge that the credit is to
>> be used to finance a transaction between the debtor
>> and the supplier."

Limb (a) of this section embraces those agreements in which creditor and supplier
are the same (for examples, see para. [**275**]). It is thus important to appreciate that
debtor-creditor-supplier agreements do not necessarily involve three parties.
Indeed this limb is confined exclusively to the two-party arrangement. It should
be observed that "supplier" means the legal supplier, not the physical supplier.
Thus where goods are let on hire-purchase by a finance company, it is the finance

company, not the dealer, who is the supplier, so that creditor and supplier are the same and the case falls within limb (*a*), not within limbs (*b*) or (*c*). [**282**]

Three-party agreements, where creditor and supplier are different people, (the word "supplier" in ss. 11 and 12 simply denotes a party to any financed transaction who is not himself the creditor) are covered by limbs (*b*) and (*c*), and the credit will inevitably take the form of a loan, whether to the debtor in cash or in payment to the supplier at the debtor's request. It is worth emphasising here that the character of the supply agreement is not relevant (see para. [**276**], *ante*), so that even a credit agreement financing the payment of advance rentals on an equipment lease may be a debtor-creditor-supplier agreement within limbs (*b*) or (*c*). [**283**]

Limb (*b*) differs from limb (*c*) in two respects. First, it is concerned with restricted-use credit agreements, that is, those in which the creditor controls the application of the credit to its intended purpose. Among agreements within limb (*b*) are credit card agreements, so far as involving third-party suppliers; check trading agreements; personal loans by finance houses for the purchase of goods from a supplier with whom the finance house has an arrangement to extend credit to the supplier's customers. Secondly, limb (*b*) applies not only where the credit agreement is made by the creditor under pre-existing arrangements with the supplier but also where it is made in contemplation of such arrangements (see further para. [**285**], *infra*). Limb (*c*), by contrast, is concerned exclusively with unrestricted-use credit agreements made under pre-existing arrangements with a third-party supplier and in the knowledge that the credit is to be used to finance the supply transaction. If there are no pre-existing arrangements between creditor and supplier, a mere contemplation of these is not sufficient to bring an unrestricted-use credit agreement within the definition. The policy reason underlying this distinction is presumably that where the creditor neither has an existing arrangement with the supplier nor controls the application of the advance, the nexus between him and the supplier is too nebulous to justify bringing it within the debtor-creditor-supplier label. But where there *is* a pre-existing arrangement between creditor and supplier, the fact that the creditor is aware of the purpose for which the advance is to be utilised provides a sufficient nexus between creditor and supplier to attach the debtor-creditor-supplier label to the transaction, even though the creditor does not control the application of the advance but pays it direct to the debtor. [**284**]

For guidance as to the meaning of "pre-existing arrangements" and "contemplation of future arrangements" we must turn to s. 187 of the Act:

> "(1) A consumer credit agreement shall be treated as entered into under pre-existing arrangements between a creditor and a supplier if it is entered into in accordance with, or in furtherance of, arrangements previously made between persons mentioned in subsection 4 (*a*), (*b*) or (*c*).
>
> (2) A consumer credit agreement shall be treated as entered into in contemplation of future arrangements between a creditor and a supplier if it is entered into in the expectation that arrangements will subsequently be made between persons mentioned in subsection (4) (*a*), (*b*) or (*c*) for the supply of cash, goods and services (or any of them) to be financed by the consumer credit agreement.
>
> (3) Arrangements shall be disregarded for the purposes of subsection (1) or (2) if—

(*a*) they are arrangements for the making, in specified circumstances, of payments to the supplier by the creditor, and

(*b*) the creditor holds himself out as willing to make, in such circumstances, payments of the kind to suppliers generally.

(4) The persons referred to in subsections (1) and (2) are—

(*a*) the creditor and the supplier;

(*b*) one of them an associate of the other's;

(*c*) an associate of one and an associate of the other's.

(5) Where the creditor is an associate of the supplier's, the consumer credit agreement shall be treated, unless the contrary is proved, as entered into under pre-existing arrangements between the creditor and the supplier."

Section 187 (3) makes it clear that cheque guarantee cards issued by a bank do not generate a debtor-creditor-supplier agreement merely because the bank undertakes to suppliers at large that it will honour cheques drawn by the card-holder up to the limit stated on the card. [**285**]

Where the question is whether a credit agreement is entered into "in contemplation of future arrangements between a creditor and a supplier" it would seem that the party whose state of mind is involved is the creditor. [**286**]

(ii) *Debtor-creditor agreement*

A debtor-creditor agreement is a consumer credit agreement providing for what Crowther termed an "unconnected loan", that is, credit not extended pursuant to or in contemplation of arrangements between creditor and supplier. Section 13 of the Act gives an unnecessarily extended definition of debtor-creditor agreement, when all it needed to say was that a debtor-creditor agreement was any regulated credit agreement other than a debtor-creditor-supplier agreement. Typical examples of a debtor-creditor agreement are the normal bank loan and overdraft, loans by moneylenders and pawnbrokers and personal loans not made pursuant to or in contemplation of arrangements between lender and supplier. [**287**]

(iii) *Relevance of the distinction*

It is not possible, in the compass of this introductory guide, to refer to all the provisions of the Consumer Credit Act in which the distinction between a debtor-creditor-supplier agreement and a debtor-creditor agreement is relevant. Suffice it to mention the six most important.

(*a*) The criteria for exemption of agreements under the Consumer Credit (Exempt Agreements) Order 1977 vary according to whether the agreement is a debtor-creditor-supplier agreement or a debtor-creditor agreement (see Chapter 10).

(*b*) It is an offence to canvass debtor-creditor agreements off trade premises (s. 49 (1)). Hence the canvassing of a loan application at the house of the prospective debtor is prohibited, but the canvassing of entry into a check trading agreement is permitted if authorised by the terms of the licence (see generally paras. [**312**] *et seq.*).

(*c*) The disclosure requirements to be made by regulations will vary according to whether the agreement is a debtor-creditor-supplier agreement or a debtor-creditor agreement.

(*d*) The debtor's exercise of a right to cancel a regulated agreement also automatically cancels a linked transaction (s. 69 (1)); and in the case of a debtor-creditor-supplier agreement the purchase or other transaction financed by the creditor is a linked transaction (s. 19 (1) (*b*)). Thus, if a finance house, pursuant to an arrangement with a motor dealer, advances to the dealer's customer the purchase price of the car being bought by the customer from the dealer, cancellation of the loan agreement with the finance house under the provisions of the Act will automatically rescind the contract of sale between the motor dealer and the customer. In such a case, the finance house is jointly and severally liable with the dealer to repay sums paid by the debtor (s. 70 (3)).

(*e*) The provisions of s. 72 relating to the return of goods on cancellation do not apply to goods purchased with a loan under a debtor-creditor agreement; and on cancellation of a debtor-creditor agreement or indeed any regulated agreement other than a debtor-creditor-supplier agreement for restricted-use credit, the agreement continues in force so far as it relates to repayment of credit and payment of interest (s. 71 (1)).

(*f*) If the debtor in a debtor-creditor-supplier transaction has a claim against the supplier in respect of misrepresentation or breach of contract, the creditor is liable jointly and severally with the supplier (s. 75)1)), with a right of indemnity against the supplier (s. 75 (2) and see Chapter 16).

[**288**]

Credit-token agreements

The next type of agreement requiring mention is the credit-token agreement. This is defined by s. 14 (2) of the Act as a regulated agreement for the provision of credit in connection with the use of a credit-token. A credit-token, as defined by s. 14 (1), is a card, check, voucher, coupon, stamp, form, booklet or other document or thing given to an individual by a person carrying on a consumer credit business, who undertakes—

(*a*) that on the production of it (whether or not some other action is also required) he will supply cash, goods and services (or any of them) on credit, or

(*b*) that where, on the production of it to a third party (whether or not any other action is also required), the third party supplies cash, goods and services (or any of them), he will pay the third party for them (whether or not deducting any discount or commission), in return for payment to him by the individual.

Examples of credit-tokens are bank credit cards enabling the holder to draw cash from a bank or to buy goods or services from a third party such as a shop having an arrangement with the bank to accept the card; cards which enable the cardholder to draw money from a cash dispenser (see s. 14 (4)); checks issued by check trading companies; trading vouchers; and credit cards issued by a shop or store authorising the holder to purchase goods from the shop or store in question and have his account debited with the price on credit terms. But a cheque card, by which a bank undertakes to suppliers generally to whom the card is produced to honour cheques drawn by its customers up to the limit stated on the card is not a credit-token, since the bank, in paying the supplier, is not paying for the goods or services but is merely honouring its guarantee of payment of the cheque. This is made clear in example 21 in Sch. 2 to the Act. [**289**]

Almost invariably, agreements relating to credit-tokens will be within the £5,000 ceiling so as to constitute regulated agreements and thus credit-token agreements. Special provisions apply in relation to credit-tokens and credit-token agreements. Credit-token agreements are regulated in various ways described in Chapter 24. But credit-tokens themselves are the subject of various provisions, and some of these apply whether the agreement under which the token is issued is regulated or unregulated, and indeed, even if there is no agreement at all. For example, the giving of unsolicited credit-tokens is prohibited (s. 51 (1)), effectively preventing any new mass mailing of credit cards. See generally Chapter 24. [**290**]

Small agreements

These are consumer credit agreements under which the credit does not exceed £30 and consumer-hire agreements in which the minimum rental does not exceed £30. The definition has already been examined in the previous chapter (paras. [**190**] *et seq.*). This category was created because, though it was not desired to exempt small agreements from the Act as a whole, it was felt that certain provisions, e.g. documentation and cancellation, would be burdensome to the creditor having regard to the small amount involved in the transaction. [**291**]

Exempt agreements

These are examined in detail in the next chapter. [**292**]

Partially regulated agreements

See para. [**188**]. [**293**]

Non-commercial agreements

See paras. [**192**], [**193**]. [**294**]

Hire-purchase and conditional sale agreements

See paras. [**198**], [**199**]. [**295**]

Multiple agreements

The neat compartmentalisation of agreements in accordance with the above classification seems exhaustive enough, without further elaboration. Unhappily, it is still not sufficient to accommodate the diversity of credit transactions. There are various types of agreement which fall into more than one category, either because the agreement is divided up into different parts belonging to different categories (one of which may indeed be outside the Act altogether) or because the agreement, though indivisible, contains terms which place it in two or more categories. Such agreements are known as multiple agreements, and these are treated as follows;

    (*a*) As regards parts of an agreement falling into different categories, each part is to be treated as a separate agreement (s. 18 (2)) and to be construed accordingly, with appropriate apportionment of any sums payable thereunder (s. 18 (4)).

(b) As regards an agreement falling into two or more categories, the agreement is to be treated as in each category (s. 18 (3)). [**296**]

Two illustrations should suffice to show what a multiple agreement is and how the statutory provisions operate on it.

> *Example 1*
>
> A opens an account with his bank which agrees to give him overdraft facilities of £500. A is told that so long as his account is kept in credit he will not have to pay any bank charges, but that if he has overdrawn he will have to pay charges of 7½p for each cheque drawn, in addition to interest at the bank's normal prevailing rate.
>
> This is a multiple agreement. That part which relates to the operating of the account while it is in credit is not a credit agreement at all and is outside the Act. That part which deals with the terms of the overdraft is a regulated agreement.
>
> (A fuller illustration of this form of multiple agreement is given in example 18 in Sch. 2 to the Act.)
>
> *Example 2*
>
> B is issued by his bank with a credit card under the terms of an agreement which entitle him to use the card to draw cash from the bank and to obtain goods and services from named supplier and cash from other named banks who have an arrangement with B's bank to accept the card. In so far as the agreement between B and his bank deals with use of the card to draw cash from the bank, it is a debtor-creditor agreement. In so far as it relates to use of the card to obtain cash from other banks, or goods or services from the named suppliers, it is a debtor-creditor-supplier agreement. The agreement thus falls into both categories and is governed by the provisions of the Act relating to both categories.
>
> (A fuller illustration is given in example 16 in Sch. 2 to the Act). [**297**]

If in the second of the above examples the credit card agreement permitted repayment by instalments and the debtor, after drawing cash from his bank and using the card to buy goods from a supplier, were to exercise a right of cancellation after making certain payments to the bank, it might be necessary to determine what instalments had accrued due to the bank as regards the cash drawn and what instalments had accrued due as regards the goods purchased, in order to apply the provisions of s. 71 (3) (see para. [**619**]); and for this purpose the court would have to exercise its power of apportionment under s. 18 (4). [**298**]

A consequence of s. 18 (2)—whereby a part of an agreement in a different category from the remaining parts is to be treated as a separate agreement—may be to attract the operation of the Act to both parts of the agreement even though, if taken as a whole, the agreement would have provided a credit in excess of £5,000 so as to be outside the Act altogether. If, for example, a creditor agrees to advance £9,000 of which £5,000 is to refinance the indebtedness of the debtor to third parties whilst the remaining £4,000 is for the debtor to use as he chooses, the £5,000 part of the loan is restricted-use credit and the £4,000 is unrestricted-use credit, so that each of these parts is deemed a separate agreement under s. 18 (2) and each is thus controlled by the Act, being within the £5,000 ceiling. [**299**]

However, by s. 18 (5) an agreement for temporary excess of an overdraft over the credit limit does not constitute a separate agreement, nor is it to be treated as providing fixed-sum credit for the excess. It thus does not create a distinct fixed-sum category from the running-account facility created by the original overdraft arrangement. See also para. [**264**]. [**300**]

Finally, s. 18 (6) provides that the Act is not to apply to a multiple agreement so far as the agreement relates to goods if under the agreement payments are to be made in respect of the goods in the form of rent (other than a rentcharge) issuing out of land. It follows that if goods are included in a lease or tenancy agreement relating to land—as in the case of a furnished letting—the lease or tenancy agreement is outside the Act in relation to the goods as well as to the land, provided that the rent attributable to the goods issues out of the land. This will be the case if there is a single rent which does not distinguish between land and goods. It is otherwise, however, if a separate sum is fixed as the rental of the goods. [**301**]

The Act does not define the word "category" for the purpose of s. 18 and its meaning is not entirely clear. There are two possible views. The first, the wider view, is that "category" embraces every class of agreement that is accorded distinct legal treatment under the Act. On this view, for example, an agreement which is partly cancellable and partly not would be within section 18, as would a hire-purchase or conditional sale agreement (accorded separate treatment by ss. 90, 91 and 133–134) and a pledge. The narrower view is that the word "category" is confined to a class of agreement within the classification created by Part II of the Act. This seems more consistent with the intention of section 18. [**302**]

Linked transactions

These are discussed in detail in Chapter 27. [**303**]

Other definitions

The above definitions all relate to the classifications of agreements under the Act. There are a number of other important definitions, scattered throughout the Act and gathered together in section 189 (1). These will be referred to at appropriate points in the chapters which follow. [**304**]

10. Exempt Agreements

Definition

Certain agreements that would otherwise fall within the definition of regulated agreements are designated as exempt agreements. An exempt agreement means an agreement specified in or under s. 16 of the Act (s. 189 (1)), and the term is used in contradistinction to regulated agreement (see the definition of "regulated agreement" in s. 189 (1)). Exempt agreements are not affected by the Act at all, except for the provision of ss. 137–140 relating to extortionate credit bargains, which apply even to exempt agreements (s. 137). [**305**]

It is necessary to distinguish an exempt agreement from a partially regulated agreement, the latter being excluded from certain provisions of the Act but otherwise remaining controlled by it in the same way as other regulated agreements. See para. [**188**]. [**306**]

Categories of exempt agreement

There are five distinct categories of exemption provided for by s. 16:

(i) Consumer credit agreements entered into by a local authority or building society as creditor and falling into one of the categories listed in s. 16 (2). [**307**]

(ii) Consumer credit agreements falling into one of the classes listed in s. 16 (2) where the creditor is not a local authority or building society but is a body specified in an order made by the Secretary of State, being a body within one of the descriptions in s. 16 (1) (insurance, friendly society, etc.) Such agreements are exempt, but the Secretary of State may in such order limit the exemption to agreements of a description specified in the order. Exempt agreements within this category (termed hereafter "named body" exemptions) have been prescribed by art. 2 of the Consumer Credit (Exempt Agreements) Order 1977, as amended by the Consumer Credit (Exempt Agreements) (Amendment) Order 1977, the Consumer Credit (Exempt Agreements) (Amendment) Order 1978 and the Consumer Credit (Exempt Agreements) (Amendment No. 2) Order 1978. Each of the exempted bodies had to make individual submission for exemption to the Department of Prices and Consumer Protection.

The order does not exclude further submissions leading to a later exemption order. The procedure for making submissions, originally set out in a circular issued by the Department in April 1975, is now contained in the Department's booklet *Exemption of certain Consumer Credit Agreements under Section 16 (1)*, published in March 1977 and reproduced in Division V. Submissions must be sent to:

Section B (PJR)
CCC 2/Consumer Credit Branch
Department of Prices and Consumer Protection
Room 2602, Millbank Tower
London SW1 P 4QU

A separate submission is necessary for each legal entity: for example, exemption to a parent company does not as such exempt its subsidiary. The submission should set out the details specified in para. 11 of the booklet. [308]

(iii) Consumer credit agreements falling into one of the classes listed in s. 16 (2) where the creditor is not a local authority or building society but is a body of a description specified in an order made by the Secretary of State, being one of the descriptions listed in s. 16 (1). The exemption under this category differs from that referred to in (ii) in that it is an exemption of a *class* rather than of a named body. No exemption order of this kind has so far been made. [309]

(iv) Consumer credit agreements exempted by order of the Secretary of State under s. 16 (5), being agreements where the number of payments to be made by the debtor does not exceed a number specified in the order or the rate of the total charge for credit does not exceed the rate so specified or an agreement has a connection with a country outside the United Kingdom. Exemptions for agreements within this category are provided by art. 3 of the Consumer (Exempt Agreements) Order 1977. [310]

(v) Consumer hire agreements of a description specified in an order made by the Secretary of State where (a) the owner is a statutory electricity, gas or water undertaking and the subject of the agreement is a meter or metering equipment, or (b) the owner is the Post Office or the Kingston-upon-Hull City Council. Exemption for agreements within this category is provided by art. 4 of the Consumer Credit (Exempt Agreements) Order 1977. [311]

Agreements within Section 16 (2)

Section 16 (1) applies only where the agreement falls within one of the cases listed in s. 16 (2). These will in practice cover almost all local authority and building society mortgages (for the definitions of "local authority" and "building society", see s. 189 (1)), and comprise the following:

(a) *A debtor-creditor-supplier agreement financing—*
    (i) *purchase of land, or*
    (ii) *the provision of dwellings on any land,*
    and secured by a land mortgage on that land.

This exemption is confined to debtor-creditor-supplier agreements (see paras. [315] *et seq.*) and thus applies only where the credit is extended by the vendor of the land (i.e. by leaving part of the purchase price outstanding on mortgage) or the house builder (i.e. by deferment of the obligation to pay for the dwelling) or by a third-party lender pursuant to arrangements with the vendor of the land or the builder of the dwelling, as the case may be. Further, the exemption does not apply to unsecured advances, nor to advances which are not secured on the land which is being purchased or on which the dwelling is being erected. On the other hand, the exemption is not lost by reason of the inclusion of other land as additional security. "Land mortgage" includes any security charged on land (s. 189 (1)) and thus embraces a rentcharge. However, no new rent charges can validly be created (Rentcharges Act 1977, s. 2). "Land" includes an interest in land (*ibid.*), whether freehold or leasehold. "Dwelling" is not defined but denotes a house, flat, maisonette or other accommodation designed wholly or mainly for living and sleeping, as opposed to business.

The exemption conferred on agreements within this category with a local authority or building society as creditor has been extended by orders under s. 16 (1) to embrace agreements in which the creditor is an insurance company, friendly society or charity listed in the orders (see paras. [315] *et seq.*). [312]

    (*b*) *A debtor-creditor agreement secured by any land mortgage*

Where the agreement is a debtor-creditor agreement and is secured by a land mortgage it is exempt whether or not the advance is made for the purchase of the land or the provision of dwellings on the land. Thus a further advance under a building society mortgage for the purpose of enabling the borrower to make improvements would be within the exemption.

If the creditor is not a local authority or building society, certain further conditions have to be satisfied before this exemption can apply. See paras. [317] *et seq.* [313]

    (*c*) *A debtor-creditor-supplier agreement financing a transaction which is a linked transaction in relation to—*
      (i) *an agreement falling within paragraph (a), or*
      (ii) *an agreement falling within paragraph (b) financing—*
        (*aa*) *the purchase of any land, or*
        (*bb*) *the provision of dwellings on any land,*
    and secured by a land mortgage on the land referred to in paragraph (a) or, as the case may be, the land referred to in sub-paragraph (ii).

This paragraph, which is obscure to the point of unintelligibility, illustrates the problems that arise when a statutory provision designed to meet a very particular situation is framed in general terms that offer no guidance as to what the provision is aimed at or, indeed, why it is there at all. Section 16 (2) (*c*) was evidently inserted to cover the situation where a building society which might normally advance only 80 per cent, say, of the price of a house agrees to provide an additional sum on the security of an insurance company bond, the premium for which is advanced by the building society.

The exemption is confined to agreements under which a local authority or building society is the creditor, no order having been made extending it to other agreements. [314]

Named body exemptions

Article 2 (1) of the Consumer Credit (Exempt Agreements) Order 1977, as amended by the Consumer Credit (Exempt Agreements) (Amendment) Orders

1977 and 1978 and the Consumer Credit (Exempt Agreements) (Amendment No. 2) Order 1978 exempts consumer credit agreements to which that paragraph applies. The exemptions are limited to agreements under which the creditor is a body specified in Part I or Part II of the Schedule, though in this respect the order would have been clearer if the word "but" had been inserted after "applies" in the second line of paras. (2) and (3) of art. 2. **[315]**

Part I of the Schedule to the above order lists insurance companies, friendly societies and charities (the only charities named are ecclesiastical bodies concerned with finance and pensions). The effect of art. 2 of the Order is to exempt consumer credit agreements entered into as creditor by any of these named bodies if, but only if, the agreement is one of the following (for convenience, the lettering and numbering of art. 2 of the Order is here adopted):

(a) *A debtor-creditor-supplier agreement falling within s. 16 (2) (a) of the Act*
This has already been examined (para. [312]). By way of example:
B contracts to purchase from an estate developer D, one of the plots comprised in the development, and by a subsequent building agreement B contracts to erect a house on the plot for D, the whole or part of the cost being advanced to B by an insurance company, I, pursuant to an agreement between I and B. If I is a company listed in Part I of the Schedule to the Order, the loan agreement between I and B is an exempt agreement under art. 2 (2) (a) (ii) of the order. **[316]**

(b) (i) *A debtor-creditor agreement secured by any land mortgage financing the purchase of land*
This follows s. 16 (2) (b) of the Act except for the added requirement that the agreement be one which finances the purchase of land, though it does not have to be the same land as that over which the mortgage is taken.

(ii) *A debtor-creditor agreement secured by any land mortgage financing the provision of dwellings or business premises on any land*
This is self-explanatory.

(iii) *A debtor-creditor agreement secured by a land mortgage financing—*
(A) *the purchase of land; or*
(B) *the provision of dwellings or business premises on any land; or*
(C) *the alteration, enlarging, repair or improvement of a dwelling or business premises on any land in a case where the creditor is the creditor under any agreement (whenever made) by which the debtor is provided with credit for any of the purposes specified in (i) and (ii) above, being an agreement relating to the land in question and secured by a land mortgage on that land*

This head of exemption is slightly more complex. The agreement only qualifies for exemption if the insurance company, friendly society or charity financing the alteration, etc. to the dwelling or business premises also financed the provision of the dwelling or premises or the purchase of the land on which they stand, and took a mortgage on that land as security for such financing. For example, if an insurance company designated in Part I of the Schedule to the Order lends money for the purchase of a house under a debtor-creditor agreement, taking a mortgage on the house as security, the agreement is exempt under art. 2 (2) (b) (i) of the Order, and if the insurance company subsequently provides finance for alterations, extensions, repairs or improvements to the house by way of a further advance under the mortgage, that new debtor-creditor agreement will likewise be exempt.

But if the original advance for the purchase had been secured on *other* land only, then though the original consumer credit agreement would still be exempt under art. 2 (2) (*b*) (i), the credit agreement relating to the alterations, etc. would not be exempt. The basic idea is to distinguish a further advance on first mortgage from a second-mortgage advance by a lender not involved in the original financing. Second-mortgage financing has generated a considerable volume of trading malpractice in recent years (see para. [**20**] and is thus deliberately excluded from the exemption. [**317**]

> (*c*) *A debtor-creditor agreement secured by any land mortgage to refinance any existing indebtedness of the debtor's, whether to the creditor or another person, under any agreement by which the debtor was provided with credit for any of the purposes specified in (i) to (iii) of (b) above*

This is self-explanatory. The exemption applies whether the refinancing is done by the original creditor, i.e. by rescheduling the debt, or by a new creditor who takes over the financing, wholly or in part. [**318**]

Part II of the Schedule to the Order lists one land improvement company and various other bodies corporate named or specifically referred to in some public general Act. A consumer credit agreement entered into by such a company as creditor is exempt only if, in addition to falling within one of the categories listed in s. 16 (2) of the Act, the agreement is of a description specified in Part II of the Schedule and is made pursuant to the enactment in question or for the purpose specified in Part II of the Schedule (art. 2 (3)). [**319**]

Exemption of other consumer credit agreements

Article 3 of the Order exempts various other categories of consumer credit agreement pursuant to s. 16 (5) of the Act, though the exemptions given under art. 3 (1) (*a*) do not apply where the agreement is one of a class falling within art. 3 (2), that is to say:

> (*a*) agreements financing the purchase of land;
> (*b*) a conditional sale or hire-purchase agreement; or
> (*c*) an agreement secured by a pledge, other than a pledge of documents of title.

Unless the agreement falls within one of these categories and is within (*a*) (i) or (ii) below it is exempt if it is an agreement of one of the following descriptions (for convenience, the lettering and numbering of art. 3 of the Order is here adopted):

> (*a*) (*i*) *Fixed-sum debtor-creditor-supplier agreement under which the number of payments to be made by the debtor does not exceed four*

This head of exemption (art. 3 (1) (*a*) (i)) covers (*inter alia*) ordinary account credit, such as the weekly grocery bill, the 28-day trade credit and the like (note that despite the existence of a current account between the parties, such agreements are for fixed-term, not running-account credit—see para. [**270**]). Several points arise under this exemption.

> (1) It is confined to debtor-creditor-supplier agreements, and thus is not applicable to an agreement for a cash loan, nor to an agreement by which a purchase-money loan is paid direct to the supplier otherwise than in pursuance of or in contemplation of arrangements between the creditor and the supplier (for a full description of debtor-creditor-supplier agreements, see paras. [**282**] *et seq.*).

99

(2) "Payment"is defined as "a payment comprising an amount in respect of credit with or without any other amount" (art. 3 (1) (*a*)). Since "credit" is defined in the Act as including a cash loan and any other form of financial accommodation (s. 9 (1)), "payment" in the Order clearly refers to a payment which operates in reduction or discharge of, or alternatively as security for, a loan or other financial accommodation already granted to the debtor. This has two consequences. First, a payment required to be made by the debtor does not count as one of the four instalments if it is unrelated to the financial accommodation he has received, e.g. (A) an insurance premium has to pay at the outset in conformity with an obligation to insure the goods to which the agreement relates; or (B) an amount forming part of the total charge for credit (Consumer Credit Act, s. 9 (4)). Secondly, a payment does not count as an instalment unless it is made in or towards discharge of (A) a loan indebtedness, that is, an indebtedness to a creditor who is not the supplier, or (B) a price obligation (i.e. an indebtedness to a supplier-creditor) which is contractually deferred to a point in time after delivery of the supply to which it relates. See Chapter 8, particularly paras. [**251**] *et seq.*

(3) The exemption does not apply to agreements financing the purchase of land or to conditional sale or hire-purchase agreements, nor to agreements secured by a pledge, other than a pledge of documents of title (art 3 (2)).

(ii) *Running-account debtor-creditor-supplier agreement which provides for the making of payments by the debtor in relation to specified periods and requires that the number of payments to be made by the debtor in repayment of the whole amount of the credit provided in each such period shall not exceed one*

In the case of running-account credit, the exemption is confined to agreements under which, for each period of credit, payment has to be made in one sum. As to what constitutes running-account credit, see paras. [**269**] *et seq.*

The most common examples of debtor-creditor-supplier running-account credit are the credit card and the budget account. Under each of these credit forms the customer is sent a monthly statement. If the agreement is one which requires him to settle the balance shown on the statement by a single payment, the agreement will be exempt under art. 3 (i) (*a*) (ii). If the agreement permits the debtor to pay by two or more instalments it will be a regulated agreement, unless falling under some other head of exemption listed below. A bank overdraft is not exempt for payment if due in one sum on demand, and not in relation to specified periods.

The exemption does not apply to agreements financing the purchase of land or to conditional sale or hire-purchase agreements, nor to agreements secured by a pledge, other than a pledge of documents of title (art. 3 (2)). [**320**]

(b) *Debtor-creditor-supplier agreement financing the purchase of land, being an agreement under which the number of payments to be made by the debtor does not exceed four*

Thus, an agreement for sale by which the vendor allows part of the purchase price to remain outstanding on mortgage will be exempt if the number of payments to be made by the buyer, *including payments of interest*, does not exceed four (art. 3 (*b*)). It should be noted that in contrast to art. 3 (1) (*a*), art. 3 (1) (*b*) defines "payment" so as to include an amount in respect of the total charge for credit. Hence if the agreement between vendor and purchaser is that the balance of the price shall be repaid in a lump sum within two years, the purchaser to make quarterly payments of interest meanwhile, the agreement will not be exempt for it requires eight payments by the debtor. On the other hand, if the period were one year, with quarterly interest, the agreement would be exempt, since the principal and the last quarter's interest would become payable at the same time, so that the number of stipulated payments would not exceed four. [**321**]

(c) *Debtor-creditor agreement as interest not exceeding maximum specified in the Order*

A debtor-creditor agreement will be exempt if the rate of the total charge for credit (calculated in accordance with regulations under s. 20 of the Act—see paras. [**501**]–[**541**]) does not exceed the higher of:

(i) the sum of 1% and the minimum lending rate determined by the Bank of England, being the latest rate in operation on the date 28 days before the date on which the agreement is made; and

(ii) 13 per cent.

Care should be taken not to misinterpret the reference to minimum lending rate in the Order. It does not as such give exemption to an agreement which, for example, fixes interest at "Bank of England minimum lending rate for the time being" (though this formula would suffice if at the date of the agreement minimum lending rate was within the higher of the above maxima, for the assumption in reg. 14 of the Consumer Credit (Total Charge for Credit) Regulations 1977 would then protect the creditor. See para. [**532**]). The first of the two alternative rates stipulated as maxima by the Order is not minimum lending rate as it fluctuates from time to time but "the latest rate in operation on the date 28 days before the date on which the agreement is made". This figure becomes established on entry into agreement. If the latest minimum lending rate 28 days before the making of the agreement was 14% the agreement will be exempt if the rate stipulated does not exceed 15%. If the agreement fixes a rate of 16%, it will not be exempt even if by the date of the agreement minimum lending rate has risen to 15%. If the latest minimum lending rate 28 days before contract was 11%, the agreement can provide interest up to 13%, as the higher of the two alternatives provided by the Order.

It is permissible to provide for a fluctuating rate—e.g. a rate varying with Finance House base rate or minimum lending rate—without losing the exemption provided that the agreement fixes as the ceiling a rate not greater than the higher of the two rates specified in the Order or the assumption provided by reg. 14 operates to ensure that this ceiling is deemed not to have been exceeded. Thus a debtor-creditor agreement will be exempt under art. 3 (1) (c) if it provides for interest at "2% above Finance House base rate for the time being or 13%, whichever is the lower". It will also be exempt if it provides for interest at "2% above Finance House base rate for the time being" and at the date of the agreement that rate is in fact within the higher of the above maxima. For an illustration, see para. [**541**], *Case 4, post*. On the other hand, the exemption is lost if the agreement provides for indexation of any part of the *principal sum* repayable by the debtor, e.g. where on a loan of £5,000 repayable at interest of 10% the agreement goes on to say that the amount repayable in respect of principal shall be £5,000 plus a percentage increase equal to the increase shown in the cost of living index between the date of the loan and the date of repayment. Indexation destroys the exemption even if the total of the increase in principal and the stipulated interest is limited to the ceiling figure of interest specified in art. 3 (1) (c). [**322**]

(*d*) *Agreements with a foreign element*
Article 3 (1) (*d*) exempts—
"any agreement made in connection with trade in goods or services between the United Kingdom and a country outside the United Kingdom or within a country or between countries outside the United Kingdom, being an agreement under which credit is provided to the debtor in the course of a business carried on by him."
This exemption is considered in Chapter 32. [**323**]

Exemption of consumer hire agreements

Article 4 of the Consumer Credit (Exempt Agreements) Order exempts two classes of consumer hire agreement. The first is a hire agreement entered into as owner by a statutory electricity, gas or water undertaking and relating to a meter or metering equipment used or to be used in connection with the supply of electricity, gas or water, as the case may be. The second is a consumer hire agreement relating to certain types of telecommunications apparatus let on hire by the Post Office or the Kingston upon Hull City Council. [**323.1**]

11. Licensing

The purpose and impact of a licensing system

No consumer legislation, however sophisticated, is likely to have more than a marginal impact if not underpinned by effective enforcement machinery. The Hire-Purchase Acts provided no mechanism whatever for systematic enforcement. The onus was placed on the individual consumer to take the initiative in invoking the Acts. In many cases he was not equipped to do so, through ignorance of his rights, timidity or inability to incur the legal costs that might be involved. The reputable trader or finance house would endeavour to comply with the law. The less scrupulous creditor, against whose activities the legislation was primarily aimed, could afford to cock a snook—provided that he stood clear of the small number of criminal offences provided by the statutes—since at worst he would lose the occasional case, and this loss was far outweighed by the benefits to be derived from diligent and persistent flouting of the statutory requirements and the recovery from uninformed debtors of sums which they could not legally have been compelled to pay. So far as moneylending was concerned, the law was theoretically stronger because of a licensing system and a battery of criminal sanctions for different types of offence. But as a method of control this also was largely ineffective, partly because the licensing system was decentralised, partly because the Acts failed to impose any duty of enforcement on any specific authority. In the result, prosecutions were infrequent and were left to the occasional initiative of a police officer; and revocation and suspension of licences was almost unknown. A survey conducted by the author in 1968 showed that of the 170 licensing authorities from whom figures were received, only one had a record of any court order in the last ten years forfeiting a certificate issued to a moneylender, while in the same period there was only one recorded instance of suspension of a licence being notified to a licensing authority. [**324**]

The Consumer Credit Act has remedied these serious weaknesses of previous legislation by entrusting the overall administration and enforcement of the Act, and of regulations under it, to the Director General of Fair Trading, and by making enforcement at local level the responsibility of Weights and Measures Authorities, who have already developed considerable expertise in this type of control under the Weights and Measures Acts, the Trade Descriptions Acts and other legislation in the public law sector. A linchpin of the enforcement machinery is the licensing

system, which will be operated centrally by the Director. Licensing has many
advantages as a method of contról. First, it provides an extremely powerful
sanction against deliberate law breaking. The offender risks not merely the loss of
an occasional civil suit or even the occasional fine but the more drastic penalty of
being put out of business altogether. It is rarely necessary for enforcement agencies
to exercise a sanction of this kind. The mere threat suffices to discourage the
licensee from sailing too close to the wind. On the other hand, a licensee who
infringes a legal right through inadvertence can be cautioned without the need for
the full rigour of the law to be applied to him. The most valuable enforcement
work of trading standards inspectors is achieved by friendly caution rather than
by prosecution. These are not the only advantages of a licensing system. The
value judgment which is inevitably involved in determining the suitability of an
applicant for the grant or renewal of a licence gives a measure of flexibility and
allows the licensing authority to take into account facts known about the applicant
which might be difficult to establish by formal evidence (it has to be said, on the
other side, that this same fact also carries a risk of injustice). Through a central
licensing system, consistency can be secured in standards of conduct imposed on
licensees and in the approach to enforcement. In addition, requirements imposed
as to the supply of documents and information by existing and prospective
licensees can be expected to produce much needed information concerning the
areas of business to which the licensing requirements relate. [**325**]

It is for these reasons that licensing has become increasingly popular with
successive governments as a method of regulating spheres of business activity.
This trend·may be expected to accelerate in the light of our entry into the Common
Market, since our partners in Europe have leaned heavily on licensing and in
certain fields the introduction of new licensing systems may become mandatory as
the result of an EEC Directive. Indeed, this is already coming about in the banking
sector, partly because of reforms shown to be necessary by the near-collapse of the
secondary banking system a few years ago, leading to a White Paper on *The
Licensing of Deposit-Taking Institutions* (Cmnd. 6584, August 1976) and partly as
the result of the EEC's First Directive on Banking dated 12th December 1977.
This requires credit institutions having their head office in one member state and
their branches in another to obtain official authorisation to conduct business, and
lays down various criteria that have to be satisfied before approval can be granted
(for a summary of the Directive, see Paolo Clarotti, "The First Directive on the Co-
ordination of Banking Legislation" (1978) 19 *Credit* 115). Consequent upon the
White Paper, and stimulated by the Directive, Parliament has passed the Banking
Act 1979, which provides for the licensing by the Bank of England of all deposit-
taking institutions other than recognised banks. [**326**]

Yet the manifest advantages of licensing should not blind one to certain dangers
endemic in this method of control. A licensing system can become administratively
burdensome if not confined within proper limits. The licensing provisions of the
Consumer Credit Act are open to objection on this ground in that (following upon
the recommendation of the Crowther Committee which perhaps went too far in
this respect) they bring within the licensing net not only those whose primary
function is to provide credit but retail suppliers of goods and services who supply
on credit terms. The effect of this has been to swell the total number of licences in
issue by a considerable figure and to dissuade the Government from its original
intention to introduce licensing for estate agents. But even given a licensing

system sufficiently restricted to allow smooth and efficient running, the use of administrative procedures, and the exercise of judicial functions by administrative organs, can lead to unfair or unjust decisions which are not easily put right. The very flexibility of the system makes it difficult for a party aggrieved by refusal or revocation of a licence to make a successful challenge on the basis of improper exercise of discretion by the licensing authority. In other countries on the Continent, the power of administrative agencies is counter-balanced by highly developed systems of administrative law, usually applied by separate administrative courts, which are much readier than our own courts have been hitherto to enquire into the manner of exercise of a discretion and which may have power to award damages against the administration for breach of duty in the exercise of administrative functions. As licensing develops in this country, we may expect to see a corresponding development in our administrative law, which, despite its considerable growth in recent years, remains fragmented and undeveloped and has a long way to go before it reaches its potential power. In this chapter, after looking at the mechanism of the licensing system created by the Consumer Credit Act, we shall examine some of the problems that this may create in the administrative law field and the approach that the courts are likely to adopt when asked to review the exercise of discretion by the Director and by the Secretary of State on appeal. It is not possible, in an introductory Guide of this kind, to give more than the broadest outline of the court's power in the licensing field. For a comprehensive analysis of the principles involved in this most difficult aspect of administrative law, the reader should turn to the late Professor de Smith's brilliant book, *The Judicial Review of Administrative Action*, the third edition of which was published in 1973. [**327**]

Licensing under the Moneylenders Acts and Pawnbrokers Acts

Licensing under the Moneylenders Acts and the Pawnbrokers Acts ended on 31st July 1977, the licensing provisions of those statutes being repealed on 1st August 1977 (Consumer Credit Act 1974 (Commencement No. 2) Order 1977, art. 5 and Sch. 3, Pt. I), this being the date which was originally intended as the first date of mandatory licensing of consumer credit businesses under the Consumer Credit Act. For administrative reasons this date had to be put back to the 1st October 1977, but in order to obviate the necessity for moneylenders to renew their licences (which expire on 31st July in each year) for a mere two months the decision was taken to end licensing under the Moneylenders Acts on 31st July 1977. The effect was to create a two-month period (August and September 1977) when a moneylender did not require a licence either under the Moneylenders Acts or under the Consumer Credit Act. Similarly, during the same period pawnbrokers did not require a licence under the Pawnbrokers Acts or the Consumer Credit Act. But most of the other provisions of the Moneylenders Acts and Pawnbrokers Acts remain unrepealed. [**328**]

The licensing system—administration and publicity

The issue, variation, renewal, suspension and revocation of licences is within the exclusive domain of the Director, subject to the rights of appeal mentioned later in this chapter. Hence for the system of local licensing hitherto operated under the Moneylenders Acts there is substituted a central licensing machinery, controlled by the Director. All matters pertaining to licensing are dealt with by the Consumer Credit Licensing Branch, Office of Fair Trading, Government Buildings, Bromyard Avenue, Acton, London W3 7BB. As originally drafted, the functions now allocated to the Director by the Act were to be performed by a separate official, the Consumer Credit Commissioner. But when the Bill was reintroduced, it was decided to merge these functions into those of the Director General of Fair Trading, and there can be little doubt that the decision to do this was sensible. To assist him in evaluating applications the Director can also draw on information from various agencies, including local weights and measures authorities, Citizens' Advice Bureaux and the like. Indeed, it was at one time obligatory for the applicant for a licence to give notice in prescribed form to his local trading standards officer who would then submit a report to the Director, but these requirements were discontinued soon after their introduction. [**329**]

To ensure adequate publicity of matters concerning licensing applications and decisions, the Director is required by s. 35 to establish and maintain a register containing particulars of—

    (*a*) applications not yet determined for the issue, variation or renewal of licences, or for ending the suspension of a licence;

    (*b*) licences which are in force, or have at any time been suspended or revoked, with details of any variation of the terms of a licence;

    (*c*) decisions given by him under the Act, and any appeal from those decisions; and

    (*d*) such other matters (if any) as he thinks fit.

The Director is further required to give general notice of the various matters required to be entered in the register, and of any changes in these made under s. 35 (1) (*d*). For a description of the register established in accordance with these provisions, see paras. [**150**] *et seq.* The Act enables the Director to establish local registers, or copies of registers, if he thinks it desirable, and to allow local search facilities (s. 35 (4), (5)) and some were initially provided but had to be withdrawn soon afterwards as an economy measure. See para. [**152**]. [**330**]

A duty is imposed on the licensee under a standard licence to notify the Director of various changes. As will be seen, the duty will not always be easily performed. A standard (but not group) licensee must give notice to the Director, within 21 working days, of any change:

    (i) in any particulars entered in the register in respect of a standard licence or the licensee under s. 35 (1) (*d*) (not being a change resulting from action taken by the Director) (s. 36 (1));

    (ii) in the officers of a body corporate licensee or in the officers of a body corporate which is a controller of the licensee (s. 36 (2) (*a*)—and see below as to the definition of "controller");

    (iii) in the officers of a licensee which is an unincorporated body of persons (*ibid.*);

    (iv) in the members of a partnership licensee, including a change on the amalgamation of the partnership with another firm, or a change whereby the number of partners is reduced to one (s. 36 (2) (*c*)).

In addition, where a body corporate licensee becomes aware that a person has become or ceased to be a controller of the licensee, then the licensee must notify the Director of that fact within 21 working days after becoming aware of it (s. 36 (2) (*b*)). To ensure as far as possible that a body corporate licensee will become aware of changes in the control or officers of its controlling company, the Act provides that the controlling company shall notify the licensee of such changes within 14 working days (s. 36 (3), (4)). "Working day" means any day other than Saturday, Sunday, Christmas Day or Good Friday and a bank holiday within s. 1 of the Banking and Financial Dealings Act 1971 (s. 189 (1)). [**331**]

For the purpose of the Act "controller", in relation to a body corporate, is defined by s. 189 (1) as a person—

(*a*) in accordance with whose directions or instructions the directors of the body corporate or of another body corporate which is its controller (or any of them) are accustomed to act, or

(*b*) who, either alone or with any associate or associates, is entitled to exercise or control the exercise of, one third or more of the voting power at any general meeting of the body corporate or of another body corporate which is its controller. [**332**]

Any person is entitled, on payment of the specified fee—

(*a*) to inspect the register (or, if so determined by the Director, a copy of the register) during ordinary office hours and to take copies of any entry, or

(*b*) to obtain from the Director a copy, certified by the Director to be correct, of any entry in the register (s. 35 (3), (4)). [**333**]

The need for a licence

A licence is required to carry on a consumer credit or consumer hire business (s. 21 (1)). The only types of credit grantor not requiring a licence for a business of this kind are (i) a local authority and (ii) a body corporate empowered by a public general Act naming it to carry on such a business. Into this latter category fall, for example, the Commission for the New Towns, the Agriculture Mortgage Corporation, the White Fish Authority and the public utilities such as gas and electricity boards. These were excluded from the licensing requirement on the ground that where Parliament has conferred powers on a body corporate under a public general Act, it would be inappropriate for an independent statutory officer (in this case, the Director General of Fair Trading) to be able to take those powers away. But such bodies remain subject to the other provisions of the Act, except in so far as their agreements are exempted under s. 16 (see Chapter 10). [**334**]

By s. 189 (1) of the Act, "consumer credit business" means any business so far as it comprises or relates to the provision of credit under regulated consumer credit agreements; and "consumer hire business" means any business so far as it comprises or relates to the bailment of goods under regulated consumer hire agreements. Here it is worth repeating the point made earlier that the provision of consumer credit or consumer hire need not itself be carried on as a business to attract the definition: it suffices that it is an *activity* regularly carried on in the course of some other business, which need have no connection with the granting of consumer credit. It follows that a company regularly making loans to its employees under regulated agreements will require to be licensed as carrying on a consumer credit business even if this is the sole extent of its involvement in the granting of credit under the regulated agreements. A similar position obtains in relation to ancillary credit businesses. See para. [**997**] and Chapter 31. The word "business" is not confined to gainful activity but embraces any regular occupation in which goods, services or facilities are regularly provided to others, e.g. free credit advisory services. On the other hand, the business of granting credit must be distinguished from the activity of regular investment. Thus, regular mortgage investment by trustees, though it may involve the lending of money, would probably not be regarded in itself as carrying on a business (though if the trustee carried on some *other* business, the regular making of loans under regulated agreements would itself constitute the carrying on of a consumer credit business, for the reason previously given). The distinction between investing and carrying on a business is well recognised in revenue law, even though not always easy to apply. [**335**]

A person is not to be treated as carrying on a particular type of business merely because occasionally he enters into transactions belonging to a business of that type (s. 189 (2)). Hence regularity of activity is necessary before that activity can be regarded as a business activity so as to attract the licensing provisions. Thus, a solicitor making *occasional* bridging loans for clients would not on that account alone be carrying on a consumer credit business. It would seem that the onus of showing that a person carries on a consumer credit or consumer hire business lies on the party asserting it. [**336**]

A licence is also required to carry on an ancillary credit business (s. 147 (1)), that is, any business so far as it comprises or relates to credit brokerage, debt-adjusting, debt-counselling, debt-collecting or the operation of a credit reference agency (s. 145 (1)). These are fully discussed in Chapter 31. [**337**]

Types of licence

By s. 22 (1) a licence may be—
- (*a*) a standard licence, that is a licence, issued by the Director to a person named in the licence on an application made by him, which, during the prescribed period, covers such activities as are described in the licence, or
- (*b*) a group licence, that is a licence, issued by the Director (whether on the application of any person or of his own motion), which, during such period as the Director thinks fit or, if he thinks fit, indefinitely, covers such persons and activities as are described in the licence. [**338**]

The standard licence is issued to a named person (s. 22 (1)) and authorises him to carry on business under the name or names specified in the licence but not under any other name (s. 24). This latter requirement is discussed in detail in paras. [**374**] *et seq*. Except in the case of a partnership or an unincorporated body of persons, a standard licence must not be issued to more than one person (s. 22 (3)). A standard licence issued to a partnership or unincorporated body is issued in the name of the partnership or body (s. 22 (4)). The effect is that each partner or member of the body for the time being is deemed to hold the licence, and changes in the partnership or in members of the body do not affect the continuance of the licence so long as (in the case of a partnership) the name of the partnership remains unchanged (see para. [**374**]). [**339**]

A standard licence differs from a group licence in that it requires an individual application, which in the normal course of events will be carefully examined to ensure that the applicant is a proper person to hold a licence (see paras. [**346**] *et seq*.). Group licences, on the other hand, do not involve the screening of individual applications. However, the fact that a person is covered by a group licence in respect of certain activities does not prevent a standard licence being issued to him in respect of those activities or any of them (s. 22 (7)). [**340**]

The initial number of standard licences to be applied for was foreseen as likely to be large, and it would have been difficult, if not impossible, for all applications to be processed before the day appointed for the commencement of the licensing requirements. This problem was dealt with in paragraph 5 (2) of the Third Schedule (see para. [**352**]). [**341**]

Group licences

Group licences are intended not, as might be thought, for members of a group of companies but for those categories of creditor or credit business where individual examination is not considered necessary in the public interest. Group licences may be issued by the Director only if it appears to him that the public interest is better served by doing so than by obliging the persons concerned to apply separately for standard licences (s. 22 (5)). The Director has power to exclude named persons from any group licence (s. 22 (6)). This is a necessary safeguard to allow the Director to exercise more immediate supervision over creditors whose activities are under suspicion, whilst leaving the group licence procedure available for the remaining members of the class. [**342**]

A group licence may be issued on the application of any person or by the Director of his own motion (s. 22 (1) (*b*)). When issued on application, it is issued to the applicant (s. 22 (8)). The Director must give general notice of a group licence, whether issued on application or by the Director of his own motion (*ibid.*). A general notice means a notice published by the Director at a time and in a manner appearing to him suitable for securing that the notice is seen within a reasonable time by persons likely to be affected by it (s. 189 (1)). [**343**]

Group licences have so far been issued to (i) The Law Society, the Law Society of Scotland and the Incorporated Law Society of Northern Ireland, in relation to solicitors holding current practising certificates; (ii) the National Association of Citizens' Advice Bureaux in respect of Citizens' Advice Bureaux registered with the Association; (iii) liquidators, receivers, trustees in bankruptcy, etc. if already holding a licence or being a licensee under a group licence; (iv) various old peoples' welfare organisations. As to the position of liquidators, receivers, trustees in bankruptcy, etc. within category (iii), see para. [**379**]. Applications for a group licence must be made in form CC 3/75 (General Notice No. 4). For the text of the licences, see Division IV. [**344**]

Categories of standard licence

The Consumer Credit Act provides seven categories of licensable activity (together with authorisation of canvassing of debtor-creditor-supplier agreements and regulated consumer hire agreements off trade premises) but for administrative purposes debt-adjusting and debt-counselling have been paired so as to reduce the number of licensing categories to six. These are as follows:

Category A—Consumer credit business
Category B—Consumer hire business
Category C—Credit brokerage
Category D—Debt-adjusting and debt-counselling
Category E—Debt-collecting
Category F—The operation of a credit reference agency

Categories A and B are defined in s. 189 (1) of the Act. See para. [**335**]. Categories

C–F are defined in ss. 145 and 146 of the Act and are described in Chapter 31.
[345]

The right to a licence

In the early versions of the Consumer Credit Bill there was no right to a licence. The Director was not obliged to issue a licence to those fulfilling stated requirements; he was merely precluded from granting a licence unless certain conditions were satisfied, but apparently retained an overall discretion to refuse a licence even where such conditions were fulfilled. This was changed by amendment as the Bill proceeded through Parliament; and the effect of s. 25 (1) of the Act is that a standard licence *must* be granted on the application of any person if he satisfies the Director that—

    (a) he is a fit person to engage in activities covered by the licence, and

    (b) the name or names under which he applies to be licensed is or are not misleading or otherwise undesirable.

Accordingly, the issue of a licence is in theory a matter of right, not of discretion. In practice, this apparently clear-cut distinction is blurred by the fact that the Director has to be "satisfied" that the two conditions are fulfilled, and in determining whether condition (a) is satisfied he may have regard to any circumstances appearing to him to be relevant (see paras. [359]–[362]). Hence the "right" to a licence, involving as it does a value judgment on the part of the Director, is in reality much more akin to an administrative discretion. Nevertheless, it is not a discretion in the full sense; the Director cannot refuse a licence on any ground other than a failure to be satisfied as to one or both of the conditions set out in s. 25 (1). Thus, he is not entitled to refuse a licence to a prospective consumer credit grantor on the ground that there are already enough consumer credit businesses in the locality to meet the needs of the local populace. This is an additional test commonly applied in the United States, but it is not a relevant issue in the treatment of applications for licences under the Consumer Credit Act. Again, while the test of the Director's "satisfaction" is plainly subjective, this does not mean that the courts are powerless to intervene where the Director's approach to the assessment of evidence is manifestly unreasonable. This point is adverted to in paragraphs [434] *et seq.* [346]

Whilst the Director *must* grant a licence if he is satisfied that the two conditions set out in s. 25 (1) have been met, it is not entirely clear that the Director is precluded from granting a licence without being so satisfied. It certainly seems to have been the intention of Parliament that the Director should not be allowed to issue licences except on compliance with the two specified conditions; and it is thought that the courts would construe the words "if he satisfies . . ." as meaning "if, and only if . . .". Any other conclusion would make it extremely difficult for a third party to upset the issue of a licence on the ground of want of *vires.* [347]

Application for a licence

Under s. 6 (2) of the Act, an application for a licence, like any other application to the Director under the Act, must—

    (i) be in writing;

     (ii) be in such form, and accompanied by such particulars, as the Director may specify by general notice; and

     (iii) be accompanied by the specified fee, that is, the fee (or reduced fee) charged by the Director with the approval of the Secretary of State and the Treasury (ss. 189 (1), 2 (4), (5)).

Strict compliance with these requirements is imperative, since otherwise the application is of no effect (s. 6 (1)). No power is conferred on the Director to waive any of these requirements; and since a standard licence can only be issued on application by the intended licensee (ss. 22 (1) (*a*), 25 (1)), it would seem that a licence granted on an invalid application is itself invalid. However, it is within the power of the Director to alleviate the consequences of this situation by making a direction under s. 40 (2) (see para. [**385**]) or an order under s. 148 (2) or s. 149 (2) (see para. [**1015**]) that regulated agreements made by the trader whilst he or the credit broker was unlicensed shall be treated as if he or the credit broker, as the case may be, had been licensed during the relevant period—always assuming that the application for such a direction or order was itself valid under s. 6 (2)! [**348**]

Who must apply

    A standard licence is required to be taken out by every person carrying on one of the designated categories of licensable business or activity (see para. [**345**]) other than (*a*) a local authority, (*b*) a body corporate empowered by a general Act naming it to carry on the business in question and (*c*) a person sufficiently covered by a group licence. [**349**]

Time for application

    The following is the licensing timetable laid down by the various commencement orders. (As to renewals, see para. [**396**]).

Category of business	Date from which licence required	Relevant Order
Debt-adjusting Debt-counselling Debt-collecting Operation of credit reference agency	3 August 1976	1975 No. 2123
Consumer credit business	1 October 1977 (except where business carried on by an individual and confined to agreements under which credit or credit limit does not exceed £30)	1977 No. 325
Consumer hire business	1 October 1977	1977 No. 325
Credit brokerage	1 July 1978 (except where business carried on by an individual and confined	1977 No. 2163

Category of business	Date from which licence required	Relevant Order
Credit brokerage —*cont.*	to introduction of applicants for credit under debtor-creditor-supplier agreements where credit under any such agreement does not exceed £30 and, in case of hire-purchase and instalment sale agreements, supplier is willing to sell for cash)	

[**350**]

Though in general the 1st October 1977 is the appointed day for the purpose of s. 21 of the Act (dealing with licensing of consumer credit and consumer hire business), this does not apply to a consumer credit business in the course of which the only regulated agreements are agreements for fixed-sum credit not exceeding £30 or agreements for running-account credit under which the credit limit does not exceed £30. For such categories of business the licensing provisions do not come into operation until a further appointed day. See Consumer Credit Act 1974 (Commencement No. 2) Order 1977, art. 2 (3) (*a*). Similarly, there is a deferment, until a day to be appointed, for a credit-brokerage business carried on by an individual where the business is confined to the introduction of individuals desiring to obtain credit under debtor-creditor-supplier agreements and in the case of any such agreement (*a*) the creditor is the legal supplier (i.e. the agreement is a hire-purchase, conditional sale or credit sale agreement), the credit does not exceed £30 and the supplier is willing to sell for cash, or (*b*) the creditor is a third party and the credit or credit limit does not exceed £30. See Consumer Credit Act 1974 (Commencement No. 4) Order 1977, art. 2. [**351**]

Application for a licence before the appointed day

Since it would obviously have been impossible for the Director and his staff to process all applications for licences made prior to the appointed day in time for them to be dealt with by that day, the Act provides that where the person carrying on any description of consumer credit business or consumer hire business applies for a licence before the appointed day in relation to a business of that description, he is deemed to have been granted on the appointed day a licence covering that business and continuing in force until the licence applied for is granted or, if the application is refused, until the end of the appeal period (Third Schedule, para. 5 (2)). There is a similar provision as to renewals. See s. 29 (4) and para. [**397**]. [**352**]

Application form

An application for a standard licence must be made in Form CC 1/75 and must be accompanied by supporting information in Form CC 2/75 (see (iv) below; and/or specimens of the forms. The form must be completed with meticulous accuracy, for the particulars it requires to be provided are pre-scribed by general notice pursuant to s. 6 (2) of the Act, and if the application is not made in the prescribed form and accompanied by the prescribed particulars it is of no effect (s. 6 (1)), so that any resulting standard licence would apparently be a nullity (see, however, para. [**348**]). Presumably the court can ignore defects that are *de minimis*, e.g. minor errors in the spelling of a name that do not mislead. The form is arranged in such a way that only the information contained on the front page (i.e. paragraphs 1–6) will be registered in the public register, this being done by the Office of Fair Trading placing on the file a photocopy of the front page of the application. The reverse side of the application form (which is not considered by the OFT to form part of the application itself for the purpose of s. 6 (1)) calls for information which will not appear in the register, and an error in which will not attract the rigours of s. 6 (1). Careful consideration must be given to the name or names under which the licensed business is intended to be carried on (question 4 on the form). See further below. [**353**]

It is an offence knowingly or recklessly to furnish information in the application form which is false or misleading in a material particular (s. 7). [**354**]

Supporting information

The application Form CC 1/75 must be accompanied by supporting information to be supplied in Form CC 2/75. This information is not prescribed by general notice under s. 6 (2), and accordingly the completion and return of Form CC 2/75 cannot be considered a "requirement" under the Act, for without either a general notice or a notice to a particular applicant under s. 6 (3) the Director has no power to insist on the information being supplied. It follows that an error in or omission from the particulars furnished in Form CC 2/75 is outside the scope of s. 6 (1) and thus does not vitiate the application. On the other hand, the fact that the form is not prescribed would not appear to preclude the Director from refusing the application on the ground of failure to furnish the completed form, as by s. 25 (1) the onus is on the applicant to satisfy the Director that he, the applicant, is a fit person to engage in activities covered by the desired licence, and without the supporting information the Director would be entitled to say that he is not so satisfied. In this sense, the requirement of s. 6 (2) that supporting information required by the Director be prescribed by general notice would appear to be directory only. [**355**]

The information given in Form CC 2/75 is not entered in the public register. It was excluded from General Notice No. 5 in order to avoid the disclosure of sensitive information, though many of the details required are in fact matters of public record. Convictions which have become spent under the Rehabilitation of Offenders Act 1974, and circumstances ancillary to offences to which such spent convictions relate, do not have to be disclosed. [**356**]

Knowingly or recklessly to furnish information in Form CC 2/75 which is false or misleading in a material particular is an offence under s. 7. [**357**]

The matters that must be taken into account by the Director in deciding whether the applicant for a licence is a fit person to carry on the licensed activity are set out in s. 25 (2), (3), as follows:

> "(2) In determining whether an applicant for a standard licence is a fit person to engage in any activities, the Director shall have regard to any circumstances appearing to him to be relevant, and in particular any evidence tending to show that the applicant, or any of the applicant's employees, agents or associates (whether past or present) or, where the applicant is a body corporate, any person appearing to the Director to be

the controller of the body corporate or an associate of any such person, has—

(a) committed any offence involving fraud or other dishonesty or violence,

(b) contravened any provision made by or under this Act, or by or under any other enactment regulating the provision of credit to individuals or other transactions with individuals,

(c) practised discrimination on grounds of sex, colour, race or ethnic or national origins in, or in connection with, the carrying on of any business, or

(d) engaged in business practices appearing to the Director to be deceitful or oppressive, or otherwise unfair or improper (whether unlawful or not).

(3) In subsection (2), 'associate', in addition to the persons specified in section 184, includes a business associate."

The above provision needs to be read in conjunction with s. 170 (2):

"(2) In exercising his functions under this Act the Director may take account of any matter appearing to him to constitute a breach of a requirement made by or under this Act, whether or not any sanction for that breach is provided by or under this Act and, if it is so provided, whether or not proceedings have been brought in respect of the breach." [358]

The first point to note about these provisions is that the matters listed in s. 25 (2) (a)–(d), wide-ranging though they are, do not cover the whole field of contemplation laid upon the Director but are merely examples of matters to which he should have regard. Any matter, whether or not set out in the list, may (indeed must) be considered by the Director so far as it is a circumstance appearing to him to be relevant to the applicant's fitness to engage in any activity for which his licence is sought. It is thus open to the Director not only to go outside the list but also to determine that the applicant is a fit person to become a licensee for some of the licensable activities to which his application relates but not others, and to limit the licence accordingly. See also para. [369]. [359]

Secondly, it is not only the conduct of the applicant himself that comes into consideration but also that of any of his employees, agents or associates, past or present. So even if the applicant himself is guiltless of any offence, his association in business with undesirable characters or his family ties with persons of doubtful repute are sufficient grounds for refusing him a licence. [360]

Thirdly, the Director can take account of both lawful and unlawful activity. The criminal acts listed in paragraph (a) were presumably selected because of their particular moral turpitude, though others could no doubt be added; and unlawful conduct may also arise under the remaining paragraphs. For example, paragraph (d) speaks of (*inter alia*) sex discrimination; and s. 29 of the Sex Discrimination Act 1975 makes it unlawful for any person concerned with the provision of goods, facilities or services to the public, including facilities by way of banking or insurance or for grants, loans, credit or finance, to discriminate against a woman who seeks to obtain or use them. Unfair or improper business practices may be taken into account even if not unlawful. Examples given during the Debates on the Consumer Credit Bill were (1) persistently selling credit to those unable to afford it; (2) persistently driving extortionate credit bargains; (3) incompetence in the management of the business; (4) deliberate use of salesmen employing high-pressure techniques to sell credit. [**361**]

The word "associate" is elaborately defined in s. 184, in a definition which embraces certain forms of business association and relatives. To ensure that for licensing purposes forms of business association not mentioned in s. 184 may be brought within the purview of the Director's scrutiny, s. 25 (3) expands the meaning of the word "associate" to include a business associate. This term is not defined (though by s. 189 (1) "business" includes a trade or profession), but presumably covers any person in collaboration with whom business of any kind is transacted. "Relative" is itself widely defined, and includes, for example, not merely a husband or wife but a *former* husband or wife and even a *reputed* husband or wife. To convey the full flavour of "associate" it is necessary to set out in s. 184 in full:

"(1) A person is an associate of an individual if that person is the individual's husband or wife, or is a relative, or the husband or wife of a relative, of the individual or of the individual's husband or wife.

(2) A person is an associate of any person with whom he is in partnership, and of the husband or wife or a relative of the individual with whom he is in partnership.

(3) A body corporate is an associate of another body corporate—

(a) if the same person is a controller of both, or a person is a controller of one and persons who are his associates, or he and persons who are his associates, are the controllers of the other; or

(b) if a group of two or more persons is a controller of each company, and the groups either consist of the same persons or could be regarded as consisting of the same persons by treating (in one or more cases) a member of either group as replaced by a person of whom he is an associate.

(4) A body corporate is an associate of another person if that person is a controller of it or if that person and persons who are his associates together are controllers of it.

(5) In this section 'relative' means brother, sister, uncle, aunt, nephew, niece, lineal ancestor or lineal descendant, and references to a husband or wife include a former husband or wife and a reputed husband or wife; and for the purposes of this subsection a relationship shall be established as if any illegitimate child, step-child or adopted child of a person had been a child born to him in wedlock." [**362**]

The proposed licensed name

A standard licence authorises the licensee to carry on a business under the name or names specified in the licence, but not under any other name (s. 24). Care must therefore be taken to provide in the answer to questions 3 and 4 of Form CC 1/75 any name under which the applicant may wish to carry on the licensable activity in question. The Office of Fair Trading will not normally accept any name which is required to be registered under the Registration of Business Names Act 1916 and has not been so registered. [**363**]

The Director must be satisfied that the name or names under which the applicant asks for a licence is or are not misleading or otherwise undesirable (s. 25 (1)). An application may be queried on this ground if (*inter alia*) a name:

(*a*) is too like the name of a licensee or too like the name under which a licensee carries on business;

(*b*) is misleading, as, for example, where it misrepresents the size of the company, its resources or its area and scope of activities;

(*c*) suggests a connection with the Crown or members of the Royal Family or suggests royal patronage (by the use, for example, of such words as: Royal, King, Queen, Princess, Crown);

(*d*) suggests a connection with a Government department, agency, statutory undertaking, local authority, or any Commonwealth or foreign government;

(*e*) suggests a connection with a large or substantial organisation;

(*f*) gives a false or misleading impression of the cost, type or ease of borrowing;

(*g*) includes any of the following words: association, bank, building society, chamber of commerce, council, co-operative, corporation, credit union, institute, insurance, international, investment trust, registrar, trust, unit trust or trustee savings.

All the above illustrations are taken from note 7 on form CC 1/75. The Director will assist applicants by giving a preliminary view as to acceptability of a name, for which purpose the applicant should write to the Consumer Credit Licensing Branch, Office of Fair Trading, Government Buildings, Bromyard Avenue, Acton W3 7BB. The name cannot be reserved and the Director retains the right to refuse a name, even if provisionally approved, when the application itself is considered. These rules closely follow those laid down by the Department of Trade and the Companies Registrar in relation to approval of the name of a projected company.

[**364**]

Quite apart from the above rules, any trader, whether an individual, a partnership or a company, may be restrained at common law from using a name (even the trader's own name) with intent to deceive the public into thinking that the business is that of another trader, and in such a case an action for damages will also lie. [**365**]

The fee

The application must be accompanied by the correct fee, otherwise it is of no effect (s. 6 (2)). The fee is prescribed by General Notice No. 1 (see Division IV) and is £45 for the first licensable category applied for, £10 for each additional category and a further £10 if the application extends to canvassing off trade premises. However, the fee charged to an applicant holding a current moneylender's licence at the time of his application is reduced by £15; and the fee to an applicant holding at the time of his application a current pawnbroker's licence is reduced by £5. Registered loan societies, friendly societies and (in Northern Ireland) credit unions do not have to pay any licence fees. [**366**]

Notice to trading standards/consumer protection officers

The requirement, when licensing was first introduced, that the applicant give

notice of his application to the relevant trading standards/consumer protection officers, and notification to the Office of Fair Trading that such notice had been given, was discontinued on 4th November 1976. In consequence the forms utilised for that purpose, namely Forms CC 10/75 and CC 11/75, and Form CC 251/76 (report by the trading standards officer on the application) are no longer in use.
[**367**]

Activities authorised by the licence

A licence covers all such activities as are described in the licence (s. 22 (1)). Where the licence is to carry on a particular type of business, it covers all lawful activities done in the course of that business, whether by the licensee or other persons on his behalf (s. 23 (1)). This means that the licensee does not as a rule have to procure separate licences for his agents or to satisfy himself that those acting on his behalf in the course of some licensable activity of their own hold a licence. However, an exception to this is made by s. 149 (1) which provides that a regulated agreement made by a debtor or hirer introduced to the creditor or owner by an unlicensed credit-broker is enforceable only on an order made by the Director under s. 148 (2) or s. 149 (2). [**368**]

A licence may limit the activities it covers, whether by authorising the licensee to enter into certain types of agreement only, or in any other way (s. 23 (2)). As previously noted, there are six groups of licensable activity (see para. [**345**]), but in general only a single standard licence will be issued to a successful applicant, specifying which of these forms of business are covered by the licence, in much the same way as a driving licence specifies the groups of motor vehicles which the licence holder is authorised to drive. [**369**]

The canvassing off trade premises of debtor-creditor-supplier agreements or regulated consumer hire agreements is covered by a licence only if, and to the extent that, the licence specifically so provides; and such provision cannot be included in a group licence (s. 23 (3)). In addition, regulations may be made specifying other activities which, if engaged in by or on behalf of the person carrying on a business, require to be covered by an express term in his licence (s. 23 (4)). [**370**]

Period of licence

When granted, a standard licence covers the activities described in the licence for a period of 3 years beginning with the date specified for that purpose in the licence, not being earlier than the date of its issue (Consumer Credit (Period of Standard Licence) Regulations 1975, reg. 2). As to renewals, see para. [**396**].
[**371**]

Publicity

Details of licences granted, and of variations made, are entered in the register and are also published in the OFT's weekly journal, *Consumer Credit Bulletin.*
[**372**]

A licensee has no duty to display his licence, either on the licensed premises or elsewhere. [**373**]

Business to be conducted under authorised name

As previously mentioned, a standard licence restricts the licensee to carrying on a business under the name or names specified in the licence. This follows a provision to similar effect in s. 1 of the Moneylenders Act 1927. A licensee under a standard licence who carries on business under a name not specified in the licence commits an offence (s. 39 (2); but this would not appear to invalidate an agreement entered into by him, whether in his licensed name or otherwise (see s. 170 (1)). It should, however, be noted, as regards a licence to a partnership, that whilst changes in the partners do not appear to affect the licence so long as the business continues to be carried on under the partnership name or names specified in the licence, if as a result of a change in a partnership the business ceases to be carried on under such name or names, the licence ceases to have effect (s. 36 (5)). In that event the provisions relating to the enforcement of agreements made by unlicensed traders would come into operation (see para. [385]). [374]

In deciding whether a licensee has committed an offence by carrying on business under a name not specified in the licence, it may be necessary to determine (1) what deviations from the licensed name are to be regarded as legally significant, and (2) whether acts done under such name are to be regarded as constituting the carrying on of a business. On this point, assistance may be derived from cases on the Moneylenders Acts, and in particular from the decisions in *Peizer* v. *Lefkowitz*, [1912] 2 K.B. 235, *Kirkwood* v. *Gadd*, [1910] A.C. 422 and *Cornelius* v. *Phillips*, [1918] A.C. 199, in which the following principles were enunciated—

(i) Slight discrepancies between the name used and the licensed name (e.g. discrepancies arising from a slight mis-spelling of the name) will not be considered to contravene the statutory requirements if they are not such as to mislead. On this basis, the court felt able, in *Peizer* v. *Lefkowitz*, to overlook a description of the lender in a promissory note as "Westminster Loan and Discount Company" when the registered name was "Westminster Loan and Discount Office". The same case decided that the materiality of a discrepancy for this purpose is a question of law, not a question of fact.

(ii) Not every act done in furtherance of a business transaction constitutes the carrying on of a business. There is a distinction between the carrying on of the business and the carrying out of transactions which make up the business (*per* Lord Mersey in *Kirkwood* v. *Gadd*). If the business as a whole is carried on in the licensed name (*Kirkwood* v. *Gadd* was in fact concerned with the authorised address, but the principle would seem to be the same), the mere fact that, for example, a different name was used in a visit to the debtor in the course of completing a transaction would not contravene the statutory provisions. As Lord Atkinson put it in *Kirkwood* v. *Gadd*: "It will, I think, suffice if such important portions, or such an important portion, of the dealing are or is transacted there [i.e. the authorised address] by communications, verbal or written, as will necessarily reveal to the borrower the identity of the money-lender ..."

[375]

Conduct of licensed business

Regulations may be made as to the conduct by a licensee of his business, and may in particular specify—

    (*a*) the books and other records to be kept by him, and
    (*b*) the information to be furnished by him to persons with whom he does
        business or seeks to do business, and the way it is to be furnished (s. 26).
Such regulations may include provisions further regulating the seeking of business by a licensee who carries on a consumer credit business or a consumer hire business (s. 54). To date, the only regulations made under this section are the Consumer Credit (Conduct of Business) (Credit References) Regulations 1977. See paras. [**1028**], [**1033**]. [**376**]

Assign ability of licence

    A licence is not assignable; nor, with certain exceptions considered later in this chapter, is it transmissible on death or in any other way (s. 22 (2)). [**377**]

Termination of licences

    By s. 37 (1) of the Consumer Credit Act, a licence held by an individual automatically terminates if he dies, is adjudged bankrupt or becomes a patient within the meaning of Part VIII of the Mental Health Act 1959. Section 37 (2) provides that in relation to a licence held by one individual or a partnership or other unincorporated body of persons, or a body corporate, regulations may specify other events relating to the licence on the occurrence of which the licence is to terminate. Such events have now been prescribed by the Consumer Credit (Termination of Licences) Regulations 1976, which also provide for deferment of termination, pursuant to s. 37 (3) (*a*), and authorise the business of the licensee to be carried on under the licence by some other person during the period of deferment, pursuant to s. 37 (3) (*b*). The schedule to the Regulations lists, in relation to England, nine 'terminating events', that is, events which are to cause a licence to terminate automatically, subject to the deferment prescribed by the regulations (see para. [**380**]). The terminating events (of which the first three are also prescribed by s. 37 (1) of the Act itself) are:

    (1) the death of the licensee;
    (2) the adjudication of the licensee as bankrupt;
    (3) the licensee becoming a patient within the meaning of Part VIII of the Mental Health Act 1959;
    (4) the approval by the court of a composition or scheme of arrangement under s. 16 of the Bankruptcy Act 1914 proposed by the licensee, being a composition or arrangement under or in pursuance of which the property of the licensee comprising the business carried on by him under the licence is assigned to a trustee;
    (5) the registration under the Deeds of Arrangement Act 1914 of a deed of arrangement executed by the licensee, being a deed under or in pursuance of which the property of the licensee comprising the business carried on by him under the licence is assigned to a trustee;
    (6) in a case where all the members of a licensee which is a partnership or other unincorporated body of persons are adjudged bankrupt, the last such adjudication;
    (7) the approval by the court of a composition or scheme of arrangement under s. 16 of the Bankruptcy Act 1914 proposed by all the members of

a licensee which is a partnership or other unincorporated body of persons, being a composition or arrangement under or in pursuance of which the property of the licensee comprising the business carried on by it under the licence is assigned to a trustee;

(8) the registration under the Deeds of Arrangement Act 1914 of a deed of arrangement executed by all the members of a licensee which is a partnership or other unincorporated body of persons, being a deed under or in pursuance of which the property of the licensee comprising the business carried on by it under the licence is assigned to a trustee. [378]

It will be observed that, contrary to what had originally been intended, the regulations do not cover corporate licensees, so that an event affecting a company, such as its liquidation or the appointment of a receiver of its assets, is not a terminating event. This is because as a result of consultations the Government became aware of certain practical difficulties that would result from extending the regulations to bodies corporate. The winding-up of a company differs in material respects from the bankruptcy of an individual or partnership. The assets, though coming under the control of the liquidator, do not vest in him; and if the liquidator exercises a power to carry on the business of a company he does so in the company's name and not (if he is wise) in his own name. In effect, the company itself continues trading, through the instrumentality of the liquidator. If the company's right to carry on a licensable activity were to come to an end twelve months after the commencement of a winding-up, the liquidator would be placed in a very embarrassing position, for he would then no longer be able to conduct the activity in the company's name but would have to do so on his own account (having first obtained a licence), thereby incurring personal liability. Such an effect would obviously militate against the success of attempts by the liquidator to keep the business afloat so as to be able to sell it off as a going concern. It is for this and related reasons that companies have been excluded from the regulations, so that a licence granted to a company does not come to an end by reason only of winding-up or the appointment of a receiver (though in a particular case it may constitute a ground for the Director to exercise his powers under the Act to revoke the licence). On the other hand, in carrying on the business of the company in liquidation or receivership the liquidator or receiver is not an employee of the company but acts under statutory powers, so that in some respects he is a principal rather than a mere agent. Moreover, there may be cases where (whether through inadvertence or otherwise) he performs licensable activities (such as entering into contracts or instituting proceedings for the recovery of debts due to the company) in his own name. It is for this reason that liquidators, receivers and the like are covered as such by a group licence (see General Notice No. 1005), though only while they are covered by a separate licence in their own right, e.g. under a standard licence or under another group licence. The purpose of insistence on the separate licensing requirement is to ensure that the liquidator, receiver, etc. is as an individual, or as a member of some organisation covered by a group licence, a responsible person suitable for carrying on a licensed activity. It may be asked why a liquidator already covered by a standard licence or a group licence should need, or derive benefit from, the group licence provided by General Notice No. 1005. The answer is that the liquidator, receiver, etc. is covered as such by the group licence in General Notice No. 1005 if the licence which the licensee holds in his own right is of *any* description, whether or not covering the activities in which he will be engaging as liquidator, receiver, etc. Thus, if a professional liquidator were to obtain in his own name a standard licence covering only the carrying on of a consumer credit business, then upon his appointment as liquidator to a particular company he would, by virtue of the group licence embodied in General Notice No. 1005, be entitled to engage not only in a consumer credit business but also in any other licensable activity involved in the liquidation, e.g. debt-collecting. [**379**]

Deferment of termination

Automatic termination of a licence, with no provision for deferment of termination, would clearly create grave problems for whoever was appointed to carry on the licensee's business. It is for this reason that the Act allows regulations to provide, and the above regulations do provide, a period of deferment during which the licence continues in force. The period of deferment is 12 months beginning with the date of the terminating event. Thus on the licensee's death, the licence previously held by him continues in force in relation to the licensed activity for a period of 12 months beginning with the date of his death. If the terminating event is bankruptcy, the period is 12 months beginning with the date of the adjudication order (this is one of the few cases in which there is no relation back to the relevant act of bankruptcy). [**380**]

Where the 12-month period of deferment expires after the expiry date of the licence itself (that is, at the end of the 3-year period prescribed as the period for a standard licence by the Consumer Credit (Period of Standard Licence) Regulations 1975), the prescribed period is notionally extended to the end of the period of deferment (reg. 4). Thus the licensee's death or bankruptcy or the occurrence of some other terminating event may have the effect of prolonging the life of the licence. [**381**]

Carrying on of licensee's business by another

Upon the occurrence of a terminating event, the business of the licensee may, during the period of deferment, be carried on by a person specified in the Schedule to the Consumer Credit (Termination of Licences) Regulations as authorised so to do. The authorisation takes effect automatically by virtue of the order and it is not necessary that the person designated should himself hold a licence under the Act. Thus, on the death of the licensee the licensed business may be carried on for 12 months from the date of death by an executor or administrator; on bankruptcy, by the trustee in bankruptcy; on the licensee becoming a patient under Part VIII of the Mental Health Act 1959, by the person authorised to carry on the business under s. 102 or 103 of that Act; on the approval of a composition or scheme of arrangement, or registration of a deed of arrangement, by the trustee appointed under or in pursuance of the composition, scheme or deed. [**382**]

The person authorised to carry on the business as above must within 2 months beginning with the date on which he becomes so authorised give notice in writing to the Director of—

  (i) his name and the address from which he is or will be carrying on the business of the licensee;

  (ii) the name and address of the licensee as specified in the licence;

> (iii) the terminating event by virtue of which he is or will be carrying on the business of the licensee and the date of that event; and
>
> (iv) the capacity in which he is or will be carrying on that business.

If he fails to comply with the above requirements, his authority to carry on the business will cease at the end of the 2-month period and will not revive until such time as he has given notice in writing to the Director of all the matters specified above (reg. 6). [**383**]

There is no provision for extending the 12-month period of deferment. This may be expected to cause problems, for there will undoubtedly be cases in which the deceased's personal representatives are unable to dispose of the licensed business within 12 months of the death (it may, indeed, be some months before the personal representative obtains a grant of probate or letters of administration). If in such a case the personal representative is himself a licensee in his own right under any description of licence he can operate within the group licence given to personal representatives under General Notice No. 1005. But where the personal representative is not himself covered by a licence, the group licence provided by that General Notice does not extend to him. Apparently the only thing he can then do if he wishes to carry on the deceased's business after the expiry of the period of deferment is to procure a standard licence in his own name for that business before the period of deferment expires. [**384**]

Consequences of carrying on unlicensed activities

A person who engages in any activities for which a licence is required when he is not a licensee under a licence covering those activities commits an offence (ss. 39 (1), 147 (1)). In addition:

> (i) a regulated agreement (other than a non-commercial agreement) made when the creditor or owner was unlicensed is enforceable against the debtor or hirer only where the Director has made an order under s. 40 which applies to the agreement (s. 40 (1));
>
> (ii) a regulated agreement made by a debtor or hirer who, for the purpose of making that agreement, was introduced to the creditor or owner by an unlicensed credit-broker is enforceable against the debtor or hirer only where the Director has made one of the orders specified in s. 149 (1);
>
> (iii) an agreement for the services of a person carrying on an ancillary credit business, if made when he was unlicensed, is enforceable against the other party only where the Director has made an order under s. 148 (2) which applies to the agreement (s. 148 (1)).

Sections 148 and 149 are dealt with in Chapter 31. The provisions applicable to an order under s. 40 are set out in subsections (2)–(5) of that section, which read as follows:

> "(2) Where during any period an unlicensed person (the 'trader') was carrying on a consumer credit business or consumer hire business, he or his successor in title may apply to the Director for an order that regulated agreements made by the trader during that period are to be treated as if he had been licensed.
>
> (3) Unless the Director determines to make an order under subsection (2) in accordance with the application, he shall, before determining the application, by notice—
>
> > (*a*) inform the applicant, giving his reasons, that, as the

case may be, he is minded to refuse the application, or to grant it in terms different from those applied for, describing them, and
(*b*) invite the applicant to submit to the Director representations in support of his application in accordance with section 34.
(4) In determining whether or not to make an order under subsection (2) in respect of any period the Director shall consider, in addition to any other relevant factors—
(*a*) how far, if at all, debtors or hirers under regulated agreements made by the trader during that period were prejudiced by the trader's conduct,
(*b*) whether or not the Director would have been likely to grant a licence covering that period on an application by the trader, and
(*c*) the degree of culpability for the failure to obtain a licence.
(5) If the Director thinks fit, he may in an order under subsection (2)—
(*a*) limit the order to specified agreements, or agreements of a specified description or made at a specified time;
(*b*) make the order conditional on the doing of specified acts by the applicant."

Section 40 came into force as regards regulated agreements made on or after 1st October 1977 (Consumer Credit Act 1974 (Commencement No. 2) Order 1977). Application for an order under s. 40 (2) must be made in form CC 5/75 (General Notice No. 9). An appeal lies to the Secretary of State against the Director's refusal to make an order under s. 40 in accordance with the terms of the application (see s. 41 and paras. [**408**] *et seq*.). [**385**]

Opposing an application for a licence

The Act makes no express provision for a third party to oppose an application for a licence. The register which the Director is required to maintain under s. 35 will record applications for a licence that have not yet been determined, and general notice of such applications is required to be given by the Director (s. 35 (2)). Armed with these sources of information as to pending applications, an objector can, of course, write to the Director setting out the grounds of his objection to the proposed licence, and the Director is entitled, though not bound, to take such objections into account in reaching his decision. The Act does not confer on an objector a right to make representations, whether written or oral; indeed it says nothing about objectors at all. Whether a person opposing the grant of a licence has a *locus standi* to challenge by *certiorari* the decision of the Director, or the decision of the Secretary of State on appeal from the Director, on the ground of want of *vires* or of improper exercise of discretion depends on his ability to establish that he is a party aggrieved in the sense of one who has a legitimate interest in the outcome of the licensing application. If he has not, then it is entirely within the discretion of the court whether it will listen to him (see para. [**433**]). [**386**]

Notification of projected refusal of application

The Director cannot refuse or restrict a licence out of hand. Section 27 (1) provides that unless he determines to issue a licence *in accordance with the application,* he must by notice (that is, by a specific notice in writing to the applicant, as opposed to a general notice)—

> "(a) inform the applicant, giving his reasons, that as the case may be, he is minded to refuse the application, or to grant it in terms different from those applied for, describing them, and
>
> (b) invite the applicant to submit to the Director representations in support of his application in accordance with section 34."

These requirements apply not only where the Director is not proposing to issue a licence at all but where he proposes to issue it in terms different from that applied for. Section 34 prescribes the manner in which the Director's invitation to the applicant to make representations is to be given. The Director must invite the applicant, within 21 days after the notice containing the invitation is given to him or published or such longer period as the Director may allow—

> (a) to submit his representations in writing to the Director, and
>
> (b) to give notice to the Director, if he thinks fit, that he wishes to make representations orally. [387]

When the "minded to refuse" notice is sent to the applicant it will be accompanied by a copy of form CC 84/75, which can be used for making written representations. The form is not, however, obligatory. The procedure for making oral and written representations is described below and is elaborated in the OFT leaflet *Licensing—Your right to make representations.* [388]

By s. 28, where the Director is minded to issue a group licence (whether on the application of any person or not), and in doing so to exclude any person from the group by name, he shall, before determining the matter—

> (a) give notice of that fact to the person proposed to be excluded, giving his reasons, and
>
> (b) invite that person to submit to the Director representations against his exclusion in accordance with section 34. [389]

Written representations

These must be submitted in due time (see para. [387]), but need not be in any particular form. They may be supported by any books, correspondence or documents the applicant considers relevant, including sworn and unsworn statements. [390]

The hearing of oral representations

As an alternative or in addition to written representations, the applicant may make oral representations; and if within the time allowed he gives notice of his desire to do so the Director must arrange a hearing (s. 34 (1)). The procedure is governed by the Consumer Credit Licensing (Representations) Order 1976, examined below. No extra fee is payable by the applicant. [391]

The Director is required by the above Order to give 21 days' notice (or such shorter period as he may think fit with the consent of the applicant) of the date, time and place of hearing (art. 3). The hearing will usually be conducted by the OFT official who signed the "minded to refuse" notice. This may in important cases be the Director himself or the Director of Consumer Credit and will in any event be an official not below the level of Principal. The hearing will take place in suitable accommodation as near as possible to the applicant's place of business, e.g. the nearest OFT regional office or accommodation offered by a local authority. The applicant may present his own case and/or arrange for it to be presented by someone else of his own choice (whether or not a professional adviser) on his behalf (see art. 4 (1)). A member of the Council on Tribunals is entitled to attend any hearing (art. 4 (2)), but the hearing is held in private and no formal procedures are laid down. The applicant is entitled to call witnesses, either to give evidence or to introduce documents for him (see art. 4 (1)); and evidence must not be excluded solely on the ground that it would not be admissible in a court of law (art. 4 (3)). If the hearing is adjourned the Director must inform the person affected a reasonable time before its resumption of the date, time and place of resumption (art. 4 (1)). [**392**]

The Director is not obliged to invite or receive representations made by parties other than the applicant (e.g. objectors to a licence), though he is entitled to do so if he wishes. If he does entertain representations from third parties, it is for him to decide whether, and to what extent, to take them into account. It would seem that neither the director nor the tribunal is obliged to inform the applicant of the Director's sources of information (see *R.* v. *Gaming Board for Great Britain, ex parte Benaim,* [1970] 2 Q.B. 417; [1970] 2 All E.R. 528), though the applicant must be told the case he has to meet (*ibid.*). [**393**]

Determination of application

The Director may determine the application in a variety of ways. He may refuse it altogether, or grant it in terms asked or grant it in terms different from those applied for, e.g. by exercising his power under s. 23 (2) to limit the activities covered by the licence (whether by authorising the licensee to enter into certain types of agreement only or in any other way) or by refusing or restricting the canvassing of regulated debtor-creditor-supplier agreements off trade premises. In such a case, s. 27 (2) provides that the Director shall issue the licence in the terms approved by him unless the applicant by notice informs him that he does not wish a licence in those terms. [**394**]

The Director must give notice of his determination to the applicant (s. 34 (3)); and by art. 6 of the Consumer Credit Licensing (Representations) Order where this is a notice of refusal of the application, or a notice that it has been granted in terms different from that applied for, it must contain a statement setting out the Director's reasons for the determination and the findings of fact on which he relies, and declaring that if the applicant wishes to appeal to the Secretary of State he must do so within the period and in the manner prescribed under s. 41 (1), that is, prescribed by the Consumer Credit Licensing (Appeals) Regulations 1976. [**395**]

Renewal of licence

If the licensee under a standard licence, or the original applicant for, or any licensee under, a group licence of limited duration, wishes the Director to renew the licence, whether on the same terms (except as to expiry) or on varied terms, he must, during the period specified by the Director by general notice or such longer period as the Director may allow, make an application to the Director for its renewal (s. 29 (1)). Such application, to be valid, must comply with the requirements of s. 6 (see para. [**348**]). The Director may of his own motion renew any group licence (s. 29 (2)). The provisions previously discussed regulating the grant of licences apply equally to renewals, except that persons originally excluded from a group licence are not entitled to be given notice of the Director's intention to continue the exclusion in respect of the renewed licence (s. 29 (3)). The Director is required to give general notice of renewal of a group licence (s. 29 (6)). [**396**]

Until the determination of an application under s. 29 (1) and, where an appeal lies from the determination, until the end of the appeal period, the licence continues in force, notwithstanding that it would otherwise expire earlier (s. 29 (4)). "Appeal period" means the period beginning on the first day on which an appeal to the Secretary of State may be brought and ending on the last day on which it may be brought or, if it is brought, ending on its final determination, or abandonment (s. 189 (1)). But the licensee only secures the benefit of this temporary continuation of the licence if he applies for renewal before the licence has expired. If he does not, he will have to apply for a new licence, and until he obtains it he will not be able to continue the relevant licensable activity. [**397**]

On the refusal of a renewal application, the Director may give directions authorising the licensee to carry into effect agreements made by him before the expiry of the licence (s. 29 (5)). The Director's determination whether to refuse or give directions under s. 29 (5) must be made at the same time as his determination to refuse to renew the licence (Consumer Credit Licensing (Representations) Order 1976, art. 5). [**398**]

Variation of licence by request

On an application made by the licensee, the Director may, if he thinks fit, by notice to the licensee vary a standard licence in accordance with the application (s. 30 (1)). In the case of a group licence issued on the application of any person, the Director, on an application made by that person, may if he thinks fit by notice to that person vary the terms of the licence in accordance with the application; but the Director must not vary a group licence under this subsection by excluding a named person, other than the person making the request, unless that named person consents in writing to his exclusion (s. 30 (2)). In the case of a group licence from which (whether by name or description) a person is excluded, the Director, on an application made by that person, may if he thinks fit, by notice to that person, vary the terms of the licence so as to remove the exclusion (s. 30 (3)). In all these cases the Director has power to act only if the application conforms to the requirements of s. 6 (see para. [**348**]). [**399**]

Compulsory variation, suspension and revocation of licences

Sections 31 to 33 of the Act deal with compulsory variation of licences by the Director, and with suspension and revocation of licences by him. The Director's power to vary a licence arises where, at a time during the currency of the licence, he is of opinion that if the licence had expired at that time he would, on an application for its renewal or further renewal on the same terms (except as to expiry), have been minded to grant the application but on different terms (s. 31 (1)). His power to suspend or revoke a licence arises where, at any time during the currency of a licence, the Director is of the opinion that if the licence had expired at that time he would have been minded not to renew it (s. 32 (1)). Suspension or revocation of a licence has more serious consequences for the licensee than refusal of an application for a licence in the first instance, since the latter merely prevents a man starting up a business in which he is not yet engaged, whilst the former deprives a man, temporarily at least, of his livelihood. Hence such a power ought not to be exercised without the fullest enquiry and the most careful sifting of the evidence. [**400**]

The procedure to be adopted by the Director is broadly the same for compulsory variation, suspension and revocation.

(1) In the case of a standard licence, the Director must by notice inform the licensee of the variation he is minded to make, or of the fact that he is minded to revoke the licence, or suspend it until a specified date or indefinitely, and must invite the licensee to submit representations in accordance with s. 34 (see para. [**387**]).

(2) In the case of a group licence, the Director must give general notice of his intention, as above, and invite any licensee to make representations in accordance with s. 34, and in addition, if the group licence was issued on application, must inform the original applicant of such intention and invite him to submit representations under s. 34.

(3) The Director must give general notice of a variation, suspension or revocation of a group licence.

(4) A variation, revocation or suspension of a licence does not take effect before the end of the appeal period. [**401**]

By s. 31 (5), if the Director is minded to vary a group licence by excluding any person (other than the original applicant) from the group by name the Director must, in addition, take the like steps under s. 28 as are required in the case mentioned in that section (see para. [**389**]). [**402**]

If the Director revokes or suspends a licence, he may give directions authorising a licensee to carry into effect agreements made by him before the revocation or suspension (s. 32 (5)), and his determination whether to give or refuse such directions must be made at the same time as his determination to revoke or suspend the licence (Consumer Credit Licensing (Representations) Order 1976, art. 5). For reasons which are not clear, no such power is conferred in relation to the variation of a licence. [**403**]

Section 33 provides for the ending of suspension as follows:

"33. (1) On an application made by a licensee the Director may, if he thinks fit, by notice to the licensee end the suspension of a licence, whether the suspension was for a fixed or indefinite period.

(2) Unless the Director determines to end the suspension in accordance with the application he shall, before determining the application, by notice—

(a) inform the applicant, giving his reasons, that he is minded to refuse the application, and

(b) invite the applicant to submit to the Director representations in support of his application in accordance with section 34.

(3) General notice shall be given that a suspension of a group licence has been ended under this section.

(4) In the case of a group licence issued on application—

(a) the references in subsection (1) to a licensee include the original applicant;

(*b*) the Director shall inform the original applicant that
a suspension of a group licence has been ended under
this section." [**404**]

Statement of reasons for determination or decision

Being a tribunal under the direct supervision of the Council on Tribunals (see para. [**132**]), the Director is under a duty to furnish a statement, either written or oral, of the reasons for any decision he makes, if requested, on or before the giving or notification of the decision, to state the reasons (Tribunals and Inquiries Act 1971, s. 12 (1)). A similar obligation is imposed on the Secretary of State as regards any decision made by him on appeal from the Director (*ibid.*). Any such statement of reasons is to be taken to form part of the decision and accordingly to be incorporated in the record (*ibid.*, s. 12 (5)). The Director or Secretary of State, as the case may be, may refuse to give a statement of reasons, or may restrict the specification of the reasons, on grounds of national security, and may also refuse to furnish the statement to a person not primarily concerned with the decision if of opinion that to furnish it would be contrary to the interests of any person primarily concerned (*ibid.*, s. 12 (2)). The duty to give reasons may also be excluded by order of the Lord Chancellor and Secretary of State, after consultation with the Council on Tribunals (*ibid.*, s. 12 (6)). [**405**]

Challenging a determination of the director

A person aggrieved by a determination of the Director has two possible avenues for challenging such determination:

(*a*) by appeal to the Secretary of State, and thence on a point of law to the High Court, pursuant to the provisions of ss. 41 and 42 of the Act (see paras. [**408**]– [**432**]);

(*b*) by application to the court to exercise its inherent jurisdiction over administrative tribunals by orders of mandamus, prohibition or certiorari (see paras. [**434**]–[**435**]). [**406**]

It will be observed that s. 41 is confined to appeals against a "determination" of the Director. What is the position if a party wishes to complain of inaction by the Director—for example, that the Director, whilst not expressly refusing an application for a licence, has simply failed to deal with the application? An inordinate delay could well be held to constitute an implied refusal so as to ground an appeal to the Secretary of State; but the uncertainty of the applicant's position in such a case might well incline the court to entertain sympathetically an application for mandamus to compel an express determination of the application.

[**407**]

Appeal to the Secretary of State

The categories of aggrieved party entitled to appeal to the Secretary of State from a determination of the Director are as follows:

TABLE

Determination	*Appellant*
Refusal to issue, renew or vary licence in accordance with terms of application	The applicant

Exclusion of person from group licence	The person excluded
Refusal to give directions in respect of a licensee under section 29 (5) or 32 (5)	The licensee
Compulsory variation, or suspension or revocation, of standard licence	The licensee
Compulsory variation, or suspension or revocation, of group licence	The original applicant or any licensee
Refusal to end suspension of licence in accordance with terms of application	The applicant
Refusal to make order under section 40 (2) in accordance with terms of application	The applicant

The appeal procedure is formal and is governed by the Consumer Credit Licensing (Appeals) Regulations 1976. This is outlined in a *Guide—Appeals from Licensing Determinations of the Director General of Fair Trading,* issued by the Department of Prices and Consumer Protection. No fee is payable on the making of an appeal. [**408**]

(i) *Notice of appeal*

The appeal must be initiated by giving a notice of appeal to the Secretary of State. The notice must be given within the period of 28 days beginning with the day on which notice of determination of the application was given by the Director (art. 2 (1)) and must comply with the requirements of the first Schedule to the Order. These are that the notice of appeal shall:

(1) identify the appellant and give his business address and his address for service of documents (if different);

(2) identify the determination by which the appellant is aggrieved; and

(3) be signed by or on behalf of the appellant.

These requirements must be strictly complied with and the time limit adhered to. The powers of the Secretary of State to overlook non-compliance with regulations and to extend time (arts. 24, 25) do not apply to a notice of appeal. Hence a notice given out of time or not complying with the requirements is ineffective and the appeal cannot proceed. Provided that the notice of appeal complies with the above requirements it need not be in any particular form. The *Guide* above referred to contains a form of notice of appeal (Form CCB/APPEALS/1A) the use of which is optional. If a notice of appeal conforming to the requirements of the order is received by the Secretary of State within the 28-day period prescribed, he must inform the appellant of its receipt and send a copy of it to the Director (art. 2 (2)). [**409**]

(ii) *Notice of grounds of appeal*

The notice of appeal will not itself set out the grounds of appeal. This requires a separate notice ("Notice of Grounds"). Why the Order should not permit a single notice intimating the appellant's intention to appeal and setting out the grounds for appeal is not clear. If, in error, a combined notice is given the appeal will not terminate for irregularity unless the Secretary of State so directs (see art. 24). The notice of grounds, if not accompanying the notice of appeal, must be given within the period allowed for giving notice of appeal (art. 3 (1)). However, whereas the time for giving notice of appeal cannot be extended, the Secretary of State has power to extend the time for giving notice of grounds, and this is presumably exercisable even after the time limit has expired. Paragraph 8 of the *Guide* states that an appellant unable to give notice of grounds within the time limit should explain the position to the Secretariat immediately and tell them what extension is needed and why. The address is:

> Consumer Credit Appeals Secretariat
> Department of Prices and Consumer Protection
> Room 171A
> 1 Victoria Street
> London SW1H 0ET
> Telephone 01–215 4197

However, the same paragraph adds: "... extension of time limits is legally permissible, but only likely to be granted in exceptional circumstances." [**410**]

The notice of grounds must comply with the requirements of the second Schedule to the order, viz. that it should:

(1) if it is not given to the Secretary of State together with the notice of appeal to which it relates, identify that notice;

(2) contain a concise statement of the grounds of appeal—

    (*a*) indicating—

        (i) any reason; and

        (ii) any finding of fact

    relied on by the Director in the notice of the determination which the appellant disputes;

    (*b*) giving particulars of any reason or fact upon which the appellant relies in relation to the matters disputed under sub-paragraph (*a*) above;

    (*c*) giving particulars of any other reason or fact on which the appellant relies; and

    (*d*) indicating any point on which he relies under sub-paragraphs (*b*) and (*c*) above which appears to him to be a point of law;

(3) state the nature of the directions which the appellant wishes the Secretary of State to give under s. 41 (3) of the Act; and

(4) be signed by or on behalf of the appellant.

As with the notice of appeal, the Secretary of State, upon receiving the notice of grounds, must acknowledge receipt and send a copy of the notice to the Director.

The appellant may amend his notice of grounds at any time before the Secretary of State gives directions for the hearing or notice dispensing with the hearing, or thereafter if so permitted by the Secretary of State or given leave during the hearing by the person appointed to hear it (see below). [**411**]

(iii) *Director's reply*

Within 14 days beginning with the day on which he is given the notice of grounds, the Director must give to the Secretary of State a copy of the appellant's application to the Director, a copy of any notice of the determination given by the Director to the appellant and of any general notice of it given by the Director and notice setting out any representations which the Director wishes to make together with a copy of any document which he wishes to produce (reg. 4). The notice and copy document are collectively termed "The Director's reply" (*ibid.*). [**412**]

(iv) *Appellant's rejoinder*

A copy of the above documents must be furnished by the Secretary of State to the appellant, together with an invitation to make a rejoinder by giving to the Secretary of State within 14 days notice setting out further representations he wishes to make and a copy of any document he wishes to produce (art. 5). The 14-day period may be extended by the Secretary of State (art. 25). [**413**]

(v) *Amendment of grounds*

The appellant may give the Secretary of State notice of amendment of his notice of grounds at any time before the Secretary of State has given notice under reg. 9 (4) that a hearing of oral representations is not necessary or has given directions under reg. 10 (1) for oral representations to be heard by an appointed person (reg. 6 (2)). The appellant is not, however, entitled to amend as of right, for the Secretary of State is required to amend the notice of grounds, in accordance with the appellant's notice to amend, only if it appears to the Secretary of State that the amendment should be made (reg. 6 (1)). If he disallows an amendment, the Secretary of State must notify the appellant, giving reasons (reg. 6 (4)). The appellant's time for giving notice of an amendment may be extended by the Secretary of State (reg. 25), in addition to which the appellant may amend at the hearing (if any) with leave of the appointed person (see (x), below). [**414**]

(vi) *Director's reply to amendment*

The Director has seven days in which to give notice setting out any representations he wishes to make on the amendment, together with a copy of any further documents he wishes to produce (reg. 7 (1)). The Director's reply is limited to matters raised by the amendment, and whilst this limitation is not expressed to apply to further documents it would seem to be implicit in the regulation. The appellant is given 7 days within which to answer the Director's further representations (reg. 7 (2)). [**415**]

(vi) *Disposal of appeal without hearing*

The appellant's appeal may be disposed of without a hearing in three different ways:

    (1) by abandonment of the appeal under reg. 23 (1);
    (2) by the Director's consent to the allowing of the appeal, in which case the Secretary of State will give the appropriate directions (reg. 8);
    (3) by the appellant giving notice to the Secretary of State, within 14 days beginning with the Secretary of State's notice of intention to give directions for the hearing, that the appellant prefers the appeal to be heard without oral representations (reg. 9 (1)). See (viii) below. [**416**]

(viii) *Contested appeal without hearing*

Where the appellant has given notice that he prefers the appeal to be disposed of without the hearing of oral representations, it does not necessarily follow that a hearing will be dispensed with. The Secretary of State may, if he so wishes, proceed to give notice to any party specifying any question which appears to him to be material and inviting that party to give, within 7 days, a notice setting out representations he wishes to make on the question; and if such a notice is given the Secretary of State must send a copy to the other party and invite a similar notice of representations from him (reg. 9 (2)). The Secretary of State may decide that oral representations are unnecessary either upon receipt of the appellant's notice under reg. 9 (1) expressing a preference for a hearing without oral representations or after taking account of any notice given to the Secretary of State under reg. 9 (2). In that event, the Secretary of State may either refer the appeal to an appointed person for consideration and report without hearing of oral representations or alternatively give directions under s. 41 (3) for disposing of the appeal (reg. 9 (4)), e.g. by directing that it be dealt with by one of his officers. In either event, appropriate notice must be given to the parties (*ibid.*). But the Secretary of State has the right to insist on an oral hearing, in which event the appeal will proceed accordingly (see (ix), below). [417]

(ix) *Disposal of appeal with hearing*

The Secretary of State, having decided that a hearing of oral representations is necessary, may direct this to take place either before an appointed person (see para. [144], *ante*) or by an officer of the Secretary of State (reg. 10 (1)), presumably an official of the Department of Prices and Consumer Protection. But the latter direction cannot be given unless the parties have been afforded an opportunity to make representations to the Secretary of State upon the proposed directions (reg. 10 (2)). In practice it is only in exceptional cases that the Secretary of State is likely to direct a hearing before one of his officers instead of before an appointed person. The provision for hearing by an officer of the Secretary of State was inserted as a precautionary measure to deal with eventualities such as an excessive workload on appointed persons or the last-minute inability of an appointed person, through illness or otherwise, to hear an appeal. The Council on Tribunals viewed with disfavour the prospect of a hearing by an officer of the Secretary of State and has been given certain assurances.

> "We questioned the need to provide in regulation 10 of the Appeals Regulations that the Secretary of State might appoint one of his own officers to hear the oral representations, and we suggested that such a person should not be appointed except with the written consent of the parties. The Department argued that there might well be difficulties in finding outside a sufficient number of highly qualified persons to conduct such hearings, but they undertook to do their best to ensure that outsiders were appointed wherever possible. They stated also that if it became necessary to appoint their own officers of the Department regularly they would be ready to draw up suitable guidelines. In the light of this, we decided not to pursue our objection, but we have reserved the right to review the situation when we have seen how the system of appointments has worked out in practice." (*Annual Report of the Council on Tribunals for 1975–76*, para. 62.)

At least 21 days' notice of the hearing must be given by the Secretary of State (reg. 12), and rules as to procedure at the hearing apply whether the hearing is before an appointed person or before an officer of the Secretary of State (reg. 10 (3)). The tribunal may in fact comprise several appointed persons. If the case is of particular importance, it is probable that at least three appointed persons will hear it. [418]

(x) *Procedural directions*

Subject to the provisions of the Act and the above regulations, the procedure to be followed in the course of an appeal except in the course of the hearing of oral representations shall be such as the Secretary of State shall direct (reg. 26). What are contemplated by this regulation are not published directions applicable to appeals generally but directions that may prove necessary or desirable in the course of a particular appeal. [419]

(xi) *Procedure at hearing*

The hearing is likely to take place either in London or at the OFT regional office most convenient to the appellant. The appointed person (and the same applies to an officer of the Secretary of State if he is hearing the appeal) must give such directions at the hearing as appear to him to be appropriate for its proper conduct (reg. 14 (1)). He is required to permit any person authorised by a party ("representative") to conduct that party's case on his behalf and must afford the parties or their representatives an opportunity of making an opening and closing statement (reg 14 (2)) He must also allow each party or its representative to call witnesses and to cross-examine the other party (if present) and his witnesses; and the appointed person must himself address any questions which appear to him to be appropriate to each party and to any witness (*ibid.*). The appointed person does not appear to have power to call witnesses of his own motion. The appellant may, with leave of the appointed person, amend his notice of grounds in the course of the hearing, though before giving leave the appointed person must first inform the Director that he is minded to do so and must give the Director an opportunity of making representations on the proposed amendment (reg. 11). If the hearing is adjourned, the appointed person must inform the parties a reasonable time before its resumption of the date, time and place of the resumption (*ibid.*). If the appellant or his representative does not appear at the hearing, the appointed person may either adjourn the hearing or, if there appears to him good reason to do so, proceed to hear the Director or his representative if he appears or proceed forthwith to prepare his report (reg 15) Presumably the effect of this regulation is that on failure of the appellant to appear the appointed person need not call upon the Director or his representative to address him but may proceed to prepare a report recommending dismissing of the appeal; but there may be cases in which he first wishes to hear the Director before proceeding. Evidence may be admitted at the hearing whether or not it would be admissible in a court of law (reg. 20). Evidence is not taken on oath. [**420**]

(xii) *Disclosure of documents*

There is no procedure for compulsory discovery. However, the Secretary of State at any time, or the appointed person during the hearing of oral representations by him, may invite any party to supply to him any document or copy thereof which appears to him material to the appeal (reg. 21 (1)). If this is supplied to the Secretary of State, he must furnish a copy to any other party. If it is given to the appointed person, he must afford any other party an opportunity to examine it or must otherwise make known its contents to that party (reg. 21 (2)). But suitable steps must be taken to exclude from any copy supplied information relating to the private affairs of a person who is not a party and the publication of which would or might in the opinion of the Secretary of State or of the appointed person prejudicially affect the interests of that person (reg. 22). If a party fails to respond to a request by the appointed person to supply an apparently material document or copy, the appointed person is presumably entitled to draw any reasonable inference from this failure and to take it into account in formulating his report.

[**421**]

(xiii) *Appointed person's report*

In preparing his report, the appointed person must take into account any representations made and evidence produced in the course of the appeal, and give to the Secretary of State a reasoned report in writing thereon and, if he has proceeded in default of appearance by the appellant, stating that fact expressly in his report (reg. 16 (2)). [**422**]

(xiv) *Dismissal of appeal after appellant's failure to appear*

The Secretary of State may, if the appellant failed to appear at the hearing, give directions dismissing the appeal (reg. 17 (1)); but unless an appointed person had proceeded in default of appearance on some prior occasion the Secretary of State must first give 7 days' notice of his intention to dismiss the appeal unless the appellant satisfies him that there was sufficient reason for the failure to appear (reg. 17 (2)). If the appellant does satisfy the Secretary of State on that score, the Secretary of State must give such directions as appear to him appropriate for a further hearing of oral representations, and the regulations will apply to such further hearing as to the original hearing (reg. 17 (3)). [**423**]

(xv) *Statement of case for opinion of High Court*

In the course of the appeal proceedings the Secretary of State may, of his own motion or at the request of any party to the proceedings, state in the form of a special case for the decision of the High Court any question of law arising in the proceedings (RSC Order 94, r. 9 (1), applicable by virtue of s. 13 (1) of the Tribunals and Inquiries Act 1971, ss. 1 and 13 (5A), the latter being added by the Consumer Credit Act 1974, s. 42 (1)). Any such party aggrieved by the refusal of the Secretary of State to state a case may apply to the High Court for an order directing him to do so (*ibid.*, r. 9 (2)). The procedure is governed by Order 56 and the case will be heard by a single judge of the Queen's Bench Division (Order 56, r. 7 (1)), as will any application for an order requiring the Secretary of State to state case (*ibid.*, r. 7 (2)). The procedure is invoked by way of originating motion (*ibid.*, rr. 8 (1), 10 (1)), and where the case is stated by the Secretary of State it must be signed by him or by a person authorised in that behalf to do so (*ibid.*, r. 9 (1)). On the hearing, the Secretary of State is entitled to appear and be heard (*ibid.*, r. 12). The case stated procedure is available only during the course of the appeal from the determination of the Director, not as a method of securing judicial review of the decision of the Secretary of State on the conclusion of the appeal. [**424**]

(xvi) *Decision of the Secretary of State*

The Secretary of State is not bound by the recommendations of the appointed person (or of his own officer where the appeal was heard by such officer), though it is to be assumed that in most cases he will act upon them. The Secretary of State's powers are wide, the Act providing that he may give such directions for disposing of the appeal as he thinks just, including directions for the payment of costs by any party to the appeal (s. 41 (3)). Thus the appellate functions of the Secretary of State cover all matters relevant to the determination appealed against, whether of fact, law (so long as the Director acted within his jurisdiction—see para. [**435**]) or the Director's exercise of his discretion. The powers of the Secretary of State to quash or vary a determination of the Director are not restricted to cases where the determination was unreasonable or against the weight of the evidence but enable the Secretary of State to substitute his own judgment for that of the Director and to make any order that the Director could have made. Thus, the Secretary of State may direct that a licence or renewal refused by the Director be granted, whether in the terms applied for or in different terms; that a licence or renewal granted by the

Director on terms different from those applied for be granted upon the terms of the application or upon any other terms that seem to the Secretary of State to be proper; that a suspension ordered by the Director should not take effect or should be for a different period; that a revocation ordered by the Director should not take effect; that directions refused by the Director under ss. 29 (5) or 32 (5) should be given or that directions given should be given in different terms; and that a rejected application for the ending of a suspension of a licence should be granted.

[**425**]

Where costs are awarded, the direction for their payment may be made a rule of court on the application of the party in whose favour the order is given (s. 41 (4)) and will then become enforceable as an order of the court. [**426**]

Since the appeal is by way of rehearing, it would seem that the Secretary of State can receive evidence not given before the Director, can determine the appeal on grounds other than those raised in the appellant's notice and can give a decision more adverse to the appellant than the determination of the Director from which he is appealing. Accordingly an appellant who appeals against the grant of a licence in terms different from those applied for may find that on appeal to the Secretary of State he is refused a licence altogether; and a period of suspension ordered by the Director can, it seems, be lengthened by the Secretary of State as well as shortened. [**427**]

(xvii) *Notice of directions disposing of appeal*

The Secretary of State, in giving directions for disposal of an appeal, is required to give notice to the parties of the directions so given in conformity with reg. 18 of the Consumer Credit Licensing (Appeals) Regulations 1976. [**428**]

(xviii) *Appeal from decision of Secretary of State*

If any person who had a right to the appeal to the Secretary of State (whether or not he has exercised that right) is dissatisfied in point of law with the decision of the Secretary of State, he may, according as rules of court may provide, either appeal from the Secretary of State to the High Court or require him to state a case for the opinion of the High Court (Tribunals and Inquiries Act 1971, s. 13 (1), (5A), as added by Consumer Credit Act, s. 42 (1)). The rules of court made under this section provide only for appeal, not for a proceeding by way of case stated, so that the latter option is not open to the aggrieved party (*Hoser* v. *Ministry of Housing and Local Government*, [1963] Ch. 428, [1962] 3 All E.R. 945). The right to appeal is given to any person (whether or not in fact aggrieved by the decision of the Secretary of State) who falls within the designated category of appellant in column 2 at the end of s. 41 of the Consumer Credit Act (see para. [**408**]), even if he had not himself appealed from the original determination of the Director. The matter cannot, of course, come before the High Court at all unless at least one person within the designated category makes an appeal from the Director which results in a decision of the Secretary of State. Hence if there is only one member of the class—as where a standard licence is applied for by and refused to a single individual—the unsuccessful applicant for the licence is the only person who can appeal to the Secretary of State, and he cannot come before the High Court *under the Act* without first obtaining a decision of the Secretary of State on appeal from the Director. If, however, more than one person within the designated categories is aggrieved, as where the Director excludes several persons or a class of persons from a group licence, then if one such person or member of the class exercises his right of appeal to the Secretary of State, the others may appeal to the High Court on a point of law from the decision of the Secretary of State, or require him to state a case, even if they did not themselves appeal against the original determination of the Director. [**429**]

The Director himself does not, of course, have any right of appeal from a decision of the Secretary of State varying his original determination, nor is he entitled to require the Secretary of State to state a case. [**430**]

The appeal procedure is prescribed by Order 94, r. 10A of the Rules of the Supreme Court (added by the Rules of the Supreme Court (Amendment) 1976 with effect from 1st April 1976), and, so far as not excluded by this rule, by the general provisions of R.S.C. Order 55. The appeal is by originating motion, notice of motion being served on the Secretary of State and, where the appeal is by a licensee under a group licence against compulsory variation, suspension or revocation of that licence, the original applicant, if any; but the court may direct notice to be served on any other person (Order 94, r. 10A (2)). The court hearing the appeal (i.e. a single Judge of the Queen's Bench Division—Order 55, r. 2), may remit the matter to the Secretary of State to the extent necessary to enable him to provide the court with such further information in connection with the matter as the court may direct (r. 10A (3)). If the court is of the opinion that the decision appealed against was erroneous in point of law, it is not to set aside or vary that decision but it is to remit the matter to the Secretary of State with the opinion of the court for hearing and determination by him (r. 10A (4)). This particular rule is made in exercise of an express power conferred by s. 13 (3) of the Tribunals and Enquiries Act 1971. [**431**]

Thus it is not the function of the court to quash a decision of the Secretary of State or to exercise its own discretion in place of his. The court simply decides the question of law and then remits the matter to the Secretary of State for hearing and determination by him in the light of the court's ruling. In this respect, the end result is very much the same as where a case is stated for the opinion of the court. The phrase "hearing and determination" suggests that when the court's ruling has been given the case comes back to the appointed person or officer of the Secretary of State by whom the appeal was originally heard, and presumably the appellant will then be given a right to make further representations in the light of the court's decision before the final report is made to the Secretary of State. But these are no doubt matters as to which the Secretary of State would give procedural directions under reg. 26 of the Consumer Credit Licensing (Appeals) Regulations 1976 (see para. [**419**]). [**432**]

The inherent power of judicial review

The jurisdiction of the court can be invoked not only by the applicant for a licence, or other party set out in the Table at the end of s. 41 (see para. [**408**]), but by anyone having a substantial interest (over and above that of the general public) in raising the matter before the court. This would appear to include a competitor, even though he had no statutory right to make representations to the Director or to appear to make representations in connection with an appeal to the Secretary of State (see *R. v. Thames Magistrates Court, ex parte Greenbaum* (1957), 55 L.G.R. 129). Exceptionally, the court might, in its discretion, accede to an application by a member of the public not having a distinct interest as an aggrieved party. [**433**]

If the Director acts in excess of jurisdiction or if, whether or not asked to do so, he gives reasons for a determination which indicate that he has erred in law or has for some reason improperly exercised or failed or refused to exercise his discretion or has adopted an approach which is manifestly unreasonable, the court may intervene by orders of certiorari and mandamus quashing the invalid determination and requiring the Director to hear and determine the application afresh according to law. [**434**]

Whether the court will decline its jurisdiction to grant certiorari or mandamus by reason of the alternative remedy available to the applicant in the form of an appeal to the Secretary of State under s. 41 depends on the circumstances. The court will not refrain from interfering if the defect in relation to the Director's determination goes to jurisdiction, for in that situation there is no valid determination against which an appeal under the statutory machinery can be made; and in any event the court will always be willing to intervene to quash a decision which the tribunal in question had no jurisdiction to make (see *Barnard* v. *National Dock Labour Board*, [1953] 2 Q.B. 18, [1953] 1 All E.R. 1113; *R.* v. *Paddington Valuation Officer, ex parte Peachey Property Corporation, Ltd.*, [1966] 1 Q.B. 380, [1965] 2 All E.R. 836). Even if the complaint is not want of jurisdiction but, e.g., the taking into account of factors not specified in the Act, or the adoption of a manifestly unreasonable approach, the court will not necessarily refuse *certiorari* because of the alternative remedy, particularly where it takes the view that *certiorari* is the most efficacious method of dealing with the matter. See generally de Smith, *op. cit.*, pp. 131–133 374–376 [**435**]

Investigation by Ombudsman

The investigatory powers of the Parliamentary Commissioner for Administration (popularly known as the Ombudsman) under the Parliamentary Commissioner Act 1967 have been extended by Order to the Director pursuant to s. 4 (2) of that Act (Parliamentary Commissioner Order 1975). But the Commissioner will not usually exercise his powers as regards those determinations of the Director which are subject to appeal to the Secretary of State or acts or omissions of the Director within the scope of judicial review (see *ibid.*, s. 5 (2)). [**436**]

12. Seeking Business

The need for pre-contract control

Whilst the regulation of the form and content of consumer credit agreements, and of the rights of the parties thereunder, is obviously of great importance, the consumer has need of protection at an earlier stage. Experience has shown that in the field of consumer credit the prospective debtor is peculiarly vulnerable to over-commitment of his resources, through a variety of factors. The first, and most obvious, is the innate attraction of being able to acquire goods or services now without having to put down the whole of the price at the outset. The second is the lack of adequate information to enable him to make an informed choice, to compare one form of credit with another, to evaluate the cost and to judge whether cheaper and better alternatives might not be available. The third is his reliance on information which in many cases is either false or, at best, misleading. The fourth is the immense pressure, both overt and covert, put upon him to buy in general and to utilise credit in particular. This pressure is exerted partly through the mass media, partly by face to face contact with salesmen and canvassers. Particularly prone to abuse are the activities of doorstep purveyors of goods and services on credit. The stories concerning some of these are legion: misrepresenting the organisations on whose behalf they are calling (a common technique used by encyclopedia salesmen to secure entry into a house was to represent themselves as calling to carry out a survey for educational purposes); misrepresentation of the nature of the proposed transaction (as by saying it was a hire-purchase agreement whereas it was a mere hiring, giving the customer no right to become the owner of the goods); foisting inferior or defective goods on the unsuspecting housewife; pressuring the housewife into signing contracts against her better judgment; and, finally, disappearing in a cloud of dust, leaving the consumer to find out at a later date that the company by whom the salesman employed was not to be traced or was impervious to demands for redress of the customer's grievances. [**437**]

Legislative control prior to the Consumer Credit Act

The legislature has been concerned about these problems, but hitherto has dealt with them only in a fragmentary manner. Pre-contract activity by moneylenders has been closely controlled since 1927. The moneylender was not permitted to employ agents or canvassers to drum up business (Moneylenders Act 1927, s. 5 (3)); he was required to conduct all business in his authorised name from his authorised address (*ibid.*, s. 1 (3)); he was prohibited from despatching unsolicited circulars inviting applications for loans (*ibid.*, s. 5 (1)); and even the permitted content of newspaper advertisements he made was tightly circumscribed (*ibid.*, s. 5 (2)). These restrictions have stemmed from a well justified concern for the consequences of uncontrolled peddling of loan credit. However, it is only the moneylender that has hitherto been caught in this way. Those exempt from the Moneylenders Acts—banks in particular—have been free to conduct business as they chose; and whilst this may have seemed reasonable enough as regards the clearing banks, the development of the secondary banks, some of whose activities were far from desirable, has shown that such an exemption is no longer acceptable. In the sphere of sale credit, control has been much less stringent. The Advertisements (Hire-Purchase) Act 1967 controlled to some extent the content of the advertisements for credit, by requiring certain essential information to appear in such advertisements; and the Hire-Purchase Act 1965 required the pre-contract disclosure of the cash price of goods offered for disposal on hire-purchase or instalment sale terms. That was the limit of statutory intervention specifically directed at pre-contract activity in relation to credit transactions. [**438**]

There are, of course, numerous statutes and regulations affecting particular types of advertising (a useful, though not exhaustive, list is contained in Appendix 4 to the Code of Advertising Standards and Practice published by the Independent Broadcasting Authority), and some of these are of especial importance to the credit industry. Reference has already been made to the Protection of Depositors Act 1963 and regulations thereunder, prospectively repealed by the Banking Act 1979. Other regulations that need to be borne in mind in relation to advertisements aimed at consumers are the following:

(i) The Consumer Transactions (Restrictions on Statements) Order 1976, as amended by the Consumer Transactions (Restrictions on Statements) (Amendment) Order 1978. This Order, made under s. 22 of the Fair Trading Act 1973, makes it an offence to purport, in notices, advertisements or contract documents, to apply in relation to consumer sale and hire-purchase transactions terms which are void under s. 6 of the Unfair Contract Terms Act 1977 or to set out the supplier's obligations in relation to the quality, fitness or description of the goods without at the same time stating that the consumer's statutory rights are not affected. The purpose of this order is to prevent the practice by which sellers invoked void exemption clauses in reliance of the buyer's ignorance of the fact that such clauses were legally ineffective. As to s. 6, see paras. [**669**] *et seq., post.* [**439**]

(ii) The Mail Order Transactions (Information) Order 1976, also made under s. 22 of the Fair Trading Act, which requires advertisements (other than radio, television or cinema advertisements) inviting in the course of business orders by post for goods for which payment is to be made before dispatched to contain in legible characters the advertiser's name and business address. [**440**]

(iii) The Business Advertisements (Disclosure) Order 1977, made under the same section of the Fair Trading Act, and requiring that advertisements by persons seeking to sell goods in the course of a business which indicate that goods are for sale and which are likely to induce consumers to buy them shall indicate clearly that the goods are to be sold in the course of a business. This order is aimed at the practice which had developed among certain business advertisers of advertising from what was or appeared to be a private address, conveying the implication that the offer was by a private seller, not a dealer. Apart from other considerations, such a practice might mislead the consumer into thinking that the resulting sale contract did not have imported into it the statutory terms implied upon a sale in the course of a business. [**441**]

Codes of advertising practice

The Independent Broadcasting Authority, pursuant to the Independent Broadcasting Authority Act 1973, controls advertising on independent television and radio and pursuant to the Act exercises responsibility for the formulation and enforcement of the Code referred to in para. [**439**], *supra*. The Code has particular rules concerning financial advertisements. Each advertisement going out on a national network in independent television is pre-screened by the copy committee of the Independent Television Companies Association and advertisements which are cleared by that committee are individually vetted by the Authority's own Advertising Control. For other media, particularly newspapers and magazines, the publishers' own professional body, the Advertising Association, has set up the Advertising Standards Authority, a company limited by guarantee which also operates a Code of Advertising Practice. Though there is no prior vetting of advertisements, complaints concerning infringement of the Code are taken up by the Code of Advertising Practice Committee, which also gives guidance to advertisers on advertising copy. For further details, see Ross Cranston, *Consumers and the Law*, Chapter 2. [**442**]

The impact of the Consumer Credit Act

The Consumer Credit Act for the first time provides for a coherent pattern of control over methods of seeking business in the consumer credit sphere. The thrust of the Act is directed at three main areas of activity, namely:

    (i) advertising;
    (ii) canvassing;
    (iii) quotations and the display of information.

The control will be exercised partly under the provisions of the Act itself, partly under regulations made pursuant to its provisions. In addition to the three specific fields of activity mentioned above, a general power is conferred by s. 54 to include in regulations under s. 26 (see para. [**376**]) provisions further regulating the seeking of business by a licensee who carries on a consumer credit business or a consumer hire business. A major feature of the Act is the importance attached to the disclosure to the consumer of information concerning the terms and cost of credit which is not only not misleading but is sufficiently clear and detailed to enable him to make an informed choice as to whether to take credit and if so, from what source.   The Act provides for pre-contract disclosure in three stages: in advertisements, in quotations and in the contract documents themselves.   Obviously the detail and precision that can be given and required become greater with each stage towards the contract.   [**443**]

The phasing of control

The general pattern is that as provisions of the Consumer Credit Act are brought into force and regulations made, corresponding provisions of the Moneylenders Acts are repealed.   At present, the legislative scene affecting the seeking of business is distinctly untidy.   The advertising provisions in Part IV of the Act itself have not yet been brought into force, and no regulations have so far been made in relation to any of the three fields of activity listed in para. [**443**].   On the other hand, s. 49 of the Act, which prohibits the canvassing of debtor–creditor agreements off trade premises, has been operative since the 1st October 1977 (Consumer Credit Act 1974 (Commencement No. 3) Order 1977), and on the same date the restrictions imposed by the Moneylenders Acts on the employment of agents and canvassers ceased to have effect (*ibid.*).   [**444**]

Advertising—the scope of control

Subject to the exceptions mentioned below, Part IV of the Act, regulating the seeking of business, applies to any advertisement, published for the purposes of a business carried on by the advertiser, indicating that he is willing—

    (*a*) to provide credit, or
    (*b*) to enter into an agreement for the bailment of goods by him (s. 43 (1)).

This subsection involves an analysis of the words "advertisement", "published" and "advertiser".   [**445**]

By s. 189 (1), "advertisement" includes every form of advertising, whether in a publication, by television or radio, by display of notices, signs, labels, showcards or goods, by distribution of samples, circulars, catalogues, price lists or other material, by exhibition of pictures, models or films, or in any other way, and references to the publishing of advertisements are to be construed accordingly.   It should be noted that under this section, unlike the definition section in the Advertisements (Hire-Purchase) Act 1967, the word "advertisement" is not confined to visual advertisements but extends to any form of advertising, visual or oral, including advertising on the radio or through loudspeaker vans or even by sales patter in a shop or showroom.   This does not, of course, mean that all types of oral communication by a prospective creditor to a prospective debtor constitute advertisements.   The test would seem to be whether the statement is made with the object of drawing attention to the facilities offered by the creditor or whether it is for the sole purpose of answering a specific enquiry without actively trying to promote business.   But even a reply to an enquiry will amount to an advertisement if couched in terms calculated to attract business.   See, for example, *R.* v. *Delmayne*, [1970] 2 Q.B. 170, [1969] 2 All E.R. 980.   [**446**]

Whilst the definition of "advertisement" does not in terms require that it be an advertisement to the public, Part IV applies only to advertisements *published* for the purpose of a business carried on by the advertiser (s. 43 (1)).   Hence to be within Part IV the advertisement must be issued or displayed either to the public at large or to an individual or individuals as a member or members of the public, not in some other capacity. A letter or circular to employees advising them of preferential credit terms available from the employer would thus not constitute an advertisement published within the Act. On the other hand, an advertisement can be published even if it is merely a letter or circular sent to a single individual, if it is sent to him as a member of the public for the purpose of attracting business. See *R.* v. *Delmayne,* above. [**447**]

An advertisement is not within the Act unless it is published for the purpose of the advertiser's business. It should, however, be borne in mind that "advertiser" is not necessarily the person who actually places the advertisement but denotes "any person indicated in the advertisement as willing to enter into transactions to which the advertisement relates" (s. 189 (1)). Accordingly if an advertisement is published by S, the seller of goods, announcing that credit facilities to buy the goods are available from F, a finance house, F is an advertiser for the purpose of the Act and the advertisement, though placed by S, is accordingly an advertisement published by F for the purpose of its business and indicating F's willingness to provide credit. This appears to be so even if the advertisement was placed without F's prior knowledge or authority, though F's responsibility for it may then be negated by s. 168 (see para. [**1053**]). S is also an advertiser, for the word "transactions" is not confined to credit transactions but includes a sale transaction to be financed by the advertised credit. [**448**]

Exempted advertisements

By s. 43 (2), an advertisement does not fall within subsection (1) if the advertiser does not carry on—

    (*a*) a consumer credit business or consumer hire business, or
    (*b*) a business in the course of which he provides credit to individuals secured on land, or
    (*c*) a business which comprises or relates to unregulated agreements where—

        (i) the proper law of the agreement is the law of a country outside the United Kingdom, and
        (ii) if the proper law of the agreement were the law of a part of the United Kingdom it would be a regulated agreement.

By s. 43 (3), an advertisement does not fall within subsection (1) (*a*) if it indicates—

    (*a*) that the credit must exceed £5,000, and that no security is required, or the security is to consist of property other than land, or
    (*b*) that the credit is available only to a body corporate.

It should be noted that one who carries on a business in the course of which he provides credit to individuals secured on land is caught by the provisions of the Act relating to advertising, even if his business is limited to transactions that are above the £5,000 ceiling and therefore outside the Act and even if the advertisement is expressed to be limited to transactions above £5,000, unless the advertisement makes it clear that security on land is not required. On the other hand, an advertisement is not within the Act if the advertiser's business is restricted to credit to bodies corporate or if the advertisement states that the credit is available only to a body corporate. An advertisement of hire facilities is outside Part IV if it indicates that the advertiser is not willing to enter into a consumer hire agreement (s. 43 (4)). Finally, the Secretary of State may by order provide that Part IV shall not apply to other advertisements of a description specified in the order (s. 43 (5)). No such order has yet been made. [**449**]

Whilst agreements entered into by building societies, local authorities and other bodies specified in s. 16 of the Act are exempt from the Act, if secured on land, in the conditions previously discussed (para. [**312**]), such creditors are nevertheless subject to the restrictions imposed by Part IV on seeking business. Thus, advertisements by local authorities and building societies offering mortgage facilities for the purchase of dwelling-houses are no more exempt than advertisements by other creditors, unless an exempting order is made by the Secretary of State under s. 43 (5). [**450**]

Form and content of advertisements

The Secretary of State is empowered by s. 44 of the Act to make regulations as to the form and content of advertisements within Part IV. Such regulations are required to contain such provisions as appear to the Secretary of State appropriate with a view to ensuring that, having regard to its subject matter and the amount of detail included in it, an advertisement conveys a fair and reasonably comprehensive indication of the nature of the credit or hire facilities offered by the advertiser and of their true cost to persons using them (s. 44 (1)). In addition such regulations may, under s. 44 (2)

(a) require specified information to be included in the prescribed manner in advertisements, and other specified material to be excluded;
(b) contain requirements to ensure that specified information is clearly brought to the attention of persons to whom advertisements are directed, and that one part of an advertisement is not given insufficient or excessive prominence compared with another.

Infringement of a regulation is an offence (s. 167 (2)). No regulations have yet been made, though these are expected in the near future. [**451**]

Appendix I to the White Paper set out in detail the contemplated requirements of regulations concerning credit and hire advertisements, dividing these into unspecific and specific advertisements. The intention was that advertisements indicating simply that credit or hire facilities were available but not giving any financial details would merely have to state that further details would be supplied without charge on request, and upon receipt of such request the advertiser would then have to supply the prescribed information, whilst specific advertisements, that is, those containing some data as to the terms or cost of credit, would themselves have to set out the full range of prescribed information. The initial consultation papers setting out the projected form of regulations were modelled on this approach, but it soon became apparent that the unspecific/specific classification was too unsophisticated to be workable, the definition of "unspecific" being so narrow, and accordingly that of "specific" so wide, that advertisers who wished merely to give a general indication of the facilities available, with one or two financial details (e.g. the cost or period of credit) would then have to set out a quantity of additional information that might be suitable for inclusion in a contract document once the terms had been agreed but simply could not be furnished at a

143

stage when there was no applicant for credit, no specific transaction on the horizon and no way of telling, in relation to a prospective application, how much credit would be applied for and of what kind. In short, the advertiser would have been expected to set out information which at that stage he could not possibly possess. It was indeed because of this difficulty that the Advertisements (Hire-Purchase) Act 1967 had provided three categories of advertisement, the required content of each category being graded according to the degree of its specificity (see R. M. Goode, *Hire-Purchase Law and Practice* (2nd Edn.), pp. 781 *et seq.*). [**452**]

It now seems likely that this concept will be adopted in advertising regulations to be made under the Consumer Credit Act, and that instead of unspecific and specific advertisements there will be a threefold division, into simple, intermediate and full advertisements, the prescribed content of an advertisement varying according to the category into which it falls. [**453**]

Whatever form the regulations ultimately take, their purpose will be threefold:

 (i) To ensure that no advertisement contains information which is misleading (s. 46 (1) of the Act prohibits this in general terms, and the regulations will proscribe specific words or expressions considered objectionable).

 (ii) To provide the reader of the advertisement with a reasonable picture (whether through typical examples or otherwise) of the terms on which credit is likely to be extended to him if he applies for it, and in particular the amount and rate of the credit charge.

 (iii) To ensure that prospective applicants for credit are made aware of the respects in which the availability and terms of credit are affected by the personal qualifications of the applicant for credit (age, occupation, place of residence, etc.) or by the fact that he is a credit buyer and not a cash buyer. [**454**]

Availability of cash terms

Section 45 of the Act provides as follows:

> "If an advertisement to which this Part applies indicates that the advertiser is willing to provide credit under a restricted-use credit agreement relating to goods or services to be supplied by any person, but at the time when the advertisement is published that person is not holding himself out as prepared to sell the goods or provide the services (as the case may be) for cash, the advertiser commits an offence."

The object of the above provisions is to outlaw advertisements purporting to show no credit charge, or an attractively modest credit charge, when the advertised supplier does not sell for cash, so that there is no method of determining the cash price and thus of verifying the stated rate or amount of the credit charge. In the absence of an exemption order under s. 43 (5), the prohibition imposed by s. 45 may seriously affect certain mail order companies whose practice is not to sell for cash but only to offer credit terms. Evidence was given to the Crowther Committee that the organisation of some mail order firms was geared exclusively to credit transactions and that the customer who insisted on paying cash was regarded as a considerable nuisance! It seems probable that an order will be made exempting, for example, advertisements relating to agreements that would, upon being entered into, be exempt agreements under the Consumer Credit (Exempt Agreements) Order 1977, such as unsecured fixed-sum debtor-creditor-supplier agreements order under which the number of payments to be made by a debtor does not exceed four (see para. [**320**]). [**455**]

Section 45, as originally drafted, aroused some anxiety in trade circles owing to the width of its provisions, and in particular the requirement that the advertised supplier must at the time of publication of the advertisement not only offer the goods or services for cash but offer them *on the same terms* except as to payment. The requirement created a difficulty due to the fact that because a supply on credit raises problems which do not occur in a cash transaction, the normal form of credit agreement will inevitably include terms (other than as to payment) that would have no place in a cash sale. In view of this, the requirement was dropped by amendment. It is now sufficient that the goods are available for cash from the designated supplier. [**456**]

To avoid an offence under s. 45 it is not sufficient that the provider of the advertised goods or services is willing to sell or provide them for cash. He must hold himself out as being prepared to do so. But if he has already sold goods or supplied services of the description in question for cash, this would normally constitute a sufficient holding out. Conversely, if he falsely holds himself out as willing to sell or provide for cash when in fact he is not, no offence is committed under s. 45, but the advertiser will be guilty of an offence under s. 46. [**457**]

False or misleading advertisements

If an advertisement within Part IV conveys information which in a material respect is false or misleading, the advertiser commits an offence (s. 46 (1)). Information stating or implying an intention on the advertiser's part which he has not got is false (s. 46 (2)). [**458**]

Advertising infringements

Section 47 (1) provides as follows:

> "Where an advertiser commits an offence against regulations made under section 44 or against section 45 or 46 or would be taken to commit such an offence but for the defence provided by section 168, a like offence is committed by—
>
> (a) the publisher of the advertisement, and
> (b) any person who, in the course of a business carried on by him devised the advertisement, or a part of it relevant to the first-mentioned offence, and
> (c) where the advertiser did not procure the publication of the advertisement, the person who did procure it."

Case (b) would include an advertising agency devising an advertisement for a client. Case (c), which at first sight may appear somewhat odd, can arise where, for example, a person is the advertiser not because he placed the advertisement but because he is named in it as the person willing to enter into the transaction to which the advertisement relates (see s. 189 (1) and para. [**448**]). [**459**]

Section 47 (2) provides an innocent publisher with a defence as follows:

> "In proceedings for an offence under subsection (1) (a) it is a
> defence for the person charged to prove that—
>
> (a) the advertisement was published in the course of a
>   business carried on by him, and
> (b) he received the advertisement in the course of that
>   business, and did not know and had no reason to
>   suspect that its publication would be an offence
>   under this Part."

A quite independent defence, available to the publisher as well as the advertiser, is provided by s. 168 of the Act, which is discussed in paragraphs [**1053**] *et seq.* [**460**]

Infringement of provisions in the Act or regulations results merely in the commission of a criminal offence and does not, under the Act, invalidate any agreement which the consumer is induced to enter into as the result of the offending advertisement (s. 170 (1)), though he may, of course, have a right to rescind the agreement at common law for misrepresentation. [**461**]

Quotations

Regulations may be made imposing on persons carrying on a consumer credit business or consumer hire business a duty to provide quotations and regulating the form and content of quotations to prospective customers (s. 52). Regulations may likewise be made requiring persons carrying on such a business to display prescribed information about the business in the prescribed manner at any premises where the business is carried on to which the public have access (s. 53). Breach of any regulations made under ss. 52 or 53 is an offence (s. 167 (2)). [**462**]

No regulations have yet been made under either section, though these are expected in the near future. [**463**]

Disclosure requirements for quotations are designed to fulfil much the same purposes as for advertisements, and the structure of the two sets of regulations, and of subsequent regulations as to the content of contract documents, is likely to be very similar. In many cases the quotation regulations will be triggered off by the advertisement, since this will either contain an offer to supply further information on request or elicit a request for such information from a prospective debtor. [**464**]

Canvassing

The Crowther Committee, while recommending the repeal of the Moneylenders Acts, was strongly against the peddling of loan credit at the doorstep, and recommended that the prohibition against canvassing of loan credit imposed by the Moneylenders Acts should be maintained in the new legislation. Sections 48–51 are concerned with the canvassing and solicitation of applications for credit. As originally drawn, these provisions were extremely stringent, and might seriously have impaired check trading, as well as making it illegal to telephone a prospective debtor except in response to his prior request. The provisions finally enacted have avoided these problems and are restricted to the mischief against which the legislation was aimed. [**465**]

In essence, canvassing consists of oral representations to the prospective debtor or hirer, or to any other individual, during an unsolicited visit for that purpose to any place other than the *business* premises of the creditor or owner, a supplier, the canvasser himself or his employer or principal or the prospective debtor or hirer. The full definition is contained in s. 48, which provides as follows: [**466**]

> "(1) An individual (the 'canvasser') canvasses a regulated agreement off trade premises if he solicits the entry (as debtor or hirer) of another individual (the 'consumer') into the agreement by making oral representations to the consumer, or any other individual, during a visit by the canvasser to any place (not excluded by subsection (2)) where the consumer, or that other individual, as the case may be, is, being a visit—
>
> > (a) carried out for the purpose of making such oral representations to individuals who are at that place, but
> > (b) not carried out in response to a request made on a previous occasion.
>
> (2) A place is excluded from subsection (1) if it is a place where a business is carried on (whether on a permanent or temporary basis) by—
>
> > (a) the creditor or owner, or
> > (b) a supplier, or
> > (c) the canvasser, or the person whose employee or agent the canvasser is, or
> > (d) the consumer." [**467**]

The following points should be noted in connection with the above provisions:

(1) If the solicitation occurs at a place where a business is carried on by one of the four categories of person listed in s. 48 (2), it is at (and not off) trade premises, even if the business is conducted there only on a temporary basis. Hence solicitation of the consumer (i.e. the prospective debtor or hirer) from a stall at a trade fair or in a tent at an agricultural show used for the purpose of the creditor's business for the duration of the fair or show is not canvassing.

(2) To solicit the consumer at his own premises is not canvassing if he carries on a business at those premises. Thus, a finance house can lawfully solicit stocking or other loan application from its dealers, even if they are not incorporated. But the position is otherwise if the debtor uses the premises exclusively for other purposes, e.g. as a residence.

(3) It is not essential to the definition of canvassing that oral representations should have been made face to face, nor that they should have been made to the consumer himself. Representations on the telephone, and representations to an individual other than the consumer, still involve canvassing the consumer if they take place during a visit by the person making them to the non-business address where the representee is and solicit the consumer's entry into the prospective regulated agreement. Thus if the caller, during the course of an unsolicited visit, speaks to the consumer on an internal telephone at the consumer's premises or speaks to his wife for the purpose of getting her to persuade the consumer to enter into the agreement, canvassing takes place. On the other hand, it is the *consumer's* entry into the agreement that it has to be canvassed, so that representations to his wife to induce *her* to enter into an agreement

147

will be canvassing of the wife, not of the consumer himself. Moreover, either the consumer or the individual to whom representations are made by way of solicitation of the consumer's entry into the agreement must be on the premises on the occasion of the visit. It is not canvassing to solicit the consumer by telephoning him *from* his own premises to another address where he then is. Further, the representations must be made during the visit, so that it is not canvassing for the trader to telephone from his own premises to the consumer's home and solicit the consumer's entry into the agreement.

(4) To give rise to canvassing within the statutory definition, the visit must be unsolicited and must be carried out for the purpose of making the oral representations to any individual (not necessarily the consumer himself) who may be at the place in question. A visit made to service an existing loan does not give rise to canvassing if, without having called for that purpose, the caller solicits a new loan application.

(5) The term "representation" includes any condition or warranty, and any other statement or undertaking, whether oral or in writing (s. 189 (1)). [**468**]

Canvassing and other solicitation of debtor-creditor agreements

It is an offence to canvass debtor-creditor agreements off trade premises (s. 49 (1)). The meaning of "debtor-creditor agreement" has been discussed earlier (paras. [**280**] *et seq.*). The effect of s. 49 (1) is to prohibit the canvassing of what Crowther termed unconnected loans, whilst permitting canvassing by check traders, credit traders, credit card issuers (but see para. [**474**] as to unsolicited credit-tokens) and persons offering hire-purchase, conditional sale, credit sale and rental facilities. [**469**]

Canvassing involves calling "otherwise than in response to a request made on a previous occasion". The request does not for the purpose have to be in any particular form. Any request, whether oral or written, which initiates the visit prevents that visit from giving rise to canvassing in breach of s. 49 (1). However, a separate offence is committed under s. 49 (2) if the request was not in writing signed by or on behalf of the person making it. The requirement of writing and signature was dealt with in this way, and not as an ingredient of the definition of canvassing, because of the relevance of that definition in other sections, e.g. s. 23 (3). [**470**]

The soliciting of agreements for overdrafts on current accounts of any description is exempt from the provisions of s. 49 (1) and (2) where:

(a) the Director has determined that current accounts of that description kept with the creditor are excluded from subsections (1) and (2), and

(b) the debtor already keeps an account with the creditor (whether a current account or not) (s. 49 (3)).

Such a determination may be made subject to such conditions as the Director thinks fit, must be made only where the Director is of opinion that it is not against the interests of debtors, and may be revoked or varied by the Director if he thinks fit (ss. 49 (4), 183). If soliciting is done in breach of a condition imposed under s. 49 (4) (a), the determination under s. 49 (3) (a) does not apply to it (s. 49 (5)). [**471**]

The Director made a determination under s. 49 (3) on the 1st June 1977 excluding current accounts of a banking character from the provisions of s. 49 (1) and (2). [**472**]

Circulars to minors

By s. 50 (1) a person commits an offence who, with a view to financial gain, sends to a minor (i.e. a person under the age of 18 years) any document inviting him to—

    (*a*) borrow money, or
    (*b*) obtain goods on credit or hire, or
    (*c*) obtain services on credit, or
    (*d*) apply for information or advice on borrowing money or otherwise obtaining credit, or hiring goods.

In proceedings under s. 50 (1) in respect of the sending of a document to a minor, it is a defence for the person charged to prove that he did not know, and had no reasonable cause to suspect, that he was a minor (s. 50 (2)). Where a document is received by a minor at any school or educational establishment for minors, the person sending it to him at that establishment knowing or suspecting it to be such an establishment is to be taken to have reasonable cause to suspect that he is a minor (s. 50 (3)). The onus lies on the sender to prove that he did not know or suspect the establishment to be a school or other establishment for minors (s. 171 (5)). These provisions are modelled on ss. 2 and 3 of the Betting and Loans (Infants) Act 1892. If a finance house, not knowing that a person is a minor, sends to him at home a circular inviting him to borrow money and the minor's parent forwards the circular to the minor at his school, no offence is committed. The finance house does not contravene s. 50 because it is within s. 50 (2) and is not the person who sent the circular to the school. The parent who is the sender of the circular, commits no offence because his despatch of the circular to the minor is not effected with a view to financial gain. Section 50 does not prohibit the *giving* of a document to a minor inviting him to borrow, merely the *sending* of such document, i.e., its transmission through the post or by some other agency, as opposed to delivering to the minor by the creditor in person. If, however, the document is sent to a minor, an offence is committed whether or not the document arrives.

[**473**]

Prohibition of unsolicited credit-tokens

It is an offence to give a person a credit-token if he has not asked for it (s. 51 (1)). "Give" means deliver or send by post (s. 189 (1)). Except where the credit-token agreement is a small debtor-creditor-supplier agreement (e.g. a check trading agreement where the credit does not exceed £30—see paras. [**189**]–[**191**]), the request does not fulfil the requirements of s. 51 (1) unless it is contained in a document signed by the person making the request (s. 51 (2)). But the unsolicited provision of a credit-token is permitted:

    (*a*) for use under a credit-token agreement already made, or
    (*b*) in renewal or replacement of a credit-token previously accepted by the

debtor under a credit-token agreement which continues in force, whether
varied or not (s. 51 (3)).

This provision is wider in scope than it may seem at first sight, and would appear
to preclude a finance house from sending a debtor who settles his agreement a
satisfaction note or letter which, on being produced by him to the finance house on
a subsequent application for credit, enables him to obtain it on favourable terms.

[**474**]

13. Rate Computation and Disclosure

Introduction

In its *Report on Consumer Credit*, the Crowther Committee strongly recommended that in consumer credit advertisements and agreements the cost of the credit, covering not only the pure interest element but all other borrowing costs (including those to be incurred by the borrower under ancillary contracts for services where the borrower was not free to choose his own supplier of such services) should be stated in terms of a true annual percentage rate, thus enabling the borrower more readily to compare the cost of borrowing from one lender with the cost of borrowing from another, and to evaluate the relative costs of different forms of credit and of contracts of different payment periods. [**475**]

The Act implements this recommendation by making provision for regulations under ss. 20 (1), 44 (1) and 60 (1). To date, regulations have been made only under s. 20. These will be analysed in detail later in this chapter, but in order to make them understandable it is first necessary to give a brief picture of the problems involved in rate disclosure and some of the more common methods hitherto used in expressing the amount of credit in terms of a percentage rate. For further details, see R. M. Goode, *Hire-Purchase Law and Practice* (2nd Edn.), Appendix A, as corrected by the Supplement, and (ed.) *Consumer Credit*, Chapter 5. [**476**]

The cost to the debtor

The essential function of rate disclosure is to provide the prospective debtor with a statment of credit costs which will enable him not merely to know the amount he is paying for the use of credit but also to compare the cost of one source or type of credit with that of others. Hence the relevant fact is the cost to the debtor, not the net return to the lender. There are many good reasons why some types of lending institution charge more than others. The charges levied by a creditor vary according to the cost to him of obtaining the money which he is to lend, the level of his overheads, the amount of commission he has to pay to brokers for introducing business, the amount and duration of typical advances, the period allowed for repayment and the risk category of the sector of the market he is serving. The English consumer credit market is highly structured in terms of interest rates, the cheapest form of finance being the bank overdraft and the dearest the moneylender's loan, with a range of intermediate rates for loans by finance houses, hire-purchase agreements, credit cards and budget accounts. But lenders' reasons for charging differential rates are of no concern to the borrower. What matters to him is what he has to pay for credit, not what profit the lender will make on the transaction; and so far as the borrower is concerned one item of cost is like another, so that, for example, the payment of land registry fees in connection with a mortgage transaction is just as unpalatable as interest on the loan itself and is thus just as appropriate for inclusion in the total charge for credit, despite the fact that from the lender's point of view this item of expenditure is not reflected in any corresponding benefit to him. [**477**]

Of course, the cost of credit is only one factor among many which the consumer has to weigh in the balance. He must also have regard to convenience (relying on sources of credit introduced by the retailer from whom he is acquiring the goods is obviously much simpler than shopping around for credit himself), the comparability of other terms of the contract and the advantages of preserving an existing line of credit for other occasions. The more sophisticated will consider in particular the term of the credit offered. In a period of inflation, with rising interest rates, a 15 per cent effective rate on a fixed-rate 24-month loan may be much better value than a 12 per cent effective rate on a loan repayable on demand. [**478**]

The flat rate

It has for many years been common, when quoting a rate of interest or charge, to quote a flat rate, that is, a rate which is applied to the original loan figure, even where the loan is to be repaid by instalments and will thus not be outstanding in full throughout the agreed period for repayment. A flat rate may be an add-on rate or a discount rate. An add-on rate is that which is applied to the sum actually handed over to the borrower, or applied for his benefit, as where the borrower borrows £100 and repays by instalments over twelve months the total sum of £110, producing a flat rate of 10 per cent. A discount rate is a flat rate applied to a figure from which the amount of the discount is deducted at the outset, as where a loan of £100 is repayable by instalments over twelve months at a discount of 10 per cent. deducted from the advance, so that the sum the borrower receives is only £90. The discount rate is 10 per cent., but the equivalent add-on rate is $\frac{10}{90} \times 100$, i.e. 11.1 per cent., since the true amount of the loan is not £100 but £90. [**479**]

Both the add-on rate and the discount rate are seriously misleading (the latter even more so than the former), since the stated rate takes no account of the diminution of the principal indebtedness through repayment by instalments but is geared throughout to the original advance (in the case of the add-on rate) or the original advance before deduction of the discount (in the case of the discount rate). Since the average amount outstanding throughout a loan contract providing for repayment by equal instalments at equal intervals is only one-half of the original advance plus one-half of one instalment, the actual annual rate (before compounding—see para. [**489**]) is nearly double the flat rate. [**480**]

It follows that if a quoted annual rate is to be at all meaningful, even as an approximation, it must be calculated in such a way as to reflect the mode of repayment; for since interest (and we shall use this term for convenience, whilst making it clear that what we are thereby referring to is the cost to the borrower, not the net return to the lender) is a function of funds in use, it is axiomatic that interest must reduce as the principal indebtedness diminishes. Where interest is not precomputed but is expressed by the terms of the contract to be payable at a given rate on the balance from time to time outstanding (as in the case of a bank overdraft), this result is produced automatically and apart from any adjustment necessary to convert a period rate which is other than a year into an effective, as opposed to a nominal, annual rate (see para. [**489**]) no computation is necessary. The difficulty arises where interest is precomputed and added to principal to produce a total sum repayable by instalments over an agreed contract period, as in the case of a hire-purchase agreement or a fixed-term personal loan. Here the rate of interest has to be extracted, and the computation depends on the manner in which it is notionally spread over the contract. [**481**]

The actuarially computed rate

There are any number of methods, of varying degrees of accuracy, by which interest may be notionally spread over a contract so as to reflect deductions in the principal indebtedness (a reasonably accurate method, if the loan period is not too long and the rate not too high, is that incorporated in the First Schedule to the Advertisements (Hire-Purchase) Act 1967), but there can be only one "true" rate, and that is a rate computed actuarially on the basis that the ratio of interest to funds in use, i.e. at the service of the borrower, is completely constant throughout the repayment period. The contract may, of course, be expressed to provide that interest shall be taken by the creditor in full at the outset (in which event it is in truth a discount) or shall be collected with the final instalment of principal or shall be spread evenly across the contract period; but such a provision is merely a convenient method of expressing the payment obligation and cannot alter the mathematical concept of interest, so that a stated rate computed on the basis of accrual of interest by any of such methods will not in fact be a true rate. [**482**].

By way of illustration, let us take a loan of £1,200 repayable without charges by 12 equal monthly payments of £100. This can be regarded as the equivalent of a series of loans for one month each, i.e. a loan of £1,200 for one month, £1,100 for one month, £1,000 for one month, and so on, the amount in the borrower's hands diminishing by £100 each month as he makes his repayments. In effect, the borrower has the equivalent of £7,800 (the sum of the amounts £1,200, £1,100 ... £100) for one month. The result of this mathematical operation is to convert a loan repayable by instalments into a loan for a single payment period. Suppose that we now vary the transaction by imposing interest charges of £300, making a total of £1,500 repayable by 12 equal monthly payments of £125. The calculation of the amount of principal outstanding at the end of each month, and thus of its equivalent expressed in terms of a single loan for one month, now becomes more complex, for it depends on the manner in which repayments are distributed as between principal and interest; but if we can find the correct method of making this distribution we shall then have notionally converted the instalment transaction into a single loan for one month at interest totally one month's interest, and the division of the latter into the former multiplied by 100 will produce the rate of charge for the period of one month. The second, and relatively easy, stage of the operation is to convert this notional period rate into its effective annual equivalent (see para. [**489**]). [**483**]

Now clearly if a single interest rate per month is to be extracted for the transaction as a whole, the interest must be distributed over the contract period in such a way that the rate of interest charged at the end of each month on the principal outstanding during that month is constant. If, for example, the charge is so distributed that the rate of interest charged on each month's loan (i.e. on the amount of principal outstanding for that month) is x per cent., then the total of the sum distributed as interest will be x per cent. of the total of the sums shown as outstanding for principal at the end of each month, and we can thus properly say that the rate of interest on the transaction as a whole is x per cent. per month. This is illustrated in the following table taken from a leading American textbook on the mathematics of instalment credit. [**484**]

TABLE I

SCHEDULE FOR ACTUARIAL METHOD

Face of Note £100. Charge £6. Cash Advance £94. Repayment 12 Monthly Payments of £8·33 each. Charge Distributed in Fixed Ratio to Monthly Unpaid Principal Balances. Fixed Ratio = ·00964994

(1) Month	(2) Cash Principal Of Which Borrower Has Use	(3) Monthly Contract Payment	(4) Charges Credited Monthly	(5) Monthly Credits to Reduce Principal	(6) Charge as Per Cent. of Cash in Borrower's Possession	(7) Accumulated Charges Credited
1	£94·00000000	£8·33	£0·90709436	£7·42290564	0·00964994	£0·90709436
2	86·57709436	8·33	0·83546376	7·49453624	0·00964994	1·74255812
3	79·08256073	8·34	0·76314196	7·57685804	0·00964994	2·50570008
4	71·50570269	8·33	0·69002574	7·63997426	0·00964994	3·19572582
5	63·86572843	8·33	0·61630045	7·71369955	0·00964994	3·31202627
6	56·15202888	8·34	0·54186371	7·79813629	0·00964994	4·35388998
7	48·35389259	8·33	0·46661216	7·86338784	0·00964994	4·82050214
8	40·49050475	8·33	0·39073094	7·93926906	0·00964994	5·21123308
9	32·55123569	8·34	0·31411747	8·02588253	0·00964994	5·52535055
10	24·52535316	8·33	0·23666818	8·09333182	0·00964994	5·76201873
11	16·43202134	8·33	0·15856802	8·17143198	0·00964994	5·92058675
12	8·26058936	8·34	0·07971419	8·26028581	0·00964994	6·00030094
Total	£621·79671198	£100·00	£6·00030094	£93·9969906	0·00964994	

Action of principal = 621·79671198 pound-months.
Monthly rate = 6/621·79671198 = ·00964994
Annual rate = ·00964994 × 12 = 11·579928% without compounding.

Source: M. R. Neifeld, *Neifeld's Guide to Instalment Computation*, pp. 176–7 (modified to show pounds sterling instead of dollars and with addition of column (6)). [**484.1**]

Here we can see that the test of the actuarial spread is satisfied in that the monthly rate is uniform at 0·964994 per cent. throughout the contract. In other words, we have reduced the loan to a series of one-month loans at a standard rate of charge, and this accurately reflects the rate of the transaction as a whole, which can be treated as the equivalent of a loan of £621·79671198 for one month at an amount of interest for that month of £6·00030094. Dividing the former by the latter produces a figure of 0·00964994 which when multiplied by 100 produces a rate of 0·964994 for one month. [**485**]

Contrast this with the figures for the same transaction in the next table, where the interest, instead of diminishing as the principal reduces, has been distributed evenly throughout the period of the contract, infringing the cardinal rule that interest is a function of funds in use and should thus diminish with the reduction of the principal. The result is that the proportion of each repayment attributed to interest is too small in the early part of the contract and too large in the latter part. The rate of monthly charge to principal outstanding during each month is not constant but fluctuates and the resultant total interest and total principal shown in columns (4) and (2) respectively are erroneous, so that the figure produced by expressing the former as a percentage of the latter is necessarily inaccurate. The effect of attributing too little of the repayment to interest and too much to principal in the early stages of the contract is to accelerate the repayment of principal artificially, reduce below the true figure the total of principal outstanding for one month (i.e. £611 instead of £622) and thus overstate the period rate by 0·017 per cent. This constant ratio formula is that used in the Schedule to the Moneylenders Act 1927 and exaggerates the period rate, an error for which the Act then over-compensates by a formula which converts that period rate into a nominal instead of an effective annual rate. [486]

TABLE 2

SCHEDULE FOR CONSTANT RATIO METHOD

Face of Note £100. Charge £6. Cash Advance £94. Repayment 12 Monthly Payments of £8·33 each. Charge Credited in Equal Amounts over Each Payment

(1) Month	(2) Cash Principal of Which Borrower Has Use	(3) Monthly Contract Payment	(4) Charges Credited Monthly	(5) Monthly Credits to Reduce Principal	(6) Charge as Per Cent. of Cash in Borrower's Possession	(7) Unpaid Debt Balance	(8) Charge Out-standing
1	£94·00	£8·33	£0·50	£7·83	0·53%	£100·00	£6·00
2	86·17	8·33	0·50	7·83	0·58	91·67	5·50
3	78·34	8·34	0·50	7·84	0·64	83·34	5·00
4	70·50	8·33	0·50	7·83	0·71	75·00	4·50
5	62·67	8·33	0·50	7·83	0·80	66·67	4·00
6	54·84	8·34	0·50	7·84	0·91	58·34	3·50
7	47·00	8·33	0·50	7·83	1·06	50·00	3·00
8	39·17	8·33	0·50	7·83	1·28	41·67	2·50
9	31·34	8·34	0·50	7·84	1·60	33·34	2·00
10	23·50	8·33	0·50	7·83	2·13	25·00	1·50
11	15·67	8·33	0·50	7·83	3·19	16·67	1·00
12	7·84	8·34	0·50	7·84	6·38	8·34	0·50
Total	£611·04	£100·00	£6·00	£94·00	0·982%	£650·04	£39·00

Action of principal = 611·04 pound-months.
Monthly rate = 6/611·04 = 0·982%.
Annual rate = 0·982 × 12 = 11·78%, without compounding.
Note: 650·04 − 39·00 = 611·04.

Source: M. R. Neifeld, *Neifeld's Guide to Instalment Computations*, p. 194 (modified to show pounds sterling instead of dollars). [486.1]

Hence we have to use the actuarial spread in order to arrive at the correct period rate. This is the first stage of the operation. The second stage is to convert the period rate into an annual rate. Here there is a choice between the nominal annual rate (used in the United States) and the effective annual rate (adopted in regulations under s. 20 of the Consumer Credit Act). [**487**]

The nominal annual rate

The nominal annual rate is produced by multiplying the period rate by the number of payment periods in a year. Thus if the actuarially calculated period rate is, for example, 1 per cent. per month, this is converted to produce an annual rate of 12 per cent. per year. In order to indicate the frequency of interest payments, financiers would quote such a rate as 12 per cent. per annum convertible monthly. This annual rate is known as the nominal annual rate, and is that used in Tables prepared by the United States Federal Reserve Board under Regulation Z, pursuant to the Consumer Credit Protection Act. Such a rate, though relatively accurate where the contract term is limited in duration and the frequency of payments is not too great, is not suitable in other cases for comparing rates payable under contracts of different length and payment frequency, since it fails to take account of the fact that a borrower who pays interest of 1 per cent. a month at the end of each month is parting with the use of the money represented by his interest payments earlier than the borrower who pays interest of 12 per cent. a year at the end of each year. The greater the payment frequency, the greater becomes the disparity between the nominal annual rate and a rate which takes this factor into account. This is clearly shown in Table 3, para. [**488.1**]. [**488**]

The effective annual rate

To produce a true comparison between a rate of interest where interest is payable annually and a rate where interest is payable at a different periodic interval, it is necessary to introduce a compounding factor into the calculation. Compounding in this context does not denote compound interest in the contractual sense, which involves the accretion of *unpaid* interest to principal at stated compounding intervals, whereas we are here discussing an interest spread such that the interest payable in respect of each payment period is *precisely* geared to funds in the borrower's hands in that period, so that there is never any unpaid interest to compound. The compounding here referred to arises from the fact that the more frequently the interest payments are made the earlier the debtor is out of the use of his money and the greater becomes the effective rate of charge. The same mathematical concepts are involved, however, as for compound interest in its normal sense. [**489**]

What has to be computed is the rate that a borrower who is required to pay interest at the end of the year would have to pay in order for him to be paying the same effective rate as the borrower who has to pay at greater or (more usually) shorter intervals. Use of compound interest tables would show, for example, that the true rate of interest paid by the borrower who pays 1 per cent. per month at the end of each month is not 12 per cent. per annum but 12·68 per cent. per annum (in other words, the borrower paying 12 per cent. interest in one sum at the end of the year is 0·68 per cent. of the principal better off than the borrower who has to pay 1 per cent. each month), and that a borrower paying $\frac{3}{13}$ per cent. a week at the end of each week would be paying a true annual rate of 12·76 per cent. The discrepancy becomes greater as the disparity between

TABLE 3

EFFECTIVE ANNUAL RATE EQUIVALENTS OF STATED NOMINAL ANNUAL AND PERIOD RATES

Nominal Annual Rate	FREQUENCY OF COMPOUNDING												
	ANNUALLY		HALF-YEARLY		QUARTERLY		MONTHLY		WEEKLY		DAILY		CONTINUOUSLY
	Period Rate	Effective Annual Rate	Period Rate	Effective Annual Rate	Period Rate	Effective Annual Rate	Period Rate	Effective Annual Rate	Period Rate	Effective Annual Rate	Period Rate	Effective Annual Rate	Effective Annual Rate
12·00	12·00	12·00	6·00	12·36	3·00	12·55	1·00	12·68	0·23	12·73	0·03	12·75	12·75
24·00	24·00	24·00	12·00	25·44	6·00	26·25	2·00	26·82	0·46	27·05	0·07	27·11	27·12
36·00	36·00	36·00	18·00	39·24	9·00	41·16	3·00	42·58	0·69	43·16	0·10	43·31	43·33
48·00	48·00	48·00	24·00	53·76	12·00	57·35	4·00	60·10	0·92	61·25	0·13	61·56	61·61
60·00	60·00	60·00	30·00	69·00	15·00	74·90	5·00	79·59	1·15	81·59	0·16	82·12	82·21

Examples: 1. A nominal annual rate of 12% convertible (i.e. to be compounded) quarterly, so that the period rate is 3% a quarter, represents an effective (annual) rate of 12·55%.

2. A rate of 3% per month represents a nominal annual rate of 36% and an effective rate of 42·58%. [**488.1**].

157

the payment intervals widens (though there is a mathematical maximum, reached by continuous compounding, beyond which the rate cannot go) and as the rate itself rises. [**490**]

In jurisdictions whose legislation imposes ceiling rates of interest (which is the case in most other countries, including the United States) the discrepancy between the nominal rate and the effective rate is no doubt considered too small to cause concern. In England, on the other hand, where no such ceiling exists, charges on hire-purchase agreements can go as high as 30 per cent. and on moneylending contracts not infrequently reach 70 per cent. or above. At these levels, the divergence between nominal and effective rates becomes striking, as indicated in Table 3, para. [**488.1**]. It is for this reason that the use of the effective rate over the nominal annual rate is to be preferred. [**491**]

To produce the effective rate a compounding factor must be built into the calculation when the period rate is converted into the annual rate. This is so not only in relation to loans repayable by instalments but even in relation to single-repayment loans, where the period at the end of which the loan is to be repaid is greater or less than a year. It is only in the case of a loan for exactly a year repayable with interest at the end of the year that a simple interest formula will produce a completely accurate rate. [**492**]

The rates of 12·68 per cent. and 12·76 per cent. given in the illustration in para. [**490**] represents the annual rate compounded annually. The phrase "compounded annually" denotes the yardstick by reference to which the period rate is being converted is a year. In other words, the annual rate compounded annually tells us what rate of interest a borrower paying at the end of a year would have to pay in order to be paying the equivalent of the borrower who pays the period rate per period. There is no mathematical magic in annual compounding. One could, for example, convert a monthly rate to the equivalent of an annual rate compounded semi-annually. The effective rate would then represent the rate which a debtor paying interest at half-yearly intervals would have to pay in order to be paying the same annual rate as the borrower who pays the contract period rate per period. But annual compounding is the conventional basis for comparison in the financial world, and is the basis employed in the regulation made under s. 20 of the Consumer Credit Act. Unlike the nominal annual rate, it produces a true comparison between rates of interest charged under contracts of different length and/or different payment frequency. [**493**]

The use of formulae

There is no mathematical formula by which the one true rate can be deduced from a stated amount of interest if the loan is repayable by more than three instalments; and for any loan other than a single-repayment loan the formula for the computation is extremely complex. Where more than three instalments are involved, the rate cannot be extracted by formula with complete precision since the equation that has to be set up contains an unknown quantity which makes the equation insoluble unless the rate desired to be ascertained is known in advance. An approximation can be obtained by eliminating the component from the formula on the basis that its quantity is so small as to make no significant difference to the result. But this is true only where the term of the contract is relatively short, and even then only up to a certain level of interest. Where these two conditions do not prevail, a completely true rate can be produced only by trial and error, by assuming a given rate as an approximation and then, if this is found to produce a figure above or below the actual amount of interest, adjusting the selected rate by a series of approximations so as to come ever closer to the right result. This can be done without undue difficulty by computer to any required degree of accuracy. [**494**]

For an explanation of the formulae used in the regulations, see para. [**529**].

[**495**]

Rate computation in revolving credit

It will be obvious that in the case of revolving credit (or running-account credit, as it is termed in the Consumer Credit Act) a true rate in the sense predicated above cannot be stated in advance, since the actual rate of interest paid by the borrower depends on the manner in which he chooses to use the credit facility. A good illustration, in relation to a budget account, will be found in paragraph 6.5.20 of the Crowther Report:

> "Thus, in the case of an account on which charges are fixed on the balance carried forward from the end of the previous account period, it is theoretically open to the customer to secure one month's credit at no charge at all by making all his purchases on the first day of each account period and paying off his indebtedness on the last day of that period. On the other hand, if such a customer were to make his purchases on the last day of the account period, he would incur the full credit charge for that period without having enjoyed any credit at all. It follows from this that the actual cost of borrowing as a rate per cent cannot be stated for revolving accounts as it can for non-revolving instalment credit; and that the statement of a range of rates, from maximum to minimum, will not assist either, since the range will be from infinity to zero—a statement which would not be particularly helpful to the consumer." [**496**]

The regulations under s. 20 adopt the solution advocated in paragraph 6.5.21 of the Crowther Report, namely to require the creditor to state in advance the basis of calculation of the credit charge (e.g. 1 per cent. per month on the balance outstanding at the end of the month) and the effective annual equivalent of the quoted period rate, on the basis of annual compounding. In other words, instead of computing the actual rate in fact paid by the customer after he has utilised the credit facility, one takes the period rate which is used as the basis of calculation of the charge and converts this into a true annual rate compounded annually, as described in paragraphs [**489**]–[**493**]. See further para. [**530**]. [**497**]

Rebates for early settlement

Section 95 of the Consumer Credit Act empowers regulations to be made providing for a debtor to be given a rebate of charges in the event of early settlement. No regulations have yet been made but they are expected in the near future. If rebates are to be calculated on a strict mathematical basis (ignoring policy questions such as whether the creditor should be given an allowance for the initial non-recurrent costs of setting up the transaction), then in computing how much of the charge remains unearned at the date of settlement it is logical to adopt the actuarial spread of charges in making the calculation. In other words, the distribution of interest for the purpose of calculating the actuarial rate also tells us what amount of interest remains unaccrued at any given point in the contract. The question of rebates is discussed fully in Chapter 20. [**498**]

The significance of the total charge for credit

We can now return to the Consumer Credit Act. Section 20 of the Act provides for regulations to be made by the Secretary of State for determining the true cost to the debtor of the credit provided or to be provided under an actual or prospective consumer credit agreement ("the total charge for credit"), and such regulations are required to prescribe:

    (*a*) what items are to be treated as entering into the total charge for credit and how their amount is to be ascertained; and

    (*b*) the method of calculating the rate of the total charge for credit. [**499**]

Determination of the total charge for credit is crucial to the working of the transactional provisions of the Act, embodied in Parts V–IX, and is relevant to many other provisions, including those contained in Part IV and relating to the seeking of business. It is because of the complexity of the problems governing the computation of the cost of credit (and particularly that part which relates to *rate* disclosure) that the implementation of the Act as a whole is proceeding at such a slow pace. The total charge for credit is relevant for (*inter alia*) the following purposes:

   (i) to determine the amount of the credit, this being material in ascertaining whether—

    (*a*) the credit is within the £5,000 ceiling;

    (*b*) the agreement is a small agreement;

    (*c*) art. 2 (3) (*a*) of the Consumer Credit Act 1974 (Commencement No. 2) Order 1977 applies (see para. [**351**]).

  (ii) to establish the effective annual percentage rate, this being material in ascertaining:

    (*a*) whether the agreement is exempt under s. 16 (5) (*b*) of the Act by virtue of art. 3 (1) (*c*) of the Consumer Credit (Exempt Agreements) Order 1977 (see para. [**322**], *ante*);

    (*b*) the rate to be quoted in advertisements, quotations and agreements, as and when regulations to such documents come into existence;

    (*c*) the amount remaining payable by the debtor under s. 69 (2) of the Act)

    (*d*) the application of ss. 69 and 70 of the Act;

    (*e*) the rebate to be allowed to the debtor for early settlement, as and when rebate regulations are made;

    (*f*) the amount to be stated in a statement of account sent, or in a settlement figure quoted, to the debtor;

    (*g*) whether the credit bargain is extortionate for the purpose of ss. 137–140;

    (*h*) what sums payable to a credit-broker otherwise than as a fee or commission are to be treated as a fee or commission under s. 155 (4). [**500**]

Regulations and tables

Regulations under s. 20 have now been made, in the form of the Consumer Credit (Total Charge for Credit) Regulations 1977. These came into operation on 1st April 1977 but will not exert their full influence until the advertising and documentation regulations have become effective, which is not likely to be before 1980. Thus the s. 20 regulations do not yet operate in relation to disclosure of the total charge for credit in advertisments or contract documents; and when, as a result of separate regulations covering the seeking of business and formalities of contract, rate disclosure does become mandatory it is likely that certain tolerances will be permitted that would not be appropriate in relation to delineation of the boundaries of transactional control (see para. [**506**]). [**501**]

Pending further regulations, the Consumer Credit (Total Charge for Credit) Regulations are relevant only to items (i) and (ii) (*a*), (*g*) and (*h*) of those listed in para. [**500**]. [**502**]

Concurrently with the regulations, rate tables have been published by HM Stationery Office for the Office of Fair Trading. These have statutory force by virtue of reg. 11 and are examined in paras. [**535**] *et seq.* [**503**]

Rate computation—general points

The ascertainment of the total charge for credit and the expression of the charge as a percentage rate raise various problems with which the regulations have had to deal, in particular:

(i) what items are to enter into the total charge for credit;

(ii) what account, if any, should be taken of the possibility of events occurring after the date of the contract which would result in the quoted rate ceasing to be the actual rate—e.g. variation of the rate of charge (whether automatic or on notice), early settlement, late payment, extension of the contract period, exercise by the debtor of a right of termination;

(iii) to what extent account should be taken of tax relief that might be available to the debtor in respect of interest or charges payable;

(iv) the method of treating items of charge which depend on factors not known or capable of quantification at the time of the agreement—e.g. charges geared to the frequency of use of a facility, such as maintenance charges, bank charges for drawing cheques pursuant to an overdraft arrangement, and the like;

(v) the mathematical basis of the computation. [**504**]

The regulations (which follow broadly the lines of Appendices I and II to the White Paper *Reform of the Law on Consumer Credit* (Cmnd. 4596, March 1971) but with significant deviations) deal with these matters:

(i) by specifying the types of charge which are to enter into or are to be excluded from the total charge for credit;

(ii) by setting out a series of assumptions on which a calculation is to be based, e.g. the assumption that the contractual provisions as to time of payment will be adhered to;

(iii) by providing formulae for the computation designed to provide the effective annual rate of charge, calculated actuarially on the basis of annual compounding. [**505**]

In fixing the boundaries of transactional control it is obviously necessary to be precise. The parties must be able to determine whether an agreement is within the Act or outside it. Hence for this purpose the rate must be calculated to one decimal point (reg. 7) strictly in accordance with the relevant formula or rate table, for to allow a tolerance or "spread" would be to permit a situation where an agreement could at one and the same time be regarded as within the Act and outside it, according to which end of the tolerance scale was adopted. On the other hand, it does not follow that this precision is necessary for statements of percentage rates in advertisements and contract documents; and almost certainly regulations providing for rate disclosure will allow a limited tolerance within which a statement of a rate will be treated as accurate, even though not providing the precise rate that would be extracted from a strict application of the relevant formula or rate table. [506]

The notional basis of the calculation

The key point to be borne in mind is that the regulations are based on what the consumer credit agreement stipulates is to happen and what, in default of such stipulation, the regulations deem to happen, not what in fact happens. The regulations thus involve the application of only two classes of factor:

    (i) the date and provisions of the consumer credit agreement,

    (ii) notional factors derived from applying one or more of the assumptions prescribed by the regulations.

Apart from the making and contents of the consumer credit agreement itself *the regulations are not concerned with actual events*. Thus the date on which the credit is in fact provided is irrelevant, as is the date on which repayments are in fact made. Other post-contract events, e.g. late delivery of goods supplied on credit, early settlement or other premature termination, default by the debtor, are all immaterial to the calculations. Hence application of the regulations is not designed to show what amount or rate of charge will in fact be paid by the debtor (for this would require a knowledge of post-contract events), but is intended to indicate the amount and rate of charge as seen at the date of the agreement, which of course must inevitably be the material date for the purpose of ascertaining whether or not the agreement is a regulated agreement and for the purpose of rate disclosure in the agreement itself. [507]

The calculation date

In considering the material date by reference to which calculations have to be made, a distinction must be drawn between computation of the *amount* of the total charge for credit and computation of the *time* at which the credit is to be treated as provided or at which the credit or total charge for credit is to be treated as repaid. The latter is, of course, relevant only to calculation of the *rate* of charge, not to the calculation of its amount. [508]

    (i) *The amount of the total charge for credit*

        The total charge for credit (i.e. the amount of the charge) may, as previously noted, comprise various factors—the finance charge itself, insurance premiums, installation and maintenance charges, and the like. As regards some of these items, the amount may be known at the time of the agreement, as regards others the amount may at that stage be unquantified.

In all cases, the date as at which the calculation of the amount of the charge must be made is the date of making of the agreement (reg. 3). Hence this is the material date for determining whether the amount of an item in the total charge for credit is known or unknown. If it is then known, it is counted. If it is unknown but falls within one of the assumptions prescribed by the regulations, the amount ascertained by application of that assumption must be taken and added to the known amounts. For example, an index-linked charge must be treated as fixed by reference to the level of the index at the time of the agreement (reg. 14). Where the amount of an item is not known at the date of making of the agreement and is not covered by one of the assumptions set out in the regulations the annual rate becomes incapable of calculation, with the result that the low-rate exemption (para. [**322**], *ante*) cannot be claimed. When regulations come to be made as to disclosure of the cost of credit in advertisements, quotations and contract documents, these will obviously have to make provision for components of the credit charge not known at the time the agreement is entered into, in so far as these are not covered by one of the specified assumptions. [**509**]

(ii) *Time at which credit is deemed to be provided*

The regulations had to be drawn so as to allow for the fact that whereas under some agreements (e.g. the typical hire-purchase agreement) the credit or advance is extended at the date of the agreement, in other cases (e.g. many loan agreements) the agreement may provide for the advance to be made at a later date. The date on which the credit is deemed to be provided is termed "the relevant date" (reg. 1 (2)). This refers to the date "on which the debtor is entitled to require provision of anything the subject of the agreement", which in the case of goods supplied on credit presumably means the date on which the debtor is entitled to delivery of the goods and in the case of a loan or other advance denotes the date on which he is entitled to receive or draw it. Where a date is specified in or determinable under the agreement at the date of its making as that on which the debtor is entitled to require provision of anything the subject of the agreement, the earliest such date is the relevant date. Thus if the debtor is given an overdraft facility, the relevant date is the earliest date at which he can draw on the account. This links up with reg. 2 (2) (*a*), by which, subject to regs. 2 (2) (*b*) and 19 each provision of credit is to be taken to be made at the earliest time provided under the transaction or, if it is to be made at not later than a specified time, at that time. In short, if the option is with the debtor to take the credit on or after a certain date, that date is the date on which the credit is deemed to be provided; if the option is with the creditor to provide the credit on or before a specified date, the date so specified is the deemed date of provision of the credit. If, in either case, the date is not so specified or determinable, the relevant date means the date of making of the agreement. This in turn links up with reg. 18. [**510**]

(iii) *The credit period*

The credit period, that is the period for which the debtor is entitled to enjoy the credit before repayment, commences with the relevant date (for this is the date on which the credit is deemed to be provided as described in (ii)) and ends on expiry of the contractual period of credit or, if this is not ascertainable at the date of making of the agreement, at the end of one year beginning with the relevant date (see definition of "credit period," reg. 1 (2)). This links up with reg. 17. [**511**]

(iv) *Time at which credit or credit charge deemed to be repaid*
    The deemed time of repayment of the credit or total charge for credit follows the same rules as those applicable to the deeemed time of provision of the credit, as described in (ii), above. Reference should again be made to the definition of "the relevant date" and to reg. 2 (2) (*a*). Rather curiously, the latter concludes by saying that where any such repayment is to be made before the relevant date, it is to be taken as made on the relevant date. It is hard to see how a credit can be deemed to be repayable before the date on which it is deemed to have been provided! What appears to be contemplated is an arrangement under which the debtor makes payments after the date of the agreement but before receiving benefits under it, as where he books a holiday with a travel firm and pays part of the cost after the agreement but before commencement of the holiday. Whatever this part of reg. 2 (2) (*a*) may mean, it is linked to and qualified by reg. 19, which provides that where it may reasonably be expected that a debtor will not make payment of a charge on the relevant date, it is to be assumed that the charge will be payable on the earliest date at which it may reasonably be expected that he will make payment. This notion of reasonable expectation seems singularly unfortunate in view of the precise calculation required by the regulations, since there could be differing reasonable views as to the expected payment date, which clearly lacks any degree of certainty, and even if the difference is only a few days it could affect the calculation and, at the boundary of the limits of transactional control under art. 3 (1) (*c*) of the Consumer Credit (Exempt Agreements) Order 1977, could occasion serious doubts as to whether the agreement in question is or is not an exempt agreement. [**512**]

Total charge for credit
    Regulation 3 of the Consumer Credit (Total Charge for Credit) Regulations 1977 provides as follows:

> "For the purposes of the Act the total charge for the credit which may be provided under an actual or prospective agreement shall be the total of the amounts determined as at the date of the making of the agreement of such of the charges specified in reg. 4 as apply in relation to the agreement but, subject to reg. 6, excluding the amount of the charges specified in reg. 5." [**513**]

    Thus the starting point is reg. 4, which defines the items included in the total charge for credit; but an item that would otherwise fall under reg. 4 is excluded if it is within reg. 5 except to the extent that it is caught by reg. 6. Through a drafting slip the regulations define "agreement" as a "consumer credit agreement", that is, an agreement for credit not exceeding £5,000 (Consumer Credit Act 1974, s. 8 (2)), whereas part of the purpose of the regulations themselves is to establish the amount of the total charge for credit and therefore of the credit. The regulations should have defined "agreement" as a *personal* credit agreement. It would seem that in order not to deprive the regulations of their intended effect it is necessary in the first instance to postulate that the agreement *may* be within the £5,000 ceiling (i.e. is a "prospective" agreement) so as to apply the regulations for the purpose of determining whether the agreement is in fact within the ceiling. [**514**]

Items included in total charge for credit

Except as provided in regs. 5 and 6, the amounts of the following charges are included in the total charge for credit in relation to an agreement—

(*a*) the total of the interest on the credit which may be provided under the agreement, and

(*b*) other charges at any time payable under the transaction by or on behalf of the debtor or a relative of his whether to the creditor or any other person,

notwithstanding that the whole or part of the charge may be repayable at any time or that the consideration therefor may include matters not within the transaction or subsisting at a time not within the duration of the agreement (reg. 4). [**515**]

Limb (*a*) of the definition is confined to interest in the strict sense, that is, a charge for credit where there is an immediate indebtedness, even though repayable in the future—e.g. interest on a loan, or on a purchase price already contracted, as opposed, for example, to a finance charge payable under a hire-purchase agreement. The latter would be covered by limb (*b*). [**516**]

Limb (*b*) is not confined to charges for the credit payable to the creditor under the credit agreement itself but (subject to regs. 5 and 6) extends to all charges payable under the "transaction", whether payable by or on behalf of the debtor himself or a relative of his and whether to the creditor or any other person. "Transaction", except in reg. 5 (1) (*c*), means an agreement, any transaction which is a linked transaction by virtue of s. 19 (1) (*a*) of the Act, any contract for the provision of security relating to the agreement and any other contract to which the debtor or a relative of his is a party and which the creditor requires to be made or maintained as a condition of the making of the agreement (reg. 1 (2)). Thus in principle, and subject to regs. 5 and 6, the total charge for credit will encompass the following:

(i) Sums payable to the creditor under the credit agreement which are not payable for use of the financial accommodation as such but are merely designed to reimburse to the creditor expenses he incurs in connection with the transaction, e.g. survey fees, legal fees, stamp duties.

(ii) Sums payable, whether to the creditor himself or to a third party, under a transaction separate from the credit agreement, being a transaction entered into by the debtor or a relative of his and required by the credit agreement to be entered into or maintained as a condition of making of the credit agreement. Into this category (subject to regs. 5 and 6) would fall sums payable to the creditor or a third party under contracts for the installation, maintenance or insurance of the property or the goods the subject of the credit agreement, whether those contracts are entered into in compliance with the credit agreement or existed at the time when the credit agreement was made and are continued in compliance with it.

(iii) Charges payable under any contract entered into by the debtor or a relative of his for the provision of security relating to the credit agreement—e.g. survey or valuation fees or legal costs payable under a charge on property given by the debtor's father as collateral security.

On the other hand, brokerage fees payable by a prospective debtor to a credit broker for negotiating an advance would not (unless made payable by the credit agreement itself) appear to enter into the total charge for credit, since entry into the credit brokerage agreement is not a requirement of the credit agreement but precedes it, and the only classes of linked transaction within the definition of "transaction" in reg. 1 (2) are those falling within s. 19 (1) (*a*) of the Act. Thus a linked transaction within s. 19 (1) (*c*)—the category into which a brokerage contract falls—is outside reg. 1 (2). The result is that credit brokerage fees are not within the terms of reg. 4; and even if that regulation was wide enough to cover them they would in any event have been within the category specifically excluded by reg. 5 (1) (*d*) (see para. [**520**], below). [**517**]

For further explanation, see the booklet issued by the Department of Prices and Consumer Protection, *Counting the cost of credit* and the separate booklet issued by the Office of Fair Trading, *The Total Charge for Credit*. [**518**]

An item within reg. 4 (*a*) or (*b*) has to be included in the total charge for credit even if the whole or part of the charge may be repayable at any time or the consideration for it may include matters not within the transaction or subsisting at a time not within the duration of the agreement (reg. 4). Thus an insurance premium payable on a policy which, in addition to covering a house the subject of the credit agreement, also covers the contents and which will continue to cover the insured property after discharge of the credit must nevertheless be brought into the computation. [**519**]

Items excluded from total charge for credit

By reg. 5 (1) the amounts of various items are not included in the total charge for credit. It is only necessary to look at reg. 5 (1) as regards a charge which would otherwise fall within reg. 4 (*vide ante*). If a charge is in any event outside the scope of reg. 4 (e.g. where it is a sum payable under a maintenance or insurance contract which the debtor enters into solely from choice), reliance on reg. 5 is unnecessary. Regulation 5 (1) excludes the following:

(*a*) *Charges payable to the creditor on default by the debtor or his relative*
        The total charge for credit does not include a charge payable under the transaction to the creditor upon failure by the debtor or a relative of his to do or to refrain from doing anything which he is required to do or to refrain from doing, as the case may be.

(*b*) *Charges payable by the creditor upon default by the debtor or his relative and recoverable from the debtor or relative*
        Where, as the result of default by the debtor, the creditor incurs charges for which the credit agreement, or any other agreement forming part of the transaction, entitled him to reimbursement from the debtor or a relative of the debtor, these do not enter into the total charge for credit. Thus if as the result of the debtor's failure to repair or to insure the subject matter of the agreement the creditor pays the premium or cost of repairs and then claims recoupment for his outlay under the terms of the credit agreement, the amount involved does not feature in the total charge for credit (but in the case of insurance, the premium originally payable by the debtor under the insurance policy will, of course, form part of the total charge for credit under limb (*b*) of reg. 4 if

the insurance was a term of the credit agreement, unless excluded by one of the heads of exclusion mentioned below).

(c) *Charges payable even if the transaction were for cash*

If the charge is one which would be payable even on a cash transaction, it is excluded from the total charge for credit. For example, installation charges imposed on a debtor under a credit agreement that would also have been charged to a cash purchaser will be excluded. Where a cash buyer would have had to pay a charge but of a lower cost than that chargeable to a debtor under a consumer credit agreement, then presumably the excess payable by the debtor enters into the total charge for credit.

Needless to say, this head of exclusion does not apply to charges on refinancing within s. 11 (1) (c) since these are obviously not applicable to those paying cash.

(d) *Charges for incidental services or benefits*

Paragraph (d) of reg. 5 (1) excludes any charge not within (c)—

(i) of a description which relates to services or benefits incidental to the agreement and also to other services or benefits which may be supplied to the debtor, and

(ii) which is payable pursuant to an obligation incurred by the debtor under arrangements effected before he applies to enter into the agreement, not being arrangements under which the debtor is bound to enter into any personal credit agreement.

This exclusion—the wording of which is decidedly imprecise—embraces, *inter alia*, (A) fees payable to credit brokers under arrangements made before application to enter into the consumer credit agreement (such fees would in any event appear to be outside the scope of reg. 4, for the reasons indicated in para. [**517**]; (B) an insurance premium payable under a policy taken out before the debtor's application for credit and covering not only the subject matter of the consumer credit agreement but other items (see also (f), below).

(e) *Certain maintenance charges*

Paragraph (e) excludes charges under arrangements for the care, maintenance or protection of any land or goods, but this exclusion is subject to reg. 5 (2), which prescribes it in two categories of case. The first is where, in pursuance of the arrangements, the services are to be performed if, after the date of the making of the agreement, the condition of the land or goods becomes or is in immediate danger of becoming such that the land or goods cannot reasonably be enjoyed or used, and the charge will not accrue unless the services are performed (reg. 5 (2) (a)). For example, the hirer of goods under a hire-purchase agreement undertakes as a term of the agreement to maintain the goods in good working order, and enters into a separate maintenance contract for that purpose with the owner or a third party. Provided that charges accrue only as and when servicing or repairs are carried out, they will be excluded by reg. 5 (2) (a) from the total charge for credit. The position is otherwise where the maintenance contract provides for a fixed or periodic charge payable irrespective of whether repairs in fact prove to be necessary or of the time when servicing is in fact carried out. In such a case, the exclusion under reg. 5 (2) (*a*) does not operate, and it is necessary to consider the second category of exclusion, provided by reg. 5 (2) (*b*). This applies also to premiums payable under contracts of insurance referred to in reg. 5 (1) (*g*) and is attracted where the three conditions listed in reg. 5 (2) (*b*) are fulfilled. These are considered in (*g*), *post*.

(*f*) *Premiums under pre-application insurance contracts*

If, before applying to enter into the consumer credit agreement, the debtor makes a contract of insurance and becomes liable to pay a premium under that contract before the date of making of the consumer credit agreement, the premium is excluded from the total charge for credit. For example, suppose that the debtor enters into a hire-purchase agreement to acquire a dish-washing machine which by the terms of the agreement is required to be kept insured, and there was already in force, before the debtor had applied to enter into the agreement, an insurance policy covering the contents of his house which would automatically extend to the item in question. The premium payable under such a policy would be excluded under this paragraph if payable before the debtor's application for credit (and if payable after that date would be exempt under para. (*d*), above).

(*g*) *Other maintenance charges and insurance premiums*

Regulation 5 (1) (*g*) provides that, subject to reg. 5 (2) (*b*), the total charge for credit is not to include "a premium under a contract of insurance other than a contract of insurance where the policy monies are, under the transaction, to be used for the repayment of the credit or of the total charge for credit." Hence provided the three conditions specified in reg. 5 (2) (*b*) are satisfied (as to which see *post*), a premium payable under an insurance policy covering goods let on hire-purchase and taken out pursuant to a requirement of the hire-purchase agreement does not form part of the total charge for credit. But the exemption does not apply to premiums payable under a policy by which the balance outstanding under the credit agreement is to be settled in the event of the debtor's death or by which payments are to be maintained during the debtor's absence from work through illness, for in both these cases the proceeds of the policy are to be used for repayment of the credit, wholly or in part. For the same reason premiums payable under an endowment policy assigned to the creditor to secure an advance under a non-exempt endowment mortgage transaction are not within the exemption. In this particular case the regulations produce a very odd effect, for as has been pointed out by Mr. John Patrick, secretary of the Consumer Credit Trade Association, they require the whole of the premium to be brought into account despite the fact that part of this is to provide the sum by which the credit is to be repaid, so that the total charge for credit becomes the same as the amount of credit repayable. The matter has been under consideration by the Department of Prices and Consumer protection, and an appropriate amendment is to be made to the regulations. [**520**]

Regulation 5 (2) (*b*) sets out three conditions for the exemption of insurance premiums under reg. 5 (1) (*g*) and of maintenance, etc., charges under reg. 5 (1) (*e*). The exemptions are given—

    (i) where provision of substantially the same description as that to which the arrangements or contract of insurance relate is available under comparable arrangements from a person who is not the creditor or a supplier or a credit-broker who introduced the debtor and the creditor; and

    (ii) where the arrangements or contract of insurance are made with a person chosen by the debtor; and

    (iii) if, in accordance with the transaction, the consent of the creditor or of a supplier or of the credit-broker who introduced the debtor and the creditor is required for the making of the arrangements or contract of insurance, where the transaction provides that such consent may not be unreasonably withheld whether because no incidental benefit will or may accrue to the creditor or to the supplier or to the credit-broker or on any other ground.

References in reg. 5 (2) to the creditor, a supplier and a credit-broker include references to his near relative, his partner and a member of a group of which he is a member and various other categories mentioned at the end of reg. 5 (2), in which "near relative" and "group" are also defined. [**521**]

The effect of the regulation is that so long as the choice of insurer or provider of maintenance or protection services is made by the debtor, then even if the debtor enters into an insurance or maintenance contract with the creditor, etc., himself, the charges payable will be excluded if comparable insurance or maintenance arrangements are available from another source and the creditor, etc., could not, under the terms of the transaction, reasonably withhold his consent to the debtor's selection of that other source. The meaning of the phrase "comparable arrangements" is not clear. Suppose, for example, that provision of similar description is available from an independent source but at substantially greater (or lower) cost or utilising a materially different procedure or documentation. Does this prevent the arrangement from being comparable? It is unfortunate that the regulations offer no guidance as to the meaning of this phrase. It is clear, however, that if there is not alternative source of supply at all (e.g. where a television supplier imposing maintenance charges is the only person who keeps a stock of spare parts) then this head of exemption cannot apply. The wording of sub-para. (*b*) (iii) is not entirely happy. In the first place, it is odd to speak of a provision being made by a "transaction"; this presumably means a provision of any agreement forming part of the transaction as defined in reg. 5 (2). Secondly, it is not clear whether the agreement in question must expressly declare that want of benefit to the creditor, etc., if the debtor makes insurance or maintenance arrangements elsewhere is not to be deemed a good reason for withholding consent. It would seem necessary for the agreement to spell this out, for withholding of consent on such a ground would not *per se* seem unreasonable as a matter of law, though in relation to the given facts of a particular case it might well be taken to be unreasonable in that case. [**522**]

Apportionment of certain life insurance premiums

Where a credit protection life policy covers two or more agreements and as regards one of them the premium would otherwise form part of the total charge for credit, the premium is to be apportioned in the proportion which the amount of credit under that agreement bears to the sum of the credit under all such agreements, and only the apportioned part is included in the total charge for credit of the agreement in question (reg. 6). [523]

Rate of total charge for credit

Both the total charge for credit and its expression as a percentage rate are relevant for the purpose of the Act and Regulations; but until the making of advertisements and documentation regulations the main function of the rate calculation is to determine whichever the low-rate exemption given by art. 3 (1) (c) of the Consumer Credit (Exempt Agreements) Order 1977 applies. The Office of Fair Trading has published a useful booklet on this question, *Exemptions for certain low-cost Credit*. [524]

The mode of expressing the total charge for credit as an annual percentage rate is prescribed by Part III of the Consumer Credit (Total Charge for Credit) Regulations 1977. In general the rate is to be taken as that derived from the application of the relevant formula given in Part III; but where the agreement is one to which an entry in a table contained in the official rate tables *exactly* applies (see further paras. [535] *et seq., post*), the applicable rate set out in that table is to be taken to be the rate determined in accordance with the regulations (reg. 11). Hence in the unlikely event of a conflict between the rate produced by formula and the relevant entry in a rate table, the latter prevails, even if it is erroneous. (This possibility is not entirely fanciful. Some entries were already the subject of correction slips when the tables were published.) This means that a creditor who relies on the erroneous entry is safe. Conversely a creditor applying the formula correctly and thus producing a result different from the erroneous entry will be in difficulty. It is to be hoped that when the advertisement and documentation regulations are made, a creditor making the correct calculation instead of using the erroneous entry will not be penalised! Both the formulae and the tables are designed to give the effective annual percentage rate, that is, the actuarial rate on the footing of annual compounding. [525]

For an explanation, see paras. [489]–[493], *ante*. The calculation is to one decimal place, further decimal places being disregarded (reg. 7). Hence for the purpose of the Act and regulations, both a rate of 20·10% and a rate of 20·19% are to be taken as 20·1%. The effect is that the rate expressed in conformity with the regulations may fall below the precise rate by up to 0·09%. [526]

The rate formulae

The formulae in the regulations, though differently expressed, are the same as those produced in the White Paper except that the short-cut formula given in the White Paper for fixed-sum credit agreements payable by equal instalments has been abandoned. The Department did consider, but ultimately rejected, a refinement which became jokingly known as the "Bonkers" formula, after its proponent Mr. Dick Bonker of the United States. The mathematics involved in the derivation of an effective annual interest rate in an instalment payment transaction are complex, involving the solution of a polynomial equation, that is, an equation with several terms, and further examination of the problem showed that the equation set up could have several roots satisfying the formula, some of which might be negative! Hence reg. 10 (4) provides that where the equation set up in this way gives more than one rate per annum, the rate to be taken is the positive rate nearest to zero or, if there is no positive rate, the negative rate nearest to zero. [**527**]

Regulation 10 sets out the calculations applicable to any agreement. The regulation does not embody a formula for a true rate but is simply an equation which will be satisfied if the stated rate is correct. The equation, though expressed in somewhat different form, is the same as that given in paras. 9.4 (i) and 11.4 (i) of the White Paper. As to the meaning of "the relevant date" referred to in the regulations, see para. [**510**], *ante*. [**528**]

The White Paper, in paras. 9.4 (ii) and 11.4 (ii), had given, for fixed-sum credit where the instalments were of equal size and were to be repaid at equal intervals over a period not exceeding 48 months, a short-cut formula which was at that time believed to give an approximation of the effective rate to the required degree of accuracy. Subsequent examination showed that the formula did not hold good outside a given range of factors, and it does not feature at all in the regulations. Accordingly to find the effective annual rate it is necessary either to use tables (as to the official tables, see paras. [**535**] *et seq.*) or a computer or one of the more sophisticated desk or pocket calculators or to establish manually, by trial and error with a series of approximations, the rate satisfying the equation given by reg. 10.
[**529**]

There is, however, no problem where there is a constant period rate of charge in respect of periods of equal length. In such a case the period rate is converted to the effective annual rate by using the formula given in reg. 8 (1). This corresponds to the formula in paras. 9.4 (iv) and (v) and 11.4 (iv) and (v) of the White Paper.
[**530**]

Equally there is no difficulty where, in an agreement for fixed-sum credit provided in a single lump sum, repayment is to be made at the end of a specified period in a lump sum. In such a case the effective annual rate can be found by using the formula in reg. 9, corresponding to that given in paras. 9.4 (iii) and 11.4 (iii) of the White Paper. [**531**]

Assumptions

The general rule, as previously stated, is that the total charge for credit and the rate of such charge are computed in the light of information available at the date of the agreement. Where matters relevant to the calculation are not known at the time of the agreement, the appropriate assumption provided by Part IV of the regulations must be applied. Part IV sets out six categories of assumption.

(i) *Assumption about index-linked rates and amounts*

Where the rate or amount of any item included in the total charge for credit, or the amount of repayment of any credit, is linked to an index or other factor, it is to be assumed that the level of the index or factor is that prevailing on the date on which the agreement is made (reg. 14). For example, if an agreement for a loan or overdraft provides that interest is to be payable on the debit balance from time to time outstanding calculated from day to day at the rate of 2% above prevailing Finance House base rate, then although the rate of interest actually charged will fluctuate as Finance House base rate goes up or down, for the purpose of calculating the total

171

charge for credit and rate of charge it will be taken as that prevailing at the
date of the agreement.

(ii) *Assumption about changes in charges*

Where the period over which the credit or any part of it to be provided
cannot be ascertained at the date of making of the agreement and the rate or
amount of any item included in the total charge for credit will change at a
stipulated time within one year beginning with the relevant date (as to
"relevant date" see para. [510], *ante*), the rate or amount is to be taken as the
highest rate or amount at any time obtaining under the transaction in that
year (reg. 15). It should be observed that this assumption applies only
where the rate or event of charge *will* change within a year of the relevant
date, not where it *may* change; and it only applies where the duration of the
credit is not known at the date of the agreement, for if it were known at that
date then, of course, the creditor would have enough information to calculate
the rate in the ordinary way and the assumption would be unnecessary.

An example of the operation of this assumption is where, under an
agreement of indefinite duration or for a loan repayable after expiry of a
stated period of notice, the annual rate of interest is expressed to be 10% for
the first six months and thereafter 18%. In determining whether the
agreement is exempt, the rate must be taken as 18%.

(iii) *Assumption about amount of credit*

Where the amount of credit which may be provided under the agreement
cannot be ascertained at the date of making of the agreement, that amount
is to be taken as £100 (reg. 16). This assumption, taken with those in (*d*) and
(*e*), below, is particularly apt for the bank overdraft. Suppose, for example,
that a bank agrees to let its customer have an overdraft facility of £500, this
to be reviewed annually. At the time of the agreement it will not be known
how much the customer will draw, nor when he will withdraw it; nor will
there be a known date for repayment, for the credit is a revolving credit and
payments to the creditor of the account go to restore the amount of the
facility that was reduced by earlier drawings. Assuming the contractual
rate to be 4% above the base rate of the bank in question, the effective rate
is obtained by taking 4% over base rate at the time of the agreement (reg.
14) and treating that as a rate applied to a loan of £100 (reg. 16) for one year
(reg. 17, *ante*), made at the time of the agreement (reg. 18, *post*).

(iv) *Assumption about period over which credit is provided*

Where the period for which credit is to be provided is not ascertainable
at the date of making of the agreement, it is to be assumed that credit is
provided for one year beginning with the relevant date (reg. 17).

(v) *Assumption about time of provision of credit*

Where the earliest date on which credit is to be provided cannot be
ascertained at the date of making of the agreement, it is to be assumed that
the credit is provided on that date. This assumption is particularly useful,
for it means that what is relevant is either the contractual date for provision
of the credit, if specified or otherwise ascertainable, or the date of the
agreement, if not so specified or ascertainable, so that the actual date on
which the credit is provided is irrelevant. Had the actual date been the

reference point, great problems would have arisen, e.g. if goods to be supplied on hire-purchase were delivered late, thus falsifying the calculation in the agreement. The assumption in reg. 18 demonstrates the essential point that all factors are viewed as at the date of the contract and in the light of its provisions, and not by reference to the events which in fact occur after the agreement and otherwise than as provided in it.

(vi) *Assumption about time of payment of charges*
Regulation 19 provides that in the case of any transaction it is to be assumed—
(*a*) that a charge payable at a time which cannot be ascertained at the date of the making of the agreement is to be payable on the relevant date or, where it may reasonably be expected that a debtor will not make payment on that date, on the earliest date on which it may reasonably be expected that he will make payment; or
(*b*) where more than one payment of a charge of the same description falls to be made at times which cannot be ascertained at the date of the making of the agreement, that the first such payment will be payable on the relevant date (or, where it may reasonably be expected that a debtor will not make payment on that date, at the earliest date on which it may reasonably be expected that he will make payment), that the last such payment will be payable at the end of the credit period and that all other such payments (if any) will be payable at equal times between such times;
as the case may require.

The reference to the date upon which payment may reasonably be expected introduces a most unwelcome element of uncertainty into an otherwise fairly precise set of temporal reference points in the regulations.
[532]
Certain other assumptions are provided by reg. 2.

(*a*) *Debtor not entitled to tax relief*
Though advertisements for credit frequently indicate the effective rate payable after tax relief on tax at the standard rate, the factual possibility of such relief must be ignored in the computation of the total charge for credit and rate of charge, which is thus to be calculated on the gross rate. It is, however, intended to amend the regulation so as to allow life insurance premiums payable under deduction of tax to be computed net of tax instead of being grossed up.

(*b*) *Agreement will run its full course*
Where the agreement provides for payment not later than a specified time or times but reserves to the creditor the right to call for payment earlier in stated events (as where a loan is repayable after 2 years with interest payable quarterly, and the creditor is allowed to call in the whole loan on demand if there is default in payment on interest), the assumption is to be made that the creditor will not exercise such right.

(*c*) *Creditor will not exercise right to vary charge*
Where the creditor is given the right to vary the amount or rate of charge upon the occurrence of an event which may occur (as opposed to an

event which *must* occur), it is to be assumed that the event will not occur.
In other words, unless the event in question is bound to occur the creditor's
right to vary the charge must be ignored. This links up with reg. 14 (see
para. [**532**] (*a*), *ante*), the only difference being that whereas the latter is
concerned with *automatic* variation through indexation, reg. 2 (1) (*c*) is
concerned with the creditor's right to vary, e.g. on notice. If the stipulated
event is bound to occur at a specified time, there is no need for any
assumption, for the actual rate can then be calculated. If the event is bound
to occur but the time of occurrence is not known in advance when the
agreement is made, the assumption in reg. 19 comes into play (see para. [**532**]
(vi), *ante*); and if, in addition, the period over which the credit is to be
provided cannot be ascertained at the date of making of the agreement, the
assumption in reg. 17 also becomes operative (see para. [**532**] (iv), *ante*).

(*d*) *Credit will be provided and repaid at earliest time*
    Subject to reg. 19, and to the special rules for running account credit (see
(*e*) *below*), each provision of credit and each repayment of the credit and of
the total charge for credit is to be taken to be made—
    (i) at the earliest time provided under the transaction,
    (ii) in a case where any such provision or repayment is to be made at or
        not later than the specified time, at that time.
and, where any such repayment is to be made before the relevant date, it is
to be made on the relevant date. At first sight, (i) and (ii) appear to be
mutually inconsistent, with no clear indication as to when one applies
instead of the other. But as pointed out earlier in relation to the time of
provision of credit (para. [**510**]) the answer would appear to depend on
whether, under the terms of the agreement, the choice as to the exact time of
provision or repayment of the credit lies with the creditor or the debtor. In
relation to the deemed time of provision of the credit, (i) will apply where the
choice lies with the debtor (as in the case of an overdraft or a budget account
facility, where the credit will be deemed to be provided at the time the
facility is opened) and (ii) will apply where it is the creditor who has the right
to determine on what day on or before the specified time the credit is to be
provided. In relation to the deemed time of repayment, the rule works in
reverse, (i) applying where it is the creditor who has the option of calling up
payment and (ii) operating where it is the debtor who has the right to defer
payment until the specified time.

(*e*) *Running-account credit with constant period rate*
    By reg. 2 (2) (*b*) where under an agreement for running-account credit a
constant period rate of charge in respect of periods of equal or of nearly
equal length is charged, it is to be assumed for the purpose of calculations
under the regulations that—
    (i) the amount of credit outstanding at the beginning of a period is to
        remain outstanding throughout the period;
    (ii) the amount of any credit provided during a period is provided
        immediately after the end of the period; and
    (iii) any repayment of credit or of the total charge for credit made during
        a period is made immediately after the end of the period.
The effect of this useful series of assumptions is that the credit charge is

calculated as if applied to the debit balance outstanding at the beginning of the credit period (as defined in reg. 1 (2)), drawings and repayments made during that period being ignored. The time at which or the balance to which the credit is in fact applied is irrelevant, as is the time at which the debtor chooses to make drawings or purchases and repayments. The consequence of this assumption is thus to apply a notional system of operating the account, and this leaves the creditor free to use any method he wishes in applying his period rate, so long as the rate is a constant rate in respect of periods of equal or nearly equal length. For an illustration, see para. [541], case 5.

The simplicity of this rule from the viewpoint of the creditor is inevitably purchased at the cost of some impairment in the effectiveness of the quoted rate as a basis for comparison. A creditor who at the end of the month applies a charge of 2 per cent. to the closing balance carried forward from the end of the preceding month, taking no account of repayments made during the month of billing, will quote exactly the same rate (i.e. 26·8%) as the creditor who, in calculating a charge at the above rate, takes account of repayments made during the month. Plainly the credit facility in the second case is potentially significantly cheaper than in the first, but as repayments to be made during a billing cycle are ignored, both are shown as involving the same rate of charge. The consumer is left to work out for himself the implications of the difference in the two charging methods.

(f) Deduction of housing subsidy

The interest payable by a borrower is to be treated as reduced by the amount of any subsidy received by him under the option mortgage scheme established by Part II of the Housing Subsidies Act 1967; and the amount of rate of total charge for credit must be calculated accordingly. [533]

Computation of time

Regulation 12 contains various rules for the computation of time. Thus a period which is to be counted in calendar months is to be taken as of a length equal to the relevant number of twelfth parts in a year (reg. 12 (5) (*a*)), i.e. where the computation is in calendar months all calendar months are treated as of equal length; a day is treated as one three hundred and sixty-fifth part of a year (reg. 12 (6)), i.e. the extra quarter of a day which might otherwise be included so as to average the increase through a leap year is ignored; and a period which is not a whole number of calendar months or a whole number of weeks is to be counted in years and days (reg. 12 (2)). [534]

Rate tables

HM Stationery Office has published for the Office of Fair Trading a set of "Consumer credit tables" in fifteen Parts which enable the user to calculate the rate of total charge for credit in conformity with the Act and the Consumer Credit (Total Charge for Credit) Regulations 1977. These have statutory force by virtue of reg. 11 (see para. [525]) and comprise the following:

> Part 1—charge per pound lent: equal weekly instalments up to one year
> Part 2—charge per pound lent: equal weekly instalments one to two years

Part 3—charge per pound lent: equal weekly instalments two years and over
Part 4—charge per pound lent: equal monthly instalments up to three years
Part 5—charge per pound lent: equal monthly instalments three years and over
Part 6—charge per pound lent: equal quarterly instalments
Part 7—charge per pound lent: equal half-yearly and yearly instalments
Part 8—charge per pound lent: single repayment up to 33 weeks/10 months
Part 9—charge per pound lent: single repayment six months and over
Part 10—charge per pound lent: annual percentage rates of 100% and over
Part 11—flat rate: equal weekly instalments
Part 12—flat rate: equal monthly instalments
Part 13—flat rate: equal quarterly, half-yearly and yearly instalments
Part 14—flat rate: single repayment
Part 15—period rate on balance outstanding: weekly, monthly, four-weekly, quarterly and half-yearly periods.

It will be seen that the tables are of three kinds:

(i)   those which convert a charge per pound lent into an effective annual rate (Parts 1–10);
(ii) those which convert a flat rate into an effective annual rate (Parts 11–14);
(iii) that which converts a period rate into an effective annual rate (Part 15).

Tables in categories (i) and (ii) presuppose a contract under which a single advance of credit is to be made and repayment is to be made by equal instalments at equal intervals commencing one interval after the advance of the credit. If any of these factors is missing these tables cannot be used. Thus if a hire-purchase agreement specifies a number of equal instalments but provides that with the last instalment a small additional sum shall be paid by way of an option fee the tables cannot be used because the instalments are no longer equal. [**535**]

The charge per pound lent is, quite simply, the credit charge or interest divided by the amount of the credit of principal, expressed in the formula $\frac{C}{P}$ and stated as a decimal fraction. Thus, if a hire-purchase agreement provides for a cash price of £1,800, a down-payment of £600 and charges of £365, C is £365, P is £1,200, and the charge per pound lent is $\frac{365}{1200} = 0.3042$. Use of the charge per pound lent tables requires, first, a knowledge of the periodicity of the payments and the duration of the agreement and secondly an entry in the relevant table which is *precisely* 0.3042. Assume that the above agreement provides for payment by monthly instalments. Then the requisite set of tables is Part 4 (which covers monthly instalments up to three years), and in the section headed 23–32 months we have to run down one of the vertical columns headed 24 until we reach the fraction 0.3042. This will be found on p. 40 of Part 4 of the tables and running from the figure 0.3042 to the extreme right of the table shows an annual rate of 30.5%. [**536**]

Suppose that the charges, instead of being £365, had been £360. Then the decimal would have been $\dfrac{360}{1200} = 0\cdot3000$, and as Table 4 does not contain an entry 0·3000 for a 24-month contract the table cannot be used, even though there are entries near that figure, i.e. on one side 0·2994 and on the other 0·3004. All we say, looking at table 4, is that the annual rate is either 30·0% or 30·1%. Hence we must instead turn to a table of flat rates (see *infra*] to see whether there is a precise corresponding entry there. A charge per pound lent can be converted to a flat rate by multiplying by 100 and dividing by the number of years of the agreement, that number being taken as the total number of payment periods divided by the number of payment periods in a year. The formula for the conversion to a flat rate thus becomes $\dfrac{C}{P} \times \dfrac{100n}{t}$ where n = the number of payment periods in a year and t the number of payment periods in the contract. Applying this conversion formula to the charge per pound lent in our revised example, we find that the flat rate is

$$\dfrac{360}{1200} \times \dfrac{100 \times 12}{24} = 15\cdot00\%.$$ We can check this by looking in the table of flat rates in Part 12 at p. 11. As it happens, there is an entry for the precise flat rate of 15·00%, and under the column headed 24 months it gives an effective rate of 30·00%. [**537**]

This shows just how misleading a flat rate quotation can be, for in the example given the effective rate is exactly double the flat rate. As the length of the contract increases the effective rate, after initially moving further from the flat rate, gradually falls back towards it. For example, a flat rate of 10% produces an effective rate of 16% on a three-month contract, rising to 19·7% at 16 months, after which it remains constant at 19·7% until 27 months, when it falls back to 19·6%. At 249 months it is 14·9%. (After 1,000 million years, the effective rate would be virtually the same as the flat rate!). As with the charge per pound lent tables, use of the flat rate tables requires, first, a knowledge of the periodicity of the payments and the duration of the agreement and secondly an entry in the flat rate table *precisely* corresponding to the flat rate. The tables are constructed to give the flat rates at intervals of 0·25%. Hence if the flat rate is not either a whole number or an exact multiple of 0·25% the flat rate tables cannot be used. For example, Creditor grants Debtor a loan of £500 repayable with £225 interest by 36 monthly instalments of £20·14. The flat rate is $\dfrac{225}{500} \times \dfrac{100 \times 12}{36} = 15\cdot00\%$. We turn to Part 12 of the tables (flat rate—equal monthly instalments) and in the section headed 29–41 months we run down the vertical left-hand column headed "Annual flat rate %" until we reach the figure 15·00. This will be found on p. 15 of Part 12 of the tables. From the figure 15·00 run horizontally to the right until reaching the column headed 36. The entry shows an effective annual rate of 29·3%.

Suppose that the interest, instead of being £225, had been £220. The flat rate would then have been $\dfrac{220}{500} \times \dfrac{100 \times 12}{36} = 14\cdot67\%$, a flat rate figure for which no entry is given in the table. The table could thus not be used for the calculation. All we can say is that the answer lies between 28·3% and 28·8%. The flat rate can be converted to the charge per pound lent by dividing by £100 and multiplying by the number of years in the agreement, that number being calculated in the manner previously described. The formula for conversion from a flat rate to a charge per

pound lent thus becomes $\dfrac{F}{100} \times \dfrac{t}{n}$ where F = the flat rate, t = the total number of

payment periods in the contract and n the number of payment periods in a year. Applying this conversion formula to the above example, we find that the flat rate

of 14·67% becomes a charge per pound lent of $\dfrac{14\cdot67}{100} \times \dfrac{36}{12} = 0\cdot4401$. We can

check this approximately by turning to the table of charges per pound lent, Part 4 where in the section 33–42 months we look for an entry 0·4401 under a column headed 36. There is no entry for this figure, though the table on p. 54 indicates that the annual rate must be either 28·6% or 28·7%. The table therefore cannot be used. The calculation must be made by machine or manually by trial and error. The answer is 28·6%. [**538**]

The *period rate* is the rate per payment period; and provided that the period rate is the same for each period of the contract and that the periods are of equal length this can be converted into the effective annual rate by use of Part 15 of the tables. Where a payment period is monthly, all months are taken as of equal length (see Consumer Credit (Total Charge for Credit) Regulations 1977, reg. 12). As explained earlier in this chapter (paras. [**488**] *et seq.*) the effective annual rate is not obtained simply by multiplying the period rate by the number of payment periods in a year, for it is necessary to introduce a compounding element in order to equate the rate of interest paid by a borrower paying annually with that of a borrower paying the period rate per period. The entries in Part 15 embody this compounding formula. The instructions in Part 15, following reg. 8 (1) of the Consumer Credit (Total Charge for Credit) Regulations 1977, set out the three types of agreement for which the tables in Part 15 are suitable, given a constant period rate and payment periods of equal length. The reasons why the tables are only suitable for these three types of agreement is that where the credit charge is not payable on the debit balance outstanding but is included in instalments of equal amount combining principal and charges, there is no formula by which the precise period rate can be extracted where the number of instalments exceeds three; and the formula for the period rate where repayment is to be made by more than a single payment is too complex to be practicable for everyday use (see para. [**494**]). [**539**]

Given the rate for a stated period, the annual percentage rate can readily be found in Part 15 of the tables by turning to the table for the period in question (1 week, 1 month, or as the case may be) and running down one of the columns headed "Period rate %" until the contractual period rate is reached. The annual percentage rate is the figure immediately to the right of it in the column headed "Annual % rate of charge". Thus a rate of ·0437 a week produces an effective annual rate of 25·4% (see the table on p. 7 of Part 15, right-hand pair of columns; and a rate of 2% per month gives an annual rate of 26·8%. If the period rate does not precisely match an entry in the tables then the tables cannot be used, and it is necessary to calculate the annual rate some other way, e.g. by calculator. For example, suppose the period rate is 1·026% a month. Page 10 of the tables in Part 15 gives an entry of 1·024% a month, equal to 13% a year and an entry of 1·032% a month, equal to 13·1% a year. We cannot tell from the table whether 1·026% a month would produce an annual rate of 13·0% or an annual rate of 13·1%, and the answer could be crucial in deciding whether the agreement was exempt under art. 3 (1) (c) of the Consumer Credit (Exempt Agreements) Order 1977, since for the purpose of this order the calculation must be precise, that is, to one decimal place, ignoring remainders. Accordingly the table cannot be used. Use of a calculator shows that a period rate of 1·026% a month produces an effective annual rate of 13·03%, which to one decimal place without remainder is 13·0%. The agreement is thus exempt if fulfilling the other conditions of art. 3 (1) (c). [**540**]

Illustrations of credit charge computation, using prescribed assumptions

A few illustrations which gather together the prescribed ingredients of the total charge for credit, prescribed assumptions and calculation of the annual percentage rate will now be given.

Case 1—Hire-purchase
O lets a lorry on hire-purchase to H. The cash price is £1,500, the deposit £500 and the balance of the cash price, with charges of £200, is payable by 24 equal monthly instalments commencing one month after the date of the agreement. The charge per pound lent is 0·2000, for which no entry is given in the charge per pound lent tables covering a period of 24 months, so that these tables cannot be used. The flat rate is $\frac{200}{1000} \times \frac{100}{2} = 10\%$, for which there is an entry in the flat rate tables on p. 11 of Part 12 showing an annual rate of 19·7%.

Case 2—Hire-purchase
The facts are as in Case 1 except that the hirer also has to pay, with the final instalment, £2 for exercise of the option to purchase. This makes the instalments unequal, with the result that none of the published tables can be used and the annual rate must be worked out by formula as indicated in Appendix 4 to *Counting the cost of credit*.

Case 3—Hire-purchase
The facts are as in Case 1 except that in addition to the finance charge there is an item of £150 representing the insurance premium for insurance of the lorry. If the insurance company was not chosen by the debtor or comparable arrangements for the provision of insurance are not available from someone other than O or a credit-broker or supplier or if O's consent to H's selection of his own insurer is necessary and there is no provision that this cannot be unreasonably withheld, the insurance premium forms part of the total charge for credit (see reg. 5 (2)), the total charge for credit thus amounts to £350 and the charge per pound lent is 0·3500, for which no entry exists in the charge per pound lent tables. These therefore cannot be used. The flat

rate is $\dfrac{350}{1000} \times \dfrac{100}{2} = 17 \cdot 5\%$, for which there is an entry in the flat rate

tables on p. 12 of Part 12, showing an annual rate of 35·3%.

Case 4—Loan
By an agreement made on 3rd January 1977, L agrees to grant B a cash loan of £1000 on 1st February 1977 at interest of 2% above Excelsior Bank base rate for the time being, payable quarterly in arrear, the loan being repayable on one month's notice. For the purpose of the regulations, the interest rate throughout is to be taken as 2% over Excelsior Bank rate ruling on 3rd January 1977, the date of the agreement (reg. 14) and it is further to be assumed that the loan will be repaid on 2nd January 1978, that is, one year from the contractual date of advance (reg. 17 and 1 (2)) and that L will not exercise his right to call in the loan earlier on notice (reg. 2 (1) (*b*) (ii)). If Excelsior Bank base rate on 3rd January 1977 was 11·5%, the annual percentage rate will be 13·5%, regardless of any fluctuations that may in fact occur in that bank's base rate during the currency of the loan. The agreement will be exempt under art. 3 (1) (*c*) of the Consumer Credit (Exempt Agreements) Order 1977 provided that the latest Bank of England minimum lending rate in operation on 6th December 1976 (i.e. 28 days before the making of the agreement) was not less than 12·5%.

Case 5—Option Account
A department store offers its customers an option account by which, instead of paying for their purchases within the time provided by their monthly statement, they can obtain credit up to a specified multiple of the amount of the monthly payment agreed with the store, a credit charge being imposed of 2% a month calculated on the debit balance carried forward from the end of the preceding month. The annual percentage rate extracted from p. 11 of Part 15 of the tables is 26·8%. The manner in which the customer chooses to use the facility—that is, the actual timing of purchases and repayments— is irrelevant, since the assumption is that purchases and repayments made during a period are made immediately after the end of that period (reg. 2 (2) (*b*)) and thus do not affect the percentage rate applied to the debit balance existing at the beginning of the period. [**541**]

14. The Formalities of Agreement

Introduction

Part V of the Act (which is inapplicable in the cases mentioned in s. 74—see para. [196]) deals with four principal matters in the following order:

(a) Pre-contract disclosure.

(b) Withdrawal from a prospective regulated agreement, and the consequences of such withdrawal on that and linked transactions.

(c) The formalities for entry into a regulated agreement.

(d) Cancellation by the debtor or hirer of a cancellable regulated agreement, and the consequences of cancellation on that and linked transactions.

Since (b) and (d) are closely related, they are dealt with in Chapter 15. The present chapter discusses the provisions of the Act relating to pre-contract disclosure and formal requirements for regulated agreements, and outlines the intended content of regulations which will fill in the detail of some of the statutory provisions and the consequences of non-compliance by the creditor or owner. [**542**]

Pre-contract disclosure

Regulations may require specified information to be disclosed in the prescribed manner to the debtor or hirer before a regulated agreement is made (s. 55 (1)). Thus, in a hire-purchase or instalment sale transaction, regulations may require advance disclosure of the cash price. Failure to comply with the regulations means that the regulated agreement is not properly executed (s. 55 (2)) and is thus enforceable only on an order of the court (s. 65 (1)). No regulations have yet been made under s. 55. [**543**]

Form and content of agreements

The provisions of the Act relating to the form and content of agreements broadly follow the pattern that was laid down in the Hire-Purchase Act 1965. The duty is imposed on the Secretary of State to make regulations as to the form and content of documents embodying regulated agreements (s. 60 (1)); and the Act itself prescribes the procedure for execution of regulated agreements and for the supply of copies of contract documents to the debtor or hirer. The regulations to

181

be made by the Secretary of State must contain such provisions as appear to him appropriate with a view to ensuring that the debtor or hirer is made aware of—
  (*a*) the rights and duties conferred or imposed on him by the agreement,
  (*b*) the amount and rate of the total charge for credit (in the case of a consumer credit agreement),
  (*c*) the protection and remedies available to him under the Act, and
  (*d*) any other matters which, in the opinion of the Secretary of State, it is desirable for him to know about in connection with the agreement (s. 60 (1)).
Such regulations may in particular—
  (*a*) require specified information to be included in the prescribed manner in documents, and other specified material to be excluded;
  (*b*) contain requirements to ensure that specified information is clearly brought to the attention of the debtor or hirer, and that one part of a document is not given insufficient or excessive prominence compared with another (s. 60 (2)).
However, a welcome flexibility is introduced into the Act—as recommended by the Crowther Report—by a provision that if, on an application made to the Director by a person carrying on a consumer credit business or consumer hire business, it appears to the Director impracticable for the applicant to comply with any requirement of regulations under s. 60 (1) in a particular case, he may, by notice to the applicant, waive or vary the requirement in relation to such agreements, and subject to such conditions (if any), as he may specify, and the Act and regulations shall have effect accordingly (s. 60 (3)). Thus, if a prospective creditor binds himself to grant a line of credit and charges a commitment fee, the Director might consider that this was a suitable case for waiving the requirement of disclosure of a rate of charge, since this is impossible to calculate until it is known how much credit will be utilised by the debtor. But a notice under s. 60 (3) may be given by the Director only if he is satisfied that to do so would not prejudice the interests of debtors or hirers (s. 60 (4)). The projected content of the regulations was indicated in some detail in Appendix II of the White Paper but the regulations have not yet been made. [**544**]

Documentation of the agreement

Section 61 of the Act lays down what has to be done in order for a regulated agreement to be properly executed. Compliance with these provisions is important because a regulated agreement that is not properly executed cannot be enforced except on an order of the court (s. 65 (1)); and for this purpose a retaking of goods or land to which a regulated agreement relates is an enforcement of the agreement (s. 65 (2)). Further, a security provided in relation to the improperly executed agreement is itself enforceable only if the court has made an order enforcing the agreement (s. 113 (2)), and if the court dismisses an application for such an order except on technical grounds the security is rendered void *ab initio* (ss. 113 (3) (*b*), 106). The rules to be followed by the court when application is made to enforce an agreement which is enforceable only on an order of the court are set out in ss. 127–128, discussed in paragraphs [**930**] *et seq.* [**545**]

For all transactions except land mortgages (which are subject to special provisions discussed in paragraphs [**577**] *et seq.*), the Act requires a regulated agreement to satisfy certain tests in order to qualify as a properly executed agreement:

(*a*) The terms must be embodied in a signed and legible document complying with the requirements of s. 61.

(*b*) A copy of the unexecuted agreement (i.e. of the document before it has crystallised into a contract) must be supplied to the debtor or hirer in accordance with s. 62, unless the unexecuted agreement is presented to the debtor or hirer personally for his signature and on the occasion when he signs the document becomes an executed agreement, in which case compliance with requirement (*c*) suffices.

(*c*) A copy of the executed agreement must be supplied to the debtor or hirer in accordance with s. 63, except where the unexecuted agreement was sent to the debtor or hirer for signature and became an executed agreement upon the occasion of such signature.

(*d*) A notice in prescribed form advising the debtor or hirer of his rights of cancellation must be included in the above copies, and where requirement (*b*) is inapplicable the notice must also be sent by post to the debtor or hirer, in accordance with s. 64.

Each of the above requirements will now be considered in turn. [**546**]

A signed document

Section 61 (1) provides that a regulated agreement is not properly executed unless—

(*a*) a document in the prescribed form itself containing all the prescribed terms and conforming to regulations under s. 60 (1) is signed in the prescribed manner both by the debtor or hirer and by or on behalf of the creditor or owner, and

(*b*) the document embodies all the terms of the agreement, other than implied terms, and

(*c*) the document is, when presented or sent to the debtor or hirer for signature, in such a state that all its terms are readily legible.

Each of these paragraphs contains various ingredients which require separate examination. [**547**]

Paragraph (a)

The first requirement of paragraph (*a*) is that there is a document in the prescribed form, that is, in the form prescribed by regulations. Such regulations will prescribe general legibility requirements similar to those currently contained in the Hire-Purchase (Documents) (Legibility and Statutory Statements) Regulations 1965. They will thus provide for the colouring of the paper used, the size and style of lettering and the prohibition of handwriting except for particulars of parties, goods and finance and any signature and date. The regulations will also prescribe the form and content of statutory notices informing the debtor of certain essential rights, such as the rights of cancellation and termination. In addition, the document must conform to regulations under s. 60 (1). Such regulations (which may either be separate or combined with the legibility, etc., regulations above referred to) will impose detailed disclosure requirements covering a wide range of information varying according to the type of credit agreement. Thus, in a debtor-creditor-supplier agreement details would have to be given of the goods, the cash price, the deposit, any advance payments, the total charge for credit expressed as a percentage rate and other information. Full details will be found in Appendix II of the White Paper. [**548**]

The document, in addition to conforming to the above legibility and information requirements, would have to contain "all the prescribed terms". This is a reference not to terms which the parties would have negotiated between themselves independently of the Act (since these are covered by s. 61 (1) (*b*)) but to contract terms which the creditor or owner will be required by regulations to include for the benefit of the debtor or hirer. The White Paper does not give any indication of what these might be, but merely a reference to "certain provisions" (White Paper, para. 46). [**549**]

Section 61 (1) (*a*) says that the document "itself" must contain all the prescribed terms. This would seem to mean that incorporation by reference to another document containing the prescribed terms is not sufficient. [**550**]

The document must be signed "in the prescribed manner" both by the debtor or hirer and by or on behalf of the creditor or owner. "The prescribed manner" will presumably embrace a prescribed signature block with wording informing the debtor or hirer of the nature of the agreement, as in the present regulations. In the case of a body corporate, it is sufficient if the document is sealed by that body (s. 189 (3)). Whilst the creditor or owner will be permitted to sign by an agent, a debtor or hirer will have to sign personally. The only exception is where the debtor or hirer is a partnership or unincorporated body. In that case it is not necessary for all the partners or members of the body to sign; one can sign on behalf of the others. Indeed there is nothing to prevent a signature on behalf of the partners or unincorporated body by a duly authorised agent who is not himself a partner or member of the body at all. [**551**]

What has to be signed is a document in the prescribed form and containing the prescribed terms and information. Accordingly a document conforming fully to the regulations must be completed before signature. Signature of a document in blank or omitting some of the prescribed details does not suffice, even if these are inserted subsequently (cf., on this point, *Eastern Distributors, Ltd.* v. *Goldring*, [1957] 2 Q.B. 600 [1957] 2 All E.R. 525). [**552**]

Paragraph (*b*)

The document must embody all the terms of the agreement, other than implied terms. Terms may be implied in fact—i.e. by inferences from the conduct of the parties—or in law, as in the case of terms implied under the Sale of Goods Act 1893 and the Supply of Goods (Implied Terms) Act 1973 relating to title to and quality of the goods. Terms of this kind need not be spelled out in the agreement unless they were the subject of express oral agreement between the parties. No time limit is prescribed for reduction of orally agreed terms to writing; and it would appear sufficient if this is done at any time before the creditor or owner has commenced proceedings or has otherwise taken steps to enforce the agreement or any security. [**553**]

Whereas terms prescribed by regulations under paragraph (*a*) must be set out in the contract document itself, the terms required by paragraph (*b*) to be embodied in the document may be so embodied by reference to another document containing those terms. This is the effect of s. 189 (4) which states that a document embodies a provision if the provision is set out either in the document itself or in another document referred to in it. [554]

The requirement that the document should "embody all the terms of the agreement" appears to create, by statute, a further exception to the parol evidence rule, i.e. the rule that extrinsic evidence is not admissible to alter, vary or contradict the terms of a written document. This rule, which is logically indefensible, has in any event been so cut down by exceptions and qualifications that it is now honoured more in the breach than in the observance. If, pursuant to the parol evidence rule, the creditor relying on a written document were to be entitled to shut out evidence from the debtor as to an orally agreed term allegedly omitted from the document, this would largely defeat the purpose of s. 61 (1) (b). [555]

It will, of course, remain a matter of evidence whether an oral statement made by the creditor to the debtor was indeed promissory in nature or whether it was a "mere" representation inducing the contract but not forming a term of it. If the statement, though not a term of the contract to which the subsequent document relates, constituted a collateral promise or warranty, the omission of the collateral term from the document would not appear to contravene s. 61 (1) (b). Thus, if a dealer were to warrant to its customer the quality of a motor car which the customer contemplated acquiring on hire-purchase and the customer were then to conclude a hire-purchase agreement with the finance house through the agency of the dealer, the warranty by the dealer, even though it would represent a promise not only by him but also by the finance house by virtue of s. 56 (2) (see para. [689]) might well be held to be not a term of the hire-purchase agreement itself but a collateral warranty by the finance house and the dealer inducing entry into the hire-purchase agreement. In such a case, omission of the promise from the hire-purchase document would not infringe s. 61 (1) (b). [556]

Paragraph (c)
Paragraph (c), requiring that the terms of the document be readily legible when presented or sent to the debtor or hirer for signature, is self-explanatory. This provision may overlap the general legibility requirements to be imposed by regulations made under s. 61 (1) (a) (see para. [548]). [557]

Supply of copy of unexecuted agreement
Section 62 lays down the duty of the creditor or owner to supply the debtor or hirer with a copy of the unexecuted agreement, that is, the document embodying the terms of a prospective regulated agreement, or such of them as it is intended to reduce to writing (s. 189 (1)). As Mr. Francis Bennion, the draftsman of the Act, has pointed out, the definition of "unexecuted agreement" is defective in that it refers only to the prospective regulated agreement, when it ought also to catch an unsigned document embodying an agreement already concluded, e.g. orally. See Bennion, *Consumer Credit Control*, para. 1 § 3060. In general, of course, as has been noted, the document itself will have to embody *all* the express terms. The requirements of s. 62 vary according to whether the contract document is presented personally to the debtor or hirer for his signature or whether it is sent to him for his signature. If the document is presented for signature but will not become an executed agreement on the occasion of such signature (i.e. where, as will usually be

the case, the agreement is not executed by both parties on the spot but will be signed by the creditor or owner at a later date), the debtor or hirer must there and then have delivered to him a copy of the unexecuted agreement and of any other document referred to in it (s. 62 (1)). It will thereafter be necessary to supply the debtor or hirer with a copy of the executed agreement under s. 63 (see para. [565]). If the document is sent to the debtor or hirer for signature, a copy of the document, and of any other document referred to in it, must be sent at the same time (s. 62 (2)). The documents need not be sent to the debtor or hirer personally. Dispatch to his solicitor or other authorised agent suffices. If, after his signature, the agreement becomes an executed agreement i.e. because the creditor or owner has already signed) no further copy need be sent. [558]

Section 62 appears to have an unfortunate lacuna in that it does not cover the case where a document is presented personally to the debtor for his signature and the debtor then takes it away with him before signing. In such a case it appears impossible to comply with s. 62, for the creditor will not be present when the debtor signs so as to be able to give him a copy immediately after signature, and the delivery of a copy with the unexecuted agreement *prior* to its signature is permitted only where the unexecuted agreement is sent for signature as opposed to being presented personally for signature. [559]

There may be some situations in which the unexecuted agreement is neither presented personally to the debtor nor sent to him. Such is the case, for example, where a form of agreement is included in a brochure available at a display stand or in a newspaper. In such situations, there is no duty to supply a copy of the unexecuted agreement at all. There is only a duty, after the debtor has returned the agreement for acceptance and this has been effected as described in paragraph [565], to supply a copy of the executed agreement within seven days thereafter, under s. 63 (2). [560]

The obligation to supply not only a copy of the contract document but also a copy of any document referred to in it might, if left in this unqualified form, create difficulties. For example, references to the Consumer Credit Act might attract an obligation to supply a copy of the Act, and a reference to an insurance policy might require the creditor to supply a copy of the policy. To avoid cases of difficulty, the Act provides for regulations to be made which may exclude specified classes of document from the supply requirements (s. 180 (3)) and may authorise the omission from a copy of certain material contained in the original, or the inclusion of such material in condensed form (s. 180 (1)). [561]

The copy supplied must be a true copy, though no doubt the court would disregard purely trivial deviations as *de minimis*. The copy must also comply meticulously with the prescribed form and prescribed requirements. If it does not, the duty of supply is not fulfilled (s. 180 (2)). [562]

Failure to comply with any of the above requirements prevents the resulting regulated agreement from being properly executed (s. 62 (3)). [563]

Supply of copy of executed agreement

If the unexecuted agreement is presented personally to the debtor or hirer for his signature, and on the occasion when he signs it the document becomes an executed agreement, a copy of this, and of any other document referred to in it, must be there and then delivered to him (s. 63 (1)). In practice, this situation will be unusual, because the debtor or hirer is almost invariably required to sign first, and in most types of credit transaction the document is not then immediately signed by the creditor or owner but is taken back by his employee, agent or intermediary for consideration or, in the case of a finance house, is sent back to the finance house, either by the debtor or hirer himself or through a dealer or retailer. Hence in the great majority of cases s. 63 (1) will not apply, and the debtor or hirer will be supplied with a copy of the unexecuted agreement under s. 62 (see para. [**558**]) *and* a copy of the agreement itself as subsequently executed, under s. 63 (2) (see para. [**565**]). [**564**]

Where s. 63 (1) does not apply, then unless the document sent to the debtor or hirer for his signature becomes an executed agreement on the occasion of such signature, a copy of the executed agreement, and of any document referred to in it, must be given to the debtor or hirer within the seven days following the making of the agreement (s. 63 (2)). "Give" means deliver or send by post (s. 189 (1)). Again, the document need not be given to the debtor or hirer personally. It suffices if it is given to his solicitor or other authorised agent. If the agreement is a cancellable agreement, the copy *must* be sent by post (s. 63 (3)). Depatch by post within the seven-day period constitutes compliance with s. 63, whether or not the copy reaches the debtor or hirer in the ordinary course of post or at all; but delay or failure of the post will prolong the debtor's right to cancel (see para. [**609**]). An agreement concluded by offer and acceptance is "made", i.e. becomes a contract, when the acceptance becomes effective. This will normally be when it is communicated to the offeror. Where the post is an authorised means of communication, acceptance takes effect from the time of posting. Hence if, for example, a prospective debtor signs a hire-purchase document which is then transmitted to the finance house for its signature, that signature alone will not (unless the document otherwise indicates) give rise to a contract. It is only when the finance house's acceptance of the debtor's offer has been communicated to the debtor that the contract becomes complete, and it is from that time that the seven days for giving of a copy starts to run. It follows that if the only communication of acceptance is by despatch of the copy of the agreement itself, such despatch will be simultaneous with the formation of the contract, and if the copy complies with regulations it will satisfy s. 63 (2). (The time at which a contract comes into existence is further discussed in paras. [**239**]–[**247**]). [**565**]

There are special rules for credit-token agreements. First, a copy of the executed agreement need not be given within the seven days following the making of the agreement if it is given before or at the time when the credit-token is given to the debtor (s. 63 (4)). In other words, the time allowed for giving of the copy of the executed agreement does not expire until seven days after the making of the agreement *or* upon giving of the credit-token to the debtor, whichever is the later.
[**566**]

Secondly, whenever, in connection with a credit-token agreement, a credit-token (other than the first) is given by the creditor to the debtor, the creditor must give the debtor a copy of the executed agreement (if any) and of any other document referred to in it (s. 85 (1)). If the creditor fails to comply with this requirement, then

   (*a*) he is not entitled, while the default continues, to enforce the agreement; and

   (*b*) if the default continues for one month he commits an offence (s. 85 (2)).
[**567**]

Again, non-compliance with the above requirements prevents the regulated agreement from being properly executed (s. 63 (5)). [**568**]

Notice of rights of cancellation
In the case of a cancellable agreement (that is, a regulated agreement which may be cancelled by the debtor or hirer under the cooling off provisions contained in s. 67—see Chapter 15), a notice in the prescribed form advising the debtor or hirer of his right to cancel must be included in every copy of the unexecuted or executed agreement supplied in accordance with ss. 62 or 63, as previously discussed. In addition, where the agreement is presented or sent to the debtor for signature and becomes an executed agreement on the spot, either because the creditor has already signed or because he does so immediately after signature by the debtor, a separate notice in prescribed form of the debtor's right of cancellation must be sent to him by post within seven days (s. 64 (1) (b)). This is subject to dispensation by the Director pursuant to regulations under s. 64 (4). But where the agreement is not concluded on the spot immediately after the debtor's signature, so that s. 63 (2) applies, there is no need to send a separate notice of cancellation rights; the inclusion of the notice in the copy of the agreement required to be sent by post suffices. The object is to ensure that the debtor is supplied with a notice of cancellation rights by post independently of any notice that may be included in a copy of the agreement handed to him when the creditor or his representative is present. Hence the debtor must be provided either with a copy of the executed agreement on the spot followed by a notice of cancellation rights by post or a copy of the executed agreement by post incorporating such notice. [**569**]

Again, there is a relaxation of the rules in relation to credit-token agreements. The seven-day time limit need not be complied with if the notice is sent by post to the debtor or hirer either with the credit-token or before the credit-token is given to the hirer (s. 64 (2)). If there is a failure to comply with the requirements of s. 64, the cancellable agreement is not properly executed (s. 64 (5)). In addition, the time limit for exercise of the right of cancellation may in consequence be indefinitely prolonged (see para. [**609**]). [**570**]

15. Withdrawal and Cancellation

General effect of statutory provisions

The Act contains various provisions as to withdrawal by an intending debtor or hirer from a prospective regulated agreement and as to cancellation by a debtor or hirer of an agreement that has actually been concluded. The purpose of the statutory provisions, as of comparable provisions of the Hire-Purchase Act 1965, is to allow the debtor a period for reflection in circumstances where, the agreement not having been signed at the business premises of the creditor or "other appropriate trade premises", there is a risk that the debtor was subjected to considerable pressure at the point of sale. [**571**]

The debtor is given a right of cancellation in circumstances similar to those provided at present by the Hire-Purchase Act 1965. There are, however, certain extensions and modifications. First, all types of consumer credit and consumer hire agreement are affected other than land mortgages. Previously the cooling off rights were confined to hire-purchase and instalment sale agreements. Secondly, the phrase "appropriate trade premises" has disappeared, though the concept remains. The cooling-off provisions will not apply if the debtor signed the agreement at premises at which a business is carried on by the creditor or owner, any party to a linked transaction (other than the debtor or hirer or a relative of his), or the negotiator. Thirdly, the debtor's right of cancellation is restricted to cases in which oral representations are made in his presence by an individual acting as or on behalf of the negotiator. Thus mail order transactions involving no personal contact with the debtor prior to the agreement will be outside the cooling off provisions. [**572**]

Regulated agreements secured on land (see para. [**577**]) are outside the cooling off provisions. This is not because Parliament did not wish to allow the debtor a period of reflection in such transactions but simply because the Land Registry wanted to avoid a situation in which a land mortgage could be cancelled after registration, thus necessitating administrative work and other difficulties in vacating the entry in the Register. Accordingly the Act, instead of allowing the debtor in a land mortgage transaction a right of cancellation, provides him with a period of reflection by a different machinery. The creditor must not send the credit agreement for signature without first sending the debtor a copy of the agreement at least seven days in advance. After this period has expired without receipt by the creditor of any notice of withdrawal by the debtor, the agreement itself may be sent to the debtor for signature. If he signs and returns the agreement, it thereupon takes effect in the usual way. During the interval between giving of the advance copy and the debtor's return of the signed agreement or the expiry of seven days after sending of the unexecuted agreement, whichever first occurs, the creditor or owner must refrain from approaching the debtor (whether in person, by telephone or letter or any other manner) except in response to a specific request by the debtor made after the advance copy has been delivered or posted to him. If any of these requirements are infringed, the agreement will be improperly executed and will be enforceable only on a court order. The requirements apply wherever the agreement was signed and even if no representations were made. [573]

Withdrawal from a proposed agreement

The right of an intending debtor or hirer to withdraw from a prospective regulated agreement is not conferred by the Act but derives from the common law rule that an unaccepted offer imposes no obligations on the offeree and may be withdrawn by the offeror at any time before acceptance unless the offeror bound himself not to withdraw by a document under seal or alternatively for valuable consideration (see para. [242]). Even in the case of a land mortgage, it is not the Act which gives the prospective mortgagor a right of withdrawal; all that the Act does is to prescribe the manner and deemed time of withdrawal, the consequences of a valid withdrawal on linked transactions (see para. [585]) and the special requirements which have to be fulfilled if the regulated agreement secured by the land mortgage is to be considered properly executed. The sanction for non-compliance with the requirements—namely that the agreement is improperly executed and is thus enforceable only on an order of the court—presupposes that a regulated agreement has come into existence despite, perhaps, some earlier notice of withdrawal by the debtor. Whether an agreement has come into existence has to be determined by application of the general law of contract, including rules as to withdrawal of an offer prior to acceptance. See further paras. [168] *et seq.* [574]

Mode of withdrawal in general

Unless a party has bound himself not to withdraw an offer (by promising under a seal or for valuable consideration to hold the offer open) he can withdraw the offer by notice to the offeree before the offeree's acceptance has been manifested by communication or conduct. In the case of a prospective regulated agreement the Act provides that the giving to a party of a written or oral notice which, however expressed, indicates the intention of the other party to withdraw from the agreement, operates as a withdrawal from it (s. 57 (2)). At common law, withdrawal of an offer is in general ineffective unless communicated to the offeree, and if sent by post takes effect not at the time of posting but at the time of receipt. If before that time there has been a proper acceptance, the withdrawal is too late and the offeror is bound. A provision in the Consumer Credit Bill that the debtor's posted notice of withdrawal should take effect on posting was dropped; and s. 69 (7), which so provides in regard to notices of cancellation, is not made applicable to a notice of withdrawal by s. 57 (1), since that section merely applies the same statutory *consequences* to withdrawal as to cancellation, and does not operate until there has been an effective withdrawal. Hence a posted notice of withdrawal is governed by the common law rule. The debtor or hirer need not necessarily serve the notice of withdrawal on the creditor or owner himself. By s. 57 (3) each of the following is deemed to be the agent of the creditor or owner for the purpose of receiving a notice under subsection (2)—

(*a*) a credit-broker or supplier who is the negotiator in antecedent negotiations, and

(*b*) any person who, in the course of a business carried on by him, acts on behalf of the debtor or hirer in any negotiations for the agreement.

Hence a prospective hirer of a motor car can give notice of intended withdrawal to the finance house which is to let the car on hire-purchase to him or alternatively to the dealer. General provisions as to the mode of service of notices, including notice of withdrawal from a prospective regulated agreement, are contained in s. 176, as to which see para. [**1095**]. [**575**]

Whilst as a matter of general contract law a party may bind himself not to withdraw an offer (as where the owner of land grants an option to purchase under seal or in consideration of payment of an option fee), a prospective debtor or hirer cannot usually bind himself to enter into an agreement that is a regulated agreement within the Consumer Credit Act. This is the effect of s. 59 (1) of the Act, which provides that an agreement is void if, and to the extent that, it purports to bind a person to enter as debtor or hirer into a prospective regulated agreement. However, as there may be transactions where this causes difficulty, power is given to make regulations excluding from s. 59 (1) agreements such as are described in the regulations (s. 59 (2)). [**576**]

Withdrawal from prospective land mortgage

It has previously been mentioned that the right conferred on a debtor or hirer, in given conditions described below, to cancel what would otherwise be a binding regulated agreement does not apply to agreements secured on land (s. 67), since this would cause administrative difficulties for the Land Registry. "Land" includes an interest in land (s. 189 (1)), and the exemption covers all forms of security in land, including rentcharges. However, no new rentcharge can now be validly created (Rentcharges Act 1977, s. 2). Where the agreement is secured on land, then instead of giving the debtor or hirer a post-contract cooling off period, what the Act does is to lay down a procedure designed to ensure that he is granted a minimum period of reflection *before* contract in which he can consider the prospective contract terms without pressure or indeed unsolicited communication of any kind from the prospective mortgagee. The statutory procedure (which will apply wherever the agreement was signed by the debtor—see para. [**573**]) involves compliance with the three primary requirements:

(1) Despatch to the debtor or hirer of an advance copy of the agreement he will later be asked to sign, and of any other document referred to in it (s. 58 (1)).

(2) Despatch to the debtor or hirer of the contract document itself not less than seven days later, for signature by debtor (s. 61 (2) (*b*)).

(3) No unsolicited communication with the debtor or hirer during the consideration period (s. 61 (2) (*c*)), that is, the period beginning with supply of the advance copy and ending seven days after despatch or

delivery of the contract document itself for signature *or* signature and return of the contract document by the debtor or hirer, whichever is the earlier (s. 61 (3)).

Breach of any of these requirements has the consequence that any resulting regulated agreement is not properly executed (s. 61 (2)), and is accordingly enforceable only on an order of the court (s. 65 (1)). Requirements (1) and (3) call for certain observations. There are also two cases, mentioned in s. 58 (2), where this special three-stage procedure does not have to be complied with (see para. [**581**]), though the transactions in question will remain exempt from the cancellation provisions. As to first mortgage transactions, see para. [**584**]. [**577**]

Despatch of the advance copy

The requirement to despatch an advance copy to the prospective debtor or hirer is contained in s. 58 (1), which provides as follows:

> "Before sending to the debtor or hirer, for his signature, an unexecuted agreement in a case where the prospective regulated agreement is to be secured on land (the 'mortgaged land'), the creditor or owner shall give the debtor or hirer a copy of the unexecuted agreement which contains a notice in the prescribed form indicating the right of the debtor or hirer to withdraw from the prospective agreement, and how and when the right is exercisable, together with a copy of any other document referred to in the unexecuted agreement."
>
> [**578**]

Several points arise in relation to s. 58 (1). First, it applies whether the land mortgage is to be given by the debtor himself or by a third party. Secondly, the test of applicability of s. 58 (1) is whether there is a prospective regulated agreement which is to be secured on land. Hence for s. 58 (1) to apply, the projected agreement must be one which, when made, will be regulated by the Act; and the intention must exist, prior to formation of the agreement, to secure it on land. If, up to the time when the regulated agreement is concluded, the transaction is intended to be unsecured, s. 58 (1) will not apply, even though the creditor may ask for and receive security subsequently—a not uncommon event in the case of loan credit. There may sometimes be a factual dispute between the parties as to whether security taken after execution of the regulated agreement was intended to be given all along (in which case s. 58 (1) would apply) or whether it resulted merely from a subsequent desire by the creditor to protect his position. Thirdly, although what has to be supplied to the prospective debtor is an advance copy of the unexecuted agreement (i.e. the *credit* agreement, which is not necessarily the mortgage document) of course the debtor must also be given an advance copy of any other document referred to in the unexecuted agreement. Hence if a finance house proposes to lend money under a loan agreement which requires a mortgage to be executed by way of security, the debtor must be supplied with advance copies of both the loan agreement and the intended mortgage, whether the mortgage is to be given by the debtor himself or by a third party. Since the object of s. 58 (1) is to supply the debtor or hirer with advance details of all the credit terms, it is thought that if a document referred to in the copy of the unexecuted agreement itself incorporates by reference provisions of another document, the two documents should be taken as together constituting the document referred to in the copy of the unexecuted agreement and copies of both such documents should therefore be supplied. Any other conclusion would enable a prospective creditor to frustrate the purpose of s. 58 (1) by including in the unexecuted agreement a reference to the terms of a short document which itself did no more than refer to a third document, and to supply the prospective debtor with merely a copy of the short document, leaving him quite unenlightened as to the precise terms to which that document would commit him. [579]

The advance copy of the unexecuted agreement must contain a notice in prescribed form indicating the right of the debtor or hirer to withdraw from the prospective agreement, and how and when the right is exercisable (s. 58 (1)). The copy must in addition conform to such other requirements as may be prescribed by regulations under s. 180 (1) of the Act. If the copy fails to meet these conditions, the duty to supply the copy is not considered satisfied (s. 180 (2)), with the consequence that any resulting regulated agreement will not be properly executed (s. 61 (2) (a)). The copy need not be served on the debtor personally. Service on an authorised agent, e.g. his solicitor, suffices. [580]

When an advance copy need not be sent

By s. 58 (2), the duty imposed by s. 58 (1) to supply an advance copy of the unexecuted agreement and of any document referred to in it does not apply to—

    (a) a restricted-use credit agreement to finance the purchase of the mortgaged land, or

    (b) an agreement for a bridging loan in connection with the purchase of the mortgaged land or other land.

The reason for these exceptions is that a purchase-money loan which is to be secured on the purchased land may need to be provided very quickly if the transaction is not to fall through, and the delays imposed by the s. 58 (1) procedure could therefore cause difficulties. Case (a) of s. 58 (2) covers the situation where the link between the loan and the purchase can be readily established because the credit agreement is a restricted-use credit agreement, so that by definition the creditor controls the application of the loan to the intended purchase (see para. [274]). Case (b) of s. 58 (2) is inserted to cover the not uncommon position that arises where, for example, a person selling his house and buying another wants temporary accommodation from his bank to tide him over in connection with his purchase pending sale of his existing home. Such temporary loans will not necessarily involve control by the bank of application of the loan monies so as to give rise to a restricted-use credit agreement satisfying case (a) of s. 58 (2). The credit may be provided by overdraft or loan which, though intended for the purchase of the new house, is provided in such a way as to leave the debtor free to utilise it as he chooses (see s. 11 (2) and para. [273]). It is for this reason that case (b) does not import the requirement that the credit agreement shall be a *restricted-use* agreement. But case (b) is restricted to bridging loans, a term which is not defined but denotes a temporary advance to bridge a period of time at the end of which the debtor is to raise the required finance from another source and repay the temporary advance. [581]

The debtor's isolation period

During the consideration period (see para. [573]) the creditor or owner (which includes an actual or deemed agent of the creditor or owner, e.g. a person who is a negotiator within s. 56) must "refrain from approaching the debtor or hirer (whether in person, by telephone or letter, or in any other way) except in response to a specific request made by the debtor or hirer after the beginning of the consideration period" (s. 61 (2) (*c*)). Compliance with this requirement (which does not apply in cases within s. 58 (2)—see para. [**581**]) is not as easy as it might appear, and there are many pitfalls for the unwary.

> *Example 1*
> The advance copy of the proposed credit agreement to be secured on land is sent to the prospective debtor, who writes by return of post to say that he approves the terms. As a matter of office routine, a member of the creditor's staff sends the debtor a printed card acknowledging receipt of his letter and saying that this is receiving attention. The effect is that the credit agreement subsequently signed by the parties is improperly executed.

> *Example 2*
> The prospective debtor consults his solicitor with instructions to act on his behalf in connection with a projected loan from a finance house on the security of a second mortgage of his house. The solicitor writes to the finance house for particulars and is sent details of the transaction, together with a copy of the proposed credit agreement. As the result of a sudden rise in minimum lending rate, the finance house finds it necessary to revise its quotation and writes to the solicitor with the new figures. The resultant credit agreement is improperly executed. The solicitor is the agent of the debtor and communication to him is equivalent to communication to the debtor, in breach of s. 61 (2) (*c*). [**582**]

If a mistake of the kind illustrated in the above examples is discovered in time, there seems no reason why the creditor should not be able to rectify the matter by beginning again and sending the debtor a fresh copy of the unexecuted agreement. This will then become the relevant copy for the purpose of establishing the commencement of the consideration period, and so long as there is no communication with the debtor during this new consideration period (except in response to a specific request made by the debtor after the commencement of that period) all will be well. [**583**]

Most first mortgage transactions exempt

The special procedure described above for agreements secured on land is, of course, confined to *regulated* agreements. It will therefore not apply to the ordinary building society or local authority mortgage, which will be exempt under s. 16 (1) of the Act (see paras. [**312**] *et seq.*). Hence most first mortgage transactions will not be affected by this procedure or indeed by the Act as a whole. The main thrust of ss. 58 (1) and 61 (2) will thus be directed at the second mortgage market. [**584**]

Consequences of withdrawal

Withdrawal of either party from a prospective regulated agreement not only terminates any outstanding offer in relation to the agreement, making this incapable of acceptance, but also operates to cancel any linked transaction (see paras. [**611**]–[**612**]) and to withdraw any offer by the debtor or hirer to enter into a linked transaction (ss. 57 (1), 69 (1)). A linked transaction cancelled in this way is to be treated as if it had never been entered into (s. 69 (4)), so that it is rescinded *ab initio*. However, regulations may be made excluding linked agreements of the prescribed descriptions from the scope of the above provisions (s. 69 (5)). Contracts of insurance, in particular, are likely to be excluded, for obvious reasons, but no regulations have yet been made under s. 69 (5). [**585**]

All the provisions relating to the consequences of cancellation of a regulated agreement—the debtor's right to repayment, the return of part-exchange goods or payment of the part-exchange allowance, and the like—apply with equal force to withdrawal from a prospective regulated agreement (s. 57 (1)), whether or not such agreement, if made, would itself have been cancellable (s. 57 (4)). These provisions are examined in detail in relation to cancellation in the following paragraphs. Whatever may have been stipulated between the parties, the creditor is not entitled to retain any sum paid by the debtor, e.g. as an earnest of good faith designed to secure that the debtor proceeded with the transaction. This applies to sums paid or payable to the creditor to cover pre-contract expenses, even if the expenses have actually been incurred. Thus, if a finance house proposing to advance money on the mortgage of the property incurs survey fees and legal costs before discovering that the property offered is unsuitable, it is not entitled to recover these from the intending borrower, despite any agreement between them, after deciding not to grant the loan, and if the latter has paid he has a right to reimbursement. This, indeed, is the case even where it is the prospective borrower himself who takes the decision to withdraw from the transaction; and the effect of s. 57 (4) is that payments he has made are repayable to him even though, had an agreement been concluded, it would have been exempt from the cancellation provisions as an agreement secured on land. Similarly, parties to linked transactions must return all payments received (for illustrations in relation to cancellation, see para. [**612**]).
[**586**]

However, although s. 57 (1) treats withdrawal from a prospective agreement as equivalent to entry into that agreement followed by cancellation of it under s. 69, this is so only for the purpose of the application of Part V of the Act. Section 57 (1) does not attract any other source of liability that would have arisen had the agreement in fact been concluded, e.g. a liability at common law to repay a pre-contract deposit paid by the debtor to an intermediary and deemed to have been received by the creditor in a balance of account as the result of his entry into the credit agreement (see para. [**99**]).

> *Example*
> H signs an agreement to take a car on hire-purchase from a finance house, F, and pays the requisite deposit to the dealer, D. Before F has signed the hire-purchase agreement, H notifies D that he does not wish to proceed with the transaction. The effect is that H's offer to take the car on hire-purchase from F is withdrawn, and D is liable under s. 70 to repay to H the amount of the downpayment, but no liability is incurred by F, for the duty of repayment that would have fallen on F if the agreement had in fact been made and then cancelled would

195

have been a duty as deemed recipient at common law, not by
virtue of s. 70 (see para. [**613**]). [**587**]

Specific mention needs to be made of the effect of withdrawal on the rights
of a debtor who has been credited with an allowance for goods tendered in part-
exchange. Section 73 (2)—which applies to withdrawal as well as cancellation
by virtue of s. 57 (1)—provides that unless, before the end of the period of 10 days
beginning with the date of cancellation, the part-exchange goods are returned to
him in a condition substantially as good as when they were delivered to the
negotiator, the debtor shall be entitled to recover from the negotiator a sum equal
to the part-exchange allowance as defined, that is, the sum agreed as the part-
exchange allowance or, if no such sum was agreed, such sum as would have
represented a reasonable allowance (s. 73 (7)). The above section—which is not,
it would appear, intended to derogate from the rights of the debtor at common
law—does not confer on the negotiator the option to retain the part-exchange
goods or pay the part-exchange allowance. It merely says that if he fails to return
the part-exchange goods in the stipulated time and condition, he incurs an
obligation to pay the part-exchange allowance. To comply with the time limit
he must return the goods "before the end of the period of 10 days beginning with
the date of cancellation", so that if notice of withdrawal is given on a Monday,
the part-exchange goods must be returned to the debtor on or before Wednesday
of the following week if the obligation to pay the part-exchange allowance is to
be avoided. But even after expiry of the 10-day period, the debtor may be
entitled to insist upon a return of the part-exchange goods *in specie*, and to sue
for damages for detention or conversion if the negotiator fails or refuses to return
them, or for conversion if he has sold them. Whether the debtor has the right to
do this depends on the terms of the part-exchange agreement, and in particular
on whether it was intended that ownership of the part-exchange goods should
pass to the negotiator immediately on delivery or whether (as will usually be the
case) the transfer of property to the negotiator was expressly or impliedly
conditional on the consumer credit agreement coming into operation. For a full
discussion of problems concerning part-exchange reference should be made to the
author's book *Hire Purchase Law and Practice* (2nd edn.) pp. 185–186 and Chapter
14. Other points concerning s. 73 are discussed in paras. [**622**] *et seq.* [**588**]

Cancellation

The right to cancel (*i.e.* rescind) a concluded agreement was first conferred by
the Hire-Purchase Act 1964 and re-enacted in the Hire-Purchase Act 1965. It was
aimed primarily at the doorstep salesman who, taking advantage of the
unsuspecting housewife, would there and then sign her up on the spot to an onerous
agreement for goods she might not be able to afford, frequently inducing her entry
into the agreeement by oral misrepresentations of various kinds, secure in the
knowledge that no-one else was present to overhear him and that the organisation
he represented would rely on the agreement to disclaim any responsibility for his
statements. The Hire-Purchase Act dealt with the matter by providing that any
hirer or buyer signing a hire-purchase or instalment sale agreement within the Act
at a place other than appropriate trade premises (i.e. broadly the premises of a
dealer or finance house) should be entitled to cancel the agreement during a period
of four days commencing with the day of receipt by post of the requisite copy of the
executed agreement. [**589**]

How widely the right of cancellation under the Hire Purchase Act was exercised is not known for certain. The indications are that it was infrequently used and that the value of the statutory provisions lay more in the fact that they *might* be used—thus discouraging certain forms of doorstep selling—than in the actual exercise of the statutory rights. The Act certainly appeared to be effective in warning off some of the more unscrupulous door-to-door sales organisations. [**590**]

The cancellation provisions of the Hire-Purchase Act were at once too wide and too narrow: too wide in that they applied even if there had been no personal contact between creditor and debtor at all, as in the case of many mail order credit sale transactions; too narrow, in that they were confined to hire-purchase and instalment sale agreements and could not be invoked in relation to other forms of credit, such as rental and loan agreements. These deficiencies have been remedied in the Consumer Credit Act. [**591**]

Section 67, which confers the right of cancellation, provides as follows:

> "A regulated agreement may be cancelled by the debtor or hirer in accordance with this Part if the antecedent negotiations included oral representations made when in the presence of the debtor or hirer by an individual acting as, or on behalf of, the negotiator, unless—
>> (a) the agreement is secured on land, or is a restricted-use credit agreement to finance the purchase of land or is an agreement for a bridging loan in connection with the purchase of land, or
>> (b) the unexecuted agreement is signed by the debtor or hirer at premises at which any of the following is carrying on any business (whether on a permanent or temporary basis)—
>>> (i) the creditor or owner;
>>> (ii) any party to a linked transaction (other than the debtor or hirer or a relative of his);
>>> (iii) the negotiator in any antecedent negotiations."

We shall examine, first, the conditions that have to be satisfied in order for the right of cancellation to arise (paras. [**593**] *et seq.*) and secondly, the two exceptions (para. [**602**]). [**592**]

It is only a regulated agreement that can be cancelled under s. 67. Exempt agreements are not cancellable; nor are agreements excluded by s. 74 from Part V of the Act, that is to say:

(a) non-commercial agreements (i.e. those not made by the creditor or owner in the course of a business carried on by him—s. 189 (1));

(b) debtor-creditor overdraft agreements, if so determined by the Director, but only if he is of opinion that such determination is not against the interests of debtors, and subject to conditions specified by him (see, however, para. [**196**] as to banks and licensed deposit-taking institutions);

(c) small debtor-creditor-supplier agreements for restricted-use credit, e.g. check trading and credit sale agreements where the credit does not exceed £30.

Further, a temporary overdraft in excess of the previously agreed limit does not give rise to a separate agreement attracting the cancellation provisions. See paragraphs [**245**], [**264**], [**300**]. [**593**]

Even if the agreement is a regulated agreement and is not excluded from Part V, it will not be a cancellable agreement unless:

(*a*) the antecedent negotiations included oral representations;

(*b*) the oral representations were made in the presence of the debtor or hirer;

(*c*) they were made by an individual acting as, or on behalf of, the negotiator.

The onus of establishing the above facts lies on the debtor or hirer. Even if all these facts are proved, the debtor or hirer will have no right to cancel if the case falls within one of the two exceptions provided by s. 67 itself (see para. [**602**]). The onus of establishing these exceptions however lies on the creditor. [**594**]

The term "antecedent negotiations" is elaborately defined in s. 56 of the Act, which is of sufficient importance to set out in full:

"(1) In this Act 'antecedent negotiations' means any negotiations with the debtor or hirer—

(*a*) conducted by the creditor or owner in relation to the making of any regulated agreement, or

(*b*) conducted by a credit-broker in relation to goods sold or proposed to be sold by the credit-broker to the creditor before forming the subject-matter of a debtor-creditor-supplier agreement within section 12 (*a*), or

(*c*) conducted by the supplier in relation to a transaction financed or proposed to be financed by a debtor-creditor-supplier agreement within section 12 (*b*) or (*c*),

and 'negotiator' means the person by whom negotiations are so conducted with the debtor or hirer.

(2) Negotiations with the debtor in a case falling within subsection 1 (*b*) or (*c*) shall be deemed to be conducted by the negotiator in the capacity of agent of the creditor as well as in his actual capacity.

(3) An agreement is void if, and to the extent that, it purports in relation to an actual or prospective regulated agreement—

(*a*) to provide that a person acting as, or on behalf of, a negotiator is to be treated as the agent of the debtor or hirer, or

(*b*) to relieve a person from liability for acts or omissions of any person acting as, or on behalf of, a negotiator.

(4) For the purposes of this Act, antecedent negotiations shall be taken to begin when the negotiator and the debtor or hirer first enter into communication (including communication by advertisement), and to include any representations made by the negotiator to the debtor or hirer and any other dealings between them." [**595**]

For present purposes we are concerned with s. 56 only so far as it relates to the debtor's right to cancel. As will be seen (para. [**689**]), it has a separate significance in relation to the liability of the creditor for the statements of his deemed agent under s. 56 (2). It will be apparent from s. 56 (4) that all regulated agreements within Part V must inevitably be preceded by antecedent negotiations. It is manifestly impossible for a regulated agreement to come into existence without some prior communication between creditor/owner and debtor/hirer. Hence s. 56

(4) somewhat expands the normal meaning of the word "negotiate". Moreover, since "communication" in s. 56 (4) is expressed to include communication by advertisement, antecedent negotiations will in many cases begin before the creditor is even aware of the debtor's existence! It may be wondered why the draftsman thought it necessary to include advertisements as a form of communication. Section 67 only comes into operation if oral representations are made in the course of antecedent negotiations, and the commencement of an oral representation must inevitably constitute a communication sufficient to start "antecedent negotiations" for the purpose of the Act, even if there had been no prior contact between the parties. The reason why advertisements are included as a communication is that the definition of "antecedent negotiations" is relevant not only to the cancellation provisions of the Act but also to the provisions of s. 56 (3), which render void an agreement purporting to make a negotiator the agent of the debtor or hirer or to relieve any person from liability for the acts of a negotiator. Hence the creditor under a regulated agreement will, for example, be liable for the misrepresentations contained in a poster or advertisement put out on his behalf by the dealer through whom the agreement was concluded and which induced the debtor's entry into the agreement, whether or not any oral representations were made. [**596**]

Though s. 56 (4) tells us when antecedent negotiations are taken to begin, it says nothing about when they are to be deemed to end, a not unimportant point in that oral statements made after the conclusion of negotiations are not within s. 67. It would seem that the terminal point is the entry of the parties (debtor and creditor or hirer and owner) into the regulated agreement. Any statement or dealing between debtor/hirer and negotiations up to that point are a part of the antecedent negotiations, a post-contract statement or dealing is not. [**597**]

Negotiations are "antecedent negotiations" only if conducted by a person within categories (a), (b) or (c) in s. 56 (1). Category (a) covers the creditor or owner (which for this purpose includes a prospective creditor or owner—see s. 189 (1)); and as a matter of agency law negotiations conducted by an agent or employee of the creditor or owner acting in the course of his agency or employment will be treated as conducted by the creditor or owner himself within category (a). A typical example of a creditor within category (a) is a finance company supplying goods under a hire-purchase agreement. Category (b) will typically cover a dealer selling goods to a finance house to be let on hire-purchase or sold on conditional sale or credit sale to the hirer or buyer introduced by the dealer to the finance house. It may be noted in passing that a housewife acting as part-time agent for a mail order house is not a credit-broker (s. 146 (5)), and is thus not a negotiator. But her negotiating acts are as agent for the mail order house as creditor, which will thus itself be the negotiator within s. 56 (1) (a); and the housewife will be acting on behalf of the negotiator within s. 67. Category (c) will embrace a supplier selling goods against a credit card or trading check and a motor dealer selling a car for cash advanced to the buyer by a finance house to whom the buyer was introduced by the dealer. (Note that a hire-purchase agreement contracted between a finance house and the debtor through the medium of the dealer from whom the goods were obtained is within category (a), not category (c), since the finance house is both creditor and legal supplier). Any person within the above categories who conducts negotiations is a negotiator within s. 56 (1), and the negotiations he conducts are antecedent negotiations for the purpose of the cancellation provisions. [**598**]

It will be observed that category (b) of s. 56 (1) does not include a credit broker engaged in negotiations for debtor-creditor credit. The reason is that such a broker is almost invariably the agent of the creditor so as to come within category (*a*) (see para. [**598**]), whereas a person selling goods to a finance house to be let on hire-purchase or sold on instalment sale in not usually considered the agent of the finance house in law but is carrying out the transaction in furtherance of his own business (see *Branwhite* v. *Worcester Works Finance, Ltd.*, [1969] 1 A.C. 552, [1968] 3 All E.R. 104), so that it was necessary to create category (*b*) in s. 56 (1) in order to bring him within the definition of a negotiator and make him a deemed agent under s. 56 (2). [**599**]

Oral representations

Once the activites constituting antecedent negotiations have been established—by demonstrating that negotiations (including communication by advertisement) have been conducted by a person who is a negotiator within s. 56 (1)—we have then to see whether such negotiations included oral representations made when in the presence of the debtor or hirer by an individual acting as, or on behalf of, the negotiator. In the absence of such face-to-face oral representations, the cancellation provisions do not apply. This is one of the respects in which the provisions differ from those of the previous legislation. [**600**]

"Representation" is defined as including any condition or warranty, and any other statement or undertaking, whether oral or in writing (s. 189 (1)). However, the cancellation provisions operate only where the representation is oral, and even then only if made when in the presence of the debtor or hirer. A telephone discussion with the debtor is thus outside s. 67. The words "in the presence of the debtor or hirer" do not require that the representation shall actually have been addressed to the debtor or hirer himself. Remarks made in his presence to a third party—e.g. his wife or a friend—designed to further his entry into the prospective agreement will be within the section. On the other hand, it would seem that the debtor must be present personally. Presence by an agent would not, it is thought, suffice. The object of the statutory provisions is to protect a prospective debtor who is subjected to sales talk in person, not by proxy. The oral representations must be made by an individual, a somewhat superfluous provision, since a body corporate has no physical voice and cannot make statements orally save through an individual. The representor may be the negotiator himself or his agent or employee acting in the course of his agency or employment. The negotiator as such need not, of course, be an individual. [**601**]

Exceptions

Apart from the general exemptions from Part V (see para. [**593**]) section 67 itself lays down two categories of case in which the cooling-off provisions are not to apply, even if all the other requirements of the section are satisfied. The first is where the agreement is secured on land or is a restricted-use credit agreement to finance the purchase of land or is an agreement for a bridging loan in connection with the purchase of land. The onus of establishing that the agreement is within this category lies on the creditor asserting it. Agreements secured on land have been discussed earlier in this chapter. They are governed by the special advance copy procedure described in paragraphs [**578**] *et seq.* Restricted-use agreements to finance the purchase of land and agreements for a bridging loan in connection with the purchase of land are excluded both from the cooling off provisions and from the advance copy requirement. They have been discussed in paragraph [**581**]. The second category of excluded agreement depends not on the character of the agreement but on the place where it is signed by the debtor or hirer. If it is signed at business premises (whether permanent or temporary) of the creditor or owner, any party to a linked transaction (see para. [**612**]) or the negotiator in any antecedent negotiations, the cooling off provisions do not apply. Thus, if a prospective hirer signs a hire-purchase agreement at the premises of the dealer or finance house, he has no statutory right of cancellation. Note, however, that (in contrast to the position under the Hire-Purchase Act 1965) this is so only where signature takes place at the business address of the finance house or dealer concerned in the transaction. Signature at the business premises of some other dealer dealing in goods of a similar description does not suffice. In such a case, the hirer will have a right to cancel, as he will also if he signs the agreement at his home, his own business premises or at the offices of his solicitor. Again, the onus is on the creditor to show that because of the place of signature the cooling-off provisions do not apply; for it is the creditor who is relying on the exception. It is not for the debtor or hirer to prove where he signed the agreement. [**602**]

Mode of cancellation

By s. 69 (1) the right of cancellation is exercised by notice (i.e. notice in writing—s. 189 (1)) served by the debtor or hirer within the prescribed time (see para. [**606**]) on:

    (a) the creditor or owner; or

    (b) the person specified in the notice under s. 64 (1) as the person to whom notice of cancellation may be given; or

    (c) a person who (whether by virtue of s. 69 (6) or otherwise) is the agent of the creditor or owner. [**603**]

"Creditor" means the person providing credit under the consumer credit agreement or his assignee; "owner" means the person who bails goods under the consumer hire agreement or his assignee (s. 189 (1)). Section 69 (6) provides that each of the following shall be deemed to be the agent of the creditor or owner for the purpose of receiving a notice of cancellation—

    (a) a credit broker or supplier who is the negotiator in antecedent negotiations, and

    (b) any person who, in the course of a business carried on by him, acts on behalf of the debtor or hirer in any negotiations for the agreement.

Thus, in a normal hire-purchase or instalment sale transaction with a finance house, the hirer or buyer can serve his notice of cancellation on the finance house or on the dealer. In a check trading transaction, the notice would normally have to be served on the check trader. A supplier would not as a rule fall within s. 69 (6) (a) as a negotiator since in general the initiative for entry into a check trading agreement is taken by the check trader, and the debtor's contact with the various suppliers in connection with the credit does not take place until afterwards. If, however, a particular supplier did in fact act as a negotiator within the definition of s. 56 (1), the debtor would be entitled to serve his notice of cancellation on that supplier. [**604**]

Paragraph (b) of s. 69 (6), by which the debtor's agent is deemed to be the creditor's agent, appears startling at first sight, but is necessary in view of the fact that there are various types of broker (particularly in the insurance world) who, though not in law the agent of the creditor, are often taken to be such by the consumer, who might thus assume that communication to them was equivalent to communication to the other party. The Act gives statutory effect to that assumption for the purpose of service of a notice of cancellation. [605]

Time limit within which notice must be served

The Hire-Purchase Act 1965 allowed a hirer or buyer a period of four days, beginning with the day of receipt of the copy of the executed agreement, within which to exercise a right of cancellation. The Consumer Credit Act effectively extends this by two days in the normal case, but introduces some variations. The time limit is laid down by s. 68. The commencement of the period in which the debtor can cancel is the date of his signature of the unexecuted agreement. The date of expiry of the period depends on whether the agreement is concluded on the spot after the debtor's signature or whether, as is the usual case, it is not concluded until later. [606]

If the agreement is concluded on the spot, the debtor (in addition to being supplied with a copy there and then) must be sent by post within seven days a notice advising him of his right of cancellation. The debtor then has until the end of the fifth day *following* the date of receipt of such notice within which to serve a notice of cancellation. Thus, if the debtor received the s. 64 (1) (b) notice on a Monday, he has until midnight on the ensuing Saturday within which to serve a cancellation notice. If, however, a s. 64 (1) (b) notice is not served on the debtor, because the Director has dispensed with this requirement pursuant to regulations under s. 64 (4) (see para. [569]), then the debtor has until the end of the fourteenth day following the day on which he signed the unexecuted agreement (s. 68 (b)).
[607]

If the agreement is not concluded on the spot after signature by the debtor—e.g. because it then has to be sent or taken for signature by the creditor—the duty of the creditor is to send not a separate notice advising the debtor of his cancellation rights but a copy of the executed agreement incorporating such a notice. The debtor then has until the end of the fifth day following receipt of such copy within which to serve his cancellation notice (s. 68 (a)). [608]

Except where s. 68 (b) applies (as the result of the Director's dispensing with service of a notice under s. 64 (1) (b)), the debtor s period of cancellation is geared to the date of his receipt of the notice under s. 64 (1) (b) or of the copy of the executed agreement, as the case may be. If the notice or copy goes astray in the post and does not reach him, his time for cancellation is indefinitely prolonged. If the creditor discovers the postal failure in time to serve a fresh notice or copy within the permitted seven days from the making of the agreement, he can rectify the situation in this way. If, however, he does not discover it until after the seven-day period has expired, it would seem that he is powerless to start the cancellation period running by service of a fresh notice or copy, since this, being served outside the time laid down by ss. 64 (1) (b) and 63 (2), could not be said to be a notice "under s. 64 (1) (b)" or a copy "under s. 63 (2)", and the receipt of such a notice by the debtor is essential to start time running against him. In such a case, all the creditor could do, if he came to enforce the agreement, would be to hope that the debtor would not exercise his right to cancel. Subject to such right, the agreement is fully enforceable as a properly executed agreement, since service by post is compliance with ss. 63 and 64 whether or not the copy or notice reaches its destination. [**609**]

If the debtor serves his cancellation notice by post, this is deemed to be served at the time of posting (s. 69 (7)), irrespective whether or when the notice arrives. [**610**]

Effect of cancellation

By s. 69 (1) service of a notice of cancellation by the debtor operates:
(i) to cancel the agreement, and any linked transaction; and
(ii) to withdraw any offer by the debtor, or his relative, to enter into a linked transaction.

Subject to s. 71 (see para. [**617**]), an agreement or transaction cancelled as above is to be treated as if it had never been entered into (s. 69 (4)). On cancellation the debtor, except in cases within s. 70 (5) (see para. [**616**]), is released from liability for any payment, whether accrued due or payable in the future, and is entitled to:
(a) repayment of sums paid under or in contemplation of the consumer credit or consumer hire agreement or linked transaction;
(b) recovery of any goods tendered in part exchange or, if not recovered within ten days in substantially the same condition as when delivered, a sum equal to the part-exchange allowance;
(c) a lien on goods received by him under the consumer credit or consumer hire agreement, pending fulfilment of (a) and (b) (ss. 70 (1), (2), 73 (2), (5)).

Further, the effect of cancellation is that any security given is to be treated as never having effect and any property lodged with the creditor or owner solely for the purposes of the security must be returned by him forthwith (s. 106, as applied by s. 113 (3)). For his part, the debtor (except in cases within s. 72 (9)—see para. [**631**]) is obliged to surrender goods received by him under the agreement, and meanwhile to retain possession of the goods and take reasonable care of them (s. 72 (4)). But where the creditor has taken security, these duties cannot be enforced against the debtor until the creditor has complied with his obligations under s. 106 (see para. [**774**]) in relation to the security (s. 113 (5)). A debtor or hirer who has cancelled an agreement pursuant to s. 69 is entitled to apply to the court for a declaration that the agreement was so cancelled (s. 142 (2)). [**611**]

Linked transactions

Linked transactions are defined in s. 19, which is examined in detail in Chapter 27. Suffice it at this stage to give a few illustrations of the types of agreement that will automatically be cancelled as the result of cancellation of the consumer credit or consumer hire agreement.

> *Example 1*
> Pursuant to a provision in a regulated hire-purchase agreement, the hirer insures the goods. Subject to any regulations that may be made under s. 69 (5), cancellation of the hire-purchase agreement automatically rescinds the insurance contract and entitles the hirer to be repaid the premium by the insurer. This is so whether or not there was any arrangement between the insurer and the owner, and indeed even though the insurer was unaware that the insurance was taken out pursuant to a

requirement of the hire-purchase agreement. The same would apply to an associated contract of maintenance entered into pursuant to a provision of the hire-purchase agreement.

Example 2
A car is bought from a motor dealer for cash paid with the aid of an advance from a finance house under a regulated loan agreement, the purchaser having been introduced to the finance house by the dealer pursuant to arrangements between them for the provision of finance for customers of the dealer. The borrower exercises his right to cancel the loan agreement. The cash sale by the dealer to the buyer, being a linked transaction, is thereby rescinded, and the buyer is entitled to recover any payment made to the dealer.

Example 3
The holder of a credit card exercises a right to cancel the credit-token agreement under which the card was issued. Assuming that the agreement is not an exempt agreement (see Chapter 10), all purchases made with the card (otherwise than to meet an emergency) are thereby automatically cancelled and the debtor is entitled to recover his payments from the creditor (i.e. the issuer of the card), except that a payment made for the issue of the card is recoverable only on surrender of the card to the issuer or a supplier (s. 70 (5)).

Section 69 (5) enables regulation to be made preserving linked transactions of the prescribed description from retrospective obliteration under s. 69 (1), (4). This saving was introduced primarily to cover situations where cancellation of a deemed withdrawal from the linked transaction might unfairly affect the debtor, e.g. by retrospectively invalidating insurance taken out on a motor vehicle comprised in a regulated or prospective agreement. For the same reason, the operation of s. 19 (3) (which provides that a linked transaction entered into before the making of the principal agreement has no effect until such time (if any) as the principal agreement is made) may be excluded by regulations (s. 19 (4)). [**612**]

Repayment to and release of the debtor

On cancellation, the debtor is entitled to recover all payments made under or in contemplation of the cancelled agreement or any linked agreement (s. 70 (1)), except that if the total charge for credit includes an item in respect of a fee or commission charged by a credit broker, the amount repayable in respect of that item is the excess over £1 of the fee or commission (s. 70 (6)). Usually, the debtor's claim for repayment must be made against the person to whom he made the payment (s. 70 (3)). But where the credit agreement is a debtor-creditor-supplier agreement and the creditor is not the supplier himself, the creditor and the supplier are jointly and severally liable for the repayment (*ibid.*). Thus, a debtor cancelling a purchase-loan agreement with a finance house concluded through the dealer supplying the goods will be entitled to recover a deposit paid to the dealer either from the dealer or from the finance house or from both together. In such a case, the finance house is entitled (subject to any agreement with the dealer) to be indemnified by the dealer for the loss it suffers in consequence of this liability, including costs reasonably incurred by the finance house in defending the hirer's claim (s. 70 (4)). Such a defence might be made, for example, where the finance house had been misled by the dealer into thinking that the agreement was signed at the dealer's premises and was thus not a cancellable agreement. Where a finance house supplies goods on hire-purchase or instalment sale, the second limb of s. 70 (3) does not apply, since the finance house is both creditor and supplier; but whilst under the first limb a deposit paid to the dealer is recoverable only from the dealer (he being "the person to whom it was originally paid"), there is also a common law right of recovery from the finance house as a deemed recipient in a balance of account (*Branwhite* v. *Worcester Works Finance, Ltd.*, [1969] 1 A.C. 552, [1968] 3 All E.R. 104). [**613**]

In addition to being entitled to repayment of sums paid, the debtor is released from liability for sums (including credit charges) payable under the cancelled agreement or any linked agreement (s. 70 (1) (*b*)). [**614**]

In the case of a debtor-creditor-supplier agreement for restricted-use credit financing the doing of work or supply of goods to meet an emergency or the supply of goods which become incorporated by the debtor into land or other goods prior to the notice of cancellation, the service of such notice retrospectively extinguishes the credit obligations of the debtor under the credit agreement or any linked transaction but leaves him liable to the supplier for the cash price of the goods or services (s. 69 (2), (3)). By an unfortunate omission, agreements for the *hire* of goods to meet an emergency (e.g. the hire of a pump to pump water from a house in a flood) are outside these provisions—which are confined to consumer *credit* agreements (see the definition of "debtor-creditor-supplier agreement" in s. 12) yet have not been excluded from s. 72 (9). The result appears to be that the hirer to whom goods are supplied under a consumer hire agreement for the purpose of meeting an emergency remains free to cancel the agreement under s. 69 and withhold or recover payments but is absolved from the duty to return the goods. This seems unfair and irrational. [**615**]

For the debtor's right to repayment of a sum paid for issue of a credit-token, see para. [**827**]. By virtue of s. 70 (5), the debtor is not released from liability for repayment of a loan made under an unrestricted-use loan agreement which continues under s. 71 (1) and is not repaid under s. 71 (2) (see para. [**617**]). [**616**]

Continuance of unrestricted-use loan agreements

Section 71 of the Act contains provisions which are deliberately designed to discourage a lender from making a cash loan under a cancellable credit agreement before expiry of the period allowed to the debtor for cancellation. The debtor who during the period allowed for cancellation receives a loan is likely to spend it immediately; and if his exercise of the right to cancel were then to involve him in immediate repayment of the loan, with interest, he could be placed in acute financial difficulty. Section 71 (1) accordingly provides that notwithstanding the cancellation of a regulated agreement, other than a debtor-creditor-supplier agreement for restricted-use credit, the agreement shall continue in force so far as it relates to repayment of credit and payment of interest. [**617**]

Section 71 (1) is in effect confined to loan agreements under which the loan is paid direct to the debtor in a form which (even though the loan may have been advanced for a specific purpose) leaves the debtor free to use it as he wishes—in other words, a loan paid direct to the debtor in money, as opposed to a credit-token.   Where the debtor exercises a right to cancel such an agreement, it nevertheless continues in force "so far as it relates to the repayment of credit and payment of interest".   The meaning of this phrase is not entirely clear.   It is reasonable to assume that it is confined to repayment of a loan already made (wholly or in part) at the date of cancellation.   Taken by themselves, the words "repayment of credit" are capable of referring to a contractual provision for repayment of a loan to be made in the future; but if the agreement as to future advances goes by the board, a provision for repayment obviously cannot operate on such future advances.   Moreover, subsections (2) and (3) make it fairly clear that the section as a whole is concerned with cash already paid to the debtor at the time of cancellation.   Hence that part of the agreement which relates to advances that have not been made at the date of cancellation, and the repayment of such advances, is retrospectively extinguished.   The creditor ceases to be bound to provide such advances and the debtor to take them.   But what of other covenants by the debtor, e.g. for the provision of security or for maintenance and insurance of an asset purchased with the loan?   It would seem that all such undertakings are extinguished—even guarantees and indemnities given in connection with the loan.   Any security given (and this would cover an agreement for security) is extinguished by s. 113 (3), which in the case of cancellation brings s. 106 into effect in relation to the security.   The other undertakings, such as maintenance and insurance, would also appear to become inoperative.   Section 71 (1) obviously contemplates that the debtor will not incur any future liability beyond repayment of the loan with interest, so that executory obligations of insurance and maintenance—whether contained in the credit agreement itself or in associated contracts—will, it seems, be extinguished.   This may seem hard on the creditor, but helps to achieve the desired objective of giving the debtor a period for reflection *before* he receives his loan.   [**618**]

Further protection for the debtor, and discouragement of the creditor from making the loan during the period allowed for cancellation, is provided by the remaining provisions of s. 71:

> "(2) If, following the cancellation of a regulated consumer credit agreement, the debtor repays the whole or a portion of a credit—
>> (*a*) before the expiry of one month following service of the notice of cancellation, or
>> (*b*) in the case of a credit repayable by instalments, before the date on which the first instalment is due, no interest shall be payable on the amount repaid.
>
> (3) If the whole of a credit repayable by instalments is not repaid on or before the date specified in subsection (2) (*b*), the debtor shall not be liable to repay any of the credit except on receipt of a request in writing in the prescribed form, signed by or on behalf of the creditor, stating the amounts of the remaining instalments (recalculated by the creditor as nearly as may be in accordance with the agreement and without extending the repayment period), but excluding any sum other than principal and interest.
>
> (4) Repayment of a credit, or payment of interest, under a cancelled agreement shall be treated as duly made if it is made to any person on whom, under section 69, a notice of

cancellation could have been served, other than a person referred to in section 69 (6) (*b*)."

The effect of s. 71 as a whole is thus to give the debtor who cancels a cash loan agreement three choices:

(*a*) to repay the loan in full without interest within the time prescribed by s. 71 (2);

(*b*) to repay part of the advance without interest within that time, and repay the balance with pro-rated interest, after receipt of a written request, over the contractual period for repayment then remaining (see para [**620**]);

(*c*) to make no repayment at all within the time prescribed by s. 71 (2), but to repay the advance, with the stipulated interest, after receipt of a written request, over the contractual period for repayment then remaining (see para. [**620**]).

But where the creditor has taken security, the debtor's duty of repayment cannot be enforced against him until the creditor has complied with the obligations under s. 106 (see para. [**774**]) in relation to the security (s. 113 (5)). [**619**]

Thus the debtor who cancels can obtain a loan free of interest for at least a month, and possibly much longer, depending on how long before expiry of the cancellation period he received the loan and the time allowed for payment of the first instalment. As is apparent from the opening lines of s. 71 (3), the time limit in s. 71 (2) (*a*) is confined to loans repayable by instalments. Section 71 (3) would seem to mean that a loan not repaid in full within the time specified in s. 71 (2) becomes repayable over the period between receipt of the request for repayment under s. 71 (3) and the contractual date for payment of the last instalment, by instalments of the frequency stipulated in the contract at interest pro-rated on an even-spread basis. A consequence of this statutory re-arrangement is, of course, that the payment period is shortened (since it does not begin until the creditor's written request for repayment has been received) so that the instalments will be larger than the amount (or in the case of a partially repaid loan, than a due proportion of the amount) stipulated in the contract.

> *Example 1*
> On 1st January 1976, pursuant to a cancellable agreement, a cash advance of £1,000 is made to A, repayable with interest of £200 over a period of 12 months by equal instalments of £100 a month commencing on 31st January 1976. On 15th January, A cancels the loan agreement but does not make any repayment by the end of that month. On 1st April A receives from the lender notice in writing under s. 71 (3) requiring repayment, on rescheduled terms set out in the notice. This will show that the total of £1,200, representing the principal and agreed interest, is now repayable over a period of 10 months ending on 31st January 1977, so that the monthly instalments become £120 instead of £100.

> *Example 2*
> The facts are as above except that A repays £400 on 28th January 1976, thus reducing the principal indebtedness to £600. For the purpose of working out the revised terms to be stated in his request of 1st April, the lender will take the period

1st April 1976 to 31st January 1977, i.e. 10 months, adjust the interest—to reflect reduction in the principal to £600 and in the payment period from 12 to 10 months—to the sum of £100 (i.e. £200 × 6/10 × 10/12) and spread the total sum of £700 (i.e. revised principal of £600 plus revised interest of £100) over the 10 months to 31st January 1977, producing revised monthly instalments of £70. [**620**]

The adjustment of interest on a partially repaid loan operates to the detriment of the creditor, since his fixed administration and overhead expenses remain constant despite what amounts to a reduction in the loan, and he might well have stipulated a higher rate of interest if at the outset the loan had been for the lower figure. In effect, the debtor who exercises a right to make a partial repayment under s. 71 (2) secures not only the benefit of freedom from interest on the part repaid but also the benefit of an interest rate originally fixed on the basis of the full amount of the loan, not on the basis of the reduced amount. [**621**]

Recovery of part-exchange goods or allowance

We have seen that on cancellation, the debtor is entitled by s. 70 (1) to repayment of any sum paid by him, or his relative, under or in contemplation of the cancelled agreement. However, there are many transactions in which an initial payment by the debtor is made wholly or partly by the crediting to him of an allowance for goods tendered in part-exchange. Section 73 (2) accordingly confers on the debtor the right to recover a sum equal to the part-exchange allowance in the circumstances previously mentioned (para. [**588**]). In the case of a debtor-creditor-supplier agreement within s. 12 (*b*)—e.g. a personal loan agreement with a finance house providing for a loan to buy a car from a motor dealer who had introduced the buyer to the finance house pursuant to an arrangement with the finance house—the negotiator and the creditor (i.e. in our example the dealer and the finance house) are jointly and severally liable for payment to the debtor of the part-exchange allowance (s. 73 (3)). But the creditor is entitled to be indemnified against this liability (s. 73 (4)) in the same way as on a liability for repayment of money paid by the debtor (see para. [**613**]). [**622**]

Debtor's lien

If the debtor or his relative is in possession of the goods comprised in the cancelled agreement, he has a lien on the goods for any sums repayable to him under s. 70 (1) of the Act (s. 70 (2)). In addition, during the ten days allowed to the negotiator for the return of the part-exchange goods, the debtor has a lien on the goods in his possession to secure return of the part-exchange goods or payment of the part-exchange allowance (s. 73 (5)). The negotiator can thus secure release of the goods from the lien either by returning the part-exchange goods or, at his option, by paying the debtor the part-exchange allowance, but after the ten-day period has expired the negotiator cannot force the debtor to accept return of the part-exchange goods and must tender a sum equal to the part-exchange goods and must tender a sum equal to the part-exchange allowance if he wishes to terminate the lien. [**623**]

Return of goods by debtor or relative

Section 72 provides for the return to the creditor or other authorised person of goods comprised in a cancelled agreement and for exercise of reasonable care in relation to the goods pending their return. The section applies where any agreement or transaction relating to goods, being—

    (*a*) a restricted-use debtor-creditor-supplier agreement, a consumer hire agreement, or a linked transaction to which the debtor or hirer under any regulated agreement is a party, or

    (*b*) a linked transaction to which a relative of the debtor or hirer under any regulated agreement is a party,

is cancelled after the debtor or hirer (in a case within paragraph (*a*)) or the relative (in a case within paragraph (*b*)) has acquired possession of the goods by virtue of the agreement or transaction (s. 72 (1)). A typical case is that of a hirer or buyer acquiring possession under a hire-purchase, conditional sale or credit sale agreement (other than a small agreement—see s. 74 (2)). Also within the provision is one who buys goods with the aid of a credit card or trading check, assuming that the credit agreement is not a small agreement. These are cases of possession by the debtor himself. Possession by a relative under a linked transaction is less likely. An example is delivery of goods to a minor on a cash sale where the price was advanced by a personal loan to the minor's parent under a regulated agreement pursuant to arrangements between the lender and the supplier. [**624**]

The Act provides that on cancellation the possessor (i.e. the debtor or relative acquiring possession under the regulated agreement or linked transaction) shall:

    (1) be under a duty, subject to any lien (see para. [**623**]), to return the goods to the other party (i.e. the person from whom he acquired possession) in accordance with s. 72, and meanwhile to retain possession of the goods and take reasonable care of them (s. 72 (4)); and

    (2) be treated as having been under a duty throughout the pre-cancellation period (i.e. the period beginning with the acquiring of possession and ending with cancellation—s. 72 (2)) to retain possession of the goods and to take reasonable care of them (s. 72 (3)).

Each of these duties requires separate examination. The exceptional cases in which such duties do not arise are discussed in paragraph [**631**]. Where security has been taken by the creditor, none of the duties is enforceable until the creditor has complied with his obligations under s. 106 (see para. [**774**]) in relation to the security (s. 113 (5)). [**625**]

The duty to restore

The obligation is to restore the goods to the person from whom the possessor acquired possession. It would seem that this refers to the *legal* supplier, not the physical supplier, so that, for example, if a person enters into a hire-purchase agreement with a finance house, he acquires possession of the goods from the finance house, not from the dealer who delivered them. The point will normally be academic, since the possessor's duty is discharged by delivering the goods (whether at his own premises or elsewhere), or by sending them, to any person on whom a notice of cancellation could have been served under s. 69, other than a person who acted for the debtor himself in negotiations for the agreement (s. 72 (6)). Thus delivery may be made:

    (i) to the creditor, that is, the person providing credit or his assignee (s. 189 (1)); or

     (ii) to any person specified in a notice of cancellation served, or incorporated in a copy of a document served, on the debtor in conformity with s. 64 (1); or

     (iii) a credit broker or supplier who was the negotiator in antecedent negotiations; or

     (iv) any agent of the creditor. [**626**]

The possessor need not return the goods to the other party's premises. It suffices if he holds them available for collection at his own premises; and he is under no duty to surrender them except pursuant to a written request signed by or on behalf of the other party and served on him either before or at the time when the goods are collected from his premises (s. 72 (5)). If the address of the possessor is specified in the cancelled agreement (as it almost invariably will be) then for the purpose of the above provisions he is only entitled, and obliged, to treat that address as his own premises (s. 72 (10)). On delivery in accordance with s. 72 (6) (*a*), the debtor's obligation to take care of the goods ceases (s. 72 (7)), and provided that he delivers to a person who is within one of the four categories mentioned in paragraph [**626**] the debtor is not concerned to see that the goods actually reach the person entitled to possession of them. If, instead of delivering the goods, he sends them to a person within such a category, he is under a duty to take reasonable care to see that they are received by the other party and not damaged in transit (e.g. he must ensure that they are propery packed and sent by an apparently competent carrier), but in other respects his duty to take care of the goods then ceases (s. 72 (7)). [**627**]

Failure by the debtor to surrender the goods in accordance with the statutory provisions exposes him to an action for damages for breach of statutory duty (s. 72 (11)). [**628**]

The duty of care

After cancellation, the possessor has a duty to take reasonable care of the goods until he has delivered or sent them pursuant to the above provisions; but his duty of care in any event comes to an end on the expiration of 21 days following the cancellation unless he has by then received a written and signed request for delivery under s. 72 (5) and has unreasonably refused or failed to comply with it (s. 72 (8)). This provision is designed to ensure that a debtor exercising a right of cancellation is not inconvenienced by having to house the goods indefinitely as the result of the other party's failure to collect. If the latter does not serve such a request within 21 days, or if having served it he does not call to collect the goods within such period, the debtor's duty to take reasonable care ceases, and his obligation in relation to the goods becomes limited to that of an involuntary bailee, viz. to refrain from causing wilful damage. [**629**]

Not only is the possessor under a duty of care after the cancellation; he is deemed to have been under a duty to retain possession of the goods and take reasonable care of them throughout the cancellation period (s. 72 (3)). This provision ensures that a debtor who cancels an agreement does not escape liability merely because restoration of the goods in proper condition had already become impossible prior to cancellation as the result of damage to or disposal of the goods. If, therefore, the debtor or other person parted with possession prior to cancellation, then whilst this might at the time have been perfectly lawful (as where the buyer under a credit sale agreement resells the goods immediately and delivers possession to his purchaser) the subsequent cancellation retrospectively places him in breach of his deemed statutory duty to retain possession, and he is liable to the other party in damages for the value of the goods. Similarly, if he damages the goods before cancellation, then even if at the time of such damage the goods were his own property (as under a credit sale agreement) he is liable under s. 72 (7) for the damage so caused. [**630**]

Exemptions

Section 72 (9) provides as follows:

> "The preceding provisions of this section do not apply to—
> (*a*) perishable goods, or
> (*b*) goods which by their nature are consumed by use and which, before the cancellation, were so consumed, or
> (*c*) goods supplied to meet an emergency, or
> (*d*) goods which, before the cancellation, had become incorporated in any land or thing not comprised in the cancelled agreement or a linked transaction."

These provisions require some explanation, as their effect is more striking than may at first sight be apparent. [**631**]

The effect of paragraph (*a*) is that the possessor of perishables has no duty to retain possession or to restore them. He may consume them or dispose of them as he thinks fit. Indeed, he will usually have little choice, since by their nature perishables are unlikely to be returnable to the supplier in suitable condition. On the other hand, consumer credit agreements relating to perishables are not excluded from the cancellation provisions, so that the debtor, having consumed the perishables, is none the less entitled to recover under s. 70 (1) the sums paid in respect of them and to obtain release from liability for sums remaining payable. In short, he can have his cake without paying for it! This may appear startling, but reflects a deliberate policy to ensure that a debtor having a right of cancellation is not inhibited from exercising that right by the prospect of incurring some financial liability. One of the typical transactions against which the provision is aimed is an agreement under which a freezer is supplied on credit together with food to stock the freezer, the food itself being supplied on credit terms. There have been many complaints concerning such transactions, and the fear was that if the consumer cancelling the freezer agreement were thereby to incur a liability to pay for the food, he might be inhibited from exercising his right of cancellation. The statutory provision is not, indeed, limited to cases of this kind but applies even where the supply of food on credit is the sole transaction. In practice, however, such agreements are uncommon, and the supplier can in any event avoid difficulty by deferring delivery until after expiration of the cancellation period or alternatively (if the circumstances warrant) by relying on the provisions of s. 69 (2) (*a*) relating to goods supplied to meet an emergency. A similar reasoning applies under s. 72 (9) (*b*) to other consumables, e.g. fuel, though in this case, since the goods do not automatically perish with the passing of time but are merely consumed through use, the debtor is only absolved of his duty to return the goods if they were in fact consumed prior to cancellation. [**632**]

The position is somewhat different in the case of goods supplied in the circumstances described in s. 72 (9) (c) and (d). Despite cancellation, the debtor to whom goods are supplied for an emergency or by whom goods are incorporated into land or other goods remains obliged to pay the cash price to the supplier (see para. [615]). Hence in these cases, exemption of the debtor from a duty to return the goods after cancellation is given simply because restoration of the goods would usually be impracticable. Goods supplied for an emergency will normally have been employed to cope with that emergency, and may continue to be needed for that purpose. Goods which become incorporated into land lose their identity as chattels and usually pass into the ownership of the owner of the land. Similarly, goods which become annexed as accessions to other chattels, and thus cannot be detached without material damage to those chattels, will in general pass to the owner of the chattels (see generally R. M. Goode, *op. cit.*, Chapter 33). Unfortunately s. 72 (9) (c) goes too far, for it includes goods supplied under a consumer hire agreement. It is hard to see the justification for allowing the hirer to retain them when he is not the owner, particularly since his exercise of the right to cancel absolves him from the duty to pay hire charges. [633]

There remains one final point. It is not entirely clear that s. 72 (9) fully achieves its objective of exempting the debtor who cancels from liability, in the cases mentioned in that sub-section, for not returning the goods. Consequent upon a change in wording in the statutory provisions as the Bill was proceeding through Parliament s. 72 (9) only excludes duties imposed by the preceding provisions of s. 72 itself. It does not in terms negate a duty imposed on the debtor at common law. Hence it is perhaps arguable that the debtor remains exposed to a claim at common law in detinue or conversion. However, it seems likely that the court would interpret s. 72 (1)–(8) as intended to be an exhaustive code of duties of care and return resulting from cancellation and thus to displace any duties that would otherwise arise at common law. Section 72 (9), in excluding those statutory duties, would therefore exclude the only duties of care and return capable of arising in the circumstances described in s. 72 (1). [634]

Loss of right to cancel

There are only two circumstances in which the statutory right to cancel is lost. The first is where the debtor fails to serve a cancellation notice within the time prescribed by s. 68 (see para. [606]). The second is where judgment has already been given against the debtor, in an action on the agreement, before he serves his cancellation notice, for the original cause of action merges in the judgment, so that the debtor's obligations thenceforth derive from the judgment, not from the agreement. See *V. L. Skuce & Co.* v. *Cooper*, [1975] I All E.R. 612, [1975] I W.L.R. 593. Factors which would at common law preclude rescission, such as inability to restore the goods through loss, consumption or disposition to a third party, do not appear to affect the statutory right of cancellation. This, indeed, is apparent from s. 72 (3) and (9). The sanction for a debtor who damages or disposes of the goods in the pre-cancellation period is not loss of the right to cancel but damages for breach of statutory duty (see para. [630]). The debtor who before cancellation consumes goods or has them incorporated in land or other goods may still cancel but is exempted from the usual consequential obligation to return the goods. Even destruction of the goods otherwise than by consumption does not affect the right of cancellation under the Act. Moreover, the right to cancel would appear to be unaffected even by the fact that at the time when notice of cancellation is given the agreement has already come to an end, e.g. through exercise by one party of a right to terminate or through frustration. It may seem odd to speak of rescinding an agreement which has ceased to exist, but there is nothing illogical in this, since the remedy of rescission operates retrospectively, cancelling the contract from the beginning and thus overriding a purported termination of the agreement by the other party. This result is reasonable, since destruction of the right of cancellation by exercise by the creditor of a power of termination would deprive the debtor of the protection which the Act intends to give him. If, for example, the owner of goods let on hire-purchase were to fail to send the debtor a notice or copy of an agreement informing the debtor of his right to cancel, and after collecting payments from the debtor were then to terminate the agreement for default, it is unlikely that the court would regard the debtor's remedy as restricted to reliance on unforceability of the agreement. Almost certainly, he would be held entitled to exercise a right to cancel, despite the owner's termination, on the ground that the time for cancellation had not begun to run against him. On the other hand, if the hirer, being aware of his right to cancel, deliberately chooses an alternative remedy by electing to terminate the agreement himself he would, it is thought, be precluded from invoking the statutory right of cancellation. [**635**]

Rescission at common law

The cancellation provisions do not in any way affect the debtor's right of rescission for misrepresentation at common law and under the Misrepresentation Act 1967. However, s. 102 (1) of the Act (re enacting in this respect s. 31 (2) of the Hire-Purchase Act 1965) facilitates exercise of such right by providing that the following are to be deemed the agent of the creditor or owner for the purpose of receiving any notice rescinding the agreement which is served by the debtor or hirer—

(a) a credit broker or supplier who was the negotiator in antecedent negotiations, and
(b) any person who, in the course of a business carried on by him, acted on behalf of the debtor or hirer in any negotiations for the agreement.

By s. 102 (2), it is provided that in s. 102 (1) "rescind" does not include—

(a) service of a notice of cancellation, or
(b) termination of an agreement under s. 99 or 101, or by the exercise of a right or power in that behalf expressly conferred by the agreement.

[**636**]

16. Misrepresentation and Breach of Contract by Supplier

1. THE BACKGROUND TO THE STATUTORY PROVISIONS

The creditor's liability for the acts of the supplier

Where the creditor and the legal supplier of goods or services are not the same—that is, where the credit takes the form of a loan as opposed to deferment of the price under a supply contract—the business *nexus* between creditor and supplier may be such that even though the loan contract and the supply contract are quite distinct, policy dictates that the creditor shall be held responsible for misrepresentations and breaches of contract by the supplier. This concept of joint and several responsibility was advocated by the Crowther Committee for cases where the credit was extended by a "connected lender", that is, a lender who makes the advance to the borrower pursuant to a regular business relationship between the lender and the supplier. [**637**]

The policy basis for the creditor's liability

The rationale for holding the creditor liable is set out in the passage in the Crowther Report which is quoted below. The Report took as a typical case the arrangements between a finance house and a dealer for the introduction of the dealer's customers to the finance house to obtain credit to buy the dealer's goods. After pointing out (para. 6.6.20) that in the typical hire-purchase transaction the liability of the finance house to the hirer stemmed from the fact that it was in a direct contractual relationship with the hirer, the Report continued (paras. 6.6.22–6.6.25):

> "But the reason for making the finance house liable for acts and defaults of the dealer up to the time the hire-purchase agreement is made can be put on a wider footing than the purely contractual nexus between the parties. Even if one ignores the legal form of the transaction, the finance company is not in the position of a purely independent lender to whom the borrower comes for a loan. To a considerable extent the finance house and the dealer are engaged in a joint venture. The finance house controls the contract documents used by the dealer in his instalment credit business. It competes keenly

with other finance houses for the privilege of obtaining the dealer's credit business. On motor vehicle business it pays the dealer a substantial commission (currently 20 per cent of the finance charge) for introducing a hire-purchase contract, thus giving the dealer a positive incentive to procure the customer's signature to a hire-purchase agreement instead of selling for cash. It provides general financial support for the dealer, the cost of which may be materially influenced by the volume of retail instalment credit business introduced to it by the dealer. When business is slack, the finance house will continually press the dealer to increase the volume of transactions put through. In every sense, therefore, the finance house relies on the dealer as a medium for promoting its own business and it cannot be equated with a wholly independent lender such as a bank approached by the borrower himself . . .

If, with all the pressure for business exerted by the lender and the financial inducements the lender offers, the seller seeks to boost sales by making false representations, or supplies goods which are defective, is it right that the lender should be able to disclaim all responsibility and insist on repayments of the loan being punctually maintained? We do not think so. We accept that the person who should bear ultimate responsibility is the seller who made the misrepresentation or supplied the defective goods, but we do not consider that it is sufficient to leave the borrower with his remedy against the seller, even assuming that with a changed legal structure the sale is made direct to the customer . . .

There are many reasons why in practice a legal right which the buyer may have against his seller is not sufficient protection. Where the seller is reputable he will usually be prepared to deal with justified complaints and rectify the matters complained of. The majority of the cases in which the buyer is likely to suffer are those where a seller is of doubtful repute and is able to continue in business only because of the financial support he receives from the lender. The buyer supplied with defective goods may find that to secure redress from such a seller he has to incur the worry and expense of litigation, in which the burden of taking the initiative lies on him; and that in some cases the seller's financial position is so poor that it is doubtful whether he will be able to meet the judgment even if the buyer is successful. The buyer's difficulties of pursuing a claim against the seller are enhanced if, whilst wrestling with the financial problems of litigation, he has to go on paying the lender under the loan agreement. Problems of this kind are particularly prevalent in relation to agreements for the installation of central heating. There have been many cases where the supplier has either not delivered at all or has provided an ineffective heating system, and has then gone into liquidation before the consumer has been able to obtain redress, so that the consumer is left to meet a liability on a loan contract entered into with a third party. Especial hardship is caused where the buyer was induced to take the goods because they were represented as capable of procuring

215

income—e.g. knitting machines—which would enable the buyer to maintain payment of the instalments due under the loan agreement. If the machine is found to be inoperable, the whole basis of the buyer's financial calculation falls to the ground." [638]

Possible forms of liability

Discussing the nature of the liability that it would be proper to impose on the connected lender, the Report went on to say (paras. 6.6.26–6.6.29);

"There are three different ways in which the borrower might be given relief against a connected lender. The first is to make the lender answerable in damages for misrepresentations made by the seller in antecedent negotiations and for breaches of any term of the agreement relating to title, fitness or quality of the goods. An alternative and intermediate measure is to provide that, while the lender shall not incur a positive liability in damages, the borrower shall, by way of defence to a claim for sums due under the loan agreement, be entitled to set off any claim that he has for such a misrepresentation or breach. The third approach is to require the borrower to pursue his remedies against the seller in the first instance, the lender becoming liable to the consumer only if the latter is unable to obtain redress from the seller because of his insolvency. This is the solution advocated by the finance houses, who accept that a seller-linked lender must accept a measure of responsibility for misrepresentation or breaches of contract by the seller, but who urge that this should be limited to the secondary liability of underwriting the seller's solvency.

We have reached the conclusion that the first of these approaches is that which should be adopted. If the borrower's claim does not arise, or is not made, until after he has repaid a substantial part of the loan a mere right of set-off will not give him adequate protection. Indeed, the borrower who pays his loan instalments promptly will be worse off than one who has been dilatory and thus has a substantial accrued indebtedness against which to exercise his right of set-off when the nature and extent of his own claim become clear. The third alternative would not in our view adequately protect the borrower. It imposes on him what is for the average consumer the heavy burden of initiating litigation instead of merely defending an action and exercising a right of set-off and counterclaim. Moreover, the obligation to pay the loan instalments while pursuing his claim against the seller may substantially diminish his ability to prosecute his claim.

We therefore recommend that where the price payable under a consumer sale agreement is advanced wholly or in part by a connected lender that lender should be liable for misrepresentations relating to the goods made by the seller in the course of antecedent negotiations and for defects in title, fitness and quality of the goods. Further, we consider that where the sale and the loan are made by separate contracts, the

> borrower should nevertheless have the right to set off against any sum payable by him under the loan contract any damages he is entitled to recover from the lender for breaches of the sale agreement by the seller.
>
> In reaching this conclusion we have been influenced by the additional fact that if the delinquent seller is worth powder and shot it ought to be easier for the lender to put pressure on him to deal with the complaint than it is for the borrower. The lender is not likely to be so inhibited by expense from suing the seller; and in most cases proceedings by the lender would be unnecessary because the lender is in a position to say to the seller that future financing facilities will be withdrawn unless the seller attends to the complaint and takes greater care in the conduct of his business." [**639**]

The Consumer Credit Act adopts the reasoning of the Crowther Report and, selecting as the basis of the creditor's liability the extension of credit by him pursuant to or in contemplation of arrangements with the supplier, provides that:

> "75. Liability of creditor for breaches by supplier
>
>   (1) If the debtor under a debtor-creditor-supplier agreement falling within section 12 (*b*) or (*c*) has, in relation to a transaction financed by the agreement, any claim against the supplier in respect of a misrepresentation or breach of contract, he shall have a like claim against the creditor, who, with the supplier, shall accordingly be jointly and severally liable to the debtor.
>
>   (2) Subject to any agreement between them, the creditor shall be entitled to be indemnified by the supplier for loss suffered by the creditor in satisfying his liability under subsection (1), including costs reasonably incurred by him in defending proceedings instituted by the debtor.
>
>   (3) Subsection (1) does not apply to a claim—
>   (*a*) under a non-commercial agreement, or
>   (*b*) so far as the claim relates to any single item to which the supplier has attached a cash price not exceeding £30 or more than £10,000.
>
>   (4) This section applies notwithstanding that the debtor, in entering into the transaction, exceeded the credit limit or otherwise contravened any term of the agreement.
>
>   (5) In an action brought against the creditor under subsection (1) he shall be entitled, in accordance with rules of court, to have the supplier made a party to the proceedings."

The precise application and effect of s. 75 are discussed later in this chapter. The essential point to make at this stage is that the creditor's liability for misrepresentations and breaches of contract by the supplier is tailored to that of the supplier, and the source of the supplier's liability is to be found not in the Consumer Credit Act but in the general law of contract and in the provisions of other statutes, notably the Sale of Goods Act 1893, as amended, the Misrepresentation Act 1967, as amended, the Supply of Goods (Implied Terms) Act 1973 and the Unfair Contract Terms Act 1977. Section 75 is not the only source of the creditor's liability for the acts of the supplier, for as the result of the agency provisions of s. 56 (discussed in the next chapter) statements made and other acts done by the supplier in antecedent negotiations may be attributed to the creditor so as to involve him in liability. [**640**]

In this chapter we shall consider, first, the circumstances in which the supplier himself would incur a liability to the debtor in the absence of any contractual provision excluding or restricting such liability; secondly, the extent to which the supplier can validly exclude or limit his liability by some suitable disclaimer or exemption clause; and thirdly, the provisions of s. 75 by which the creditor is made jointly and severally with the supplier. [**641**]

2. THE SUPPLIER'S LIABILITY FOR MISREPRESENTATION

An actionable misrepresentation is a false statement of fact (including a statement of belief or intention where this is not held by the maker of the statement) which is intended to and does induce the representee to enter into a contract with the representor in reliance on the truth of the statement but which is not at the time of its making intended to be a promise forming a term of the contract. The distinction between a "mere" representation inducing, but not forming part of, the contract and a statement constituting a term of the contract is more easily expressed than applied. At common law, the issue was whether a reasonable onlooker would assume that the maker of the statement intended to warrant its truth or make it as a promise (in which case the statement would have contractual force) or whether, in the eyes of the reasonable onlooker, the maker of the statement was simply asserting a fact without intending to be bound by the statement. The distinction between a "mere" representation and a contract term was formerly of great importance in that while a fraudulent misrepresentation always gave rise to a claim for damages in tort for deceit, a misrepresentation made in good faith merely entitled the representee to rescind the contract, and as a rule conferred no remedy in damages, even if the statement were negligently made. There was no claim in contract (for the complaint was not breach of contract but misrepresentation) and no claim for negligence, for until recently the tort of negligence was not conceived as designed to compensate for pure economic loss. Only where reliance on the negligent statement led to the representee suffering physical injury to his person or damage to his property was a claim for negligence available, in the absence of some fiduciary relationship between the parties, but the distinction between a mere representation and a contract term has now lost much of its importance, for two reasons. First, the House of Lords held in *Hedley Byrne & Co. Ltd.* v. *Heller & Partners, Ltd.,* [1964] A.C. 465, [1963] 2 All ER 575 that, contrary to what had previously been understood to be the law, there was no distinction in principle between loss resulting from physical injury or damage and pure economic loss, and that liability for negligence could be imposed whenever there was a special relationship between representor and representee in the sense that the representee was led to rely on the representation by virtue of the special knowledge or expertise professed by the representor, the latter knowing or having reason to know that his representation was likely to be acted upon. The *Hedley Byrne* principle has been held capable of applying not only to a representation inducing the representee to enter into a contract with a third party (*McInerney* v. *Lloyds Bank, Ltd.,* [1974] 1 Lloyds Rep. 246) but even to a representation inducing the representee to contract with the representor (*Esso Petroleum Co., Ltd.* v. *Mardon,*

[1976] Q.B. 801, [1976] 2 All E.R. 5, and cf. *Howard Marine and Dredging Co., Ltd.* v. *A. Ogden & Sons (Excavations), Ltd.,* 1978 Q.B. 574, [1978] 2 All E.R. 1134; *Midland Bank Trust Co., Ltd.* v. *Hett, Stubbs and Kemp,* [1978] 3 All E.R. 571). Secondly, s. 2 of the Misrepresentation Act 1967 in given conditions entitles the representee to damages even for a non-fraudulent misrepresentation, unless the representor can show that it was not made negligently (see para. [**646**]). [**642**]

Sometimes the courts experienced a difficulty in that a false statement made prior to a written contract, and plainly intended to have the character of a promise or warranty, was not incorporated into the written document, so that the representee might be barred by the parol evidence rule (see para. [**555**]) from asserting that the statement formed part of the contract embodied in the document. How was the court to give effect to the promise or warranty in such a case? The judicial solution was to treat the statement as a collateral promise or warranty generating a distinct contract, the maker of the statement promising to perform, or warranting the truth of the statement, in consideration of the representee entering into the main contract. Since the promise or warranty thus formed the essential obligation of a contract entirely distinct from that embodied in the document, it was not caught by the parol evidence rule and could be proved in the usual way. The device of the collateral contract, or collateral warranty, was also useful to give a remedy where the false statement induced the representee to enter into a contract not with the representor but with a third party. For example, if a motor dealer were to make a false statement about the quality of a car for the purpose of inducing a prospective customer to acquire it on hire-purchase from a finance house introduced by the dealer, the dealer's warranty could not be treated at common law as a term of the hire-purchase agreement, since the dealer was not a party to that agreement, but it could be accorded force as a collateral warranty generating a separate contract for the breach of which the customer would have a remedy in damages. See, for example, *Andrews* v. *Hopkinson,* [1957] 1 Q.B. 229, [1956] 3 All E.R. 422, and para. [**697**]. [**643**]

Even a wholly innocent misrepresentation (i.e. a misrepresentation made in good faith and without negligence) entitled the innocent party at common law to rescind the contract. Rescission is not the same as termination. A contract terminated for breach puts an end to future obligations without disturbing accrued rights and liabilities (though in the case of a total failure of consideration the innocent party has a right to recover all his payments), and the innocent party's remedy consequent upon such termination is usually damages. Rescission of a contract, on the other hand, cancels it from the beginning, so that it is treated as if it had never existed. The consequence is that both parties must as nearly as possible be restored to their *status quo,* so that each is entitled to recover payments made and property transferred under the rescinded contract. If for some reason restitution is not possible—e.g. because a third party has acquired an interest in the subject matter of the contract—then the innocent party usually loses the right to rescind. It should be noted that the innocent party's right after rescission to recover payments made is a right not to damages but to restitution. What is involved is not compensation to the innocent party for loss he has suffered through the contract not proceeding but return by the guilty party of benefits conferred on him by the contract, which the law will not allow him to retain once the contract has become ineffective through rescission. The distinction between restitution and damages is not always appreciated, and indeed was overlooked in the original version of what is now s. 75 (1) of the Consumer Credit Act (see para. [**681**]). [**644**]

We have mentioned one barrier to rescission, namely the inability of a party to give restitution. There were other barriers at common law, e.g. election by the innocent party to affirm the contract, completion of performance of the contract by one party (so that it became an executed contract), and incorporation of the misrepresentation as a term of the contract, in which case the better view was that the innocent party was restricted to his common law remedy and lost his equitable right to rescind. [**645**]

The Misrepresentation Act 1967

The Misrepresentation Act 1967 has made a number of changes to the common law rules. First, it removes two of the bars to rescission, by providing that the innocent party retains the right to rescind even if the misrepresentation has become a term of the contract and even if the contract has been performed (s. 1). Secondly, the Act confers on the innocent party a right to damages (either in addition to or in lieu of rescission) for negligent misrepresentation, the onus being placed on the representor to show that he had reasonable ground to believe and did believe up to the time that the contract was made that the facts represented were true (s. 2 (1)). Thirdly, it confers on the court (except in the case of a fraudulent misrepresentation) the power to require the innocent party to accept damages in lieu of rescission, even if the innocent party has already exercised a right to rescind (s. 2 (2)). Finally, the Act renders ineffective any term of a contract (i.e. of *any* contract, whether it be the contract induced by the misrepresentation or an entirely separate contract) purporting to exclude or restrict liability for misrepresentation or remedies available to the innocent party for misrepresentation, except so far as that term satisfies the requirement of reasonableness as stated in s. 11 (1) of the Unfair Contract Terms Act 1977, the onus being on those claiming that the term satisfies that requirement to show that it does (Misrepresentation Act 1967, s. 3, as amended by Unfair Contract Terms Act 1977, s. 8 (1)). [**646**]

3. TERMS IMPLIED BY LAW IN FAVOUR OF THOSE CONTRACTING FOR GOODS OR SERVICES

We must now consider briefly the terms implied by law in favour of those to whom goods or services are to be supplied under a contract, and the principal remedies available for breach of those terms. The question whether, and if so to what extent, such terms and remedies can be cut down by exemption clauses in the contract in question is discussed later (paras. [**659**] *et seq.*) [**647**]

Terms implied in favour of buyer

The Sale of Goods Act 1893, as amended by the Supply of Goods (Implied Terms) Act 1973, imports into a contract of sale a set of implied terms in favour of the buyer in relation to the goods. These are:

(a) an implied condition that the seller has a right to sell or will have a right to sell at the time the property is to pass (Sale of Goods Act 1893, s. 12 (1));

(b) an implied warranty that the goods are free, and will remain free until the time when the property is to pass, from any charge or encumbrance not disclosed or known to the buyer before the contract is made and that the buyer will enjoy quiet possession (*ibid.*);

(c) in the case of a sale by description or sample, an implied condition that the goods shall correspond with the description or sample (ss. 13, 15);

(d) where the seller sells goods in the course of a business, an implied condition that the goods are of merchantable quality, except as regards defects specifically drawn to the buyer's attention before the contract is made or, if the buyer examines the goods before the contract is made, defects which that examination ought to reveal (s. 14 (2));

(e) where the seller sells goods in the course of a business and the buyer, expressly or by implication, makes known to the seller (or, where the purchase price is payable wholly or in part by instalments and the goods were previously sold by a credit-broker to the seller, to that credit-broker) any particular purpose for which the goods are being bought, an implied condition that the goods supplied under the contract are reasonably fit for that purpose, whether or not that is a purpose for which such goods are commonly supplied, except where the circumstances show that the buyer does not rely, or that it is unreasonable for him to rely, on the seller's skill or judgment (s. 14 (3), as prospectively amended by the Consumer Credit Act 1974, s. 192 and Sch. 4, para. 3).
[**648**]

Buyer's remedies for breach
Where the implied term broken by the seller is a warranty, the buyer can sue for damages, the normal measure of damages being the amount by which the value of the goods as warranted exceeds their value as delivered (Sale of Goods Act 1893, s. 53 (3)). Alternatively, the buyer can set up the breach of warranty in diminution or extinction of the price (s. 53 (1)) and, if his loss exceeds the price, can sue for the balance as damages (s. 53 (4)). Where the term broken is a condition, the buyer can either affirm the contract, treat the breach of condition as a breach of warranty and claim damages or reject the goods as not tendered in conformity with the contract. If he exercises a right to reject, the effect is that the seller has not made delivery in accordance with the contract. If the seller still has time to deliver, he can perform by a fresh tender of goods that do conform to the contract *Borrowman, Phillips & Co.* v. *Free and Hollis* (1878), 4 Q.B.D. 500; *E.E. and Brian Smith, Ltd* v *Wheatsheaf Mills, Ltd.*, [1939] 2 K.B. 302). Where the contract is for the sale of unascertained goods, the seller can cure the defective tender either by altering or repairing the goods originally tendered so as to make them in conformity with the contract or by tendering other goods of the contract description; for although the seller may have purported to appropriate the original goods to the contract, yet if the buyer lawfully rejects them the appropriation becomes ineffective (for it did not accord with the contract and cannot be forced on the buyer), with the result that the seller becomes free, if there is still time, to appropriate different goods. But where the contract is for the sale of specific goods, a new tender of other goods is not permitted without the buyer's consent, for the contract goods are those identified and agreed upon at the time of the contract and no other. [**649**]
If it is too late for the seller to put the matter right (either because the contract

time of delivery was of the essence and has expired or because a reasonable time for delivery has already elapsed), or if the seller is unwilling or unable to make a fresh tender, the buyer can treat the contract as repudiated, and either sue for damages for non-delivery (s. 51 (1)) or bring a quasi-contractual claim for recovery of the price (to the extent he has paid it) on the basis of a total failure of consideration. The buyer is not obliged to accept a credit note; he is entitled to the return of his money or to damages, whichever of the above two remedies he prefers. The normal measure of damages is the amount by which the market price at the contract date for delivery (or if none, at the time of refusal to deliver) exceeds the contract price (s. 51 (3)). [**650**]

As a rule, the buyer loses his right to reject (and is accordingly limited to damages) if the contract of sale is not severable and he has accepted the goods or a part of them (s. 11 (1) (*c*)). He is deemed to have accepted where he intimates to the seller that he has accepted them or where (having had a reasonable opportunity to examine the goods) he takes delivery and does any act in relation to the goods which is inconsistent with the ownership of the seller or, after the lapse of a reasonable time, retains the goods without intimating to the seller that he has rejected them (ss. 35, 34). But s. 11 (1) (*c*) does not apply to conditional sale agreements which are agreements for consumer sales (Supply of Goods (Implied Terms) Act, s. 14 (1)). Moreover, a breach of condition of a consumer conditional sale agreement is to be treated as a breach of warranty (so as to bar the right to reject and treat the contract as repudiated) only if it would have fallen to be so treated had the condition been contained or implied in a corresponding hire-purchase agreement as a condition to be fulfilled by the owner (s. 14 (2)). "Corresponding hire-purchase agreement" means, in relation to a conditional sale agreement, a hire-purchase agreement relating to the same goods as the conditional sale agreement and made between the same parties and at the same time and in the same circumstances and, as nearly as may be, in the same terms as the conditional sale agreement (s. 15 (4)). The effect of s. 14 (2) of the Supply of Goods (Implied Terms) Act is that technical rules in the Sale of Goods Act as to deemed acceptance do not apply, and the question whether the buyer has accepted the goods is to be determined by reference to the more liberal common law principles applicable to hire-purchase agreements (see para. [**654**]). [**651**]

The buyer of defective products may also have rights under other legislation, e.g. for breach of regulations made under the Health and Safety at Work etc. Act 1974 (*ibid.*, s. 47 (2)) or the Consumer Safety Act 1978 (*ibid.*, s. 6 (1)). [**652**]

Terms implied in favour of hirer on hire-purchase

These are set out in ss. 8–11 of the Supply of Goods (Implied Terms) Act 1973 and correspond to the terms implied under the Sale of Goods Act in favour of the buyer under a contract of sale. But the hirer remains entitled to the benefit of any wider common law terms (other than as to quality or fitness), so far as not excluded by the contract (see s. 15 (5)). Thus, although under s. 8 (1) the owner is not required to have a right of disposal until the time when the property is to pass to the hirer, the duty at common law is to have a right to dispose at the time of delivery to the hirer under the hire-purchase agreement (*Mercantile Union Guarantee Corporation, Ltd.* v. *Wheatley*, [1938] 1 K.B. 490, [1937] 4 All E.R. 713). The hirer can invoke this wider common law rule unless the agreement otherwise provides. [**653**]

The remedies of the hirer where the owner commits a breach of the implied terms relating to the goods comprised in the hire-purchase agreement are broadly the same as those of the buyer under a conditional sale agreement. But the technical rules embodied in the Sale of Goods Act as to deemed acceptance of the goods by the buyer in a contract of sale do not apply to hire-purchase agreements. Accordingly the hirer will usually lose his right to reject only if he elects to affirm the contract with knowledge of the breach. See *Farnworth Finance Facilities, Ltd.* v. *Attryde*, [1970] 2 All E.R. 774, [1970] 1 WLR 1053, and *Guarantee Trust of Jersey, Ltd.* v. *Gardner* (1973), 117 Sol. Jo. 564. For a comprehensive treatment, see R. M. Goode, *Hire-Purchase Law and Practice* (2nd Edn.) Chapter 20. [654]

Terms implied in favour of hirer on simple hire
These are broadly the same as for hire-purchase. The old rule that a bailee could not dispute his bailor's title (*Biddle* v. *Bond* (1865), 6 B. & S. 225) has now been abolished through the combined effect of the Torts (Interference with Goods) Act 1977, s. 8 and RSC Order 15, r. 10A, made pursuant to that section, and it would seem that an implied condition as to title is now to be imported into contracts of hire. [655]

The hirer's remedies for breach are again broadly the same as under a hire-purchase agreement, but because the contract is not one under which he has the right to acquire the goods there will be a difference in the measure of damages. See R. M. Goode, *op. cit.*, pp. 891–897. [656]

A consumer hire agreement is not, of course, a credit agreement within s. 75, but may well be a transaction financed by a debtor-creditor-supplier agreement to which s. 75 applies (see para. [283]). [657]

Terms implied in contracts for services
In general, a contract for the provision of services imports an obligation on the promisor of the services to perform them with reasonable care and to exercise that measure of skill which he professes himself to possess or which he will be taken as so professing by virtue of his calling. But the terms of the contract may be such as to show a strict obligation to ensure that the promised services will produce their intended effect (*Greaves & Co. (Contractors), Ltd.* v. *Baynham Meikle & Partners*, [1975] 3 All E.R. 99, [1975] 1 W.L.R. 1095); and where the contract also involves the supply of materials—as in building contract—then as to the materials the common law imports the same strict terms of fitness for purpose and merchantable quality as are implied in contracts of sale (*Gloucester County Council* v. *Richardson*, [1969] 1 A.C. 480, [1968] 2 All E.R. 1181). [658]

4. EXEMPTION CLAUSES

In principle, a party undertaking a contractual obligation is free to qualify the obligation, or his liability for breach of it, by a term of that or some other contract. But for many years now the courts have been concerned over the use of exemption clauses, particularly in standard-term contracts with consumers in which the individual consumer has little or no opportunity to negotiate but is obliged to accept the contract as it stands. Hence the courts developed a battery of weapons to control exemption clauses; and these have now been greatly strengthened by the provisions of the Unfair Contract Terms Act 1977. **[659]**

The judicial control of exemption clauses

The courts have found many ways to strike down exemption clauses considered unfair or unreasonable, and for the most part these remain unaffected by the Unfair Contract Terms Act. The first question, of course, is whether the exempting stipulation has contractual force at all. If it is embodied in a document which the profferee did not regard, and could not reasonably have been expected to regard, as a contract document, the exempting stipulation will be ineffective unless brought to the profferee's notice at or before the time he entered into the contract (*Chapelton* v. *Barry U.D.C.*, [1940] 1 K.B. 532, [1940] 1 All E.R. 356). Alternatively, the court may find that the attempt by the *proferens* to rely on a notice disclaiming liability comes too late to cut down the other party's rights, since the contract has already been concluded (*Olley* v. *Marlborough Court Ltd.*, [1949] 1 K.B. 532, [1949] 1 All E.R. 127; *Thornton* v. *Shoe Lane Parking, Ltd.*, [1971] 2 Q.B. 163, [1971] 1 All E.R. 686). Again, what would otherwise have been an effective exemption clause in a standard-term contract may be held to have been overridden by a prior oral representation to the effect that the exemption clause would not apply or which is otherwise inconsistent with the provisions of the exemption clause (*Mendelssohn* v. *Normand, Ltd.*, [1970] 1 Q.B. 177, [1969] 2 All E.R. 1215; *J. Evans & Sons (Portsmouth)* v. *Andrea Merzario, Ltd.*, [1976] 2 All E.R. 930, [1976] 1 W.L.R. 1078). Another useful judicial device is the *contra proferentem* rule, by which a document will be construed strictly against the party who prepared it or presented it. This rule has enabled the court to treat an exemption clause as inapt to cover situations which, on ordinary rules of construction, might otherwise have been held to be within the scope of the clause. For example, an exemption clause or indemnity purporting to exclude or indemnify against "all liabilities" will be construed *contra proferentem* as intended to cover strict liability only (assuming the case is one in which strict liability could arise) and will not encompass liability for negligence, even if the word "whatsoever" is added after "liability" (*Smith* v. *South Wales Switchgear, Ltd.*, [1978] 1 All E.R. 18, [1978] 1 W.L.R. 165). **[660]**

Two principles evolved by the courts deserve particular mention, namely the doctrines of fundamental term and fundamental breach. Under the former, every contract has an essential core, a fundamental term which cannot be excluded without in substance negating the contract altogether. Accordingly an exemption clause will not be construed as intended to cut down that which has been presented as the fundamental obligation. For example, the duty to supply goods corresponding with their contract description is a fundamental term and as such cannot be effectively cut down by an exemption clause. Of course, the parties are free to agree on as broad or narrow a description as they choose; but if the *proferens* presents the contract in such a way that the fundamental term appears as x, he will not be allowed to rely on the exemption clause as asserting that the fundamental obligation is in truth limited to y. For example, a dealer selling a motor car and setting out details of the vehicle in the sale document will not (quite apart from statute) be able to rely on a clause excluding conditions and warranties as entitling him to proffer a machine which may or may not function as a motor car. **[661]**

The separate, though related, doctrine of fundamental breach has generated a mass of litigation, and even now it is difficult to state the doctrine with complete certainty. In essence, a party who commits a fundamental breach, that is, a breach which by its nature or consequences is so serious as to frustrate the commercial purpose of the contract, will not be allowed to fall back on an exemption clause unless (a) the innocent party elects to affirm the contract despite the breach *and* (b) the breach is one which as a matter of construction is covered by the exemption clause. The ineffectiveness of the exemption clause where the innocent party elects, or is as a matter of practicality constrained, to treat the contract as discharged by the breach now appears to represent a settled rule of law, though this has been modified by s. 9 of the Unfair Contract Terms Act 1977 (see para. [**671**]), and is not merely a rule of construction of the contract. It is based on the illogical premise that because the contract as a whole has ended, the exemption clause necessarily ceases to be operative. The reasoning is facile, however, for it is a common feature of contracts to provide for post-termination rights, duties and immunities, as in the case of provisions in a contract of employment restricting the employee from competition and from use of his employer's trade secrets after the contract of employment has ended. But where the innocent party elects to affirm the contract, he thereby lets in all his terms, including the exemption clause, and this will protect the party in breach if as a matter of construction the cause is apt to cover the breach in question. Though this aspect of the doctrine is a rule of construction, the court is unlikely in practice to find that an exemption clause was intended to be so wide in scope as to exclude liability before a fundamental breach. [**662**]

The particular feature of the doctrine of fundamental breach (and one which distinguishes it from the separate doctrine of fundamental term) is that the validity of the exemption clause is tested not by reference to the facts existing at the time of the contract but in the light of the consequences of the breach and other post-contract events and behaviour of the parties right up to the time of the proceedings. Further, in deciding whether the contract has been broken in some fundamental respect the court looks at the contract *apart from the exemption clause.* It is only at the second stage, when the court has decided that the breach is indeed fundamental, that recourse is then had to the exemption clause for the purpose of seeing whether it affords protection from liability as a matter of construction, and even this does not fall to be considered except in the event of the innocent party affirming the contract. [**663**]

Among the authorities for these propositions are *Suisse Atlantique Société d'Armement Maritime S.A.* v. *N.V. Rotterdamsche Kolen Centrale,* [1967] 1 A.C. 361, [1966] 2 All E.R. 61; *Harbutts 'Plasticine' Ltd.* v. *Wayne Tank and Pump Co., Ltd.,* [1970] 1 Q.B. 447, [1970] 1 All E.R. 225; *Farnworth Finance Facilities, Ltd.* v. *Attryde,* [1970] 2 All E.R. 774, [1970] 1 W.L.R. 1053; *Kenyon, Son and Craven Ltd.* v. *Baxter, Hoare & Co., Ltd.,* [1971] 2 All E.R. 708, [1971] 1 W.L.R. 519; *Wathes (Western), Ltd.* v. *Austin's Menswear, Ltd.,* [1976] 1 Lloyd's Rep. 14; and *Photo Production, Ltd.* v. *Securicor Transport, Ltd.,* [1978] 3 All E.R. 146, [1978] 1 W.L.R. 856. [**664**]

The Unfair Contract Terms Act

This Act, misnamed because it is not confined to contracts, nor does it give the courts a general power to re-open contracts merely because they are unfair, came into force on 1st February 1978 and does not apply to agreements made before that date but otherwise governs liability for any loss or damage suffered on or after that date (s. 31 (2)). The Act applies both to contractual exemption clauses and to disclaimers of tortious liability by notice. It is for the most part confined to business liability as defined by s. 1 (3). Contract terms and notices purporting to exclude or restrict liability for death or personal injury resulting from negligence are void (s. 2 (1)). In other cases, the term or notice will be ineffective except insofar as it satisfies the test of reasonableness. Section 3 of the Act lays down general provisions as to liability in contract.

> "(1) This section applies as between contracting parties where one of them deals as consumer or on the other's written standard terms of business.
> (2) As against that party, the other cannot by reference to any contract term—
>> (*a*) when himself in breach of contract, exclude or restrict any liability of his in respect of the breach; or
>> (*b*) claim entitled—
>>> (i) to render a contractual performance substantially different from that which was reasonably expected of him, or
>>> (ii) in respect of the whole or any part of his contractual obligation, to render no performance at all,
> except in so far as (in any of the cases mentioned above in this subsection) the contract term satisfies the requirement of reasonableness."

The phrase "dealing as consumer" is defined in s. 12 and despite appearances encompasses the status of both parties to the contract, not merely the "consumer". A person deals as consumer if he does not make or hold himself out as making the contract in the course of a business, the other party does make the contract in the course of a business and, where the contract involves the supply of goods, they are of a type ordinarily supplied for private use or consumption and are not being sold by auction or competitive tender. "Written standard terms of business" is not defined but presumably denotes any terms of business regularly used by a party as his terms of business, whether they were formulated by him or by a trade association or other third party for his use. For example, both builders and developers regularly using the JCT form of building contract would thereby be adopting its terms as their own written standard terms of business. Where in any given transaction buyer and seller both use standard terms so that there is a battle of the forms, the overriding terms will usually be those of the seller, on the basis that a purported acceptance of the buyer's offer but on different terms amounts to a counter-offer which the buyer will usually be found to have accepted by conduct. The buyer's conditions may still operate so far as not inconsistent with the seller's standard terms, in which case each party will be dealing by reference to the other's standard terms of business. [**665**]

It is to be observed that where a party deals on the other's written standard terms of business s. 3 applies whether or not the transaction is a consumer transaction. Accordingly a great many business contracts, including contracts between companies, large and small, are governed by s. 3. [**666**]

Section 3 (2) (*a*) is clear enough, though it should be borne in mind that "exclude or restrict any liability" has an extended meaning by virtue of s. 13. Paragraph (*b*) (i) of s. 3 (2) encapsulates the fundamental breach concept and may be regarded as the contract counterpart of the concluding lines of s. 13 (1) covering exclusion of liability in tort. The scope of para. (*b*) is unclear, but it is at least arguable that it is wide enough to encompass contractual provisions empowering a party to terminate a contract, whether for breach or otherwise, since the effect of lawful termination is that the party concerned is absolved from the duty of further performance. Certainly *force majeure* clauses appear to be within the scope of s. 3 (2) (*b*). [**667**]

Where s. 3 applies, the exempting term will not be effective except insofar as it satisfies the requirement of reasonableness. The effect of this provision is far from clear. Reasonableness is required to be tested in the light of the circumstances which were, or ought reasonably to have been, known to or in the contemplation of the parties when the contract was made (s. 11 (1)). Thus in contrast to the position under the Supply of Goods (Implied Terms) Act 1973 (where the question was not whether the term was reasonable but whether *reliance* on it was reasonable) post-contract events are *prima facie* to be ignored in determining whether the exemption clause satisfies the reasonableness test. But what is the position where, as seen at the time of the contract, the clause would be reasonable for some events and not reasonable for others, and the particular event that occurs is one for which, as seen at the time of the contract, it would be reasonable to provide an exemption from liability? It would seem that the court can and should give effect to the exemption clause in such circumstances, for it satisfies the requirement of reasonableness to the extent that it is aimed at the event that occurred, and the phrase "except insofar as ... the contract term satisfies the requirement of reasonableness)" suggests that where the court is able to apply the term without rewriting the contract, it is free to do so to the extent that the term is reasonable. The court will not, of course, do the work of the parties for them, and a clause seeking to impose on the court the burden of redrafting an exemption clause so as to narrow it to what is reasonable is likely to be doomed to failure. On the other hand, this problem does not arise if (*a*) the exemption clause as a whole can be applied without severance, leaving to be severed or distinguished merely those events that are reasonably covered by the clause from those that are not, the court looking at the particular event that has in fact occurred, or (*b*) the exempting provisions are so framed as to be susceptible to the blue pencil test, so that those parts which go beyond what is reasonable can be struck out without making nonsense of the contract or distorting its provisions or effect. [**668**]

Section 6 substantially re-enacts the Supply of Goods (Implied Terms) Act 1973 in relation to exemption clauses, except that reasonableness is tested as at the date of contract (s. 11 (1)), a wider range of clauses is caught (s. 13 (1)) and the coverage of international transactions is broadened (s. 26 (3) (*a*)). It should be borne in mind that s. 6, in dealing with contracts of sale and hire-purchase, complements and does not displace s. 2 and 3. [**669**]

The implied undertakings of the seller or owner (we shall hereafter use the term "supplier" to cover both) as to title, quiet possession and freedom from encumbrances cannot be excluded or restricted (s. 6 (1)), though the supplier can limit his obligation by contracting to transfer only such title as he or a third party may have (s. 12 (2)). As against a person dealing as consumer (see s. 12 and para.

227

[**665**]) any provision purporting to exclude or restrict the implied undertakings as to correspondence with description or sample, merchantable quality or fitness for purpose is void (s. 6 (2)); and as against a person dealing otherwise than as consumer, the provision is effective only so far as it satisfies the requirement of reasonableness. Section 7 contains similar provisions affecting hiring agreements. In determining reasonableness, the court is required to apply the guidelines laid down in Sch. 2, namely any of the following which appear to be relevant:

- (a) the strength of the bargaining positions of the parties relative to each other, taking into account (among other things) alternative means by which the customer's requirements could have been met;
- (b) whether the customer received an inducement to agree to the term, or in accepting it had an opportunity of entering into a similar contract with other persons, but without having to accept a similar term;
- (c) whether the customer knew or ought reasonably to have known of the existence and extent of the term (having regard, among other things, to any custom of the trade and any previous course of dealing between the parties);
- (d) where the term excludes or restricts any relevant liability if some condition is not complied with, whether it was reasonable at the time of the contract to expect that compliance with that condition would be practicable;
- (e) whether the goods were manufactured, processed or adapted to the special order of the customer.

In all cases, whether or not involving s. 6, the onus of showing that a contract term or notice satisfies the requirement of reasonableness lies on those claiming that it does (s. 11 (5)); and it is for those claiming that a party does not deal as consumer to show that he does not (s. 12 (3)). [**670**]

For the most part, the Act leaves untouched the common law rules concerning exemption clauses. However, an important modification is introduced by s. 9 (1) which provides:—

> "Where for reliance upon it a contract term has to satisfy the requirement of reasonableness, it may be found to do so and be given effect accordingly notwithstanding that the contract has been terminated either by breach or by a party electing to treat it as repudiated." [**671**]

The provisions of the Act cannot be evaded by the use of unreasonable indemnity clauses (s. 4 (1)), secondary contracts (s. 10) or the choice of a foreign law when the contract would otherwise have been governed by the law of any part of the United Kingdom (s. 27 (2) (a)). [**672**]

5. LIABILITY OF CREDITOR FOR MISREPRESENTATION OR BREACH OF CONTRACT BY SUPPLIER

Having examined the duties of the suppliers of goods and services at common law and by statute, and the conditions in which those duties can be qualified or excluded by contract or notice, we can now turn to the Consumer Credit Act and see in what circumstances the creditor or owner will be liable for the defaults of the supplier. [**673**]

In considering the creditor's liability for misrepresentations or breaches of contract by the supplier, it is necessary to distinguish the case where the creditor is himself the legal supplier—as where a finance house buys goods from a dealer and lets them on hire-purchase, or agrees to sell them on instalment sale to the dealer's customer—from the case where the sale is by the dealer himself, the purchase price being advanced by the finance house or other creditor by way of loan. Where a finance house disposes of goods under a regulated hire-purchase or instalment sale agreement, it is liable for misrepresentations made by the dealer in the course of antecedent negotiations, since the dealer is the negotiator by virtue of s. 56 (1) (*b*) (see para. [**596**]), and the negotiations are accordingly deemed to have been conducted by him as agent for the finance house as well as in his actual capacity (s. 56 (2)). The meaning of "negotiator" and "antecedent negotiations" has been fully discussed earlier (para. [**595**]). Section 56 (2) applies also where a finance house, pursuant to a pre-existing arrangement or in contemplation of a future arrangement with the dealer, lends money under a regulated agreement to enable the borrower to buy the goods from the dealer, who is then a negotiator under s. 56 (1) (*c*). But in this case s. 56 (2) (which is considered in more detail in the next chapter) is reinforced by section 75, which provides as follows:—

> "(1) If the debtor under a debtor-creditor-supplier agreement falling within section 12 (*b*) or (*c*) has, in relation to a transaction financed by the agreement, any claim against the supplier in respect of a misrepresentation or breach of contract, he shall have a like claim against the creditor, who, with the supplier, shall accordingly be jointly and severally liable to the debtor.
>
> (2) Subject to any agreement between them, the creditor shall be entitled to be indemnified by the supplier for loss suffered by the creditor in satisfying his liability under subsection (1), including costs reasonably incurred by him in defending proceedings instituted by the debtor.
>
> (3) Subsection (1) does not apply to a claim—
>
>   (*a*) under a non-commercial agreement, or
>   (*b*) so far as the claim relates to any single item to which the supplier has attached a cash price not exceeding £30 or more than £10,000.
>
> (4) This section applies notwithstanding that the debtor, in entering into the transaction, exceeded the credit limit or otherwise contravened any term of the agreement.
>
> (5) In an action brought against the creditor under subsection (1) he shall be entitled, in accordance with rules of court, to have the supplier made a party to the proceedings."

Several points arise in connection with this section. [**674**]

Types of agreement within section 75

Section 75 (1) is confined to cases in which the creditor and the supplier are different persons, i.e. where the credit takes the form of a loan financing a supply transaction between the debtor and a third party as supplier. Accordingly the section has no application to, say, a hire-purchase agreement between the debtor and a finance house, for though the goods may have been physically supplied by the dealer who introduced the credit transaction, the legal supplier is the finance house, and the debtor's claim against the finance house is for breach of its direct obligations as supplier. It follows, of course, that the right of indemnity given against the supplier has no relevance in this situation. If the finance house, on being sued by the debtor for defects in the goods supplied under the hire-purchase agreement, wishes to have recourse to the dealer from which it bought the goods, it must base its claim against the dealer on the contract of sale and/or any representations or warranties made by the dealer, and not on s. 75. [**675**]

The next point to note is that since s. 75 applies only to debtor-creditor-supplier agreements, it is by definition confined to regulated agreements (see s. 12). Thus no claim can be made against the creditor where the consumer credit agreement is an exempt agreement. Similarly, s. 75 does not apply where the credit agreement was made before the 1st April 1977, for such an agreement is not a regulated agreement (Consumer Credit Act 1974, Sch. 3 para. 1, as applied by the Consumer Credit Act 1974 (Commencement No. 2) Order 1977, art. 2 (1)). This order removes a doubt that might otherwise have arisen as to the retrospectivity of s. 75, the Act itself being silent on the point and the Sch. 3 raising conflicting presumptions where no rule is laid down (see para. [**1076**]). [**676**]

A controversy has arisen as to the effect of the order in relation to bank credit cards. The banks have taken the position that s. 75 does not apply to the use of a card if it was issued pursuant to a credit card agreement made before 1st April 1977. This view would appear to be unfounded. In the case of a unilateral contract established by a running-account credit agreement, there is a separate acceptance of the creditor's continuing offer each time the facility is utilised, so that on each occasion when the debtor uses the card a distinct contract is generated, governed by the terms of the running-account agreement (see para. [**245**]). It follows that s. 75 applies as regards any misrepresentation or breach of contract by a supplier who accepts the card on or after 1st April 1977, even though the document governing relations between the issuing bank and the cardholder was issued before that date. It seems quite clear that s. 75 is concerned with a credit agreement financing a specific transaction, and not merely with a general "agreement" prescribing standard terms for any future supply transaction the debtor might choose to enter into. Under pressure from the Office of Fair Trading the banks have in fact agreed to accept voluntarily joint and several liability even in relation to credit card agreements made before 1st April 1977, but only up to the sum advanced in connection with the relevant supply transaction. [**677**]

It is only claims against the supplier for misrepresentation or breach of contract that give rise to a concurrent claim against the creditor. Thus no claim can be made against the creditor under s. 75 (though a claim may be admissible by virtue of s. 56) in respect of a liability of the supplier so far as this arises from breach of statutory duty or in tort for negligence or fraud otherwise than in respect of a misrepresentation. Moreover the liability of the creditor is confined to cases where the transaction with a supplier on which the claim is based is the transaction financed by the debtor-creditor-supplier agreement. Accordingly the creditor is not, for example, liable for the supplier's breach of an ancillary maintenance contract unless the maintenance services as well as the contract for the supply of the related goods are being financed by the creditor. [**678**]

Quantum of the creditor's liability

It is worth underlining the point that the liability of the creditor to the debtor under s. 75 is co-terminous with the liability of the supplier to the debtor for misrepresentation or breach of contract. To the extent to which the supplier effectively excludes or restricts his liability, the exclusion or restriction enures for the protection of the creditor in any claim made against him under s. 75. Conversely, insofar as a purported exclusion or restriction of liability in the supply contract is ineffective to protect the supplier, the creditor will not be able to avail himself of it; nor will he be able to invoke a term of the *credit* agreement purporting to exclude or restrict the statutory rights of the debtor under the supply contract, for this is caught by s. 10 of the Unfair Contract Terms Act 1977 (see para. [**672**]).

[**679**]

It is thought that a creditor sued under s. 75 can exercise any right of set-off vested in the supplier, as well as any right of set-off available to the creditor in his own right. If this were not the case, the supplier would effectively be deprived of his right of set-off against the debtor, for upon the debtor suing the creditor the latter would have a right of indemnity against the supplier under s. 75. [**680**]

The liability of the creditor is not (as it was in an earlier version of the Consumer Credit Bill) limited to cases where the debtor's claim against the supplier is in the form of damages. Thus, if the debtor exercises a right to rescind the sale agreement for misrepresentation and pursues a restitutionary remedy for recovery of payments he has made, then whilst the finance house would not be a proper party to a claim for rescission (which can only be made against the other contracting party) it is jointly and severally liable to give restitution by paying back to the debtor sums paid by him under the rescinded agreement, whether those sums were paid to the finance house or to the supplier. [**681**]

The creditor's liability under s. 75 (1) arises even if the debtor, in entering into the supply transaction, exceeded the credit limit or otherwise contravened any term of the agreement (s. 75 (4)). Thus if a debtor enjoying a credit card facility which enables him to pay by instalments utilises the card to purchase goods which prove defective, he has a claim against the issuer of the card under s. 75 even though the purchase may have taken his debit balance above the limit for which he was entitled to use the card under his agreement with the issuer. [**682**]

Parties liable under section 75

The debtor can pursue his claim under s. 75 (1) against the supplier, the creditor or both. An unsatisfied judgment against one does not bar proceedings against the other (*Blyth* v. *Fladgate*, [1891] 1 Ch. 337; and see now the Civil Liability (Contribution) Act 1978, s. 3). It would seem that a claim under s. 75 must be made against the original creditor, not an assignee, despite the definition of "creditor" in s. 189 (1). On the other hand, there seems no reason why a claim available against the original creditor under s. 75 should not be set off against a claim by the assignee, if the requisite conditions for pleading a set-off are satisfied. [**683**]

Creditor's right of indemnity

Subject to any agreement between them, the creditor is entitled to be indemnified by the supplier for loss suffered by the creditor in satisfying his liability under s. 75 (1), including costs reasonably incurred by him in defending proceedings instituted by the debtor (s. 75 (2)). For this purpose, the creditor is entitled, when sued by the debtor, to have the supplier made a party to proceedings in accordance with rules of court (s. 75 (5)) i.e. by third-party notice under RSC Order 16 or CCR Order 12. [**684**]

Exemptions from section 75

Section 75 (1) does not apply in any of the circumstances listed in s. 75 (3) (see para. [**640**]). Section 75 (3) would appear to apply to contracts for the supply of services as well as contracts for the supply of goods. However some difficulty is likely to be occasioned by s. 75 (3) (*b*). What constitutes an "item" for the purpose of this paragraph? If several goods are supplied under a single sale contract and are individually priced, s. 75 (1) will not apply to any article priced at £30 or less. Similarly, if any part of an article is individually priced at £30 or less, s. 75 (1) will not apply to that part, even if the rest of the article is within the section. But can the debtor invoke s. 75 (1) if his complaint is that the article as a whole is defective because of (and only because of) a defective part priced at not more than £30. Again, if the supply contract is for the execution of, say, building works in accordance with a priced specification and because of defects in the quality or performance of an article or item of work priced at £25 the debtor incurs substantial expenditure in having remedial work carried out, is his claim to be treated as relating to that item as such or is it simply a claim for defective performance of an entire contract? Still more difficult is the case where the claim arises because of defects in two or more items, one of which is priced at £30 or under. The exemption given by s. 75 (3) applies "so far as" the claim relates to the latter item—but how is the claim to be apportioned? Clearly s. 75 (3) raises some tantalising problems and one can only speculate on the outcome if these are ever litigated. [**685**]

Foreign supply contracts

The fact that the supply contract is governed by foreign law would not appear to affect the creditor's liability under s. 75 of the Act, assuming that the credit agreement is itself within the Act. Thus, a bank issuing a credit card under a regulated consumer credit agreement will be liable under s. 75 if the cardholder uses the card abroad to purchase goods or obtain services and the supplier commits a misrepresentation or breach of contract. This may seem hard; but it has to be remembered that liability is imposed on the creditor only as the result of the credit being extended pursuant to or in contemplation of arrangements between him and the supplier, and it is therefore for the creditor to exercise care in selecting overseas suppliers with whom to conclude arrangements. Indeed, it can be argued that the consumer needs even greater protection in dealings with a foreign supplier than with a trader in his own country, for the problems of litigating abroad are formidable. However, the fact that the supply transaction is governed by foreign law may indirectly assist the creditor, for his liability is tailored to that of the supplier, and the latter's duties under the applicable foreign law may be less onerous, and his ability to exclude them may be greater, than in the case of a supply contract governed by English law. A creditor sued under s. 75 in respect of breaches under a foreign supply contract should, however, remember that so far as English civil procedure is concerned foreign law is presumed to be the same as

English law unless otherwise proved, and if the foreign law is less stringent as regards the supplier's duties it should be properly pleaded and established by evidence at the trial. [**686**]

17. Agency

This chapter discusses the circumstances in which the creditor or owner may incur a liability for, or be legally bound by, the acts and omissions of those who are to be deemed his agents for the purpose of the Consumer Credit Act. For brevity, "creditor" will be used to describe the creditor or owner, and "debtor" to denote the debtor or hirer, unless otherwise indicated. [**687**]

1. AGENCY AT COMMON LAW

At common law, the creditor is bound by the acts of his agent acting within the scope of the agent's actual, apparent (ostensible) or usual authority. The extent to which the dealer through whom a hire-purchase agreement is concluded with a finance house is to be considered the agent of the finance house has been briefly discussed in Chapter 4, and a detailed analysis is given in R. M. Goode, *Hire Purchase Law and Practice* (2nd Edn.) Chapter 13. For principles of agency in relation to other types of transaction, reference should be made to standard texts on agency, in particular *Bowstead on Agency* (14th Edn.), G. H. L. Fridman, *Law of Agency* (4th Edn.), *Powell's Law of Agency*, and to the Agency titles in Halsbury's Laws of England (4th Edn.), Vol. I and *Chitty on Contracts* (24th Edn.) Chapter 1. [**688**]

2. AGENCY UNDER THE CONSUMER CREDIT ACT

Negotiations
The Act provides that negotiations with the debtor in a case falling within s. 56 (1) (*b*) or (*c*) shall be deemed to be conducted by the negotiator in the capacity of an agent of the creditor as well as in his actual capacity (s. 56 (2)). Example of deemed agents under section 56 (1) (*b*) and (*c*) have been given in Chapter 15, which also contains a discussion of the meaning of "antecedent negotiations" and the time when such negotiations are to be considered as beginning and ending (see paras. [**596**]–[**597**]). [**689**]

It would seem that when s. 56 (2) treats negotiations as conducted by the negotiator in the capacity of agent for the creditor, it also intends that such negotiations shall be deemed to have been contracted in the course and within the scope of the deemed agency. That is to say, the words "in the capacity of" import a deemed authority from the creditor to conduct the negotiations, so making it unnecessary to consider whether, for example, representations made by the negotiator in the course of negotiations were within or outside the scope of his actual or apparent authority. If this interpretation of the section were not correct, a serious difficulty would arise, for the agency created by the Act is, of course, purely notional, and what acts could be treated as performed in the course and scope of an agency that might not in fact exist? Hence to give effect to s. 56 (2) we have to assume that acts done and statements made by the negotiator in the antecedent negotiations are authorised by the creditor, whether or not they would have been treated at common law as within the negotiator's actual, apparent or usual authority. The inevitable conclusion is that in this situation the usual fetters on the power of an agent to commit his principal do not apply, and that provided the debtor to whom the representations are made acts in good faith he can treat the negotiator's representations as those of the creditor himself, however fanciful and extravagant they may be and whether or not they are of a kind which a person in the position of a negotiator would ordinarily be authorised to make by a person in the position of the creditor. [**690**]

What, then, are the consequences of the deemed agency arising under s. 56 (2)? In principle, the creditor is bound by the statements of the negotiator and incurs a non-excludable liability for the wrongful statements (and probably other wrongful acts—see para. [**698**]) of the negotiator in the course of the negotiations, whether they are wrongful because they infringe the Act or for any other reason. This creates a curious position in relation to attempts to exclude or restrict liability (see para. [**701**]) and also raises a nice question as to the creditor's liability in tort for the pre-contract negligence of the negotiator (see para. [**700**]). [**691**]

It would seem that s. 56 is not triggered off unless the agreement which is under negotiation is in fact concluded, but that once this has happened the section then latches on to the pre-contract statements and dealings of the negotiator. As to this, see paras. [**699**] *et seq.* [**692**]

Statements by the negotiator

(i) *Types of statement within the deemed agency*
Plainly the creditor is bound by promises made by the negotiator, and is answerable for the negotiator's false or misleading statements, so far as made in the course of negotiations and not subsequently displaced (see para. [**695**]), for the making of statements is the essence of negotiation. Indeed, s. 56 (4) says in terms that antecedent negotiations include any representations made by the negotiator to the debtor, and "representation" includes any condition or warranty (s. 189 (1)). Of course, the statement will not be a condition or warranty at the time it is made (for *ex hypothesi* the parties are still in negotiation), and s. 56 (4) must be read as meaning that negotiations include pre-contract statements made by the negotiator to the debtor whether or not they are then intended as, or later become, terms of the credit agreement. "Representation" thus covers a pre-contract statement which was not intended as a promise and does not become a term of the

contract; a pre-contract statement which was not at the time of its making intended
as a promise but is later incorporated as a term of the contract; and a statement
which at the time of its making was intended as a promise, whether or not it
features in the contract when this is finally concluded. Moreover, a representation
does not have to be express. It may be implied by conduct, and even silence may
constitute a representation, as where the prospective debtor makes a comment
concerning the apparent good quality of the goods in the presence of the negotiator,
who says nothing to disillusion him. [**693**]

(ii) *Classifying the negotiator's statement*
    The precise classification of the negotiator's statement may be far from easy.
In particular, there is some difficulty in ascribing to a deemed agent an intention to
make a promise or offer as a term of a projected contract with a deemed principal
when no agency may in fact exist. For example, H enters into a hire-purchase
agreement with a finance house, F, to acquire on hire-purchase a car supplied by a
dealer, D, through whom the agreement was concluded, D having stated in the
course of negotiations that the car had travelled only 10,000 miles when in fact it
had covered 40,000 miles. At common law, the dealer is probably not the agent of
the finance house for the purpose of this representation, and it is unlikely that this
statement was intended as a promise on behalf of the finance house. There are,
however, at least six different ways in which such a statement could be classified:—
  (*a*) As a mere representation not intended to be a promise by D either on
         behalf of F or on his own behalf.
  (*b*) As a promise on behalf of F forming a term of the hire-purchase
         agreement.
  (*c*) As a promise on behalf of F constituting an overrriding warranty or
         collateral contract between F and H and representing the consideration
         for H's entry into the hire-purchase agreement.
  (*d*) As a promise by D solely on his own behalf, generating a collateral
         contract between himself and H (see para. [**697**]).
  (*e*) As both a promise by D on his own behalf and a mere representation on
         behalf of F.
  (*f*) As both a promise by D on his own behalf and a promise on behalf of F
         as a term of the hire-purchase agreement or alternatively as a term of a
         collateral contract between F and H.
Of these various alternatives, only (*d*) is ruled out by the Act, by virtue of s. 56
(2). The theoretical answer, of course, is that it all depends on D's intention when
making the statement; but this does not advance the argument greatly, for D's
actual intention is usually a matter of conjecture and in practice has to be ascribed
to him by a robust finding of fact by the judge. In most cases, it may not matter
greatly which avenue of redress is pursued, since if one thing is certain it is that in
one way or another the debtor will almost invariably be able to fix liability on the
creditor. But the quantum of the debtor's claim may be affected by the ground on
which it is based; and quite apart from this, formidable problems confront a
pleader who wishes to cover all possibilities in his pleading. [**694**]

(iii) *Misrepresentation not incorporated as a contract term*
    Where the debtor is induced to enter into the credit agreement as the result of
the negotiator's misrepresentation, then whether this misrepresentation relates to
the terms of the credit agreement (e.g. the cost of the credit) or to the description,

quality or condition of the goods, or to any other facet of the intended transaction, the debtor is entitled to rescind the credit agreement by notice either to the creditor or to the negotiator (s. 102 (1)), and having rescinded may recover any deposit or other monies paid from the person to whom it was paid (which may include the creditor himself, in a balance of account, even though paid to the negotiator—see para. [**99**]) and any goods tendered in part-exchange or their price as represented by the part-exchange allowance. As to part-exchange transactions generally, see R. M. Goode, *op. cit.*, Chapter 14. In addition, the creditor will be liable in tort for a fraudulent misrepresentation by the negotiator, though a claim in deceit will not lie where the negotiator's statement is made in good faith and the creditor, though aware that the facts are not as represented, did not know and had no reason to suppose that the representation would be made (*Armstrong* v. *Strain*, [1952] 1 K.B. 232, [1952] 1 All E.R. 139). On the other hand, if the misrepresentation, though in good faith, was negligent, the creditor will be liable in damages under s. 2 (1) of the Misrepresentation Act and probably also under the *Hedley Byrne* principle (see *Esso Petroleum Co., Ltd.* v. *Mardon*, [1976] Q.B. 801, [1976] 2 All E.R. 5), the statutory remedy providing the advantage that the onus lies on the creditor of disproving negligence.

To be actionable, the misrepresentation must still have had force at the time of the credit agreement. Accordingly if before then the creditor has learned the true facts or has otherwise ceased to rely on the false statement, the creditor will not incur any liability in respect of it. [**695**]

(iv) *Misstatement as a term of contract with the creditor*
The misstatement may start life as an intended contract term or it may begin as a mere representation and be incorporated as a contract term later, in which event the debtor will have the option of pursuing remedies for misrepresentation on the one hand (rescission, restitution, etc.) or for breach of contract (termination, damages, etc.) on the other. Whether the statement constitutes a term of the credit agreement itself or a term of a collateral agreement between debtor and creditor is largely academic, though it may have some relevance, e.g. for the purpose of determining whether the document recording the credit agreement contains all the terms as required by s. 61 of the Act (paras. [**547**] *et seq.*). [**696**]

(v) *Misstatement as a warranty by the negotiator on his own behalf*
Quite apart from the effect of the statement as a deemed statement by the creditor himself, it may be held to constitute a collateral warranty involving the negotiator in personal liability if it proves false. See, for example, *Andrews* v. *Hopkinson*, [1957] 1 Q.B. 229, [1956] 3 All E.R. 422; *Brown* v. *Sheen and Richmond Car Sales, Ltd.*, [1950] 1 All E.R. 1102; and R. M. Goode, *Hire-Purchase Law and Practice* (2nd Edn.) pp. 638 *et seq.* [**697**]

Other acts of the negotiator
The phrase "antecedent negotiations" is not confined to representations but embraces "other dealings" between the negotiator and the debtor (s. 56 (4)). The word "dealings" would seem to encompass any act by the negotiator which promotes or furthers the projected regulated agreement (cf. s. 58 (3) of the Hire Purchase Act 1965). It would appear to include delivery of the goods in anticipation of the making of the credit agreement and steps in or towards the

conclusion of ancillary contracts, e.g. of installation, maintenance or insurance. If this be right, then the delivery of dangerous goods by the negotiator to the debtor before the making of the credit agreement may, when such agreement is made, involve the creditor in liability in tort for negligence whether or not the negotiator made any representation to the debtor concerning the goods (see *infra*). [**698**]

The time factor under section 56

It would seem that s. 56 does not become operative unless the projected regulated agreement to which the negotiations relate actually comes into being. If no agreement of any kind results between the prospective creditor and the prospective debtor, the negotiations are outside s. 56. If an agreement does result, s. 56 will apply so long as the agreement can be said to be one to which the negotiations "relate", even if it is not on the terms provisionally settled between the prospective debtor and the negotiator. [**699**]

More difficult is the question whether the creditor is liable for physical injury or damage suffered by the debtor before entry into the credit agreement, as the result of the negligent statements or acts of the negotiator. For example, if a motor dealer, D, in anticipation of the making of a hire-purchase agreement between H and F relating to a motor car to be supplied by D, negligently delivers the car to H in an unsafe condition, with the result that H suffers injury before F has signed the hire-purchase agreement, does the coming into force of the agreement render F liable for D's negligence? If the claim were to rest in contract, the answer would be no, for the hire-purchase agreement operates only from the time of its making (see *Newlands* v. *Argyll Insurance Co., Ltd.* (1959) S.R. (N.S.W.) 130, the facts of which are given in R. M. Goode, *op. cit.* pp. 149–150). But F's liability for the acts of D under s. 56 is not merely *ex contractu*, but can arise in tort also, and once D's negligence becomes attributed to F as the result of F's entry into the hire-purchase agreement it would seem to follow that F is liable for that negligence even though the injury or damage occurred before the agreement was made. Thus s. 56, like s. 16 of the Hire Purchase Act 1965 produces the unusual situation that the making of the contract between F and H enlarges H's rights in tort. [**700**]

Exclusion of liability

An agreement is void if and to the extent that it purports in relation to an actual or prospective regulated agreement—

(a) to provide that a person acting as, or on behalf of, a negotiator is to be treated as the agent of the debtor or hirer, or

(b) to relieve a person from liability for acts or omissions of any person acting as, or on behalf of, a negotiator (s. 56 (3)).

At first sight, this appears to create the paradoxical situation that the creditor could not effectively exclude liability for the acts of his negotiator even if he could validly have exempted himself from liability for defective performance of the acts himself. Such a result can scarcely have been the intention of the legislature, and it is submitted that s. 56 (3) (b) merely prevents the creditor from contracting out of his *vicarious* liability for the acts and omissions of his negotiator and does not preclude him from excluding a purely *personal* liability that would otherwise be imposed on him by reason of his own breach of duty committed through the medium of his deemed agent. The distinction between vicarious liability and personal liability is well established in the law of tort, though often difficult to apply. Of course, the ability of the creditor to exclude or limit his personal liability may be restricted by other provisions of the Consumer Credit Act or by other legislation (e.g. the Unfair Contract Terms Act 1977) or rules of common law (see paras. [**660**] *et seq.*). [**701**]

Notices

The Act provides that—

(*a*) a creditor-broker or supplier who is the negotiator in antecedent negotiations, and

(*b*) any person who, in the course of a business carried on by him, acts on behalf of the debtor or hirer in any negotiations for the agreement,

is to be deemed the agent of the creditor for the purpose of receiving a notice of withdrawal by the debtor from a prospective agreement (s. 57 (3)), a notice of cancellation by the debtor under s. 69 of the Act (s. 69 (6)) and a notice rescinding the agreement otherwise than under section 69 (s. 102). As to the effect of s. 175 in relation to the receipt of notices by such deemed agents, see para. [**1093**]. [**702**]

Misuse of credit facilities

Section 83 (1) provides that the debtor under a regulated consumer credit agreement shall not be liable to the creditor for any loss arising from the use of the credit facility by another person not acting, or to be treated as acting, as the debtor's agent. The Act contains no provision by which any person is to be treated as the debtor's agent, and accordingly the reference must be to cases of ostensible authority or agency by estoppel at common law. [**703**]

18. The Supply of Information

The need to know
A key feature of protection for the consumer in credit transactions is the supply of information before, upon and after entering into the contract, which will make him aware of his essential statutory rights and keep him informed as to the state of his account with the creditor. The Consumer Credit Act thus contains numerous provisions designed to ensure that the debtor or hirer is suitably informed. Similar protection is given to a surety. There is also one case in which the duty goes the other way, and the obligation is imposed on the debtor or hirer to supply information to the creditor or owner. [**704**]

Pre-contract disclosure
We have already discussed the provisions of Part IV relating to advertisements, quotations and the display of information (see Chapter 12) and the provisions of Part V as to the disclosure of information before the making of a regulated agreement and in documents embodying a regulated agreement (see Chapter 14). The duty to supply copies of the contract document, and of documents referred to in it, has also been noted (Chapter 14). In addition the Act provides for the supply of information to the debtor or hirer during the currency of the agreement. Under some provisions, the duty is to provide information on request; under others, it is automatic. The nature of the information to be provided depends upon whether the agreement is a consumer credit or consumer hire agreement, and in the former case whether it is for fixed-sum credit or running-account credit. Regard should also be had to the entirely distinct duty imposed by s. 97 to supply a settlement figure on request (see para. [**711**]) and by s. 110 to supply the debtor or hirer with a copy of any security instrument (para. [**713**]). [**705**]

Fixed-sum credit
Section 77 provides as follows:
>"(1) The creditor under a regulated agreement for fixed-sum credit, within the prescribed period after receiving a request in writing to that effect from the debtor and payment of a fee of 15 new pence, shall give the debtor a copy of the executed

agreement (if any) and of any other document referred to in it, together with a statement signed by or on behalf of the creditor showing, according to the information to which it is practicable for him to refer—

    (*a*) the total sum paid under the agreement by the debtor;

    (*b*) the total sum which has become payable under the agreement by the debtor but remains unpaid, and the various amounts comprised in that total sum, with the date when each became due; and

    (*c*) the total sum which is to become payable under the agreement by the debtor, and the various amounts comprised in that total sum, with the date, or mode of determining the date, when each becomes due.

    (2) If the creditor possesses insufficient information to enable him to ascertain the amounts and dates mentioned in subsection (1) (*c*), he shall be taken to comply with that paragraph if his statement under subsection (1) gives the basis on which, under the regulated agreement, they would fall to be ascertained.

    (3) Subsection (1) does not apply to—

    (*a*) an agreement under which no sum is, or will or may become, payable by the debtor, or

    (*b*) a request made less than one month after a previous request under that subsection relating to the same agreement was complied with.

    (4) If the creditor under an agreement fails to comply with subsection (1)—

    (*a*) he is not entitled, while the default continues, to enforce the agreement; and

    (*b*) if the default continues for one month he commits an offence.

    (5) This section does not apply to a non-commercial agreement."

It is in the creditor's own interest to ensure that the information supplied in a statement under s. 77 (1) is correct, since the statement is binding on him (s. 172 (1)). If, therefore, the creditor informs the debtor that the outstanding balance is £100 when it is in fact £500, the debtor is entitled to a termination statement (see para. [**712**]) on tendering £100. This is subject, however, to the powers of the court under s. 172 (3) to direct such relief (if any) to be given to the creditor, or owner as appears to the court to be just (see para. [**1090**]). [**706**]

Running-account credit

In the case of running-account credit, s. 78 (1) imposes a similar duty to supply information on request, save that the information to be supplied is:

    (*a*) the state of the account, and

    (*b*) the amount, if any, currently payable under the agreement by the debtor to the creditor, and

    (*c*) the amounts and due dates of any payments which, if the debtor does not draw further on the account, will later become payable under the agreement by the debtor to the creditor.

The same qualifications and exceptions are provided by s. 78 (2) and (3) as are furnished by s. 77 (2) and (3) in relation to fixed-sum credit; and a statement under s. 78 (1) is binding under s. 172 (1) in the same way as a statement under s. 77 (1), and subject to the same relief. [**707**]

In addition, where running-account credit is provided there is a duty to furnish periodic statements of account automatically, whether or not requested by the debtor. Section 78 of the Act further provides—

"(4) Where running-account credit is provided under a regulated agreement, the creditor shall give the debtor statements in the prescribed form, and with the prescribed contents—

(*a*) showing according to the information to which it is practicable for him to refer, the state of the account at regular intervals of not more than twelve months, and

(*b*) where the agreement provides, in relation to specified periods, for the making of payments by the debtor, or the charging against him of interest or any other sum, showing according to the information to which it is practicable for him to refer the state of the account at the end of each of those periods during which there is any movement in the account.

(5) A statement under subsection (4) shall be given within the prescribed period after the end of the period to which the statement relates.

(6) If the creditor under an agreement fails to comply with subsection (1)—

(*a*) he is not entitled, while the default continues, to enforce the agreement; and

(*b*) if the default continues for one month he commits an offence."

But apart from the general exception in respect of non-commercial agreements (s. 78 (7)), the duty to supply information automatically is also excluded in the case of small agreements (*ibid.*). Moreover, a statement under s. 78 (4) is not caught by s. 172 (1) and is therefore not binding on the creditor under that section, though it may in certain cases bind the creditor as a matter of general law. [**708**]

Consumer hire

Section 79 (1) provides:

"The owner under a regulated consumer hire agreement, within the prescribed period after receiving a request in writing to that effect from the hirer and payment of a fee of 15 new pence, shall give to the hirer a copy of the executed agreement and of any other document referred to in it, together with a statement signed by or on behalf of the owner showing, according to the information to which it is practicable for him to refer, the total sum which has become payable under the agreement by the hirer but remains unpaid and the various amounts comprised in that total sum, with the date when each became due."

The same exemptions from this duty are given as in s. 77 (3) and (5), and the same sanctions for infringement are imposed as in ss. 77 (4) and 172 (1) (see para. [**706**]). [**709**]

Whereabouts of goods

Where a regulated agreement, other than a non-commercial agreement, requires the debtor or hirer to keep goods to which the agreement relates in his possession or control, he must, within seven working days after he has received a request in writing to that effect from the creditor or owner, tell the creditor or owner where the goods are (s. 80 (1)). "Working day" is defined in s. 189 (1) (see para. [**332**]). If the debtor or hirer fails to comply with s. 80 (1) and the default continues for 14 days, he commits an offence (s. 80 (2)). [**710**]

Information as to settlement figure

Section 97 provides as follows:

"(1) The creditor under a regulated consumer credit agreement, within the prescribed period after he has received a request in writing to that effect from the debtor, shall give the debtor a statement in the prescribed form indicating, according to the information to which it is practicable for him to refer, the amount of the payment required to discharge the debtor's indebtedness under the agreement, together with the prescribed particulars showing how the amount is arrived at.

(2) Subsection (1) does not apply to a request made less then one month after a previous request under that subsection relating to the same agreement was complied with.

(3) If the creditor fails to comply with subsection (1)—

(a) he is not entitled, while the default continues, to enforce the agreement; and

(b) if the default continues for one month he commits an offence."

At first sight, this section would appear to overlap completely with ss. 77 and 78, which require the creditor to supply the debtor on request with (*inter alia*) a statement of the total sum remaining payable under the agreement. It must, however, be remembered that this is not necessarily the same as the settlement figure called for by s. 97, which must be calculated so as to take into account any statutory rebate to which the debtor will be entitled by virtue of regulations under s. 95 (see para. [**734**]). Such regulations can only provide for a rebate in relation to a consumer credit agreement, not a consumer hire agreement. It is for this reason that s. 97 is itself confined to consumer credit agreements. [**711**]

A statement under s. 97 (1) binds the creditor under s. 172 (1) in the same way as under s. 77 (1) (see para. [**706**]). [**712**]

Security instrument

Section 110 provides as follows:

"(1) The creditor or owner under a regulated agreement, within the prescribed period after receiving a request in writing to that effect from the debtor or hirer and payment of a fee of 15 new pence, shall give the debtor or hirer a copy of any security instrument executed in relation to the agreement after the making of the agreement.

(2) Subsection (1) does not apply to—

   (a) a non-commercial agreement, or

   (b) an agreement under which no sum is, or will or may become, payable by the debtor or hirer, or

   (c) a request made less than one month after a previous request under subsection (1) relating to the same agreement was complied with.

(3) If the creditor or owner under an agreement fails to comply with subsection (1)—

   (a) he is not entitled, while the default continues, to enforce the security (so far as provided in relation to the agreement); and

   (b) if the default continues for one month he commits an offence." [713]

Sureties

Sections 107–109 require the creditor, within the prescribed period after receiving a request in writing to that effect from a surety and payment of a fee of 15 new pence, to provide the surety with the same statement as could have been called for by the debtor under ss. 77–79, and in addition to supply a copy of the executed agreement (if any) and of any other document referred to in it, together with a copy of the security instrument (if any). "Security instrument" will normally denote the contract of guarantee itself (see the definition of "security instrument" in s. 105 (2) and of "security" in s. 189 (1), discussed in para. [764]–[765]), but would also embrace any other form of security document taken by the creditor, whether from the surety, the debtor or another surety. The same exceptions apply, and the same sanctions are imposed, *i.e.* unforceability of the security (so far as provided in relation to the agreement) while the default continues and the commission of an offence if the default continues for one month. A statement given to the surety under s. 107 (1) (c), 108 (1) (c) or 109 (1) (c) is binding under s. 172 in the same circumstances as described for a statement under s. 77 (1) (see para. [706]). [714]

Termination statement

From time to time a debtor under a completed credit agreement may have need of written evidence to show that he has completed his payments. Some creditors automatically provide this; other do not unless requested; whilst some even decline altogether to furnish completion certificates. To remedy this difficulty, s. 103 of the Consumer Credit Act provides as follows:

"(1) If an individual (the 'customer') serves on any person (the 'trader') a notice—

   (a) stating that—

      (i) the customer was the debtor or hirer under a regulated agreement described in the notice, and the trader was the creditor or owner under the agreement, and

      (ii) the customer has discharged his indebtedness to the trader under the agreement; and

      (iii) the agreement has ceased to have any operation;

and

    (*b*) requiring the trader to give the customer a notice, signed by or on behalf of the trader, confirming that those statements are correct,
the trader shall, within the prescribed period after receiving the notice, either comply with it or serve on the customer a counter-notice stating that, as the case may be, he disputes the correctness of the notice or asserts that the customer is not indebted to him.

    (2) Where the trader disputes the correctness of the notice he shall give particulars of the way in which he alleges it to be wrong.

    (3) Subsection (1) does not apply in relation to any agreement if the trader has previously complied with that subsection on the service of a notice under it with respect to that agreement.

    (4) Subsection (1) does not apply to a non-commercial agreement.

    (5) If the trader fails to comply with subsection (1), and the default continues for one month, he commits an offence."

A notice given by a trader under s. 103 (1) (*b*) is binding on him (s. 172 (2)), subject to the provisions of s. 172 (3) (see para. **1090**)). [**715**]

19. Variation of Agreements

Introduction

In general, the parties to a consumer credit or consumer hire agreement are free to vary it as they think fit, as in the case of other contracts. However, in the consumer credit field special care needs to be exercised by the creditor to ensure:

(a) that he does not, by concluding a binding variation, discharge a surety who has guaranteed the debtor's obligations;

(b) that the variation does not infringe any applicable hire-purchase or hiring Control Order;

(c) that the variation agreement accords with such formalities as may be prescribed by or under the Consumer Credit Act;

(d) that he is aware of the effect of the variation under the Act. [**716**]

The general principles governing the variation of credit agreements have been analysed in some detail by the author in *Hire-Purchase Law and Practice* (2nd Edn.), Chapter 15. The same work deals with the restrictions on variation imposed by the Hire-Purchase and Credit Sale Agreements (Control) Order and the Control of Hiring Order (see *op. cit.*, pp. 968–970, 987–988), and whilst the Orders there referred to are the 1969 Orders, the same reasoning affects current Orders which are in almost identical language. As regards the general law, a surety is usually discharged by a variation in the agreement to which his guarantee relates, unless the variation was made with his consent or the contract of guarantee contains provisions preserving his liability. Hence an agreement to substitute goods or to reschedule payments would release the surety (see generally R. M. Goode, *op. cit.*, pp. 494 *et seq*). [**717**]

General effect of variations under the Act

The consequences of a contractual variation of a regulated agreement are dealt with by s. 82 which provides as follows:

"(1) Where, under a power contained in a regulated agreement, the creditor or owner varies the agreement, the variation shall not take effect before notice of it is given to the debtor or hirer in the prescribed manner.

(2) Where an agreement (a "modifying agreement") varies or supplements an earlier agreement, the modifying agreement

246.

shall for the purposes of this Act be treated as
    (*a*) revoking the earlier agreement, and
    (*b*) containing provisions reproducing the combined effect
        of the two agreements,
and obligations outstanding in relation to the earlier agreement shall accordingly be treated as outstanding in relation to modifying agreement.

(3) If the earlier agreement is a regulated agreement but (apart from this subsection) the modifying agreement is not then, unless the modifying agreement is for running-account credit, it shall be treated as a regulated agreement.

(4) If the earlier agreement is a regulated agreement for running-account credit, and by the modifying agreement the creditor allows the credit limit to be exceeded but intends the excess to be merely temporary, Part V (except section 56) shall not apply to the modifying agreement.

(5) If—
    (*a*) the earlier agreement is a cancellable agreement, and
    (*b*) the modifying agreement is made within the period
        applicable under section 68 to the earlier agreement,
then, whether or not the modifying agreement would, apart from this subsection, be a cancellable agreement, it shall be treated as a cancellable agreement in respect of which a notice may be served under section 68 not later than the end of the period applicable under that section to the earlier agreement.

(6) Except under subsection (5A), a modifying agreement shall not be treated as a cancellable agreement.

(7) This section does not apply to a non-commercial agreement."

The effect of this section (which came into force on 1st April 1977 by virtue of the Consumer Credit Act 1974 (Commencement No. 2) Order 1977) is not altogether easy to determine, and we shall consider different aspects in the following paragraphs. [**718**]

The need for notice

Section 82 (1) of the Act provides that where, under a power contained in a regulated agreement, the creditor or owner varies the agreement, the variation is not to take effect before notice of it is given to the debtor or hirer in the prescribed manner. This provision is confined to cases where the creditor has an *option* to vary. It does not embrace automatic variation pursuant to the terms of the agreement itself, e.g. under a provision that interest shall be charged at 2% above Finance House base rate for the time being. [**719**]

Where the provisions of a regulated agreement do empower the creditor to vary it, then before the variation can become effective notice of it must be given to the debtor or hirer in the prescribed manner, that is, in conformity with the requirements of the Consumer Credit (Notice of Variation of Agreements) Regulations 1977. Section 82 (1) applies only where the power of variation is contained in the regulated agreement itself. This allows the possibility of restricting the scope of s. 82 by transferring to a separate agreement variation provisions which are not a necessary part of the regulated agreement itself. For example, if maintenance charges are imposed, with power in the creditor to vary maintenance charges, the inclusion of such provisions in the regulated agreement itself attracts the operation of s. 82 (1) and the above regulations, whereas if such provisions are omitted and embodied in a separate maintenance agreement that contract is a linked transaction, not a regulated agreement, and is thus outside the scope of s 82 (1). **[720]**

Contents of notice

The notice of variation must in all cases set out particulars of the variation (reg. 2 (*a*)). **[721]**

Service of notice

The general rule is that the notice must be served on the debtor or hirer not less than 7 days before the variation takes effect (reg. 2 (*b*)). There is, however, a special procedure where, both before and after the variation, the amount of interest payments charged under the agreement is determined by reference to the amount of the balance outstanding, established at daily intervals, and the variation is a variation of the rate of interest payable under the agreement. The typical case is the clearing bank overdraft, which is calculated on a daily basis on the debit balance from time to time outstanding, the rate of interest being geared to the bank's prevailing base rate which, of course, it is free to vary as it thinks fit. It would be extremely cumbersome and expensive if, every time a clearing bank raised or lowered its rate base, it had to give specific notice to every customer whose account was overdrawn. The regulations thus provide an alternative procedure for serving the notice. By reg. 3 (2) the requirements of service will be deemed satisfied where—

    (*a*) the notice of variation—
        (i) is published in at least three national daily newspapers, in each case being printed in a type not less than 3 mm in height and occupying a space of not less than 100 sq. cm; or
        (ii) if it is not reasonably practicable so to publish it, is published in the Gazette; and
    (*b*) if it is reasonably practicable to do so, the notice of variation is prominently displayed, so that it may easily be read, in a part (if any) open to the public of the premises of the creditor where the agreement to which the variation relates is maintained.

For the purpose of the regulations, an agreement is to be treated as maintained on those premises where the debtor habitually approaches the creditor (or would so approach him if the need arose) in order to secure that transactions are carried out or arrangements are made under the agreement (reg. 1 (3)). **[722]**

Variation revokes and reproduces

English law has long recognised the distinction between a variation of an agreement and a novation. A variation preserves the original agreement but amends it in one or more particulars; a novation replaces it entirely. The distinction was significant under the Hire-Purchase Act 1965 (see R. M. Goode, *op. cit.*, Chapter 15) and remains significant for the purpose of the Control Orders, which differentiate between variation of an agreement and substitution of another agreement (*op. cit.*, Chapter 46). But for the purpose of the Consumer Credit Act, the distinction between variation and novation is obliterated. Where an agreement varies or supplements an earlier agreement, the Act applies as if the modifying agreement revoked the earlier agreement and reproduced the combined effect of the two agreements (s. 82 (2)). Again, it is submitted that s. 82 (2) applies only where there is an entirely distinct variation agreement concluded after the making of the original agreement. A variation of a term taking effect automatically under the provisions of the original agreement is not within s. 82 (2), since it arises independently of any subsequent agreement between the parties and does not require the assent of either of them in order to come into operation. The example previously given of a variable interest rate is a case in point. Section 82 (2) is also inapplicable to an entirely new agreement which does not alter or add to an existing agreement. [**723**]

If the earlier agreement is a regulated agreement, the modifying agreement will also be a regulated agreement, even if the effect of the variation would otherwise have been to take the modifying agreement outside the scope of the Act (see s. 82 (3)). Hence in general, the principle is: once a regulated agreement, always a regulated agreement. The only exception is where the modified agreement is for running-account credit (*ibid.*). In that case, it will be regulated only if it meets the ordinary definition of a regulated agreement. Conversely, if the earlier agreement was not a regulated agreement but the effect of the variation is to bring the modifying agreement within the definition of a regulated agreement, it will constitute a regulated agreement for the purpose of the Act. [**724**]

As a rule, a modifying agreement is not cancellable, wherever it may have been signed (see s. 82 (6)). If, however, the earlier agreement was a cancellable agreement and the modifying agreement is made within the time allowed by s. 68 for cancellation of the earlier agreement, the modifying agreement (even if it would not otherwise have been a cancellable agreement) becomes cancellable within the original time for cancellation (s. 82 (5)). In other words, on modification of the cancellable agreement before the time for cancellation of that agreement has expired the right of cancellation continues in relation to the modified agreement but the time for cancellation does not begin again and remains that prescribed for the original agreement. [**725**]

Since, under s. 82 (2), the modifying agreement is deemed to revoke the original agreement and obligations outstanding under the original agreement are to be treated as outstanding instead under the combined provisions, it would seem to follow that even if the original agreement was made before the coming into force of the Act, the provisions of the Act apply to the original unvaried terms carried over into the modifying agreement as well as to the new terms, if the modifying agreement was made on or after the day appointed for the coming into operation of s. 82. [**726**]

Formalities governing modifying agreement

The broad intention of s. 82 is that the provisions of the Act shall apply as if the combined terms (both the unvaried terms of the original agreement and the new terms) had been agreed at the time and in the manner of making of the new agreement. Hence, subject to s. 82 (4), (5) and (6) and to any special provisions that may be made for modifying agreements by regulations made under ss. 60 and 61, the formalities prescribed by Part V will apply in relation to all the terms, and not merely the new terms. Whether this will mean that the whole of the combined terms will have to be set out in a new document, instead of simply having the unvaried terms of the original agreement incorporated by reference to the document embodying that agreement, remains to be seen. [**727**]

Approval of temporary excess overdraft

By s. 82 (4), if the earlier agreement is a regulated agreement for running-account credit, and by the modifying agreement the creditor allows the credit limit to be exceeded but intends the excess to be merely temporary, Part V of the Act (except s. 56) is not to apply to the modifying agreement. This provision has been discussed in para. [**264**]. [**728**].

Variation of agreement by court

Part IX of the Act confers on the court wide powers to modify and adjust regulated agreements. These are discussed in Chapter 30. [**729**].

20. Early Settlement and Voluntary Termination by Debtor or Hirer

Early settlement

The debtor under a regulated consumer credit agreement is entitled at any time, by notice to the creditor and the payment to the creditor of all amounts payable by the debtor to him under the agreement (less any rebate allowable to him under s. 95), to discharge the debtor's indebtedness under the agreement (s. 94 (1)). It should be noted that this provision is confined to consumer credit agreements and does not extend to consumer hire agreements, where early settlement (as opposed to early termination—see para. [756]) does not arise. The notice must be in writing (see definition of "notice" in s. 189 (1)) but need not be signed or be of any minimum length (see para. [732]). Although in general payment includes tender (s. 189 (1))—a fact relevant, for example, to the question whether goods have become protected goods under s. 90 (7)—the opening words of s. 189 (1) show that this is only the case "unless the context otherwise requires", and it is obvious that an unaccepted tender will not discharge the debtor's indebtedness so as to allow him to claim a release from payment of the balance outstanding under the agreement. If the agreement under which tender of the outstanding balance is made is a hire-purchase or conditional sale agreement, it would seem that the property in the goods passes to the hirer or buyer upon the tender being made even if it is not accepted (see *City Motors (1933) Pty., Ltd.* v. *Southern Aerial Super Service Pty., Ltd.* (1961), 35 A.L.J.R. 206; *Motor Mart, Ltd* v. *Webb*, [1958] N.Z.L.R. 773) and that the hirer or buyer remains liable for payment of the amount tendered but can, if sued, make a payment into court with a plea of tender, under RSC Order 18, r. 16 (High Court) or CCR Order 9, r. 4 (9) (County Court). See generally R. M. Goode, *Hire-Purchase Law and Practice* (2nd Edn.) pp. 242–243. [730]

A notice under s. 94 (1) may embody the exercise by the debtor of any option to purchase goods conferred on him by the agreement, and deal with any other matter arising on, or in relation to, the termination of the agreement (s. 94 (2)). [731]

The notice can be given at any time. It does not have to be of any minimum length and can be given to take effect immediately, if accompanied by payment of the outstanding balance less the statutory rebate. Equally, the debtor appears to

251

be entitled to specify any future settlement date he chooses, provided that it is not later than the contractual date for completion of payment. [732]

On settlement, the debtor is entitled to a termination statement under s. 103 as previously described (para. [715]). [733]

Rebate for early settlement

Regulations may provide for the allowance of a rebate of credit charges under a regulated consumer credit agreement where the debtor's indebtedness is settled ahead of time, whether this is by payment under s. 94 or on refinancing, on breach of the agreement (e.g. under an acceleration clause) or for any other reason (s. 95 (1)). Indeed, regulations under s. 95 (1) need not be confined to early settlement of the agreement as a whole but may prescribe a rebate where *any sum* becomes payable by the debtor before the time fixed by the agreement. [734]

They may also provide for calculation of the rebate by reference to any sums paid or payable by the debtor or his relative under or in connection with the agreement (whether to the creditor or some other person), including sums under linked transactions and other items in the total charge for credit. [735]

No regulations have yet been made under s. 95 but they are expected shortly. When made they will have retrospective effect, applying to an agreement whenever made (Sch. 3, para. 35), but only if it is a regulated agreement. Section 95 is thus effectively confined to agreements made on or after 1st April 1977, the appointed day for the purpose of regulated agreements (Consumer Credit Act 1974 (Commencement No. 2) Order 1977, art. 2 (1)). [736]

A brief explanation of the factors involved in the rebate question may be helpful at this point. [737]

Early settlement of a credit transaction is a common occurrence in the case of purchase-money credit and usually arises because the asset purchased with the credit is sold (as in the case of a house) or traded in by way of part exchange (as with a motor vehicle). Where charges are precomputed, it is the practice for finance houses to allow the debtor a rebate of charges in the event of early settlement (if charges are not precomputed but are calculated on the balance from time to time outstanding the question of rebating does not, of course, arise); but the debtor, expecting a rebate which is *pro rata* to the unexpired period of the agreement, is usually unpleasantly surprised to discover that it is a great deal less. For example, a debtor liable for total charges of £100 on a 24-month contract and settling the agreement after 12 months would no doubt expect to be allowed a rebate of £50, but the figure he will be quoted is likely to be a mere £26, and if the finance house imposes a three-month loading (i.e. treats the settlement date as three months later than it actually is) to allow for the initial costs of setting up the transaction, the rebate will probably come down to a derisory £15. [738]

But a debtor who was familiar with the concept of interest as a function of funds in use (see chapter 2, para. [481]) would be less startled, if no less unhappy, at this outcome, for he would realise that since interest reduces as the principal diminishes, by far the greater part of the interest is earned in the first half of the transaction period. In other words, the balances of principal outstanding at the end of each payment period falling within the first twelve months amount to a total which is obviously very much larger than the total of the balances in the second twelve months and thus attracts a correspondingly greater proportion of the total interest. This is clear from Table 1, para. [485]. [739]

We have previously noted that for the purpose of obtaining a completely accurate statement of the effective rate of interest payable by the debtor in an instalment transaction it is necessary to distribute the interest charge over the period of the contract actuarially, that is, in such a way that the ratio of interest charged at the end of each payment period to the principal sum outstanding during that period remains constant throughout the contract (see para. [**482**]). It might seem logical to apply the same distribution for the purpose of computing the rebate for early settlement, on the basis that the proper rebate is the amount of interest still remaining to be earned at the date of settlement and the actuarial spread tells us precisely what interest has accrued due up to the end of any given payment period and what still remains unearned. This would be a perfectly valid approach if the creditor incurred no overheads or other expenditure in connection with the transaction (for his income would then be pure interest, or profit, and could properly be subjected to the actuarial rule) or if the spread of costs incurred by the creditor exactly matched the actuarial spread of income. But this, of course, does not happen. The creditor's costs are not distributed according to some neat mathematical formula, but depend on the nature and timing of a vast range of different outlays, each of which has its own time pattern. For example, dealers' commissions, legal costs, survey fees, in connection with the setting up of the transaction are non-recurrent and are incurred at the outset; wages, rent and other overheads are spread over the whole period of the contract but are likely to rise during that period because of inflation; and defaults, terminations and repossessions, followed by proceedings to enforce payment, attract expenditure at a later stage of the transaction the timing of which is to a considerable degree outside the creditor's control. [**740**]

In short, whereas for the purpose of rate disclosure one is looking at the cost to the debtor, who is not concerned with the makeup of the creditor's expenses, when it comes to rebates it is necessary to have regard to the creditor's position also, for what is now involved is not a mathematical concept of interest but a policy decision as to what is fair to both parties. Ideally, the creditor should be reimbursed his direct and indirect costs, leaving the pure profit element to be spread actuarially to produce a rebate figure, but there is no accurate way of calculating either the amount or the accrual of the creditor's costs on a specific transaction, and the complexities involved in any attempt to do so would be almost insuperable. [**741**]

In practice, finance houses do not adopt the actuarial rule (which is difficult to compute without mechanical aids) but employ the direct ratio method, more commonly known as the Rule of 78, for the purpose of calculating rebates, with or without some loading to take account of setting up costs. [**742**]

The following explanation of the rule of 78, taken from Appendix A to the author's work *Hire-Purchase Law and Practice* (2nd Edn. as amended by the Supplement), indicates its impact on the rebate calculation:

> "*The Direct Ratio Method or Rule of* 78
> This method of spreading charges is widely used owing to its simplicity and the fact that it gives a close approximation to an actuarial rate. The rule of 78 assumes that charges are spread in the ratio which the number of instalments remaining to be paid bears to the total number of instalments in the contract. Thus on a twelve-month contract where payment is to be made by equal monthly instalments $\frac{12}{78}$ of the charge is treated as earned in the first month, $\frac{11}{78}$ in the second month,

$\frac{10}{78}$ in the third month, and so on. This method is known as the rule of 78 because the sum of the numbers one to twelve is 78. Looked at another way the rule of 78 assumes that on a twelve-month contract where payment is to be made by equal monthly instalments the number of instalments remaining to be paid is constantly diminishing, so that the principal outstanding in the first month is twelve times as large as that outstanding in the last; in the second month is eleven times as large as that in the last month; and so on; and the charges are treated as spread in the same way.

The rule of 78 is also used as a convenient method of calculating rebates for early settlement. Thus if on a twelve-month contract providing for blended payments of principal and charges in twelve equal monthly instalments the debtor pays in full at the end of the ninth month he would, under the rule of 78, be given a rebate equivalent to the charges that would have been earned during the remaining three months, i.e. $\dfrac{3+2+1}{78} = \dfrac{1}{13}$ of the total charge. The term "rule of 78" is applied to all cases where this method of spread is adopted, whatever the contract length, but the figure 78 is, of course, applicable only to a twelve-month contract. For a 24-month contract the series is $24 + 23 + 22 \ldots 1$ and the sum of the series is 300. For a 36-month contract the series is $36 + 35 + 34 \ldots 1$ and the sum of the series is 666. The formula for calculating the sum of the series is $\dfrac{n}{2}(n + 1)$ where n is the number of terms in the series." [**743**]

The rule of 78 is reasonably simple (the formula for the rebate is $C \times \dfrac{t(t + 1)}{n(n + 1)}$ where C represents the credit charge, t the number of payment periods still to run at the date of settlement and n the total number of payment periods in the contract) and within certain limits as to transaction period and rate it represents a tolerable approximation to the actuarial formula. It was thus recommended by the Crowther Committee as an appropriate basis for computing rebates; and the initial intention of the Government was to adopt this recommendation but to allow a three-month loading. See Appendix B to the White Paper *Reform of the Law on Consumer Credit*. More recently, the Department of Prices and Consumer Protection appears to have had second thoughts, and it is now likely that for transactions extending beyond a specified period or involving an effective rate of charge above a stated rate the actuarial formula will be made obligatory. The underlying policy of this approach appears to be that the quoted effective rate of charge should be the same whether the agreement runs its full course or is settled ahead of time. It seems probable that the creditor will still be allowed a loading factor, but not, perhaps, on as rigid a basis as the three-month rule proposed in the White Paper. [**744**]

A still more vexed question is the figure to which the rebate calculation should be applied. For the purpose of rate disclosure all borrowing costs are in principle taken into account to form the total charge for credit, whether or not reflected at the other end as income of the lender. It does not necessarily follow that it would be appropriate to apply the rebate calculation to the whole of this figure. For example, the creditor might well argue that he ought not to be required to give a rebate in respect of legal fees, stamp duties and other non-recurrent costs which are not spread over the contract period but are once-for-all outlays making no contribution to his overheads and not in any way recoverable from those to whom they are paid. As against this, the Government may take the position that undue complexity should be avoided and that creditors should have, or be able to acquire, a sufficient knowledge of typical patterns of expenditure and debtor behaviour to programme this into their calculations when fixing their rates. [**745**]

Effect of early settlement on linked transactions

The early settlement of a regulated consumer credit agreement automatically discharges the liability of the debtor, and any relative of his, under a linked transaction, except as regards a debt which has already become payable (s. 96 (1)). But this does not apply to a linked transaction which is itself an agreement providing the debtor or his relative with credit (s. 96 (2)). [**746**]

Voluntary termination by debtor

The provisions discussed in the preceding paragraphs deal with the debtor's right to discharge his indebtedness by completing payments ahead of time. But the hirer or buyer under a regulated hire-purchase or conditional sale agreement has an alternative right to terminate the agreement without completing payments under it. This right, and the liability of the debtor who exercises it, are governed by ss. 99 and 100 of the Act, re-enacting provisions formerly contained in ss. 27 and 28 of the Hire-Purchase Act 1965. [**747**]

At any time before the final payment by the debtor under a regulated hire-purchase or regulated conditional sale agreement falls due, the debtor is entitled to terminate the agreement by giving notice to any person entitled or authorised to receive the sums payable under the agreement (s. 99 (1)). It will be remembered that "conditional sale agreement" is not confined to the conditional sale of goods but covers the conditional sale of land as well (s. 189 (1)). However, by s. 99 (3) the debtor ceases to be entitled to terminate a conditional sale agreement relating to land after title to the land has passed to the debtor. [**748**]

The debtor's right to terminate a conditional sale agreement relating to goods is lost if the property in the goods is transferred to a person who does not become the debtor under the agreement (s. 99 (4)). This provision, re-enacting s. 27 (2) of the Hire-Purchase Act 1965, is designed to cover the eventuality of a conditional sale agreement which provides for the debtor to acquire title before he has made all the payments called for by the agreement, e.g. after payment of 50 per cent. Such an agreement would be unusual, but if the buyer, having acquired ownership, were then to resell he would lose his right of termination. The right to terminate would equally be lost where title had passed from the conditional buyer to a third party by virtue of some exception to the *nemo dat* rule, e.g. under Part III of the Hire-Purchase Act 1965. But s. 99 (4) does not cover the case of a debtor who assigns his rights under the conditional sale agreement; for the assignee then becomes the debtor (see definition of "debtor" in s. 189 (1)). [**749**]

Section 99 (5), re-enacting s. 27 (3) of the Hire-Purchase Act 1965, provides as follows:

> "Subject to subsection (4), where a debtor under a conditional sale agreement relating to goods terminates the agreement under this section after the property in the goods has become vested in him, the property in the goods shall thereupon vest in the person (the "previous owner") in whom it was vested immediately before it became vested in the debtor;
>
> Provided that if the previous owner has died, or any other event has occurred whereby that property, if vested in him immediately before that event, would thereupon have vested in some other person, the property shall be treated as having devolved as if it had been vested in the previous owner immediately before his death or immediately before that event, as the case may be."

The effect of this provision is that exercise of a power of termination by a debtor who has acquired title and still owns the goods at the time of his notice to terminate revests ownership in the conditional seller or his successor in interest. Thus, if by the time of termination by the debtor, the conditional seller has transferred the property in the goods to another, they will vest in the transferee; if he has become bankrupt, they will pass to his trustee in bankruptcy; and if he has died they will vest in his personal representative. If the conditional seller is a company which has gone into liquidation, property revests in the company itself, since liquidation does not of itself divest a company of its property or transmit it to the liquidator. [**750**]

Liability of debtor on voluntary termination

Termination of an agreement under s. 99 (1) does not affect any liability accrued due before the termination (s. 99 (2)). Hence the creditor is entitled to recover arrears of instalments and damages for any other breach of the agreement (the failure to take reasonable care of the goods is, in addition, covered expressly by s. 100 (4)—see below). Apart from his accrued liability the debtor is liable, unless the agreement provides for a smaller payment, or does not provide for any payment, to pay to the creditor the amount (if any) by which one-half of the total price exceeds the aggregate of the sums paid and the sums due in respect of the total price immediately before the termination (s. 100 (1)). Where the creditor was required under the agreement to carry out any installation and the agreement specifies an installation charge as part of the total price, the reference in s. 100 (1) to one-half of the total price is to be construed as a reference to the aggregate of the installation charge and one-half of the remainder of the total price (s. 100 (2)). Thus, if the total price is £850 of which £30 is specifically identified in the agreement as the installation charge, the sum to which the debtor can be required to make up his payments (subject to s. 100 (3)—see para. [**752**]) is

$$£30 + \frac{£850 - 30}{2} = £440. \quad [\mathbf{751}]$$

If in any action the court is satisfied that a sum less than the amount specified in s. 100 (1) would be equal to the loss sustained by the creditor in consequence of the termination of the agreement by the debtor, the court may make an order for payment of that lower sum (s. 100 (3)). The word "loss" appears to mean loss calculated on the footing that but for the termination by the debtor the creditor would have received the total price (see R. M. Goode, *op. cit.*, pp. 406–407). But, for a different view, see A. G. Guest, *Law of Hire-Purchase*, para. 609. [**752**]

If the debtor has contravened an obligation to take reasonable care of the goods or land, the amount payable by him must be increased by the sum required to recompense the creditor for that contravention (s. 100 (4)). [**753**]

If the agreement itself confers an express power of termination, it may not be easy to decide whether the notice given by the debtor is to be construed as an exercise of his contractual right (which would not attract the liability under s. 100) or his statutory rights under s. 99 (which would attract such liability). The court would probably construe the notice as evincing an intention to select the alternative least burdensome to the debtor, in accordance with the principle enunciated in *Withers* v. *General Theatre Corporation, Ltd.*, [1933] 2 K.B. 536. [**754**]

Return of goods

Where the debtor, on the termination of the agreement, wrongfully retains possession of goods to which the agreement relates, then in any action brought by the creditor to recover possession of the goods from the debtor, the court, unless it is satisfied that having regard to the circumstances it would not be just to do so, must order the goods to be delivered to the creditor without giving the debtor an option to pay the value of the goods (s. 100 (5)). The word "wrongfully" in this context presumably means without the consent of the creditor. Section 100 (5), though part of a section which in all other respects is confined to termination by the debtor is not by itself expressly so confined, but would almost certainly be construed as inapplicable to termination by the creditor (see para. [**904**]). [**755**]

Termination of hiring agreement

Sections 99 and 100 are confined to termination by a hirer or buyer under a hire-purchase or conditional sale agreement. The position of a hirer under a hiring agreement who wishes to terminate is governed by s. 101, which (subject to exceptions designed to exclude equipment leasing—see para. [**758**]) gives the hirer under a consumer hire agreement a cut-off point at 18 months. The object is to prevent hirers from being locked into burdensome contracts for long periods, possibly committing themselves to a total rental amounting to many times the value of the goods. Section 101 (1) therefore provides that the hirer under a regulated consumer hire agreement is entitled to terminate the agreement by giving notice (i.e., written notice) to any person entitled or authorised to receive the sums payable under the agreement. By s. 101 (3) the notice cannot be given to expire earlier than 18 months after the making of the agreement (this is not necessarily 18 months from commencement of the period of hire). Subject to this the minimum period of notice, unless the agreement provides for a shorter period, is as follows:

(1) If the agreement provides for the making of payments by the hirer to the owner at equal intervals, the minimum period of notice is the length of one interval or three months, whichever is less (s. 101 (4)).
(2) If the agreement provides for the making of such payments at differing intervals, the minimum period of notice is the length of the shortest interval or three months, whichever is less (s. 101 (5)).

(3) In any other case, the minimum period of notice is three months (s. 101 (6)).

The consumer hirer appears to be entitled to fix any termination date he wishes, provided that it allows the minimum 18 months period specified above, is of the requisite minimum length and has an expiry date not later than the date fixed by the agreement for expiry of the period of hire. Even if the hiring agreement is modified, the 18-month period after which the hirer can terminate runs from the date of the original agreement (s. 101 (9)). **[756]**

Liability of hirer on termination

Termination of an agreement under s. 101 (1) does not affect any liability accrued due under the agreement before the termination (s. 101 (2)). It would seem that any provision in the agreement purporting to impose an additional liability on the hirer (e.g. by way of compensation for loss of future rentals) is void (s. 173 (1), (2)). **[757]**

Exclusion of right to terminate

The proposal to give the hirer under a regulated consumer hire agreement the right to bring the agreement to an end after 18 months caused considerable anxiety to equipment leasing companies, whose rental terms were customarily tailored to leases of four years and upwards. From the viewpoint of a leasing company, an equipment lease is essentially a financial operation, in which the rentals are so structured as to secure the payment to the company, over the minimum period of the lease, of sums equal to the capital cost of the equipment plus the desired return on capital, after taking due account of corporation tax, capital allowances and regional development grant. In order for equipment leasing to be viable, it is essential that the lessor shall be committed to a minimum leasing period sufficient to generate enough rentals for the above purpose. Theoretically, rentals *could* be spread over a period as short as 18 months, but no lessee would be willing to do business on this basis, since the ability to spread what is in essence the capital cost of the equipment with charges over at least a four-to five-year period is a *raison d'être* of the transaction from the lessee's point of view, and payment of the total rent over 18 months would in many cases be impossible for him. The 18 month cut-off point thus placed seriously at risk leasing to unincorporated bodies—in particular sole traders and partnerships—where the rentals did not exceed £5,000. The industry wanted the government to grant leasing of goods for business purposes a blanket exemption from the Act, but this the government, like its predecessor, steadfastly refused to do, in the light of many complaints received showing that the small trader was just as much in need of protection as the private individual. **[758]**

The solution was therefore to select the characteristics of that part of the leasing business that had not been found to generate abuse, and to use these characteristics as the criteria for exemption from s. 101. It is on this basis that s. 101 (7) exempts from the termination provisions:

> "(a) any agreement which provides for the making by the hirer of payments which in total (and without breach of the agreement) exceed £300 in any year, or

  (*b*) any agreement where—
   (i) goods are bailed or (in Scotland) hired to the hirer for the purposes of a business carried on by him, or the hirer holds himself out as requiring the goods for those purposes, and
   (ii) the goods are selected by the hirer, and acquired by the owner for the purposes of the agreement at the request of the hirer from any person other than the owner's associates, or
  (*c*) any agreement where the hirer requires, or holds himself out as requiring, the goods for the purpose of bailing or hiring them to other persons in the course of a business carried on by him."

Category (*a*) is effective to exclude a large number of equipment leases. Indeed, with inflation it may also exclude many ordinary rental transactions. Category (*b*) covers the traditional equipment lease under which the intended lessee conducts negotiations direct with the manufacturer or other supplier, selects the equipment and then asks the leasing company to buy the equipment and let it to him on lease. It should be noted that category (*b*) does not apply to the case of a lease by the manufacturer himself, for the goods must have been "acquired" by the owner for the purpose of the agreement. Category (*c*) exempts leases to a lessee whose business involves sub-leasing, e.g. a lease of a fleet of motor vehicles to a car hire firm with permission to sub-hire to the end user. [**759**]

  To cover the possibility of other types of leasing contract for which the termination provisions would cause unintended difficulties, s. 101 (8) provides that if, on an application made to the Director by a person carrying on a consumer hire business, it appears to the Director that it would be in the interest of hirers to do so, he may by notice to the applicant direct that s. 101 shall not apply to consumer hire agreements made by the applicant, and subject to such conditions (if any) as the Director may specify, the Act is to have effect accordingly. [**760**]

21. Security

Introduction

The Consumer Credit Act embodies the first attempt to provide a coherent pattern of rules governing the taking and enforcement of security given in connection with a consumer credit or consumer hire transaction. Hitherto, apart from the Bills of Sale Acts (see Chapter 1) there have been merely a few scattered provisions in the Moneylenders Acts and Hire-Purchase Acts relating to security. Part VIII of the Consumer Credit Act is devoted exclusively to security; and there are various other provisions which also bear on the rights of the secured party *vis-à-vis* the debtor and sureties. [**761**].

The security provisions of the Act are for the most part confined to relations between the creditor on the one hand and the debtor and sureties on the other. Third party rights are affected only to a minor degree, and these must largely be determined by reference to rules of common law and equity and to other legislation affecting security by individuals, e.g. the Bills of Sale Acts (for written chattel mortgages generally), the Mortgaging of Aircraft Order (for aircraft mortgages) and the Law of Property Acts, Land Charges Acts and Land Registration Acts (for mortgages of land). [**762**]

The Consumer Credit Act seeks to control security taken in relation to a regulated agreement by:

(a) providing for the form and content of securities;
(b) requiring specified information and documents to be supplied to sureties;
(c) controlling the realisation or other enforcement of securities;
(d) preventing evasion of the Act through use of a security;
(e) providing that in various circumstances securities shall become ineffective, i.e., void *ab initio*;
(f) making special provision for pledges, in replacement of the Pawnbrokers Acts 1872–1960.

Each of these will be considered in turn. [**763**]

"Security"; "security instrument"; "surety"

The term "security", in relation to an actual or prospective consumer credit agreement or consumer hire agreement, or any linked transaction, means a mortgage, charge, pledge, bond, debenture, indemnity, guarantee, bill, note or other right provided by the debtor or hirer, or at his request (express or implied), to secure the carrying out of the obligations of the debtor or hirer under the agreement (s. 189 (1)). It will be seen that the term is thus given the widest connotation, embracing not only real security (mortgage, charge, pledge) but personal security (bond, guarantee, indemnity, bill, note). The only qualification is that to fall within the statutory definition the security must be provided by or at the request of the debtor or hirer. Thus, a guarantee of the hirer's obligations under a hire-purchase agreement with a finance house is a security if given, for example, by the hirer's friend at the hirer's request but not if given by a dealer as part and parcel of a master agreement with a finance house or pursuant to a request by the finance house. [**764**]

A document which, in conformity with the requirements of s. 105 (1) (see para. [**766**]) expresses the terms of a security provided in relation to a regulated agreement is termed by the Act a "security instrument". Since those requirements do not apply to a security provided by the debtor or hirer himself (see para. [**766**]), it follows that "security instrument" is limited to documents embodying a security given by a third party at the request of the debtor or hirer. The term "surety", which in ordinary legal usage denotes a guarantee, has a much wider meaning under the Act, being defined as "the person by whom any security is provided, or the person to whom his rights and duties in relation to the security have passed by assignment or operation of law" (s. 189 (1)). Hence except where the Act otherwise indicates, "surety" covers not only a guarantor but the principal debtor if he provides a security. [**765**]

Any security provided in relation to a regulated agreement is required by s. 105 (1) to be expressed in writing. This provision does not apply to security provided by the debtor or hirer himself (s. 105 (6)), but a similar effect will be achieved by regulations under s. 105 (9) (see para. [**767**]). In some cases, a security provided by a third party will be part and parcel of the consumer credit or consumer hire agreement, as where the agreement incorporates a guarantee or indemnity or where a third party joins in the credit agreement to give a mortgage or charge. In other cases, the third party's security is distinct. Either way, it will have to be expressed in writing. This is a departure from the previous law, which required contracts of guarantee and certain types of mortgage to be *evidenced* by a note or memorandum in writing but permitted them to be *made* orally. [**766**]

The requirement of writing applies only to a security provided in relation to a regulated agreement, as opposed to an exempt agreement or an agreement which is not a consumer credit or consumer hire agreement at all; and, as we have seen, even a security provided in relation to a regulated agreement is not within s. 105 (1) if provided by the debtor or hirer himself. Regulations under s. 60 (1) are required to include provision requiring documents embodying regulated agreements also to embody any security provided in relation to a regulated agreement by the debtor or hirer (s. 105 (9)). This does not mean that the regulations must necessarily require the security to be set out in the credit agreement itself. Section 105 (9) will be sufficiently complied with if the regulations provide for the credit agreement to refer to some other document containing the terms of the security—see s. 189 (4). The effect of such regulations will be that even security provided by the debtor or hirer himself will have to be in writing—whether in the credit or hire agreement or in a separate document— if provided in relation to a regulated agreement. There is no exemption from this requirement. Even security given by way of deposit of documents of title will have to be embodied in a document, since whilst pledges of documents of title are exempt from the provisions of ss. 114–122 relating to pledges (see s. 114 (3) and para. [**782**]), they are not excluded from the scope of s. 105 (9). Where security is provided in connection with a *prospective* regulated agreement, the security does not become subject to Part VIII (other than s. 113 (6)) until the regulated agreement is actually made. In such case, the security is not enforceable until after the making of the regulated agreement (s. 113 (6)); and until that time the person providing the security is entitled, by notice to the creditor or owner, to require that s. 106 shall apply to the security (*ibid.*; and see para. [**774**]). [**767**]

By s. 105 (2) regulations may prescribe the form and content of security instruments (i.e., third party security documents—see para. [**765**]) to be made in compliance with s. 105 (1) and by s. 105 (3) may in particular —

(a) require specified information to be included in the prescribed manner in documents, and other specified material to be excluded;

(b) contain requirements to ensure that specified information is clearly brought to the attention of the surety and that one part of a document is not given insufficient or excessive prominence compared with another.

Section 105 gives no power to regulate the form and content of a security document given by the debtor, but such a document could, it seems, be the subject of regulations under s. 179 relating to secondary documents. [**768**]

Other formalities

By s. 105 (4), (5) a security instrument is not properly executed (and is therefore enforceable only on an order of the court—s. 105 (7)) unless—

(a) a document in the prescribed form itself containing all the prescribed terms and conforming to regulations under sub-section (2), is signed in the prescribed manner by or on behalf of the surety, and

(b) the document embodies all the terms of the security, other than implied terms, and

(c) the document, when presented or sent for the purpose of being signed by or on behalf of the surety, is in such a state that its terms are readily legible, and

(d) when the document is presented or sent for the purpose of being signed by or on behalf of the surety there is also presented or sent a copy of the document, and

(e) where the security is provided after, or at the time when, the regulated agreement is made, a copy of the executed agreement, together with a copy of any other document referred to in it, is given to the surety at the time the security is provided, and

(f) where the security is provided before the regulated agreement is made, a copy of the executed agreement, together with a copy of any other document referred to in it, is given to the surety within seven days after the regulated agreement is made.

It will be seen that the surety need not sign the guarantee personally. Signature on his behalf suffices. [**769**]

It will be recalled that the requirements of s. 105 (4) and (5) apply only to a security instrument as defined in s. 105 (2) (see paras. [**765**]–[**766**]). Security provided by the debtor or hirer will, by virtue of s. 105 (9), be governed by regulations under s. 60 (1). [**770**]

Consequences of non-compliance

The consequences of non-compliance with the statutory provisions are potentially severe. Subsection (7) and (8) of s. 105 provide as follows:

"(7) If—

(*a*) in contravention of subsection (1) a security is not expressed in writing, or

(*b*) a security instrument is improperly executed,

the security (so far as provided in relation to a regulated agreement) is enforceable against the surety on an order of the court only.

(8) If an application for an order under subsection (7) is dismissed (except on technical grounds only) section 106 (ineffective securites) shall apply to the security."

It is to be observed that the sanctions prescribed by the above subsections will apply not only non-compliance with s. 105 (1), (4) but also to a failure to comply with regulations under s. 60 (1) as to embodying of security by the debtor or hirer in the executed agreement; for non-compliance with such regulations will render the regulated agreement (including the security it embodies) improperly executed (s. 61 (1) (*a*)). [**771**]

In all these cases, the security will be enforceable only on an order of the court. The principles to be applied by the court in dealing with an application for an enforcement order in the above circumstances are set out in s. 127 (see para. [**931**]). If an application for an order is dismissed otherwise than on technical grounds, the security becomes retrospectively invalidated and all the other consequences prescribed by s. 106 (see para. [**774**]) will apply. An application is to be taken to be dismissed on technical grounds if the court so certifies (s. 189 (5)). This provision, if construed as requiring the court to determine whether in ordinary parlance the defect was to be considered technical, could occasion the court considerable difficulty. A procedural defect in making the application—as by inadvertent failure to comply with a rule of court or by defect in a pleading—could readily be treated as a mere technical defect. But what if the action in which the application to enforce the security is made is dismissed because, for example, the creditor had omitted to serve a notice of default, or had served an invalid notice or had begun his action prematurely, by miscalculating the date of expiry of the requisite default notice? In a popular sense, these might well be considered mere technical defects, yet they are all matters which prevent the creditor from establishing his cause of action. It is thought that s. 189 (5) is intended to give the court a wide discretion to overlook irregularities that do not furnish a meritorious defence for the debtor or hirer, and that accordingly the court is not obliged to apply the dictionary meaning of "technical grounds" but can treat any ground of dismissal of an application as if it were technical and certify accordingly. On the other hand, the spirit of s. 189 (5) would seem to require that the court should not give a certificate where the ground of dismissal is a substantial and meritorious ground of defence to the application. Moreover, even if the court has certified a ground for dismissal as technical, the debtor or hirer is entitled to apply for a declaration that the creditor or owner is not entitled to do the thing for which he requires the enforcement order; and if the court makes such a declaration as respects any regulated agreement, no application for an enforcement order in respect of that thing can thereafter be entertained (s. 142 (1)), and s. 106 becomes applicable to any security provided in relation to that agreement (s. 113 (3) (*d*)).

[772]

Enforcement without court order

Strangely, except where s. 106 is applied to the security (*vide supra* and *post* para. [774]) the Act imposes no specific sanction on a secured creditor who proceeds to realise or otherwise enforce his security without the requisite court order. Indeed, s. 170 (1) provides that a breach of any requirement of the Act shall not as such incur any civil or criminal sanction except as provided by the Act. This does not mean that the creditor can ignore s. 105 (7) with impunity, for there is always the ultimate sanction of suspension or revocation of his licence, a penalty that can be imposed for any breach of the Act and, indeed, for any improper business practice, whether unlawful or not (s. 25 (2) (*b*), (*d*)), and whether or not any sanction for the breach is provided (s. 170 (2)). But the absence of a specific provision as to the consequences of improper enforcement without an order of the court does create potential problems for the debtor. It is true that a measure of protection is given by s. 170 (3), which preserves the court's power to grant an injunction; but "the court" usually denotes the county court (s. 189 (1)), whose power to grant an injunction, derived from s. 74 of the County Courts Act 1959, is (except in the case of land) exercisable only if the injunction is claimed as ancillary to some other relief which is within the jurisdiction of the court (*De Vries* v. *Smallridge*, [1928] 1 K.B. 482; *Kenny* v. *Preen*, [1963] 1 Q.B. 499, [1962] 3 All E.R. 814; *Arnbridge (Reading), Ltd.* v. *Hedges*, [1972] C.L.Y. 551), though a purely nominal money claim has been held sufficient for this purpose (*Hatt & Co. (Bath), Ltd.* v. *Pearce*, [1978] 2 All E.R. 474, [1978] 1 W.L.R. 885). Hence a debtor claiming an injunction against a creditor who has enforced, or threatens to enforce, a security (other than a land mortgage) in breach of s. 105 (7) should ensure that the claim is made ancillary to some form of substantive relief, such as a declaration under s. 142 of the Act. Alternatively, the debtor can simply seek a declaration under s. 142 and then rely on the declaration as applying s. 106 to the security (s. 113 (3) (*d*)) so as to nullify it *ab initio*. As to actions concerning land, see para. [820]. As to the position of a purchaser where an improper sale is made, see para. [775]. [773]

Invalidation of securities

Section 106 provides that where, under any provision of the Act, that section is applied to any security provided in relation to a regulated agreement (see para. [776]), then subject to s. 177—

> "(*a*) the security, so far as it is so provided, shall be treated as never having effect;
> (*b*) any property lodged with the creditor or owner solely for the purposes of the security as so provided shall be returned by him forthwith;
> (*c*) the creditor or owner shall take any necessary action to remove or cancel an entry in any register, so far as the entry relates to the security as so provided; and

> (*d*) any amount received by the creditor or owner on realisation of the security shall, so far as it is referable to the agreement, be repaid to the surety." [**774**]

Section 177 provides two exceptions from s. 106. By s. 177 (1) nothing in the Act affects the right of proprietor of a registered charge (within the meaning of the Land Registration Act 1925), who—

(*a*) became the proprietor under a transfer for valuable consideration without notice of any defect in the title arising (apart from s. 177) by virtue of the Act, or

(*b*) derives title from such a proprietor.

This subsection is very limited in scope. It protects the first registered proprietor of a charge, a transferee from such a proprietor who is himself registered as proprietor of the charge and a person to whom a mortgagee (whether of registered or unregistered land) sells in exercise of his power of sale, but does not protect the holder of an unregistered charge over registered land (e.g. a charge protected by entry of notice of deposit or caution) or the transferee of such a charge who is not himself entered as proprietor, nor the transferee of a mortgage of unregistered land. Section 177 (1) also does not protect a proprietor carrying on a business of debt-collecting (s. 177 (3)). Hence one whose business consists, for example, of taking assignments of mortgages is caught by the full rigours of s. 106. Where, by virtue of the exemption under s. 177 (1), a land mortgage is enforced which would otherwise be treated as never having effect, the original creditor or owner is liable to indemnify the debtor or hirer against any loss thereby suffered by him (s. 177 (4)). The second exception is furnished by s. 177 (2), which provides that nothing in the Act is to affect the operation of s. 104 of the Law of Property Act 1925. The effect of s. 104 is that a purchaser from a mortgagee exercising a power of sale under that Act is not, either before or on conveyance, concerned to see or inquire whether the power of sale has been properly and regularly exercised (s. 104 (2)), provided that such purchaser did not take with notice of the irregularity (*Bailey* v. *Barnes*, [1894] 1 Ch. 25) or collude with the mortgagee to obtain the property at an undervalue (*Haddington Island Quarry Co., Ltd.* v. *Huson*, [1911] A.C. 722). Any person damnified by an unauthorised or improper or irregular exercise of the power can recover damages from the person exercising the power (s. 104 (2)). Hence if a mortgagee under a mortgage caught by s. 106 of the Consumer Credit Act nevertheless enforces the mortgage by exercising a power of sale conferred by s. 101 of the Law of Property Act 1925, the purchaser gets a good title, but the debtor can recover damages, if he can show that he has suffered loss. For a discussion of further points arising under these provisions, see R. M. Goode, "*The Consumer Credit Act 1974*" [1975] C.L.J. 79 at pp. 112–113, esp. n. 85, and J. E. Adams, "*Mortgages and the Consumer Credit Act 1974*" (1974) 39 Conv. (N.S.) 94.

[**775**]

Section 106 applies in the following cases to a security provided in relation to a regulated agreement:

(*a*) Where an application to the court to enforce the security where it is not expressed in writing or is improperly executed is dismissed by the court otherwise than on technical grounds (s. 105 (8)).

(*b*) Where the regulated agreement is cancelled under s. 69 (1) or becomes subject to s. 69 (2) or is terminated under s. 91 (s. 113 (*a*), (*b*)).

(c)   Where the Director dismisses otherwise than on technical grounds an application under s. 40 (2) for an order that the regulated agreement made by a trader when unlicensed should be treated as if he had been licensed (s. 113 (3) (c)).

(d)   Where the Director dismisses otherwise than on technical grounds an application for an order under s. 149 (2) that the regulated agreement made with a debtor introduced by an unlicensed credit-broker had been licensed (*ibid.*).

(e)   Where the court dismisses otherwise than on technical grounds an application under s. 65 (1) to enforce the regulated agreement when improperly executed (*ibid.*).

(f)   Where the court dismisses an application under s. 124 (1) or (2) to enforce the regulated agreement or security, being an agreement or security in respect of which a negotiable instrument has been taken or negotiated in breach of s. 123 of the Act (ss. 113 (3) (c), 124 (3)).

(g)   Where the court, on application by the debtor or hirer, makes a declaration under s. 142 (1) that the creditor or owner is not entitled to enforce the regulated agreement (s. 113 (d)). But in this case, if the declaration relates to a part only of the regulated agreement, s. 106 applies to the security only so far as it concerns that part (s. 113 (4)).

(h)   Where the security is provided in relation to a prospective agreement and before the agreement is made the person providing the security gives notice to the creditor or owner requiring that s. 106 shall apply to the security (s. 113 (6)). [776]

Where a security is provided in relation to an actual or prospective linked transaction, the above provisions apply as if references to the agreement with references to the linked transaction and as if references to the creditor or owner were references to the person (other than the debtor or hirer or his relative) who is a party, or prospective party, to the linked transaction (s. 113 (8)). [777]

Provision of information to surety

The provisions of ss. 107–109 relating to information to be provided to a surety have already been discussed (para. [714]). [778]

Default notice

Since a guarantee is a security, enforcement of a guarantee falls within s. 87 (1) (e) of the Consumer Credit Act, so that no steps can be taken to sue a guarantor under a guarantee given in connection with a regulated agreement until the requisite default notice has been served on the debtor under s. 87 (1) and a copy served on the surety under s. 111 (1) and the period for payment has expired without payment being made (see para. [893]). Curiously there is no similar requirement in s. 76 (1) in the case of enforcement for non-breach events though a separate limb of s. 76 (1) partially covers the point by requiring service of a seven-day notice before recovery of possession of any goods or land; but enforcement by other means is not within s. 76, nor is security over choses in action, e.g. a life policy or a debt, so that in these cases enforcement otherwise than for breach is permissible without any prior notice other than such as may be prescribed by the security instrument itself. [779]

Enforcement and realisation of securities

A land mortgage securing a regulated agreement is enforceable on an order of the court only (s. 126). Again, no sanction is provided for enforcement in breach of this provision and the same difficulties arise as in relation to s. 105 (see para. [**773**]). The creditor's right to enforce and realise other valid and properly executed securities will be governed by regulations under s. 112 of the Act and by the general law and such other legislation as may be relevant, e.g. the Bills of Sale Acts. However, paragraph 1 of s. 7 of the Bills of Sale Act (1878) Amendment Act 1882 (which entitles the grantee of a security bill of sale to seize the goods on default of payment) is, by s. 7A of that Act, as added by paragraph 1 of the Fourth Schedule to the Consumer Credit Act, made inapplicable to a default relating to a bill of sale by way of security for the payment of money under a regulated agreement within s. 87 (1) of the Consumer Credit Act—

    (a) unless the restriction imposed by s. 88 (2) of that Act (expiry of default notice) has ceased to apply to the bill of sale; or

    (b) if, by virtue of s. 89 of that Act (remedying of breach of debtor), the default is to be treated as not having occurred.

Where paragraph 1 of s. 7 does apply, application by the debtor for relief under the proviso to s. 7 of the Act of 1882 must be made to the County Court, not the High Court (Bills of Sale Act (1878) Amendment Act 1882, s. 7A, as added by Consumer Credit Act, Fourth Schedule, para. 1). [**780**]

The first two subsections of s. 113 provide as follows:

"(1) Where a security is provided in relation to an actual or prospective regulated agreement, the security shall not be enforced so as to benefit the creditor or owner, directly or indirectly, to an extent greater (whether as respects the amount of any payment or the time or manner of its being made) than would be the case if the security were not provided and any obligations of the debtor or hirer, or his relative, under or in relation to the agreement were carried out to the extent (if any) to which they would be enforced under this Act.

(2) In accordance with subsection (1), where a regulated agreement is enforceable on an order of the court or the Director only, any security provided in relation to the agreement is enforceable (so far as provided in relation to the agreement) where such an order has been made in relation to the agreement, but not otherwise."

The effect of this provision is that a creditor cannot, by enforcing a security, recover more than he could have done under the regulated agreement itself. By reason of the definition of "security" (see para. [**764**]), this section applies not only to enforcement of a real security such as a mortgage but also enforcement of a guarantee or indemnity. However, where an indemnity is given in a case where the debtor or hirer is a minor, or is otherwise not of full capacity, the reference in s. 113 (1) to the extent to which his obligations would be enforced is to be read in relation to the indemnity as a reference to the extent to which they would be enforced if he were of full capacity (s. 113 (7)). Breach of s. 113 attracts no sanction; the debtor's only remedy is to seek an injunction (see para. [**773**]). [**781**]

Pledges

Sections 114–122 of the Act provide a new code for pawnbroking, replacing the Pawnbrokers Acts 1872–1960. Strictly speaking, ss. 114–122 are not limited to pawnbrokers but apply to any creditor who takes an article in pawn under a regulated agreement (s. 114 (1)), other than a non-commercial agreement (s. 114 (3) (*b*)). But pledges taken by creditors who are not pawnbrokers usually take the form of a pledge of documents of title, and since such pledges together with pledges of bearer bonds are excluded from ss. 114–122 (s. 114 (3) (*a*)), it is only pawnbrokers who are likely to be substantially affected by these sections. [**782**]

The expression "document of title" is not defined by the Act, but in this context plainly denotes a document of title to goods, as opposed to land, since only goods are susceptible of pledge, and title deeds, if deposited as such for the purpose of security over the land and not merely as pieces of paper and wax "savour of the realty" and are not personal chattels (see *Swanley Coal Co.* v. *Denton*, [1906] 2 K.B. 873). As to what documents are documents of title to goods, see para. [**197**]. [**783**]

Formalities of contract

Section 114 (1) requires the creditor to issue a pawn-receipt to the pledgor at the time of receipt of the pledge by the creditor. Sections 62–64 of the Act (discussed in Chapter 7) apply to regulated agreements for a pledge as to any other regulated agreement. But the sanction for non-compliance is still more powerful, since a creditor under a regulated agreement to take an article in pawn who infringes ss. 62–64 or s. 114 (1) commits an offence (s. 115). [**784**]

Pledges from minors

A person who takes any article in pawn from an individual whom he knows to be, or who appears to be and is, a minor commits an offence (s. 114 (2)). [**785**]

Redemption period

The combined effect of subsections (1)–(3) of s. 116 appears to be that the pawnor can redeem the pawn until the occurrence of whichever of the following events is the latest, viz.:

(*a*) the expiry of six months from the taking of the pledge; or

(*b*) the expiry of termination of the period fixed by the parties for the duration of the credit secured by the pledge (taking into account, it is assumed, any acceleration clause coming into force under the agreement after expiry of the notice of default served under s. 87); or

(*c*) expiry of such longer period as the parties may agree; or

(*d*) realisation of the pawn by the pawnee under s. 121 (para. [**792**]) or forfeiture of the pledge to the pawnee under s. 120 (1) (*a*) (see para. [**791**]). [**786**]

No special charge may be made for redemption of a pawn after the end of the redemption period, and charges in respect of the safekeeping of the pawn must not be at a higher rate after the end of the redemption period than before (s. 116 (4)).
[**787**]

Redemption procedure

On surrender of the pawn-receipt, and payment of the amount owing, at any time when the pawn is redeemable, the pawnee must deliver the pawn to the bearer of the pawn-receipt (s. 117 (1)), except where he knows or has reasonable cause to suspect that the bearer of the pawn-receipt is neither the owner of the pawn nor authorised by the owner to redeem it (s. 117 (2)). The pawnee making delivery under the provisions of s. 117 (1), or refusing to make delivery where the person demanding delivery does not comply with s. 117 (1), incurs no liability in tort to any person (s. 117 (3)). [**788**]

Loss of pawn-receipt

As under the Pawnbrokers Acts, the person entitled to redeem the pledge who through loss or other reason is not in possession of the pawn-receipt may redeem the pawn by tendering a prescribed form of statutory declaration or, in the case of a pawn which is security for fixed-sum credit not exceeding £15 or running-account credit on which the credit limit does not exceed £15, a prescribed form of written statement (s. 118). [**789**]

Unreasonable refusal to deliver pawn

If a person who has taken a pawn under a regulated agreement refuses without reasonable cause to allow the pawn to be redeemed, he commits an offence (s. 119 (1)). The onus lies on the pawnee to prove that he had reasonable cause to refuse to allow the pawn to be redeemed (s. 171 (6)). [**790**]

Consequences of failure to redeem

Where the pawn is security for a fixed-sum credit not exceeding £15 or running-account credit on which the credit limit does not exceed £15 and the redemption period is six months, the property in the pawn passes to the pawnee automatically at the end of the six-month period if the pawn has not then been redeemed (s. 120 (1) (*a*)). In any other case, the pawn is realisable by the pawnee (s. 120 (1) (*b*)) by sale in accordance with s. 121 (see para. [**792**]). Where the debtor or hirer is entitled to apply to the court for a time order under s. 131, an additional five days following the end of the redemption period must expire before the property in the pawn passes to the pawnee, or the pawn becomes realisable by the pawnee, as the case may be (s. 120 (2)). [**791**]

Realisation of pawn

Section 121 provides for realisation of the pawn as follows:
> "(1) Where a pawn has become realisable by him, the pawnee may sell it, after giving to the pawnor (except in such cases as may be prescribed) not less than the prescribed period of notice of the intention to sell, indicating in the notice the asking price and such other information as may be prescribed.
>
> (2) Within the prescribed period after the sale takes place, the pawnee shall give the pawnor the prescribed information in writing as to the sale, its proceeds and expenses.
>
> (3) Where the net proceeds of sale are not less than the sum which, if the pawn had been redeemed on the date of the sale, would have been payable for its redemption, the debt secured by the pawn is discharged and any surplus shall be paid by the pawnee to the pawnor.

(4) Where subsection (3) does not apply, the debt shall be treated as from the date of sale as equal to the amount by which the net proceeds of sale fall short of the sum which would have been payable for the redemption of the pawn on that date.

(5) In this section the "net proceeds of sale" is the amount realised (the "gross amount") less the expenses (if any) of the sale.

(6) If the pawnor alleges that the gross amount is less than the true market value of the pawn on the date of sale, it is for the pawnee to prove that he and any agents employed by him in the sale used reasonable care to ensure that the true market value was obtained, and if he fails to do so subsections (3) and (4) shall have effect as if the reference in subsection (5) to the gross amount were a reference to the true market value.

(7) If the pawnor alleges that the expenses of the sale were unreasonably high, it is for the pawnee to prove that they were reasonable, and if he fails to do so subsections (3) and (4) shall have effect as if the reference in subsection (5) to expenses were a reference to reasonable expenses."

Quite apart from this section, the pawnee may have or acquire rights of sale under ss. 12 and 13 of the Torts (Interference with Goods) Act 1977 where the pawnor fails to collect the goods on or before the due date for redemption. [**792**]

Negotiable instruments

The use of bills of exchange in connection with consumer credit transactions has long been a source of concern and was the subject of evidence to the Crowther Committee. Typically, the problem arose where a consumer wishing to have central heating or double glazing installed in his home gave the supplier, prior to the work being put in hand, a promissory note or bill of exchange in favour of the supplier providing for payment of the price with interest or charges by stated instalments, the whole to became due on default in payment of any instalment. The note or bill would then be discounted by the supplier to a finance house, so that the burden of the credit extension did not fall on the supplier. If, as not uncommonly occurred, the installation proved defective or if it was never provided at all—which sometimes happened because the supplier became insolvent—the consumer seeking to withhold payment of the note or bill would find himself legally bound to pay the finance house, despite the supplier's breach, because the finance house was a holder in due course and therefore took the note or bill free of defences, pursuant to s. 38 (2) of the Bills of Exchange Act 1882. In such cases the consumer, having temporarily withheld payment, might then find himself liable to pay the full outstanding balance immediately as a result of the provision in the bill or note for acceleration of payment in the event of failure to pay an instalment.

[**793**]

The Consumer Credit Act does not attempt to disturb the privileged position of a holder in due course. What it does is to restrict the taking and negotiation of negotiable instruments in connection with a regulated agreement in such a way as to make it difficult for these to come into the possession of a holder in due course (or indeed any holder) other than a bank; and usually the bank would be acting as agent for collection of the instrument on behalf of the original creditor. [**794**]

The Act achieves the desired result in three ways. First, it provides that the creditor or owner shall not take a negotiable instrument, other than a bank note or cheque, in discharge of any sum payable by the debtor or hirer under a regulated agreement or by any person as surety in relation to the agreement (s. 123 (1)). Whether a post-dated cheque is within this exemption is not entirely clear. Though a post-dated cheque is undoubtedly a negotiable instrument (see Bills of Exchange Act 1882, s. 13 (2)), it is not, at the time of delivery to the payee, a cheque as defined by s. 73 of that Act since it is not payable on demand. It is, however, submitted that the word "cheque" should not in this context be construed too technically but should be interpreted in accordance with current usage as covering a post-dated cheque, the essential ingredient being that it is drawn on a banker and does not involve acceptance. Since the instrument is not accepted (i.e. there can be no question of dishonour by non-acceptance), its issue cannot involve the drawer in any legal liability before the specified date, and when this is reached the instrument becomes a demand instrument and thus a cheque in the full sense.

[**795**]

A bill of exchange marked "not negotiable" is not, of course, a negotiable instrument and is thus not caught by the prohibition contained in s. 123. Such an instrument is outside the mischief at which the section is aimed, namely the creation of holder in due course status which would expose the debtor to liability on an instrument despite a total failure of the consideration for which it was supplied. The prohibition of negotiable instruments is also inapplicable to a postal order, which is not a negotiable instrument. [**796**]

Secondly, the Act precludes a creditor who has taken a cheque as payment (which is permitted by s. 123 (1)) from negotiating this except to a bank within the meaning of the Bills of Exchange Act 1882, i.e., a person or body or persons carrying on the business of banking. This is effective to prevent any person, other than a bank, from becoming a holder in due course, since the definition of "holder in due course" in s. 29 (1) of the Bills of Exchange Act requires that he be a person to whom the bill has been negotiated. A bill is negotiated when transferred from one person to another in such a manner as to constitute the transferee the holder of the bill (Bills of Exchange Act, s. 31 (1)). A bearer bill is negotiated by delivery, an order bill, by indorsement of the holder completed by delivery (*ibid.*, s. 31 (2), (3)). Transfer of a bill otherwise than by negotiation (e.g. by assignment or charge, as where a factoring agreement or floating charge embodies an equitable assignment sweeping up bills and notes of the supplier or chargor) is not prohibited, since the transferee cannot then be a holder in due course (indeed he cannot be a holder at all) and thus cannot bring an action on the bill unless he takes a statutory assignment of the holder's rights in conformity with s. 136 of the Law of Property Act 1925. He can then sue as assignee, but takes subject to all equities and defences of which the debtor could have availed himself against the original payee, so that the mischief against which the Act is aimed is thus prevented.

Thirdly, the creditor or owner cannot take a negotiable instrument as security, but only as conditional payment (s. 123 (3)). He will be regarded as taking the negotiable instrument as security for discharge of a sum if the sum is intended to be paid in some other way, and the negotiable instrument is to be presented for payment only if the sum is not paid in that way (s. 123 (4)). [**797**]

Exemption from s. 124

The Secretary of State may, by order, provide that s. 123 shall not apply where the regulated agreement has a connection with a country outside the United Kingdom (s. 123 (6)). No such order has yet been made. However, s. 129 is confined to negotiable instruments taken as payment, or as security for payment, of sums payable under a regulated agreement, and thus does not apply where the agreement is an exempt agreement (as to which see Chapter 10); and one category of exempt agreements is that made in connection with trade in goods or services with a country, or between two countries, outside the United Kingdom. See the Consumer Credit (Exempt Agreements) Order 1977, art. 3 (1) (*d*) and para. [**1049**]. [**798**]

Consequences of breach

After any contravention of s. 123 has occurred in relation to a sum payable as mentioned in s. 123 (1) (*a*), the agreement under which the sum is payable is enforceable against the debtor or hirer on an order of the court only (s. 124 (1)). If the application is dismissed by the court otherwise than on technical grounds, a security taken in relation to the agreement becomes void *ab initio* under s. 106 of the Act (see s. 113 (3) (*b*), and para. [**774**]). Similarly, after contravention of s. 123 in relation to a sum payable by any surety, the security is enforceable on an order of the court only (s. 124 (2)); and if an application to enforce the security is dismissed otherwise than on technical grounds, s. 106 becomes applicable to the security (s. 124 (2)). [**799**]

Section 125 (1) provides that a person who takes a negotiable instrument in contravention of s. 123 (1) or (3) is not a holder in due course, and is not entitled to enforce the instrument. But this disability is restricted to the creditor or owner himself, since it is only a taking of the negotiable instrument by the creditor or owner that contravenes s. 123 (1) or (3). If the creditor or owner negotiates a cheque in contravention of s. 123 (2), his doing so constitutes a defect in title within the meaning of the Bills of Exchange Act (Consumer Credit Act, s. 125 (2)), with the result that if he negotiates the instrument to any person taking with notice of the contravention, such person does not become a holder in due course (see Bills of Exchange Act, s. 29 (1) (*b*)). If, however, the creditor negotiates the instrument to a person who takes in good faith and without notice of the creditor's contravention of s. 123 of the Consumer Credit Act, then provided that such person fulfils the other requirements of a holder in due course under s. 29 of the Bills of Exchange Act he takes free from the defect in title generated by the contravention (Bills of Exchange Act, s. 38 (2)) and can enforce the instrument as such in the usual way. (Consumer Credit Act, s. 125 (4)). In that event, the debtor or hirer is entitled to be indemnified by the creditor or owner in respect of the liability incurred to the holder in due course (s. 125 (3)). [**800**]

22. Guarantees and Indemnities

Introduction

The contract of guarantee has long been the Cinderella of the law. Legislation, apart from requiring such contracts to be evidenced by a note or memorandum in writing (Statute of Frauds 1677, s. 4; Hire-Purchase Act 1965, s. 22 (1)) and conferring a limited measure of protection under the Hire-Purchase Act 1965, has done little for the guarantor, and it has been left to the courts to safeguard his interests by developing various grounds for his release, e.g. the variation of the principal agreement without his consent or the impairment of securities taken by the creditor. [**801**]

If this is true of guarantors, it is applicable with even greater force to indemnifiers. A guarantor is one whose liability is secondary, i.e. dependent on that of the principal debtor. He incurs no liability until the debtor has made default, and unless otherwise provided by the contract of guarantee can repudiate the guarantee if the principal contract to which the guarantee relates is invalid or unenforceable. On the other hand, the liability of an indemnifier under a contract of guarantee (which does not require to be evidenced in writing where it is governed by the Hire-Purchase Act 1965) is a principal liability and not in any way dependent on default by the principal debtor or on the validity of the contract entered into by the debtor. The classic exposition of the difference is the example given in *Birkmyr* v. *Darnell* (1704), 1 Salk. 27. A says to B: "Supply goods to C and if he does not pay you I will." That is a contract of a guarantee. A says to B: "Supply goods to C and I will see that you are paid." That is a contract of indemnity. The difference between the two contracts produces substantial legal consequences, yet in most cases it is totally unreal. If the obligations of the indemnifier have the same content as those of the principal debtor, it is mere sophistry to say that the indemnifier's liability is not dependent on the principal debtor's default; for performance of their respective obligations falls due at the same time and if the principal debtor meets his obligations, there will be no remaining liability to which the indemnity can attach. [**802**]

The Hire-Purchase Act assimilated the treatment of guarantees and indemnities as regards the limited range of safeguards conferred on the guarantor by that Act. The Consumer Credit Act goes much further, and when its various provisions relating to guarantees and indemnities are drawn together they will be found to

273

provide a reasonably comprehensive pattern of protection for guarantors and indemnifiers. The Act does not in fact refer to a "guarantor" or an "indemnifier" but to a "surety", i.e., the person by whom any security is provided, or the person to whom his rights and duties in relation to the security have passed by assignment or operation of law (s. 189 (1)). Moreover, in looking at the statutory provisions the reader should bear in mind that the Act rarely uses the words "guarantee" and "indemnity". Instead it refers to "security". This usage is unfortunate since it confuses the genus with the species. A guarantee or indemnity is a form of security, but the term "security" as defined in s. 189 (1) embraces many other security forms, including mortgages. By using the word "security" when what was meant was "guarantee or indemnity" the Act raises doubts as to the full impact of some of its provisions. [803]

Formal requirements

The provisions of the Act relating to the form and contents of securities, including guarantees and indemnities, have been discussed in the previous chapter (paras. [766] *et seq.*). [804]

Supply of information and documents to surety

For the right of a surety to information and documents, see paragraph [714].
[805]

Notice of default

Service of a notice of default on the debtor or hirer in accordance with s. 88 is necessary before any security (including a guarantee or indemnity) can be enforced (s. 87 (1) (e)). Where such a notice of default is served on the debtor or hirer, a copy must be served on any surety (s. 111 (1)), otherwise the security becomes unenforceable against the surety, except on a court order, in respect of the breach or other matter to which the notice relates (s. 111 (2)). But no time limit is laid down for compliance with s. 111 (1), so that the creditor can avoid the disability imposed by s. 111 (2) by serving the copy of the notice of default before stating proceedings, or taking extra-judicial steps, to enforce his claim against the surety. Moreoever, it is only the matters specified in the notice of default that cannot be relied on against the surety without service of a copy of the notice of default. Hence if the debtor remedies the breach under s. 89 and subsequently commits a fresh breach in respect of which a new notice of default is served on him, it is only a copy of the new notice that needs to be served on the surety. Section 111 applies also to notices under ss. 76 (1), 98 (1), but unlike s. 87 (1) neither of these provisions applies to the enforcement of a security as such, so that where the creditor proceeds to enforce a guarantee on some ground other than the debtor's breach, no notice need be served on the debtor under s. 76 and accordingly no question arises of service of a copy on the surety under s. 111. [806].

Limitation of liability to that of principal debtor

A consequence of s. 113 (1) (discussed in para. [781]) is that notwithstanding any provision of the guarantee or indemnity itself, the creditor or owner cannot recover from the guarantor or indemnifier a sum greater than the recoverable from the debtor or hirer himself. This goes much further than the common law rule, which can be excluded by agreement (see para. [809]). [807]

An exception is provided in relation to contracts of indemnity (but not contracts of guarantee) by s. 113 (7), to which reference has been made earlier (para. [781]). [808]

Unenforceability of guarantee or indemnity

At common law, the liability of a guarantor, unlike that of an indemnifier, is *prima facie* co-terminous with that of the principal debtor, so that if for any reason the contract entered into by the principal debtor is void or unenforceable the guarantee is affected to the same extent. But whereas at common law this principle may be excluded by the terms of the guarantee, s. 113 (1) of the Act prevents the guarantor from incurring a liability which would not fall on the debtor or hirer. If the regulated agreement, though not void, is enforceable only on an order of the court, then until such order has been made the guarantee is likewise unenforceable (s. 113 (2)). This is, of course, entirely distinct from the statutory rule that if the guarantee itself is not properly executed, an order of the court must be obtained to enforce the guarantee, so far as it is provided in relation to the regulated agreement (s. 105 (6)). It should be noted that if the debtor under a regulated debtor–creditor agreement, or a debtor–creditor–supplier agreement for unrestricted-use credit, exercises a right to cancel but elects under s. 71 to leave the whole part of the credit outstanding, all guarantees, indemnities and other forms of security are extinguished, and the credit agreement continues as an unsecured agreement (see para. [618]). [809]

If a defaulting debtor in respect of whose liability a guarantee has been given obtains a time order, then during the currency of the order the breach is deemed not to have occurred (s. 130 (5) (c)), with the result that the right to proceed against the surety for the debtor's breach is suspended so long as the order remains effective. [810]

Negotiable instruments

If the creditor or owner contravenes the provisions of s. 123 relating to the taking or negotiation of a negotiable instrument, the surety is protected in the same way as the debtor, since the security cannot be enforced except on an order of the court (s. 124 (2)—see para. [799]). [811]

Extortionate bargains

The provisions of the Act relating to extortionate credit bargains (see Chapter 30) ensure for the protection of the surety as well as of the debtor or hirer in respect of whose obligations the guarantee or indemnity was given. [812]

Continuance of common law rules

Nothing in the Act affects the principles evolved at common law for the protection of guarantors. See generally R. M. Goode, *op. cit.*, Chapter 22. [813]

23. Land Mortgage Transactions

Application of Act

In principle, the Act regulates all forms of consumer credit and consumer hire agreement, and does not cease to apply merely because the agreement is secured on land or the credit is extended for the purchase of land. But land mortgages extended by certain types of creditor (notably local authorities and building societies) are for the most part exempt under s. 16 (1), and the Secretary of State has by order extended the exemption to certain mortgages entered into as creditor by other classes specified in s. 16 (1) (see paras. [**315**] *et seq.*). However, whilst total exemption is limited to cases within s. 16, consumer credit agreements which are secured by a land mortgage or under which the credit is extended in connection with the purchase of land are in given conditions exempted from certain specific parts or provisions of the Act (see below). "Land" includes an interest in land (s. 189 (1)), and the term "land mortgage" includes any security charged on land (*ibid.*), and thus embraces a rentcharge, but it is no longer possible to create a valid rentcharge (Rentcharges Act 1977, s. 2). [**814**]

Advertisements

Advertisements of credit facilities which would otherwise be outside Part IV of the Act may be brought within it if the advertiser carries on a business of a type mentioned in s. 43 (2) (see paras. [**449**], [**450**]). [**815**]

Withdrawal and cancellation

The right of cancellation conferred by s. 67 does not apply to (i) a regulated agreement secured on land; or (ii) a restricted-use credit agreement to finance the purchase of land; or (iii) an agreement for a bridging loan in connection with the purchase of land. Instead, the Act provides the debtor (except in cases (ii) and (iii), above) with a period of reflection by prescribing a special documentation procedure and an isolation period in which the debtor must not be disturbed by unsolicited communications (see Chapter 15). However, the debtor's right to withdraw from a prospective regulated agreement applies the cancellation provisions of the Act to the agreement, any linked transaction and any other thing done in anticipation of the making of the agreement as if it had been made and then cancelled under s. 69

(s. 57 (1)), and this is so even though the agreement would not itself have been cancellable if made (s. 57 (4)). This may have unfortunate consequences for the prospective creditor who has incurred survey fees or legal costs in connection with the projected transaction. See para. [**586**]. [**816**]

Entry on land

Except under an order of the court, the creditor or owner is not entitled to enter any premises to take possession of goods subject to a regulated hire-purchase agreement, regulated conditional sale of agreement or regulated consumer hire agreement (s. 92 (1)). It would seem that s. 92 (1) applies even to entry on the land of a third party, thus restricting the common law right to recapt from a third party's land goods placed there by the third party's trespass.

Entry in contravention of this provision is actionable as a breach of statutory duty (s. 92 (3)). It is not, however, a breach to enter with the consent of the debtor or hirer given at the time (s. 173 (3)). [**817**]

Recovery of land

At any time when the debtor is in breach of a regulated conditional sale agreement relating to land, the creditor is entitled to recover possession of the land from the debtor, or any person claiming under him, on an order of the court only (s. 92 (2)). The possession in breach of s. 92 (2) is actionable as a breach of statutory duty (s. 92 (3)) unless with the consent of the debtor given at the time of repossession (s. 173 (3)). Conditional sale agreements relating to land are uncommon, since a vendor who agrees to leave part of the purchase price outstanding almost invariably does so not by preserving the legal title until payment but by taking a mortgage from the purchaser to secure the balance of the price. Section 92 (2) does not cover mortgages of land, which are in any event enforceable only on an order of the court (s. 126), though no sanction is provided for enforcement without the requisite court order (see para. [**820**]). [**818**]

Buyer's termination of conditional sale agreement comprising land

The statutory right of a buyer under a conditional sale agreement to terminate it at any time by notice (s. 99 (1)) applies to a conditional sale agreement relating to land (see definition of "conditional sale agreement" in s. 189 (1)). But the right of termination ceases to be exercisable after title to the land has passed to the buyer (s. 99 (3)). Accordingly, sub-ss. (4) and (5) of s. 99 (see paras. [**749**]–[**750**]) are restricted to conditional sale agreements relating to goods. [**819**]

Enforcement of land mortgage

A land mortgage securing a regulated agreement is enforceable (so far as provided in relation to the agreement) on an order of the court only (s. 125). However, by a curious omission no sanction is provided for enforcement without a court order, e.g. by repossession or sale; and s. 170 (1) precludes an action for damages for breach of statutory duty where this is not expressly provided. Hence the debtor's only remedy is to apply to the court for an injunction, this being outside the scope of s. 170 (1) (see s. 170 (3)). As a rule, the county court can only grant an injunction by way of ancillary relief (see para. [**773**]). However the county court now has jurisdiction to grant such an injunction as the primary relief provided that the net annual value for the rating of the premises does not exceed the current limit on jurisdiction in s. 51 of the County Courts Act 1959, i.e. £1,000 (see *ibid.*, s. 51A, added by the Administration of Justice Act 1977, s. 14). The court clearly has power to restrain a threatened breach; and even if the debtor's application is not made until after the breach has occurred, the court would seem to have power to grant a mandatory injunction to restore the *status quo*, except where this would affect the rights of an innocent third party, e.g. a *bona fide* purchaser from the mortgagee. See further para. [**775**]. [**820**]

24. Credit-token Agreements

Definition

A credit-token agreement is defined in s. 14 (1), discussed in paragraph [289]. As there noted, the term "credit-token" covers bank and other credit cards, trading checks and trading vouchers, but not bank cheque guarantee cards. Special provisions apply to credit-tokens and credit-token agreements (see paras. [290], [566]–[568]) which will now be examined in more detail. [821]

Unsolicited credit-tokens prohibited

The provisions of s. 51 prohibiting unsolicited credit-tokens have been mentioned earlier (para. [474]). [822]

Supply of copy of executed agreement

As a rule, a copy of the executed consumer credit or consumer hire agreement must be sent to the debtor or hirer within seven days following the making of the agreement (s. 63 (2)—and see Chapter 14). But in the case of a credit-token agreement, it suffices that the copy is given before or at the time when the credit-token is given to the debtor (s. 63 (4)). The requirements on the issue of new credit-token agreements have been mentioned earlier (para. [567]). [823]

Notice of cancellation

Where, in the case of a cancellable agreement, the agreement is presented or sent to the debtor for signature and becomes an executed agreement on the spot, a separate notice in prescribed form setting out the debtor's right of cancellation must usually be sent to him by post within seven days (s. 64 (1) (b)—and see para. [569]). But in the case of a credit-token agreement, it suffices if the copy is sent by post either before the credit-token is given to him or with the credit-token (s. 64 (2)). [824]

Acceptance of credit-token

The debtor incurs no liability under a credit-token agreement for use made of the credit-token by any person unless the debtor had previously accepted the

279

credit-token, or the use constituted an acceptance of it by him (s. 66 (1)). By s. 66 (2), the debtor accepts a credit-token when—

    (*a*) it is signed, or
    (*b*) a receipt for it is signed, or
    (*c*) it is first used,

either by the debtor himself or by a person who, pursuant to the agreement, is authorised by him to use it. The debtor would not, it is thought, be treated as having signed a receipt for a credit-token unless the receipt is given for the credit-token as such, and not merely for the package containing it. Hence a receipt for a registered or special delivery letter containing a credit-token does not thereby constitute signature of receipt for the token itself unless the delivery receipt expressly refers to the token. [**825**]

Cancellation of credit-token agreement

The right of cancellation applies to credit-token agreements, in the circumstances set out in s. 67, in the same way as to other regulated agreements. On cancellation, the debtor is entitled (subject to s. 70 (5)—see below) to recover payments made to the creditor either from the creditor himself or from the various suppliers in respect of whose accounts the debtor has made payment to the creditor (s. 70 (3)). For the purpose of determining to which of such accounts payments made by the debtor to the creditor relate, the court will, under common law rules, have regard to any appropriation made by the debtor; but in the absence of such appropriation the court will presumably apply the rule in *Clayton's Case* (1816), 1 Mer. 572, and treat each payment as made in reduction of the earliest account first. [**826**]

There is, however, a special rule applicable to credit-token agreements. The debtor is not entitled to repayment of a sum payable for the issue of the credit-token, or to release from liability for payment of such sum, until the credit-token has been returned to the creditor or surrendered to a supplier (s. 70 (5)). The limited effect of this provision should be noted. It applies not to sums paid or payable in respect of goods or services acquired with the token but only to a sum paid or payable for the *issue* of the token. It is thus directed at those check trading agreements which require the debtor to pay the check trader a sum of money for the privilege of having the trading checks issued to him. [**827**]

Misuse of credit-token

By s. 83 (1), the debtor under a regulated consumer credit agreement is not liable to the creditor for any loss arising from use of the credit facility by another person not acting, or to be treated as acting, as the debtor's agent. This provision is not confined to misuse of credit-tokens (it could, for example, cover pledge of a debtor's credit by another but it does not apply to forgery of a cheque or any other misuse of an instrument within s. 4 of the Cheques Act 1957 (s. 83 (2)) and is most likely to arise from theft or other unauthorised use of a credit card or other credit-token. But s. 84 sets out various cases in which the debtor can be made liable, within the limits laid down by that section, for loss to the creditor arising from misuse of the credit-token. The rules embodied in s. 84 may be summarised as follows:

(1) Subject to (2) and (3) below, the debtor can be made liable (either by virtue of the credit-token agreement or in tort for negligence):

   (i) without limit, for loss to the creditor from use of the credit-token by a person who acquired possession of it with the debtor's consent (s. 84 (2)), even if the particular use was not with the debtor's consent;

   (ii) to the extent of £30 (or the credit limit if lower) for loss to the creditor from use of the credit-token during the period when it is not in the possession of an authorised person (s. 84 (1)), i.e. the debtor, the creditor and any person authorised by the debtor to use the token (s. 84 (7)).

(2) No liability for unauthorised use is incurred by the debtor under (1) unless there are contained in the credit-token agreement in the prescribed manner particulars of the name, address and telephone number of a person stated to be the person to whom notice is to be given under s. 84 (3) (s. 84 (4)).

(3) Once the debtor has given notice to the creditor that the token is lost or stolen or is for any other reason liable to be misused, he ceases to incur any further liability in respect of the token (s. 84 (3)), even within the £30 limit. Such notice may be given orally or in writing (s. 84 (3)) and takes effect when received (s. 84 (5)); but where it is given orally, and the agreement so requires, it is to be treated as not taking effect if not confirmed in writing within seven days (*ibid.*). This allows the creditor, by appropriate provision in the agreement, to safeguard himself against false assertions by the debtor that he gave oral notification of loss. If, therefore, the credit-token agreement requires oral notice of loss to be confirmed in writing within seven days and the debtor fails to give any written confirmation at all, his liability continues to accrue up to the maximum of £30 or the credit limit if lower. If, where there is such a requirement, the debtor does give written confirmation but this does not reach the creditor until, say, ten days after the oral notice was given, the debtor is liable, within the above limit, for all unauthorised purchases made up to the date of receipt of the written confirmation, but incurs no liability for purchases made thereafter.

(4) Any sum paid by the debtor for the issue of the credit-token, to the extent (if any) that it has not been previously offset by use made of the credit-token, is to be treated as paid towards satisfaction of any liability under s. 84 (1) or (2) (s. 84 (6)).

(5) Where two or more credit-tokens are given under one credit-token agreement, the provisions of s. 84 apply to each credit-token separately (s. 84 (8)). [**828**]

25. Leasing, Hire and Rental Agreements

Nature of agreement

A leasing (or hire or rental) agreement is an agreement for the hire of goods which does not provide for ownership of the goods to pass to the lessee. The terms "leasing", "hire", "contract hire" and "rental" have different business connotations (see R. M. Goode, *Hire-Purchase Law and Practice* (2nd Edn.), p. 880) but are legally interchangeable, the distinctions being purely functional and having no legal significance. Nevertheless, as we shall see, there is one provision of the Consumer Credit Act, namely s. 101, in which Parliament has endeavoured to isolate transactions which in the business world would be termed "equipment leasing" and to exclude these from the provisions of that section conferring on the hirer the right to bring the agreement to an end after 18 months. In all other respects, the Act draws no distinction between these different forms of hiring agreement; and in discussing the provisions of the Act we shall employ the statutory term "consumer hire agreement", drawing attention to the fact that except where the hirer is a body corporate this term covers all forms of hiring subsumed under the above labels.

[**829**]

Legal control of hiring agreements

Prior to the Consumer Credit Act, hiring agreements were free from legal controls other than those imposed as a measure of economic regulation by control orders, which continue in force (see para. [**31**]). The Consumer Credit Act, embodying the recommendations of the Crowther Committee, brings such agreements for the first time within the scope of consumer protection legislation under the description "consumer hire agreement". [**830**]

Scope of the Act

The Act applies to all consumer hire agreements as defined by s. 15 (see para. [**158**]), other than agreements exempted by order of the Secretary of State under s. 16 (6) (see para. [**323.1**]). Except as indicated below, the provisions relating to consumer credit agreements apply equally to consumer hire agreements. It should be noted that unlike consumer credit agreements, consumer hire agreements are by

282

definition (s. 15) limited to goods and do not extend to the hire or services or the letting of land. [**831**]

Formalities of contract

No distinction is drawn by the Act between regulated consumer credit agreements and regulated consumer hire agreements in relation to the formalities of contract, though the disclosure requirements to be imposed by regulations will obviously have to reflect differences between the two forms of agreement. [**832**]

Implied terms

The Consumer Credit Act does not contain any provision as to implied terms in consumer hire agreements, but at common law there are implied terms as to correspondence with description, fitness and merchantable quality, as well as quiet possession and probably also title in view of the provisions of s. 8 of the Torts (Interference with Goods) Act 1977, and these implied terms cannot be excluded or restricted except so far as permitted by s. 7 of the Unfair Contract Terms Act 1977. [**833**]

Information and documents

The hirer's right to information and documents under s. 79 of the Act has been previously discussed (para. [**709**]), as has the hirer's duty under s. 80 to inform the owner, on request, of the whereabouts of the goods comprised in the agreement which the hirer is required to keep in his possession or control (para. [**710**]), and the owner's duty under s. 109 to supply information to a surety (para. [**706**]). [**834**]

Misuse of credit facilities

The provisions of s. 83 (para. [**828**]) are not applicable to the misuse of consumer hire facilities. [**835**]

Termination of hiring agreement

The provisions of ss. 99 and 100 conferring a right on the hirer or buyer to terminate a hire-purchase or conditional sale agreement by notice in writing, and restricting his liability on such termination, have no application to consumer hire agreements. Instead, a more restricted right of termination, with limitation of liability to that accrued prior to termination, is conferred by s. 101. This has been fully discussed in paras. [**756**]–[**760**]. [**836**]

Recovery of hired goods

The provisions of ss. 90 and 91 relating to protected goods do not apply to goods comprised in a consumer hire agreement. The owner remains free to exercise a contractual right to repossess, subject to—

(i) service of the requisite notice under s. 76 (1) if the period of hire has not expired (s. 76 (2));
(ii) service of the requisite default notice under ss. 87 and 88, and its expiry without the default having been remedied within the specified time;

(iii) exercise by the court of its powers under Part IX of the Act (see Chapter 22);
(iv) exercise by the court of its general equitable jurisdiction to grant relief against forfeiture (see para. [**840**]).

It is thought that a default notice complying with s. 88 will *ipso facto* constitute at the same time a notice complying with s. 76 (1). [**837**]

Instead of exercising power to repossess, the owner can apply to the court for an order for delivery of the goods, with or without the option to the hirer to pay their value. Such an order is made not under the Consumer Credit Act (for the statutory orders provided by s. 133 are confined to hire-purchase and conditional sale agreements) but under s. 3 of the Torts (Interference with Goods) Act 1977, which applies generally to claims for wrongful interference with goods. It is within the discretion of the court whether to make an order for delivery of the goods without giving the hirer the option to pay their value (*ibid.*, s. 3 (3) (*b*)). Apart from this, the choice of relief is with the owner (*ibid.*), so that if he does not seek, or the court is not prepared to grant, an order for delivery without giving the hirer the option to pay the value of the goods, it is for the owner to choose between an order for delivery which does give such an option and an award of damages. If the court does make an order for delivery of the goods, with or without an option to the hire to pay their value, it may impose conditions (*ibid.*, s. 3 (6)). A similar power is conferred by the Consumer Credit Act, under which the operation of an order for the delivery of the goods may be made conditional on the doing of specified acts by the owner or hirer (s. 135 (1) (*a*)) or may be suspended until such time as the court subsequently directs or until the occurrence of a specified event or events (s. 135 (1) (*b*)), e.g. non-payment of sums ordered to be paid by the hirer as a condition of suspension of the order. But the court's power to suspend the operation of an order s. 135 (1) (*b*) may not be exercised so as extend the period for which the hirer is entitled to possession under the terms of the consumer hire agreement (s. 135 (3)). It would seem to follow that the court cannot vary the agreement under s. 136 so as to prolong the period of hire beyond that provided by the agreement. See also s. 135 (2). [**838**].

Consequences of repossession or order for delivery

The owner who repossesses goods or obtains an order for their delivery incurs some risk in so doing in that the court's power under s. 132 to order return of payments to the hirer and his release from liability then becomes exercisable (see paras. [**841**], [**947**]. [**839**]

Relief against forfeiture

The court has an inherent equitable jurisdiction to grant the hirer relief against forfeiture of a hiring agreement in cases where it would be harsh and unconscionable for the owner to refuse the hirer an opportunity to tender late performance, subject, however, to application for relief being made promptly and to the hirer showing he can within a reasonable time discharge arrears and remedy other breaches. See generally *Barton Thompson & Co., Ltd.* v. *Stapling Machines Co.*, [1966] Ch. 499, [1966] 2 All E.R. 222; *Starside Properties, Ltd.* v. *Mustapha*, [1974] 2 All E.R. 567. This jurisdiction would seem to be unaffected by the Consumer Credit Act. [**840**]

Extortionate credit bargains

The provisions of ss. 137–140 relating to extortionate credit bargains do not apply to hiring agreements. In most cases, however, the hirer under a consumer hire agreement will be adequately protected from the consequences of an oppressive agreement by the provisions of s. 132, which empower the court to order total or partial repayment of rentals to the hirer, and release of the hirer from all or part of any future liability under the agreement, in any case where the owner repossesses the goods or obtains an order for their return; and this is so whether the repossession or order results from termination by the owner for the hirer's default or termination by the hirer himself. The strength of s. 132 is thus reinforced by s. 101 of the Act, which, with certain exceptions, empowers the hirer to terminate the agreement despite the absence of any contractual right of termination. In addition, the court has a wide discretion as to time orders under ss. 129 and 130. Whilst an order for return of the goods cannot be suspended so as to allow the debtor a right to remain in possession beyond the contractual period of hire (s. 135 (3)), no such limitation is imposed on the court in relation to the time it can allow the hirer for payment where possession of the goods by the hirer beyond the contract period of hire is not thereby involved. [**841**]

26. Agreements for Services

The need for control

It is a remarkable fact that until the advent of the Trade Descriptions Act 1968, there were no general statutory provisions conferring on the aggrieved consumer redress for non-performance or defective performance of contracts for the supply of services; and even the Trade Descriptions Act is limited to sanctions for false or misleading statements as to services, the making of which constitutes an offence under that Act (s. 14 (1)) and entitles any person who thereby suffers loss to apply for a compensation order under s. 1 of the Criminal Justice Act 1972. The lack of attention devoted to services by the legislature did not pass unnoticed in the Crowther Report:

> "Consumer protection legislation has tended to concentrate on transactions involving the disposition of goods. Agreements for the provision of services have so far received little attention from the legislature, although they give rise to equally serious forms of hardship and abuse. We consider that the extension of legislation to deal with this situation is long overdue" (para. 6.8.2.). [**842**]

In accordance with the Crowther Committee's recommendations the Consumer Credit Act takes in agreements for the provision of services and facilities on credit as well as contracts for the supply on credit of goods and land. [**843**]

Application of the Act

Only those provisions of the Act relating to consumer credit (as opposed to consumer hire) affect the supply of services. The Crowther Report drew a distinction between the sale of services (i.e. the supply of services on a particular occasion only, as in the case of holidays and hotel accommodation) and the hire of services (i.e. the provision of services which are continuous and for which the consumer pays as he goes along). The Report recommended that both forms of contract should be controlled, the sale of services on credit being equated as far as possible with the sale of goods, whilst the hire of services, not being a credit transaction, should be treated in broadly the same way as the hire of goods. The

Act does not wholly implement this recommendation. It embraces contracts for the supply of services on credit within the definition of "consumer credit agreement", but does not touch the hire of services at all, except in relation to linked transactions (see para. [845]) and agreements with a credit-broker, debt-adjuster or debt-counsellor (see s. 156 and para. [227]). The provisions relating to "consumer hire agreements" are confined to contracts for the hire of goods. [844]

The distinction between contracts for the provision of services on credit and contracts under which the acquirer of the services pays as he goes along has been exemplified in paragraph [227]. The former are within the Act; the latter are outside it except insofar as the agreement for services is a linked transaction within s. 19 of the Act (see Chapter 27). [845]

Extent of control

Except for those provisions of the Act which are peculiar to hire-purchase and conditional sale agreements (see para. [198]) or which otherwise refer exclusively to goods or land, the Act applies to advertisements of services on credit and to regulated consumer credit agreements relating to services in the same way and to the same extent as advertisements of goods on credit and regulated consumer credit agreements relating to goods. Provisions relating exclusively to goods or land, apart from those mentioned in para. [198], are s. 72 (see para. [849]), with which must be read s. 57 (1), ss. 114–122 (pledges) and s. 126 (enforcement of land mortgages). [846]

Implied terms

The Consumer Credit Act does not import into contracts for services any terms in favour of the debtor, but certain terms are implied at common law (see para. [658], *ante*), and the creditor's ability to exclude or restrict them is limited by the Unfair Contract Terms Act 1977, and in particular by ss. 2 and 3 (see paras. [665] *et seq.*). [847]

To the extent to which the supplier does effectively exclude or limit his liability in a contract for services, this enures for the benefit of a creditor who would otherwise incur a liability under s. 75 of the Act (see paras. [679] *et seq.*). [848]

Withdrawal and cancellation

Whilst a debtor who, having received goods prior to entry into a regulated agreement or before expiry of the period allowed for cancellation of a cancellable agreement, must surrender the goods on exercising his right of cancellation, the "return" of services already provided to a debtor who withdraws from a prospective agreement or who cancels a cancellable agreement is obviously not possible. Accordingly the provisions of s. 72 of the Act (discussed in paras. [624] *et seq.*) are inapplicable to services supplied on credit. The consequence is that if the provider of the services is rash enough to furnish them before contract or before expiry of the time allowed for cancellation, he must accept the fact that the debtor, having had the benefit of the services, can by withdrawal (s. 57 (1)) or cancellation (s. 70 (1)) disclaim liability for payment and recover any payments he has made. The only exceptions are those prescribed by s. 69 (2) (*a*) (see para. [615]). [849]

Appropriation of payments

The provisions of s. 81 (2), providing for a statutory appropriation of payments where the debtor under two or more regulated agreements with the same person fails to appropriate himself under s. 81 (1), do not apply to a regulated consumer credit agreement for the provision of services unless it or the other agreement is an agreement in relation to which security is provided (see s. 81 (2) (c)) or the other agreement is a hire-purchase, conditional sale or consumer hire agreement.   [**850**]

27. Linked Transactions

Introduction

In preceding chapters, we have examined in some detail the rights and duties of one who is the debtor under a consumer credit agreement or the hirer under a consumer hire agreement. So far, we have concentrated attention on such rights and duties as may arise in relation to the credit or hire agreement itself. But if that agreement is a debtor-creditor-supplier agreement, it cannot be divorced from the supply transaction which it financed. Moreover, the debtor may have entered into other, ancillary, contracts, e.g. maintenance or insurance, which may be affected by the impact of the Act on the regulated agreement to which they are linked. The draftsman has in fact taken considerable trouble to work out the effect which different events occurring in relation to a regulated agreement are to have on these linked transactions. This is of great importance; for if, for example, a debtor who had taken out insurance or life assurance pursuant to a requirement of a cancellable regulated agreement were to remain bound by his contract with the insurers after cancellation of the regulated agreement, he would be placed in a most unfortunate position, the prospect of which might well discourage him from exercising his right to cancel. The Act deals with this and various other problems arising in relation to linked transactions in the manner described below. [**851**]

Definition of linked transaction

This is contained in s. 19 (1) and (2), which provide as follows:

> "(1) A transaction entered into by the debtor or hirer, or a relative of his, with any other person ('the other party'), except one for the provision of security, is a linked transaction in relation to an actual or prospective regulated agreement of which is does not form part (the 'principal agreement') if—
> > (a) the transaction is entered into in compliance with a term of the principal agreement; or
> > (b) the principal agreement is a debtor-creditor-supplier agreement and the transaction is financed, or to be financed, by the principal agreement; or
> > (c) the other party is a person mentioned in subsection (2), and a person so mentioned initiated the transaction by suggesting it to the debtor or hirer, or his relative,

who enters into it—
  (i) to induce the creditor or owner to enter into the principal agreement, or
  (ii) for another purpose related to the principal agreement, or
  (iii) where the principal agreement is a restricted-use credit agreement, for a purpose related to a transaction financed, or to be financed, by the principal agreement.

(2) The persons referred to in subsection (1) (c) are—
  (a) the creditor or owner, or his associate;
  (b) a person who, in the negotiation of the transaction, is represented by a credit-broker who is also a negotiator in antecedent negotiations for the principal agreement;
  (c) a person who, at the time the transaction is initiated, knows that the principal agreement had been made or contemplates that it might be made." [**852**]

The Act refers to a linked "transaction", not "agreement". The word "transaction" is not defined, but is plainly wider than "agreement". In *Greenberg* v. *I.R. Comrs.*, [1972] A.C. 109, [1971] 3 All E.R. 136, it was said that "the word 'transaction' is normally used to denote some bilateral activity but it can be used to denote an activity in which only a single person is engaged" (*per* Lord Reid, at p. 149) and that "its ordinary meaning is 'proceeding' or 'action' or, in particular, 'business deal'" (*per* Lord Simon, at p. 159). It is thus clear that the phrase "linked transaction" covers not only the ancillary agreement itself but any acts done or to be done (whether by one party or both) by way of implementation of the agreement. However an agreement for the provision of security is expressly excluded by the opening words of s. 19 (1). Accordingly, a mortgage given to secure a regulated agreement is not a linked transaction, nor is a guarantee or indemnity entered into on the insistence of the creditor. Thus, whilst a life policy taken out by the debtor pursuant to a requirement of a regulated agreement is a linked transaction, the charging of such policy to the creditor, being a transaction for the provision of security, is not a linked transaction (see Second Schedule, example 11). [**853**]

It should be noted that a transaction may be a linked transaction even though the parties to it were not the same as the parties to the regulated agreement to which the transaction is linked. It suffices if they are parties connected by a relationship which falls within one of the categories mentioned in s. 19 (1) or (2). The purpose of the provisions is to prevent evasion through use of persons associated with one of the parties to the regulated agreement; and in defining the types of association which are to attract the statutory provisions, the Act casts its net far and wide. The reach of the net depends on whether the transaction falls within category (a), (b) or (c) of s. 19 (1). Even where it is the debtor or hirer himself who is a party to the linked transaction, if the other party is not the creditor or owner he may well be unaware of the existence of the principal agreement. The status of a transaction as a linked transaction does not in any way depend on knowledge by the third party that such transaction is entered into with him by the debtor or hirer for the purposes of or in compliance with the regulated agreement. See further paragraph [**862**]. [**854**]

It is clear from s. 96 (2) that a linked transaction may itself be a credit transaction; and there seems no reason why a regulated agreement should not be a linked transaction in relation to another regulated agreement, as where a bank advances money to a prospective debtor under a hire-purchase agreement to enable him to pay the necessary deposit. Indeed it is quite possible to have two regulated agreements each of which is a linked transaction in relation to the other. [**855**]

Category (*a*)

Into category (*a*) fall transactions entered into by the debtor or hirer, or a relative of his, with any other person in compliance with a term of the regulated agreement. Thus if, in compliance with a hire-purchase agreement, the hirer insures the goods, the contract of insurance is a linked transaction. Similarly, a maintenance agreement entered into by the hirer pursuant to the hire-purchase agreement is a linked transaction, whether entered into with the owner or with a third party. The fact that no arrangement or business relationship between the creditor and the third party exists or is contemplated is irrelevant to the application of category (*a*). The position would be the same if the insurance or maintenance contract were taken out not by the debtor but by a relative of his, that is, an associate as defined in s. 184 (1) (see s. 189 (1) and para. [**362**]). [**856**]

Category (*a*) obviously applies only where the regulated agreement is made first. A transaction made prior to the regulated agreement cannot be a linked transaction in category (*a*), though it may well fall within category (*b*) or category (*c*). [**857**]

Category (*b*)

This category brings in the definition of "debtor-creditor-supplier agreement" in s. 12, and thus entails a regulated agreement to finance a transaction with a supplier and entered into by the creditor under pre-existing arrangements, or in contemplation of future arrangements, with the supplier. The following are illustrations of linked transactions within category (*b*).

(1) A finance house, pursuant to an arrangement with a motor dealer, grants a personal loan to the dealer's customer to enable that customer to buy a motor vehicle from the dealer. The loan is applied for that purpose. The sale by the dealer to the customer is a linked transaction.

(2) The debtor under a check-trading agreement uses checks to buy goods from a supplier who has an arrangement with the check-trader to accept as payment checks issued by the check-trader. The purchase made by the debtor from the supplier is a linked transaction.

(3) The holder of a bank credit card uses it to pay for the cost of a flight on an airline which recognises the card, pursuant to arrangements between the bank and the airline. The contract of carriage by air between the cardholder and the airline is a linked transaction.

Section 19 (1), when defining a linked transaction, excludes a transaction which forms part of the regulated agreement itself. Hence an agreement in which the creditor is himself the supplier of the goods or services—e.g. a hire-purchase agreement—is not a linked transaction, even though it would otherwise fall within category (*b*) of that subsection. [**858**]

Category (c)

This category subdivides into three. In each case, the other party is a person within s. 19 (2) and initiates the transaction by suggesting it to the debtor or hirer, or his relative.

Category (c) (i)

The debtor or hirer, or his relative, on the suggestion of the creditor or owner or other person of a kind mentioned in s. 19 (2), enters into the transaction to induce the creditor or owner to enter into the principal agreement. Into this category would fall, for example, insurance and maintenance contracts which, though not made compulsory under a term of the regulated agreement itself, are orally stipulated by the creditor as a prerequisite of his entry into the agreement.

Category (c) (ii)

This is a somewhat wider category, where the debtor or hirer, or his relative, on the suggestion of the creditor or owner, or of another person of a kind mentioned in s. 19 (2), enters into the transaction for another purpose linked to the principal agreement. If a person enters into an agreement with a tour operator for a holiday on credit and at the tour operator's suggestion takes out a policy of assurance covering death or disability whilst travelling or insures against the risk of a wasted payment as a result of his having to cancel the holiday through illness, such insurance transactions are linked transactions within category (c) (ii).

Category (c) (iii)

This category is confined to cases where the principal agreement is a restricted-use credit agreement. Category (c) (iii) is somewhat difficult to envisage at first sight, involving (a) a transaction entered into on the suggestion of the creditor etc., which is (b) entered into for a purpose related to another transaction, which in turn is (c) financed or to be financed by the restricted-use credit agreement. However category (c) (iii) is less formidable than it seems. It is primarily concerned with an ancillary contract for the provision of goods or services not as a condition of the creditor's entry into the regulated agreement nor as a term of that agreement or for the purposes of the agreement but in order to provide or facilitate a use of the goods or services acquired with the finance provided under the principal agreement. An example is a maintenance agreement entered into with the supplier of a television set from whom the debtor has brought it on credit sale (this is within (c) (iii) rather than (c) (ii) because its purpose is related to the use of the television set, not to the credit by which the purchase of this was financed). Another case is where the debtor, on the suggestion of the creditor, buys food to stock a deep-freeze which he is acquiring on credit from the creditor. The contract for the purchase of the food (whether or not itself a credit agreement) is a linked transaction within (c) (iii). [859]

Impact of the Act on linked transactions

The definition of "linked transaction" is relevant for the following reasons.

(1) Charges payable under any transaction which is a linked transaction within s. 19 (1) (a) are required to be treated as part of the total charge for credit (see para. [517]).

(2) A linked transaction entered into before the making of the regulated agreement to which it relates has no effect until such time (if any) as that agreement is made (s. 19 (3)), unless the linked transaction is of a description exempted by regulations from this provision (s. 19 (4)). Some insurance contracts are likely to be excluded under s. 19 (4), for much the same reason as in the case of cancellation (see para. [**612**]).

(3) Withdrawal of a party from a prospective regulated agreement operates as a withdrawal from a linked transaction (ss. 57 (1), 69 (1)); and cancellation of a cancellable agreement by the debtor or hirer operates to cancel any linked transaction and to withdraw any offer by him, or his relative, to enter into a linked transaction (s. 69 (1)). For examples, see para. [**612**]. But regulations may exclude linked transactions of the prescribed description from the above provisions (s. 69 (3)). Again, certain insurance contracts are likely to qualify for such exclusion (see para. [**612**]).

(4) On cancellation of any linked transaction, any sum paid by the debtor or hirer or his relative is repayable, and any sum which but for the cancellation would have become payable by the debtor or hirer or his relative ceases to be payable, under the provisions of s. 70, and subject to the exemption in s. 70 (5), previously discussed (para. [**617**] *et seq.*). If the linked transaction relates to goods, the debtor or hirer or relative has a duty, under the provisions of s. 72 and subject to the exceptions in s. 72 (9), to surrender the goods to the other party to the linked transaction and meanwhile to retain possession of them and take reasonable care of them (see paras. [**624**] *et seq.*).

(5) Regulations under s. 95 (1) prescribing rebates for early settlement of a regulated consumer credit agreement (paras. [**734**] *et seq.*) may provide for calculation of the rebate by reference to any sums paid by the debtor or his relative under or in connection with the agreement (whether to the creditor or some other person) including sums under linked transactions (s. 95 (2)).

(6) Where for any reason the indebtedness of the debtor under a regulated consumer credit agreement is discharged before the time fixed by the agreement, he, and any relative of his, is at the same time discharged from any liability under a linked transaction, other than a debt which has already become payable (s. 96 (1)). But this does not apply to a linked transaction which is itself an agreement providing the debtor or his relative with credit (s. 96 (2)), or to linked transactions excluded by regulations (s. 96 (3)). It should be noted that s. 97 (1) applies only to early settlement and not, for example, to termination by the debtor under s. 99 or by the creditor for breach.

(7) The provisions of s. 113—preventing evasion of the Act through use of security (see para. [**781**] *et seq.*)—apply to security provided in relation to an actual or prospective linked transaction as they do to security provided in relation to the actual or prospective regulated agreement (s. 113 (8)).

(8) The provisions of s. 173, dealing with attempted contracting out of the statutory provisions for the protection of the debtor or hirer or his

relative (para. [1091]) apply to a linked transaction as well as to the regulated agreement.

(9) The power under s. 179 (1) to make regulations as to the form of secondary documents (para. [1096]) applies to documents or things issued in connection with linked transactions. [860]

Mention should also be made of certain other provisions of the Act which, though not confined to linked transactions, will almost invariably affect them. These are s. 75 (relating to the creditor's liability for misrepresentations and breaches of contract by the supplier—see paras. [674] *et seq.*) and s. 139 (relating to the reopening of extortionate agreements—see paras. [966] *et seq.*). [861]

A significant feature of the provisions discussed above is that if the other party to the linked transaction is not the creditor himself by a third party, the linked transaction may suddenly become inoperative without the third party being aware of the fact. Indeed, it is quite possible for a person to be a party to a linked transaction with a debtor without knowing of the principal agreement to which the transaction is linked (see para. [854]). This may well cause considerable complications in the unscrambling of linked transactions, particularly where there is a dispute between the debtor and creditor as to whether the regulated agreement has been effectively terminated, cancelled or affected in some way having a bearing on the linked transaction. [862]

Improperly executed agreements and securities

The fact that an agreement or security has been, or is to be deemed, improperly executed so as to be enforceable only on an order of the court appears to have no impact on the enforceability of a linked transaction. Indeed, apart from s. 139 relating to extortionate credit bargains (see paras. [966] *et seq.*), there is no provision of the Act which gives the court special powers over linked transactions which are not themselves regulated agreements. In particular, the provisions of Part IX (other than ss. 139–142) are restricted to the making of orders in relation to regulated agreements and securities. [863]

Extortionate credit bargains

The powers of the court to re-open a credit agreement under ss. 137–140 arise where the court finds a credit bargain extortionate. "Credit bargain" means not only the credit agreement itself but also, where one or more other transactions are to be taken into account in computing the total charge for credit, those other transactions taken together with the credit agreement (s. 137 (2) (*b*) (ii)). In re-opening the agreement the court may, for the purpose of relieving the debtor or a surety from payment of any sum in excess of that fairly due and reasonable, make various orders under s. 139 (2) and may in particular—

(*a*) direct accounts to be taken between any persons,

(*b*) set aside the whole or part of any obligation imposed on the debtor or a surety by the credit bargain or any related agreement,

(*c*) require the creditor to repay the whole or part of any sum paid under the credit bargain or any related agreement by the debtor or a surety, whether paid to the creditor or any other person. [864]

An order may be made under s. 139 (2) notwithstanding that its effect is to place a burden on the creditor in respect of an advantage unfairly enjoyed by another person who is a party to a linked transaction (s. 139 (3)). Hence, if, for example, the total charge for credit imposed by a credit agreement relating to goods includes as a component the cost to the creditor of procuring servicing of the goods under a maintenance contract with a third party, and the court takes the view that the maintenance charge is extortionate, the court may require the creditor to repay the whole or any part of the sum paid under the credit agreement even though the effect may be that the creditor has to carry the burden of having paid, or incurred a liability to pay, sums due to the third party under the extortionate maintenance agreement. [**865**]

28. Agreements with more than one Debtor/Hirer or Creditor/Owner

The problem stated

In the preceding analysis of the Consumer Credit Act, it has been assumed that each regulated agreement involves one person as debtor or hirer, another as creditor or owner. In practice, it not infrequently happens that there are two or more debtors or hirers (either specifically named or constituting members of a partnership that is a debtor or hirer) or two or more creditors as owners. In situations such as these, complex questions arise, e.g. as to the liability of the co-debtors or co-hirers *inter se* and *vis-a-vis* the creditor or owner, and as to the procedure to be adopted where the creditor or owner wishes to terminate the agreement against all the debtors or hirers. These problems, discussed by the author elsewhere in relation to co-hirers under hire-purchase agreements (see R. M. Goode, *Hire-Purchase Law and Practice* (2nd Edn.), Chapter 21) were not touched on in the Hire-Purchase Act 1965. The Consumer Credit Act, however, has two provisions dealing with the matter, s. 185 (concerning an agreement with more than one debtor or hirer) and s. 186 (concerning an agreement with more than one creditor or owner). The effect of the statutory provisions is in some respects obscure, partly because the provisions are very general in character and do not link up with any specific requirements of the Act. [**866**]

Agreements with more than one debtor or hirer

Section 185, as amended by s. 38 of the Banking Act 1979, provides as follows:

> "(1) Where an actual or prospective regulated agreement has two or more debtors or hirers (not being a partnership or an unincorporated body of persons)—
>> (a) anything required by or under this Act to be done to or in relation to the debtor or hirer shall be done to or in relation to each of them; and
>> (b) anything done under this Act by or on behalf of one of them shall have effect as if done by or on behalf of all of them;
>> [(c) a dispensing notice which is operative in relation to an agreement shall be operative also in relation to

any subsequent agreement which, in relation to the earlier agreement, is a modifying agreement.]

(2) Notwithstanding subsection (1) (*a*), where running-account credit is provided to two or more debtors jointly, any of them may by a notice signed by him (a "dispensing notice") authorise the creditor not to comply in his case with section 78 (4) (giving of periodical statement of account); and the dispensing notice shall have effect accordingly until revoked by a further notice given by the debtor to the creditor:
Provided that:

    (*a*) a dispensing notice shall not take effect if previous dispensing notices are operative in the case of the other debtor, or each of the other debtors, as the case may be;

    (*b*) any dispensing notices operative in relation to an agreement shall cease to have effect if any of the debtors dies.

(3) Subsection (1) (*b*) does not apply for the purposes of section 61 (1) (*a*) or 127 (3).

(4) Where a regulated agreement has two or more debtors or hirers (not being a partnership or unincorporated body of persons) section 86 applies to the death of any of them.

(5) An agreement for the provision of credit, or the bailment or (in Scotland) the hiring of goods, to two or more persons jointly where—

    (*a*) one or more of those persons is an individual, and

    (*b*) one or more of them is a body corporate,

is a consumer credit agreement or consumer hire agreement if it would have been one had they all been individuals; and the body corporate or bodies corporate shall accordingly be included among the debtors or hirers under the agreement.

(6) Where subsection (5) applies, references in this Act to the signing of any document by the debtor or hirer shall be construed in relation to a body corporate as referring to a signing on behalf of the body corporate." **[867]**

Acts to be done to or in relation to debtor or hirer

Leaving on one side partnerships and unincorporated bodies (discussed in paras. **[876]**–**[877]**), the general effect of s. 185 (1) (*a*) is that where there are two or more debtors or hirers:

    (*a*) pre-contract disclosure prescribed by regulations under s. 55 (1) must be given to all the debtors or hirers, unless otherwise provided by such regulations;

    (*b*) the regulated agreement must be signed by each debtor or hirer personally;

    (*c*) the copies prescribed by ss. 62 and 63, and the notice prescribed by s. 64, must be supplied to each debtor or hirer in accordance with those sections;

    (*d*) sums repayable under ss. 57 (1), 70 and 73 in respect of a transaction from which the debtors or hirers have withdrawn or which they have exercised their right to cancel (see para. [**870**]) are repayable to all of them;

(e) information and documents to be provided to a debtor or hirer under ss. 77–79 must be supplied to all;

(f) a notice under s. 76 or notice of default under s. 87 or of termination under s. 98 must be served on all the debtors or hirers;

(g) a statutory rebate allowable by regulations under s. 95 must be allowed to all the debtors or hirers. [**868**]

It seems clear that failure to comply with the above statutory provisions as regards all the debtors or hirers involves a contravention of those provisions, even if they have been complied with as regards some of the debtors or hirers. [**869**]

When examined more closely, some of the effects listed above are much more difficult to apply than the simplistic wording of s. 185 (1) (a) would suggest. Consider first the documentation requirements of ss. 62 and 63. If the unexecuted agreement is sent to one debtor for signature but presented to the other, which of the alternative procedures laid down in these sections applies? Common sense would suggest that for the former debtor, the procedure laid down for documents sent for signature applies, and for the latter debtor the procedure prescribed for documents presented for signature operates. But s. 185 (1) (a) appears to preclude such a simple solution. Next, let us consider the question of cancellation, which also raises difficulties under s. 185 (1) (b) (see para. [**873**]). If one of the debtors serves a notice of cancellation (and this would seem to be effective as a notice by all), are repayments under ss. 57 (1) or 70 to be made to the debtor by whom the payment was made in the first instance or are they to be made to all the debtors by way of a joint remittance? Apparently the latter. Again, a sum equal to the part-exchange allowance and payable under s. 73 must, it seems, be paid to all the debtors, not merely to the debtor who tendered the part-exchange goods to which the allowance relates. The assumption apparently is that the debtors must sort out these matters among themselves afterwards. [**870**]

The only relief provided in respect of s. 185 (1) (a)—except in the case of a partnership or unincorporated body—is that where there are joint debtors on a running-account, any of them may by dispensing notice under s. 185 (2) waive the requirement that he be supplied automatically with the periodic statements of account prescribed by s. 78 (4). But the obligation must remain to supply such accounts to at least one joint debtor. Accordingly if all the joint debtors give dispensing notices, the last of these is ineffective (s. 185 (2), proviso). [**871**]

Acts to be done by or on behalf of the debtor or hirer

The effect of ss. 185 (1) (b) is that:

(a) service by one debtor or hirer of a notice of cancellation under s. 69 or a notice of termination under ss. 99 or 101 operates as cancellation or termination by all the debtors or hirers;

(b) early settlement by one debtor under s. 94 constitutes settlement on behalf of all;

(c) a request for information and documents by a debtor or hirer under ss. 77–79 constitutes a request by all, which must accordingly be complied with in regard to all;

(d) supply of information by one debtor or hirer as to the whereabouts of goods, pursuant to s. 80, constitutes compliance with that section by the other debtors or hirers as well;

(e) an application by one debtor or hirer to the court under s. 129, or by one hirer under s. 132, operates as an application by all.

On the other hand, a breach by one debtor or hirer of his statutory obligations is not a breach by all by virtue of s. 185 (1) (b), since a breach is not a thing done "under" the Act for the purpose of s. 185 (1) (b) but is a contravention of the Act. It may, however, constitute a breach by all the debtors as a matter of general law. [872]

Just as difficulties arise in applying s. 185 (1) (a), so also they arise in connection with s. 185 (1) (b). If one debtor signs a regulated agreement at his own home, while another signs at the creditor's premises, is the agreement (if otherwise fulfilling the requirements of a cancellable agreement) cancellable under s. 67? Apparently it is, since the debtor who signed at home fulfils the requirements of s. 67 and by virtue of s. 185 (1) (b) service of a notice of cancellation by him is service for all. What if one debtor wishes to cancel and the other does not? Seemingly, the former's notice of cancellation is effective despite the opposition of the latter. Nice questions arise where one debtor serves a termination notice under s. 99 whilst at the same time the other applies under s. 129 for further time to remedy a breach of the agreement! [873]

What emerges from this analysis is the undesirability of trying to regulate a number of diverse situations by a general catch-all provision not worked out in relation to each situation individually. It would have been very much better if Parliament in its wisdom had let the subject matter of s. 182 (and of s. 183) to be dealt with by regulations. [874]

There are in fact two cases, set out in s. 185 (3), in which the draftsman has addressed his mind to specific sections that might otherwise have been caught by s. 185 (1) (b). That subsection does not apply for the purpose of s. 61 (1) (a), so that signature of the regulated agreement by one debtor or hirer does not constitute signature for all, and each of the debtors or hirers must sign individually. As a corollary, the court cannot make an enforcement order in respect of a regulated agreement not signed by all the debtors or hirers, since s. 185 (1) (b) is made inapplicable for the purpose of s. 127 (3). [875]

Partnerships

Section 185 does not apply where the debtor is a partnership. Section 61 (4) establishes that the regulated agreement need not be signed by all (or indeed any) of the partners. It suffices if it is signed on behalf of the firm by a partner or by any other person authorised for that purpose. The effect on the partnership of other acts done by or to a partner has to be determined by general agency principles and by the Partnership Act 1890. By s. 6 of the Partnership Act, the firm and all the partners are bound by any act or instrument relating to the firm's business done or executed in the firm's name, or in any other way showing an intention to bind the firm, by any person thereto authorised, whether a partner or not. Moreover, as a matter of agency law the acts of a partner within the scope of his actual, apparent or usual authority bind the partnership. If, therefore, a partner signs a regulated agreement on behalf of the firm and the agreement is one which is on the face of it entered into for the purposes of the partnership business and is the type of agreement which it would be usual for a firm engaged in that type of business to make, the agreement will bind the firm. But in the case of a non-commercial firm, a partner has no implied authority to borrow money, to accept, make or indorse negotiable instruments other than cheques, or to mortgage or pledge partnership property; and even in a commercial partnership, a partner has no implied authority to give a guarantee on behalf of the firm. It follows that in these cases the mere fact that a person is a partner does not give him ostensible authority to do any of these acts on behalf of the firm, though the firm will be bound if the partner in question has been held out as having authority. If a partner has, or is held out as having, authority to enter into a regulated agreement or linked transaction, then no doubt the court will readily infer authority, or ostensible authority, on his part to cancel or terminate the agreement or transaction, or to give or receive notices in respect of it, on behalf of the firm. The firm will similarly be bound by such acts when within the usual authority of the partner concerned. [876]

Unincorporated bodies
   Similarly the ability of a member of an unincorporated body to bind the body as a whole depends on agency principles. There is however the added complication that whilst a partnership, though juridically not a legal *persona*, is for certain purposes recognised by the law as a distinct legal entity, an unincorporated association has no status distinct from that of its members, so that the membership as a whole can only be bound by acts which they have collectively authorised, or ostensibly authorised, one of their number to carry out. In the case of a members' club, authority to act would normally be conferred by rules of the club adopted by the members and by decisions taken at meetings held in conformity with the rules. Ostensible authority to manage the affairs of an association generally (as opposed to ostensible authority to conclude a specific transaction) is not easy to establish in the case of an unincorporated association, so that if the committee of a club contracts without authority, the remedy of the other party to the contract will usually be an action against the committee members personally. See further J. F. Keeler (1971), 34 M.L.R. 615. [877]

Body corporate as one of joint debtors or hirers
   The provisions of s. 185 (5) (see para. [867]) are limited to joint debtors and joint hirers and thus appear to exclude transactions in which the liability of the debtors or hirers is joint and several. In the latter case, the agreement will be a consumer credit or consumer hire agreement as regards the individuals but not as regards the bodies corporate. The distinction may appear surprising but has a certain logic. A joint liability is indivisible, and therefore could scarcely be regulated by the Act as regards some parties but not others. Hence all parties are brought within the Act by s. 185 (5). A joint and several liability creates both a joint obligation and several obligations on the part of the various co-contractors, so that there is no difficulty in limiting the application of the Act to those debtors or hirers who are individuals. Whether in a given case the liability is joint only or joint and several depends on the absence or presence of words of severance. See R. M. Goode, *op. cit.*, p. 471. [878]

Agreements with more than one creditor or owner

The case of several creditors or owners is dealt with summarily by s. 186 as follows:

> "Where an actual or prospective regulated agreement has two or more creditors or owners, anything required by or under this Act to be done to, or in relation to, or by, the creditor or owner shall be effective if done to, or in relation to, or by, any one of them."

Hence one of several creditors or owners can perform all or any of the following acts on behalf of the other or others:

(a) supply pre-contract information to a prospective debtor or hirer pursuant to regulations under s. 55 (1);

(b) sign a regulated agreement;

(c) supply documents to the debtor or hirer in accordance with ss. 62–64 and s. 110 of the Act;

(d) repay sums payable under ss. 70 and 57 to a debtor or hirer who has exercised his right of cancellation or has withdrawn from a proposed transaction;

(e) supply information and documents to the debtor or hirer in accordance with ss. 77–79 and to a surety in accordance with ss. 107–109;

(f) serve a notice under s. 76 or a default notice under s. 87 or notice of termination under s 98;

(g) institute proceedings for the recovery of protected goods in conformity with the requirements of s. 90.

These powers are exercisable by such creditor or owner whether or not he has actual or ostensible authority from his co-creditors or co-owners, though if he exercises the powers in excess of authority he may incur a liability to such co-creditors or co-owners. But it is only those acts *required by the Act* that fall within s. 186. Hence this section cannot be invoked to support, for example, a variation of the regulated agreement made by one creditor or owner without the consent of the others. Whether such variation is effective depends on the ordinary principles of agency previously mentioned. [879]

Just as s. 186 empowers an actual or prospective creditor or owner to perform acts on behalf of the other or others, so also it makes acts required by the Act to be done to, or in relation to, the creditor or owner or prospective creditor or owner effective if done to, or in relation to, one such creditor or owner. Such acts would include:

(a) service of a notice of withdrawal under s. 57 or of cancellation under s. 69;

(b) making of a request for information under ss. 77–79;

(c) giving of notice of intended early settlement under s. 94 and payment under that section;

(d) giving of notice of termination under s. 99 or s. 101. [880]

Proceedings against a joint debtor or hirer

By s. 3 of the Civil Liability (Contribution) Act 1978 judgment recovered against any person liable in respect of any debt or damage is not to be a bar to any action, or to the continuance of an action, against any other person who is (apart from any such bar) jointly liable with him in respect of the same debt or damage. This abolishes the rule in *Kendall* v. *Hamilton* (1879), 4 App. Cas. 504, by which judgment against a joint debtor, even if remaining unsatisfied, barred proceedings against the other. The rule never applied to debtors jointly and severally liable, and even in the case of joint liability an exception was provided by rules of court to allow judgment in default of appearance of default or under RSC Order 14 against one defendant jointly liable without releasing the other defendant (RSC Order 13, r. 1; Order 19, rr. 2–6; Order 14, r. 5; CCR Order 5, r. 3 (3)). [**881**]

29. Remedies of Creditor or Owner on Default

Nature and range of remedies

Where a debtor or hirer commits a breach of a regulated agreement, the remedies of the creditor or owner depend partly on the common law, partly on the terms of the regulated agreement itself, and of any security instrument made in connection with it, and partly on the Consumer Credit Act and regulations thereunder. [**882**]

Remedies conferred or implied by law

The remedies for default given by the common law to the creditor or owner, insofar as not provided for by the credit or security agreement itself, vary according to the nature of the transaction see paras. [**103**] *et seq., ante.* Under all forms of agreement—whether conditional sale, hire-purchase, credit sale, rental or secured or unsecured loan—the creditor is entitled to sue (i) for each sum payable under the agreement as it falls due; (ii) for damages for loss suffered as the result of a breach other than non-payment. Other remedies given or implied by law (as opposed to an express contractual provision) vary according to the nature of the credit agreement. [**883**]

In the case of breach of a conditional sale, hire-purchase or hiring agreement, where the term broken is a condition (i.e. a major term) or the breach evinces an intention on the part of the debtor or hirer to repudiate the contract or produces consequences so serious as to frustrate the commercial purpose of the contract, the seller or owner has the option to treat the contract as at an end and recover damages on that basis, or to affirm the contract, in which event his claim is limited to damages for such loss (if any) as he can establish. Where the debtor or hirer did not have a right to terminate the agreement himself—as in the case of a conditional sale agreement or a hiring for a fixed term—the damages recoverable by the creditor or owner who elects to treat the contract as terminated will include the loss of profit resulting from premature termination, i.e. loss of the profit (duly discounted to allow for any acceleration of payment) that would have been made by him if the contract had run its full course. Where the agreement is a hire-purchase agreement giving the hirer a right to terminate at any time, then logically the owner's damages on accepting the hirer's repudiation should not exceed the amount (if any) for which the hirer would have become liable if he himself had exercised the power of termination conferred on him. But by an anomaly established in *Yeoman Credit, Ltd.* v. *Waragowski*, [1961] 3 All E.R. 145, [1961] 1 W.L.R. 1124, as modified by *Yeoman Credit, Ltd.* v. *Maclean*, [1962] 1 W.L.R. 131 and *Overstone, Ltd.* v. *Shipway*, [1962] 1 All E.R. 52, [1962] 1 W.L.R. 117, the owner is in such a case held entitled to recover the unpaid balance of the hire-purchase price less the sum fixed as the fee for exercise of the option to purchase and a discount to allow for acceleration of payment (see para. [104], *ante*). In addition, the conditional seller or owner who terminates the agreement by acceptance of the other party's repudiation becomes entitled to make a claim for delivery of the goods or payment of their value and damages for their detention or alternatively damages for the value of the goods. See para. [838]. [884]

In the event of breach of a credit sale agreement, the seller is usually restricted to an action for the price, and (in the absence of an acceleration clause in the agreement) must wait for each instalment to fall due before he can sue for it. His statutory right of resale under ss. 39 and 48 of the Sale of Goods Act 1893 ceases to be exercisable when both the property in the goods and possession have passed to the buyer. [885]

On default in payment of a loan, the lender can recover the instalments in arrear, but must usually wait to sue for each instalment as it falls due, in the absence of an acceleration clause in the loan agreement entitling him to call up the outstanding balance. If he has taken a mortgage as security, he has in addition all the remedies accorded to a mortgagee by the common law and by the Law of Property Act 1925. These include possession, sale, appointment of a receiver and an application to the court for foreclosure. The availability of these remedies depends partly on whether the mortgage is of goods or of land, partly on whether it is legal or equitable and partly on whether it is under seal or under hand only. [886]

Remedies conferred by the agreement

The credit agreement itself may, and almost invariably does, contain express provisions conferring a range of remedies on the creditor in the event of the debtor's default. Within limits, and subject to statutory provisions of the kind we are about to consider, the law gives effect to the contract. Thus at common law the court will uphold provisions which:

    (i) call up the outstanding balance in the event of a breach by the debtor;

    (ii) empower the creditor to terminate the agreement in specified events, *e.g.* if the debtor commits a breach of the agreement or allows a judgment to remain outstanding against him for more than a stated period or has execution levied on his goods (but a contractual power of termination is arguably capable of falling within s. 3 (2) of the Unfair Contract Terms Act 1977—see para. [667]);

    (iii) empower the creditor to remedy breaches himself and charge the debtor with the cost;

    (iv) confer on the creditor powers of repossession and sale of goods or property comprised in the agreement or security;

    (v) fix in advance the damages to be paid for a breach, if the sum fixed is a reasonable pre-estimate of the loss likely to flow from the breach (see below). [887]

In fact the common law has always adopted a very liberal attitude towards creditors' rights in general and self-help in particular. But even at common law (including for this purpose rules of equity) there are certain limitations on freedom of contract. Thus a mortgagee's right to redeem the mortgaged property cannot be cut off except by sale or foreclosure, whatever the mortgage may provide; and if realisation of the security produces a surplus, this is payable to the debtor (in the absence of any other incumbrances affecting the property) notwithstanding any agreement to the contrary. Again, whilst it is open to the parties to stipulate in the contract a sum to be paid as liquidated damages in the event of a breach, the sum so fixed must, as seen at the date of the contract, be a reasonable pre-estimate of the loss likely to flow from the breach and not a penalty imposed to deter the debtor from breaking the contract or to give the creditor an additional windfall in the event of breach. On this basis, provisions in hire-purchase agreements purporting to give the owner, on termination for breach, a right to recover sums over and above accrued arrears and interest have been repeatedly struck down by the courts as contrary to the rule against penalties, though occasionally they have been upheld where the court was satisfied that the contractual provision was a reasonable attempt to assess in advance loss that might be suffered as the result of the goods depreciating at a faster rate than covered by the instalments. See, for example, *Bridge* v. *Campbell Discount Co., Ltd.*, [1962] A.C. 600, [1962] 1 All E.R. 385; *Anglo-Auto Finance Co., Ltd.* v. *James*, [1963] 3 All E.R. 566, [1963] 1 W.L.R. 1042; and other cases explored in detail in R. M. Goode, *op. cit.*, Chapter 18. [**888**]

Broad effect of the Consumer Credit Act

The Consumer Credit Act, adopting and strengthening provisions previously contained in the Hire-Purchase Act, imposes various restrictions on contractual remedies, notably by:

- (a) requiring at least seven days' notice of an intention by the creditor or owner to invoke (otherwise than on the ground of a breach) an acceleration clause or to recover possession of goods or land or treat any right conferred on the debtor or hirer by the agreement as terminated, restricted or deferred (s. 76 (1)—see paras. [**890**] *et seq.*);
- (b) requiring the creditor or owner to serve at least seven days' notice of default before exercising, by reason of a breach on the part of the debtor or hirer, any of the above rights or enforcing any security, so as to give the debtor an opportunity to remedy the breach if it is remediable (ss. 87–89—see paras. [**893**] *et seq.*) or to apply to the court for a time order under s. 129 (see paras. [**892**] *et seq.*) or for equitable relief against forfeiture (see para. [**840**]);
- (c) requiring the creditor or owner to give at least seven days' notice before terminating a regulated agreement otherwise than by reason of a breach by the debtor or hirer (s. 98—see paras. [**902**]–[**903**]);
- (d) prohibiting enforcement of a right to recover possession of protected goods except on an order of the court (s. 90 (1));
- (e) restricting the exercise of contractual rights that would otherwise be exercisable by reason of the death of the debtor or hirer (s. 86);

(*f*) nullifying a contractual provision purporting to make the debtor liable to pay default interest at a rate exceeding the contract rate (s. 93—see para. [**924**]);

(*g*) limiting the liability of a hirer under a regulated hire-purchase or conditional sale agreement who, pursuant to s. 99, terminates the agreement (s. 100—see paras. [**751**] *et seq.*);

(*h*) prohibiting enforcement of an improperly executed agreement or security without an order of the court (ss. 65 (1), 105 (6)—see paras. [**545**] *et seq.*);

(*i*) regulating the redemption and realisation of pawns (ss. 116–121—see paras. [**782**] *et seq.*);

(*j*) prohibiting, except on an order of the court, enforcement of a regulated agreement or security in respect of which a negotiable instrument has been taken or negotiated in contravention of s. 123 (see paras. [**794**] *et seq.*);

(*k*) prohibiting enforcement of a land mortgage otherwise than on an order of the court (s. 126—see para. [**820**]);

(*l*) conferring wide powers on the court to give relief to a defaulting debtor or hirer by orders under Part IX of the Act in proceedings brought in respect of a consumer credit or consumer hire agreement or security (see Chapter 30);

(*m*) empowering the court to re-open a credit agreement with an individual (whether a regulated agreement or not and whether a consumer credit agreement or not) where the credit bargain is extortionate (ss. 137–140—see Chapter 30);

(*n*) nullifying contractual provisions inconsistent with a provision for the protection of the debtor or hirer or his relative or any surety contained in the Act or in any regulation made under the Act or imposing on any such party a liability greater than that specified in such a provision (s. 173—see para. [**1091**]);

The matters referred to in paragraphs (*g*)–(*n*) are dealt with elsewhere in this book, at the paragraph numbers indicated. The present chapter will be devoted to an examination of the provisions referred to in paragraphs (*a*)–(*f*). The provisions of s. 176 of the Act laying down general rules as to the service of notices and other documents are discussed in Chapter 35. [**889**]

Duty to give notice before taking certain action

Section 76 of the Act provides as follows:

"(1) The creditor or owner is not entitled to enforce a term of a regulated agreement by—

(*a*) demanding earlier payment of any sum, or

(*b*) recovering possession of any goods or land, or

(*c*) treating any right conferred on the debtor or hirer by the agreement as terminated, restricted or deferred,

except by or after giving the debtor or hirer not less than seven days' notice of his intention to do so.

(2) Subsection (1) applies only where—

(*a*) a period for the duration of the agreement is specified in the agreement, and (*b*) that period has not ended when the creditor or owner does an act mentioned in subsection (1),

but so applies notwithstanding that, under the agreement, any party is entitled to terminate it before the end of the period so specified.

(3) A notice under subsection (1) is ineffective if not in the prescribed form.

(4) Subsection (1) does not prevent a creditor from treating the right to draw on any credit as restricted or deferred and taking such steps as may be necessary to make the restriction or deferment effective.

(5) Regulations may provide that subsection (1) is not to apply to agreements described by the regulations.

(6) Subsection (1) does not apply to a right of enforcement arising by reason of any breach by the debtor or hirer of the regulated agreement." [**890**]

It will be observed that s. 76 does not apply to a right of enforcement arising by reason of a breach by the debtor or hirer. Where it is desired to exercise a remedy for a breach, s. 87 (relating to default notices) comes into play. But s. 76 is available to control the exercise of remedies conferred by the agreement in events which, though not technically breaches, are for practical purposes equated with breaches by the agreement. For example, a provision that the full balance shall immediately become payable, or that the creditor shall be entitled to terminate the agreement and/or to repossess the goods, if the debtor or hirer becomes bankrupt or has execution levied against his assets or allows a judgment to remain unsatisfied against him for more than a given period, is not within s. 87, since none of the specified events is a breach, but is controlled by s. 76. In the result, seven days' notice, in prescribed form, must be given of the intention of the creditor or owner to invoke the provision. There are, however, three qualifications. First, s. 76 does not apply where at the outset the credit is repayable on demand, as in the case of the traditional bank overdraft. A distinction must, however, be made between a credit repayable on demand because no period is specified for the duration of the credit agreement (such a case is exempt from s. 76) and an agreement to give credit for a specified period with an overriding right to the creditor to make demand for payment at any time (such a case remains governed by s. 76). Secondly, the creditor or owner can, without serving such notice treat the right to draw on a credit as restricted or deferred and take such steps as may be necessary to make the restriction or deferment effective. Accordingly a bank does not have to give notice before terminating or suspending an overdraft facility; and a credit card issuer can without notice exercise a right to terminate a card holder's entitlement to his credit card and can make that termination effective by notifying suppliers that a stop has been placed on the card and that it should not be accepted. Thirdly, regulations under s. 76 (5) may exempt specified agreements from the notice requirements. Curiously, s. 76 (1) does not cover the enforcement of security as such, though if the security comprises goods or land s. 76 (1) (*b*) requires the service of a seven-day notice before recovery of possession. [**891**]

It would seem that s. 76 (1)(*c*) is confined to termination, restriction or deferment of a specific right or rights of the debtor or hirer and is not applicable to termination of the agreement as a whole, this being governed by s. 98. It is apparent from s. 87 (1) (*a*) and (*d*) that the Act does not consider termination of an agreement as a whole to be adequately covered by a provision dealing merely with termination of a right.   On the other hand, while s. 98 is the section controlling termination of an agreement otherwise than for breach, enforcement of the contractual consequences of that termination is regulated by s. 76, insofar as the consequences are of a kind specified in s. 76 (1).   Hence an owner who wishes to exercise a contractual right to terminate a hire-purchase agreement, and recover possession of the goods by reason of the fact that the hirer has allowed judgment obtained against him by a third party to remain unsatisfied for more than a given period, must give at least seven days' notice of termination under s. 98 (1) and at least seven days' notice of his intention to repossess under s. 76 (1) (b).   There seems no reason why the two notices should not be combined in one document or why the two seven-day periods should not run concurrently.   If the goods are protected goods, then repossession without the defendant's consent requires a court order (see paras. [**840**] *et seq.*).   It should be noted that whereas a debtor or hirer can extinguish the operation of a default notice under s. 87 by remedying the breach or paying specified compensation, there is no way in which he can procure the extinguishment of a notice served under s. 76 or s. 98.   He can however apply to the court for a time order under s. 129 (see paras. [**905**] *et seq.*) or for equitable relief against forfeiture (see para. [**840**]).   [**892**]

Default notice

Sections 76 and 98, referred to earlier, deal with the exercise of contractual rights otherwise than on the ground of default by the debtor or hirer.   Section 87 controls the exercise of remedies on a breach.   By s. 87 (1), service of a default notice in accordance with s. 88 is necessary before the creditor or owner can become entitled, by reason of a breach by the debtor or hirer, to terminate the agreement, demand earlier payment of any sum, recover possession of any goods or land, treat any right conferred on the debtor or hirer by the agreement as terminated, restricted or deferred, or enforce any security.   No notice is necessary, however, if the creditor or owner merely wishes to sue for accrued arrears or for damages, unless he intends to proceed against a surety, in which case he is enforcing a security for the purpose of s. 87 (1) (e) and must serve a default notice on the debtor or hirer (whether or not he is joined in the proceedings) and a copy on the surety (s. 111 (1)).   [**893**]

If the debtor or hirer has died, the default notice can be served on his executor (even before probate) as the "debtor" or "hirer" within s. 189 (1) or, if there is no executor, on the person to whom letters of administration were granted; but it is unnecessary to serve in this way, since service will be validly effected if addressed to the debtor or hirer and sent by post to, or left at, his address last known to the creditor or owner (s. 176 (1)–(6)).   This is so even if the creditor or owner was aware at the time that the debtor or hirer has died (s. 176 (6)).   Service in this way is necessary where the debtor or hirer died intestate and it is desired to serve a notice of default prior to letters of administration, since it is not permitted to serve a default notice on the Probate Judge, even though the estate is vested in him pending the grant (s. 176 (7)—and see para. [**916**]).   It is to be observed that s. 87 is considerably wider than its predecessor, s. 25 of the Hire-Purchase Act 1965. Section 87 applies to all types of breach, whether taking the form of a default in payment or a breach of some other provision. Moreover, s. 87 is not confined to cases where a remedy of the kind described in s. 87 (1) is conferred expressly by the agreement, but also controls the exercise of such a remedy (other than termination, restriction or deferment of a right under s. 87 (1) (*d*)) where given by general contract law, e.g. the right to treat the agreement as repudiated by reason of a major breach. [**894**]

There are three cases where a notice need not be served:

(1) Section 87 (1) does not prevent the creditor from treating the right to draw upon any credit as restricted or deferred, and taking such steps as may be necessary to make the restriction or deferment effective (s. 87 (2)). This matches a corresponding exception to s. 76, discussed in paragraph [**891**].

(2) Regulations may provide that s. 87 (1) is not to apply to agreements described by the regulations (s. 87 (4)).

(3) Where a breach triggers off another provision of the agreement (as where the full outstanding balance is made payable on default in payment of an instalment), non-compliance with such provision does not necessitate (and indeed cannot be the subject of) a distinct default notice; it suffices that a default notice was served, and not complied with, in respect of the breach which makes the provision operative (s. 88 (3)). (For a further illustration of the impact of s. 88 (3), see para. [**900**]). [**895**]

The doing of an act by which a floating charge becomes fixed is not enforcement of a security (s. 87 (3)). A floating charge becomes fixed on the appointment of a receiver or on commencement of winding up of the chargor company or on the occurrence of any other event which by the terms of the charge causes it to crystallise. Section 87 (3) makes it clear that no notice is required to be given under s. 87 (1) (*e*) of any act which causes the floating charge to crystallise, though notice will, of course, be required if the act falls within one of the other categories listed in s. 87 (1). Section 87 (3) will rarely apply to a floating charge given by the debtor himself, since except where s. 185 (5) applies (see paras. [**867**], [**878**]) the debtor will be an individual (bodies corporate being outside the protection of the Act) and the Bills of Sale Act (1878) Amendment Act 1882, s. 5, precludes the granting of a security bill of sale over after-acquired chattels. There are certain statutory exceptions, both under the 1882 Act itself and under other legislation (e.g. Part II of the Agricultural Credits Act 1928 as regards agricultural charges by farmers) but save in such exceptional cases a floating charge by an individual over future chattels will usually be ineffective, and a floating charge by an individual over after-acquired land, though legally permitted, is of limited practical value, since until the land is acquired there is no machinery for registering the charge so as to give public notice of it. On the other hand, a floating charge might well be given by a body corporate at the request of an individual debtor (e.g. for the purpose of securing a guarantee given by the body corporate) and s. 87 (3) would enable a receiver to be appointed without service of a seven-day notice on the debtor under s. 87 (1). [**896**]

Form and contents of default notice

By s. 88 (1), the default notice must be in the prescribed form and specify—

(*a*) the nature of the alleged breach;

(*b*) if the breach is capable of remedy, what action is required to remedy it and the date before which that action is to be taken;

(*c*) if the breach is not capable of remedy, the sum (if any) required to be paid
        as compensation for the breach, and the date before which it is to be paid.
A date specified under s. 88 (1) must be not less than seven days after the date of
service of the default notice, and the creditor or owner must not take action such
as is mentioned in s. 87 (1) before the date so specified or (if no requirement is made
under sub-s. (1) before those seven days have elapsed (s. 88 (2)).   [**897**]

The above provisions closely follow s. 146 (1) of the Law of Property Act 1925
(prescribing the notice to be served by a landlord before forfeiting a lease otherwise
than for non-payment of rent), save that instead of the "reasonable time" allowed
to the lessee under s. 146 for remedying the breach, s. 88 (2) allows the debtor or
hirer the period specified in the default notice, with a minimum of seven days.
With this qualification, and subject to certain fundamental differences between the
legal treatment of goods and that of land (see (3) below), cases on s. 146 of the Law
of Property Act provide a useful guide to the interpretation of s. 88 of the Consumer
Credit Act, the effect of which may accordingly be summarised as follows:

(1) For a breach to be capable of remedy within s. 88 (1) (*b*), it must, by
     implication, be completely remediable within a reasonable time (see
     Rugby School (Governors) v. *Tannahill*, [1935] 1 K.B. 87; *Egerton* v.
     Esplanade Hotels London, Ltd., [1947] 2 All E.R. 88). But the fact that a
     breach is not capable of being remedied within the minimum seven-day
     period prescribed by s. 88 (2) does not on that account make it
     irremediable (see para. [**898**]).

(2) Bankruptcy, if it is a breach of the agreement at all, is an irremediable
     breach (*Civil Service Cooperative Society* v. *McGrigor's Trustee,* [1923] 2 Ch.
     347, *per* Russell, J., at p. 356) but it is unusual for a credit agreement to
     provide that the debtor shall not become bankrupt. Bankruptcy is
     usually specified not as a breach of the agreement but as a ground for
     exercise of remedies under it (see para. [**891**]), and will thus normally be
     caught by ss. 76 and 98, not by s. 87.

(3) Although it has been held that a covenant against assignment or sub-
     letting in a lease of land is irremediable (*Scala House and District Property
     Co., Ltd.* v. *Forbes,* [1974] Q.B. 575, [1973] 3 All E.R. 308), it is submitted
     that this is not necessarily so in the case of an agreement relating to
     goods. The grant of a lease of land confers an estate on the lessee and an
     assignment or sub-letting, even if unlawful, is effective to vest a term of
     years in the assignee or sub-lessee. But ownership of goods is indivisible,
     so that no "estate" vests in the hirer or conditional buyer, merely
     contractual rights accompanied by possession. If the hirer or buyer
     wrongfully assigns or sub-lets, the assignment or sub-letting will usually
     have no impact on the rights of the owner or seller, so that the breach
     does not affect him and can be remedied by the hirer or buyer regaining
     possession, if he is able to do so.

(4) The creditor need not claim compensation for an irremediable breach if
     he does not wish to do so. This is clear from the words "if any" in s. 88
     (1) (*c*), and would in any event follow as a matter of general law (see
     Rugby School (Governors), v. *Tannahill*, [1935] 1 K.B. 87; *Lock* v. *Pearce*,
     [1893] 2 Ch. 271).

(5) Even if the breach is irremediable and the creditor does not wish to
     claim compensation, he must serve a default notice specifying the breach,

in order to give the debtor an opportunity of considering his position (see *Civil Service Cooperative Society* v. *McGrigor's Trustee*, [1923] 2 Ch. 347; *Horsey Estate, Ltd.* v. *Steiger*, [1899] 2 Q.B. 79). Such a requirement is by no means otiose, since even though the debtor is *ex hypothesi* unable to comply with the default notice, his attention is thereby directed to the consequences of failure to comply (see para. [**901**]) and he is given an opportunity to apply to the court for relief in the form of a time order under s. 129 (1) (see paras. [**935**] *et seq.*) or equitable relief against forfeiture (see para. [**840**])

(6) A default notice specifying several breaches is not invalidated by reason of the fact that some of the alleged acts of default have not in fact been committed or, though committed, are not breaches of the agreement. It suffices that at least one of the specified defaults has been committed and constitutes a breach (*Pannell* v. *City of London Brewery Co.*, [1900] 1 Ch. 496, approved by the House of Lords in *Fox* v. *Jolly*, [1916] 1 A.C. 1; *Blewett* v. *Blewett*, [1936] 2 All E.R. 188).

(7) On the other hand, where several breaches are specified all of which have in fact been committed, the time allowed for remedial action must be sufficient to allow all the defaults to be remedied, otherwise the notice will be totally invalid and will not be upheld even as to the breaches which could reasonably be rectified within the specified time (*Wykes* v. *Davis*, [1975] Q.B. 843, [1975] 1 All E.R. 399, applying *Shepherd* v. *Lomas*, [1963] 2 All E.R. 902, [1963] 1 W.L.R. 962).

(8) A default notice cannot validly specify a non-continuing breach that has been waived, e.g. by acceptance of rent with knowledge of the breach (*Jacob* v. *Down*, [1900] 2 Ch. 156). [**898**]

In contrast to a notice under s. 146 (1) of the Law of Property Act 1925, a default notice served in compliance with s. 87 of the Consumer Credit Act must not merely require the debtor or hirer to remedy a remediable breach but must specify what action is required to remedy it and the date by which that action is to be taken (s. 88 (1) (*b*)). It would seem to follow from s. 88 (2) that the creditor or owner need not allow more than seven days for remedying of the breach. But a breach which is incapable of being remedied within that time, or within any other time specified in the section which is less than a reasonable time, is not on that account an irremediable breach so as to be outside s. 88 (1) (*b*); for in determining whether a breach is remediable the court must, it is submitted, consider what would be a reasonable time for remedying it (see point (1) of para. [**898**]), not such limited time as the creditor or owner may choose to allow within the restriction imposed by s. 88 (2). It should be borne in mind, when reading these provisions, that the fact that a breach is not remediable does not debar the court from granting relief to the defaulting debtor or hirer (see paras. [**840**], [**935**] *et seq.*). [**899**]

Whereas s. 146 of the Law of Property Act 1925 enables the lessor to specify a sum required as compensation for the breach even if it is a remediable breach, s. 88 (1) only speaks of compensation in the paragraph dealing with irremediable breaches. But s. 88 (1) merely prescribes the minimum content of a default notice. There seems no reason why compensation for loss cannot be claimed in a default notice even in the case of a remediable breach. In such case, no time limit for payment of the compensation need be specified, unless such payment is itself the remedial action required; for it is only in cases of irremediable breach that s. 88

(1) (*c*) requires a date to be specified for payment of compensation. This causes no hardship to the debtor or hirer, for the taking of the remedial action specified under s. 88 (1) (*b*) suffices to extinguish the breach, under s. 89, even if the specified compensation for loss has not then been paid. Such loss is recoverable by action without service of any fresh notice of default (see s. 88 (3)). [**900**]

The default notice must contain information in the prescribed terms about the consequences of failure to comply with it (s. 88 (4)). When making a requirement as to remedial action, or as to compensation for an irremediable breach, the default notice may include a provision for the taking of action such as mentioned in s. 87 (1) at any time after the restriction imposed by s. 88 (2) will cease, together with a statement that the provision will be ineffective if the breach is duly remedied or the compensation duly paid (s. 88 (5)). If before the date specified for that purpose in the default notice the debtor or hirer takes the action specified under s. 88 (1) (*b*) or (*c*) the breach is to be treated as not having occurred (s. 89).   [**901**]

Notice of termination otherwise than for breach

Section 98 (1) provides that the creditor or owner is not entitled to terminate a regulated agreement except by or after giving the debtor or hirer not less than seven days' notice of termination. This provision has been mentioned earlier (para. [**892**]). The notice under s. 98 need not be drawn so as to terminate the agreement automatically on expiry of the period specified in the notice. The creditor or owner may, if he wishes, state simply that he reserves the right to give notice of termination at any time after expiry of the s. 98 notice. As mentioned previously (para. [**892**]), a notice under s. 98 cannot be rendered ineffective by any action on the part of the debtor or hirer comparable to the remedial action provided by ss. 88 and 89 in relation to a notice of default. The remedy of the debtor or hirer who wishes to avoid the consequences of termination of the agreement is to apply to the court for a time order under s. 129 of the Act (see paras. [**935**] *et seq.*) or for equitable relief against forfeiture (see para. [**840**]).   [**902**]

The provisions of s. 98 (2)–(6), limiting the operation of s. 98 (1) and providing for notices to be in the prescribed form, exactly match those of s. 76 (2)–(6), discussed in paras. [**890**]–[**891**].   [**903**]

Debtor's liability on termination of hire-purchase or conditional sale agreement

The liability of a debtor under a hire-purchase or conditional sale agreement who exercises his right under s. 99 to terminate the agreement is limited by s. 100 of the Act (see paras. [**751**] *et seq.*). By a curious omission, the Consumer Credit Act contains no counterpart to the provision in s. 29 (2) (*c*) of the Hire-Purchase Act 1965 restricting the debtor's monetary liability on termination by the creditor to what it would have been on termination by the debtor. But probably a contractual provision seeking to impose on the debtor, upon termination by the creditor, a liability greater than that imposed by s. 100 of the Consumer Credit Act would be struck down as a penalty. Similarly, in assessing a claim for unliquidated damages the court, in fixing the loss resulting from the debtor's breach, would obviously have regard to the fact that he could himself have terminated the agreement under s. 99, with consequent restriction of liability under s. 100.   [**904**]

Recovery of protected goods

Sections 90 and 91 of the Act, re-enacting in somewhat different form the provisions of ss. 33 and 34 of the Hire-Purchase Act 1965, preclude the creditor under a hire-purchase or conditional sale agreement from recovering possession of protected goods from the debtor without the latter's consent, except on an order of the court, and entitle the debtor to recover all his payments, and to be released from further liability, if the creditor infringes this prohibition (see R. M. Goode, *Hire-Purchase Law and Practice* (2nd edn.) pp. 413–421). The restrictions imposed by ss. 90 and 91 are additional to those imposed by other provisions of the Act. Hence the creditor cannot begin proceedings for recovery of possession under s. 90 unless the requisite default notice prescribed by s. 87 has been served and has expired without the debtor remedying the breach. In addition, the creditor must comply with the requirements of s. 134 in order to establish adverse possession so as to ground an action in tort or on the contract for failure of the debtor to deliver up the goods (see paras. [**909**]–[**910**]). [**905**]

Meaning of "protected goods"

Goods are "protected goods" if falling within s. 90 (s. 90 (7)). The basic provision is s. 90 (1), which provides as follows:

> "At any time when—
> > (*a*) the debtor is in breach of a regulated hire-purchase or a regulated conditional sale agreement relating to goods, and
> > (*b*) the debtor has paid to the creditor one-third or more of the total price of the goods, and
> > (*c*) the property in the goods remains in the creditor,
> the creditor is not entitled to recover possession of the goods from the debtor except on an order of the court."

But s. 90 (1) does not apply, or ceases to apply, to an agreement if the debtor has terminated, or terminates the agreement (s. 90 (5)). Hence exercise by the debtor of a right of termination, whether conferred by the agreement or by the Act, extinguishes his right to rely on s. 90 (1) and removes the barrier created by that section to recovery of possession by the creditor, though it does not preclude the debtor from applying for relief in the form of a time order under s. 129 (1) (see paras. [**935**] *et seq.*). To exclude the debtor's protection under s. 90 (1), his act of termination must be a genuinely voluntary and informed act as opposed, for example, to despatch of a letter of termination dictated by the creditor to which the debtor did not really address his mind (*United Dominions Trust (Commercial), Ltd.* v. *Ennis*, [1968] 1 Q.B. 54, [1967] 2 All E.R. 345). A wrongful repudiation of the agreement by the hirer which is accepted by the creditor would seem to be outside the scope of s. 90 (5), since what brings the agreement to an end in such a case is not the debtor's own repudiatory act but the owner's acceptance of it as discharging the contract. Cf. *F. C. Finance, Ltd.* v. *Francis* (1970), 114 Sol. Jo. 568. [**906**]

The provisions of s. 90 (1) are confined to hire-purchase and conditional sale agreements. They cannot be invoked by a hirer under a consumer hire agreement. His protection is given in other ways, notably by application to the court for a time order under s. 129 (see paras. [**935**] *et seq.*) or for relief against forfeiture in equity (see para. [**840**]) or, if the goods are repossessed or are ordered to be returned to the owner, for an order for repayment and/or release from liability under s. 132 (see para. [**947**]). Moreover, unlike s. 33 of the Hire-Purchase Act 1965, s. 90 (1) of the Consumer Credit Act limits protected goods to those comprised in the regulated hire-purchase or conditional sale agreement at a time when the debtor is in breach of the agreement. It follows that even where the debtor has paid or tendered one-third of the total price, the owner remains entitled to seize goods if the debtor is not then in breach of the agreement but some event other than a breach which is stipulated in the agreement as a ground for repossession (e.g. levy of execution by a third party against the debtor's assets) has occurred. This is a surprising diminution of the protection previously given under s. 33 of the Hire-Purchase Act 1965 and is probably due to an oversight. In practice, it is unlikely to affect the debtor, since it is extremely unusual for a non-breach ground of possession to arise where the debtor is not already in default of some obligation under the agreement. [**907**]

In order for the goods to be protected goods, the debtor must have "paid" one-third or more of the total price (s. 90 (1) (*b*)); but "paid" includes "tendered" (s. 189 (1)). There is a special provision as to successive agreements (see paras. [**914**] *et seq.*). Where the agreement requires the creditor to carry out any installation, and specifies an installation charge as part of the total price, the reference to one-third of the total price is to be construed as a reference to the aggregate of the installation charge and one-third of the remainder of the total price (s. 90 (2)). Hence if the total price is £900, of which the installation charge is £60. the one-third requirement is met once the debtor has paid or tendered $£60 + \dfrac{£900 - £60}{3} = £340$. By s. 189 (1), "installation" means—

(*a*) the installing of any electric line or any gas or water pipe,
(*b*) the fixing of goods to the premises where they are to be used, and the alteration of premises to enable goods to be used on them,
(*c*) where it is reasonably necessary that goods should be constructed or erected on the premises where they are to be used, any work carried out for the purpose of constructing or erecting them on those premises.

"Electric line" has the meaning given by the Electric Lighting Act 1882 (Consumer Credit Act, s. 189 (1)), that is, "a wire or wires, conductor, or other means used for the purpose of conveying, transmitting or distributing electricity with any casing, coating, covering, tube, pipe, or insulator enclosing, surrounding or supporting the same or any part thereof, or any apparatus connected therewith for the purpose of conveying, transmitting, or distributing electricity or electric currents" (Electric Lighting Act, s. 32). The modification made by s. 90 (2) to the one-third formula applies only where the creditor *is required under the agreement* to carry out the installation. If the agreement imposes no obligation on the creditor to install, but merely fixes an installation charge if he does install, the normal formula applies, so that in our illustration the goods would become protected goods (in the event of a breach by the debtor) after payment or tender of £300. [**908**]

Proof of adverse detention

A creditor bringing an action in tort or in contract for return of the goods by the debtor must ordinarily show that the debtor has without lawful justification failed or refused to surrender the goods after demand by the creditor, so that the debtor's continued possession is in defiance of the creditor's right to possess. At common law, there are no special requirements in relation to the creditor's demand for surrender of the goods, other than that the demand must be unconditional and must describe the goods in a manner sufficient to enable them to be identified. The demand may thus be made in writing or orally. But in the case of protected goods, or of any other goods recoverable only on an order of the court, it is necessary to make special provision for establishing adverse detention, for in the absence of such provision the debtor would be entitled to say that in remaining in possession he was not acting in defiance of the creditor's right to possess but was merely invoking the right conferred by the Act to require the creditor to obtain a court order (see *Smart Brothers, Ltd.* v. *Pratt*, [1940] 2 K.B. 498, [1940] 3 All E.R. 432, *per* MacKinnon, L. J., at p. 437). Section 134 (1) of the Act accordingly provides as follows:

> "Where goods are comprised in a regulated hire-purchase agreement, regulated conditional sale agreement or regulated consumer hire agreement, and the creditor or owner—
>
> (a) brings an action or makes an application to enforce a right to recover possession of the goods from the debtor or owner, and
>
> (b) proves that a demand for the delivery of the goods was included in the default notice under section 88 (5), or that, after the right to recover possession of the goods accrued but before the action was begun or the application was made, he made a request in writing to the debtor or hirer to surrender the goods,
>
> then, for the purposes of the claim of the creditor or owner to recover possession of the goods, the possession of them by the debtor or hirer shall be deemed to be adverse to the creditor or owner." [**909**]

Section 134 (1) in effect re-enacts s. 48 of the Hire-Purchase Act 1965 but with a significant modification. Under s. 48, a written request to surrender could not be made until after the right to recover possession of the goods had accrued due but before proceedings for possession. Since the right to possession did not accrue until after expiry of the requisite default notice, it followed that the request to surrender could not be incorporated in the default notice itself but had to be made separately in writing after the default notice had expired. Section 134 (1) allows the creditor the alternative of including the request to surrender in the notice of default. If he omits to do this, he must wait until after expiry of the default notice before making a separate written request. It should be noted that s. 134 is not confined to protected goods but extends to all claims for recovery of goods under a regulated hire-purchase, conditional sale or consumer hire agreement. This extension is necessary to cover other cases where the goods are recoverable only on an order of the court, e.g. because the agreement was improperly executed. Where the creditor has a right to repossess without a court order, he has no need to rely on s. 134 and can make his demand in any way permitted at common law, though he must, of course, have a right to possession at the time of demand and must therefore wait for expiry of any requisite notice of default or notice under s. 76 or s. 98. [**910**]

Section 134 (2) provides that in sub-s. (1) "the debtor or hirer" includes a person in possession of the goods at any time between the debtor's or hirer's death and the grant of probate or administration. Accordingly a creditor or owner who, after the

315

death of the debtor or hirer, wishes to establish adverse possession on the part of
the person in possession prior to the grant of probate or administration may
comply with s. 134 (1) by making a written request to surrender to the person in
possession.   [911]

Repossession with consent permitted

Section 33 of the Hire-Purchase Act 1965 did not preclude recovery of
possession as such, but merely *enforcement* of a right to recover possession.
Acceptance of a surrender by the hirer was therefore permissible (*Mercantile Credit
Co., Ltd.* v. *Cross*, [1965] 2 Q.B. 205, [1965] 1 All E.R. 577), so long as the debtor's
consent to the repossession was truly free and voluntary (*ibid.*). Section 90 (1) of
the Consumer Credit Act, on the other hand, provides that "the creditor is not
entitled to recover possession of the goods from the debtor except on an order of
the court".   At first sight, this may appear to preclude even acceptance of a
voluntary surrender by the debtor or hirer.   However, s. 173 (3) states that a
provision of the Act under which a thing may be done in relation to any person on
an order of the court or the director only shall not be taken to prevent its being
done at any time, with that person's consent given at that time, though the refusal
of such consent is not to give rise to any liability.   Hence recovery of possession
with consent of the debtor *given at the time* is not a contravention of s. 90 (1); but
a consent given in advance, e.g. in the agreement itself, is not within s. 173 (3) and
will not by itself protect the creditor from liability if he repossesses without a court
order.   What if the debtor simply abandons the goods? The position under s. 33 of
the Hire-Purchase Act 1965 was clear.   By the act of abandonment, the debtor
made it plain that he did not wish to retain possession, so that repossession of the
abandoned goods was not "enforcement" of a right to repossess (*Bentinck, Ltd.* v.
Cromwell Engineering Co., [1971] 1 Q.B. 324, [1971] 1 All E.R. 33).   But s. 90 (1) of
the Consumer Credit Act has dropped the word "enforce", so that the creditor has
to rely on s. 173 (3).   Though not as explicit as it might be, this seems sufficient to
protect the creditor who repossesses abandoned goods, since the debtor's
abandonment implies a consent to repossession by the creditor and such implied
consent would continue to subsist up to the date of repossession, thus fulfilling the
requirement of s. 173 (3) that there should be consent at that time.   [912]

Repossession from third party

Where the debtor has not abandoned the protected goods or terminated the
agreement, recovery of the goods by the creditor without the debtor's consent is a
contravention of s. 90 (1) whether the goods are repossessed from the debtor
himself or from some third party to whom the debtor has entrusted them. Thus,
repossession of a motor vehicle from a garage where the debtor has deposited the
vehicle for repair is equivalent to recovery of possession from the debtor himself
(*Bentinck, Ltd.* v. *Cromwell Engineering Co., supra*).   [913]

Application of section 90 (1) to successive agreements

Section 90 (3), re-enacting in somewhat different form provisions previously
contained in s. 47 of the Hire-Purchase Act 1965, provides as follows:

> "in a case where—
> (a) subsection (1) (a) is satisfied, but not subsection (1) (b),
>   and

(b)   subsection (1) (b) was satisfied on a previous occasion
        in relation to an earlier agreement, being a regulated
        hire-purchase or regulated conditional sale agree-
        ment, between the same parties, and relating to any
        of the goods comprised in the later agreement
        (whether or not other goods were also included),
subsection (1) shall apply to the later agreement with the
omission of paragraph (b)."

The purpose of this provision is to ensure that a debtor who has paid one-third of
the total price under a regulated hire-purchase or conditional sale agreement,
thereby prospectively (i.e. subject to his default — see s. 90 (1) (a)) securing protection
under s. 90 (1) for all the goods comprised in the agreement, does not lose that
protection as regards some of the goods by coming to an agreement with the
creditor that those goods shall be transferred to a new agreement (with or without
additional goods), payments under the original agreement being attributed to the
remaining goods.   But for s. 90 (3), the consequence of the transfer would be that
to secure protection again for the goods transferred to the new agreement, the
debtor would have to pay a sum equal to one-third of the total price fixed by the
new agreement.   The effect of s. 90 (3) is to ensure that once one-third of the total
price has been paid under the original agreement the transferred goods will be
automatically protected under the new agreement when the debtor is in breach of
that agreement, whether or not one-third of the total price payable under the new
agreement has been paid or tendered.   It is not necessary for this purpose that
condition (a) of s. 90 (1) (i.e. default by the debtor) should have been satisfied in
relation to the original agreement in order for the transferred goods to be protected
under the new agreement.   [**914**]

   If the later agreement is a modifying agreement (as defined by s. 82—see para.
[**718**] and *infra*), s. 90 (3) applies with the substitution, for the second reference to
the later agreement, of a reference to the modifying agreement (s. 90 (4)).   The
effect of this provision is that where an agreement varies or supplements a
regulated hire-purchase or conditional sale agreement under which one-third of the
total price has been paid, s. 90 (1) applies to the two agreements together (as
notionally combined by s. 82 (2)) without the one-third requirement having to be
satisfied in relation to the combined agreements.   In consequence, if default is
made by the debtor under the agreements as combined, then not only will the
goods comprised in the original agreement be protected but any goods added by
the later agreement will be protected as well, regardless of the sum (if any) paid
under the modifying agreement.   Any successive agreement will constitute a
modifying agreement except where the original agreement, instead of being merely
varied or supplemented, is discharged altogether by, or on or before the making of,
the later agreement.   [**915**]

Application of section 90 (1) on death of debtor

   The Third Schedule to the Hire-Purchase Act 1965 contained complicated
provisions designed to ensure that where goods had become protected goods before
the death of the hirer or buyer, his estate should be protected against repossession
of the goods by the owner or seller prior to a grant of probate or letters of
administration of the estate (see R. M. Goode, *op. cit.*, pp. 558–574).   The extremely

intricate provisions have been swept away and replaced by the admirably short and simple provisions of s. 90 (6):

> "Where subsection (1) applies to an agreement at the death of the debtor, it shall continue to apply (in relation to the possessor of the goods) until the grant of probate or administration ..."

This elegant solution to a problem made unnecessarily complicated by the Hire-Purchase Act 1965 means that goods which are protected goods at the death of the debtor cannot after his death and until a grant of probate or letters of administration be recovered from the person in possession of them without the consent of "the debtor" except on an order of the court. (As to service of the requisite default notice after the death of the debtor or hirer, see para. [**894**].) The executor of a debtor who dies testate becomes "the debtor" immediately upon the death, by virtue of the definition of "debtor" in s. 189 (1), since the debtor's rights pass to him by operation of law even before probate, though the court will not usually allow him to enforce such rights prior to a grant. Accordingly if at the death the goods are in possession of some third party, e.g. a repairer, the executor as "the debtor" can give his consent to collection of the goods from the third party, but a purported consent by any other person is not effective (see *Peacock* v. *Anglo-Auto Finance Co., Ltd.* (1968), 112 Sol. Jo. 746). Where the debtor dies intestate, his administrator becomes "the debtor" upon the grant of letters of administration. Until then the debtor's rights vest in the Probate Judge (Administration of Justice Act 1925, s. 9), i.e. the President of the Family Division of the High Court (*ibid.*, s. 55; Administration of Justice Act 1970, s. 1 (1), (6)). It should be noted that s. 90 (6) of the Consumer Credit Act operates only where the debtor was in breach of the agreement at the date of his death, for it is only during the continuance of a breach that the goods can be protected goods (see s. 90 (1) (*a*)). It follows that if the debtor, having paid or tendered one-third of the total price, dies without being in breach of the agreement at the date of his death, the goods will not become protected goods unless a default occurs after the death in payment of instalments or in performance of other obligations imposed by the agreement. Such a default will make the goods protected goods (assuming that the other requirements necessary for this have been fulfilled); and if the creditor repossesses them before probate or letters of administration have been taken out, he infringes s. 90 (1), as applied to the person in possession by s. 90 (6). [**916**]

Even if the goods are not protected goods at the date of death of the debtor or hirer, enforcement of contractual rights arising by reason of the death is restricted by ss. 86 and 128 (see paras. [**922**]–[**923**]). [**917**]

Effect of contravention of section 90

Section 91 provides that if goods are recovered by the creditor in contravention of s. 90

(*a*) the regulated agreement, if not previously terminated, shall terminate, and

(*b*) the debtor shall be released from all liability under the agreement, and shall be entitled to recover from the creditor all sums paid by the debtor under the agreement. [**918**]

The above consequences ensue whether the creditor repossesses all the goods comprised in the regulated agreement or only some of them. If he repossesses some only, he becomes entitled to take possession of the remaining goods thereafter. The agreement is brought to an end by the first repossession (s. 91 (*a*)), and exercise of the court's power to make a time order under s. 129 or an order under s. 133 does not arise, since the owner is not seeking (and indeed cannot seek) judicial enforcement of the agreement and the debtor's liability under the agreement is extinguished, and he is entitled to recover all his payments. If the debtor wishes to establish beyond doubt that s. 91 has come into operation so as to bring the agreement to an end, he can apply to the court for a declaration to that effect (s. 142 (2)). [**919**]

Termination of the agreement under s. 91 attracts the operation s. 106 to a security provided in relation to the agreement (s. 113 (3)), with the result that (*inter alia*) the security (including any guarantee or any indemnity) is deemed never to have had effect and the surety is entitled to repayment of sums he has paid (see para. [**774**]). [**920**]

Section 170 (1) makes it clear that the above remedies are exhaustive. Thus the debtor from whom the goods are repossessed in contravention of s. 90 cannot, for example, bring proceedings in tort for wrongful interference with goods (and see, on this point, *Carr* v. *James Broderick & Co., Ltd.,* [1942] 2 K.B. 275, [1942] 2 All E.R. 441). [**921**]

Rights exercisable by reason of death of debtor or hirer

The creditor or owner under a regulated agreement is not entitled, by reason of the death of the debtor or hirer, to do an act specified in paragraphs (*a*) to (*e*) of s. 87 (1) if at the death the agreement is fully secured (s. 86 (1)). The term "fully secured" is not defined but apparently means that the value of the security is adequate to cover all the obligations of the debtor or hirer remaining to be performed at the date of his death. The value judgment thus involved in determining whether s. 86 (1) applies may create difficulty, particularly where the security is not real security but personal security in the form of a guarantee or indemnity. Hence the creditor or owner should not launch proceedings under s. 86 (2) (see below) unless he is confident that he can establish the inadequacy of his security. If at the date of the death the agreement is unsecured or partly secured, the creditor or owner must, by s. 86 (2), obtain an order of the court if he wishes to do any of the acts specified in paragraphs (*a*) to (*e*) of s. 87 (1). The court can only make an enforcement order if the conditions specified in s. 128 are fulfilled (see para. [**933**]). [**922**]

The scope of s. 86 (1) and (2) is in fact fairly limited. It is restricted to cases where the right to do an act of the kind specified in paragraphs (*a*) to (*e*) of s. 87 (1) becomes exercisable *by reason of* the death of the debtor or hirer, that is, where the act is done under a power conferred by the agreement which is exercisable on the death of the debtor or hirer or exercisable at will and exercised at any time after his death (s. 86 (6)). Moreover, three additional limits on the operation of s. 86 (1) and (2) are imposed by sub-ss. (3), (4) and (5), which provide as follows:

> "(3) This section applies in relation to the termination of an agreement only where—
> (*a*) a period for its duration is specified in the agreement, and
> (*b*) that period has not ended when the creditor or owner purports to terminate the agreement,
> but so applies notwithstanding, that, under the agreement, any

party is entitled to terminate it before the end of the period so specified.

(4) This section does not prevent the creditor from treating the right to draw on any credit as restricted or deferred and taking such steps as may be necessary to make the restriction or deferment effective.

(5) This section does not affect the operation of any agreement providing for payment of sums—

(a) due under the regulated agreement, or

(b) becoming due under it on the death of the debtor or hirer,

out of the proceeds of a policy of insurance on his life."

Subsections (3) and (4) follow the wording of s. 26 (2) and (4) and have the same meaning (see paras. [**890**]–[**891**]). Section 86 (6) (b) is rarely likely to arise, which is just as well, for its effect is remarkable. If for example, a regulated agreement is fully secured by a mortgage which is enforceable at will, the debtor's death puts an end to the creditor's contractual right to enforce the mortgage, and it would seem that even the court is powerless to come to the mortgagee's aid. It is ironic that this result comes about only when the agreement is "fully secured". A mortgage by which a regulated agreement is partially secured is enforceable by an order of the court (s. 86 (2)). [**923**]

Default rate of interest not to exceed contract rate

Section 93 of the Act provides as follows:

"The debtor under a regulated consumer credit agreement shall not be obliged to pay interest on sums which, in breach of the agreement, are unpaid by him at a rate—

(a) where the total charge for credit includes an item in respect of interest, exceeding the rate of that interest, or

(b) in any other case, exceeding what would be the rate of the total charge for credit if any items included in the total charge for credit by virtue of section 20 (2) were disregarded." [**924**]

30. Judicial Control

Introduction

Part IX of the Act is devoted to judicial control of regulated agreements and securities given in connection with such agreements. It also confers on the court wide powers to re-open extortionate credit bargains; and these powers are exercisable in relation to *any* credit agreement in which the individual is the debtor, even if the credit agreement is outside the scope of the Act. Part IX bears little resemblance to the provisions of the Hire-Purchase Act 1965 (ss. 33–49) which it is designed to replace; and those who have become accustomed to working with the former legislation may initially experience some difficulty in finding in Part IX the equivalents of orders available under the previous legislation. For example, no reference to postponed orders for specific delivery of protected goods will be found in Part IX, but the powers conferred on the court will in fact enable such orders to be made in the same way as under the Hire-Purchase Act 1965 (see para. [**938**]). Indeed, the court's powers are very much wider under Part IX, since they are exercisable not only in actions concerning protected goods but in any action or application concerning a regulated agreement or a security given in connection with a regulated agreement. [**925**]

For the purpose of the Act, "the court" means the county court (s. 189 (1)). It follows that in addition to any jurisdiction it possesses independently of the Act, the county court has exclusive jurisdiction as regards all the matters listed in paragraph [**927**], other than the re-opening of extortionate credit agreements. In respect of these it has exclusive jurisdiction over applications by the debtor or a surety where the agreement is a regulated agreement or an agreement for fixed-sum credit not exceeding £2,000 or running-account credit with a credit limit not exceeding £2,000 (s. 139 (5) as amended by the County Courts Jurisdiction Order 1977, art. 2), but in other cases relating to extortionate credit agreements it has jurisdiction concurrently with the High Court (s. 139 (1)). But an action or application brought in the High Court which by virtue of the Act ought to have been brought in the county court is not to be treated as improperly brought but it is to be transferred to the county court (s. 141 (2)). The effect of the above provisions is to remove (effective from the appointed day, 16th May 1977) a sizeable area of jurisdiction from the High Court, which, under the Hire-Purchase Act 1965, has been able to entertain all actions other than actions for recovery of

321

protected goods and actions to recover goods where less than one-third of the hire-purchase price or total purchase price had been paid or tendered. Even a claim for, say, £4,000 arrears under a regulated agreement, where no claim is made for recovery of the goods, will henceforth be within the exclusive jurisdiction of the county court. [926]

Summary of court's powers

The powers of the court under Part IX, each of which will be examined in detail in this chapter, may be summarised as follows:

(i) To hear and determine any action by the creditor or owner to enforce a regulated agreement or any security relating to it or any action to enforce any linked transaction against the debtor or hirer or his relative.

(ii) To make or refuse orders enforcing agreements and securities which, under the provisions of the Act, are enforceable only on an order of the court (see paras. [930] *et seq.*).

(iii) To make a time order allowing the debtor or hirer or a surety to pay any sum owed under a regulated agreement or a security by instalments or extending the time for remedying of any other breach (see paras. [935] *et seq.*).

(iv) To make a protection order preserving any property of the creditor or owner, or property subject to any security, from damage or depreciation pending the determination of proceedings, including an order restricting or prohibiting use of the property of giving directions as to its custody (see para. [946]).

(v) To order repayment to a hirer under a consumer hire agreement of the whole or any part of any sum paid by him, and his release from liability for any sum payable by him, in respect of the goods where these have been repossessed by the owner or where an order has been made for their delivery to the owner (see para. [947]).

(vi) Upon an application for a time order or an enforcement order in relation to a regulated hire-purchase of conditional sale agreement, or in proceedings by the creditor to recover possession of the goods comprised in such an agreement, to make an order:
  (a) directing return of the goods to the creditor (see paras. [931] *et seq.*); or
  (b) by way of a transfer (or "split") order, transferring title to certain of the goods to the debtor and directing return to the creditor of the remaining goods (see paras. [955] *et seq.*).

(vii) To make conditional or suspend the operation of any term of an order made in relation to a regulated agreement (see paras. [931] *et seq.*).

(viii) To include in any order made under the Act such provision as the court thinks just for amending any agreement or security in consequence of a term of the order (see para. [950]).

(ix) To re-open a credit agreement where the credit bargain is extortionate and provide various forms of consequential relief to the debtor or a surety (see paras. [966] *et seq.*).

(x) To make certain types of declaratory order (see para. [995]).

(xi) To make such orders in relation to agreements for credit brokerage, debt-adjusting or debt-counselling as the court may be empowered to make as the result of regulations made by the Secretary of State under s. 156 of the Act (see para. [**1023**]). [**927**]

In addition, the court retains all the powers it would possess apart from the Act, except to the extent to which those powers are excluded or restricted by the provisions of Part IX. [**928**]

Exclusive jurisdiction of county court

The exclusive jurisdiction of the county court, derived partly from s. 141 of the Act, partly from the definition of "court" in s. 189 (1) of the Act, has been noted in paragraph [**926**], where it was also pointed out that an action or application within such exclusive jurisdiction but brought or made in the High Court is nevertheless valid, the sole effect being that it must be transferred to the county court (s. 141 (2)). As to the particular county court that must be selected for the commencement of proceedings within the Act, see para. [**994**]. [**929**]

Enforcement orders in cases of infringement

Section 127 (3) precludes the court from making an enforcement order under s. 65 (1) in the case of non-compliance with s. 61 (1) (*a*) unless a document (whether or not in the prescribed form and complying with regulations under s. 60 (1)) itself containing all the prescribed terms of the agreement was signed by the debtor or hirer (whether or not in the prescribed manner). In other words, failure to set out all the prescribed terms in the contract document, or failure to procure signature by the debtor or hirer of a document containing those prescribed terms, cannot be dispensed with by the court, so that in these cases the agreement is perpetually unenforceable. The court is also precluded by s. 127 (4) of the Act from making an enforcement order in the case of a cancellable agreement if—

(*a*) a provision of s. 62 or 63 was not complied with, and the creditor or owner did not give a copy of the executed agreement, and of any other document referred to in it, to the debtor or hirer before the commencement of the proceedings in which the order is sought, or

(*b*) section 64 (1) was not complied with. [**930**]

Save in the three cases mentioned in paragraph [**930**], the court, on entertaining an application for which an order is required by reason of infringement (*i.e.* of ss. 61–64, 105 (1) or (4), 111 (1) or 123), is to dismiss the application if, but only if, it considers it just to do so having regard to—

(i) prejudice caused to any person by the contravention in question, and the degree of culpability for it; and

(ii) the powers conferred on the court by ss. 127 (2), 135 and 136 (s. 127 (1)).

The court may consider that it would be unjust to dismiss the application if, for example, the infringement had not seriously affected the debtor or hirer or a surety or if the adverse consequences of the infringement can be substantially eradicated by exercise of the court's powers to give relief under s. 127 (reduction or discharge of sum payable by debtor or hirer to compensate him for prejudice suffered through the contravention) s. 135 (imposition of condition or suspension of order) or s. 136 (amendment of agreement or security in consequence of a term of the order).   If the court makes an enforcement order in cases within s. 127 (3) (as it has power to do if the only contravention of s. 61 (1) (*a*) was failure to ensure that the document was in the prescribed form or complied with regulations under s. 60 (1) or was signed by the debtor or hirer otherwise than in the prescribed manner), the court may direct that the regulated agreement is to have effect as if it did not include a term omitted from the document signed by the debtor of hirer (s. 127 (5)).   [**931**]

Orders where no infringement involved

There are three cases in which an order (which is not technically an "enforcement order" within s. 181 (1)) is necessary under the Act even though the creditor or owner has not infringed any of the statutory requirements.   These are:

> (i) exercise by an unsecured or partly secured creditor or owner of certain rights arising by reason of the death of the debtor or hirer (s. 86 (2)—see paras. [**922**] *et seq.*);
> (ii) recovery of protected goods without the consent of the debtor (s. 90 (1)—see paras. [**905**] *et seq.*);
> (iii) enforcement of a land mortgage (s. 126—see para. [**820**]).   [**932**]

By s. 128, the court is to make an order under s. 86 (2) if, but only if the creditor or owner proves that he has been unable to satisfy himself that the present and future obligations of the debtor or hirer under the agreement are likely to be discharged.   [**933**]

The Act contains no provisions dealing specifically with the approach to be adopted by the court in dealing with actions for recovery of protected goods or for enforcement of a land mortgage.   Sections 129–131 and 133–136 confer the widest discretion on the court as to the orders it can make in entertaining an application involving a regulated agreement or security, and the few restrictions that do exist (*i.e.* in ss. 130 (3), 133 (3) and 135 (3)) are not peculiar to actions for recovery of protected goods or for enforcement of a land mortgage.   [**934**]

Time orders

Section 129 (1) provides as follows:

> "If it appears to the court just to do so—
>> (*a*) on an application for an enforcement order; or
>> (*b*) on an application made by a debtor or hirer under this paragraph after service on him of—
>>> (i) a default notice, or
>>> (ii) a notice under section 76 (1) or 98 (1); or
>> (*c*) in an action brought by a creditor or owner to enforce a regulated agreement or any security, or recover possession of any goods or land to which a regulated agreement relates,
> the court may make an order under this section (a 'time order')."

An "enforcement order" is defined in s. 189 (1) as an order made under ss. 65 (1),

105 (7) (*a*) or (*b*), 111 (2) or 124 (1) or (2).   By s. 129 (2) a time order must provide for one or both of the following, as the court considers just—

(*a*) payment by the debtor or hirer or any surety of any sum owed under a regulated agreement or a security by such instalments, payable at such times, as the court, having regard to the means of the debtor or hirer and any surety, considers reasonable;

(*b*) the remedying by the debtor or hirer of any breach of a regulated agreement (other than non-payment of money) within such period as the court may specify.

Where in accordance with rules of court an offer to pay any sum by instalments is made by the debtor or hirer and accepted by the creditor or owner, the court may in accordance with rules of court make a time order under s. 129 (2) (*a*) giving effect to the offer without hearing evidence of means (s. 130 (1)).   [**935**]

The court's power to make a time order is qualified, in relation to a regulated agreement secured by a pledge, by s. 130 (3), which precludes the court from making a time order in such a case if, by virtue of regulations made under s. 76 (4), 87 (3) or 99 (4), service of a notice is not necessary for enforcement of the pledge.
[**936**]

It will be seen that the power to make time orders is not confined to actions for the recovery of protected goods but (subject to s. 130 (3)—see para. [**936**]) extends to almost every type of action concerning a regulated agreement or goods or land comprised in a regulated agreement of a security given in relation to a regulated agreement.   The power to make an instalment order under s. 129 (2) (*a*) goes no further than the court's existing power to make instalment orders under s. 99 of the County Courts Act 1959.   However, a time order under s. 129 (2) (*a*) is more powerful in its impact, since it attracts the operation of the supplemental provisions embodied in s. 130, including those of s. 130 (2) empowering the court, in the case of a hire-purchase or conditional sale agreement, to deal with sums not becoming payable until after the date of the order.   Moreover, the making of an *application* for a time order suffices to enable the court to exercise its special powers under s. 133 of the Act (see paras. [**948**] *et seq.*).   Section 129 (2) (*b*) has a still more radical effect, as will be seen below.   [**937**]

It has been mentioned earlier that the Consumer Credit Act does not in terms provide for the making of a postponed order for specific delivery of the type hitherto available under s. 35 (4) (*b*) of the Hire-Purchase Act 1965.   However, the Consumer Credit Act has not abolished the court's power to make a postponed order, but has merely scattered the ingredients of such an order over different sections.   The court can produce the effect of the old-style postponed order by combining a time order under s. 129 with a return order under s. 133 (1) (*b*) (i) and a suspension of the operation of that order, under s. 135 (1) (*b*) (ii) (see para. [**945**]), for so long as the debtor complies with the requirements of the time order.   If the debtor completes payment of the total price in pursuant to the time order and fulfils "any other necessary conditions" (by which is presumably meant conditions specified in the agreement as necessary for ownership to pass to him) the creditor's title to the goods vests in the debtor (s. 133 (5)).   In the case of goods comprised in a regulated consumer hire agreement, the court cannot make a return order under s. 133 (1) (*b*) (i) (since the section is confined to hire-purchase and conditional sale agreements) but can make an order for delivery under the Torts (Interference with Goods) Act 1977 (see para. [**838**]) and can suspend the operation of that order under s. 135 (1) (*b*). [**938**]

Effect of time order

The effect of a time order is spelled out in s. 130 (4) and (5) as follows:

"(4) Where, following the making of a time order in relation to a regulated hire-purchase or conditional sale agreement or a regulated consumer hire agreement, the debtor or hirer is in possession of the goods, he shall be treated (except in the case of a debtor to whom the creditor's title has passed) as a bailee or (in Scotland) a custodier of the goods under the terms of the agreement, notwithstanding that the agreement has been terminated.

(5) Without prejudice to anything done by the creditor or owner before the commencement of the period specified in a time order made under section 129 (2) (*b*) ('the relevant period')—

(*a*) he shall not while the relevant period subsists take in relation to the agreement any action such as is mentioned in section 87 (1);

(*b*) where—

(i) a provision of the agreement ('the secondary provision') becomes operative only on breach of another provision of the agreement ('the primary provision'), and

(ii) the time order provides for the remedying of such a breach of the primary provision within the relevant period,

he shall not treat the secondary provision as operative before the end of that period;

(*c*) if while the relevant period subsists the breach to which the order relates is remedied it shall be treated as not having occurred." [**939**]

Statutory bailment

Section 130 (4)—which corresponds to s. 38 (1) of Hire-Purchase Act 1965 though the scope of s. 130 (4) is much wider—does not, strictly speaking, resuscitate a terminated hire-purchase, conditional sale or consumer hire agreement but makes the debtor or hirer in possession a statutory bailee under the terms of the agreement, as controlled by a time order under s. 129 or consequential amendment under s. 136. This means that subject to such order, the obligations of the debtor or hirer under the terminated agreement are notionally revived, so that from the making of the time order payments again accrue due under the agreement (as controlled by the time order), other obligations (*e.g.* as to maintenance or insurance) are restored, and these continue in force while the debtor remains in possession, even, it seems, if the time order is later revoked. So far as payment obligations are concerned, the notional accrual of payments under the agreement will rarely arise, since each payment will be fixed by the time order itself which, in the case of hire-purchase or conditional sale agreement but not any other type of agreement, can deal with future instalments as well as arrears (s. 130 (2)). If the time order is revoked, then presumably payments accrued under the time order prior to revocation are enforceable by virtue of the order whilst the agreement again becomes fully operative according to its terms in relation to periods arising after revocation of the time order. [**940**]

Freezing of rights

The effect of s. 130 (5) (which is restricted to time orders providing for the remedying of non-monetary breaches and is thus of somewhat limited importance—see para. [**943**]) depends on whether the regulated agreement is still in force at the commencement of the period allowed by the time order for remedying of the breach or whether it has already been terminated by that date. If the agreement is still in force, the time order in effect freezes the creditor's remedies for the period specified in the time order (as varied by any variation order made under s. 130 (6)) until the time order is revoked by the court under s. 130 (6). Thus the creditor is, during the specified period, disabled from terminating the agreement or exercising any of the other rights enumerated in s. 87 (1). This restriction operates not only in relation to a breach for the remedying of which time is allowed by the time order but any other breach, including fresh breaches committed during the currency of the time order itself. The creditor's remedy in such a case is to apply for revocation of the time order. In addition, none of the rights listed in s. 87 (1) or any other rights expressed to arise on breach of a contractual provision which the time order allows the debtor time to remedy within a given period can be treated as arising before the end of that period. If the breach in question is remedied within such period, it is to be treated as not having occurred, with the result that in the absence of any other unremedied breach the agreement continues in force as if nothing had happened. If the breach is not remedied within the time stipulated in the time order, or if the time order is revoked, the restraints imposed by s. 130 (5) are removed and subject to the powers of the court to vary the time order under s. 130 (6) or to make a new time order or exercise its other powers under Part IX, the creditor can proceed to enforce his contractual rights in the ordinary way. He is still, of course, obliged to obtain an enforcement order for those rights which, under the provisions of the Act, are enforceable only on an order of the court. Where the creditor has duly terminated the agreement prior to the making of the time order and/or exercised other remedies such as the right to repossess, the position is more complex. Section 130 (5) is expressed to be "without prejudice to anything done by the creditor or owner before the commencement of the period specified in a time order made under s. 129 (2) (*b*)". If the agreement has been terminated prior to the commencement of that period, a time order under s. 129 (2) (*b*) does not disturb the termination but it does prevent the creditor from exercising any consequential right of repossession until expiry of the period in question. If during that period the breach is remedied, it is treated as not having occurred, and the debtor continues in possession as statutory bailee under the terms of the agreement, despite its termination, by virtue of s. 130 (4). Where, however, the creditor has repossessed the goods before the commencement of the period allowed in the time order for remedial action, the time order does not entitle the debtor to have the goods returned to him. Its sole effect in such a case is to freeze remedies not already exercised so as to allow the debtor or hirer to remedy the breach within the period specified in the order. In this situation, no statutory bailment is created under s. 130 (4), which is restricted to cases where the debtor is still in possession after the making of the time order.   [941]

As a result of s. 130 (5), it would seem that during the period for remedial action specified in a time order under s. 129 (2) (*b*) the creditor or owner is precluded even from serving a notice of default under s. 87 in respect of other breaches. On the other hand, a default notice served prior to the commencement of the period continues to run during that period, and can accordingly be relied upon by the creditor or owner on revocation of the time order, and acted upon immediately if the time specified in the default notice has then expired.   [942]

The freeze imposed by s. 130 (5) is limited to time orders under s. 129 (2) (*b*), i.e. time orders which provide for the remedying of a breach other than non-payment of money. Since default in payment is by far the most common breach complained of by creditors, s. 130 (5) will only operate in a minority of actions. A time order which is made solely under s. 129 (2) (*a*) and is thus restricted to fixing payment by instalments does not by itself restrict the creditor's remedies for default and, if no other order is made, leaves the creditor free to seize the goods (unless they are protected goods) or to bring an action for recovery of the goods. But on the debtor's application for a time order, or on the creditor's application for recovery of possession of the goods, the court's powers under s. 133 (1) become exercisable, so that the court may, for example, make an order for the return of the goods suspended so long as the payments fixed by the time order continue to be made. The powers under s. 133 (1) are not, however, exercisable in relation to consumer hire agreements, and goods comprised in such agreements cannot be protected goods for the purpose of s. 90. Accordingly where the hirer under a consumer hire agreement defaults in payment and fails to comply with a default notice served on him in accordance with s. 87, the hirer cannot invoke the Act to stop the owner from exercising a right to seize the goods, even if the court has made a time order providing for payment of the arrears by instalments. The only remedies open to the hirer in such a case are (*a*) to invoke the court's equitable jurisdiction to grant relief against forfeiture (see para. [840]) or (*b*) to apply to the court for an order for repayment of monies under s. 132 (see para. [947]). This latter provision is in fact a powerful inducement to owners not to act unreasonably in the enforcement of their rights of repossession.   [943]

Variation and revocation of time order

The court may vary or revoke a time order on the application of any person affected by it (s. 130 (6)). Revocation of a time order removes the restrictions imposed by s. 130 (5) (see para. [940]), since the "relevant period" referred to in that sub-section (i.e. the period allowed the debtor for remedying of a non-monetary breach) ceases to subsist when the time order is revoked. The creditor can thereupon proceed to exercise his remedies in the ordinary way, subject to the other provisions of the Act (see para. [941]). A default notice served prior to the date of commencement of a period stipulated in a time order under s. 129 (2) (*b*) but not expired before that date nevertheless continues to run so as to be available to the creditor or owner on revocation of the time order (see also para. [942]).   [944]

Breach of time order

If a time order for payment of a sum by instalments is made under s. 129 (2) (*a*) and the debtor or hirer defaults in payment of an instalment fixed by the order, the creditor or owner can forthwith issue execution for the whole of such sum then remaining unpaid or for such part as he wishes, not being less than £3 or the amount of one monthly instalment or four weekly instalments, whichever is the greater (C.C.R. Order 25, r. 13 (5)). But the debtor or hirer can prevent such execution by tendering the instalment or instalments in arrear prior to issue of the warrant of execution (*ibid.*, proviso), in which case the time order continues in force. In the case of a hire-purchase or conditional sale agreement where a return order has been made under s. 133 (1) (*b*) (i) but suspended under s. 135 (1) (*b*), default in payment under the time order entitles the creditor to have the return order executed immediately, without further order of the court, if the suspension was made under s. 135 (*b*) (ii) and was expressed to be until default in payment; but if the suspension was expressed to be under s. 135 (*b*) (i), i.e. until such time as the court would subsequently direct, the return order cannot be executed until a further order of the court has been made lifting the suspension. This also applies to an order under the Torts (Interference with Goods) Act 1977 for delivery of goods comprised in a consumer hire agreement but suspended under s. 135 (1) (*b*). The position is the same where the debtor or hirer fails to remedy a non-monetary breach within the period stipulated in a time order made under s. 129 (2) (*b*). [**945**]

Protection orders

The court, on the application of the creditor or owner under a regulated agreement, may make such orders as it thinks just for protecting any property of the creditor or owner, or property subject to any security, from damage or depreciation pending the determination of any proceedings under this Act, including orders restricting or prohibiting use of the property or giving directions as to its custody (s. 131). This re-enacts s. 35 (3) of the Hire-Purchase Act 1965. Quite independently of s. 131, the court has a general power under rules of court to make orders for the sale of perishables, etc. and for the detention, preservation, inspection, surveying, measuring and weighing of any property the subject of an action or as to which any question may arise therein (C.C.R., Order 13, rr. 11, 12— see also *ibid.*, r. 10). [**946**]

Repayment to consumer hirer

Where the owner under a regulated consumer hire agreement recovers possession of goods comprised in the agreement otherwise than by action or in proceedings relating to such an agreement obtains an order for delivery of the goods, the hirer may apply to the court for repayment of the whole or part of any sum paid by him to the owner in respect of the goods and for cessation of any obligation to pay the whole or part of any sum owed by him to the owner in respect of the goods; and if it appears to the court just to do so, having regard to the extent of the enjoyment of the goods by the hirer, the court must grant the application in full or in part (s. 132). These provisions, which may appear somewhat Draconian, are designed to enable the court to alleviate hardship that may be suffered by a hirer locked into a harsh consumer hire agreement that enables the owner, on repossessing for a default, to receive a windfall at the expense of the hirer. A graphic illustration of this type of case is *Galbraith* v. *Mitchenall Estates, Ltd.*, [1965] 2 Q.B. 473, [1964] 2 All E.R. 653, where the plaintiff, a working gardener and handyman, signed a hiring agreement relating to a caravan which he required as a home for his wife and family, and made a downpayment of £550·10·0, incurring an obligation under the agreement to pay 60 rentals of £12·10·0 every month over a five-year period. After five months, the defendants terminated the agreement owing to the non-payment of any instalments by the plaintiff, and after repossessing the caravan they sold it for £775 and would, indeed, have obtained even more but for the damage caused by mishandling by the repossession agents. The original retail price of the caravan was £1,050. Hence after only five months, the defendants had received, with the down-payment, a total sum of over £250 above the retail price of the caravan, whilst the only benefit that the hirer had received from his initial payment of £550·10·0 was five months' occupation of the caravan. Nevertheless the judge felt constrained by authority to refuse him relief in the absence of unconscionable conduct at the time of the making of the agreement. Section 132 of the Consumer Credit Act would enable the court to grant such relief in a case of this kind. The section is particularly necessary in view of the fact that the provisions of the Act relating to extortionate credit bargains (see paras. [**961**] *et seq.*) are not applicable to consumer hire agreements. [**947**]

Special powers of the court

Section 133 of the Act, taken in conjunction with s. 135, enables the court to make the same range of orders as it was empowered to make under s. 35 (4) of the Hire-Purchase Act 1965. There is, however, the striking difference that whereas the powers under s. 35 (4) were exercisable only in proceedings by the owner or seller for recovery of protected goods, the powers under s. 133 of the Consumer Credit Act may be exercised in relation to any goods comprised in a regulated hire-purchase or conditional sale agreement if it appears to the court just to do so—

    (*a*) on an application for an enforcement order or a time order; or
    (*b*) in an action by the creditor to recover possession of goods to which the agreement relates.

This is the case even where it was the debtor himself who terminated the agreement; in such a case the discretion of the court to refuse an order for specific delivery is restricted by s. 100 (5) of the Act, but this restriction is of somewhat limited impact in view of the provisions of s. 133 (5) (see para. [**953**]). It should be noted that the powers under s. 133 are exercisable only in relation to regulated hire-purchase and conditional sale agreements, not in relation to regulated consumer hire agreements. [**948**]

Types of special order that may be made

The court may, under the provisions of s. 133 (1) (*b*)—

    (i) make an order (a "return order") for the return to the creditor of goods to which the agreement relates;
    (ii) make an order (a "transfer order") for the transfer to the debtor of the creditor's title to certain goods to which the agreement relates ("the transferred goods"), and the return to the creditor of the remainder of the goods.

But the court cannot suspend an order requiring the debtor to deliver up goods unless satisfied that the goods are in his possession or control (s. 135 (2)), nor suspend an order against a hirer under a consumer hire agreement so as to entitle him to remain in possession for longer than the contractual period of hire (s. 135 (3)). [**949**]

Amendment of agreement or security
The court may in an order by it under the Act include such provision as it considers just for amending any agreement or security in consequence of a term of the order (s. 136). It would seem that termination of an agreement does not preclude a variation order under s. 136 in cases where the agreement is notionally revived under s. 129 (4). [**950**]

Return order
The first type of order listed in s. 133 (1) is an order for the return to the creditor of goods to which the agreement relates. The order may be immediate and unqualified or, under s. 135 (1), it may be made subject to a suspension (though only if the goods are in the debtor's possession or control—see paras. [**949**], [**954**]) or condition. Again, the order may direct return of goods without giving the debtor an option to pay their value (an order described in the Hire-Purchase Act as an order for *specific* delivery) or it may allow the debtor the option of paying the value of the goods if he fails to return them within the time stipulated by the order. However, where a debtor, having exercised his statutory right to terminate the agreement under s. 99, wrongfully retains possession, then in proceedings by the creditor to recover possession the court is obliged to order delivery of the goods to the creditor without giving the debtor an option to pay their value, unless the court is satisfied that having regard to the circumstances it would not be just to do so (s. 100 (5)). But this provision is of limited significance in view of the debtor's rights under s. 133 (4) (see para. [**953**]). The effect of contravention of a return order is considered in paragraph [**958**]. [**951**]

It is in relation to return orders that the court is most likely to exercise its discretion to make a conditional or suspended order. Of the two, the conditional order in favour of the creditor is, perhaps, the less likely, though it allows the court great flexibility in arriving at a just result. For example, if the court, though minded to make a return order, considers that the value of the goods exceeds the unpaid balance due under the agreement, so that sale of the returned goods by the creditor would produce a surplus, the court can make it a condition of the order that any such surplus shall be paid to the debtor. The more common form of order is likely to be (as under the Hire-Purchase Act) a suspended order (the equivalent of the postponed order provided by the Hire-Purchase Act), e.g. an order for delivery (with or without an option to the debtor to pay the value of the goods), suspended on condition that the debtor pays the arrears and future sums falling due by instalments specified in the order. If the debtor completes the payments due under the agreement and fulfils any other conditions necessary under the agreement for the transfer of ownership to him he acquires title (s. 133 (5)). If he defaults in payment, the creditor can immediately proceed to execute the order if the suspension was expressed to be until non-payment, pursuant to s. 135 (*b*) (ii). If, however, the suspension was in the form provided by s. 135 (*b*) (i), i.e. "until such time as the court subsequently directs", the creditor cannot enforce the return order immediately but must apply for the suspension to be lifted. [**952**]

Whilst the court can deprive the debtor of an option to pay the value of the goods instead of returning them to the creditor, little is achieved by so doing, since the Act provides that notwithstanding the making of a return order the debtor may at any time before the goods enter the possession of the creditor, on payment of the balance of the total price and the fulfilment of any other necessary conditions, claim the goods ordered to be returned to the creditor (s. 133 (4)). [**953**]

The court has no power to suspend the operation of a term requiring the delivery up of goods by the debtor, or indeed by any other person, unless satisfied that the goods are in his possession or control (s. 135 (2)). Under the Hire-Purchase Act, where the owner or seller applied for an order for delivery and did not oppose the postponing of the operation of the order, many courts would make an order without any affirmative evidence that the goods were in the possession or control of the hirer or buyer. Such practice could no doubt be justified on the footing that since the requirement of possession or control was intended for the protection of the owner or seller, it was open to him to waive the requirement; and no doubt the same practice will be followed in dealing with s. 135 (2) of the Consumer Credit Act.
[**954**]

Transfer order

The second type of order that may be made under s. 133 (1) is a transfer order. This is the type of order previously provided by s. 35 (4) (c) of the Hire-Purchase Act 1965, and commonly known as a "split" order. By such an order, the court transfers to the debtor the creditor's title to certain goods and directs return of the remainder of the goods to the creditor. However, as under the Hire-Purchase Act, the court can make a transfer order only where the sum paid by the debtor exceeds the part of the total price referable to the transferred goods by an amount equal to at least one-third of the unpaid balance of the total price (s. 133 (3)). The object of this provision is to compensate the creditor for having to accept the return of used goods under the order. For the purpose of s. 133, the part of the total price referable to any goods is the part assigned to those goods by the agreement or (if no such assignment is made) the part determined by the court to be reasonable (s. 133 (7)). In practice, an agreement comprising several goods will usually show a single *total price*, and only the *cash* price of each article will be separately stated. In determining for the purposes of s. 133 how much of the total price has been paid ("the paid-up sum"), the court may—

(a) treat any sum paid by the debtor, or owed by the creditor, in relation to the goods as part of the paid-up sum;
(b) deduct any sum owed by the debtor in relation to the goods (otherwise than as part of the total price) from the paid-up sum,

and make corresponding reduction in amounts so owed (s. 133 (2)). [**955**]

The above provisions may be illustrated by a simple example. Let us suppose that a hire-purchase agreement is made comprising a gas cooker and a refrigerator at a total price of £400, that this is apportioned, either in the agreement (which is unlikely) or by the court as to £225 to the cooker and £175 to the refrigerator, and that the debtor has made payments totalling £250. The court can order transfer of the refrigerator to the debtor, since the payments he has made exceed the price referable to the refrigerator by £75, and this is more than one-third of the unpaid balance of the total price (viz. £50). The court cannot order transfer of the cooker to the debtor, since the excess of payments over the price referable to the cooker is only £25, which is less than one-third of the unpaid balance of the total price. Whilst the court cannot reduce the one-third margin in favour of the creditor the margin may be greater than one-third and in practice will almost invariably be so, since it will only be by coincidence that payments exceed the price referable to the transferred goods by exactly one-third of the unpaid balance to the total price. Under the Hire-Purchase Act, there was no power to order the creditor to refund any excess of payments by the debtor over and above the one-third margin. In theory, the court can deal with this under s. 135 (1) (a) of the Consumer Credit Act by making such refund a condition of the transfer order; but since transfer orders are unusual and are not likely to appeal to the creditor, such a condition would in practice be likely to produce a stalemate. [**956**]

Notwithstanding the making of a transfer order, the debtor may at any time before the goods enter the possession of the creditor, on payment of the balance of the total price and the fulfilment of any other necessary conditions, claim the goods ordered to be returned to the creditor (s. 133 (4)). [**957**]

Debtor's failure to return goods

By s. 133 (6) if, in contravention of a return order or transfer order, any goods to which the order relates are not returned to the creditor, the court, on the application of the creditor, may—

(a) revoke so much of the order as relates to those goods, and
(b) order the debtor to pay the creditor the unpaid portion of so much of the total price as is referable to those goods.

The computation of the part of the total price referable to the goods is made in conformity with s. 133 (7) (see para. [**955**]). [**958**]

Suspended orders in relation to consumer hire agreements

The court's power to suspend the operation of an order is not restricted to orders under s. 133 but extends to any order made by the court in relation to a regulated agreement. However, in the case of a consumer hire agreement the court cannot use its power of suspension so as to extend the hirer's right to possession beyond the contractual period of hire (s. 135 (3)). [**959**]

Variation of orders

The court's power under s. 129 (6) to vary a time order has already been noted (see para. [**944**]). In addition, the court may vary a suspension or condition imposed by s. 135 (1), upon application by any person thereby affected (s. 135 (4)). [**960**]

Extortionate credit bargains

The court has long had an equitable jurisdiction to set aside harsh and unconscionable bargains, but this power (which appears to be unaffected by the Consumer Credit Act—see para. [**992**]) has in the main been devoted to upsetting sales at an undervalue by poor or uninformed vendors, and improvident bargains made by expectant heirs or reversioners, and has rarely been invoked successfully in the last half century. For a recent unsuccessful attempt to upset an index-linked money obligation in a mortgage, see *Multiservice Bookbinding, Ltd.* v. *Marden,* [1978] 2 All E.R. 489, [1978] 2 W.L.R. 535, which contains a general review of the equitable jurisdiction to re-open unconscionable mortgage transactions. Section 1 of the Money-lenders Act 1900 conferred on the court in any proceedings by a moneylender for recovery of the loan or enforcement of a security, or in any proceedings by a buyer or surety for relief, power to re-open the transaction where there was evidence that the interest or other charges were excessive and that the transaction was harsh and unconscionable or otherwise such that a court of equity would give relief. This provision was later strengthened by s. 10 (1) of the Moneylenders Act 1927, which created a presumption that interest was excessive, and the transaction harsh and unconscionable, if the rate of interest exceeded 48 per cent. *per annum.* Hence where interest was above 48 per cent., the onus was on the lender to refute that presumption; in other cases, the onus lay on the borrower to show that the interest was excessive. [**961**]

The utility of the above provisions in the consumer credit field was limited, since quite apart from the fact that moneylenders could usually advance a justification for their charges in terms of risk and the relatively small amount of the loan, borrowers normally failed to defend proceedings brought against them. Moreover the statutory provisions were confined to moneylending transactions within the Moneylenders Act. They did not catch other forms of credit, such as hire-purchase or instalment sale agreements; nor did they control loan transactions where the lender did not carry on moneylending as a business or was deemed by s. 6 of the Act of 1900 not to be carrying on the business of moneylending, *e.g.* because he was a banker. [**962**]

The only other legal control over interest rates was that imposed by the Pawnbrokers Acts, which laid down a tariff of charges that could be made by pawnbrokers. [**963**]

The Crowther Committee, whilst recommending retention of the 48 per cent. formula in the Moneylenders Act 1927, as opposed to the fixing of an inflexible ceiling rate, advocated that this should be extended over the whole field of consumer credit, and that the consumer should be protected from consistent overcharging in various other ways, as by use of the licensing system and by a requirement that a lender regularly charging more than 48 per cent. *per annum* should send quarterly returns to the Consumer Credit Commissioner (see Crowther Report, paragraph 6.6.9). [**964**]

The Consumer Credit Act, though adopting the first part of the Crowther Committee's recommendations by extending control of extortionate credit bargains to cover all types of credit agreement with an individual as debtor, abandons the 48 per cent. formula altogether. What the Act does is to provide guidelines for the court in determining whether a credit bargain is extortionate, but to put the onus of showing that the credit bargain is not extortionate on the creditor in all cases (however low the rate of interest or charge) where the debtor or a surety asserts in proceedings that the bargain is extortionate (see para. [**984**]).   [**965**]

The power to re–open

If the court finds a credit bargain extortionate, it may re-open the credit agreement so as to do justice between the parties (s. 137 (1)). For this purpose, "credit agreement" means any agreement between an individual ("the debtor") and any other person ("the creditor") by which the creditor provides the debtor with credit of any amount (s. 137 (2) (*a*)). It is important to note that, in contrast to other provisions of the Act, the court's powers under s. 137 are not confined to regulated agreements but apply to all credit agreements of any kind—whether exempt agreements or agreements which are otherwise outside the Act altogether, e.g. because the credit exceeds £5,000—where the debtor is an individual. "Individual", it will be recalled, includes a partnership and an unincorporated association (s. 189 (1)). But only *credit* agreements can be re-opened. There is no power to re-open *hire* agreements under s. 137, though the court can provide substantial relief under s. 132 as regards goods comprised in a consumer hire agreement which are repossessed by or ordered to be returned to the owner (see para. [**947**]). There is no power under the Act to grant any relief to the hirer under a hiring agreement which is not a consumer hire agreement.   [**966**]

By s. 137 (1) (*b*), "credit bargain"—

(i) where no transaction other than the credit agreement is to be taken into account in computing the total charge for credit, means the credit agreement, or

(ii) where one or more other transactions are to be so taken into account, means the credit agreement and those other transactions taken together.

Hence in determining whether a credit *agreement* is to be re-opened, the court looks not only at that agreement but at all other agreements to be taken into account in computing the total charge for credit, e.g. the maintenance and insurance contracts entered into pursuant to a term of the credit agreement where the debtor is not free to choose the insurer or the supplier of the maintenance service (see paras. [**515**] *et seq.*). The purpose of bringing such associated contracts within the definition of "credit bargain" is, of course, to prevent the creditor from evading the Act by keeping his charges under the credit agreement itself at a reasonable level while loading the charges payable under ancillary contracts. The effect of s. 137 (1) (*b*) (ii) is to require the court to take account of the total charge for credit, whether the charge arises wholly under the credit agreement or partly under that agreement and partly under the ancillary contract or contracts. Section 137 (1) speaks only of re-opening the credit *agreement*; but s. 137 (2) empowers the court, in re-opening the agreement, to set aside the whole or part of any obligation imposed on the debtor or a surety by the credit bargain or any related agreement (see para. [**984**]). The words "related agreement" are not defined.   [**967**]

The word "bargain" is not wide enough to cover prior loan transactions settled by means of the credit extended under the agreement in respect of which the court's reopening powers are being invoked. Accordingly the fact that the loan under the current transaction stems from a prior transaction or series of transactions imposing extortionate terms does not constitute a ground for reopening the current transaction, nor does it by itself afford a defence to the creditor's claim in respect of that transaction. On the other hand, there is nothing to prevent the debtor from counterclaiming for reopening of the earlier transactions notwithstanding that they have been settled (see para. [**988**]).   [**968**]

How the court's jurisdiction is invoked

By s. 139 (1) the credit agreement may be reopened under the above provisions:

(a) on an application for the purpose made by the debtor or any surety to the High Court or county court; or

(b) at the instance of the debtor or a surety in any proceedings to which the debtor and creditor are parties, being proceedings to enforce the credit agreement, any security relating to it, or any linked transaction; or

(c) at the instance of the debtor or a surety in other proceedings in any court where the amount paid or payable under the credit agreement is relevant.   [**969**]

When a credit bargain is extortionate

By s. 138 (1) a credit bargain is extortionate if it—

(a) requires the debtor or a relative of his to make payments (whether unconditionally, or on certain contingencies) which are grossly exorbitant, or

(b) otherwise grossly contravenes ordinary principles of fair dealing.

The Act sensibly does not attempt to define "grossly exorbitant" or "grossly contrary to ordinary principles of fair dealing" but instead lays down a set of guidelines for the court in determining whether a credit bargain is extortionate. These are examined in paras. [**977**] *et seq.* But first we must look at the underlying concept of the "extortionate credit bargain" and see what it is that this phrase seeks to encapsulate.   [**970**]

Unconscionability

The Moneylenders Acts, in describing transactions which the court was to be empowered to reopen, employed the phrase "harsh and unconscionable", and the word "extortionate" would seem to mean much the same thing. Indeed, in *Castle Phillips Finance Co., Ltd.* v. *Khan* (1978), unreported (Croydon county court), His Honour Judge Perks, in quoting this work, expressed the view that the meaning was precisely the same. "Extortionate", like "harsh and unconscionable", signifies not merely that the terms of the bargain are stiff, or even unreasonable, but that they are so unfair as to be oppressive. This carries with it the notion of morally reprehensible conduct on the part of the creditor in taking grossly unfair advantage of the debtor's circumstances. This element of moral culpability, in the form of abuse of power of bargaining position, is adverted to in a number of cases under the Moneylenders Acts (see, for example, *Samuel* v. *Newbold*, [1906] A.C. 461; *Poncione* v. *Higgins* (1904), 21 T.L.R. 11; *Bonnard* v. *Dott* (1906), 21 T.L.R. 491; and the Western Australian case of *W. F. Lean, Ltd.* v. *Dale* (1936), 39 W.A.L.R. 22), as well as in decisions concerning the power of equity to set aside unconscionable bargains (see, for example, *Multiservice Bookbinding, Ltd.* v. *Marden*, [1978] 2 All E.R. 489, *per* Browne-Wilkinson J., at p. 502). See further Lord Meston's *Law Relating to Moneylenders* (5th Edn.), Chapter XII and Dr. Clifford Pannam's *The Law of Money Lenders in Australia and New Zealand*, Chapter 17. [971]

It seems clear that ss. 137–140 do not cover the whole of the ground occupied by the equitable power of the court to set aside bargains, and that this power remains exercisable independently of the Act. See para. [992]. [972]

The time as at which the bargain is to be tested

The question is whether the credit bargain is extortionate, not whether it has become unprofitable through a drop in the level of interest rates not whether the creditor has acted unconscionably in enforcing it. The court has adequate powers to grant relief to the debtor from the consequences of unconscionable enforcement. Whether the credit bargain is extortionate has to be determined as at the date of the credit agreement, not in the light of subsequent events. See *Harris* v. *Clarson* (1910), 27 T.L.R. 30 and *Harrison* v. *Gremlin Holdings Pty., Ltd.* (1961), 78 W.N. (N.S.W.) 711. [973]

The terms to be examined

Once the allegation has been made that the credit bargain is extortionate, the court must approach the question by examining the terms of the transaction constituting the credit bargain and then determining whether, in the light of the statutory guidelines and other factors external to the contract, the credit bargain is or is not extortionate. The external factors to be taken into consideration are discussed in paras. [978] *et seq.* At this point, we are concerned merely with the types of contractual provision to which the court is likely to devote particular attention when considering the question. [974]

The fundamental point is that whilst the most typical form of unconscionable stipulation is that which imposes an exorbitant credit charge, this is but one factor among many, and the court must have regard to the terms of the bargain as a whole, both monetary and non-monetary. Even though no single item taken in isolation is extortionate, the contract taken overall may nevertheless constitute an extortionate transaction. [975]

Among the specific terms to which the court is likely to have regard (and for this purpose also the decisions under the Moneylenders Acts are helpful) are the following:—

(i) The amount and rate of the total charge for credit—a factor to be weighed against interest rates prevailing at the time of the contract, the risk of default and the value of any security taken by the creditor (s. 138 (2) (*a*), (4) (*b*), and paras. [977] *et seq.*).

(ii) The benefit to be derived by the creditor from other sources, e.g. discounts from suppliers against the price of goods or services financed by the credit.

(iii) The amount payable by the debtor to brokers or other intermediaries, so far as not already reflected in the total charge for credit.

(iv) The severity of the default provisions, and in particular:
 (*a*) the nature and gravity of the events specified as attracting the creditor's default remedies;

(*b*) the monetary liability sought to be imposed on the debtor (the fact that the contractual provision is in any event unenforceable as a penalty would not appear to preclude the court from taking it into account under s. 137, and indeed is clearly a relevant factor, though not conclusive, since the degree of unfairness required to attract the rule against penalties is significantly less than is necessary to make the bargain extortionate);

(*c*) any forfeiture provisions contained in the contract—e.g. provisions entitling the creditor to repossess goods, to enforce a security or to confiscate a deposit paid to secure the performance of the debtor's obligations;

(v) The amount of rebate to be allowed for early settlement or on refinancing. The inadequacy of the rebate may be an element, though in due course this will be taken care of by regulations under s. 95 of the Act.

(vi) The duration of the contract commitment. *Semble*, the burden sought to be imposed by a long-term contract is relevant even if the debtor has a statutory right of termination under s. 99 of the Act, if such right has not been made a term of the contract.

(vii) The extent to which the debtor is required, as a term of the credit agreement or as a condition of his being granted the credit, to enter into or to maintain ancillary contracts that are burdensome to him (see, for example, the solus agreement involved in *Esso Petroleum Co., Ltd.* v. *Harper's Garage (Stourport), Ltd.*, [1968] A.C. 269, [1967] 1 All ER 699). [**976**]

Statutory guidelines

These are laid down in sub-ss. (2)–(5) of s. 138, which provide as follows:

"(2) In determining whether a credit bargain is extortionate, regard shall be had to such evidence as is adduced concerning—

(*a*) interest rates prevailing at the time it was made,
(*b*) the factors mentioned in subsections (3) to (5), and
(*c*) any other relevant considerations.

(3) Factors applicable under subsection (2) in relation to the debtor include—

(*a*) his age, experience, business capacity and state of health; and
(*b*) the degree to which, at the time of making the credit bargain, he was under financial pressure, and the nature of that pressure.

(4) Factors applicable under subsection (2) in relation to the creditor include—

(*a*) the degree of risk accepted by him, having regard to the value of any security provided;
(*b*) his relationship to the debtor; and
(*c*) whether or not a colourable cash price was quoted for any goods or services included in the credit bargain.

(5) Factors applicable under subsection (2) in relation to a linked transaction include the question how far the transaction was reasonable required for the protection of debtor or creditor, or was in the interest of the debtor." [**977**]

The court is only *obliged* to take into account those factors listed above on which evidence is adduced, though it remains *entitled* to take account of other matters, e.g. facts of which it can take judicial cognisance and which therefore do not require to be established by evidence. [**978**]

The statutory provisions do not indicate in which direction a particular factor should incline a court to move. In some cases, this is not difficult to infer. It may be assumed, for example, that if the debtor is immature, senile, mentally unstable or lacking in business experience, or if his relationship with the creditor is such that he is accustomed to relying on the creditor's advice or otherwise acting under his influence, this will go to support a contention that the credit bargain is extortionate, for the court may then be ready to assume that a high rate of charge was imposed not so much because the debtor was a poor risk but because the creditor was taking advantage of the debtor's mental state or ability or lack of experience or of the relationship between them. [**979**]

But what if the debtor suffers physical ill-health or is under acute financial pressure? On the one hand, these are conditions which make him particularly vulnerable to acceptance of a harsh agreement; but on the other hand, it is these self-same conditions that may generate a pressing need for financial assistance, whilst making it difficult for the debtor to obtain credit because of his poor income prospects. Such is sometimes the case, for example, where a householder who is heavily in debt borrows money at higher rates not for some extravagance but to pay the electricity bill and thus avoid disconnection of the electricity supply. Is the existence of pressures of this kind to be taken as strengthening the likelihood that the bargain is extortionate or, on the contrary, as showing that because of the need and the risks involved the interest rate, though high, is not unreasonable? No hard and fast rules can be laid down, but a useful test is to ask whether, on the available evidence, the creditor has used the debtor's circumstances as an opportunity to take a grossly unfair advantage by imposing terms that go far beyond what is reasonable for his profit and protection or whether on the other hand his terms are genuinely intended to reflect the degree of risk involved. If the evidence is so evenly balanced that the court is unable to reach a conclusion one way or another, the bargain must be held extortionate (see para. [**985**]). [**980**]

There is a potential difficulty for credit grantors in that as a rule tariffs of interest rates and finance charges are constructed not according to the personal characteristics or finances of a particular debtor (since the assessment of a separate rate for each individual transaction would be quite impracticable for all except the smallest credit granting institutions) but on the basis of external factors, e.g. the cost of money, the nature of the goods to be acquired with a purchase-money credit (such as hire-purchase or conditional sale) and whether such goods are new or second-hand. Inevitably, therefore, there will be some debtors on whom, by reason of the factors mentioned in s. 138 (3), rates fixed by a standard tariff will bear more hardly than in the case of other debtors. The court should, it is submitted, seek to avoid a result in which the use of standard charges which are reasonable in themselves is jeopardised because of the prospect that particular debtors may, on account of their own personal circumstances, find their specific agreements burdensome to them. In short, in deciding whether the presence of one of the factors mentioned in s. 138 makes a credit bargain extortionate, the court should consider whether such factor influenced the rate of charge or the other terms of the credit bargain. If it did not, then in general it would seem reasonable to hold that the credit bargain is not made extortionate by reason only of that factor. This approach, which leaves credit-granting institutions free to continue the convenient practice of establishing and maintaining standard rates, is consistent with the requirement built into s. 138 (1) that for a credit bargain to be extortionate, the charges must be "grossly exorbitant" or the agreement must otherwise "grossly" contravene the ordinary principles of fair dealing.   [**981**]

The other factors referred to in s. 138 (2)–(4) do not call for further comment, except in relation to the factor mentioned in s. 138 (4) (*c*), namely "whether or not a colourable cash price was quoted for any goods or services included in the credit bargain". This factor was mentioned in order to alert the court to the possibility that part of an apparently reasonable credit charge may in fact be concealed in an inflated cash price, as where goods are sold on credit sale at a specified price greater than would ordinarily be charged by a person selling goods of the like description for cash (cf. s. 45 of the Act, discussed in paras. [**455**] *et seq.*). The effect of inflating the cash price is twofold. First, it enables the creditor to receive the same return while reducing the charge component of the total price. Secondly, it reduces the proportion which such charges bear to the cash price, so that the stated rate of charge is still more misleading.   [**982**]

Other factors

The statutory guidelines, though covering a wide range of circumstances, do not purport to be exhaustive. Other factors which the court might regard as relevant are: the extent to which the debtor appeared to understand the nature and terms of the commitment he was undertaking; whether he received, or had access to, independent advice before entering into the transaction; the extent to which the creditor held out inducements or temptations to the debtor to persuade him to make the contract, or otherwise foisted the credit upon the debtor (a malpractice particularly prevalent some years ago in the field of second-mortgage lending); and the existence of any moral pressure on the debtor to enter into the commitment, e.g. to help a parent, a child or other close relative (cf., in relation to guarantees, *Lloyds Bank, Ltd.* v. *Bundy*, [1975] Q.B. 326, [1974] 3 All E.R. 757).   [**983**]

Onus of proof

If, in proceedings referred to in s. 141 (1), the debtor or any surety alleges that the credit bargain is extortionate it is for the creditor to prove the contrary (s. 171 (5)). This provision applies however low the rate of interest or charge and even if it is a rate which makes the credit agreement an exempt agreement under regulations made pursuant to s. 16 (5) (*b*).   [**984**]

The question whether a credit bargain is extortionate, though involving the determination of certain facts, would seem to be a question of law (see *Abrahams* v. *Dimmock*, [1915] 1 K.B. 662, a decision on s. 1 (1) of the Money-lenders Act 1900). The burden of proof imposed on the creditor by s. 171 (7) of the Act would appear to be the *legal* burden of proof, that is, the onus of persuading the court at the end of the day that on the evidence before it the credit bargain was not extortionate.

This onus arises only where the debtor alleges that the credit bargain is extortionate (s. 171 (7)); but once the allegation has been made the ultimate persuasive burden lies on the creditor, and if the evidence is evenly balanced the debtor will succeed. On the other hand, the onus would seem to be on the debtor to discharge the *evidential* burden of proving a particular fact on which he seeks to rely as attracting one of the elements listed in s. 138, particularly where that fact lies exclusively within his own knowledge. If he fails to adduce evidence establishing that fact on a balance of probabilities, then it will not feature as an element when the court comes to decide whether the creditor has discharged the legal burden of proof. For example, suppose that under a given consumer credit agreement interest is payable at the rate of 75% per annum and the debtor seeks to contend that the creditor took advantage of the debtor's lack of business experience or mental infirmity through age. It is for the debtor to show that he lacked business experience or was of a given age and in a poor state of mental health at the time of the agreement and (in so far as the creditor's knowledge of these facts is relevant—see para. [**981**]) that they were known to the creditor. If the debtor fails to adduce evidence establishing these matters on a balance of probabilities, they will be ignored when the issue comes to be decided at the end of the trial, but the court remains free to conclude that the creditor has failed to show on a balance of probabilities that a rate of 75% was not in any event extortionate in the circumstances. Conversely, even if the debtor shows that to the knowledge of the creditor he, the debtor, was old and infirm, the judge may still be persuaded by the creditor that the interest rate was fixed at 75% not because the creditor was unfairly taking advantage of the debtor's state of health and want of experience but because it was a fair return having regard to the degree of risk involved in the transaction. In short, the evidential burden of establishing a particular fact lies on the party asserting it, whether he be the debtor or creditor; the ultimate burden of satisfying the court that in the light of all the evidence the bargain was not extortionate lies on the creditor when once an allegation to this effect has been made by the debtor in proceedings covered by s. 139 (1). [**985**]

Nature of relief given

Section 139 (2) provides as follows:

> "In reopening the agreement, the court may, for the purpose of relieving the debtor or a surety from payment of any sum in excess of that fairly due and reasonable, by order —
>
>   (*a*) direct accounts to be taken, or (in Scotland) an accounting to be made, between any persons,
>
>   (*b*) set aside the whole or part of any obligation imposed on the debtor or a surety by the credit bargain or any related agreement,
>
>   (*c*) require the creditor to repay the whole or part of any sum paid under the credit bargain or any related agreement by the debtor or a surety, whether paid to the creditor or any other person,
>
>   (*d*) direct the return to the surety of any property provided for the purposes of the security, or
>
>   (*e*) alter the terms of the credit agreement or any security instrument."

An order may be made under s. 139 (2) notwithstanding that its effect is to place a burden on the creditor in respect of an advantage unfairly enjoyed by another person who is a party to a linked transaction (s. 139 (3)). An illustration of the effect of this provision is given in para. [**865**]. [**986**]

An order under section 139 (2) is not to alter the effect of any judgment (s. 139 (4)). Hence, once the creditor has obtained judgment against the debtor for recovery of a loan or enforcement of a security, the debtor is obliged to meet the judgment and cannot secure his discharge by reliance on s. 139 (2). Such a principle is necessary in order to ensure the finality of judicial proceedings. But the court retains its normal power, by virtue of statutes, rules of court and its inherent jurisdiction, to set aside a judgment in a proper case, as where it is a judgment entered in default of appearance (R.S.C. Order 13, r. 9) or defence (R.S.C. Order 19, r. 9; C.C.R. Order 37, r. 3) or given in the absence of the defendant (R.S.C. Order 35, r. 2; C.C.R., Order 37, r. 2) or set aside consequent on an order for a new trial (R.S.C. Order 59, r. 11; County Courts Act 1959, s. 113 (1); C.C.R. Order 37, r. 1). [**987**]

Retrospective effect

The power of the court under ss. 137–140 of the Act to reopen a credit bargain as extortionate became exercisable on and after the 16th May 1977 (Consumer Credit Act 1974 (Commencement No. 2) Order 1977, art. 2 (2)), and applies to agreements and transactions whenever made (Consumer Credit Act 1974, Sch. 3, para. 42). The court can thus reopen transactions made before the 16th May 1977, and indeed transactions made before the passing of the Act itself, and this notwithstanding that prior to the 16th May 1977 the debtor had a right to apply under the Moneylenders Acts or the transaction to be reopened. Moreover, the fact that a transaction has been completed and discharged by payment before application for relief is made is no barrier to the court's powers (see *B. S. Lyle, Ltd. v. Pearson,* [1941] 2 K.B. 391, [1941] 3 All E.R. 128, a decision under s. 1 (1) of the Money-lenders Act 1900), so that the protection given by ss. 137–140 cannot be evaded by the device of refinancing on reasonable terms a prior loan or series of loans extended at a usurious rate of interest *(ibid.).* Nevertheless, the court will have regard to the time that has lapsed since the closing of the transaction sought to be reopened and will not ordinarily be minded to set aside transactions closed a long time ago in the absence of special circumstances, such as deception or similar malpractice on the part of the creditor (see *Stone* v. *Hamilton,* [1918] 2 I.R. 193). [**988**]

Procedure

On 16th May 1977, when ss. 137–140 became operative (see para. [**988**], above) Ords. 83 and 84 of the Rules of the Supreme Court (relating respectively to actions by moneylenders and actions arising out of hire-purchase or conditional sale agreements) became inoperative (Rules of the Supreme Court (Amendment No. 2) 1976, rr. 10 and 11), the old Ord. 83 being replaced by a new order which prohibits the entry of default judgment without leave after the debtor or surety has served a notice under Ord. 83, r. 2, of his desire to have a credit agreement reopened (Ord. 83, r. 3 (1)). Application for leave must be made by summons supported by affidavit and must be served on every other party to the proceedings even if that party has not entered appearance or has no address for service (r. 3 (2)). A summons for leave to enter judgment in default of appearance must not be issued until after the time limited for appearance (r. 3 (3)). On the hearing of the application the court may exercise its powers under ss. 137–140, whether or not the debtor or surety has entered an appearance or appears at the hearing, and if it refuses leave to enter judgment the court can make any order it could have made if the application had been for judgment under Ord. 14, r. 1 (r. 4). [**989**]

The County Court (Amendment No. 2) Rules 1976 likewise make provision for the reopening of credit agreements where the application is made in the County Court. The procedure is prescribed by a new Ord. 46, r. 22, added by r. 7 of the 1976 Rules. An application to a County Court under s. 138 (1) (*a*) of the Consumer Credit Act for a credit agreement to be reopened must be made by originating application (Ord. 46, r. 22 (1)). The debtor or surety desiring to have a credit agreement reopened must give notice to that effect to the registrar and every other party within 14 days of the service of the originating process on him. Once he has served this notice, he is deemed to have delivered a defence or answer and no default judgment may be entered under Ord. 10, r. 2. The new rule came into force on 16th May 1977. [**990**]

Unregulated credit agreements

Section 140 provides that where the credit agreement is not a regulated agreement expressions used in ss. 137–139 which, apart from s. 140, apply only to regulated agreements, are to be construed as nearly as may be as if the credit agreement were a regulated agreement. The drafting of this section is defective, since there is only one expression used in ss. 137–139 which is peculiar to a *regulated* agreement, namely a "linked transaction", but there are several expressions applicable only to *consumer credit* or *consumer hire* agreements (which are not necessarily regulated agreements, since they may be exempt under s. 16), i.e. "creditor", "debtor", "security" and "surety". Obviously the court must employ in relation to these expressions the same approach as is required by s. 140 in relation to linked transactions. [**991**]

The court's inherent equitable jurisdiction

In *Castle Phillip Finance Co., Ltd.* v. *Khan* (see para. [**971**]) the court upheld an argument by the creditor that the Consumer Credit Act, as successor to the Moneylenders Acts, now provided a complete code on that branch of the law dealing with the reopening of unconscionable transactions and that there was no longer any jurisdiction to refuse to enforce a moneylending contract that did not offend against the terms of the Act. But this proposition is too sweeping and is not supported by the authorities cited for it, namely *Earl of Aylesford* v. *Morris* (1873), 8 Ch. App. 484 and *Samuel* v. *Newbold*, [1906] A.C. 461. In general, a statute conferring rights and remedies will not be interpreted as displacing rights and remedies established at common law unless the statute manifests an intention to occupy the whole field. Equity recognised at least two distinct grounds for upsetting moneylending transactions. The first was that the transaction was harsh and unconscionable, and this, as previously noted (para. [**971**]) involved a finding that the lender had been guilty of moral turpitude in taking a grossly unfair advantage of the debtor. But a quite distinct rule emerged as regards bargains

343

with expectant heirs, for these would be set aside in equity unless the purchaser or lender could prove that the bargain in question was fair, just and reasonable (*Earl of Aylesford* v. *Morris, supra*) and in the case of a loan this was so even if the lender did not take security over the expectancy but merely lent money on the strength of it (*ibid.*). Though by statute a sale or loan on the security of a reversion is no longer voidable merely by reason of undervalue (Law of Property Act 1925, s. 174, re-enacting the Sale of Reversions Act 1867), the statutory provisions do not apply to loans made on the credit of the borrower's expectancy where no security over that expectancy is taken, and transactions involving such loans remain within the equitable rule and are liable to be set aside unless the creditor discharges the onus of showing that they are fair and reasonable. [**992**]

Section 1 (1) of the Money-lenders Act 1900 covered both heads of equitable jurisdiction, for it conferred on the court power to reopen a transaction not only where it was "harsh and unconscionable" but also where it was "otherwise such that a court of equity would give relief". This made academic the question whether any residual equitable jurisdiction survived the Act, for after some controversy it was settled that the two limbs of the section were independent of each other (*Samuel* v. *Newbold, supra*). By contrast, ss. 137–140 of the Consumer Credit Act are confined to those transactions of a kind previously described as harsh and unconscionable and do not extend to that species of so-called equitable fraud by which unfairness in dealings with an expectant heir is presumed unless the contrary is proved and moral delinquency on the part of the creditor is in no way a necessary element (*Rae* v. *Joyce* (1892), 29 L.R. Ir. 500, *per* Walker L.C. at p. 519). Accordingly, whilst it is extremely unlikely that the court will treat a credit bargain as unconscionable in equity if it is not extortionate for the purpose of the Consumer Credit Act, it is submitted that it retains a residuary equitable jurisdiction and that one such case where this might well be invoked is where the bargain, though not unconscionable in the normal sense, is a bargain with an expectant heir in a case outside s. 174 of the Law of Property Act and the creditor is not able to prove that is is fair and reasonable. [**993**]

Selection of county court by creditor

Section 49 of the Hire-Purchase Act 1965 provided that actions by the owner or seller for recovery of protected goods or actions for recovery of goods brought before one-third of the hire-purchase price or total purchase price had been paid or tendered, were to be brought into the county court district in which the hirer or buyer "resides or carries on business, or resided or carried on business at the date on which he last made a payment under the hire-purchase agreement or conditional sale agreement". No such provisions are contained in the Consumer Credit Act, and the place of commencement of proceedings is left to be governed by Order 2 of the County Court Rules. [**994**]

Declaratory orders

In addition to its general power to grant declarations (which unless otherwise provided by statute is exercisable only where the declaration is claimed as ancillary to a claim that is otherwise within the county court's jurisdiction—*De Vries* v.

344

Smallridge, [1928] 1 K.B. 482), the county court may make various declaratory orders under s. 142 of the Consumer Credit Act, which provides as follows:

> "(1) Where under any provision of this Act a thing can be done by a creditor or owner on an enforcement order only, and either—
>
> > (a) the court dismisses (except on technical grounds only) an application for enforcement order, or
> >
> > (b) where no such application has been made or such an application has been dismissed on technical grounds only, an interested party applies to the court for a declaration under this subsection,
>
> the court may if it thinks just make a declaration that the creditor or owner is not entitled to do that thing, and thereafter no application for an enforcement order in respect of it shall be entertained.
>
> (2) Where—
>
> > (a) a regulated agreement or linked transaction is cancelled under section 69 (1), or becomes subject to section 69 (2), or
> >
> > (b) a regulated agreement is terminated under section 91,
>
> and an interested party applies to the court for a declaration under this sub-section, the court may make a declaration to that effect." [**995**]

31. Ancillary Credit Businesses

The control

Part X of the Consumer Credit Act regulates various kinds of ancillary credit business whose activities are connected to the provision of credit or hire facilities to individuals. The broad effect of Part X is:

    (i) to subject all these forms of business to the licensing provisions of Part III of the Act;

    (ii) to impose in relation to certain classes of ancillary credit business the same kind of requirements and restrictions as to the seeking of business as are imposed in relation to consumer credit and consumer hire businesses by Part IV of the Act;

    (iii) to restrict to the sum of £1 brokerage fees recoverable by credit-brokers in cases where no credit agreement ensues within six months after the introduction effected by the credit-broker;

    (iv) to provide for regulations as to ancillary credit agreements;

    (v) to provide the consumer with various forms of protection in relation to information filed with credit reference agencies. [**996**]

"Ancillary credit business"

By s. 145 (1) an ancillary credit business is any business insofar as it comprises or relates to—

    (*a*) credit brokerage,

    (*b*) debt-adjusting,

    (*c*) debt-counselling,

    (*d*) debt-collecting, or

    (*e*) the operation of a credit reference agency.

Each of these forms of activity is defined, and we shall examine the definitions in the following paragraphs. A general point to note about this sub-section is that it is not confined to cases where a person is carrying on the business of credit brokerage, debt-adjusting, etc. *Any* business is within s. 145 "so far as it comprises or relates to" one of the five designated categories of activity; and except in the case of a credit reference agency it is not necessary that these activities shall themselves constitute a business. It suffices that they form part of or are related to a business, of whatever kind. Thus if a company regularly introduces employees to

346

banks or building societies for the purpose of procuring loans for house purchase, the company will be a credit broker even if it receives no commission from either party and its sole concern is to promote the welfare of its staff. Similarly an accountant who regularly gives advice to debtors about liquidation of debts due under consumer credit agreements is to be considered carrying on an ancillary credit business relating to debt-counselling. In short, though the Act speaks of "ancillary credit business" what it is regulating is an *activity* (whether or not itself a business) that is comprised in or is related to some business which for the most part may not have any connection with the activity at all. Only credit reference agencies would seem to be an exception because the definition of credit reference agency in s. 145 (8) itself incorporates a reference to the carrying on of a business.

[**997**]

Credit brokerage

Credit brokerage is in essence the effecting of introductions of individuals seeking credit or goods on rental to those whose business involves the grant of consumer credit or consumer hire facilities or who themselves carry on business as credit-brokers. The definition of credit brokerage contained in s. 145 (2)–(4) is so framed as to control not only introductions to creditors and owners extending such facilities under regulated agreements but also introductions to creditors and owners offering those facilities under certain classes of exempt agreement and certain types of unregulated agreement. For example, a person who, in the course of his business, regularly introduces to a building society individuals seeking mortgages is a credit-broker for the purpose of the Act even if all the agreements resulting from his introduction are exempt agreements and even if the business of the building society is confined to granting credit under exempt agreements or agreements outside the Act. [**998**]

Credit-brokers within the statutory definition cover not only the traditional type of loan and mortgage broker but a vast range of other credit intermediaries, including motor dealers and retail shops and stores who introduce retail customers to finance houses for hire-purchase, credit sale, conditional sale or rental facilities or personal loans; solicitors who regularly engage in negotiating advances for non-corporate clients; and estate agents who as part of their business introduce prospective house purchasers to building societies or other prospective mort-gagees. There are two qualifications. First, barristers, and solicitors engaging in contentious business, are not on that account to be treated as carrying on the business of credit brokerage or indeed any ancillary business (s. 146 (1), (2)). Secondly, s. 146 (5) provides that for the purposes of s. 145 (2), introductions effected by an individual by canvassing off trade premises either debtor-creditor-supplier agreements falling within s. 12 (*a*) or regulated consumer hire agreements shall be disregarded if—

(*a*) the introductions are not effected by him in the capacity of an employee, and

(*b*) he does not by any other method effect introductions falling within s. 145 (2).

Hence agents engaged by check traders to canvass trading check applications are not on that account credit-brokers, nor are housewives who as part-time agents for mail-order companies canvass applications from those wishing to acquire goods on credit sale from the companies concerned. [**999**]

347

Where an application for credit is transmitted through several brokers or intermediaries, it is thought that only the broker who negotiates with the creditor is a credit-broker in relation to the resulting transaction. Thus for licensing purposes the creditor need be concerned only with the broker with whom he is actually dealing in relation to the application, not with intermediaries earlier in the chain. [**1000**]

Debt-adjusting

Section 145 (5) provides as follows:

> "Subject to section 146 (6), debt-adjusting is, in relation to debts due under consumer credit agreements or consumer hire agreements—
>
> (*a*) negotiating with the creditor or owner, on behalf of the debtor or hirer, terms for the discharge of a debt, or
>
> (*b*) taking over, in return for payments by the debtor or hirer, his obligation to discharge a debt, or
>
> (*c*) any similar activity concerned with the liquidation of a debt."

Again, the scope of this definition is much wider than appears at first sight. It covers not only those whose main business is that of debt-adjustment but (subject to s. 146 (6)—see para. [**1008**]) solicitors and accountants who negotiate on behalf of clients in respect of debts owed by such clients to third parties, and banks who as part of their business provide overdrafts to customers in replacement of overdrafts previously outstanding from such customers to other banks. Moreover, the definition centres on activities in relation to consumer credit and consumer hire agreements, whether or not regulated. [**1001**]

It would seem to fall within the definition of debt-adjusting the activity in question must be aimed at some rearrangement (whether legally binding or otherwise) of the debt, e.g. by negotiating on behalf of the debtor for time to pay or by taking over responsibility for the debt and procuring reimbursement from the debtor. Thus a motor dealer who, when taking in part-exchange goods held on hire-purchase, obtains a settlement figure from the finance house owning the goods and discharges this out of the agreed part-exchange allowance, is not on that account a debt-adjuster. Debt-adjusting also appears at first sight to be confined to activity concerning the discharge of monetary obligations that have actually accrued due under the agreements in question, as opposed to action or advice on the discharge of future instalments. But it is unlikely that the phrase "debts due" is intended to bear this narrow meaning. A similar phrase in other statutes has been held to apply equally to debts that are contracted but payable in the future (see, for example, *Flint* v. *Barnard* (1888), 22 Q.B.D. 90; *Re Fastnedge, ex parte Kemp* (1874), 9 Ch. App. 383; and cf. *Irish Land Commission* v. *Massereene*, [1904] 2 I.R. 502). It is thought that s. 145 (5) is concerned not only with debts actually due but with sums payable in the future under an existing contract and also with sums *allegedly* due; for it is scarcely conceivable that the section would be held inapplicable to steps taken to adjust sums which for one reason or another are not legally recoverable from the supposed debtor. [**1002**]

As with credit brokerage, there are certain exemptions. A barrister engaged for clients in negotiating settlement of debts is not a debt-adjuster (s. 146 (1)); nor is a solicitor *insofar as he is thereby engaging in contentious business* (s. 146 (2)). This qualification largely stultifies the exemption given to solicitors. It means that solicitors whose negotiations on behalf of the debtors are successful in avoiding proceedings require to be licensed as debt-adjusters to conduct such negotiations, whereas solicitors conducting negotiations on behalf of the debtor in respect of debts which are or become the subject of an action are not thereby acting as debt-adjusters and do not require to be licensed! Fortunately, solicitors holding a practising certificate are covered by a group licence (see para. [344]). Further exemptions from the definition of debt-adjusting are contained in s. 146 (6) (see para. [1007]). [1003]

Debt-counselling

Subject to s. 146 (6) (see para. [1008]), debt-counselling is the giving of advice to debtors or hirers about the liquidation of debts due under consumer credit agreements or consumer hire agreements (s. 145 (6)). First this covers any debt-counsellor who regularly advises for reward, whether he be a full-time debt-counsellor, a solicitor (if advising in relation to non-contentious business), an accountant or a banker. Secondly, by virtue of the definition of "business" in s. 189 (1) of the Act, the term "debt-counsellor" includes those whose *profession* is the giving of advice of the kind above mentioned. It is immaterial that such advice is given without fee or other reward. Thus, Citizens' Advice Bureaux, Neighbourhood Law Centres and other free legal advice organisations are debt-counsellors within the Act even though giving advice without charge. But Citizens' Advice Bureaux are covered by a group licence (see para. [344]). [1004]

Debt-counselling like debt-adjusting, is not confined to advice on overdue debts (see para. [1002]). On the other hand, s. 145 (6) is plainly concerned with advice in relation to sums payable or supposedly payable under existing contracts, so that it would not, for example, be debt-counselling to give advice to those about to enter into a consumer credit or consumer hire agreement. [1005]

Debt-collectors

Subject to s. 146 (6) (see para. [1008]), debt-collecting is the taking of steps to procure payment of debts due under consumer credit agreements or consumer hire agreements (s. 145 (7)). Once more, this definition is not confined to the commercial debt-collection organisation but covers, for example, solicitors collecting debts for clients without recourse to proceedings and professional receivers and liquidators of companies (but not trustees in bankruptcy—see para. [1008]). However, a group licence is available for such persons (see paras. [344], [379]. Also within the term "debt-collector" are those who collect debts which they have purchased (see para. [1008]). As to the meaning of debts, see para. [1002]. [1006]

Exclusions

Section 146 (6) provides that it is not debt-adjusting, debt-counselling or debt-collecting for a person to do anything in relation to a debt arising under an agreement if—

    (a) he is the creditor or owner under the agreement, otherwise than by virtue of an assignment, or

(b) he is the creditor or owner under the agreement by virtue of an assignment
made in connection with the transfer to the assignee of any business other
than a debt-collecting business, or

(c) he is the supplier in relation to the agreement, or

(d) he is a credit-broker who has acquired the business of the person who was
the supplier in relation to the agreement, or

(e) he is a person prevented by sub-s. (4) from being treated as a credit-
broker, and the agreement was made in consequence of an introduction
(whether made by him or another person) which, under sub-s. (4), is to be
disregarded.

It should be observed that the exemption in favour of the creditor or owner is
confined to the original creditor or owner or one who becomes such by operation
of law (e.g. on death or bankruptcy of the original creditor or owner) as opposed to
assignment of the debt. Paragraph (c) of s. 146 (6) appears to be confined to cases
where the credit takes a loan form, so that creditor and supplier are different
people, for where they are the same the case is within para. (a). Para. (c) would thus
cover, for example, a dealer who sells goods for cash advanced by a finance house
and acts as agent for the finance house in collecting payment but would not cover
a dealer collecting instalments for a finance house under a hire-purchase agreement,
for though the dealer may have been the physical supplier of the goods the legal
supplier is the finance house. This restriction appears not to have been intended
(see F. A. R. Bennion, *Consumer credit control* §1240A). [**1007**]

Though it is arguable that an assignee of a debt, whilst excluded from the
exemption in s. 146 (6) (a), qualifies under s. 146 (6) (c) where the debt takes the
form of a price deferment (for under s. 189 (1) "supplier" includes an assignee), this
would seem to be a case where the definition of "supplier" is displaced by a contrary
intention, for it is unlikely that in excluding assignees from para. (a) Parliament
intended to allow them in by the back door under para. (c). See to the same effect
F. A. R. Bennion, *loc. cit.* Accordingly those who buy debts at a discount and in due
course proceed to collect in the debts thereby become debt-collectors. These
include not only commercial buyers of bad debts but also finance houses discounting
hire-purchase, instalment sale and rental agreements from dealers; factors who
factor debts outstanding from sole traders or partnerships; professional receivers
appointed by debenture holders (this would seem to be so even though they are as
a matter of law agents of the mortgagor company to whom the debts are owed);
and professional liquidators (since the property of a company in liquidation,
including debts owed to it, remains vested in the company and does not pass to the
liquidator so as to make him the creditor by operation of law). The licence required
by the professional liquidator as a debt-collector is, of course, quite distinct from
any licence required by the company of which he is appointed liquidator in respect
of the consumer credit or ancillary credit activities of that company. On the other
hand, the professional trustee in bankruptcy does not become a debt-collector
solely by reason of collecting in debts due to the bankrupt's estate, since he becomes
the creditor otherwise than by assignment, the property of the bankrupt vesting in
him automatically by operation of law under the provisions of s. 18 of the
Bankruptcy Act 1914. [**1008**]

Credit reference agencies

A credit reference agency is a person ("person" includes a company—see

Interpretation Act 1978, Sch. 1) carrying on a business comprising the furnishing of persons with information relevant to the financial standing of individuals, being information collected by the agency for that purpose (s. 145 (8)). [1009]

Already the definition of "credit reference agency" has caused more anxiety and discussion than almost any other definition in the Act. This is largely because although in general an organisation needing a licence for a consumer credit or consumer hire business loses little by obtaining additional licences for various ancillary credit businesses which it might at some stage wish to undertake (the fee involved is only £10 for each individual category), to hold the status of a credit reference agency involves a prospective duty to supply information on credit status which the organisation in question might well prefer to keep confidential. The definition of "credit reference agency" in s. 145 (8) is somewhat peculiar in that whilst s. 145 (1) lists a series of business activities, and s. 145 (1) (e) in its natural sense would denote the operation of a credit reference agency as a business activity, s. 145 (8) defines "credit reference agency" as a *person* carrying on the designated activity. This gives a somewhat odd meaning to the phrase "the operation of a credit reference agency" in s. 145 (1) (e). The drafting of s. 145 (8) would have been much more felicitous if the words "a person carrying on" had been omitted. As it stands, s. 145 (1) (e) does not readily interlock with s. 145 (8), and the combination of the two subsections produces a distinctly tautologous provision. [1010]
as it "comprises or relates to" a designated activity—so that an activity done in the course of a business which does not have as one of its objects the carrying on of that activity is nevertheless caught—s. 145 (8) deals with a person carrying on a business "comprising" the furnishing of persons with information relevant to the financial status of individuals, being information collected by the agency for that purpose. The use of the word "comprises", in contrast to "comprises or relates to" in s. 145 (1), suggests that the designated activity, if not itself the "business" referred to in the phrase "any business" in s. 145 (1), must in its own right have the characteristics of a business if it is to be covered by the provisions relating to a credit reference agency. In other words, those provisions are not attracted merely because information, etc., is regularly furnished in the course of some other business. It is necessary that the information-furnishing activity should itself constitute a business. This would appear to mean that the activity must be carried on as a business objective in itself and not solely in furtherance of the objectives of some other business. Accordingly, the regular exchange of credit status information among members of a group of companies does not constitute the business of a credit reference agency even if the information is collected, wholly or in part, for the purpose of such dissemination. It is interesting to note in this connection that the statement concerning groups of companies in the revised edition of the OFT's leaflet "Do you need a Licence?" is somewhat more cautious ("you may be regarded as a credit reference agency ...") than the original edition ("you will be regarded as a credit reference agency if ..."). On the other hand, if a company is set up within a group as a district trading entity with the specific business objective of collecting information for the purpose of disseminating it to other members of the group, it will usually be a credit reference agency, despite the fact that it does not furnish information to the outside world. [1011]

Certain other ingredients of the definition of credit reference agency should be noted.

(1) The information must be collected *for the purpose* of furnishing it to others. Thus the fact that a bank or other organisation, having collected information for its own purposes, furnishes it to others in response to a request, does not make it a credit reference agency.

(2) The business must comprise the furnishing of "persons" with information. This indicates at least some degree of plurality of intended recipients. So a bank which includes as part of its advertised services to its customers the taking up of bank references on the customers of other banks is not on that account a credit agency, for in collecting information from another bank it is doing so not for the purpose of furnishing it to "persons" but simply to pass it on to the particular customer who asked for it.

(3) The information must be relevant to the financial standing of "individuals" and must be information "collected" for the purpose of being furnished. This implies a degree of system in the *gathering* and *collation* of items of information covering a number of individuals, as opposed to a series of isolated acts of *obtaining* information covering a single individual. Hence a motor dealer whose customer wishes to obtain a car on hire-purchase from a finance house and who procures for submission to the finance house information relevant to that customer's financial standing is not "collecting" information but merely obtaining information; and the fact that he performs the same activity in relation to a number of customers does not alter the situation, for such information is not gathered together for the purpose of being furnished to persons but each item of information is obtained in isolation because of its possible relevance to a particular transaction with a particular finance house.

[**1012**]

Licensing of ancillary credit business

The provisions of Part III (except s. 40) apply to an ancillary credit business as they apply to a consumer credit business. The licensing system (fully described in chapter 11) is now fully operative as regards all categories of ancillary credit business, except that under the Consumer Credit Act 1974 (Commencement No. 4) Order 1977 there is deferment, to a day to be appointed, for a credit brokerage business conducted by an individual which is confined to introductions resulting in credit under debtor-creditor-supplier agreements not exceeding £30. In the case of hire-purchase and instalment sale transactions, the deferment applies only where the trader is willing to sell the goods for cash. There is no deferment for corporate credit brokers, nor for credit brokers whose business includes the introduction of customers desiring debtor-creditor credit or consumer hire facilities. [**1013**]

Certain categories of ancillary credit trader are covered by a group licence. Thus solicitors holding practising certificates enjoy the benefit of a group licence for all types of ancillary credit business except that of a credit reference agency; and citizens' advice bureaux are covered by a group licence for debt-adjusting and debt-counselling. [**1014**]

Agreement for services of unlicensed trader

An agreement for the services of a person carrying on an ancillary credit business (the "trader"), if made when the trader was unlicensed, is enforceable against the other party (the "customer") only where the Director has made an order under s. 148 (2) which applies to the agreement (s. 148 (1)). The trader or his successor in title may apply to the Director for an order that agreements within s. 148 (1) are to be treated as if made when the trader was licensed (s. 148 (2)). Before refusing an application in the terms in which it is made the Director must, under s. 148 (3), give the trader reasons for the intended refusal and invite representations in accordance with s. 34. See paras. [**387**] *et seq.*, as to the similar procedure in regard to applications by those carrying on a consumer credit or consumer hire business. Section 148 (4) provides that in determining whether or not to make an order under s. 148 (2) in respect of any period the Director shall consider, in addition to any other relevant factors—

    (*a*) how far, if at all, customers under agreements made by the trader during that period were prejudiced by the trader's conduct,

    (*b*) whether or not the Director would have been likely to grant a licence covering that period on an application by the trader, and

    (*c*) the degree of culpability for the failure to obtain a licence.

By s. 148 (5), if the Director thinks fit, he may in an order under s. 148 (2)—

    (*a*) limit the order to specified agreements, or agreements of a specified description or made at a specified time:

    (*b*) make the order conditional on the doing of specified acts by the trader.

[**1015**]

Section 148 (1) came into operation, as regards credit brokerage business, in relation to agreements made on or after 1st July 1978 (Consumer Credit Act 1974 (Commencement No. 4) Order 1977) and, as regards other ancillary credit businesses, in relation to agreements made on or after 3rd August 1976 (Consumer Credit Act 1974 (Commencement No. 2) Order 1977). An application for an Order under s. 148 (2) must be made in form CC6A/77 (General Notice No. 8). The fee is £10 (General Notice No. 1, item 19). [**1016**]

Regulated agreements made on introduction of unlicensed credit-broker

It behoves creditors to ensure that credit-brokers from whom they obtain business are duly licensed. Section 149 (1) and (2) provides as follows:

    "(1) A regulated agreement made by a debtor or hirer who, for the purpose of making that agreement, was introduced to the creditor or owner by an unlicensed credit-broker is enforceable against the debtor or hirer only where—

        (*a*) on the application of the credit-broker, the Director has made an order under section 148 (2) in respect of a period including the time when the introduction was made, and the order does not (whether in general terms or specifically) exclude the application of this paragraph to the regulated agreement, or

        (*b*) the Director has made an order under subsection (2) which applies to the agreement.

    (2) Where during any period individuals were introduced to a person carrying on a consumer credit business or consumer hire business by an unlicensed credit-broker for the purpose of making regulated agreements with the person carrying on that business, that person or his successor in title may apply to

353

the Director for an order that regulated agreements so made
are to be treated as if the credit-broker had been licensed at the
time of the introduction."

The procedure to be adopted where the Director is minded to refuse the application,
the factors he is to take into account and the limitations and conditions he may
impose in any order he makes, follow the language of s. 148 (3)–(5), with the
omission of s. 148 (4) (*b*). [**1017**]

Section 149 came into force as regards credit brokerage businesses on 1st July
1978 (Consumer Credit Act 1974 (Commencement No. 4) Order 1977). An
application for an Order under s. 149 (2) must be made in form CC7/75 (General
Notice No. 10). The fee is £10 (General Notice No. 1, item 19). [**1018**]

Appeals

A disappointed applicant is given a right to appeal to the Secretary of State,
and thence on a point of law to the High Court, pursuant to s. 41 as applied by
s. 150. See generally paras. [**406**] *et seq.* [**1019**]

Seeking business

Sections 151–154 broadly apply the provisions of Part IV (relating to
advertising, canvassing, quotations, the display of information and regulations for
the conduct of business) to the seeking of business by those engaged in the business
of credit brokerage, debt-adjusting and debt-cancelling. Section 154 makes it an
offence to canvass off trade premises (as defined by s. 153) the services of a person
carrying on a business of credit brokerage, debt-adjusting or debt-cancelling.
[**1020**]

Brokerage fees

Evidence was given to the Crowther Committee of serious abuses in the
charging of commission by brokers for supposedly undertaking to endeavour to
procure a loan, knowing that there was little or no prospect of their succeeding.
Perhaps the most remarkable case was the charging of a £20 survey fee to arrange
the survey of a council house tenanted by the debtor to see if this would be suitable
security for a second (!) mortgage! Section 155 tackles this problem by providing
that if within six months following the introduction of an individual to a
prospective creditor the introduction does not result in the individual's entry into
a relevant agreement (as defined by the section) the whole of the brokerage fee
except for the sum of £1 shall cease to be payable or, as the case may be, shall be
recoverable, by the individual. [**1021**]

Section 155 (1) became operative, as regards mortgage brokerage, on the
passing of the Act on 31st July 1974 and, as regards other brokerage activities, on
1st April 1977, the day appointed for regulated agreements, but appears to have
been widely ignored by credit-brokers. The Director-General of Fair Trading has
indicated that mortgage-brokers who persistently flout s. 155 may be refused
licences (see *The Times*, 20th April 1977). [**1022**]

Section 155 (4), which treats as a fee or commission any other item entering
into the total charge for credit, was technically in force on 31st July 1974, but
could not be applied until the making of regulations under s. 20 of the Act. These

regulations (the Consumer Credit (Total Charge for Credit) Regulations 1977) were made on 28th February 1977 and came into operation on 1st April 1977, but it would seem that s. 155 (4) takes effect from its commencement, and not from the time of coming into operation of the regulations under s. 120, and can thus be invoked by the debtor even in relation to a brokerage contract made before 1st April 1977. [**1023**]

Entry into agreements

Regulations may make provision, in relation to agreements entered into in the course of a business of credit brokerage, debt-adjusting or debt-counselling, corresponding, with such modifications as the Secretary of State thinks fit, to the provision which is or may be made by or under s. 55, 60, 61, 62, 63, 65, 127, 179 or 180 in relation to agreements to which those sections apply (s. 156). [**1024**]

Credit records

The Crowther Committee devoted much attention to problems arising in connection with credit records, and in particular the difficulties facing a consumer who did not know why he was being refused credit facilities and against whom adverse information might have been filed that was in some way erroneous or indeed should have been filed not against him at all but against some other person with whom he had been confused (see Crowther Report, paras. 9.1.9–9.1.28). Further study of these problems was made by the Younger Committee on Privacy, which recommended (*inter alia*) that an individual should have a legally enforceable right of access to information held about him by a credit reference agency (see *Report of the Committee on Privacy* (Cmnd. 5012, July 1972), Chapter 9, and in particular paragraph 275). [**1025**]

The recommendation of the Younger Committee has been adopted in strengthened form by the Consumer Credit Act, which confers on an individual the following rights:

(i) The right to obtain from a creditor, owner or negotiator (and from a prospective creditor or owner) the name and address of any credit reference agency from whom the former has, during antecedent negotiations, applied for information about the individual's credit standing (s. 157 (1)—see paras. [**1027**], [**1028**].

(ii) The right to obtain from the credit reference agency a copy of the file relating to him, on tender of prescribed particulars and a fee of 25p (s. 158 (1)—see paras. [**1029**] *et seq*.).

(iii) The right to require erroneous information on the file to be removed or amended (s. 159—see paras. [**1031**] *et seq*.).

In addition, regulations under s. 26 of the Act (as applied by s. 147 (1)) may include provisions regulating the collecting and dissemination of information by credit reference agencies (s. 147 (2)). [**1026**]

Disclosure of name and address of agency

Section 157 provides as follows:

"(1) A creditor, owner or negotiator, within the prescribed period after receiving a request in writing to that effect from the debtor or hirer, shall give him notice of the name and address of any credit reference agency from which the creditor, owner or negotiator has, during the antecedent negotiations, applied for information about his financial standing.

(2) Subsection (1) does not apply to a request received more than 28 days after the termination of the antecedent negotiations, whether on the making of the regulated agreement or otherwise.

(3) If the creditor, owner or negotiator fails to comply with subsection (1) he commits an offence."

"Creditor" and "owner" include a prospective creditor and a prospective owner, and "debtor or hirer" includes a prospective debtor or hirer (s. 189 (1)). The prescribed period is 7 days (Consumer Credit (Credit Reference Agency) Regulations 1977, reg. 3 (a)). Section 157 (1) applies as regards requests made on or after 16th May 1977 (Consumer Credit Act 1974) (Commencement No. 2) Order 1977. [**1027**]

To ensure that the credit-broker who conducted negotiations has the information which will enable him to supply the necessary details to the debtor or hirer, so far as not already supplied by the creditor or owner himself, the Consumer Credit (Conduct of Business) (Credit References) Regulations 1977 provide that not later than he informs a credit-broker that he is not willing to make a regulated agreement, a creditor or owner shall, unless he informs the debtor or hirer directly that he is not willing to make the agreement, inform the credit-broker of the name and address of any agency from which he has during the negotiations relating to the proposed agreement applied for information about the financial standing of the debtor or hirer (reg. 2). Rather curiously, the regulations do not impose on a credit-broker who consults a credit reference agency a similar obligation to inform the creditor of the name and address of the agency so consulted. A credit-broker who is a negotiator must, at the same time as he gives notice of any agency which he himself consulted, give the debtor or hirer notice of the name and address of any agency of which he has been informed by the creditor or owner under reg. 2 (reg. 3), but by s. 157 (2) of the Act this obligation does not apply to a request received more than 28 days after the termination of the antecedent negotiations. Regulation 4 of the above regulations imposes the same duties on a credit-broker who is not the negotiator as regards requests made by the debtor or hirer within 28 days after the termination of negotiations. [**1028**]

Supply of copy of file

Subject to s. 160 (see para. [**1030**]) a credit reference agency, within the prescribed period after receiving a request in writing to that effect from any individual (the "consumer") and such particulars as the agency may reasonably require to enable them to identify the file, and a fee of 25p, must give the consumer a copy of the file relating to him kept by the agency (s. 158 (1)). Section 158 is operative as regards requests for information received on and after the 16th May 1977 (see Consumer Credit Act 1974 (Commencement No. 2) Order 1977, and ss. 159 and 160 are triggered off accordingly. The prescribed period is 7 working days (Consumer Credit (Credit Reference Agency) Regulation 1977, reg. 3). By "file" is meant, in relation to an individual, all the information about him kept by a credit reference agency, regardless of how the information is stored, and "copy of the file", as respects information not in plain English, means a transcript reduced into plain English (s. 158 (5)). This latter provision is designed to cover, for example, information which is in coded form or which consists of expressions or abbreviations familiar to those in the trade but not readily comprehensible by others. When giving a copy of the file, the agency must also give the consumer a statement in the prescribed form of his rights under s. 159 (s. 158 (2)), relating to the correction of wrong information (see para. [1031]). The form is that prescribed by Schedule 1 to the above regulations. If the agency does not keep a file relating to the consumer it must give him notice of that fact, but need not return any money paid (s. 158 (3)). If the agency contravenes any provision of s. 158 it commits an offence (s. 158 (4)). [1029]

Alternative procedure for business consumers

The above provisions, if left in unqualified form, might seriously have hampered the ability of a credit reference agency to provide an effective service to his subscribers concerning business consumers, *i.e.* debtors or hirers who were sole traders or partnerships. The particular difficulty envisaged by the trade was that since supply of a copy of the complete file would almost inevitably reveal the agency's sources of information, those sources, having given the information in confidence, might decline to provide such information in the future. To deal with this situation the Director is empowered, upon an application by a credit reference agency, to direct that s. 160 of the act shall apply to that agency (s. 160 (1)). The Director may only accede to such an application if he is satisfied—

(a) that compliance with s. 158 in the case of consumers who carry on a business would adversely affect the service provided to its customers by the agency, and

(b) that having regard to the methods employed by the agency and to any other relevant factors, it is probable that consumers carrying on a business would not be prejudiced by the making of the direction.

The application must be made in form CC301/75 (see General Notice No. 3) and must be accompanied by the fee of £25 (General Notice No. 1, item 23). Upon granting the application the Director will state in his direction what information is to be given by the credit reference agency to business consumers as an alternative to supplying a copy of the file. If thereafter the agency receives a request from a business consumer under s. 158 (1), then instead of supplying a copy of the file under that section it may, under s. 160 (3), elect to deal with the matter by giving notice to the consumer of intention to proceed under s. 160. This notice must be given within 7 working days of receipt of the consumer's request (Consumer Credit (Credit Reference Agency) Regulations 1977, reg. 3 (a)). Within the same period (though not necessarily at the same time as giving the above notice) the agency must give the consumer such information included in or based on entries in the file as is required by the direction, together with a statement of the consumer's rights under ss. 159 and 160 of the Act (see para. [1031]) in the form prescribed by the 2nd Schedule to the above regulations. Failure to comply with any of these requirements is an offence (s. 160 (6)). If the consumer is dissatisfied with the information supplied under s. 160 (3) and within 28 days of receiving it, or such longer period as the Director may allow, gives notice to the Director accordingly, satisfies the Director that he has taken reasonable steps to remove the cause of his dissatisfaction and pays the specified fee, the Director may then direct the agency to supply a copy of the file (s. 160 (4)), and may himself disclose to the consumer such of the information on the file as he thinks fit (*ibid.*). The notice by the consumer to the Director need not be in any particular form, and there is at present no fee (see General Notice No. 1, item 25). [**1030**]

Removal or correction of wrong information

Section 159, reinforced by the Consumer Credit (Credit Reference Agency) Regulations 1977, contains elaborate provisions by which the consumer can require incorrect information on the file to be removed or amended and satisfy himself that the necessary corrective action has in fact been taken by the credit reference agency. The procedure is the same for business consumers as for private consumers. However, the business consumer, having not been supplied with a copy of the file but only with information required by the Director's direction under s. 160, may be unable to judge the accuracy of that information without further data that may have been withheld under the Director's dispensation. In such case, he should within 28 days of receipt of the information invoke the procedure laid down by s. 160 (4) (see para. [**1030**]). [**1031**]

Under s. 159 (1) a consumer given information under s. 158 who considers that an entry in his file is incorrect, and that if it is not corrected he is likely to be prejudiced, may give notice to the agency requiring it either to remove the entry from the file or to amend it. Within 28 days after receiving such notice the agency must by notice inform the customer that it has removed the entry from the file or amended the entry or taken no action, and if the notice states that the entry has been amended it must include a copy of the file so far as it comprises the amended entry (s. 159 (2)). Where the notice states that the entry has been removed, then (assuming that this is a truthful statement) that is an end to the matter. But in any other case—that is, where the notice indicates that the entry has merely been amended or that no action has been taken, or where the consumer does not receive the notice within 28 days after expiry of the time for its dispatch—the consumer may by notice require the agency to add to the file an accompanying notice of correction not exceeding 200 words, and to include a copy of the notice of correction when furnishing information included in or based on that entry (s. 159 (3)). All these notices must be in writing (see the definition of "notice" in s. 189 (1) of the Act. The agency then has 28 days within which to send the consumer notice that it has received the consumer's notice of correction and intends to comply with it (s. 159 (4)). If the consumer does not receive this further notice within 28 days or it appears to the agency that it would be improper for it to publish a notice of correction because it is incorrect or unjustly defames any person or is frivolous or scandalous, the consumer or the agency, as the case may be, may in the prescribed manner and on payment of the specified fee apply to the Director who may make such order on the application as he thinks fit (s. 159 (5)). Failure to comply with the order within the period specified in it is an offence (s. 159 (6)). By reg. 4 (2) of the above regulations the consumer's application must state the name and address of the agency and of the consumer and must give an indication of when the notice of correction under s. 159 (3) was given by the consumer to the agency. If the application is by a consumer it must in addition give particulars of the entry in the file or of the information received by him and must state why he considers the entry or information to be incorrect and why, if it is not corrected, he considers that he is likely to be prejudiced (reg. 4 (3)). These requirements are, somewhat unnecessarily, reiterated in General Notice No. 11, which adds that the consumer's application must be in writing. If the application is by an agency it must, under reg. 4 (4) be accompanied by—

    (*a*) a copy of the file given by the agency to the consumer or, as the case may be, of the information included in or based on entries in the file given under s. 160 (3) of the Act by the agency to a consumer who carries on a business;

    (*b*) a copy of the notice of correction; and

    (*c*) a copy of related correspondence and other documents which have passed between the agency and the consumer;

and must state the grounds upon which it appears to the agency that it would be improper for it to publish the notice of correction. The application must be made in form CC 314/77 (General Notice No. 12), and should be accompanied by supporting information in form CC 315/77, but this latter form is not prescribed by General Notice, so that an inaccuracy in the information supplied does not vitiate the application under s. 6 (1) of the Act. There is no prescribed form for an application by a consumer; it suffices that the application contains the information prescribed by the regulations as set out above. No fee is at present payable on an application under s. 159 (5), whether it be made by the consumer or by the agency (see General Notice No. 1, item 24). [1032]

Information to third parties about correction of entries

Within 10 working days after (*a*) notice by the agency under s. 159 (2) of the Act that it has removed an entry or (*b*) notice by the agency under s. 159 (4) that it has received a notice of correction under that subsection and intends to comply with it, or (*c*) the expiration of the period specified in an order of the Director under s. 159 (5) of the Act as that within which it is to be complied with, the agency must, under reg. 5 (1) of the Consumer Credit (Conduct of Business) (Credit References) Regulations 1977 supply particulars detailed by reg. 5 (2) to each person to whom at any time since the date 6 months immediately preceding the receipt by it of the request, particulars and fee referred in s. 158 (1) of the Act, it furnished information relevant to the financial standing of the consumer concerned. [1033]

Defamation and qualified privilege

If a credit reference agency publishes (i.e. communicates to a third party) a defamatory statement concerning a consumer which is untrue, then if the statement is in writing the consumer may (subject to certain defences) sue for damages for libel, even if he has suffered no special damage; and if the statement is oral, the consumer may (subject to the same defences) sue for damages for slander on showing that he has suffered special damage or that the imputation is made against him in the way of his business or office or conveys that he has committed a criminal offence or suffers from an existing contagious or infectious disease or, in the case of a woman, that she is unchaste. [1034]

Among the various defences to an action for defamation are justification and qualified privilege. Justification is a plea that the defamatory statement complained of is true; and if this be the case, it is a complete defence to a civil claim for libel, though not to a prosecution for criminal libel. Even if the defamatory

statement is untrue, the defendant may be able to defeat the plaintiff's claim by
establishing that the statement was made on an occasion of qualified privilege.
The principal classes of statement attracting qualified privilege, apart from reports
of Parliamentary, judicial and certain other public proceedings and professional
communications between solicitor and client, are (i) statements made by the
defendant under a legal, moral or social duty to communicate them and so made to
a person having a corresponding interest or duty to receive the statements; and (ii)
statements made by the defendant in the protection of some lawful interest and
made to a third party who has a corresponding legal, moral or social duty to
protect that interest. But in both cases, the privilege is qualified only, and
accordingly subsists only so far as the defamatory statement is made honestly and
without "malice" (i.e. improper motivation) and the publication of it is no wider
than is reasonable for the fulfilment of the duty or the protection of the interest in
question. [**1035**]

Whether trade protection societies and other credit reference agencies are
entitled to plead qualified privilege in answer to a claim based on their publication
to third parties of defamatory statements concerning individuals on their files has
never been finally settled. In *Macintosh* v. *Dun*, [1908] A.C. 390, the Judicial
Committee of the Privy Council held that the privilege was not available to a trade
protection society which carried on business as such for profit, whether its income
was derived from subscriptions or from charges made on the occasion of each
supply of information. The distinction drawn in this case between protection
societies who (while making charges to cover their expenses) do not conduct
business for profit and provide information as a service to their subscribers and
protection societies operating as commercial concerns selling information to any
who wish to buy it derived support from dicta in judgments of the House of Lords
in *London Association for Protection of Trade* v. *Greenlands, Ltd.*, [1916] 2 A.C. 15.
Nevertheless, *Macintosh* v. *Dun* (which is of persuasive authority only in an English
court) almost certainly overstated the case if it decided that the profit motive
inevitably and in all circumstances negates the existence of a social or legal duty
to communicate. Plainly a duty of communication imposed by statute must be
observed; and even at common law, the communication made by the defendant
may be made pursuant to a duty to do so, despite the fact that he carries on the
business of disseminating information for profit. See *Watt* v. *Longsdon*, [1930] 1
K.B. 130, *per* Scrutton, L.J., at p. 148. We take up this matter further in paragraph
[**1039**]. [**1036**]

The Younger Report (para. 275), in recommending that a person refused credit
on the basis of an agency report should be entitled to have details of the filed
information and its sources, went on to say:

> " 'A pre-requisite of these arrangements would be the extension
> of qualified privilege to profit-seeking, commercial credit
> bureaux. A convenient moment for providing this protection
> would arise when the Faulks Committee on the law of
> defamation reports.' " [**1037**]

The Consumer Credit Act, though implementing that part of the Younger
Committee's recommendations calling for disclosure of the filed information to the
consumer, contains no provision extending qualified privilege to publications of
credit reference agencies run for profit. The first version of the Consumer Credit
Bill had in fact provided for qualified privilege to apply to the publication of any

defamatory matter relating to the financial standing of an individual where published to a licensed credit reference agency for the purposes of its business or published by such an agency in the course of its business. But as a result of opposition in Committee, this provision was dropped. It is thus clear that the absence of any provision in the Consumer Credit Act extending qualified privilege to defamatory statements published by organisations conducted for profit is a deliberate policy decision, not merely a postponement of consideration of the matter pending the report of the Faulks Committee. [**1038**]

What, then, is now the position of a credit reference agency controlled by the Consumer Credit Act? No difficulty arises concerning supply to the Director of a copy of the file in accordance with a direction made under s. 160 (4). This is mandatory, and manifestly attracts qualified privilege, even if the agency business be conducted for profit. It is equally clear that despatch to the consumer of information on his file containing statements defamatory of a third party does not attract qualified privilege by reason of any duty imposed by the Consumer Credit Act, since the duty is to supply a copy of "the file" and by s. 158 (5) this means, in relation to the individual who asks for it, all the information *about him*, but does not extend to information concerning others. But what are the rights of the consumer as regards defamatory statements made *about him* by or to a creditor reference agency run for profit? No duty is imposed *by the Act* to supply such information. It is, however, submitted that despite *Macintosh* v. *Dun* such a communication, if made to a prospective credit grantor or other person having a legitimate interest in receiving it, is to be considered made on a privileged occasion. Time and again, the courts have rightly criticised a creditor for failing to make proper enquiries concerning the financial position of the debtor before giving him credit. The failure to pursue such enquiries not only makes the creditor the author of his own misfortune but produces highly undesirable social consequences through the extension of credit to whose who are not creditworthy and lack either the ability or the will to repay what they borrow. The public interest therefore requires that information held by reputable agencies concerning the financial standing of prospective debtors should be readily available to prospective creditors. Equally, it is in the public interest that such agencies shall be able to perform their function by collecting necessary information from reputable sources without thereby rendering the providers of such information liable in damages for defamatory statements honestly made. The reputability of credit reference agencies engaged in the consumer credit sector will be secured by the licensing provisions of the Consumer Credit Act, as applied by s. 147, which also empowers regulations made under s. 26 of the Act to regulate the collection and dissemination of information by credit reference agencies. It is therefore submitted that information honestly and without malice published by a licensed credit reference agency to a prospective creditor or prospective owner, or to a negotiator, or published to a licensed credit reference agency by a reputable source, attracts qualified privilege even if the agency business is conducted for profit. [**1039**]

32. Agreements with a Foreign Element

Where a credit agreement is concluded involving some foreign element—as where the creditor carries on business in England and the debtor is overseas or where the credit is to be provided in England but both parties are resident abroad—then in any proceedings brought in this country based on the agreement two questions are likely to arise:

    (1) Does the court have jurisdiction to entertain the claim?

    (2) If so, what law governs the agreement and the rights of the parties to it? And in particular, is the agreement controlled by the Consumer Credit Act and regulations made thereunder? [**1040**]

Jurisdiction

At present, the court will assume jurisdiction if the defendant is served while within the jurisdiction (i.e. England, Wales and Berwick on Tweed), even if he does not ordinarily reside there or if he submits to the jurisdiction (either by express agreement or by entering an unconditional appearance to the writ or summons) or if the originating process is served on the defendant outside the jurisdiction pursuant to leave granted under RSC Order 11 or CCR Order 8. These rules will be radically changed when the United Kingdom becomes a party to the European Convention of 27th September 1968 on Jurisdiction and the Enforcement of Judgments in Civil and Commercial Matters. The Convention provides special rules as to jurisdiction in matters relating to instalment sales and loans, the general principle being that the creditor may be sued either in his own State or in that of the debtor, whilst the debtor may be sued only in his own State, contracting out being permitted only in specified conditions (see arts. 13–15). [**1041**]

An agreement to submit to the jurisdiction of a foreign court in a case where the contract is governed by the Unfair Contract Terms Act 1977 is brought within the purview of the Act by s. 13 (1) (a). *Aliter* an agreement to submit to foreign arbitration (see s. 13 (2)). [**1042**]

Choice of law

The fact that a court in England has jurisdiction to entertain the claim does not, of course, mean that it will necessarily apply English law. The applicable law is governed by English conflict of laws rules. In general, the rights of the parties under a contract are governed by the proper law of the contract, that is, the law which the parties must be taken to have intended to apply to it (*Vita Food Products Inc.* v. *Unus Shipping Co., Ltd.,* [1939] A.C. 277, [1939] 1 All E.R. 513). If the contract designates the law which is to control it, that law will be the proper law. If the contract is silent and the intention of the parties cannot be gleaned from the language and style of the document, the proper law will be that of the State having the closest connection with the contract. For this purpose, various factors are taken into account, including the place where the contract was made and the place of intended performance. [**1043**]

In general, the parties are free to select whatever law they choose to govern their rights and duties under the contract, and it is not necessary that the State whose law is selected shall have any connection with the contract (*Vita Food Products Inc.* v. *Unus Shipping Co., Ltd., supra*). There are, however, certain limitations on the efficacy of a choice of law clause. In the first place, it may be displaced by a mandatory choice of law clause in a statute applicable to the transaction. Secondly, the contract may be as a matter of construction of a statute be held to be within its scope, despite the foreign element involved, and in that event it is the duty of the court to give effect to the statute notwithstanding that the proper law of the contract is not English. Thirdly, the court will not give effect to the proper law of the contract (whether expressly chosen by the parties or otherwise) if this would produce a result contrary to the public policy of English law. Finally, the court will ignore a choice of law clause if satisfied that the choice was not made *bona fide* but was intended to evade the mandatory requirements of the law of a foreign state with which the contract has the closest connection. [**1044**]

Conversely, the fact that the proper law of the contract is English does not necessarily mean that it is governed by the English statute under consideration, for the statute may as a matter of construction be held not to apply to transactions possessing the particular foreign element involved. For an Australian decision to this effect in relation to a hire-purchase agreement, see *Kay's Leasing Corporation Pty., Ltd.* v. *Fletcher* (1964), 116 C.L.R. 124. [**1045**]

The Consumer Credit Act

In view of the strong consumer protection policy underlying the Consumer Credit Act, it would seem that in principle any of its provisions relating to the performance of an act or the execution of a document will apply where the act is performed or the document executed in England, notwithstanding any foreign element involved. Thus in principle, formalities of contract and rights of withdrawal and cancellation apply to a consumer credit agreement signed by the debtor in England; and restrictions on repossession of goods and enforcement of securities operate to prevent a repossession or enforcement in breach of the Act of goods or securities situated in England at the time when recovery or enforcement is sought. Indeed, the court is likely to apply the Act to any agreement made in England by a debtor residing or carrying on business in England so far as the agreement relates to the provision of credit in England and is otherwise within the ambit of the statute. See, for example, *English* v. *Donnelly*, 1958 S.C. 494, and R. M. Goode, *op. cit.,* pp. 994 995. This view derives support from s. 16 (5) of the

Act, which empowers the Secretary of State to exempt from the Act agreements having a connection with a country outside the United Kingdom; for *exclusio unius inclusio alterius*. [**1046**]

Where the credit agreement is governed by the Consumer Credit Act the law applicable to a connected supply transaction would appear to be irrelevant. Thus a bank issuing a credit card under an agreement providing for payment by instalments is liable under s. 75 for misrepresentation or breach of contract by the supplier even if the supply transaction was foreign e.g. a stay in an hotel in France. See para [**686**]. [**1047**]

Pursuant to s. 16 (5), certain agreements involving a foreign element have been made exempt agreements (Consumer Credit (Exempt Agreements) Order 1977, art. 3 (1) (*d*)), with the result that they are largely uncontrolled by the Consumer Credit Act, though they remain governed by the provisions relating to extortionate credit bargains (ss. 137–140). [**1048**]

Article 3 (1) (*d*) exempts—

> "any agreement made in connection with trade in goods or services between the United Kingdom and a country outside the United Kingdom or within a country or between countries outside the United Kingdom, being an agreement under which credit is provided to the debtor in the course of a business carried on by him."

This exemption is limited to business debtors. Given that the credit is being extended to the debtor in the course of a business carried on by him the agreement will be exempt if made in connection with trade in goods or services which does not take place exclusively within the United Kingdom. This exemption would thus cover an agreement by which:

   (i) a British exporter sells goods on credit from the United Kingdom to a foreign buyer;

  (ii) a British company having a factory in France sells goods on credit from that factory to a French or German buyer;

 (iii) a British bank advances money to a partnership firm carrying on business in the United Kingdom to finance the import of goods from abroad;

 (iv) a British bank advances money to a partnership firm carrying on business in the United Kingdom against payments to be received by the firm from overseas customers to whom the firm has supplied goods or services.

It does not follow that an agreement with a foreign element is caught by the Act outside the categories of exemption provided by the Act or the Order, for the creditor may be able to show that under English conflict of laws rules (*vide supra*) the contract is not governed by English law at all. Even where the agreement is an exempt agreement within the above Order it may be advantageous to establish that English law does not apply, for as indicated above an exempt agreement is not totally excluded from the operation of the Act but remains subject to the provisions relating to extortionate credit bargains. [**1049**]

The Unfair Contract Terms Act

The importance of this Act in relation to credit agreements has already been mentioned (paras. [**665**] *et seq.*). The Act does not apply to international transactions for the supply of goods (s. 26), nor to contracts which would be governed by foreign law but for a contract term adopting the law of some part of the United Kingdom (s. 27 (1)). On the other hand, the Act applies notwithstanding any contract term applying foreign law where—

(a) the term appears to the court or arbitrator to have been imposed wholly or mainly for the purpose of enabling the party imposing it to evade the operation of the Act; or

(b) in the making of the contract one of the parties dealt as consumer (see s. 12) and he was then habitually resident in the United Kingdom, and the essential steps necessary for the making of the contract were taken there, whether by him or by others on his behalf (s. 27 (2)).

The phrase "essential steps necessary for the making of the contract" is not, perhaps, the happiest, but would appear to mean that both offer and acceptance must have occurred within the United Kingdom. [**1050**]

The application of s. 27 (2) of the Unfair Contract Terms Act does not, of course, mean that the whole contract is governed by English law, merely that the Act will apply to the contract even if it is in other respects controlled by foreign law as the result of an effective choice of law clause. It would seem that s. 27 (2) applies only where the contract is one which would have been governed by English law but for a foreign choice of law clause. [**1051**]

33. Offences and Enforcement

Offences

The Act creates thirty-five offences. These, with mode of prosecution and penalty, are tabulated in the Second Schedule to the Act. They include not only offences referred to in the preceding chapters but infringement of regulations (s. 167 (2)), impersonation and obstruction of enforcement authority officers, and supply of false information to such officers, in contravention of the provisions of Part XI discussed in the present chapter. The Act also makes it an offence (in s. 7) to supply false information to the Director. The duty of enforcement and the power to prosecute for offences are conferred on the Director and on local weights and measures authorities (see paras. [**1059**] *et seq.*). [**1052**]

Defences

Section 168 provides as follows:

> "(1) In any proceedings for an offence under this Act it is a defence for the person charged to prove—
>> (a) that his act or omission was due to a mistake, or to reliance on information supplied to him, or to an act or omission by another person, or to an accident or some other cause beyond his control, and
>> (b) that he took all reasonable precautions and exercised all due diligence to avoid such an act or omission by himself or any person under his control.
>
> (2) If in any case the defence provided by subsection (1) involves the allegation that the act or omission was due to an act or omission by another person or to reliance on information supplied by another person, the person charged shall not, without leave of court, be entitled to rely on that defence unless, within a period ending seven clear days before the hearing, he has served on the prosecutor a notice giving such information identifying or assisting in the identification of that other person as was then in his possession."

This section reproduces almost verbatim s. 24 of the Trade Descriptions Act 1968, though the first line of s. 168 (1) (*a*) refers to "his act or omission" rather than "the commission of the offence" in order to avoid the paradox of predicating an offence when, by reason of the defence given, there is no offender. The controversial decision of the House of Lords in *Tesco Supermarkets, Ltd.* v. *Nattrass*, [1972] A.C. 153; [1971] 2 All E.R. 127, establishes that a company charged with an offence may be able to treat even one of its own employees as "another person" within s. 168 (1) (*a*) where the employee is not a director or other person of such seniority or responsibility as to represent the controlling mind and will of the company but is merely a junior executive or employee (whether or not exercising supervisory functions) who is the instrument for executing company policy as dictated by his superiors. Hence if a company institutes an effective system to avoid the commission of an offence, delegating to competent employees the duty to see that the system is scrupulously adhered to by junior staff, an infringing act or omission committed by a junior member of the staff does not defeat a defence under s. 168 (1) even if resulting from failure of the superior employee to exercise proper supervision. The company is entitled to contend that such employee, as well as the junior he was supposed to supervise, is "another person" within s. 168 (1) (*a*) and that accordingly it is not the company that has failed to exercise due diligence within s. 168 (1) (*b*). Similar principles apply to any large-scale organisation, even if not in corporate form. [**1053**]

By "mistake" in s. 168 (1) (*a*) is meant the mistake of the person charged, not of some other person (*Birkenhead and District Co-operative Society, Ltd.* v. *Roberts*, [1970] 3 All E.R. 391; [1970] 1 W.L.R. 1497). Hence if the act or omission which is the subject of the prosecution is alleged to be due to the default of a third party, the defendant cannot avoid the requirements of s. 168 (2) by relying on that default as a "mistake" of the third party attracting a distinct head of defence. The combined effect of this decision and that of the House of Lords in *Tesco Supermarkets, Ltd.* v. *Nattrass, supra*, is that a company prosecuted for the mistaken act or omission of an executive or employee who does not represent the controlling mind and will of the company, and is thus "another person" within s. 168 (1) (*a*), cannot plead that act or omission as a "mistake" within s. 168 (1) (*a*) but must rely fairly and squarely on the defence of "act or default of another person" and for that purpose comply with the requirements of s. 168 (2) (*Butler* v. *Keenway Supermarkets, Ltd.*, [1974] Crim. L.R. 560). [**1054**]

The purpose of s. 168 (2) is to enable the prosecution to test the validity of the defence of "act or default of another person" by calling that other person as a witness. The subsection has the incidental effect that if the act or omission of such person resulting in the act or omission of the defendant is itself an offence under the Act, that other person can be identified and prosecuted for that offence. It should, however, be noted that s. 23 of the Trade Descriptions Act 1968 (which provides that where the commission by any person of an offence under the Act is due to the act of default of another, that other shall be guilty of an offence) has no counterpart in the Consumer Credit Act. Accordingly the mere fact that the act or omission of A causes B to omit an act required by the statutory provisions or to perform an act prohibited by such provisions, does not of itself make A guilty of an offence. It must be shown that A himself contravened a specific provision of the Consumer Credit Act, either as a principal or as an accomplice under criminal law through aiding and abetting or counselling and procuring the offence or as one who consents to or connives at the offence within s. 169 (see para. [**1056**]). [**1055**]

Offences by body corporate

Section 169 of the Act provides that where at any time a body corporate commits an offence under the Act with the consent or connivance of, or because of neglect by, any individual, the individual commits the like offence if at that time—

    (a) he is a director, manager, secretary or similar officer of the body corporate, or

    (b) he is purporting to act as such an officer, or

    (c) the body corporate is managed by its members, of whom he is one.

This provision is the counterpart of s. 20 (1) of the Trade Descriptions act 1968. By "manager" is meant one who manages the affairs of the company, not, for example, the manager of a particular shop or store in a chain of shops or stores owned by the company. See the decision of the Divisional Court in *Tesco Supermarkets, Ltd.* v. *Nattrass*, [1971] 1 Q.B. 133; [1970] 3 All E.R. 357, which on this point was not challenged in the House of Lords. [**1056**]

No further sanctions for breach of Act

A breach of any requirement made (otherwise than by any court) by or under the Act incurs no civil or criminal sanction as being such a breach, except to the extent (if any) expressly provided by or under the Act (s. 170 (1)). This provision does not prevent the grant of an injunction, or the making of an order of certiorari, mandamus or prohibition (s. 170 (3)). [**1057**]

Notification of convictions to Director

The original version of the Consumer Credit Bill conferred on the Court power to endorse the licence of a person convicted by that Court of an offence under the Act. This provision was subsequently dropped. Section 166 merely provides that where a person is convicted of an offence or has a judgment given against him by or before any court in the United Kingdom and it appears to the court—

    (a) having regard to the functions of the Director under this Act, that the conviction or judgment should be brought to the Director's attention, and

    (b) that it may not be brought to his attention unless arrangements for that purpose are made by the court,

the court may make such arrangements notwithstanding that the proceedings have been finally disposed of. [**1058**]

Enforcement of Act

A specific duty to enforce the Act is imposed on "the enforcement authorities", i.e. the Director and local weights and measures authorities (s. 161 (1)). Consequent on the re-organisation of local government effected by the Local Government Act 1972, the number of local weights and measures authorities (as defined by s. 201 (2) and (3) of that Act) has been reduced to about 100 and the area of each such authority has in consequence been greatly increased. [**1059**]

Whereas under the Weights and Measures Act 1963, a local weights and measures authority must appoint weights and measures inspectors to perform the

functions of the authority in its area, no such requirement applies to functions of local weights and measures authorities under the Trade Descriptions Act or the Consumer Credit Act. Hence whilst in most cases such authorities will no doubt delegate the task of enforcement of the Consumer Credit Act to weights and measures inspectors, as they have done in relation to their functions under the Trade Descriptions Act, they are not obliged to do so, and may empower any officer of the authority to enforce the provisions of the Consumer Credit Act.
[**1060**]

It has been a common practice for local weights and measures authorities to combine or make joint arrangements in exercising their functions under the Weights and Measures Act 1963 and the Trade Descriptions Act 1968, in reliance on powers previously contained in s. 37 of the Weights and Measures Act. The powers conferred by s. 37 have now been brought to an end by s. 201 (5) of the Local Government Act 1972, but that Act empowers any local authority (including, of course, a local authority which is a weights and measures authority) to arrange for the discharge of any of its functions by another local authority (s. 101 (1) (*b*)), and for two or more authorities to discharge any of their functions jointly (s. 101 (5)) and for that purpose to appoint joint committees (s. 102 (1)). Hence local weights and measures authorities continue to have ample powers to act in concert in the performance of their functions, including those imposed upon them by the Consumer Credit Act. [**1061**]

Local enforcement

In general, prosecutions by a local enforcement authority will be confined to contraventions arising within the area of the authority, though an authority is technically not debarred from launching a prosecution in respect of an offence committed in the area of another authority. Offences of a purely local character will usually be left by the Director to the initiative of local enforcement authorities, whilst his own staff will deal mainly with more widespread contraventions—*e.g.* advertising infringements in national newspapers— and with cases (whether local or otherwise) which in his opinion raise important questions of general policy. To ensure that the Director is kept in the picture as to local enforcement, and to avoid a multiplicity of prosecutions by different authorities arising from the same act of infringement committed in different areas, s. 161 (2) of the Consumer Credit Act (borrowing from s. 130 (1) of the Fair Trading Act 1973, which replaced s. 30 (2) of the Trade Descriptions Act 1968) provides as follows:

> "Where a local weights and measures authority in England or Wales propose to institute proceedings for an offence under this Act (other than an offence under section 162 (6), 165 (1) or (2) or 174 (5)) it shall, as between the authority and the Director, be the duty of the authority to give the Director notice of the intended proceedings, together with a summary of the facts on which the charges are to be founded, and postpone institution of the proceedings until either—
> (*a*) 28 days have expired since that notice was given, or
> (*b*) the Director has notified them of receipt of the notice and summary." [**1062**]

The duty to give notice to the Director is a duty only as between the authority and the Director, so that non-compliance with s. 161 (2) cannot be set up as a defence to a prosecution. It should also be noted that the local enforcement authority does not require the *consent* of the Director to institute proceedings. It suffices that the Director has been notified of the intended prosecution and given a summary of the facts and that such notification and summary were given at least twenty-eight days prior to the institution of proceedings or have been acknowledged by the Director. The Director does not appear to have any power under the Act to require a local enforcement authority to prosecute or to desist from an intended prosecution, unless such power can be inferred from s. 1 (1) (c) of the Act, which seems doubtful. However, every local weights and measures authority is obliged, whenever the Director requires, to report to him in such form and with such particulars as he requires on the exercise of their functions under the Act (s. 161 (3)). Moreover, the Director (or indeed anyone) can make a complaint to the Secretary of State that the functions of a local weights and measures authority under the Act are not being properly discharged in any area, and the Secretary of State may thereupon order a local inquiry, the results of which must be reported back to the Secretary of State and published by him with such observations on it (if any) as he thinks fit (s. 161 (4), (5)). [1063]

Powers of entry, inspection and seizure

As under the Weights and Measures Act and the Trade Descriptions Act, wide powers are conferred on a duly authorised officer of an enforcement authority to inspect foods, enter any premises (other than those used only as a dwelling), require the production of books and documents and take copies, and seize and detain goods (s. 162 (1)). Banks are not exempt from subjection to these provisions (see, however, para. [1067]), but a barrister or solicitor cannot be compelled to produce a document containing a privileged communication made by or to him in that capacity, nor can the powers conferred by s. 162 be used to seize any such document in his possession (s. 162 (7)). The enforcement provisions relate to suspected *breaches* of the Act, thus covering purely civil breaches as well as criminal offences. [1064]

To be able to enter premises and inspect goods under s. 162 (1) (a) it is not necessary that the inspector shall have grounds for suspecting the commission of an offence. It suffices that his entry or inspection was "in order to ascertain whether a breach of any provision of or under this Act has been committed". This presumably covers a breach of a regulation under the Act as well as a breach of the Act itself. [1065]

The powers given in s. 162 (1) where an inspector wishes to ascertain whether a breach has been committed, appear to be exercisable as regards *any* breach, whether or not it is a breach attracting a separate sanction under the Act. [1066]

By s. 162 (5) regulations may provide that, in cases described by the regulations, an officer of a local weights and measures authority is not to be taken to be duly authorised for the purpose of s. 162 unless authorised by the Director. Such cases have now been prescribed by the Consumer Credit (Entry and Inspection) Regulations 1977, which provide that unless authorised by the Director an official of a local weights and measures authority is not to be taken as a duly authorised officer so far as concerns the exercise of any power under s. 162 (1) (b) (d) and (e) in relation to any banking books or documents (except, in the case of 162 (1) (d), a book or document with respect to which the debtor has given his written consent) or any consumer hire agreement under which the owner is the Post Office or the Kingston-upon-Hull City Council or any book or document containing particulars relating to such agreement. [**1067**]

Section 163 (1) provides that where in exercising his powers under s. 163 an officer of an enforcement authority seizes and detains goods and their owner suffers loss by reason of—

(*a*) that seizure, or

(*b*) the loss, damage or deterioration of the goods during detention,

then, unless the owner is convicted of an offence under the Act committed in relation to the goods, the authority shall compensate him for the loss so suffered. Any dispute as to the right to or amount of any compensation under s. 163 (1) is to be determined by arbitration (s. 163 (2)). Such an arbitration is governed by the Arbitration Act 1950, and involves reference to a single arbitrator (*ibid.*, ss. 6, 31 (1)). If a party fails to concur in the appointment of an arbitrator, or the arbitrator refuses to act, and such failure or refusal continues for seven days after service of a notice to the other party, or to the arbitrator, as the case may be, to appoint or concur in the appointment of the arbitrator, an arbitrator may be appointed by the High Court or a Judge thereof (*ibid.*, s. 10). [**1068**]

Section 164 of the Act, like s. 27 of the Trade Descriptions Act provides that an enforcement authority may—

(*a*) make, or authorise any of their officers to make on their behalf, such purchases of goods; and

(*b*) authorise any of their officers to procure the provision of such services or facilities or to enter into such agreements or other transactions,

as may appear to them expedient for determining whether any provisions made by or under the Act are being complied with. The power to test goods extends to goods seized under the Act, and in that event the person from whom they are seized must be informed of the test results (s. 164 (3)). Where any test leads to proceedings under the Act, the enforcement authority must, under s. 164 (4)

(*a*) if the goods were purchased, inform the person they were purchased from of the test results, and

(*b*) allow any person against whom the proceedings are taken to have the goods tested on his behalf if it is reasonably practicable to do so. [**1069**]

Obstruction of authorised officer

It is an offence wilfully to obstruct an officer of an enforcement authority acting in pursuance of the Act or to fail to comply with any requirement properly made by such an officer under s. 162 of the Act or give such an officer (so acting) other assistance or information he may reasonably require in performing his functions under the Act (s. 165 (1)). The giving of information knowing it to be false is also an offence (s. 165 (2)). But a person cannot be required to answer any question or give any information if to do so might incriminate that person or (where that person is married) the husband or wife of that person (s. 165 (3)).

[**1070**]

Wide though the provisions are, they are not unlimited. An offence is committed only where the officer is, in one of the ways indicated above, obstructed in the performance of his functions under the Act. Hence if, for example, an authorised officer calls for the production of books when reasonably suspecting that a particular act has been committed and in the erroneous belief that such an act would contravene the statutory provisions when as a matter of law it would not, refusal to produce the books to him would not be an offence (see, for example, *John* v. *Matthews*, [1970] 2 Q.B. 443, [1970] 2 All E.R. 643, a decision on s. 29 (1) (*a*) of the Trade Descriptions Act 1968). [**1071**]

False information to the Director

A person who, in connection with any application or request to the Director under the Act, or in response to any invitation or requirement of the Director under the Act, knowingly or recklessly gives information to the Director which, in a material particular, is false or misleading, commits an offence (s. 7). [**1072**]

Consumer advice powers of local authorities

By s. 201 (8) of the Local Government Act 1972, a local weights and measures authority may make, or assist in the making of, arrangements to provide advice to or for the benefit of consumers of goods and services within the area of the authority. This is a very useful provision which many authorities are expected to invoke. [**1073**]

34. Commencement, Repeals and Transitional Provisions

Commencement

The transitional and commencement provisions of the Consumer Credit Act are contained in ss. 182 (2), 192 and Sch. 3. The Act was passed on the 31st July 1974, and all provisions not deferred until a day to be appointed came into force on that date (Sch. 3, Note). The rest of the Act is being brought into operation in phases, on days appointed by order of the Secretary of State; and any such order is required to include a provision amending Sch. 3 so as to insert an express reference to the day appointed (s. 192 (2)). Similarly, the Secretary of State may by order provide for the coming into operation of the amendments contained in Sch. 4, and the repeals contained in Sch. 5, and these amendments and repeals will have effect only as provided by an order so made (s. 192 (4)). Where a power to make regulations or orders is exercisable by the Secretary of State, regulations or orders made in the exercise of that power may, by s. 182 (2),

(a) make different provisions in relation to different cases or classes of case, and

(b) exclude certain cases or classes of case, and

(c) contain such transitional provisions as the Secretary of State thinks fit.

An interesting effect of this subsection is that it enables the Secretary of State to prolong indefinitely the exclusion of specified categories of agreement from the impact of the Act and to vary the transitional provisions that would otherwise apply under Sch. 3. In addition, s. 182 (2) provides a means of avoiding problems in cases where it is doubtful whether a particular provision is or is not retrospective, e.g. s. 75 (see paras. [**1076**], [**1077**]). [**1074**]

Amendments and repeals

The general approach has been to phase out existing legislation as corresponding provisions of the Consumer Credit Act are brought into force. Thus, the provisions of the Moneylenders Acts as to licensing and canvassing have been repealed with the coming into force of the sections of the Consumer Credit Act dealing with these matters (in the case of licensing, the repeal was for administrative reasons made to take effect two months before licensing under the Consumer Credit Act began—see para. [**328**]). There are some curiosities in this phased approach. For example, it is not clear why the Moneylenders Acts could not have been immediately repealed in relation to loans to companies, since such loans are outside the Consumer Credit Act (except where an individual is joined as debtor—s. 185 (5)), so that the repeal is not dependent on the bringing into force of any related provisions under the Act. Nevertheless, loans to companies by moneylenders within the Moneylenders Acts are still regulated by those Acts, except as to particular provisions (licensing, canvassing, etc.) replaced by the Consumer Credit Act. [**1075**]

Retrospectivity—some general points

The extent of the backward reach of the Act is complicated by two main factors. First, where Sch. 3 lays down a rule at all, this may involve any one of four different reference points, namely:

(a) the date of making of an agreement or transaction, or the giving of a notice, however long ago and whether before or after the passing of the Act;

(b) the passing of the Act (31st July 1974);

(c) the date on or after which an agreement must have been made in order to constitute a regulated agreement, i.e. 1st April 1977 (see para. [**166**]); or

(d) the day appointed for the purpose of the provision in question.

Secondly, when providing a rule in Sch. 3 the draftsman has not used a consistent formula, and has thus left doubt as to the position in those cases where Sch. 3 is silent. In some places, the Schedule provides that the relevant section, on being brought into force on an appointed day, is to have effect in relation to agreements or transactions made before the appointed day (see, for example, paras. 4, 16 (2), 35 and 37 (2), dealing respectively with ss. 20, 76, Part VII and ss. 107–110 of the Act). Had this formula been used throughout there would have been no difficulty, for the clear inference would then be raised that a section was not to operate in relation to agreements or transactions made before the appointed day unless expressly so stated. Unhappily there are other parts of Sch. 3 in which the reverse formula is used, by a provision that a stated section is *not* to affect agreements, etc., made before the appointed day (see, for example, paras. 3, 7 and 45, dealing respectively with ss. 19 (3), 40 and 148 (1) of the Act). These provisions raise exactly the opposite inference, namely that a section *is* to have retrospective effect unless otherwise stated. Hence where a paragraph in the Schedule says nothing, one way or the other, as to retrospectivity, the position is far from clear. For example, would s. 75, on coming into operation, impose liability in relation to agreements made on and after the 1st April 1977 (the day appointed for an agreement to be a regulated agreement) or would it be confined to agreements made on and after the day appointed for s. 75 itself? In the case of s. 75 the doubt has been removed by the terms of the order bringing it into force, art. 2 (2) of the Consumer Credit Act 1974 (Commencement No. 3) Order 1977 providing that s. 75 applies only in relation to agreements made on or after the day appointed for the section, namely the 1st July 1977. It is to be hoped that a similar technique will be employed in future commencement orders. [**1076**]

It is thought that on balance a section is not to be treated as having retrospective effect unless so stated. The majority of the paragraphs in Sch. 3 dealing with retrospectivity do so by specifying the cases in which the section is to have retrospective effect, rather than the cases in which it is not to have that effect; and as a general canon of statutory interpretation there is a presumption against retrospectivity. Of course, there is nothing to prevent the Secretary of State from making an order which fixes as the appointed day a date earlier than that of the order itself. In this sense, he is free to be as retrospective as he pleases. **[1077]**

In the following passages, the paragraph numbers given in parentheses are the numbers of the relevant paragraphs in Sch. 3, except where otherwise indicated.

[1078]

Provisions affecting pre-Act transactions

The following provisions of the Act apply to agreements "whenever made" and thus control even agreements made before the passing of the Act, whether or not such agreements are still current.

(a) Section 20, relating to regulations as to the total charge for credit (para. 4). It was necessary to make s. 20 retrospective in order (*inter alia*) to give effect to other provisions of Sch. 3 relating to agreements that would have been regulated agreements if made on the stated appointed day; for since some agreements are exempt (and thus not regulated) where the total charge for credit does not exceed a stated rate (para. **[322]**), it was necessary to ensure that the s. 20 regulations could be applied to such agreements, whenever made, for the purpose of determining whether they would have been regulated agreements if made on the appointed day.

(b) Section 56 (3), nullifying agreements precluding the agency of, or liability for the acts or omissions of, a negotiator (para. 12 (2)). Such agreements are void whenever made; but the retrospectivity here involved has been indirectly limited by the fact that s. 56 (3) is confined to agreements purporting to make stipulations in relation to an actual or prospective regulated agreement, that is, an agreement made on or after the 1st April 1977.

(c) Sections 137–140, relating to the reopening of extortionate credit bargains (para. 42). This has been discussed earlier (para. **[988]**). **[1079]**

Provisions for which appointed day is on or after 1st April 1977

As noted earlier, several sections are made to apply to "an agreement made before the day appointed for this paragraph where the agreement would have been a regulated agreement if made on that day." The effect of this wording appears to be that an agreement made before the day appointed for the purpose of the relevant section is controlled by that section where the appointed day for it is on or after the 1st April 1977 (the appointed day for a regulated agreement—para. 1) provided that when the section comes into force the agreement is still a regulated agreement. Presumably the draftsman contemplated that there would be at least some sections brought into force before the appointed day for regulated agreements but affecting prospective regulated agreements, and in such cases agreements made before the relevant appointed day would not have been caught by the section in question. In fact, no appointed day prior to the 1st April 1977 has been fixed for any section relevant to an actual or prospective regulated agreement, so that unless a future order fixes as the commencement date for such a section a date prior to the 1st April 1977 (an unlikely eventuality) agreements brought within this particular transitional formula will be governed by the relevant section whenever made, so that the section will have the same retrospective effect as if the phrase "whenever made" had been used, except in relation to agreements that have ceased to be regulated agreements on the appointed day in question.

> *Example*
> Suppose that 1st January 1979 were to be fixed as the appointed day for s. 95, relating to rebates for early settlement. Then a debtor under an agreement made in January 1977 who settled ahead of time would be entitled to the statutory rebate, despite the fact that the agreement was made before the day appointed for regulated agreements (1st April 1977) if in all other respects the agreement meets the definition of a regulated agreement; for it would have been a regulated agreement if made on the 1st January 1979 and would thus be caught by s. 95 (para. 35). **[1080]**

However, a slightly troublesome point is raised by the drafting of this transitional formula. Suppose that in the above example the agreement had been made on the 1st May 1977. Would it then be caught by s. 95? A difficulty arises in that the formula refers to "an agreement made before the day appointed for the purposes of this paragraph where the agreement *would have been* a regulated agreement if made on that day", whereas in our altered example the agreement was *in fact* a regulated agreement. Strictly construed, it would thus be outside the formula. It is, however, submitted that this was not the intention of the draftsman, and that the formula should be interpreted as covering agreements that were regulated when made, provided that they are still regulated on the appointed day in question. **[1081]**

Sections falling within this formula, and thus covering agreements whenever made if they were regulated when made or would still have been regulated if made on the appointed day, are:

(a) Section 76, dealing with notices to be served before a creditor or owner exercises certain contractual rights otherwise than by reason of breach (para. 16 (2)).

(b) Sections 83 and 84, restricting the debtor's liability for misuse by others of credit facilities or credit-tokens, (para. 20 (2), but not as regards losses arising before the day appointed for the purposes of those sections (para. 20 (4)).

(c) Section 85, relating to the creditor's duty to supply documents on issue of new credit-tokens (para. 21 (2)).

(d) Section 86, imposing restrictions on exercise of remedies arising by reason of the death of the debtor or hirer (para. 22 (2)).

(e) Sections 87 and 88, relating to default notices (para. 35).

(f) Section 92, relating to entry on premises for the purpose of repossessing goods comprised in a hire-purchase or conditional sale agreement (para. 35).

(g) Sections 94–97, relating to rebates for early settlement (para. 35).

(*h*) Section 98, requiring at least seven days' notice before termination of an agreement otherwise than for default (para. 35).

(*i*) Sections 107–109, requiring information to be supplied to sureties (para. 37 (2)).

(*j*) Section 110, requiring a copy of a security instrument to be supplied to a debtor or hirer (*ibid.*).

(*k*) Section 111, relating to service of a copy of a default notice on a surety (para. 38 (2)). [**1082**]

Other retrospective provisions

There are two other provisions which are retrospective in effect, though the formula used is slightly different, namely:

(*a*) section 19, relating to linked transactions (para. 2), other than s. 19 (3) (para. 3);

(*b*) section 185 (2), relating to notices by a joint debtor dispensing with periodic statements of account (para. 49). [**1083**]

Provisions not retrospective

(i) *Retrospectivity expressly excluded*

Sections of the Act coming into operation on appointed days but expressly excluded in relation to acts and agreements made before the appointed days in question (or in some cases, before the day appointed for the purpose of para. 1 of Sch. 3) include the following:

(*a*) Part III of the Act, relating to licensing (paras. 5, 44).

(*b*) Part IV of the Act, as regards advertisements (para. 8).

(*c*) Section 51 (1), as regards the issue of credit-tokens before the appointed day (para. 11).

(*d*) Section 56, as regards antecedent negotiations in relation to consumer credit or consumer hire agreements made before the day appointed under para. 1 (para. 12 (1)), i.e. the 1st April 1977

(*e*) section 75, relating to the liability of a creditor for misrepresentations and breaches of contract by the supplier. By virtue of para. 1 of Sch. 3 this does not impose any liability on a creditor under a credit agreement made before the day appointed for the purpose of para. 1, i.e. the 1st April, 1977; and the relevant commencement order restricts the backward reach of s. 75 still further, by confining it to agreements made on or after the 1st July 1977 (Consumer Credit Act 1974 (Commencement No 3) Order 1977).

(*f*) Sections 83–84, in relation to losses arising before the appointed day (para. 20 (4)).

(*g*) Sections 90 and 91, relating to protected goods. These sections will not apply to goods comprised in a hire-purchase or conditional sale agreement made before the day appointed for the purposes of Part VII of the Act, so that in relation to such agreements the restrictions on repossession will not apply (para. 35).

(*h*) Section 93, which restricts default interest under a regulated agreement to the contract rate. This will not apply to agreements

377

made before the day appointed for the purposes of Part VII of the Act (para. 35).

(*i*) Sections 99–101, relating to the right of termination of a hirer or buyer under a hire-purchase or conditional sale agreement, and his liability on termination. These will not apply to agreements made before the day appointed for the purposes of Part VII (para. 35).

(*j*) Section 102, relating to agency for receiving notices of rescission. This will similarly not apply to agreements made before such appointed day (para. 35.)

(*k*) Section 148 (1), in relation to agreements made by a trader before the day appointed for the purposes of para. 44 (para. 45).

(*l*) Section 149, as to introductions effected by a credit-broker before the day appointed for the purposes of para. 44 (para. 46).

(*m*) Section 151 (1), (2), in relation to advertisements published before the appointed day (para. 47). [**1084**]

(ii) *Retrospectivity implied negated*

For reasons stated earlier (para. [**1077**]) it may be concluded that where a paragraph in Sch. 3 lays down no rule as to retrospectivity one way or the other, the section to which it refers is not to have retrospective effect. If this be right, then other sections which operate only in relation to acts done on or after the relevant appointed day include the following:

(*a*) Section 57, as to the consequences of withdrawal from an agreement, where the withdrawal takes place before the appointed day.

(*b*) Section 58, as to the procedure to be followed in relation to a prospective land mortgage.

(*c*) Section 59, as to agreements made before the appointed day.

(*d*) Sections 61–65, as to the formalities of contract and the consequences of non-compliance.

(*e*) Sections 67–73 as cancellation by the debtor or hirer and its consequences.

(*f*) Section 81, as to payments made by the debtor before the appointed day.

(*g*) Section 82, as to variations by the creditor before the appointed day.

(*h*) Section 105, as to the form and content of securities.

(*i*) Sections 114–122 relating to pledges.

(*j*) Sections 123–125 relating to negotiable instruments.

(*k*) Section 126, relating to the enforcement of land mortgages.

Of course, the order fixing the appointed day may itself produce a retrospective effect by specifying a date earlier than that of the order itself. [**1085**]

35. Consumer Credit In The EEC

The European Commission has for some years been working on proposals for a Directive on consumer credit, and a draft Directive is now being considered by the Council of the EEC. This is modelled on the Consumer Credit Act in their underlying concepts but is much shorter and more general in terms, leaving most of the detail to be worked out by national legislation. There are some striking points of departure from the Consumer Credit Act. In particular, the draft Directive contains no financial ceiling for control but in principle extends to any credit agreement between a business creditor and a consumer not relating to the acquisition of land or buildings. In short, the draft Directive employs a "purpose of use" test (credit for private purposes as opposed to credit for business), not a financial ceiling, as the principal criterion for delineating the boundaries of control. Moreover, in various respects the proposed Directive is less stringent than the Consumer Credit Act so far as the liability of the creditor is concerned. For example, the creditor's liability for breach by the supplier would be imposed only where the consumer's claim was for recovery of the price, not where it was for damages. [**1086**]

If the Directive is made it will be the duty of member States to enact legislation to give effect to it. Fortunately the Directive is unlikely to necessitate any changes to the Consumer Credit Act, since member States are left free to negotiate with the European Commission upper and lower limits for transactions that are to fall within the legislation, and they are also at liberty to enact or retain legislation which gives greater protection to the consumer than would be given by the Director. To date, the proposals do not contain any form of protection which is not already conferred on the consumer by the Consumer Credit Act; and provided that the Commission is prepared to accept the upper limit of £5000 and the lower limit (for complete or partial exemption) of £30 fixed by the Act, the Directive will have no impact on English consumer credit law. [**1087**]

379

36. Miscellanea

A concluding assortment for those who have stayed the course!

Onus of proof

Section 171 provides as follows:

"(1) If an agreement contains a term signifying that in the opinion of the parties section 10 (3) (*b*) (iii) does not apply to the agreement, it shall be taken not to apply unless the contrary is proved.

(2) It shall be assumed in any proceedings, unless the contrary is proved, that when a person initiated a transaction as mentioned in section 19 (1) (*c*) he knew the principal agreement had been made, or contemplated that it might be made.

(3) Regulations under section 44 or 52 may make provision as to the onus of proof in any proceedings to enforce the regulations.

(4) In proceedings brought by the creditor under a credit-token agreement—

    (*a*) it is for the creditor to prove that the credit-token was lawfully supplied to the debtor, and was accepted by him, and

    (*b*) if the debtor alleges that any use made of the credit-token was not authorised by him, it is for the creditor to prove either—

        (i) that the use was so authorised, or

        (ii) that the use occurred before the creditor had been given notice under section 84 (3).

(5) In proceedings under section 50 (1) in respect of a document received by a minor at any school or other educational establishment for minors, it is for the person sending it to him at that establishment to prove that he did not know or suspect it to be such an establishment.

(6) In proceedings under section 119 (1) it is for the pawnee to prove that he had reasonable cause to refuse to allow the pawn to be redeemed.

(7) If, in proceedings referred to in section 139 (1), the debtor or any surety alleges that the credit bargain is extortionate it is for the creditor to prove the contrary."

Of these various provisions, the last subsection, relating to extortionate bargains, is likely to occasion the most difficulty (see paras [**894**] *et seq.*). In each case, what is referred to is the legal burden of proof, that is, the burden of persuading the court at the end of the day that on a balance of probabilities the fact asserted is true. See para. [**895**]. [**1088**]

Binding nature of statements and notices

The effect of s. 172 (1) is that subject to the power of the court to give relief under s. 172 (see para. [**1090**]), a statement by a creditor or owner is binding on him if given under—

sections 77 (1), 78 (1) and 79 (1) (provision of information to debtors and hirers);
section 97 (1) (information to debtor as to figure for early settlement);
sections 107 (1), 108 (1) (c), 109 (1) (c) (provision of information to sureties).

By section 172 (2) a notice given by a trader to a customer in compliance with s. 103 (1) (b) (relating to termination statements) or asserting under s. 103 that the customer is not indebted to him, is binding on the trader, subject, again, to the provisions of s. 172 (3) (see para. [**1090**]). [**1089**]

The provisions of s. 172 could operate very harshly on a creditor or trader sending a statement or notice understating the indebtedness of the debtor or customer or erroneously stating that no sum was outstanding. Errors of this kind are inevitable in the light of human frailty, coupled with the enormous volume of credit business and the problems of feeding information into, and extracting information from, the computers that have become the standby of the modern financial world. Some margin of error is allowed for in the sections listed in s. 172 (1), since these sections only require the creditor's statement to show specified amounts "according to the information to which it is practicable for him to refer". This allows a certain amount of latitude where, for example, the creditor would have difficulty in furnishing information that was completely up to date, but it does not cover errors in accounts. Section 172 (3) deals with this problem by empowering the court, when a statement or notice relied on in proceedings is shown to be incorrect, to direct such relief (if any) to be given to the creditor or owner from the operation of s. 172 (1) and (2) as appears to the court to be just.

[**1090**]

No contracting out of Act

Section 173 of the Act deals with contracting out. The marginal note misleadingly describes the effect of the section as forbidding contracting out. This is true only in the sense that a contract term inconsistent with a provision for the protection of the debtor or hirer or his relative is void (s. 173 (1)). The inclusion of a void exclusion clause is not as yet a criminal offence, except in relation to terms made void by s. 6 of the Unfair Contract Terms Act 1977 (see para. [**439**]). Nothing in s. 173 (1) prevents a thing being done in relation to any person which would ordinarily require an order of the court or the Director if that person gives his consent at the time (s. 173 (3)). **[1091]**

Confidentiality of information

Section 174 contains provisions prohibiting the disclosure of information obtained under or by virtue of the Act about any individual or any business except with the consent of the individual or of the person for the time being carrying on the business (s. 174 (1)). Certain exceptions to this rule are made by s. 174 (3). Disclosure of information in contravention of s. 174 is an offence (s. 174 (5)).

[1092]

Duty of deemed agents

Section 175 provides that where under the Act a person is deemed to receive a notice or payment as agent of the creditor or owner under a regulated agreement, he shall be deemed to be under a contractual duty to the creditor or owner to transmit the notice, or remit the payment, to him forthwith. The effect of this enigmatic provision is obscure. It is a general principle of agency law that where an agent receives notice of a fact which he owes a duty to communicate to his principal, the latter is deemed to have received notice of that fact as from the time when he would have received notice if the agent had duly performed his duty to communicate (*Proudfoot* v. *Montefiore* (1867), L.R. 2 Q.B. 511). But it is far from clear how this principle is to be applied in relation to those provisions of the Consumer Credit Act to which s. 175 is relevant. There is no provision in the Act at all making any person a deemed agent of the creditor or owner to receive a payment, so that the reference to payment in s. 175 appears to be totally without effect. There are only three provisions by which a person is deemed to receive a notice as agent of the creditor or owner, namely ss. 57 (3), 69 (6) and 102 (1), relating respectively to the debtor's or hirer's withdrawal from a prospective regulated agreement, cancellation of a regulated agreement and asserted right of rescission of a regulated agreement otherwise than by service of notice of cancellation. Section 69 (7) provides that "whether or not it is actually received by him, a notice of cancellation sent by post to a person shall be deemed to be served on him at the time of posting". (This section does not apply to notice of withdrawal (see para. [**575**]).) It is scarcely conceivable that the Act intended to cut down the protection formerly available to the debtor or hirer by restricting the operation of s. 69 (7) to a notice posted to the creditor or owner personally, so as to exclude posting to the deemed agent under ss. 69 (6) and 57 (4); for the consequence of this would be that a notice of cancellation posted by the debtor to the deemed agent would not be considered given to him until received by him, and if it failed to arrive then it would not constitute notice to the creditor or owner. A notice under s. 102 is not deemed to be given at the time of posting, so that as regards such a notice the principle in *Proudfoot* v. *Montefiore* could be invoked. The effect would be that the principal would be deemed to have received the notice at the time he would have received it if it had been transmitted by the agent "forthwith". This does not mean instantaneously—for the law does not command the impossible— but at the earliest available moment. The same applies to a notice under s. 57 (1).

[1093]

It is therefore submitted that in relation to a notice of cancellation served under

s. 69 of the Act, s. 175 does not change what has always been assumed to be the effect of s. 12 of the Hire-Purchase Act 1965, that notice to the deemed agent is notice to the creditor or owner and therefore if sent by post takes effect when posted to the agent. If this be right, the only effect of s. 172 in relation to a notice of cancellation (as opposed to a notice of withdrawal) would seem to be to confer on a creditor or owner who suffers loss through failure of the deemed agent to perform his deemed contractual duty a right to damages as for breach of contract.

[1094]

Service of documents

Section 176 sets out detailed rules as to the method of service of documents required to be served under the Act. Subsections (5) and (6) have the effect (*inter alia*) that a default notice given after the death of the debtor or hirer is validly served if addressed to him, even if the creditor or owner knows that he has died (and see para. [**894**]). These are self-explanatory, and the only comment that needs to be made is that (save in the case of s. 176 (5)) s. 176 deals only with the *mode* of service, not the deemed *time* of service. As previously noted, a notice of cancellation under s. 69, if sent by post, is deemed to be served at the time of posting (see para. [**1093**]). Other notices sent by post, *e.g.* a notice of withdrawal under s. 57, are governed by s. 7 of the Interpretation Act 1978 (re-enacting s. 26 of the Interpretation Act 1889), which provides that where an Act authorises or requires a document to be served by post, whether the expression "serve" or the expression "give" or "send", or any other expression, is used, then unless the contrary intention appears the service shall be deemed to be effected by properly addressing, prepaying and posting a letter containing the document. The same section goes on to state that unless the contrary is proved, service is deemed to have been effected at the time at which the letter would be delivered in the ordinary course of post.

Though the matter is not beyond doubt, it would seem that if the creditor can show that a notice of withdrawal posted by the debtor or hirer never reached the creditor or other proper addressee, it will be ineffective (see *Maltglade, Ltd.* v. *St. Albans R.D.C.*, [1972] 3 All E.R. 129, [1972] 1 W.L.R 1230; *Thomas Bishop, Ltd.* v. *Helmville, Ltd.*, [1972] 1 Q.B. 464, [1972] 1 All E.R. 365; and *R.* v. *London County Quarter Sessions Appeals Committee, ex parte Rossi,* [1956] 1 Q.B. 682, [1956] 1 All E.R. 670); and that if the creditor or other addressee proves that the notice was received later than the date on which it would have reached him in the ordinary course of post it is deemed to have been given at the date of its receipt but failing such proof is deemed, under s. 7 of the Interpretation Act 1978, to have been received at the time it would have been delivered in the ordinary course of post. Certainly it was the intention of Parliament to treat the notice of withdrawal as effective when received, rather than when given, since the original version of the Consumer Credit Bill providing for it to take effect when posted was dropped as the result of protests at this disparity of treatment between the parties (see H.C. Deb. 19th July 1974, cols. 877–878). The proposition that the notice takes effect on receipt also derives support from the opening words of s. 57 (3) ("Each of the following shall be deemed to be the agent of the creditor or owner for the purpose of *receiving* a notice under subsection (2) . . .") and from the fact that at common law revocation of an offer is not achieved by mere posting of a letter of revocation but takes effect only on receipt by the offeree (*Byrne* v. *Van Tienhoven* (1880), 5 C.P.D. 344. [**1095**]

Regulations and orders

Sections 179–182 empower regulations to be made:

(*a*) as to the form and contents of credit-cards, trading checks and other such "secondary documents" (s. 179);

(*b*) as to the form, content and supply of copies of documents referred to in the Act (s. 180);

(*c*) amending the Act so as to increase or reduce sums mentioned in various provisions, including the £5,000 limit of application of the Act (s. 181) (but such regulations require an affirmative resolution of each House of Parliament (s. 181 (2));

(*d*) to differentiate between cases and classes of case in any regulations made (s. 182). [**1096**]

Distress for rent by debtor's or hirer's landlord

Schedule 5 to the Consumer Credit Act removes bills of sale and hire-purchase and conditional sale agreements (whether within or outside the Act) from s. 4 (1) of the Law of Distress Amendment Act 1908, and thus leaves the creditor under a hire-purchase agreement or bill of sale free, like any other owner, to save his goods from distress by the debtor's landlord, by serving on the landlord the declaration prescribed by s. 1 of that Act. However, the Act as a whole (and thus the protection given to the creditor by s. 1) is excluded as regards a hire-purchase, conditional sale or consumer hire agreement (even if outside the Consumer Credit Act) which has not been terminated, except (as regards an agreement within the Consumer Credit Act) during the period between service of a default notice and the date on which the notice expires or is complied with (Consumer Credit Act, Sch. 4, para. 5). Accordingly the landlord's common law right to distrain on goods on the demised premises, whether or not belonging to the tenant, will continue to apply to goods held by the tenant under a hire-purchase, conditional sale or consumer hire agreement (whether within or outside the Act) unless the agreement has been terminated or is an agreement within the Act in respect of which a default notice is still current. [**1097**]

Bankruptcy of debtor or hirer

Where a person holding goods under a hire-purchase, conditional sale or consumer hire agreement within the Consumer Credit Act becomes bankrupt, the goods will not be treated as the property of the bankrupt (and will thus be outside the reputed ownership clause embodied in s. 38 of the Bankruptcy Act 1914) during the currency of a default notice under the Consumer Credit Act (Bankruptcy Act 1914, s. 38A, added by the Consumer Credit Act, Sch. 4, para. 6). Hence the creditor or owner will not be affected by s. 38 provided that a default notice is still running (i.e. has not expired or been complied with) at the commencement of the bankruptcy, that is, on the date of the earliest act of bankruptcy committed within the three months preceding the date of presentation of the bankruptcy petition (Bankruptcy Act 1914, s. 37). In any event, the widespread use of hire-purchase and rental has greatly reduced the impact of the reputed ownership provisions. See R. M. Goode, Hire-Purchase Law and Practice (2nd edn.), pp. 577–578, 718–720. [**1098**]

Index

All references are to paragraph numbers

All references are to paragraph numbers

BANK—*contd.*
"holder in due course", as, 794, 796
licensing of deposit-taking institutions, 326
Moneylenders Acts, exempt from, 7, 38, 438
secondary, growth of, 7, 438
trustee savings banks, 41

BANK OVERDRAFT,
debtor-creditor agreement, as, 266, 287
Director, exemption determined by, 196, 471, 593
exemption from Part V of Act, 196, 264, 593, 728
nature of, 266
non–purchase–money revolving credit, as, 79
notice of creditor's intention to exercise remedies, 889, 891
offer and acceptance, 170, 245
regulated agreement, as, 297
running-account credit, as agreement for, 79, 264, 300, 728
soliciting of agreements for, on current accounts, 471–472
temporary excess,
no separate agreement where, 245, 264, 300, 593, 728
termination or suspension of overdraft facility, 891
unilateral contract, as, 245

BANKRUPTCY
breach of agreement, whether amounts to, 891, 898
conditional seller, of, 750
debt-collection by trustee in, 1008
licensee, of, 378, 382
termination on ground of, 103, 891

BARRISTERS,
ancillary credit business provisions, exempt from, 999, 1003

BILLS OF EXCHANGE,
negotiation of, 796–797. *See also* NEGOTIABLE INSTRUMENTS

BILLS OF SALE ACTS,
Act 1878, 3, 8, 16, 761
Amendment Act 1882, 3, 8, 780
bill of sale over after-acquired property, 3
charge on chattels, 84
Consumer Credit Act, unaffected by, 30, 31
enforcement of securities, and, 780
industrial and provident societies, charge by, 54
repeal of, proposals for, 17.
third party rights in secured transaction, 30, 762

BLOCK DISCOUNTING,
agreements, 46, 69, 230
debt collection, as, 1006, 1008

BODY CORPORATE,
advertisement that credit only available to, 449
associate, as, 362
"controller" of, 331, 332

BODY CORPORATE—*contd.*
debtor, as, outside scope of Act, 172
floating charge by, 896
joint debtor or hirer, as, 172, 867, 878
licensee, as, 331, 332, 379
liquidation of, 379
meaning of, 172
offences by, 1056
public general Act, empowered by,
licence not required by, 334
mortgage transactions as exempt agreements, 319
sealing by, 551

BREACH OF STATUTORY DUTY,
co-debtor, by, 872
damage to goods, where, 630, 635
failure to surrender goods on cancellation, for, 628, 630, 635

BRIDGING LOANS
advance copy of unexecuted agreement not required in, 581
cancellation provisions not applicable to, 592, 602, 816

BROKERAGE FEES,
total charge for credit, and, 1023
transaction abortive, recoverable if, 1021
See also CREDIT-BROKER; CREDIT BROKERAGE

BUILDING SOCIETY,
advertisement by, 450
land mortgage transaction as exempt agreement, 45, 307, 312–314, 450, 584, 814

BUSINESS,
advertisements, disclosure requirements for, 441
associate, 358, 362
carrying on of a, what constitutes, 335–336, 375
conduct of, by licensee, 376
leasing of goods for purposes of, 758, 759
name,
Mail Order Transactions (Information) Order 1976, 440
registration of, 363–365
premises,
canvassing on, 466–468
signing of agreement at, 592, 602
unfair or improper practices, 358, 361

CANCELLATION,
cancellable agreements, variation of, 718, 725
cooling-off period, 606–609, 635
credit-token agreement, of, 570, 612, 826–827
declaration of, by court, 611, 995
effect of,
care, exercise of reasonable, 611, 625, 629, 630, 860
co-debtors, repayments to, 868, 869
debtor released from liability, 611, 614, 615, 860

All references are to paragraph numbers

All references are to paragraph numbers

All references are to paragraph numbers

EXTORTIONATE CREDIT BARGAINS—
contd.
exempt consumer credit agreements, 966,
1048
expectant heirs, bargains with, 992, 993
extortionate, meaning of, 971
foreign transactions, 1048
guarantee or indemnity, where, 812
High Court, jurisdiction of, 926, 969, 989
judgment against debtor, effect of, 987
jurisdiction of court,
County Court, 926, 969, 990
equitable, 992–993
High Court, 926, 969, 989
linked transactions, and, 861, 865
maintenance and insurance contracts, inclusion of, 967
Moneylenders Acts, and, 961–962
onus of proof, 965, 984–985, 1088
orders made by court, 864–865, 986
procedure, 989 990
provisions of Act as to, 158, 965
relief given where, 864, 986
re-open credit agreement, power to, 864,
966–968
jurisdiction, how invoked, 969
repayment to debtor, order for, 864, 986
retrospective effect of, 988
standard rates of charges, use of, 981
surety, provisions to protect, 812
terms of transaction, examination of, 974–
976
time at which bargain tested, 973
unconscionable bargains, 971
unregulated credit agreements, 991

FACTORING AGREEMENT,
negotiable instruments swept up by, 796

FACTORS ACT 1889,
title, transfer of, 13, 16, 31, 91

FAIR TRADING ACT 1973,
Director,
powers of, 31, 126
report of, 131

FEE,
licence, for, 348, 366

FINANCE HOUSE,
activities of, credit, 32, 42–43
block discounting agreements, 46, 69, 230
dealer as agent of, 99
debt-collector, as, 1008
European Federation of Finance House
Associations (Eurofinas), 57
Finance Houses Association, 57
hire-purchase agreement with, 67, 613
cancellation, liability on, 613
holder in due course, as, 793
HP Information Ltd., 57, 59
indemnity to, where liability for repayment, 613, 622
instalment sales, involvement in, 67
liability of, for acts of supplier, 638, 674
loan by,
part-exchange allowance, liability to
pay, 622

FINANCE HOUSE—*contd.*
loan by—*contd.*
personal, 68, 72
purchase of goods, for, 284, 858
meaning of, 42
revolving credit by, supplier-connected, 43
satisfaction note or letter from, 474
store accounts, involvement in, 43, 77
supplier-connected credit by, 42, 43
Voluntary Code for, 7

FIXED-SUM CREDIT,
agreement,
information and documents, duty to
supply, 706
statement of information binding, 706
amount of, 259–260
definition of, 269
examples of, 269
rate disclosure in advertisements, 272
running-account credit, distinguished from
261, 269–272, 1090

FIXTURES,
bailment of goods, whether, 180

FLOATING CHARGE,
fixing of, 896
industrial and provident society, by, 54
negotiable instruments swept up by, 796

FOOD,
freezer, purchased to stock, 632, 859

FOREIGN TRANSACTIONS,
advertisements, exempted, 449
application of Act to, 200–201, 1046
credit card issued in UK and usable abroad,
200, 686
creditor, liability of, for acts of supplier,
686
European Convention on Jurisdiction and
Enforcement of Judgments, 1041
exempt consumer credit agreement, as,
201, 310, 323, 1048
jurisdiction of court, 1040–1042
negotiable instruments, restrictions on, 798
Unfair Contract Terms Act, under, 1042,
1050, 1051

FORFEITURE,
relief against, 108, 840, 889, 898, 902, 907
hiring agreement, of, 837, 840, 889, 907

FORMALITIES,
modifying agreement, of, 727
regulated agreement, of, 542–568. *See also*
REGULATED AGREEMENT

FRAUD,
applicant for licence, by, 358
Fraudulent Conveyances Act 1571, 1
fraudulent misrepresentation, 642, 695

FREEZER,
supply of, with food, 632, 859

FRIENDLY SOCIETY,
credit, provision of, by, 53
debtor, as, Act applies to, 172
exempt consumer credit agreement by, 53,
316

All references are to paragraph numbers

LAND—*contd.*
lease or tenancy agreement for, and goods, 181, 301
recovery of, 818
registered charge, saving for, 775
restricted-use credit agreements to finance purchase of, 275, 279, 581
time order for recovery of possession of, 935, 937

LAND MORTGAGE,
advance copy of unexecuted agreement,
documents, incorporation of, 579
notice of withdrawal rights, 578, 580
not required, when, 581
requirement of, 577–580
advertisements, whether exempted, 450, 815
application of Act to, 814
bridging loan, agreement for, 581, 592, 600
building society, transactions by, 45, 312–314, 450, 584
cancellation provisions not applicable to, 592, 602, 816
communication during consideration period for debtor,
examples of, 582
prohibition against, 573, 582
rectification, 583
cooling off provisions not applicable to, 573, 577, 592, 602, 816
creditors, classes of, 814
endowment mortgages, 86
enforcement of,
court order, by, 780, 818, 820, 889, 932, 934
improperly executed, where, 573, 574, 577
exempt agreements, transactions as, 45, 307, 308, 312–314, 317, 318, 450, 584, 814
forms of legal mortgage, 85
invalidation of securities, and, 775
local authority, transactions by, 45, 307, 312–314, 450, 584
meaning of, 312, 814
power of sale by mortgagee, 775
purchase money, 195, 581, 592, 602
remedies of mortgagee, 886, 888
repayment mortgages, 86
second, 20, 87, 584
security and third party rights, 762
withdrawal procedure, 574, 577–585, 816. *See also* WITHDRAWAL

LAW CENTRE,
debt-counsellor, as, 1004

LAW OF DISTRESS AMENDMENT ACT 1908, 31

LAW SOCIETY,
group licence issued to, 344, 1014

LAYBY SALE,
credit transaction, whether, 217–219

LEASE,
assignment of,
agreement for, 233–235
covenant against, 898

LEASE—*contd.*
breach, whether capable of remedy, 898
equipment, termination of, 758, 759
land and goods, of, outside Act, 181, 301
land, of, not credit agreement, 233

LEASING AGREEMENT. *See* CONSUMER HIRE AGREEMENT

LEGAL ADVICE,
debt-counselling, as, 1004

LEGIBILITY,
document embodying regulated agreement, of, 547, 548, 557

LEGISLATION,
comparative analysis of, 92
tables of structure of,
after 1974 Act, 25, 28, 31
prior to 1974 Act, 26, 27

LENDING,
Crowther Committee, recommendations of, on, 17, 18, 23
Security Act, and, proposed, 17, 18, 23, 30

LICENCE. *See also* LICENSING
activities authorised by, 368–370
limitations on, 369, 394
ancillary credit business, for, 337, 369, 996, 1013–1014
appeals from determination of Director *See* APPEAL
application for,
appointed day, before, 341, 352
associates and relatives of applicant, 358–362
determination of, by Director, notice of, 395
false information, 354, 357
fee, 348, 366
fit person, whether applicant, 346, 358–362
information in support of, 355–357
invalid, 348
name, suitability of licensed, 346, 363–364
opposition to, 386
representations in support of, 387–393
statutory requirements, 348
trading standards officers, notice to, 367
assignability of, 377
canvassing off trade premises, 370, 394
consumer credit business, for, 334, 335
consumer hire business, for, 335
display of, 373
fee, 348
grant of, in terms different from application, 388, 394
group. *See* GROUP LICENCE
licensee. *See* LICENSEE
name, business to be conducted under authorised, 339, 374–375
need for, 334
not required, when, 334
opposition to grant of, 386
period of, 371
publicity for, 372–373

All references are to paragraph numbers

All references are to paragraph numbers

All references are to paragraph numbers

OFFENCES—*contd.*
  prosecutions by local enforcement author-
    ities, 1062
  sanctions for breach of Act, no further,
    1057

OFFER,
  bank overdraft, where, 170, 245
  hire-purchase agreement, in, 240
  loan, where application for, 240
  running-account credit, where agreement
    for, 271
  withdrawal of, 574, 575, 576

OFFICE OF FAIR TRADING,
  guidance, notes for, on 1974 Act, 130
  trading standards officers, duties of, 148

OMBUDSMAN,
  investigation by, 436
  Parliamentary Commissioner Order 1975,
    436

ONUS OF PROOF, 984–985, 1088

OPTION,
  purchase, to,
    early settlement, where, 731
    not consumer hire agreement, 182
  renew, to, in consumer hire agreement, 183,
    190

ORDERS. *See also* REGULATIONS
  Act of 1974, under, 1074
  Director, by, 137
  Secretary of State, by, 124

OVERDRAFTS. *See* BANK OVERDRAFT

OWNER. *See also* CREDITOR
  business premises of, signing at, 592, 602
  cancellation, notice of, to, 603, 604
  debt-collection by, 1007
  meaning of, 165, 604
  more than one, agreement with. *See*
    CREDITOR
  negotiations by, 595, 598
  signature by or on behalf of, 547, 551

PAROL EVIDENCE RULE,
  collateral contract not caught by, 643
  exclusion of, 555

PART-EXCHANGE,
  agreement, terms of, 588
  allowance, payment of, 588, 611, 622–623,
    810
    indemnity for creditor, 622
  goods,
    detention or conversion of, 588
    return of, 588, 611, 623
  instalment sale, in, constitutes credit agree-
    ment, 212

PARTIALLY   REGULATED
    AGREEMENTS,
  categories of, 188
  exempt agreements, distinguished from,
    306
  small agreements as. *See* SMALL
    AGREEMENTS

PARTNERSHIP,
  acts of partner, liability for, 876
  authority of partners, 876
  licensee, change in members of, 331, 374
  name of, effect of change in, 339, 374
  signature of, 551, 876
  standard licence, issue of, to, 339, 374, 378

PAWN. *See* PLEDGE
  receipt,
    issue of, 784
    loss of, 789

PAWNBROKER,
  Acts 1872–1960, repeal of, 30, 31, 119, 328,
    763, 782
  charges, permitted, 963
  consumer credit, provision of, by, 47
  licence of, 328
  loan by, 287
  provisions relating to, 782

PENALTIES,
  liquidated damages, and, 888, 904, 976

PERCENTAGE RATE,
  annual, recommendations of Crowther
    Committee, 475
  regulations on, 476

PERSON,
  definition of, 173

PERSONAL CREDIT AGREEMENT,
  definition of, 158

PLEDGE,
  delivery of pawn on redemption, 788
    refusal of, 790, 1088
  documents of title, of, 197, 782
  forfeiture of, 786, 791
  formalities of regulated agreement for, 784
  minor, from, 785
  nature of, 82
  pawn-receipt, 784, 789
  provisions relating to, 763, 782
  realisation of pawn, 786, 792, 889
    proceeds of sale, 792
  redemption of pawn,
    charges, and, 787
    failure to redeem, consequences of, 791
    period of, 786
    procedure, 788, 889
  time order by court, 791, 936

POST,
  acceptance, communication of, by, 240,
    565
  cancellation,
    notice of, service of, 610, 1093, 1095
    rights of, notice of, 609
  executed agreement, copy of, sent by, 565
  notice, service of, by, 1093–1095
  withdrawal of offer by, 575

POSTER,
  antecedent negotiations, as part of, 596

POSTPONED ORDER,
  specific delivery of protected goods, for,
    925, 938

PRE-PAYMENT,
goods, for, not credit transaction, 215–216

PRIVACY. *See* CREDIT REFERENCE AGENCIES, information held by

PROHIBITION,
order of, 1057

PROSPECTIVE AGREEMENT. *See* AGREEMENT

PROTECTED GOODS,
adverse possession, proof of, 905, 909–911
consent, repossession with, 912
meaning of, 906, 907
one-third of total price paid, where, 906 908, 914, 915
postponed order for specific delivery of, 925, 938
recovery of
contravention of Act, effect of, 918–921
court order for, 198, 889, 892, 905, 932, 934
death of debtor, where, 911, 916
debtor in breach, whether, 907, 916
default notice before, 905
joint creditors, by, 879
modifying agreement, where, 915
successive agreements, 914, 915
termination, and right of, 906, 918–920
third party, from, 913
request to surrender, 909, 910
transitional provisions of Act, 1084

PROTECTION ORDER,
preserve property from damage or depreciation, to, 927, 947

PUBLICATION,
advertisement, of, 447
liability of publisher, 459, 460

PUBLIC UTILITIES,
application of Act to, 334
consumer hire agreements, 311
licence needed by, 334

QUALIFIED PRIVILEGE,
credit reference agency, whether entitled to, 1036, 1038–1039

QUOTATIONS,
regulations as to, 462–464

RACIAL DISCRIMINATION, 358, 462–464

RATE OF CHARGE,
calculation of. *See* INTEREST

REASONS,
statement of, for determination or decision, 405

REBATE,
early settlement, for,
calculation of, 734–745
actuarially computed rate of charge, 498, 740–742, 744
direct ratio method, 742–744
total charge for credit as basis for, whether, 745
Rule of 78, by, 742–744

REBATE—*contd.*
early settlement, for—*contd.*
creditor, costs of, 740, 741
explanation of, 737–741
extortionate credit bargain, and, 976
joint debtors or hirers, to, 868
linked transactions, where, 735, 746, 860
regulations on, 711, 734, 736
right to, 738–739

RECORDS,
licensee, by, 376

REDEMPTION,
mortgage, of, 888
pawn, of, 786–791. *See* PLEDGE

REFORM OF LAW ON CONSUMER CREDIT. *See* WHITE PAPER

REGISTER,
entry in,
amendment and removal of, 154
copy of, 153, 333
establishment of, 150
inspection of, 153, 333
licences, of, 151, 330, 386
changes of particulars entered, 331, 332
location of, 152
security interests, of, 17, 19, 23

REGULATED AGREEMENT. *See also* CONSUMER CREDIT AGREEMENT, CONSUMER HIRE AGREEMENT
antecedent negotiations, 595–599
cancellation, notice of rights of, 546, 569, 570, 607
definition of, 117, 155, 156
documentation of, 546–557. *See also* DOCUMENT
executed,
supply of copy of, 546, 564, 565
credit-token agreement, 566
post, by, 565
execution of, 545, 546
form and content of documents, regulations as to, 544
importance of, 157
improperly executed, enforcement of. *See* ENFORCEMENT
information to be included in documents, 544
modifying agreement, and, 718, 724
partially. *See* PARTIALLY REGULATED AGREEMENTS
pre-contract disclosure, 543, 705
signing of. *See* SIGNATURE
unexecuted,
copy of, supply of, 546, 558, 562
documents referred to in, supply of, 561
not presented personally or sent, 560
unlicensed credit-broker, made on introduction of, 1017, 1019
unlicensed person, by, order under section 40 where, 348, 385
variation of. *See* VARIATION
void agreement binding person to enter prospective, 576

All references are to paragraph numbers

All references are to paragraph numbers

All references are to paragraph numbers

All references are to paragraph numbers

415